THE HISTORY AND SOCIOLOGY OF
GENOCIDE

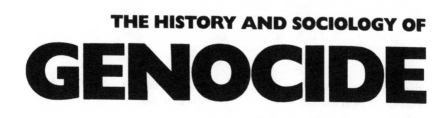

THE HISTORY AND SOCIOLOGY OF
GENOCIDE

ANALYSES AND CASE STUDIES

FRANK CHALK & KURT JONASSOHN

PUBLISHED IN COOPERATION WITH THE

MONTREAL INSTITUTE FOR GENOCIDE STUDIES

YALE UNIVERSITY PRESS NEW HAVEN & LONDON

Designed by Richard Hendel
Set in Times Roman and Gill type
by Marathon Typography Service, Inc.,
Durham, NC

Library of Congress Cataloging-in-
Publication Data
Chalk, Frank Robert, 1937–
  The history and sociology of genocide:
analyses and case studies / Frank Chalk and
Kurt Jonassohn.
    p. cm.
"Published in cooperation with the Montreal
Institute for Genocide Studies."
Includes bibliographical references (p.   ).
ISBN 0-300-04445-3 (alk. paper). —
ISBN 978-0-300-04446-1 (pbk. : alk. paper)
1. Genocide—History. I. Jonassohn, Kurt.
II. Institut montréalais des études sur le
génocide. III. Title.
HN8.C44   1990
304.6′63—dc20   89-27381
                           CIP

The paper in this book meets the guidelines
for permanence and durability of the Committee on Production Guidelines for Book Longev-
ity of the Council on Library Resources.

10 9

IN MEMORY OF

Alfred Chalk

(b. Lodz, 1901–d. Miami Beach, 1986)

and for

Jennie Klein Chalk

and

Florence and Joseph Hackman

.   .   .

To Shlomo Jannai, who escaped,

and to Richard and Frieda Jonassohn,

who did not

If we could learn to look instead of gawking,

We'd see the horror in the heart of farce,

If only we could act instead of talking,

We wouldn't always end up on our arse.

This was the thing that nearly had us mastered;

Don't yet rejoice in his defeat, you men!

Although the world stood up and stopped the bastard,

The bitch that bore him is in heat again.

—Epilogue to *Der Aufhaltsame Aufstieg des Arturo Ui*

[*The Resistible Rise of Arturo Ui*], Bertold Brecht.

Translated by George Tabori.

CONTENTS

Part III.   **Bibliographies**

Genocides and Genocidal Massacres Discussed in the Text

1a 1b 1c	3000 –1000 B.C.	Antiquity, several cases
2	416 B.C.	Melos
3	146 B.C.	Carthage
4a 4b 4c	13th century	Mongols, several cases
5	13th century	Albigensian Crusade
6	1630s	Pequots in New England
7	1640s	Hurons in Ontario
8	early 17th century	Christians in Japan
9	19th century	Tasmanians
10	early 19th century	Shaka Zulu in Southern Africa
11	19th century	Yuki in northern California

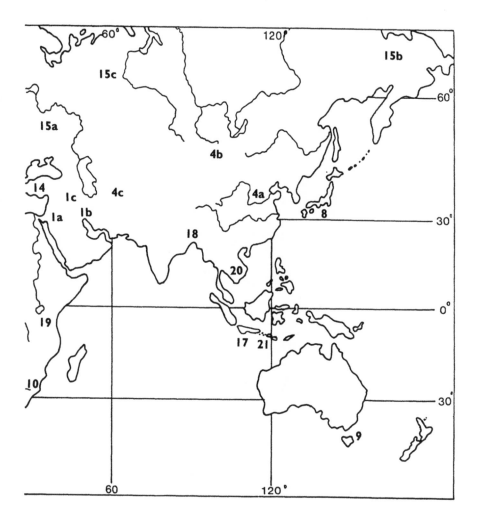

12	19th century	Cheyennes in Colorado
13	early 20th century	Hereros in South-West Africa
14	1915	Armenians in Turkey
15a		
15b	mid-20th century	Soviet Union, several cases
15c		
16a		
16b	mid-20th century	Nazi Germany, several cases
16c		
17	1965–66	Indonesia
18	1971	Bangladesh
19	1972	Burundi
20	1975–78	Cambodia
21	1975–	East Timor
22	20th century	Amazonian Indians

PREFACE

This work consists of three parts. Part I presents our conceptual framework; part II contains a series of case studies; and part III contains a topically organized bibliography that also includes all sources referred to in part I.

Part I includes a brief but critical review of the available literature. This is followed by our own definition of genocide and a typology of genocides. It concludes with some remarks on the problems encountered in doing research on this topic.

Part II contains a set of case studies that have been put together in full awareness of several limitations that the reader should note. The most important of these require some comment.

No generally accepted definition of genocide is available in the literature. We shall discuss some of the differences among the various definitions that have been formulated, and we shall also discuss why a definition of the phenomenon to be studied is important. In order to illustrate this point, we have included a number of cases that may or may not be considered genocide, depending on which definition one adopts.

Genocide has been practiced in all regions of the world and during all periods of history. The particular cases of genocide presented in part II are not intended to be either exhaustive or representative. They simply are the cases that we have selected to illustrate different types of genocide.

A further limitation has been imposed by the available literature. For obvious reasons, we have limited ourselves to materials available in English. In addition, we have had to restrict ourselves to cases for which we could find fairly short selections that could be understood even though they were being taken out of their original context. In a few cases we were able to find short published papers that were written to be read by themselves. In a few other cases we provide short summaries ourselves. These essays are intended as starting points for further exploration.

In part III, we have provided some bibliographical references for each case. They are intended as a "starter kit" leading to additional literature relevant to the particular aspect that you would like to explore further.

We would like to acknowledge the valuable contributions of students and colleagues who have commented on earlier versions of this book. We have greatly benefited from their interest and their comments. We want to add a very special thanks to Helen Fein, David Kirk, Leo Kuper, Franziska Shlosser, and Anton Zijderveld, and to the members of the Thursday Club and the Faculty Workshop on Mass Killing in History for their interest and encouragement. We also want to thank those students who have served as our research assistants, especially Michael McDevitt, Sonia Poulin, and Jan Stewart. We are grateful to Linden Rogers and Donna Whittaker for their enthusiastic and skilled typing.

Encouragement and financial assistance from Deans Charles Bertrand, June Chaikelson, and Donat Tadeo periodically revived our flagging spirits. Our research was enormously facilitated by the cheerful cooperation of the library staff at Concordia University, and especially by the Inter-Library Loans Department and Gail Flicker.

We also thank those authors and publishers who so kindly granted permission to reproduce materials as well as Charles Grench and Lawrence Kenney of Yale University Press for their constant support and editorial insight.

Finally, we want to acknowledge our very special debt to Norman Cohn, who has been our intellectual mentor through his writings and during his several visits to Montreal, as well as on our visits to London and Wood End. His unfailing encouragement has been an inspiration to us. Some of the ideas in this volume have been so thoroughly explored between us that we are no longer sure who holds paternity rights. However, the two coauthors cheerfully accept responsibility for this published version and welcome comments, suggestions, and criticisms from readers.

March 1989

THE
CONCEPTUAL
FRAMEWORK

INTRODUCTION

A significant, albeit often ignored, difference exists between everyday discourse and scientific discourse. The language we use in everyday usage does not require and does not benefit from precise definitions; this is so because we want to communicate not only information, but also feelings, attitudes, and opinions. Scientists too have feelings, attitudes, and opinions, of course, but they also have an overriding need to separate them from their data, concepts, and research findings. Therefore, the scientist requires a language that includes precise definitions of the terms he uses and that separates the cognitive content of his communication from the emotional and evaluative content.

This distinction between everyday discourse and scientific discourse is becoming increasingly difficult to establish and maintain for several reasons: the spread of education, of the mass media, and of the popularization of science allows scientific terminology to filter into daily discourse. In this process it acquires new meanings that detract from its utility in scientific language. The problem is compounded in the case of concepts that acquire a political loading; when this happens, the polemical use of a term may overshadow its original meaning and increase the difficulty of precise communication.

The term *genocide* has become an almost classic illustration of this process. The term was coined only during World War II by Raphael Lemkin, and its most widely accepted definition is that contained in the United Nations Convention on Genocide (see Appendix A). The horrible nature of the events it was meant to describe and the widespread disapproval of the perpetrators of these events have given the term a heavy negative loading; the association of genocide with a particular ideology has added a political meaning. Before long the term came, in general usage, to refer to other disapproved of events and ideas, even if no killing was intended or involved. Such diverse phenomena as family planning, abortion, medical research, language regulation in schools, the establishment of Indian reservations, and so forth have all been referred to as genocidal by some authors. Used in this manner, the term becomes devoid of all cognitive content and communicates nothing but the author's disapproval.

We must emphasize that we use the term *genocide* only as it is defined below.

This does not imply an absence of feelings, attitudes, and opinions—these can be expressed separately. But since we take it for granted that we are all against genocide, we might as well get on with the scholarly work. In the context of this work a precise definition is of crucial importance in clarifying which events are being studied and what they have in common. A great many horrible events befall humanity: from wars and massacres to epidemics, famines, and natural disasters. However, neither our understanding of them nor our exploration of possible means of prediction and prevention will be facilitated by lumping them all together.

In our comparative approach to the study of genocide, a clear definition of the term allows us to collect cases of "a form of one-sided killing" and to exclude those cases that do not fit this definition. Even within the group thus included, there are significant differences; therefore we have developed a typology that allows us to compare like events and to exclude unlike events. Our attempt, which has undergone several reformulations, is by no means a final one; but it represents our current thinking. The importance of such a typology does not lie in a pedantic need to impose neatness and order on the colorful diversity of the real world. It lies in the need of comparative research to examine cases that are on some basis comparable. Which basis of comparison is used as the organizing principle of a typology is not at all arbitrary, but must be decided in terms of the results it produces. When a typology does not contribute anything to the results of research, it must be discarded because a typology is useful only insofar as it produces such results.

In part I, we present some definitions of genocide and some of the typologies that have been proposed in the literature, including our own. However, our conceptual approach is anything but eclectic. The reader will find that we do not deal with several of the conceptual approaches that can be found in the literature. If these are sins of omission, they are quite deliberate. In using a historical and comparative approach, we focus on the attempt to identify the social conditions and situations in which genocide is likely to occur. To identify the relevant parameters is a first step in the prevention of future genocides. It is now clear that the adoption of the United Nations Convention on Genocide has not prevented genocide, for several have occurred since then. A number of people have argued that the establishment of an early warning system would be a better approach to prevention. But surely the establishment of such a system presumes the availability of a number of reasonably reliable indicators. In our opinion, there has not been nearly enough research done on the preconditions of genocide to specify such indicators with any degree of reliability. Our choice of cases is intended to emphasize the social conditions and situations in which genocide is likely or unlikely to occur because we think that it is in this area that such indicators are most probably to be found.

We close part I by briefly raising some problems concerning the evaluation of evidence based on historical sources. Here, the contemporary world view and the nature of communication must be taken into account. Such problems of historical method become important when one is trying to discover what actually happened; they are absolutely crucial if one means to ascribe intent and impute motives.

The Brutishness of the Past and Collective Denial

Our study of genocide has forced us on many occasions to confront the brutishness of most human societies in the past and the changing value placed on human life. Not very long ago many human societies sacrificed human beings to propitiate the gods, to protect the living against their displeasure, and to reassert the corporate unity of society. Human sacrifice existed throughout the ancient world, buttressed by religions that promised a good life in the afterworld to the sacrificial victim as well as the favor of the gods in this world for those who carried out the ritual slayings. The recent discovery by archeologists excavating at Carthage of the remains of six thousand infants sealed in individual sacrificial urns gives credence to the reports of commentators in the ancient world that the Carthaginian aristocracy gave its youngest sons to the priests for sacrifice to win the favor of the gods of war. In many societies human sacrifice continued until the society embraced an ethic that ennobled the individual in this world and adopted a code of behavior that placed this new ethic above the need to satisfy the grim appetite of the gods for human blood (Davies 1981, 280). Nigel Davies, who traces this change among the ancient Hebrews, credits them with transforming the "concept of life-giving . . . into that of self-giving." He contends that once the ancient Hebrews came to see God as good and just, human sacrifice ceased (ibid., 66).

Yet even in those societies that abandoned human sacrifice, daily life was coarse and brutal for all but the very few. The great French historian Fernand Braudel reminds us that famines and epidemics were so common that "they were incorporated into man's biological regime and built into his daily life" (Braudel 1967, 38). In western Europe, which was favored by nature, "famine disappeared at the close of the eighteenth century, or even later" (ibid., 39).

Sixteenth-century European towns worked out elaborate stratagems to divert armies of starving peasants from their gates. In the sixteenth and seventeenth centuries, France and England developed new institutions to control the poor, displaced peasants who flocked to their cities and to harness their labor. The physically fit poor of Paris were often chained together in pairs and forced to clean the sewers, while the poor of London were held in poorhouses under the new authority of the Poor Laws and put to work at menial labor. Conditions for the mass of the people were even worse, according to Braudel, in China and India, where famines struck more frequently and with greater severity than in Europe.

Peasants in Europe who reacted to their misery by stealing food or property were made to feel the full vengeance of the law. Death or maiming were the usual penalties until the late Middle Ages. Medieval penalties for such crimes were codified in the German Empire in the *Constitutio Criminalis Carolina* of 1532, which was representative of European practice. After specifying such penalties as hanging in chains, beheading or burial alive, and impaling for the graver crimes, the *Carolina* takes up less serious crimes such as theft. For these offenses it "prescribes afflictive punishment—flogging, pillorying, cutting off ears, chopping off fingers, cutting out the tongue—usually accompanied by a sentence of banishment" (Langbein 1977, 40).

As Wedgwood reminds us, the coming of war often brought little change for the average European; she describes living conditions in the seventeenth century just before the Thirty Years' War:

The insecurity and discomfort of life encouraged irresponsibility in the ruler. Wars brought with them no immediate upheaval since they were fought largely by professional armies, and the civilian population—except in the actual area of fighting—remained undisturbed at least until the need for money caused an exceptional levy on private wealth. Even in the actual district of the conflict the impact of war was at first less overwhelming than in the nicely balanced civilization of to-day. Bloodshed, rape, robbery, torture and famine were less revolting to a people whose ordinary life was encompassed by them in milder forms. Robbery with violence was common enough in peace-time, torture was inflicted at most criminal trials, horrible and prolonged executions were performed before great audiences; plague and famine effected their repeated and indiscriminate devastations.

The outlook even of the educated was harsh. Underneath a veneer of courtesy, manners were primitive; drunkenness and cruelty were common in all classes; judges were more often severe than just, civil authority more often brutal than effective, and charity came limping far behind the needs of the people. Discomfort was too natural to provoke comment; winter's cold and summer's heat found European man lamentably unprepared, his houses too damp and draughty for the one, too airless for the other. Prince and beggar were alike inured to the stink of decaying offal in the streets, of foul drainage about the houses, to the sight of carrion birds picking over public refuse dumps or rotting bodies swinging on the gibbets. On the road from Dresden to Prague a traveller counted 'above seven score gallowses and wheels, where thieves were hanged, some fresh and some half rotten, and the carcasses of murderers broken limb after limb on the wheels'.

The pressure of war on such a society had to be intensified and prolonged before any popular outcry was evoked, and by then the matter was usually beyond control. [Wedgwood, 13–14]

In western Europe, following the enormous population losses of the Thirty Years' War and the start of the effort to populate overseas colonies, human life came to be more highly valued. In the mid-seventeenth century, England and France moderated their use of capital punishment in cases of crimes against property. As the number of executions in England diminished, the English turned to the transportation of convicts to the colonies for terms of labor as indentured servants. At the same time, France and other Mediterranean countries found it increasingly useful to sentence physically fit convicted felons to life sentences as oarsmen on naval galleys. (The argument in this paragraph follows Langbein, chapter 2.)

This coarseness and brutality of human existence throughout much of history was a subject that hardly ever appeared in the curricula of our schools. The good news was reported; the bad news was not. The great massacres of the past lay beyond the range of the telescopes designed to focus upon evidence that justice always triumphed. In high school and university textbooks, Athens flourished, but the massacre of the men of Melos was rarely mentioned. The Romans destroyed Carthage and Corinth, but the fate of their people was not discussed. The authors of history textbooks hardly ever reported what the razing of an ancient city meant for its inhabitants. In other words, the fate of millions of human beings who died unnatural deaths as defenseless civilians was invisible and will remain so unless archeologists are able to produce such evidence at this late stage.

Our review of the history of genocide and its neglect has led us to the conclusion that until very recently scholars participated in a process of pervasive and self-imposed denial. Many factors entered into this process of collective denial. Throughout most of recorded time, it was the victors who wrote the history of their conquests, and even the victims of mass exterminations accepted their fate as a natural outcome of defeat. The idea of human rights is relatively new in

Western society; even today, many parts of the world still emphasize duties more than rights. The Enlightenment tradition of viewing human beings as inherently good and rational also played a part in the denial, as did the rise of nationalism and fear of stirring up ethnic enmity. The slaughter of people of *other* races, religions, and nationalities barely offended anyone's sensibilities.

It took the shocks of the twentieth century to reverse the process of collective denial; the gap between practice and ideals simply became too great to support the intellectual foundations of such denial. The Jews who survived the Holocaust refused to meekly accept the Nazis' assault on their right to exist. They recorded their experiences for posterity. At the end of World War II, the victorious Allied powers tried and executed top Nazi leaders judged guilty of crimes against humanity, an action that created a new interest in the history of crimes against civilians. Parochialism and nationalism were undermined by the spread of the democratic ideal after the war and by the increasing sophistication of the mass of the people that resulted from the greater access to higher education. Increasingly, journalists in the West have cast themselves in the role of adversaries to the holders of power and as spokesmen for the underdog in national and international affairs; many social historians have joined them in this novel conception of their calling. Throughout most of history only the rulers made news; in the twentieth century, for the first time, it is the ruled who make the news. Emboldened by this freer, more sympathetic atmosphere, other victims of past exterminatory campaigns—the Armenians, the Ukrainians, and the Gypsies, for example—have begun to tell their stories. Ultimately, even scholars awakened to the paucity of studies examining and analyzing the phenomenon of genocide in history.

Genocide: Origins of a Concept

When we began our work on genocide in 1979, we could count on the fingers of one hand the number of scholars who had written comparatively about genocide. A small group of writers had taken up the work started by Raphael Lemkin in a chapter on genocide in his book *Axis Rule in Occupied Europe*, published during World War II. In this pioneering scholarly essay on genocide, Lemkin coined the term and linked it to a number of historical events. Under Lemkin's definition, genocide was the coordinated and planned annihilation of a national, religious, or racial group by a variety of actions aimed at undermining the foundations essential to the survival of the group as a group. Lemkin conceived of genocide as "a composite of different acts of persecution or destruction" (Lemkin, 92). His definition included attacks on political and social institutions, culture, language, national feelings, religion, and the economic existence of the group. Even nonlethal acts that undermined the liberty, dignity, and personal security of members of a group constituted genocide if they contributed to weakening the viability of the group. Under Lemkin's definition, acts of ethnocide—a term coined by the French after the war to cover the destruction of a culture without the killing of its bearers—also qualified as genocide.

Lemkin also pioneered the development of a typology of genocide—a set of types classifying actual cases of genocide—based on the intent of the perpetrator. In his chapter on genocide, he sketched the outline of an evolutionary development incorporating three types of genocide. The aim of the first genocides —which he related to wars of extermination in antiquity and the Middle Ages— was the total or nearly total destruction of victim groups and nations. A second type of genocide, one that had emerged in the modern era, was characterized by the destruction of a culture without an attempt to physically destroy its bearers. Nazi-style genocide comprised the third type. It combined ancient and modern forms of genocide in a new type in which some groups were selected for immediate annihilation while others were designated for ethnocidal assimilation (Lemkin 79–82).

In his early work, Lemkin treated genocide as a problem in international affairs, not anticipating that twentieth-century genocide would increasingly become a problem of the state killing groups of its *own* citizens. In 1946, thanks to Lemkin's prodding, the United Nations for the first time considered the issue of preventing and punishing genocide. The General Assembly passed the following resolution:

Genocide is the denial of the right of existence of entire human groups, as homicide is the denial of the right to live of individual human beings; such denial of the right of existence shocks the conscience of mankind, results in great losses to humanity in the form of cultural and other contributions represented by these groups, and is contrary to moral law and to the spirit and aims of the United Nations. Many instances of such crimes of genocide have occurred, when racial, religious, political and other groups have been destroyed, entirely or in part. The punishment of the crime of genocide is a matter of international concern.

The General Assembly Therefore, Affirms that genocide is a crime under international law which the civilized world condemns, and for the commission of which principals and accomplices—whether private individuals, public officials or statesmen, and whether the crime is committed on religious, racial, political or any other grounds—are punishable. [Kuper 1981, 23]

In this early resolution, the United Nations significantly narrowed Lemkin's definition of genocide by downplaying ethnocide as one of its components, but, at the same time, it broadened the definition by adding a new category of victims — "political and other groups" — to Lemkin's list. Soviet and Eastern bloc delegates protested against the inclusion of political groups. They argued that "because of their mutability and lack of distinguishing characteristics [political groups] did not lend themselves to definition, [which] would weaken and blur the whole Convention" (ibid., 26, quoting the Polish delegate). The Great Powers seem to have made a behind-the-scenes compromise to preserve the remainder of the Genocide Convention. Political groups were excluded from the definition of genocide by a vote of the delegates.

We take up the issue of defining victim groups in our own definition of genocide later. Here we want to note that the problem of defining political groups can be solved. Since many of the political victim groups (for example, "enemies of the people") were mythical to begin with, it is futile to search for rational and objective boundaries to define them. Yet millions of human beings have died because of their alleged membership in these "mutable" groups. How can one set out the boundaries of a political group that may exist only in the minds of the perpetrators of genocide? We shall argue later that the solution lies in using *the perpetrator's* definition of the victim group.

On December 9, 1948, the United Nations adopted the Genocide Convention, incorporating the following definition:

Article II
In the present Convention, genocide means any of the following acts committed with intent to destroy, in whole or in part, a national, ethnical, racial or religious group, as such:

(a) Killing members of the group;
(b) Causing serious bodily or mental harm to members of the group;
(c) Deliberately inflicting on the group conditions of life calculated to bring about its physical destruction in whole or in part;
(d) Imposing measures intended to prevent births within the group;
(e) Forcibly transferring children of the group to another group.

Thus, the United Nations definition of genocide was born.* Although it marked a milestone in international law, the UN definition is of little use to scholars.

*The checkered history of the UN Convention on Genocide and its non-application is summarized in Leo Kuper's *Genocide*, chap. 2. For the complete text of the UN Convention for the Prevention and Punishment of the Crime of Genocide, see Appendix A.

First, it makes no distinction between violence intended to annihilate a group and nonlethal attacks on members of a group. "Killing members of the group" and "deliberately inflicting . . . conditions of life calculated to bring about its physical destruction in whole or in part" are commingled in the definition with causing "mental harm to members of the group" and "forcibly transferring children of the group to another group". Second, for reasons that we have already noted, the United Nations intentionally excluded the deliberate annihilation of political groups and social classes from its definition of genocide.

Although some scholars have noted these flaws, they have deferred to the fact that the UN definition is the only internationally recognized definition of genocide, and they have for this reason treated it as a given in their work. The lack of rigor in the UN definition of genocide is responsible for much of the confusion that plagues scholarly work in the field.

However, although the UN condemnation of genocide has undoubted symbolic value, it has never had any practical effect. There are several reasons for this. In negotiating the convention the member countries wanted to make sure that it applied only to the losers of World War II. The framers of the convention realized that the compromise wording was not adequate, but they accepted it because they thought that getting a bad convention passed would be better than none at all. (This is a debatable proposition, but this is not the place for such a debate.)

Another reason for its ineffectiveness is the nature of the United Nations itself. It is composed of sovereign member countries who are interested in using it as a political platform, but who are strongly opposed to the establishment of international judiciary and policing powers that would override their own sovereign powers. Since the perpetrators of genocidal killings are almost always sovereign states, it seems unlikely that the UN member countries would act against one of their own—and they have not yet done so, in spite of the fact that there has been no lack of opportunities.

Finally, it was left to an editor of the *Wall Street Journal* (rather than to a scholar or human rights activist) to point out that the wording of the convention is so restrictive that not one of the genocidal killings committed since its adoption is covered by it; thus, the victims of post–World War II genocides would not have benefited even if there were in existence an international body to enforce the convention (*Wall Street Journal*, Feb. 24, 1986, 12).

The major problem with the convention is its narrow definition of what constitutes a victim group, and potential perpetrators have taken care to victimize only those groups that are not covered by the convention's definition. The result is that none of the genocidal killings that have occurred since the adoption of this convention have been denounced by the United Nations as genocides. Thus, increasingly the United Nations has become a club of sovereign states that protects its members from interference in their sovereign affairs. Genocides are kept out of the news through the control of information channels, justified as the defense of a regime, or through outright denial. At its most ridiculous, we find the United States and other Western powers supporting the seating of representatives of the murderous Khmer Rouge instead of the ruling Vietnamese-backed government because American foreign policy requires the nonrecognition of the fruits of the Vietnamese invasion of Kampuchea. Similarly, when Indonesia occupied East Timor and killed an estimated one-third of its population, the United Nations voted at least eight times in support of self-determination for East Timor; none of these resolutions have been implemented, and the United Nations has not asked Indonesia to do anything about implementing them. The perpetrators' allies cooperate in their defense, and so the collective denial spreads. As this club includes more and more members who have been perpetrators (and their allies), the chances of amending the convention, or even of just naming a perpetrator in a vote of condemnation, rapidly approach zero. The United Nations, once a body that condemned the practice of genocide, is rapidly becoming one that condones it. Any hopes for the prevention of such killings in the future need to be placed elsewhere.

A Review of the Literature

Jessie Bernard seems to have been the first social scientist to incorporate genocide into a coherent analysis. In her book *American Community Behavior* (1949), she developed a conceptual framework to deal with processes of interaction at the local level. In her last chapter she argued that the processes of competition, conflict, organization, disorganization, and control are as real at the international level as they are at the local level. In discussing racial and ethnic competition and conflict she not only cites the work of Lemkin, but also incorporates genocide as the ultimate weapon for resolving a conflict. Her overall conceptual scheme may have been too rigid to endure, even in her own work. But a whole generation went by before genocide reappeared in works of serious analysis by social scientists.

However, during this interval, Pieter N. Drost, a Dutch law professor with extensive experience in the Dutch East Indies, wrote a major work assessing the UN Convention. Presenting his conclusions in two lengthy volumes published in 1959, Drost assailed the omission of political and other groups from the UN definition of genocide, accurately predicting that governments would thoroughly exploit this obvious loophole in the convention. Rejecting the notion that the victims of genocide were limited to racial, religious, national, and ethnic groups, Drost proposed that the United Nations redefine genocide as "the deliberate destruction of physical life of individual human beings by reason of their membership of any human collectivity as such" (Drost, 2:125). Drost also called attention to the long history of genocide and devoted several pages to a survey of genocides from the days of the ancient Romans to the modern era of European colonial expansion (Drost, 1:211–15).

From the publication of Drost's volumes until the early 1970s there was almost no scholarly comparative research on genocide. Since then, several authors have produced books and articles initiating serious theoretical discourse on the subject. In *Du Cannibalisme au Génocide*, Hervé Savon voiced his skepticism about the utility of the UN definition as a tool for sociologists, noting that it really belongs to the language of law and ethics, not to the realm of sociological analysis. He also alleged a peculiarity in the wording of the UN definition —an implication that the actions it described had appeared for the first time only around the middle of the twentieth century. Instead of inducing a general principle or law from the observation of the many instances of annihilation that were only too well represented in the history of humanity, the authors of the convention, Savon maintained, appeared to have constructed their definition of genocide through reasoning by analogy from the most recent case of genocide. It was as if, having stated in their preamble that genocides had occurred in all periods of history, the authors of the convention had forgotten the preamble when they drafted article II, defining genocide (Savon, chap. 1).

Insisting, like Lemkin and Drost, on the long pedigree of the modern practice of genocide, Savon developed a typology for classifying actual cases. His categories are genocides of substitution, devastation, and elimination. These types of genocide take their meaning from the outcome of the genocidal killings (ibid.). Although Savon's work rekindled interest in the problems of genocide, unfortunately his typology based on outcomes fails to illuminate the events leading up to genocide and the possible methods of halting the process.

In 1976, Irving Louis Horowitz tackled the subject in a short volume titled *Genocide*, which he revised and reissued in 1980 under the title *Taking Lives: Genocide and State Power*. As the new title suggests, Horowitz viewed genocide as a fundamental policy employed by the state to assure conformity to its ideology and to its model of society. He amended the UN definition to emphasize that genocide was "a structural and systematic destruction of innocent people by a state bureaucratic apparatus" (Horowitz 1980, 17). His discussion of the role of the state in genocide and his critique of the failure of modern social science to confront the most pressing social issues of the day are an important contribution. The major feature of Horowitz's thesis in *Taking Lives* was a continuum of modern societies in which the level of state-induced repression of the right to dissent and to be different is the key variable (ibid., chap. 4). This continuum ranges from genocidal societies at one extreme, through less repressive and liberal societies at the center, to permissive societies at the other extreme. Horowitz's typology was based primarily on twentieth-century cases. His approach focused on outcomes and did little to explain the process whereby an authoritarian state resorted to genocide; and it did not account for pre-twentieth-century genocides. Moreover, as Horowitz himself admitted, a typology based on internal repression cannot by itself explain those genocides conducted in foreign countries.

In his more recent essay "Genocide and the Reconstruction of Social Theory," Horowitz (1984) notes that a totalitarian society is a necessary precondition of the genocidal process, and he also points out that it is not a sufficient one. Horowitz believes that national culture plays a much more important role in genocide than the ideology of the state. He suggests that a totalitarian ideology may make class, race, or religion ineradicable sins, thus increasing the potential for genocide, but that the decision to eradicate these sins by committing genocide is largely a function of national culture. Although he does not offer a new typology of genocide in this work, Horowitz is clearly interested in discovering and investigating the common elements in the national cultures of totalitarian states that have resorted to genocide.

Vahakn Dadrian, too, set aside the UN definition and like Savon and Horowitz devised a new definition of genocide for the purpose of scholarly research and analysis. Following Lemkin in emphasizing the intent of the perpetrator, Dadrian proposed the following:

> Genocide is the successful attempt by a dominant group, vested with formal authority and/or with preponderant access to the overall resources of power, to reduce by coercion or lethal violence the number of a minority group whose ultimate extermination is held desirable and useful and whose respective vulnerability is a major factor contributing to the decision for genocide. [Dadrian 1975]

Dadrian's definition of genocide, emphasizing the degree and type of disparity between the power of the perpetrator group and the victim group, establishes the matrix for his five-category typology of genocide: (1) cultural genocide, in which assimilation is the perpetrator's aim; (2) latent genocide, in which the perpetrator's activities have unintended consequences, such as civilian deaths during bombing raids or the accidental spread of disease during an invasion; (3) retributive genocide, designed to punish a segment of a minority that challenges a dominant group; (4) utilitarian genocide, using mass killing to obtain control of economic resources; and (5) optimal genocide, in which the chief aim of the perpetrator is the total obliteration of the group, as in the Armenian and Jewish holocausts.

Dadrian's article raises many of the major conceptual problems facing investigators of genocide. To name only a few, he addresses the failure of scholars and public officials until recently to recognize genocide as a social problem and discusses the related question of collective perception; he notes the difficulties of using a newly defined concept to analyze events that transpired hundreds and even thousands of years ago; and he pinpoints questions of methodology such as the reliability of evidence.

Although it has many merits, Dadrian's approach poses difficulties for us. His typology of genocide suffers from inconsistencies between its categories and the inclusion of cases of pure ethnocide. The lumping together of intended and unintended genocide serves to weaken the rigor of his typology. While we have learned a great deal from Dadrian's discussion of the importance of perpetrator intent and his effort to create a social science definition of genocide, we have not been able to apply his typology in our own work.

In 1983–84, the sociologist Helen Fein presented a preliminary definition and a very useful typology of genocide in connection with her proposals for various types of humanitarian intervention to halt genocides (Fein 1984). In Fein's definition, "Genocide is the calculated murder of a segment or all of a group defined outside of the universe of obligation of the perpetrator by a government, elite, staff or crowd representing the perpetrator in response to a crisis or opportunity perceived to be caused by or impeded by the victim." Fein introduced a new four-part typology in which she characterized genocides as (1) developmental, in which the perpetrator intentionally or unintentionally destroys peoples who stand in the way of the economic exploitation of resources; (2) despotic, which are designed to eliminate a real or potential opposition, as in a new, highly polarized, multiethnic state; (3) retributive, in which the perpetrator seeks to destroy a real opponent; and (4) ideological, a category embracing cases of genocide against groups cast as enemies by the state's hegemonic myth or by its need to destroy victims who can be portrayed as the embodiment of absolute evil.

Fein's work marks a notable effort to replace the UN definition of genocide with a more analytically rigorous concept. Her use of the term "calculated murder," if consistently adhered to, would exclude from consideration cases of ethnocide and Dadrian's "latent genocides," while also removing from consideration those categories of nonlethal persecution that are stipulated in the UN Convention. Fein introduced a number of inconsistencies to her analysis that required clarification. She contended that her use of the term *genocide* conformed to the UN definition even though her definition was restricted to "calculated murder." On the other hand, she conformed to the UN definition by excluding political groups from the category of genocides but found, understandably, that she could not ignore political groups when imagining scenarios of future genocides and treated them under the rubric "ideological slaughters" instead. One other ambiguity in Fein's discussion also merited clarification. Nothing in her definition seemed to exclude the killing of soldiers in wartime battles or the wartime killing of civilians in attacks on enemy cities and towns.

In 1988, Fein resolved many of these problems by devising a revised sociological definition of genocide:

> Genocide is a series of purposeful actions by a perpetrator(s) to destroy a collectivity through mass or selective murders of group members and suppressing the biological and social reproduction of the collectivity. This can be accomplished through the imposed proscription or restriction of reproduction of group members, increasing infant mortality, and breaking the linkage between reproduction and socialization of children in the family or group of origin. The perpetrator may represent the state of the victim, another state, or another collectivity. [Fein 1988]

Fein's explanation of her new definition shows that she has decided to include political and social groups as victims and to exclude deaths resulting from warfare. She insists that individuals and not only states and other authorities can be perpetrators of genocides, pointing to the killings of indigenous peoples in Paraguay and Brazil by individual settlers. By omitting the term "one-sided mass killing" from her definition, she intends to eliminate any possibility that members of a victim group can be excluded because they rebelled against a perpetrator of genocide and to open the door to cases of bilateral genocidal killings arising during a civil war, such as the war in Lebanon (ibid.). While we believe that states rather than individual settlers are primarily responsible for the killings of indigenous peoples in Latin America, that "one-sided killing" includes situations in which an objectively powerless group resists genocide, and that the casualties of civil wars are not victims of genocide, there is no doubt that Fein's sociological definition is an important contribution to the effort to develop a definition of genocide that conforms to the realities of the contemporary mass killings of civilians.

Leo Kuper has contributed more to the comparative study of the problem of genocide in the twentieth century than anyone since Raphael Lemkin. In his monograph *Genocide* (1981), Kuper presents a comprehensive analysis of genocidal processes and motivations and confronts the difficulties of defining genocide. After delivering a devastating critique of the UN definition, the political compromises that shaped it, and the organization's morally bankrupt record of nonenforcement, Kuper reluctantly accepts the UN handiwork on the grounds that its definition is internationally recognized and may one day become the basis for more effective preventive action by the United Nations. Kuper hopes that his book will serve to put the United Nations under mounting pressure from international opinion and recall it to its duty.

Kuper's analysis of modern genocides clusters the motives of the perpetrator around three categories: (1) genocides designed to settle religious, racial, and ethnic differences; (2) genocides intended to terrorize a people conquered by a colonizing empire; and (3) genocides perpetrated to enforce or fulfill a political ideology (Kuper 1981, 11–18). He is particularly worried about the increasing frequency of genocidal events in the modern period. Since modern genocides, as he defines them, usually occur within nation-states that have the character of plural societies, the creation of new multiethnic states during the period of colonization and decolonization becomes particularly significant for his analysis.

Kuper does not ignore the groups excluded by the UN definition. He discusses the victims of state-organized, politically motivated mass killings in Stalin's Soviet Union, in Indonesia, and in Kampuchea under the heading "related atrocities." He suggests that each of these cases would have been labeled a genocide if the UN definition had included political groups.

In a later book, *The Prevention of Genocide* (1985), Kuper's major focus is on the need for new international pressure groups, legal institutions, and agreements to facilitate positive and timely measures against genocides before they can be carried to completion. He presents a thoughtful discussion of the major obstacles to implementation of the UN Convention, emphasizing the interplay of state interests and values. Kuper once more accepts the definition of genocide in the UN Convention, although he is still critical of the omission of political mass murder and brings it into his analysis of genocide, noting that the concepts of genocide as put forth in the UN Convention and in the cases he considers under instances of political mass murder shade into each other.

Kuper also revises his typology of genocide and presents it in its fullest form to date. He divides genocide into two main groups: "domestic genocides arising on the basis of internal divisions within a society, and genocides arising in the course of international warfare." The four types of domestic genocide are (1) genocides against indigenous peoples; (2) genocides against hostage groups, a category that includes the Holocaust; (3) genocide following upon decolonization of a two-tier structure of domination; and (4) genocide in the process of struggles by ethnic or racial or religious groups for power or secession, greater autonomy, or more equality. Kuper notes that there are few places left where the genocides following decolonization can be repeated and suggests that they are really a special case of the genocide described in type 4.

Under genocides of international warfare Kuper includes the United States's nuclear destruction of Hiroshima and Nagasaki, the Chinese invasion and occupation of Tibet, the Indonesian invasion and occupation of East Timor, and the American war in Vietnam. Standing outside his typology of genocide because they do not fall within the UN definition are cases of political mass murder. Here Kuper deals with the genocidal massacres of ethnic, racial, and religious minorities in plural societies perpetrated by despotic governments who rely on political formulas or legitimating ideologies. Within this vast category, Kuper includes many of the mass murders committed by the governments of the Soviet Union, Nazi Germany, Equatorial Guinea, Uganda, Kampuchea, Indonesia, and other states.

Kuper's books are the most useful contribution to the literature on genocide thus far, but there are several aspects of his treatment that we find awkward. First, because he uses the UN definition of genocide, he includes a number of cases in his discussion that have no salient characteristics in common. This is a handicap in a comparative study of genocide. Although Kuper is aware of the problem, instead of excluding certain cases of large-scale killing that fall outside the boundaries of the UN definition, he includes them under the categories of genocidal massacre and related atrocities. Wherever these cases involve the attempt to destroy a class or social group, Kuper must omit them from his typology of genocide. Kuper also equates Turkish and Nazi genocides with the U.S. bombing of Dresden, the dropping of atomic bombs on Japan, and American intervention in Vietnam (Kuper 1981, 17, 46, 102). Yet the United States never intended to annihilate Germans, Japanese, and Vietnamese as groups, whereas the leaders of the Turkish and Nazi states made the killing of Armenians and Jews ends in themselves. Kuper's failure to note this distinction is responsible for the awkwardness of this part of his argument.

Second, in his analysis Kuper treats plural societies as being particularly vulnerable to genocide (ibid., 17, 54, 57–83). We believe that the plural character of a society is at best an intervening variable. It is new states or new regimes attempting to impose conformity to a new ideology that are particularly likely to practice genocide. When tensions between the traditional society and the new regime escalate, it is the plural character of a society that is most likely to provide the social cleavages that define the perpetrator and victim groups.

Robert Melson is a scholar with a particular interest in genocidal processes. Following in the footsteps of Leo Kuper and Helen Fein, he has recently attempted to identify the parallels in the genocides inflicted on Armenians and

Jews (Melson 1986). Melson's thesis is summarized in this excerpt from his conclusion:

We would suggest that four factors preceding the Armenian genocide may be at work in other cases as well. First, the victimized group is a communal minority that was tolerated but was by no means considered as equal to the majority. Indeed, it was a communal group that had historically experienced some persecution and contempt at the hands of the larger society. Second, despite this history—or perhaps because of it—for some years preceding the genocide, the group that will come to be victimized adapts with relative success to the modern world and undergoes progress in the social, economic, cultural and political spheres. This social mobilization creates new tensions between this minority and segments of the majority who find its progress to be both illegitimate and threatening to the old order which was based on inequality. Third, the victimized group comes to be identified, either geographically or ideologically, with the enemies of the larger society and state. This identification may be real or may be imputed to the minority, but a link is established between an external and an internal threat. Fourth, the larger society and the state experience a series of significant military and political disasters that undermine their security and worldview.

Together these factors allow for the emergence of an ideology that links the crisis of the state and the majority to the social mobilization or progress of the minority and to its outside connections with the state's enemies. The progress of the minority is seen as having been gained at the expense of the majority and the targeted group is blamed for the disasters engulfing the state and the larger society. In the grip of its new ideology the state radically redefines its identity and decides to eliminate the offending communal group from the social structure.

It is this fateful convergence of a minority's renaissance and its connections to the outside world with the majority's disasters, fear of external aggression, and transformation of ideology and identity that seems to us to be at the core of both the Armenian and Jewish genocides. [ibid., 79–80]

Melson proposes that his model is relevant to most state-sponsored domestic genocides. He envisions a simpler process in other cases in which "a settler regime confronts a technologically less advanced people," where the victims are seen as existing outside the social and moral order of the perpetrators from the very beginning of contact.

Yehuda Bauer has underscored the unique aspects of the Holocaust in the history of genocide by proposing that we redefine our conception of genocide to recognize the differences that he perceives between the Holocaust and other genocides (Bauer 1984). Starting with the assertion that Raphael Lemkin actually offered two rather contradictory definitions of genocide, only one of which can be applied to the Jews, Bauer emphasizes that Hitler's plans for the Jews of Europe differed markedly from the fate that he intended for Europe's Czechs, Poles, Serbs, and other Slav nations. In Bauer's view, only the Jews were marked for total and immediate biological annihilation. The other victims of Nazi racial policy were doomed to live their lives as helots, slave laborers working for the benefit of the Reich. In the case of these non-Jewish helot groups, argues Bauer, mass killing was intended to destroy their leaders and to terrorize survivors, policies meant to discourage revolts among the helots and devastate their cultural roots.

After considering briefly a number of cases of mass killing in history, Bauer arrives at his major proposition, his argument that two different crimes were erroneously subsumed under the term *genocide* in Lemkin's writings and in the UN Convention. The first crime, says Bauer, should be called genocide and should refer to

the planned destruction, since the mid-nineteenth century, of a racial, national, or ethnic group as such, by the following means: (a) selective mass murder of elites or parts of the population; (b) elimination of national (racial, ethnic) culture and religious life with the intent of "denationalization"; (c) enslavement, with the same intent; (d) destruction of national (racial, ethnic) economic life, with the same intent; (e) biological decimation through the kidnapping of children, or the prevention of normal family life, with the same intent. [ibid., 213]

The second crime Bauer calls holocaust, meaning "the planned physical annihilation, for ideological or pseudo-religious reasons, of all the members of a national, ethnic, or racial group" (ibid.).

Under genocide, Bauer includes "the Nazi policies towards the Czechs, Poles, or Gypsies . . . and Soviet policies toward the Chechens, Volga Germans, or Tatars." He also includes "the policies of American settlers toward many native American tribes" and "it would probably also include the cases of the Hutus, the Biharis and the Ibos" (ibid.). Under holocaust, Bauer lists only the Nazi attempt to destroy the Jews of Europe. Although the term may apply in the future to groups that have not yet become victims, the case of the Jews, in Bauer's view, is "the most thoroughgoing to date, the only case where holocaust would appear fully applicable" (ibid., 214).

Summarizing his survey of relevant cases, Bauer visualizes a "kind of continuum of evil that would lead from 'mass murder' in recent times through 'genocide' to 'holocaust' ('shoah').'' The closest parallel to the Nazi attack on the Jews is the case of the Turkish assault on the Armenians in 1915, notes Bauer, who concludes by pointing out that the differences between the Holocaust and the Armenian massacres are less important than the similarities (ibid., 216–17).

In contrast to Yehuda Bauer, who argues that the UN definition of genocide is too broad for scholarly purposes and wishes to narrow it, Lyman Legters, who has studied the applicability of the UN definition to Soviet mass killing, finds it too narrow in one crucial respect—the exclusion of socioeconomic classes. Legters generally prefers a narrow definition of genocide. He emphasizes approvingly that the current UN definition restricts the crime of genocide to attacks on "identifiable groups—national, ethnic, [and] religious—of sufficient scope and import as to threaten the survival of that group in recognizable form." In his view, the victim group must be numerous and crucial enough that its loss "threatens the survival of the parent group" (Legters 1984, 62–63). On the whole, Legters prefers that the definition remain exclusive rather than inclusive. He endorses the exclusion from the definition of the crime of genocide of the destruction of "people randomly chosen or implicated," of political groups (the notion strikes him as "too slippery"), and of the victims of nonlethal attempts to bring about the liquidation of a group (for example, assaults on the culture of a group or deportation from its traditional territory). Legters also notes that the Soviet Gulag is already covered by the current UN definition of genocide in the case of Stalin's attacks on Soviet nationalities and minorities (for example, "the Baltic peoples, ethnic groups from the Caucasus and the Crimea, Jews, Christians, and other identifiable groups . . . so conspicuously over-represented in the camps").

Legters strongly dissents from the current UN definition of genocide in regard to its failure to take into account that "different social orders have diverse ways of classifying their own populations" and that class—a category excluded from the UN definition of genocide—"is the primary classificatory device of socialist systems" (ibid., 65). Legters argues that Stalin's elimination of kulaks (those supposedly wealthy peasants whom Stalin labeled petty bourgeois) and their families during the forced collectivization of agriculture in the late 1920s and early 1930s was a clear case of genocide. The Soviet state apparatus, he reminds us, targeted persons called kulaks as members of a "class inimical to socialism and the proletariat" and sought their physical destruction.

Legters concludes that the definition of genocide must be broadened to include victims selected on the basis of their membership in an allegedly hostile class. He argues that if the term *genocide* is to be universal in its import, it must take account of other than ethnic and religious styles of classification. If an allegedly socialist society, whose primary form of classification is that of class, either targets or invents a class with extermination in prospect, that program must count as genocide lest the term lose its continuing pertinence for the contemporary world in all its variety. [ibid.]

In his essay of 1987 on the twentieth century as an age of genocide, Roger W. Smith presents a five-part typology of genocide based on the motives of the perpetrator. The overlap between Smith's categories and the types established earlier by Kuper, Fein, and ourselves suggests that in spite of their occasional differences students of genocide are close to a consensus about the essential components of the core cases in the field. Smith's categories are (1) retributive genocide, which is based on the desire for revenge (for example, the conquests of Genghis Khan); (2) institutional genocide, frequently incidental to military conquest and prevalent in the ancient and medieval worlds; (3) utilitarian genocide, motivated by the desire for material gain and common in the colonial expansions of the sixteenth to nineteenth centuries as well as in the genocides of development devastating small aboriginal groups in the twentieth century; (4) monopolistic genocide, originating from the desire to monopolize power, particularly in plural societies (for example, Bangladesh and Burundi); and (5) ideological genocide, motivated by the desire to impose a particular notion of salvation or purification on an entire society and most commonly found in the twentieth century (for example, the Armenians, the Soviet Union, the Holocaust, and Cambodia).

Smith emphasizes the changing historical pattern in the various motives of the perpetrators of genocide. The victims of modern genocides are usually selected according to who they are, whereas those of earlier genocides were generally chosen because of where they were or what they had. Many other students of genocide—Kuper, Fein, and ourselves among them—have come to virtually the same conclusion.

The work of the scholars briefly summarized in this review of the literature reinforces our view of the importance of genocides committed to implement a belief, ideology, or theory. The work of the past fifteen years demonstrates the value of a comparative and historical framework for the study of genocide and the need for a rigorous definition of genocide appropriate to scholarly analysis. We note that even Benjamin Whitaker, a special rapporteur for the Commission on Human Rights, recommended badly needed revisions of the definition of genocide in the UN Convention. In July 1985, Whitaker recommended expanding the definition of genocide in the Genocide

Convention to protect political, economic, and social groups. "In an era of ideology," Whitaker observed, "people are killed for ideological reasons" (Whitaker 1985).

The Definition of Genocide

Having dealt above with several definitions of genocide and with our critiques of them, in this section we formulate and elaborate our own definition. It is deliberately restrictive. We have rejected the UN definition as well as others proposed because we want to confine our field of study to extreme cases. Thus, we hope that the term *ethnocide* will come into wider use for those cases in which a group disappears without mass killing. The suppression of a culture, a language, a religion, and so on is a phenomenon that is analytically different from the physical extermination of a group.

We have considered the utility of coining a new term and have rejected this possibility partly because we have not been able to think of an adequate alternate term and partly because the term *genocide* is by now so widely accepted. For the purposes of our research we have adopted the following definition:

Genocide is a form of one-sided mass killing in which a state or other authority intends to destroy a group, as that group and membership in it are defined by the perpetrator.

The terms of this definition require some comment. We start with a *form* of one-sided killing because we want to emphasize that there are many forms of mass killings and that we are proposing to deal with only one of them. We emphasize *one-sided* to indicate that we are dealing with cases in which there is no reciprocity; while the perpetrator intends to wipe out the victim group, the latter have no such plans. The term *mass killing* is meant to denote those cases in which all of the members of a group were labeled as victims, notwithstanding the fact that historically the extermination of 100 percent of a victim group is very rare. A distinction must be made here between the intent to destroy all of the members of a victim group and the empirical methods by which this may be achieved. We mean to exclude from consideration here those cases of mass killing, massacres, riots, and so forth that had a lesser aim, no matter how objectionable such cases are.

The term *one-sided mass killing* is also essential in order to exclude from our analysis the casualties of war, whether military or civilian. When countries are at war, neither side is defenseless. Although individually the civilians may be defenseless, they are part of the group or nation that is at war. In our analysis, the group is the operable unit of analysis because we are concerned with the behavior of groups rather than individuals. Although our case materials include genocides that occurred during or after a war, these are not to be interpreted as exceptions because they do not concern the victims of combat. The genocide of the Armenians occurred during World War I, that of the Gypsies and Jews during World War II; but in neither case were the victims killed as a result of warfare. Similarly, when we include the victims of the Assyrians, the Mongols, and the Romans in Carthage, we do not mean to deal with war casualties, but with the killing of the entire population after the outcome of the war had already been decided.

A further implication of *one-sided* is that the victim group has no organized military machinery that might be opposed to that of the perpetrator. Even in those cases in which the victims engaged in attempts to oppose the power of the perpetrators, the very hopelessness of such attempts underscores the one-sidedness of these mass killings. Isolated attempts to oppose the perpetrator —the Warsaw Ghetto uprising or the defense of Van, for example—serve more to assert the solidarity of the victims than to defeat the perpetrator.

Our definition of genocide also excludes civilian victims of aerial bombardment in belligerent states. In this we differ from Jean-Paul Sartre and Leo Kuper. Kuper writes, "I cannot accept the view that . . . the bombing, in time of war, of such civilian enemy populations as those of Hiroshima, Nagasaki, Hamburg, and Dresden does not constitute genocide within the terms of the [UN] convention" (Kuper 1981,1985). We base our dissenting position on the fact that in this age of total war belligerent states make all enemy-occupied territory part of the theater of operations regardless of the presence of civilians. Civilians are regarded as combatants so long as their governments control the cities in which they reside. This practice was started by the Italians and the Germans, and it became the practice of both sides in World War II. It seems unfair to single out the Allies for their bombings without mentioning Guernica and Warsaw, Rotterdam and Brest, and Rouen and London. On the other hand, the rules of war clearly entitle enemy civilians living in territory occupied by the victor to certain protections, including freedom from arbitrary killing, which would seem to place the Nazi killing of Jews, Gypsies, and others in a quite different category from wartime bombings.

In taking this view, we find ourselves in agreement with Telford Taylor, who has written,

[Hiroshima and Nagasaki, Hamburg and Dresden] were certainly not "genocides" within the meaning of the Convention, which limits genocide to "acts committed with intent to destroy . . . a national, ethnical, racial or religious group, as such." Berlin, London and Tokyo were not bombed because their inhabitants were German, English or Japanese, but because they were *enemy* strongholds. Accordingly, the killing ceased when the war ended and there was no longer any enemy.

The term *group*, in our usage, may present some difficulties. We realize that the culturally defined meaning of a group and group membership was quite different in antiquity and throughout history before the rise of nationalism. In ancient times the victims of genocide, as we have defined it, were likely to be the residents of a city-state in conflict with a rival power. Whole races, cultures, religions, or ethnic groups were generally not singled out for killing. Indeed, these concepts hardly existed in the ancient world. Thus, even if the Romans killed the residents of the city of Carthage after the fall of that city in 146 B.C. they did not also seek the elimination of the Phoenicians, who had founded and peopled Carthage. The Romans defined the residents of Carthage as a group, recognizing that Carthage had long before become independent of Phoenicia. Nor did the Romans try to kill Carthaginians living in Numidia and other nearby states on the grounds that they were Carthaginians and must die. Those Carthaginians living in the hinterland were not considered by the Romans as part of the victim group because they were not viewed as guilty of rebellion or as likely rivals for power once the city of Carthage and most of its residents had been destroyed. A crucial aspect of our definition of genocide is the definition of the group used by the perpetrator.

Another difficulty may arise when the definition of the perpetrator does not agree with conventional usage. In many cases, the victim group is a real one, in the sense that it is defined by generally agreed-upon criteria of the culture of the time. But, in keeping with W. I. Thomas's famous dictum that if people define a situation as real it is real in its consequences, a group may be any collectivity of people that is so defined by the perpetrator of a genocide. (A more detailed discussion of this point will be found below in the elaboration of our typology.)

To the extent that a group of people has been targeted by the perpetrator, it is of crucial importance to these victims whether membership has been defined by the perpetrator as voluntary or as ascribed. Thus, individual Armenians sometimes could have saved themselves by converting to Islam, whereas the Nazis defined Jews in racial laws that left no room for individual decisions to opt out.

Because our definition leaves open the nature of the victim group, it allows the inclusion of groups that were excluded from the UN Convention. Further, it allows the inclusion of groups that had not previously been considered under the UN Convention as potential victim groups (for example, the retarded, the mentally ill, and homosexuals, as in Nazi Germany, or city dwellers in Pol Pot's Cambodia) and groups that have no existence outside a perpetrator's imagination (for example, demonic witches in Western Europe and "wreckers" and "enemies of the people" in Stalin's Russia), but whose fate was no less tragic, for all that.

Genocides are always performed by a *state or other authority*. In the twentieth century, the perpetrator is almost always the state because authority and power are highly centralized and the modern means of communication are so efficient that such centralization can be effectively imposed. The addition of *or other authority* was found necessary to deal with some cases in which the perpetrator was a local authority other than the state.

Finally, a word about *intent*. The inclusion of the criterion of intent is common to most of the definitions found in the literature. It is essential in order to exclude those cases in which the outcome was neither planned nor predicted. It thus excludes not only natural disasters, but also those mass deaths that were the result of some human action that did not have this intent (for example, the spread of diseases as a result of migration).

As we said above, our definition is deliberately restrictive in order to facilitate analysis. It excludes all cases that do not clearly fit our definition. A problem that remains to be dealt with concerns those actual cases that fit part of our definition, but not all of its restrictions. What do we do with those cases of "one-sided mass killing" in which there was no intent to destroy the entire group? How do we deal with cases of an intent to destroy a group that was in fact destroyed, though only a small part of it was actually killed?

Since we suspect that many such cases are analytically instructive, we think we should not ignore them, at least not until sufficient research has accumulated to permit a more clear-cut decision. We have resolved this dilemma by including them under the label *genocidal massacres*. It should, however, be clearly understood that this is not a category designed to allow the inclusion of every case of massacre or communal violence. The cases of genocidal massacre should fit several dimensions of our definition.

The term *genocidal massacre* will also be applied to a number of cases that seem to be a combination of genocide and ethnocide, that is, there is no intent to kill the entire victim group, but its disappearance is intended. In these cases, a part of the victim group will be killed in order to terrorize the remainder into giving up their separate identity or their opposition to the perpetrator group or both.

We have defined genocide because we assume that it is a definable form of human behavior. But it must be remembered that the very term *genocide* was coined only in the middle of the twentieth century. This raises questions about the applicability of the term to earlier periods of history, and about the judgmental and moral loadings that have become attached to it.

No problem lies in applying the term to those phenomena that seem to fit the definition—assuming the reliability of the evidence—no matter when these phenomena occurred. A more serious problem is raised by the moral loading attached to the term. Western liberalism, as it has developed since the Enlightenment, raises the issue of moral relativism in historical and comparative studies. Thus, we take it for granted today that we are all against genocide whenever and wherever it occurred. But this obscures our knowledge of how it was perceived by contemporaries. In some societies, it was perceived as cruel and harsh punishment, even by the standards of the day. In other societies, it was fatalistically accepted as the fate of the losers and the weak. There were even societies in which it was seen—at least by the perpetrators—as the just and justified outcome of previous actions. But since the late Middle Ages, it has increasingly been thought of as inconsistent with the values and attributes of a fully human society. This inconsistency has resulted until recently in what we have called the *collective denial* of the prevalence of genocidal events; that is, the ignoring of these events in historical reporting, or their glossing over by the use of vague or ambiguous terminology.

From the perspective of the victims, the most prevalent perception seems to have been a fatalistic acceptance that is hard to understand in the post-Holocaust era with its increasing emphasis on equality and human rights. Our current existential, or even future-oriented, Zeitgeist makes it difficult to appreciate the brutishness of values and living conditions and the acceptance of inequality throughout most of human history. Life was short, disease was rampant, and food, clothing, and shelter were almost always problematic—even at a minimal level. In many cultures, improvements were not looked for or expected in this life, but rather in the afterlife or in another incarnation. Thus, the terrible things that happened to people were accepted as being in the nature of life in this "vale of tears."

Some Preconditions for Genocide

The most painful question about genocide is, How is it possible for people to kill other people on such a massive scale? The answer seems to be that it is not possible, at least not as long as the potential victims are perceived as people. We have no evidence that a genocide was ever performed on a group of equals. The victims must not only not be equals, but also clearly defined as something less than fully human.

Historically and anthropologically peoples have always had a name for themselves. In a great many cases, that name meant "the people" to set the owners of that name off against all other peoples who were considered of lesser quality in some way. If the differences between the people and some other society were particularly large in terms of religion, language, manners, customs, and so on, then such others were seen as less than fully human: pagans, savages, or even animals. The greater the perceived gap between the people and the out-group, the less were the values and the standards of the people applicable to the out-group.

Thus, in order to perform a genocide the perpetrator has always had to first organize a campaign that redefined the victim group as worthless, outside the web of mutual obligations, a threat to the people, immoral sinners, and/or subhuman. Even after such a campaign of vilification and dehumanization the actual performance of the mass killing seems to have required a good deal of coercion and centralized control. Unfortunately, we lack adequate data on the actual behavior of the perpetrators in most cases. But it seems that mass killing is extremely difficult for ordinary people to carry out; it requires the recruitment of pathological individuals and criminals. Thus, the reputedly blood-thirsty Mongols under Genghis Khan seem to have been reluctant to carry out his orders when the entire population of a city was to be wiped out. He had to make sure that his orders were obeyed; to do this he divided the estimated population of the city by the number of his troops to determine how many each soldier had to kill, and then ordered each soldier to cut an ear off each victim and deliver the ears to his superior officer for counting. Both the Turks and the Nazis had to deal with symptoms of psychological breakdown when attempting to use regular troops for mass killing. Given such reluctance on the part of most ordinary people in all societies to carry out a mass slaughter of defenseless victims, it becomes clearer why the performance of a genocide has always required a high degree of centralized authority and quasi-bureaucratic organization. The only exceptions probably occur when the victim group is numerically small, such as the indigenous tribes wiped out by colonizing settlers.

Having said all this, one might be tempted to turn the question around and ask why such killings should have been so difficult, particularly in premodern times, when human life was not highly valued. In spite of this, the performance of a genocide required, first, the dehumanization of the victims, and second, a strong, centralized authority and bureaucratic organization.

A Typology of Genocide

Throughout our work we have felt it important to develop a typology that would allow us to group those phenomena that could be meaningfully compared. We found that typologies available in the literature were unsatisfactory for a variety of reasons—some of which we have discussed above. We have devised several typologies ourselves and discarded them for similar reasons. Our present thinking has resulted in a fourfold typology, based on the motives of the perpetrator. This typology is presented here as a heuristic device; its validity can arise only from its usefulness in further research. But it seems to us that in the comparative research on genocide a crucial distinction is to be made in terms of the motives of the perpetrator. Therefore, our current *typology* classifies genocides according to their motive:

1. to eliminate a real or potential threat;
2. to spread terror among real or potential enemies;
3. to acquire economic wealth; or
4. to implement a belief, a theory, or an ideology.

In any actual case, more than one of these motives will be present. We propose to assign each case of genocide to one of these types by deciding which of the four motives was the dominant one.

A number of other dimensions may be considered as bases for constructing a typology. While we have temporarily rejected them in favor of our simpler typology based only on motives, we consider them to be important dimensions to be explored in future research. Here we indicate briefly what these other bases are.

Type of society.   One kind of typology deals with the nature of the societies in which genocides have occurred. The earliest of these was proposed by Jessie Bernard (1949) in her effort to develop a continuum of accommodation for racial and ethnic conflicts in the international community (see p. 12). More recently Irving Louis Horowitz (1980) has developed a continuum of modern societies. His key variable is the extent to which the state permits or represses dissent and the right to be different. His eight types range from genocidal to permissive societies (see pp. 13–14). The weakness of these efforts lies in their tautological nature; that is, a society is assigned a type or category on the basis of outcomes, not on the basis of characteristics that lead to specific outcomes. It is exactly this kind of perceived discrepancy between the character of a society and its actions that led to the worldwide incredulity when the first news of Hitler's Final Solution became public. Such an outcome seemed at the time incongruous because it was not in accord with expected behavior—behavior appropriate to a modern, Western, developed society.

Types of perpetrator. Throughout history most genocides were committed by empires to eliminate a threat, to terrorize an enemy, or to acquire and keep wealth. Another way of putting this is to say that they were committed in the building and maintaining of empires. These types of genocides have become rare in the twentieth century. Our fourth type, committed to implement an ideology, has become most frequent and seems to be associated with the rise of new regimes and states (Larner 1981). It would require a great deal of research to discover the nature of the link between the rise of the nation-state and the increase in genocides. Is it a matter of imposing a new discipline on a recalcitrant population, or is it the enforced implementation of a new ideology? As will be seen, this dichotomy of empire versus nation-state overlaps with some of the dimensions described below.

Types of victims. In the first three types of genocides in our typology the victim groups were usually located outside the perpetrator society. This had significant effects on the genocidal process. Thus, it was not necessary to dehumanize the victim group. All societies have considered outsiders as less than equal or less than fully human. In our fourth type the victim group has usually been found within the perpetrator society (especially in the twentieth century). It is this phenomenon that made it necessary first to identify the victim group as separate from the larger society, and second, to isolate and segregate it. This has to be done in such a way that the members of the perpetrator society accept the new definition; if they fail to do so, the genocide will also fail.

Types of groups. This base for constructing a typology has been much discussed ever since the UN Convention included only four types of groups in its definition. Various authors have suggested the inclusion of economic, political, or social groups or all three. As shown in our definition above, we avoid this problem entirely by using the perpetrator's definition of the victim group. However, another important distinction must be considered: that between real groups and pseudo-groups. The former can be identified by an outside observer, while the latter can be identified only by the perpetrator. The outside observer can identify such groups only after the victimization has started. The transition cases here, as we have noted, include the victims of the Great Witch-Hunt, and, in modern times, Stalin's persecution of the "enemies of the people" is a classic case. This distinction is particularly relevant to efforts at prevention because the victim group can be identified by outsiders only after the victimization has been carried out, or at least started.

Types of accusation. Much has been written about the various reasons for persecution. There seems to be a close connection between the type of group that is being victimized and the type of offense that it is being accused of. The distinction that seems important here is whether the accusation is based on verifiable fact or whether it is a pseudo-accusation that has no reality outside the frame of reference of the perpetrator. Thus, heretics usually did not deny their deviant beliefs while witches confessed to conspiracy with the devil only under torture.

In the context of genocide it is necessary to differentiate clearly between individual and collective guilt. Confessions may be extracted from individuals, but the perpetrator always victimizes a group that is accused of collective guilt. Therefore, the confessions to be extracted placed little emphasis on what the victim had done, focusing rather on the identities of the co-conspirators, that is, the members of the group.

Types of results for the perpetrator society. The bulk of the literature deals with the results of genocide for the victims, but little deals with the results for the perpetrators. For those of us who have an interest in prediction and prevention this should be a serious issue because it might lead to avenues of preventive action.

Historically, the results for the perpetrator society seem to be directly related to their motives. Genocides committed to eliminate threats, to spread terror, or to acquire wealth are motivated by concrete situations. To the extent that these situations are perceived as pressing problems by the perpetrator state, successful genocides eliminate the problem and materially enrich the perpetrator. That is, the threatening group is eliminated or terrorized into subservience, and the economic wealth is in fact acquired. In ideological genocides, however, the motive is much more abstract: it may be to enforce conformity, to purify the race, to legitimate a new regime, or to homogenize a nation-state. Such abstract motives are much harder to realize and the resulting abstract benefits have no direct relation to material costs. This seems to account for the historical fact that such ideological genocides are always carried out at tremendous costs to the perpetrator society—notwithstanding the fact that individuals may have enriched themselves (see pp. 415–21).

It bears repeating that any typology must be evaluated in terms of the results it aids in producing. Clearly, the most important results would be those that help us predict and prevent genocides in the future.

During a faculty workshop on mass killings some of our friendly critics suggested several other bases for typologies. The one most frequently mentioned was the scale of casualties. Regardless of whether this is done in numbers or in percentages, it has not been shown that any meaningful research results would be arrived at by using this method. Similarly, it has been suggested that the method of killing and its technological sophistication or the organizational complexity of such killing operations might be treated as important variables. However, it seems doubtful that these aspects would yield anything beyond descriptive categories. This is not meant to be a flippant statement; it merely reflects a conviction that the major reason for doing comparative research on genocides is the hope of preventing them in the future. Such prevention will pose difficult applied problems, but first it must be based on an understanding of the social situations and the social structures and processes that are likely to lead to genocides. Only by acquiring such knowledge can we begin to predict the likely occurrence of genocides and direct our efforts toward prevention.

A Historical Summary

We do not know when the first genocide occurred. It seems unlikely that early man engaged in genocide during the hunting and gathering stage. While we have no direct evidence, this seems a reasonable assumption because man lived in quite small groups, and overall population densities were extremely low (1 person per 10 km^2 of habitable terrain according to the estimates of McEvedy and Jones 1978, 14).

After the discovery of agriculture, the world divided into nomads and settlers. This marked the start of systematic conflict in the form of food raiding by the nomads. The nomads quickly learned to raid their settled neighbors at harvest time for their food stores; however, they had no interest in exterminating them because they planned to repeat their raids in subsequent years. The settlers may have had much better reason to do away with the nomads, but they had neither the means nor the skills to do so.

As the settlers learned to improve their agricultural techniques and produce significant surpluses, they were able to support cities, rulers, and armies. They accumulated wealth, engaged in significant trade, and began to build city-states and empires. With these developments, the scene changed dramatically. Conflicts arose over wealth, trade, and trade routes. Wars were fought over the access to wealth and over the control of transportation networks—to use a modern term. At first, these conflicts were probably in the nature of brigandry and robbery. Soon they escalated to wars between states. However, these warring peoples often discovered that their victories were temporary: the defeated peoples withdrew long enough to rebuild their resources and their armies and then tried to recoup their losses and avenge their defeat. This pattern became so common that it soon appeared that the only way to assure a stable future was to eliminate the defeated peoples once and for all. After the battle, they were killed or sold into slavery or dispersed. The elimination of a potential future *threat* (our type I genocide) appears to be the reason for the first genocides in history. Genocides seem to have been common throughout antiquity, especially in the Middle East, where trade routes connecting Asia, Africa, and Europe crossed.* The Assyrians were expert practitioners; about a number of the peoples whom they vanquished we know little more than their names (Jastrow 1971). The empire of the Hittites was destroyed during the eleventh century B.C. so efficiently that not even the location of their capital was known until an inspired German archeologist unearthed it almost by accident in the nineteenth century (Gurney 1975). Perhaps the best-known example of this type of genocide is the destruction of Carthage (Warmington 1960). The so-called Punic Wars between Carthage and Rome lasted well over a century (264–146 B.C.) and were fought mostly over the control of the Mediterranean trade and economy. These wars were incredibly costly in terms of materiel and lives, even by modern standards. After Rome barely won the Second Punic War (218–201 B.C.), it decided that Carthage had to be eliminated once and for all. Following the Third Punic War (149–146 B.C.) the victorious Romans massacred great numbers of Carthaginians and sold many into slavery; they destroyed the city. Looking at the available evidence from antiquity, one might develop a hypothesis that most wars at that time were genocidal in character. Such genocide to eliminate a threat we consider as type I.

The evidence from antiquity is often contradictory, ambiguous, or missing. Such evidence as we have consists almost exclusively of written materials that were produced by the victims or by the perpetrators. When we have accounts from both sides, which rarely happens, they tend not to confirm each other's evidence. It may well be that as-yet-undiscovered evidence will shed new light on how and why entire peoples have disappeared. Such disappearances in themselves are not evidence of genocide because they may have been due to a variety of processes, from migration to assimilation. However, if we should ever develop an archeology of genocide, we may acquire more conclusive proof of what happened to the populations of cities that were destroyed and to whole peoples that have disappeared. One case that illustrates such possibilities is the extermination, reported by Iranian historians, of whole populations by the Mongols under Genghis Khan; these reports were thought to be exaggerated because they originated with the victims. They gained renewed credibility, however, when archeologists unearthed the pyramids of skulls that Iranian historians had described (Boyle 1968).

*Detailed information on the cases mentioned in this section will be found in part II, and sources will be found in the topically organized bibliography in part III.

An archeology of genocide would be particularly important when one deals with peoples who did not leave a written record or whose written records have so far resisted all efforts at decoding. Archeologists have discovered traces of disappeared civilizations in many parts of the world. One can only speculate about what happened to them. Some of them may have fallen victim to epidemics or to natural disasters. But it seems reasonable to assume that some of them disappeared by genocide after being defeated in war. Actually, the most likely scenario seems to be a combination of genocide and ethnocide, for genocides have rarely been totally successful; usually there are some survivors. But if a people has disappeared from history, we need to ask, What happened to the survivors? The most likely explanation is that they integrated into the victorious society, either voluntarily (assimilation) or by force (ethnocide). In addition to the large number of such cases that seem to have occurred in the Middle East, we cite here a few others from different parts of the world. Of course, the question of what type of genocide may have occurred does not make sense in situations in which we are not even sure that a genocide did in fact happen.

The Anasazi Indian pueblo culture in Chaco Canyon, New Mexico, produced the Southwest's most elaborate native architecture. Archeologists have unearthed samples of their building skills in Pueblo Bonito; but they have found no evidence of how and why these people disappeared.

When the first Europeans arrived in New Zealand in the late eighteenth century, they found it inhabited by a Polynesian people, the Maori, who had a vigorous and warlike culture. They seem to have replaced an earlier people about whom we know practically nothing. It seems likely that the conquering Maori fought them upon discovering their land on one of their voyages because they wanted to settle there. If any survived, they were integrated into Maori society either voluntarily or by force.

The people of Easter Island are known to us only through their original sculptures, which have fascinated explorers and tourists for years. Even so, we know practically nothing about these artistic people and what happened to them.

Finally, we cite the experience of the Hurons in central Canada, about whom quite a lot is known (see, for instance, Trigger 1976). In the seventeenth century, they became the victims of the Iroquois. But there seems to be no evidence that the Iroquois intended to annihilate them. A few of the survivors of the Iroquois' raids fled to New France to seek the protection of the French colonial power; most were absorbed into other tribes, primarily the Iroquois. It is not clear what the actual mix of assimilation and ethnocide was in this case.

In the modern period, cases of genocide motivated by real or perceived threats are less common. In fact, genocide as a reaction to external threat seems to have disappeared. Now it has become one way of dealing with internal threats. One of the earliest such cases occurred in Japan in the seventeenth century, during the Tokugawa period. Early voyages by Europeans brought not only traders but also missionaries, whose efforts to convert the Japanese to Christianity proved to be surprisingly successful, especially among unemployed warriors and poor peasants. When these two groups formed an alliance during one of the frequent peasant revolts, the establishment felt sufficiently threatened to resort to genocide.

The twentieth century has produced several such cases. In Burundi we encounter the less frequent situation of a ruling minority, the Tutsi, feeling threatened. The majority Hutu seemed to gain too much power as a result of the introduction of elections. Having seen the Hutu gain the upper hand in the control of neighboring Rwanda, the Tutsi of Burundi resorted to genocidal massacres in order to maintain their traditionally dominant position. In Bangladesh we observe another case in which the introduction of democratic elections threatened to upset the established power structure. The election results assured Bangladesh a voice in government that the Pakistani government was not prepared to accept. In order to maintain sole control of the country it resorted to genocidal massacres of the Bangladeshi elite and intellectuals. But this turned out to be one of the rare cases in which the genocide did not achieve its intended result. Rather, it convinced the Bangladeshis that they would never have a say in their government and that their only option was to separate and establish their own, independent country. This they accomplished. The last case to be cited here is that of Indonesia, for which we have a great deal of conflicting information. The most widely accepted interpretation of the events of 1965–66 is that the army establishment felt threatened by the growing influence of the Communist party. A minor and unsuccessful coup attempt was used to outlaw the party and to kill or arrest most of its members. The genocide was so successful that the military, who have been in power ever since, have used this method again to deal with later events.

The second type of genocide—that carried out to terrorize real or potential enemies—probably is a somewhat later invention. To conquer others and keep them subjugated requires large armies and a permanent investment in a large occupying force. The Assyrians probably deserve credit for realizing that the creation of terror is far more efficient as well as effective. They are reported to have surrounded beleaguered cities with piles of skulls and with impaled corpses in order to terrorize their opponents into surrendering. Somewhat later, Athens massacred the men of Melos in order to show their allies that they expected their orders to be carried out. Genghis Khan, about two thousand years later, refined this technique (Saunders 1971). He offered his prospective conquests the choice of submitting or of being exterminated. If they did not submit, the threat was ruthlessly carried out. Although there were never more than about one million Mongols, by using these methods Genghis Khan was able to establish an empire that comprised most of the then-known world from China to central Europe.

Much later, in a different part of the world, Shaka used genocide not only to build his Zulu empire, but also to discourage any thought of opposition. In the twentieth century the USSR organized a man-made famine in the Ukraine to terrorize both kulaks and nationalists into conforming with Moscow's dictates. The most recent example of this use of terror occurred in Ethiopia, where a man-made famine served similar ends.

Our third type of genocide, that committed to acquire *economic wealth*, probably originated in antiquity also. People looking for greater wealth than their own territory could provide found it in the possession of others. When such wealth was in the form of fertile land and other primary resources, it could not be carried off as loot but could only be acquired by occupation of the land and enslavement or extermination of the indigenous population. This was probably one of the motives when a city-state or an empire sought to expand.

In the modern period, genocides of this type were associated with the discovery and settlement of the New World and the establishment of colonial dependencies by several European powers. Europe's expansion into the Americas, Asia, and Africa produced a number of genocides intended to acquire and keep economic wealth (type 3), usually in the form of land. There are strong similarities among the fate of the Pequots of New England (1637), several of the Indian tribes of Virginia (seventeenth and eighteenth centuries), and the Hereros of South-West Africa (1904–07). In contrast, little evidence of genocides exists in early South America, where colonizing Europeans needed a large labor supply for their mines and plantations.

Extensive killings resulted from European expansion when frontier settlers embarked on campaigns to destroy the native occupants of the land. Such devastations were often opposed by governments, but their feeble efforts to protect the natives were overwhelmed by the settlers' persistent attempts to annihilate their aboriginal neighbors. These were cases of genocidal massacre. Among its victims were the Caribs, the Tasmanians, the Beothuks of Newfoundland, several Indian tribes of California, and some of the tribes of the Brazilian Amazon. However, a far larger number of natives were the victims of disease, devastation of their environment, alcohol, and forced labor under lethal conditions. Surprisingly, we find that a colony like Indonesia, which successfully fought for its independence after World War II, now is using genocide as a method for its own expansion at the expense of indigenous populations.

These three types of genocide, all relating to the building and maintaining of empires, have largely disappeared from history for the simple reason that modern states have become so large that it is no longer possible for the victor to exterminate the defeated enemy. The three types, particularly genocides committed to facilitate access to wealth, persist only where the victim population consists of a small tribe living in relative isolation. In the twentieth century, several such cases have been reported in South America. The three types have several things in common: they are associated with empires, they are primarily of historical interest, and their victims were either enemies or subject peoples.

The fourth type of genocide, that committed *to implement a belief, theory, or ideology*, differs from the first three in that its primary victims are citizens of the perpetrator state rather than aliens; it is also of much more recent origin. The persecution of peoples for their religious beliefs has, of course, been going on for a long time, although it did not usually result in genocide. The best known of such persecutions are those carried out by the Inquisition, an institution that existed for over five hundred years. While the Inquisition only rarely committed genocide, it will be included in the case materials because it invented and perfected methods that are still used today in places where people are victimized for their actual or imputed beliefs.

The fourth type of genocide differs from the others in its result for the perpetrator: for the first three types, genocide arguably produced tangible benefits for the perpetrator state; in the fourth type, genocide was carried out in spite of tremendous costs to the perpetrator state, costs that can be measured in economic, political, and developmental terms—notwithstanding the fact that a number of individuals may have enriched themselves from the misfortunes of the victims.

Although type 4 genocides are a modern phenomenon perpetrated by nation-states, many of the methods used were developed during several transitional cases that happened long ago. In the twelfth and thirteenth centuries the Cathars were a heretical group in the Languedoc, a region covering the southern third of present-day France. They gained widespread support not only among the common people, but also among the aristocracy, especially at the court of the Count of Toulouse. After making vain efforts to preach to them, Pope Innocent III called for a crusade that became known as the Albigensian Crusade, after the town of Albi, the center of heresy. This is a transitional case because from the point of view of the king, Philip the Fair of France, it was an opportunity to expand his realm, while from the point of view of the pope it was necessary to eliminate heretics who did not recognize his authority. The papacy's need to deal with heresy in its realm also led to the establishment of the Inquisition, which from the beginning was misused to satisfy worldly aims rather than the purposes for which it was established.

In the early fourteenth century, the king of France was in desperate need of money to finance his expansionary wars. The Knights of the Temple were a very rich order that had lost its raison d'être since the end of the Crusades. The king and his minister conspired to arrest members of the order in France and to accuse them of heresy. Finally, he succeeded in having the order abolished. This case does not qualify as a genocide because only in France were a significant number of Templars killed. As in other cases of heresy, confessions were extracted by torture; the few who were able to resist such torture were condemned as unrepentant heretics, and those who retracted their extorted confessions were condemned as relapsed heretics.

These cases are important because persecution by torture, forced confessions, and guilt by association leading to imprisonment and death have become standard methods in many genocidal processes of the twentieth century.

An even more important transitional case is the Great Witch-Hunt of Europe because the victim groups here were an invention of the perpetrators. Its thousands of victims were burned at the stake not as witches, but for demonic witchcraft, that is, for *conspiring* with the devil. Many people doubted it at the time, and everybody today doubts that there ever was such a conspiracy, that a coven of witches ever met the Devil on a mountaintop to have sexual intercourse with him or to plot against God. However, although neither the group nor the conspiracy it was accused of had any reality in verifiable fact, the results were real enough: the accused were burned at the stake.

A note on torture is in order here. European legal codes were largely based on Roman canon law. Conviction under this legal system was based strictly on the evidence of two eyewitnesses or on a confession. Torture was an administrative procedure, intended to elicit a confession when no eyewitnesses were available and when no confession was volunteered; no matter how much it hurt, its intent was not punishment but the extraction of a confession. Since, by definition, there could hardly be eyewitnesses to witches' covens, torture to obtain a confession was the only alternative. The use of torture fell into disuse only when the law changed to permit convictions based on circumstantial evidence (Langbein 1977). This does not, of course, obviate the illegal use of torture in the twentieth century.

The question arises as to why a perpetrator would invent a pseudo-group of victims when real groups are always readily at hand. Christina Larner has suggested that the victimization of a pseudo-group for a pseudo-conspiracy serves to legitimate a new regime that is trying to impose a new discipline on a recalcitrant population. A real group would not serve this purpose nearly as well because it might be able to defend itself, because it might be able to enlist the support of sympathizers, and because its victimization might thus threaten the unity of the realm. We suspect that Stalin knew exactly what he was doing when he labeled his victims *enemies of the people* and *wreckers*. The research on this hypothesis remains to be done, but it is challenging in the light of the number of twentieth-century genocides that have been perpetrated by new regimes against pseudo-groups that are accused of pseudo-offenses.

All of the type 4 genocides, with the exception of the early transitional cases, occurred in the twentieth century. Among the early transitional cases, in addition to those mentioned above, were the lethal persecution of Christians in the Roman Empire, the slaughter of the non-Christian inhabitants of Antioch and Jerusalem during the Crusades, and the persecutions of the Marranos and Moriscos by the Inquisition in Spain. All are transitional cases involving religious persecution. Other targets of type 4 genocides are the Armenian victims of Pan-Turkic ideology and the Jews and the Gypsies who became the victims of Nazi race theories.

In the twentieth century these type 4 genocides reached their full development as the world came to be dominated by new nation-states or old ones with new regimes. Many such regimes were based on secular ideologies that had much in common with earlier religious belief systems: they specified not only a perfected future—analogous to earlier millenarian movements—but also the means of attaining this goal. Once such an ideology became established, it could not tolerate nonadherents or critics, lest they "pollute" society and jeopardize the perfected future. It is in one's dealings with such groups that the intermediate cases mentioned above become important. Only the terminology changed: heretics became reactionaries; sinners became enemies; and conversion became reeducation. What did not change was that the accuser defined the group and the accusation, that people were found guilty by virtue of having been accused, and that the holy grail of a perfected future justified any means of persecution.

The first of these twentieth-century cases was the persecution of the Armenians in Turkey in 1915. The Ottoman Empire had disintegrated, and the new regime adopted a Pan-Turkic ideology. The Armenians were the largest non-Turkic group left; living in the Turkish heartland, they prided themselves on a history and a culture considerably older than those of the Turks. This proved an intolerable situation to the Young Turk government. The onset of World War I provided an excuse—that the Armenians were disloyal and collaborated with the enemy—and an opportunity for the Turks to eliminate the Armenians while the rest of the world was preoccupied with the war.

Shortly after, the Russian revolution established a totalitarian regime in the USSR whose ideology was based on the role of the workers and the withering away of the state. In the name of this ideology, a series of genocides and genocidal massacres were committed, lasting until after World War II.

In the 1930s the Nazis came to power in Germany and implemented their theory of racial purity with a series of laws and regulations that defined who was a Jew and who was a Gypsy. Their ideology staked the future not only of Germany but of the whole world on the purity of an Aryan race. By a whole sequence of steps the Jews were forced out of the web of mutual obligations that forms the social structure of any society. But it was only during World War II that this process escalated into what came euphemistically to be known as the Final Solution.

After World War II a Communist revolution took place in China, and it established a people's republic under Mao Tse-tung. Because of the tight control over communication and the limited and controlled access permitted to foreigners, little is known about the internal events that ensued in China. Scholarly analysis of the killings in China and Tibet will have to await the availability of better information.

The final case to be mentioned here is the genocide that occurred in Cambodia under Pol Pot. Here is an ideological imperative that has no room for the foreign, urban, and intellectual influences in society and sees salvation in a return to primitive agriculture and communal living. Refugees tried to tell the world what was happening in Cambodia, but they were accused by some respected intellectuals of spreading anti-Communist propaganda. The only reason we know more of the details of the tortures and killings that occurred is that the Vietnamese occupiers, who had ousted Pol Pot's regime, found it good propaganda to admit foreigners and to make some of the documents available.

These twentieth-century genocides are marked by a strange irony. In the earlier cases, the perpetrators unabashedly performed their evil deeds for the greater glory of god, country, and the ruling elites—not necessarily in that order. The ordinary people and the victims of their genocides counted for very little. Now, the perpetrators claim to rule in the name of the people, to rule for the welfare of the masses, and they find it essential to kill—often secretly—large numbers of the very people in whose name they claim to rule.

On Methods of Research and the Imputation of Motives

So far we have presented issues dealing with definitions and typologies—issues of a theoretical nature. This is not to be misunderstood.

Definitions and typologies are not in themselves theory, but an integral part of theorizing because theory is inevitably concerned with phenomena as they have been defined and classified.

We address here some issues dealing with research methods. We do not discuss the general issues that have to be considered in every research project because they are adequately covered in many textbooks. We shall restrict ourselves to those aspects of the methods of research that seem to us to have a special significance in comparative and historical research on genocide.

The search for data on genocide in all periods of history is impeded by what we have called the *collective denial* that anything of the kind has in fact occurred. With rare exceptions, scholarship ignores such events or tries to gloss over them by using innocuous terminology.

When dealing with antiquity, we find archeologists excavating cities that have disappeared without giving much attention to the fate of their populations. At later periods, we have reports of cities being "razed," without any indication of what actual behavior is denoted by this term. When we do have additional description, it seems that "razing" may mean anything from the destruction of the city's defenses to its complete leveling. In either case, we are usually told little about the fate of the population. In the twentieth century, we find that the complete control by totalitarian regimes over the means of communication can not only introduce code words such as Final Solution, but also suppress records of what actually happened, as in the case of Stalin's exterminatory campaigns in the USSR.

We shall return to these problems of data collection when discussing specific cases. Here, it may suffice to point to four types of difficulties encountered in research on genocide:

1. Evidence is difficult to obtain because throughout most of history records were either not kept, have not yet been found, or did not survive.
2. When records do exist, they originate either with the perpetrator or with the victims; rarely do we have records from both.
3. When we do have records from the perpetrator and from the victim, they are often so different that it is difficult to discover what actually did happen.
4. The reliability of the records presents another problem. We have evidence of genocides that have occurred but were not reported. Even more curious, we have reports of genocides in antiquity that did not in fact occur at all.

Thus, research on specific cases of genocide has to be done systematically; evidence must be not only gathered but also evaluated very carefully. There is simply no substitute for careful, rigorous, and meticulous research methods. These must include the cross-checking of sources, the verification of the authenticity of documents, and a knowledge of the background of witnesses. In technical language, these are matters that affect the reliability and validity of the data.

If it is difficult in many cases to establish what actually happened, it is even more difficult to establish what the intentions of the perpetrators were. Only sometimes did they themselves announce their aims and motives. Hervé Savon (1972, 26–27) has argued that intent is of proper concern to the moralist and to the jurist, but not to the scholar. In his view, the scientist should try to establish what social structures and social processes lead inevitably to genocide and in what situations. We agree with this goal of research, but we do not see how such processes can be examined while the intentions of the actors are ignored. As most definitions of genocide now recognize, intent is part of the essence of genocide. The inclusion of intent makes our task infinitely more complex because we shall have to impute intent where the stated intent served polemical ends and was meant to distract attention from the real objective. A further reason for including intent in the analysis of structures and processes is a theoretical consideration apparently ignored by Hervé Savon: the effects of social structures are never fully deterministic on the actors; their interests and intentions can motivate them to counteract such anticipated effects, to ignore them, or to reinforce them. Therefore, we consider intent a crucial part of the definition, no matter how problematic it may be in other respects.

This is not the place for a detailed technical discussion on methods of imputing intent. We shall return to this issue in the context of specific cases, but here we merely enumerate some of the possibilities, not all of which will be applicable in each specific case:

1. When there is sufficient evidence of a fully articulated ideology or belief system, both motivation and intention may be derived from its normative parameters.

2. When the perpetrators openly stated their intentions, one needs to verify the extent to which these are polemical or programmatic statements meant to hide intentions rather than to make them explicit. When the perpetrator's intentions are reported by the victims, it is equally important to verify their reports.

3. In other cases, intent may be imputed by analyzing the inherent logic of the situation and of the processes occurring in this environment.

4. A major difficulty of analysis and definition is presented by those cases in which the actor engages in action that inevitably leads to genocide as an unanticipated consequence. Sociologists refer to this as a "structural effect," and we must frankly admit that we have yet to decide on how to deal with such effects within our conceptual framework.

Clearly we are not using terms like *motive* and *intent* in their purely psychological meaning. Neither do we imply that they are always explicit in the awareness of the actors. In our present thinking, an action is "intended" even when it is carried out for different purposes but the perpetrator is likely to know that genocide is the inevitable or probable by-product of a planned action. This complicated subject can best be dealt with in the context of case studies.

APPENDIXES TO PART I

A. Convention on the Prevention and Punishment of the Crime of Genocide

[United Nations, 9 December 1948]

The Contracting Parties,

Having Considered the declaration made by the General Assembly of the United Nations in its resolution 96 (I) dated 11 December 1946 that genocide is a crime under international law, contrary to the spirit and aims of the United Nations and condemned by the civilized world;

Recognizing that at all periods of history genocide has inflicted great losses on humanity; and

Being convinced that, in order to liberate mankind from such an odious scourge, international co-operation is required,

Hereby agree as hereinafter provided:

ARTICLE I

The Contracting Parties confirm that genocide, whether committed in time of peace or in time of war, is a crime under international law which they undertake to prevent and to punish.

ARTICLE II

In the present Convention, genocide means any of the following acts committed with intent to destroy, in whole or in part, a national, ethnical, racial or religious group, as such:

(a) Killing members of the group;

(b) Causing serious bodily or mental harm to members of the group;

(c) Deliberately inflicting on the group conditions of life calculated to bring about its physical destruction in whole or in part;

(d) Imposing measures intended to prevent births within the group;

(e) Forcibly transferring children of the group to another group.

44

ARTICLE III

The following acts shall be punishable:

(a) Genocide;

(b) Conspiracy to commit genocide;

(c) Direct and public incitement to commit genocide;

(d) Attempt to commit genocide;

(e) Complicity in genocide.

ARTICLE IV

Persons committing genocide or any of the other acts enumerated in article III shall be punished, whether they are constitutionally responsible rulers, public officials or private individuals.

ARTICLE V

The Contracting Parties undertake to enact, in accordance with their respective Constitutions, the necessary legislation to give effect to the provisions of the present Convention and, in particular, to provide effective penalties for persons guilty of genocide or of any of the other acts enumerated in article III.

ARTICLE VI

Persons charged with genocide or any of the other acts enumerated in article III shall he tried by a competent tribunal of the State in the territory of which the act was committed, or by such international penal tribunal as may have jurisdiction with respect to those Contracting Parties which shall have accepted its jurisdiction.

ARTICLE VII

Genocide and the other acts enumerated in article III shall not be considered as political crimes for the purpose of extradition.

The Contracting Parties pledge themselves in such cases to grant extradition in accordance with their laws and treaties in force.

ARTICLE VIII

Any Contracting Party may call upon the competent organs of the United Nations to take such action under the Charter of the United Nations as they consider appropriate for the prevention and suppression of acts of genocide or any of the other acts enumerated in article III.

ARTICLE IX

Disputes between the Contracting Parties relating to the interpretation, application or fulfillment of the present Convention, including those relating to the
responsibility of a State for genocide or for any of the other acts enumerated in
article III, shall be submitted to the International Court of Justice at the request
of any of the parties to the dispute.

ARTICLE X

The present Convention, of which the Chinese, English, French, Russian
and Spanish texts are equally authentic, shall bear the date of 9 December 1948.

ARTICLE XI

The present Convention shall be open until 31 December 1949 for signature on
behalf of any Member of the United Nations and of any non-member State to
which an invitation to sign has been addressed by the General Assembly.

The present Convention shall be ratified, and the instruments of ratification
shall be deposited with the Secretary-General of the United Nations.

After January 1950 the present Convention may be acceded to on behalf of
any Member of the United Nations and of any non-member State which has
received an invitation as aforesaid.

Instruments of accession shall be deposited with the Secretary-General of the
United Nations.

ARTICLE XII

Any Contracting Party may at any time, by notification addressed to the Secretary-
General of the United Nations, extend the application of the present Convention
to all or any of the territories for the conduct of whose foreign relations that
Contracting Party is responsible.

ARTICLE XIII

On the day when the first twenty instruments of ratification or accession have
been deposited, the Secretary-General shall draw up a *procès-verbal* and trans-
mit a copy thereof to each Member of the United Nations and to each of the
non-member States contemplated in article XI.

The present Convention shall come into force on the ninetieth day following
the date of deposit of the twentieth instrument of ratification or accession.[1]

Any ratification or accession effected subsequent to the latter date shall become

1. The Convention entered into force on 12 January 1951.

effective on the ninetieth day following the deposit of the instrument of ratification
or accession.

ARTICLE XIV

The present Convention shall remain in effect for a period of ten years as from
the date of its coming into force.

It shall thereafter remain in force for successive periods of five years for such
Contracting Parties as have not denounced it at least six months before the
expiration of the current period.

Denunciation shall be effected by a written notification addressed to the
Secretary-General of the United Nations.

ARTICLE XV

If, as a result of denunciations, the number of Parties to the present Convention
should become less than sixteen, the Convention shall cease to be in force as
from the date on which the last of these denunciations shall become effective.

ARTICLE XVI

A request for the revision of the present Convention may be made at any time by
any Contracting Party by means of a notification in writing addressed to the
Secretary-General.

The General Assembly shall decide upon the steps, if any, to be taken in
respect of such request.

ARTICLE XVII

The Secretary-General of the United Nations shall notify all Members of the
United Nations and the non-member States contemplated in article XI of the
following:
  (a) Signatures, ratifications and accessions received in accordance with
      article XI;
  (b) Notifications received in accordance with article XII;
  (c) The date upon which the present Convention comes into force in
      accordance with article XIII;
  (d) Denunciations received in accordance with article XIV;
  (e) The abrogation of the Convention in accordance with article XV;
  (f) Notifications received in accordance with article XVI.

ARTICLE XVIII

The original of the present Convention shall be deposited in the archives of the
United Nations.

A certified copy of the Convention shall be transmitted to each Member of the United Nations and to each of the non-member States contemplated in article XI.

ARTICLE XIX
The present Convention shall be registered by the Secretary-General of the United Nations on the date of its coming into force.
Here follow the signatures on behalf of: —

Australia	11 December, 1948
Belgium	12 December, 1949
Bolivia	11 December, 1948
Brazil	11 December, 1948
Burma	30 December, 1949
Byelorussia (with reservations)	16 December, 1949
Canada	28 November, 1949
Chile (with reservations)	11 December, 1948
China	20 July, 1949
Colombia	12 August, 1949
Cuba	28 December, 1949
Czechoslovakia (with reservations)	28 December, 1949
Denmark	28 September, 1949
Dominican Republic	11 December, 1948
Ecuador	11 December, 1948
Egypt	12 December, 1948
El Salvador	27 April, 1949
Ethiopia	11 December, 1948
France	11 December, 1948
Greece	29 December, 1949
Guatemala	22 June, 1949
Haiti	11 December, 1948
Honduras	22 April, 1949
Iceland	14 May, 1949
India	29 November, 1949
Iran	8 December, 1949
Israel	17 August, 1949
Lebanon	30 December, 1949
Liberia	11 December, 1948
Mexico	14 December, 1948
New Zealand	25 November, 1949
Norway	11 December, 1948

Pakistan	11 December, 1948
Panama	11 December, 1948
Paraguay	11 December, 1948
Peru	11 December, 1948
Philippine Republic	11 December, 1948
Soviet Union (with reservations)	16 December, 1949
Sweden	30 December, 1949
Ukraine (with reservations)	16 December, 1949
United States of America	11 December, 1948
Uruguay	11 December, 1948
Yugoslavia	11 December, 1948

B. U.S. Senate Ratification of the UN Genocide Convention

February 19, 1986

Resolved (two-thirds of the Senators present concurring therein), That the Senate advise and consent to the ratification of the International Convention on the Prevention and Punishment of the Crime of Genocide, adopted unanimously by the General Assembly of the United Nations in Paris on December 9, 1948 (Executive O, Eighty-first Congress, first session), Provided that:

I. The Senate's advice and consent is subject to the following reservations:
(1) That with reference to Article IX of the Convention, before any dispute to which the United States is a party may be submitted to the jurisdiction of the International Court of Justice under this article, the specific consent of the United States is required in each case.
(2) That nothing in the Convention requires or authorizes legislation or other action by the United States of America prohibited by the Constitution of the United States as interpreted by the United States.

II. The Senate's advice and consent is subject to the following understandings, which shall apply to the obligations of the United States under this Convention:
(1) That the term "intent to destroy, in whole or in part, a national, ethnical, racial, or religious group as such" appearing in Article II means the specific intent to destroy, in whole or in substantial part, a national, ethnical, racial or religious group as such by the acts specified in Article II.
(2) That the term "mental harm" in Article II(b) means permanent impairment

of mental faculties through drugs, torture or similar techniques.

(3) That the pledge to grant extradition in accordance with a state's laws and treaties in force found in Article VII extends only to acts which are criminal under the laws of both the requesting and the requested state and nothing in Article VI affects the right of any state to bring to trial before its own tribunals any of its nationals for acts committed outside a state.

(4) That acts in the course of armed conflicts committed without the specific intent required by Article II are not sufficient to constitute genocide as defined by this Convention.

(5) That with regard to the reference to an international penal tribunal in Article VI of the Convention, the United States declares that it reserves the right to effect its participation in any such tribunal only by a treaty entered into specifically for that purpose with the advice and consent of the Senate.

III. The Senate's advice and consent is subject to the following declaration: That the President will not deposit the instrument of ratification until after the implementing legislation referred to in Article V has been enacted.

C. The Definition of Genocide in the Canadian Criminal Code†

Hate Propaganda

Advocating genocide

281.1 (1) Every one who advocates or promotes genocide is guilty of an indictable offence and is liable to imprisonment for five years.

"Genocide"

(2) In this section "genocide" means any of the following acts committed with intent to destroy in whole or in part any identifiable group, namely:

    (a) killing members of the group, or

    (b) deliberately inflicting on the group conditions of life calculated to bring about its physical destruction

        . . . . .

(4) In this section "identifiable group" means any section of the public distinguished by colour, race, religion or ethnic origin.

† Extracted from Department of Justice, Government of Canada, *Office Consolidation of the Criminal Code, R.S.C., 1970, cc. C-34, C-35* (Ottawa: Information Canada, 1972).

D. The Definition of Genocide in the Criminal Code of the United States

S. 1851
One Hundredth Congress of the United States of America
At the Second Session
Begun and held at the City of Washington on Monday,
January 25, 1988
An Act
To Implement the International Convention on the Prevention and Punishment
of Genocide

Be it enacted by the Senate and House of Representatives of the United States of America in Congress assembled,

SECTION 1. SHORT TITLE
This Act may be cited as the "Genocide Convention Implementation Act of 1987 (the Proxmire Act)".

SECTION 2. TITLE 18 AMENDMENTS
(a) In General. —Part I of title 18, United States Code, is amended by inserting after chapter 50 the following:
CHAPTER 50A—GENOCIDE
Sec.
1091. Genocide
1092. Exclusive remedies.
1093. Definitions.

Sec. 1091. Genocide
(a) Basic Offense. —Whoever, whether in time of peace of in time or war, in a circumstance described in subsection (d) and with the specific intent to destroy, in whole or in substantial part, a national, ethnic, racial, or religious group as such—
(1) kills members of that group;
(2) causes serious bodily injury to members of that group;
(3) causes the permanent impairment of the mental faculties of members of the group through drugs, torture, or similar techniques;
(4) subjects the group to conditions of life that are intended to cause the physical destruction of the group in whole or in part;

(5) imposes measures intended to prevent births within the group; or

(6) transfers by force children of the group to another group; or attempts to do so, shall be punished as provided in subsection (b);

(b) Punishment for Basic Offense. — The punishment for an offense under subsection (a) is—

(1) in the case of an offense under subsection (a) (1), a fine of not more than $1,000,000 and imprisonment for life; and

(2) a fine of not more than $1,000,000 or imprisonment for not more than twenty years, or both, in any other case.

(c) Incitement Offense. — Whoever in a circumstance described in subsection (d) directly and publicly incites another to violate subsection (a) shall be fined not more than $500,000 or imprisoned not more than five years, or both.

(d) Required Circumstance for Offenses — The circumstance referred to in subsections (a) and (c) is that—

(1) the offense is committed within the United States; or

(2) the alleged offender is a national of the United States (as defined in section 101 of the Immigration and Nationality Act [8 U.S.C. 1101]).

(e) Nonapplicability of Certain Limitations. — Notwithstanding section 3282 of this title, in the case of an offense under subsection (a) (1), an indictment may be found, or information instituted, at any time without limitation.

Sec. 1092. Exclusive remedies

Nothing in this chapter shall be construed as precluding the application of State or local laws to the conduct proscribed by this chapter, nor shall anything in this chapter be construed as creating any substantive or procedural right enforceable by law by any party in any proceeding.

Sec. 1093. Definitions

As used in this chapter—

(1) the term "children" means the plural and means any individuals who have not attained the age of eighteen years;

(2) the term "ethnic group" means a set of individuals whose identity as such is distinctive in terms of common cultural traditions or heritage;

(3) the term "incites" means urges another to engage imminently in conduct in circumstances under which there is substantial likelihood of imminently causing such conduct;

(4) the term "members" means the plural;

(5) the term "national group" means a set of individuals whose identity as such is distinctive in terms of nationality or national origins;

(6) the term "racial group" means a set of individuals whose identity as such is distinctive in terms of physical characteristics or biological descent;

(7) the term "religious group" means a set of individuals whose identity as such is distinctive in terms of common religious creed, beliefs, doctrines, practices, or rituals; and

(8) the term "substantial part" means a part of a group of such numerical significance that the destruction or loss of that part would cause the destruction of the group as a viable entity within the nation of which such group is a part.

CASE STUDIES

INTRODUCTION

In part II we present readings on selected cases of mass killings. The cases are presented in rough chronological order. The reader is invited to examine each case with a view to determining the appropriateness of our definition and typology of genocide. Frequently more than one type may be considered appropriate when it is not obvious which one presents the best fit.

We have selected cases that span history from antiquity to the twentieth century. These cases represent different cultures and societies. The situations and the processes leading up to the genocides are also diverse. The range and the variability of these situations and processes raise important questions about their consequences and their potential for escalating to genocide.

In our own work, we have divided genocides into four types, according to whether the motive was the desire to eliminate a real or potential threat, to terrorize real or potential enemies into submission, to acquire wealth, or to implement a belief, theory, or ideology. These four motives are not mutually exclusive, but it seems to be the case that one of them is the dominant motive in any particular historical event. We have left it to the reader to determine whether and to what extent a case fits into one of these types.

The selections included here are based on the following considerations: (1) we wanted to show that genocide has occurred throughout history and that it has occurred in all parts of the world; and (2) we have tried to select cases for which we were able to find brief readings in English. If we could not find an appropriate reading, we have prepared our own summary of the case. No exhaustive presentation of all genocides in history is intended or is indeed possible. Other cases might have been selected; no particular bias is intended by our choices. Neither the length of the selections nor their number is meant to reflect a judgment on the importance of a particular case.

In some of these cases there is barely enough material available to decide whether a genocide occurred. In other cases we found such a wealth of material that it was difficult to decide what to include.

ON CASES FROM ANTIQUITY

We do not know when the first genocide occurred. We can only point to circumstantial evidence. Therefore, this first section will deal not with a specific case, but with a period in which many genocides are likely to have been part of the conflicts among city-states and empires. Some early evidence comes from Homer, who has Agamemnon say: "My dear Menelaus, why are you so chary of taking men's lives? Did the Trojans treat you as handsomely as that when they stayed in your house? No; we are not going to leave a single one of them alive, down to the babies in their mothers' wombs — not even they must live. The whole people must be wiped out of existence, and none be left to think of them and shed a tear." (Homer, 118)

We do not know whether we should take Homer literally because societies in antiquity were organized in an extremely hierarchical manner. What mattered were the ruling and the religious elites, and in most cases they were identical. Thus, the Assyrians were ruled by a king who was also the personal representative on earth of their main god, Assur. Ordinary people counted for little, although they produced the wealth with which their rulers built palaces and temples and conducted their wars. Such historical materials as we have deal with the ruling elites and rarely mention the rest of society. In fact, the workers and the peasants and the slaves were not considered as part of society at all. We know that empires have disappeared and that cities were destroyed, and we suspect that some wars were genocidal in their results; but we do not know what happened to the bulk of the populations involved in these events. Their fate was simply too unimportant. When they were mentioned at all, they were usually lumped together with the herds of oxen, sheep, and other livestock. The "people" probably consisted only of the ruling elite and perhaps their troops; ordinary workers and peasants were considered as chattel. They may have survived successive empires in their suffering anonymity.

The historical evidence we have is extremely difficult to interpret. Official documents were composed in great abundance, but they were not written as historical fact. In a world dominated by religion, they were intended to record how the kings obeyed the commands of their god and to glorify the king's stewardship of god's mandate on earth. However, different kings seem to have thought of themselves as implementing quite different mandates: some defined their mandate as conquering their neighbors and expanding their empire, while others prided themselves on a peaceful reign. The following excerpts illustrate this:

Assurnasirapli II (883–859 B.C.) conducted many wars; there are many reports of conquests, tribute, destruction of cities and villages by fire, slaughter of enemies, and resettlement of prisoners. With the rich loot he built palaces and financed the artistic flowering of Niniveh and Assur. Resistance was a crime punished with extreme cruelty, and escape did not usually work because the chase was conducted with all available resources. Prisoners were spared only when people were needed to resettle an area or to replenish his troops. For example, to terrorize a besieged city he would erect a pyramid of skulls in front of the city gate and circle the city with impaled prisoners. [Ebeling and Meissner, 1:214–20, trans. K. Jonassohn]

The entry "Friedenfürst" (peace king) points to some kings whose records make no reference to their wars, only to their temple building and other peaceful activities. It seems that they wanted to be remembered for their peaceful reign. Their wars are known only from "foreign" sources. [Ebeling and Meissner, 3:114–15, trans. K. Jonassohn]

The entry "Gefangener" (prisoner) points out that during the time of the Assyrians whole peoples were driven out of their homelands and resettled in another territory. [Ebeling and Meissner, 3:181, trans. K. Jonassohn]

Sennacherib reached the limits of despotic willfulness when, in 689 B.C., he made up his mind to erase rebellious Babylon from the face of the earth. Having forced his way into the city, he slaughtered the inhabitants one by one, until the dead clogged the streets. Private dwellings were methodically destroyed. The towered temple of E-saglia was toppled into the Arachtu canal. Finally, water was diverted into the city, and streets, squares, and houses were drowned in the artificial flood. Even then Sennacherib's lust was not appeased. He would have the city vanish, at least symbolically, from the very sight of mankind. To this end he caused loads of Babylonian earth to be loaded on boats and carried to Tilmun, where they were scattered to the four winds. [Ceram, 306]

Are we to take such information at face value? In the case of Assyria most of it comes from inscriptions, many of which were so placed that they were unlikely to be read by ordinary mortals, that is, on the foundations of buildings or high up on the face of a mountain. Some archeologists have argued that such official inscriptions were meant to be personal reports of the king to Assur. Like some contemporary administrators, they reported their achievements, but not their failures, and even falsified their reports by turning failures into achievements. Perhaps the most noteworthy example of this kind of reporting comes to us from Egyptian history: it concerns the purported victory of the Egyptians under Ramses II over the Hittites. The report was widely accepted as factual until the lost capital of the Hittites was discovered in the nineteenth century, and evidence surfaced that it was really the Hittites who had won. Much later, following their last war, the capital of the Hittites was not only destroyed but also burned. As a result, the clay tablets in their archives were baked and thus well preserved for posterity. These records were eventually deciphered and found to contain not only the Hittites' version of the battle, but also copies of the peace treaty signed with Egypt. Scholars now agree that the Egyptian version of the battle was probably written even before it took place because it was unthinkable that a court historian would report that Ramses should have lost a battle. In fact, following their victory, it was the Hittites who wrote the first "modern" peace treaty. This treaty considered the two warring empires as equals and even included an exchange of prisoners, an unprecedented sign of mutual respect. Indeed, the treaty was so successful that it resulted in seventy-five years of peace between the Hittites and the Egyptians.

The Hittites lived during the middle of the second millennium B.C. At the height of their empire they conquered Babylon and destroyed it, which spelled the end of Hammurabi. In matters of military genius, political organization, legislation, and administration of justice, Hittite civilization was far ahead of its time. Unfortunately, a great deal remains unknown about the Hittites as well as about other peoples of their time. One scholar describes how the Hittites are thought to have acted following a victory in battle:

> Treatment of the enemy depended on whether he surrendered willingly or resisted to the last. A city conquered by force of arms was the legitimate prey of the victorious army and was generally looted and burned to the ground. The devastated site was sometimes declared forever accursed and dedicated to the Storm-god by a solemn ritual, as a result of which it was thought to become the grazing-ground of the divine bulls Seris and Hurris. Future settlers would defy this taboo at their peril. The inhabitants of such a conquered place would be transplanted, with their cattle, to Hattusas (their capital) and distributed as serfs among the Hittite officers and dignitaries. But there is no evidence that they were otherwise ill-treated. There is a complete absence of that lust for torture and cruelty which characterizes the annals of the Assyrian kings in their victories.

In the event of an early surrender by the enemy the Hittite king was usually content to accept his oath of allegiance. [Gurney, 115]

The Hittites may have been an exception. Perhaps they really did not commit any genocides. However, the sudden and thorough way in which they themselves have disappeared makes it seem probable that they were one of its many victims. The Medes and the Babylonians appear to have been quite unrestrained in their tactics of conquest:

In the summer the Medes . . . then turned south down the Tigris to besiege Assur. In a successful assault the walls were breached and the city was captured and looted, the majority of the principal inhabitants being massacred and others taken prisoner. [Ceram, 14]

The allies marched up the Tigris against Niniveh. . . . The final assault took place in Ab (August) when the city fell and was heavily punished, the city and the temple being looted and the whole turned into the desolate hillocks of ruins and debris which still characterizes most of the site. (612 B.C.) [Wiseman, 16–17]

668–626 Assurbanapal destroyed Thebes. . . . In 648 Babylon was conquered. In 639 Susa (Elam) was destroyed. . . . Internal unrest and Scythian incursions weakened the state. Cyaxares of Media and Nabopolassar of Babylonia conquered and destroyed all Assyrian cities (Ashur 614, Nineveh 612, Charran (Haran) 608). The population was wiped out, the land laid waste. [Kinder and Hilgemann, 1:31]

A contrary view, expressed by H. W. F. Saggs in *Everyday Life in Babylonia and Assyria* (122–23), argues that Assyrian savagery has been vastly exaggerated. The Assyrians themselves encouraged such exaggeration in order to terrorize the enemy and facilitate their conquests. Saggs also argues that, to the extent it was successful, this tactic really saved lives. We do not find this argument very convincing; what Saggs refers to as savagery was not considered as such in its day. The sophisticated politics of peace that we seem to find among the Hittites was the exception rather than the rule.

The most detailed record of ancient history that survives is, of course, the Old Testament. It contains a number of cases that we would today consider genocides—not because of the casualties of war but because of the extermination of noncombatant women and children. We cite these cases not because we consider them to be factual, which they clearly are not; otherwise the Amalekites would appear as victims only once. For us the importance of these reports lies in the factual manner in which they refer to genocides—indicating that it was not considered an unusual event at that time.

Then came Amalek and fought with Israel in Rephidim.

And Moses said unto Joshua, choose us out men, and go out, fight with Amalek: Tomorrow I shall stand on the top of the hill with the rod of God in mine hand.

So Joshua did as Moses had said to him, and fought with Amalek: and Moses, Aaron and Hur went up to the top of the hill.

And it came to pass, when Moses held up his hand, that Israel prevailed: and when he let down his hand, Amalek prevailed.

But Moses' hands were heavy; and they took a stone, and put it under him, and he sat thereon; and Aaron and Hur stayed up his hands, the one on the one side, and the other on the other side; and his hands were steady until the going down of the sun.

And Joshua discomfited Amalek and his people with the edge of the sword.

And the Lord said unto Moses, write this for a memorial in a book, and rehearse it in the ears of Joshua: for I will utterly put out the remembrance of Amalek from under heaven.

And Moses built an altar, and called the name of it Jehovahnissi:

For he said, Because the Lord hath sworn that the Lord will have war with Amalek from generation to generation. [Exodus 17 : 8–16]

Remember what Amalek did unto thee by the way, when ye were come forth out of Egypt;

How he met thee by the way, and smote the hindmost of thee even all that were feeble behind thee, when thou was faint and weary; and he feared not God.

Therefore it shall be, when the Lord thy God hath given thee rest from all thine enemies round about, in the land which the Lord thy God giveth thee for an inheritance to possess it, that thou shalt blot out the remembrance of Amalek from under heaven; thou shalt not forget it. [Deuteronomy, 25 : 17–19]

Thus said the Lord of hosts, I remember that which Amalek did to Israel, how he laid wait for him in the way, when he came up to Egypt.

Now go and smite Amalek and utterly destroy all that they have, and spare them not; but slay both man, and woman, infant and suckling, ox and sheep, camel and ass.

.   .   .   .   .

And Saul smote the Amalekites from Havilah until thou comest to Shur, that is over against Egypt.

And he took Agag the king of the Amalekites alive, and utterly destroyed all the people with the edge of the sword. [1 Samuel, 15 : 2–8]

And it came to pass, when David and his men were come to Ziklag on the third day, that the Amalekites had invaded the south, and Ziklag, and smitten Ziklag, and burned it with fire.

And had taken the women captives, that were therein: they slew not any, either great or small, but carried them away, and went on their way.

So David and his men came to the city, and, behold, it was burned with fire; and their wives, and their sons, and their daughters, were taken captives.

.   .   .   .   .

But David pursued, he and four hundred men: for two hundred abode behind, which were so faint that they could not go over the brook Besor.

.   .   .   .   .

And when they had brought him down, behold, they were spread abroad upon all the earth, eating and drinking, and dancing, because of all the great spoil that they had taken out of the land of the Philistines, and out of the land of Judah.

And David smote them from the twilight even unto the evening of the next day: and there escaped not a man of them, save four hundred young men, which rode upon camels, and fled.

And David recovered all that the Amalekites had carried away: and David rescued his two wives.

And there was nothing lacking to them, neither small nor great, neither sons nor daughters, neither spoil, nor any thing that they had taken to them: David recovered all. [1 Samuel, 30 : 1–19]

(For other cases reported in the Old Testament, see Deuteronomy 2 : 32–34 and 3 : 1–7, Joshua 6 : 20–21, and 2 Kings 15, 16.)

The following excerpt from an article by E. A. Speiser (33) gives an idea of the upheavals among the peoples of the ancient Near East. At the same time it illustrates the way in which such history can be written without paying attention to the actual fate of the people living at that time.

Mesopotamia was, of course, the proverbial Babel; Sumerians and Semites, plainsmen and mountaineers, waged unending wars for the possession of the fertile valley. This was the situation during the best part of the third millennium. But it is a different world that confronts us in the succeeding period. There had been centuries of comparative quiet about the turn of the millennium: the golden ages of Hammurabi and of the Twelfth Dynasty of Egypt. Hither Asia had acquired in the meantime a veneer of racial equilibrium, with the Semites holding the balance of power. And then the storm broke loose.

It is not within the compass of this essay, much less within the competence of the author, to trace the ensuing events to their possible ultimate causes. To locate the original force that was soon to start an avalanche sweeping everything before it; uprooting peoples here and depositing them far from their original seats; driving Indo-Europeans into Anatolia and Cassites to the heart of Babylonia, with a powerful wedge of Hurrians in between; a force that abated long enough to permit the feeble amenities of the Amarna age, only to blaze another trail of destruction in annihilating empires and sending wave upon wave of Peoples of the Sea against the shores of the Mediterranean; all this presents an awesome task which is today as fascinating as it is dangerous.

The evidence for genocide in antiquity is circumstantial, inferential, and ambiguous, and it comes to us exclusively from the perpetrators. We believe that genocide was a relatively common event, for the following reasons: (1) whole empires and peoples have disappeared, and it seems very unlikely that all of them could have disappeared in a short time solely through enslavement and/or assimilation; (2) the reports of extreme cruelty (judged by modern standards) and of extermination are common enough to suggest that such events were not considered to be extraordinary; (3) the religions of most societies in antiquity, as different as they were in other respects, commanded their adherents to exterminate certain groups of nonbelievers or enemies; and (4) since the nineteenth century a great many destroyed cities have been excavated without producing evidence of what happened to their populations; many of these sites are hills, or tels, representing a succession of cities built on the same site, each one built after the previous one had been destroyed. Hardly any of them seem to produce information about what happened to their population—which reinforces the thought that we really do need an archeology of genocide.

MELOS

In 478 B.C., Athens rallied the Greek city-states to liberate Greeks from Persian rule and to resist the expansion of the Persian empire. Athens quickly gained control of the Delian League, the alliance system coordinating the war against Persia. Overcoming almost insurmountable odds, the Athenians and their allies defeated the Persians. The Athenians exacted taxes from the league's members long after they had checked the Persian thrust. They built a large navy to enforce the collection of tribute from their former allies and to guard the maritime trade routes responsible for their prosperity. Revolts against Athenian control occurred frequently; in the second half of the fifth century B.C., Athens suppressed rebellions in several states, including Samos, Byzantium, and Mytilene.

In 416 B.C., while warring with Sparta and the Peloponnesian League, the Athenians demanded assistance from the people of Melos (also known as Milo). Melos is a mountainous island approximately fifty-eight square miles in area that lies southeast of the Greek mainland in the Aegean Sea. It had flourished as a center of early Aegean civilization because of its deposits of obsidian and its strategic location between the Greek mainland and Crete, but it lost its arms-making importance when bronze replaced obsidian as the material of choice for the manufacture of weapons.

Lacking a large standing army capable of garrisoning the islands dotting the Aegean and the Mediterranean, the Athenians deployed their navy in a campaign of terror and intimidation aimed at preserving and expanding their empire. When the Melians, who were descended from Spartan colonists, rejected Athens's demand for assistance in the Peloponnesian War, the Athenians laid siege, marking their victory by executing all the men of the island, enslaving the women and children, and dispatching Athenian citizens (known as cleruchs) to repopulate Melos. By this brutal act of annihilation, the Athenians hoped to terrorize into submission other peoples contemplating resistance or rebellion. According to some authorities, the Carthaginians (whom we discuss in the next chapter) suffered the same fate as the Melians.

It was Thucydides who firmly embedded the slaughter of the Melians in the memory of Western civilization by including their story in his history of the Peloponnesian War. Most modern commentators are in accord with the characterization of his Melian Debate as "severe in its detachment, written from a purely intellectual point of view, unencumbered with platitudes and moral judgements, cold and critical," and with the description of Thucydides himself as "a complete and ruthless realist" (Connor, 151, quoting J. B. Bury and Russell Meiggs). Yet, as W. Robert Connor points out, Thucydides implies his condemnation of the sentence imposed on the Melians in two important ways: first, in presenting a detailed and lengthy version of the negotiations between the Athenians and the Melians that contrasts sharply with the compression of every other part of book 5 of *The Peloponnesian War*, he gives special prominence to the obliteration of Melian society (Connor, 147); second, by taking pains to show the Athenian commanders advising the Melians to submit to the logic of raw power regardless of what was right, Thucydides reveals them as repudiating their own national identity as "the opponents of despotism and of the enslavement of the Greeks" (Connor, 157). As his contemporaries would have read the Melian Debate, it led inevitably to the conclusion that the Athenians had "cut themselves off from some of their sources of strength and come to resemble their ancient enemy, the Persians" (Connor, 157).

Thucydides was not the only Greek author to remind his audience that the Athenians had blotted out the Melians. Aristophanes, the greatest of the Greek comic dramatists, also drew attention to their end. In *The Birds*, a play he wrote for a war-weary Athenian audience in 416 B.C. (the year of the genocide), Aristophanes satirized Athens by visualizing it as a utopian city built in the air by birds. One of his characters, inspired by a proposal to give supreme power in the universe to birds, manifests the hubris of the Athenians: "As for the gods," he blithely declares in an early version of the play, "if they object or get in your way, you can wipe them out with a Melian famine" (Aristophanes, 22 and footnote).

We have selected the case of Melos because we have relatively good documentation on it. We have no reason to believe that it was unique in the annals of ancient Greece.

THE MELIAN DEBATE†

Next summer Alcibiades sailed to Argos with twenty ships and seized 300 Argive citizens who were still suspected of being pro-Spartan. These were put by the Athenians into the nearby islands under Athenian control.

†From Thucydides, *The Peloponnesian War*, trans. Rex Warner (Harmondsworth, Middlesex: Penguin Books, 1954), 358–66. Reprinted by permission.

The Athenians also made an expedition against the island of Melos. They had thirty of their own ships, six from Chios, and two from Lesbos; 1,200 hoplites, 300 archers, and twenty mounted archers, all from Athens; and about 1,500 hoplites from the allies and the islanders.

The Melians are a colony from Sparta. They had refused to join the Athenian empire like the other islanders, and at first had remained neutral without helping either side; but afterwards, when the Athenians had brought force to bear on them by laying waste their land, they had become open enemies of Athens.

Now the generals Cleomedes, the son of Lycomedes, and Tisias, the son of Tisimachus, encamped with the above force in Melian territory and, before doing any harm to the land, first of all sent representatives to negotiate. The Melians did not invite these representatives to speak before the people, but asked them to make the statement for which they had come in front of the governing body and the few. The Athenian representatives then spoke as follows:

Athenians: So we are not to speak before the people, no doubt in case the mass of the people should hear once and for all and without interruption an argument from us which is both persuasive and incontrovertible, and should so be led astray. This, we realize, is your motive in bringing us here to speak before the few. Now suppose that you who sit here should make assurance doubly sure. Suppose that you, too, should refrain from dealing with every point in detail in a set speech, and should instead interrupt us whenever we say something controversial and deal with that before going on to the next point? Tell us first whether you approve of this suggestion of ours.

The Council of the Melians replied as follows:

Melians: No one can object to each of us putting forward our own views in a calm atmosphere. That is perfectly reasonable. What is scarcely consistent with such a proposal is the present threat, indeed the certainty, of your making war on us. We see that you have come prepared to judge the argument yourselves, and that the likely end of it all will be either war, if we prove that we are in the right, and so refuse to surrender, or else slavery.

Athenians: If you are going to spend the time in enumerating your suspicions about the future, or if you have met here for any other reason except to look the facts in the face and on the basis of these facts to consider how you can save your city from destruction, there is no point in our going on with this discussion. If, however, you will do as we suggest, then we will speak on.

Melians: It is natural and understandable that people who are placed as we are should have recourse to all kinds of arguments and different points of view. However, you are right in saying that we are met together here to discuss the safety of our country and, if you will have it so, the discussion shall proceed on the lines that you have laid down.

Athenians: Then we on our side will use no fine phrases saying, for example, that we have a right to our empire because we defeated the Persians, or that we have come against you now because of the injuries you have done us—a great mass of words that nobody would believe. And we ask you on your side not to imagine that you will influence us by saying that you, though a colony of Sparta, have not joined Sparta in the war, or that you have never done us any harm. Instead we recommend that you should try to get what it is possible for you to get, taking into consideration what we both really do think; since you know as well as we do that, when these matters are discussed by practical people, the standard of justice depends on the equality of power to compel and that in fact the strong do what they have the power to do and the weak accept what they have to accept.

Melians: Then in our view (since you force us to leave justice out of account and to confine ourselves to self-interest)—in our view it is at any rate useful that you should not destroy a principle that is to the general good of all men —namely, that in the case of all who fall into danger there should be such a thing as fair play and just dealing, and that such people should be allowed to use and to profit by arguments that fall short of a mathematical accuracy. And this is a principle which affects you as much as anybody, since your own fall would be visited by the most terrible vengeance and would be an example to the world.

Athenians: As for us, even assuming that our empire does come to an end, we are not despondent about what would happen next. One is not so much frightened of being conquered by a power which rules over others, as Sparta does (not that we are concerned with Sparta now), as of what would happen if a ruling power is attacked and defeated by its own subjects. So far as this point is concerned, you can leave it to us to face the risks involved. What we shall do now is to show you that it is for the good of our own empire that we are here and that it is for the preservation of your city that we shall say what we are going to say. We do not want any trouble in bringing you into our empire, and we want you to be spared for the good both of yourselves and of ourselves.

Melians: And how could it be just as good for us to be the slaves as for you to be the masters?

Athenians: You, by giving in, would save yourselves from disaster; we, by not destroying you, would be able to profit from you.

Melians: So you would not agree to our being neutral, friends instead of enemies, but allies of neither side?

Athenians: No, because it is not so much your hostility that injures us; it is rather the case that, if we were on friendly terms with you, our subjects would regard that as a sign of weakness in us, whereas your hatred is evidence of our power.

Melians: Is that your subjects' idea of fair play—that no distinction should be made between people who are quite unconnected with you and people who are mostly your own colonists or else rebels whom you have conquered?

Athenians: So far as right and wrong are concerned they think that there is no difference between the two, that those who still preserve their independence do so because they are strong, and that if we fail to attack them it is because we are afraid. So that by conquering you we shall increase not only the size but the security of our empire. We rule the sea and you are islanders, and weaker islanders too than the others; it is therefore particularly important that you should not escape.

Melians: But do you think there is no security for you in what we suggest? For here again, since you will not let us mention justice, but tell us to give in to your interests, we, too, must tell you what our interests are and, if yours and ours happen to coincide, we must try to persuade you of the fact. Is it not certain that you will make enemies of all states who are at present neutral, when they see what is happening here and naturally conclude that in course of time you will attack them too? Does not this mean that you are strengthening the enemies you have already and are forcing others to become your enemies even against their intentions and their inclinations?

Athenians: As a matter of fact we are not so much frightened of states on the continent. They have their liberty, and this means that it will be a long time before they begin to take precautions against us. We are more concerned about islanders like yourselves, who are still unsubdued, or subjects who have already become embittered by the constraint which our empire imposes on them. These are the people who are most likely to act in a reckless manner and to bring themselves and us, too, into the most obvious danger.

Melians: Then surely, if such hazards are taken by you to keep your empire and by your subjects to escape from it, we who are still free would show ourselves great cowards and weaklings if we failed to face everything that comes rather than submit to slavery.

Athenians: No, not if you are sensible. This is no fair fight, with honour on one side and shame on the other. It is a rather a question of saving your lives and not resisting those who are far too strong for you.

Melians: Yet we know that in war fortune sometimes makes the odds more level than could be expected from the difference in numbers of the two sides. And if we surrender, then all our hope is lost at once, whereas, so long as we remain in action, there is still a hope that we may yet stand upright.

Athenians: Hope, that comforter in danger! If one already has solid advantages to fall back upon, one can indulge in hope. It may do harm, but will not destroy one. But hope is by nature an expensive commodity, and those who are risking their all on one cast find out what it means only when they are already ruined; it never fails them in the period when such a knowledge would enable them to take precautions. Do not let this happen to you, you who are weak and whose fate depends on a single movement of the scale. And do not be like those people who, as so commonly happens, miss the chance of saving themselves in a human and practical way, and, when every clear and distinct hope has left them in their adversity, turn to what is blind and vague, to prophecies and oracles and such things which by encouraging hope lead men to ruin.

Melians: It is difficult, and you may be sure that we know it, for us to oppose your power and fortune, unless the terms be equal. Nevertheless we trust that the gods will give us fortune as good as yours, because we are standing for what is right against what is wrong; and as for what we lack in power, we trust that it will be made up for by our alliance with the Spartans, who are bound, if for no other reason, then for honour's sake, and because we are their kinsmen, to come to our help. Our confidence, therefore, is not so entirely irrational as you think.

Athenians: So far as the favour of the gods is concerned, we think we have as much right to that as you have. Our aims and actions are perfectly consistent with the beliefs men hold about the gods and with the principles which govern their own conduct. Our opinion of the gods and our knowledge of men lead us to conclude that it is a general and necessary law of nature to rule wherever one can. This is not a law that we made ourselves, nor were we the first to act upon it when it was made. We found it already in existence, and we shall leave it to exist for ever among those who come after us. We are merely acting in accordance with it, and we know that you or anybody else with the same power as ours would be acting in precisely the same way. And therefore, so far as the gods are concerned, we see no good reason why we should fear to be at a disadvantage. But with regard to your views about Sparta and your confidence that she, out of a sense of honour, will come to your aid, we must say that we congratulate you on your simplicity but do not envy you your folly. In matters that concern themselves or their own constitution the Spartans are quite remarkably good; as for their relations with others, that is a long story, but it can be expressed shortly and clearly by saying that of all people we know the Spartans are most conspicuous for believing that what they like doing is honourable and what suits their interests is just. And this kind of attitude is not going to be of much help to you in your absurd quest for safety at the moment.

Melians: But this is the very point where we can feel most sure. Their own self-interest will make them refuse to betray their own colonists, the Melians, for that would mean losing the confidence of their friends among the Hellenes and doing good to their enemies.

Athenians: You seem to forget that if one follows one's self-interest one wants to be safe, whereas the path of justice and honour involves one in danger. And, where danger is concerned, the Spartans are not, as a rule, very venturesome.

Melians: But we think that they would even endanger themselves for our sake and count the risk more worth taking than in the case of others, because we are so close to the Peloponnese that they could operate more easily, and because they can depend on us more than on others, since we are of the same race and share the same feelings.

Athenians: Goodwill shown by the party that is asking for help does not mean security for the prospective ally. What is looked for is a positive preponderance of power in action. And the Spartans pay attention to this point even more than others do. Certainly they distrust their own native resources so much that when they attack a neighbour they bring a great army of allies with them. It is hardly likely therefore that, while we are in control of the sea, they will cross over to an island.

Melians: But they still might send others. The Cretan sea is a wide one, and it is harder for those who control it to intercept others than for those who want to slip through to do so safely. And even if they were to fail in this, they would turn against your own land and against those of your allies left unvisited by Brasidas. So, instead of troubling about a country which has nothing to do with you, you will find trouble nearer home, among your allies, and in your own country.

Athenians: It is a possibility, something that has in fact happened before. It may happen in your case, but you are well aware that the Athenians have never yet relinquished a single siege operation through fear of others. But we are somewhat shocked to find that, though you announced your intention of discussing how you could preserve yourselves, in all this talk you have said absolutely nothing which could justify a man in thinking that he could be preserved. Your chief points are concerned with what you hope may happen in the future, while your actual resources are too scanty to give you a chance of survival against the forces that are opposed to you at this moment. You will therefore be showing an extraordinary lack of common sense if, after you have asked us to retire from this meeting, you still fail to reach a conclusion wiser than anything you have mentioned so far. Do not be led astray by a false sense of honour—a thing which often brings men to ruin when they are faced with an obvious danger that somehow affects their pride. For in many cases men have still been able to see the dangers ahead of them, but this thing called dishonour, this word, by its own force of seduction, has drawn them into a state where they have surrendered to an idea, while in fact they have fallen voluntarily into irrevocable disaster, in dishonour that is all the more dishonourable because it has come to them from their own folly rather than their misfortune. You, if you take the right view, will be careful to avoid this. You will see that there is nothing disgraceful in giving way to the greatest city in Hellas when she is offering you such reasonable terms—alliance on a tribute-paying basis and liberty to enjoy your own property. And, when you are allowed to choose between war and safety, you will not be so insensitively arrogant as to make the wrong choice. This is the safe rule—to stand up to one's equals, to behave with deference towards one's superiors, and to treat one's inferiors with moderation. Think it over again, then, when we have withdrawn from the meeting, and let this be a point that constantly recurs to your minds—that you are discussing the fate of your country, that you have only one country, and that its future for good or ill depends on this one single decision which you are going to make.

The Athenians then withdrew from the discussion. The Melians, left to themselves, reached a conclusion which was much the same as they had indicated in their previous replies. Their answer was as follows:

Melians: Our decision, Athenians, is just the same as it was at first. We are not prepared to give up in a short moment the liberty which our city has enjoyed from its foundation for 700 years. We put our trust in the fortune that the gods will send and which has saved us up to now, and in the help of men—that is, of the Spartans; and so we shall try to save ourselves. But we invite you to allow us to be friends of yours and enemies to neither side, to make a treaty which shall be agreeable to both you and us, and so to leave our country.

The Melians made this reply, and the Athenians, just as they were breaking off the discussion, said:

Athenians: Well, at any rate, judging from this decision of yours, you seem to us quite unique in your ability to consider the future as something more certain than what is before your eyes, and to see uncertainties as realities, simply because you would like them to be so. As you have staked most on and trusted most in Spartans, luck, and hopes, so in all these you will find yourselves most completely deluded.

The Athenian representatives then went back to the army, and the Athenian generals, finding that the Melians would not submit, immediately commenced hostilities and built a wall completely round the city of Melos, dividing the work out among the various states. Later they left behind a garrison of some of their own and some allied troops to blockade the place by land and sea, and with the greater part of their army returned home. The force left behind stayed on and continued with the siege.

About the same time the Argives invaded Phliasia and were ambushed by the Phliasians and the exiles from Argos, losing about eighty men.

Then, too, the Athenians at Pylos captured a great quantity of plunder from

Spartan territory. Not even after this did the Spartans renounce the treaty and make war, but they issued a proclamation saying that any of their people who wished to do so were free to make raids on the Athenians. The Corinthians also made some attacks on the Athenians because of private quarrels of their own, but the rest of the Peloponnesians stayed quiet.

Meanwhile the Melians made a night attack and captured the part of the Athenian lines opposite the market-place. They killed some of the troops, and then, after bringing in corn and everything else useful that they could lay their hands on, retired again and made no further move, while the Athenians took measures to make their blockade more efficient in future. So the summer came to an end.

In the following winter the Spartans planned to invade the territory of Argos, but when the sacrifices for crossing the frontier turned out unfavourably, they gave up the expedition. The fact that they had intended to invade made the Argives suspect certain people in their city, some of whom they arrested, though others succeeded in escaping.

About this same time the Melians again captured another part of the Athenian lines where there were only a few of the garrison on guard. As a result of this, another force came out afterwards from Athens under the command of Philocrates, the son of Demeas. Siege operations were now carried on vigorously and, as there was also some treachery from inside, the Melians surrendered unconditionally to the Athenians, who put to death all the men of military age whom they took, and sold the women and children as slaves. Melos itself they took over for themselves, sending out later a colony of 500 men.

CARTHAGE

In 150 B.C., the Roman Senate decided to go to war with the North African city-state of Carthage. A year later, Roman troops laid siege to the city, setting the stage for one of the bloodiest episodes in ancient history. After three years of siege, famine, and disease, Carthage fell, and the Romans burned and leveled the city. Carthaginians from other colonies were never again allowed to settle in the city. These are the facts that historians agree upon. Very little is known about the fate of those Carthaginians who survived the fall of the city. Indeed, Carthage is one of the last cases, so typical of antiquity, of a city being razed without providing a clue as to the fate of the inhabitants. What we do know is a result of evidence coming to us only from the perpetrators. The victims' side of the story is simply not known.

Rome and Carthage had fought each other in two previous Punic Wars (264–241 B.C. and 218–201 B.C.). Each time the cost to Rome in men, money, and materiel had been enormous. Hannibal, the audacious Carthaginian general who marched his army from Spain almost to the walls of Rome, nearly made good his boast to dine in the Capitol, but the Romans finally drove him back. The Roman victory at the conclusion of the Second Punic War was complete. Carthage accepted terms of peace that crippled its military power and drained its economy. Under these circumstances, few analysts in the ancient world would have predicted another Roman attack on Carthage. It was not until 150 B.C. that a crisis developed between the two former enemies. When the Carthaginians ignored a Roman order to turn the other cheek to attacks from Numidia, the Senate decreed that they must abandon their coastal homeland and move at least ten miles' distance from the sea. Rejecting the Roman ultimatum, the Carthaginians rearmed and mounted a vigorous defense of their territory, but they were vanquished thanks to the doggedness and brilliance of the Roman commander, Scipio Aemilianus.

The total destruction of Carthage by the Romans in 146 B.C. was an act so extreme that it shocked even the most hardened commentators and historians in the ancient world. When we began our search for early genocides, Carthage headed our list of probable examples. Further research has demonstrated to us the difficulties of making an unqualified assertion of genocide for a very large number of cases of which Carthage is representative. The problems we encountered in our research on Carthage exemplify the complexity of evaluating ancient sources, discovering what happened, and sorting out the motives of the perpetrators.

Genocides like the Holocaust, in which the perpetrators meticulously recorded their acts in documents that were captured and made available to researchers, are extremely rare. Much more typical of the problems faced by researchers is the incomplete and ambiguous historical record on the fate of the Carthaginians. To begin with, Roman accounts of the struggle have been lost or preserved only in fragmentary form. Polybius—the Greek historian of Roman politics who was probably an eyewitness to the burning of Carthage—claimed that the Roman Senate seized the first plausible excuse it could find to declare war, but he only hinted at the Romans' motives for destroying the city. Most of the manuscript containing his account of the Senate's decision for war has disappeared, and no other authoritative report on the Senate's debates has survived. What little we do know about the Senate's deliberations comes to us from the work of other writers who summarized the missing sections of Polybius's histories before they vanished.

Translating the few surviving ancient Greek sources into modern languages without distorting the sense of the original narratives poses another problem for researchers on genocide. One reputable modern translation of Polybius has the Achaean exile declaring that the Carthaginians were "utterly exterminated by the calamity which overtook them" (*Polybius*, vol. VI, fragments of book 38, I). However, on closer examination the Greek passive verb on which "extermination" rests is actually a term first used in Greek tragedies, where it meant "to disappear, to make something dark, to extinguish the life-light, or to put in the shadows," expressions with a resonance different from "exterminate," at least to our post-Holocaust sensibilities.

A long list of scholars has argued that the Romans set out to destroy Carthage and the Carthaginians. In 1927, Michael Rostovtzeff wrote in his masterful history of the ancient world, "the Romans, without any provocation, challenged Carthage again to war, ruthlessly and needlessly destroyed that flourishing city, and put to death most of the population" (Rostovtzeff, 76). Following in his footsteps, Raphael Lemkin listed Carthage as the first of his "classical examples of wars of extermination." Today, we are less certain that the Carthaginians were the victims of a genocide. Our definition of genocide would be satisfied if the Romans had deliberately killed the survivors of the siege after their conquest of the city. A careful reading of the original sources in translation indicates that the enormous number of deaths among the inhabitants of Carthage was probably a consequence of the famine and epidemics attributable to the siege. (In the selection that follows, B. H. Warmington suggests that 150,000 Carthaginians died out of a total population of 200,000.) We have narratives indicating that the Romans enslaved survivors of the siege, but none of the classical authors claim that the Romans killed survivors in cold blood or that the annihilation of the inhabitants of Carthage was one of Rome's motives for going to war. It is also worth noting that specialists like Warmington, who draw their evidence from the original sources, can make only an educated guess at the prewar population of Carthage and that estimates of the number of survivors are even more problematic. All we really know is that, after the Roman siege, old Carthage and its original inhabitants disappeared from history. Even the tale once known to every schoolchild of the Romans sowing the ruins of Carthage with salt has been challenged by R. T. Ridley as a myth (Ridley, 144).

The ambiguity of the evidence about Rome's treatment of the Carthaginians stimulated us to investigate the customary treatment that the Romans meted out to their vanquished enemies. Scattered among the primary sources, we found many fragmentary descriptions of Roman behavior toward the civilians who lived in conquered cities. Although Roman commentators were generally at pains to demonstrate the sense of fair play and evenhandedness of their soldiers when a city fell, the variety of examples presented in the sources is almost overwhelming; the cases range all the way from instances of extreme generosity to the outright slaughter of survivors. On closer examination, a pattern emerges from the chaos inherent in such fragmentary accounts of empire building over an enormous area and a long period of time. In general, the inhabitants of captured cities expected to be raped, pillaged, or murdered by the Romans and quite often Roman actions justified these fears. The determining factor in Roman policy was Rome's plan for the exploitation of the survivors and their territory. The Romans generally behaved pragmatically. If they wanted to create a client-state, they treated survivors generously; if they could not find a way to make use of their vanquished foes where they lived, they robbed, enslaved, or killed them. In the ancient world, killing all the men was often a measure aimed at destroying the military potential of a rival. It seems highly unlikely that the Romans simply released the men who survived the siege of Carthage.

Thus, we found that if we wanted to identify Rome's intentions toward the Carthaginians in order to better assess how the Romans might have treated survivors of the final battle for Carthage, we also had to investigate Rome's motives for launching the Third Punic War. Here, too, we encountered difficulties. Although most historians assert that the Romans intended to destroy the city of Carthage from the outset of the crisis leading up to war, they vigorously disagree with each other about Rome's motives. The huge gap in the evidence and the ambiguity of the evidence that has survived encourages widely differing interpretations based, in part, on the emphasizing of different actors. The major interpretations of the historians can be classified under four headings:

1. *Economic gain.* Michael Rostovtzeff has argued that the Roman Senate struck for economic reasons, guided by the desire of wealthy Roman landowners to eliminate competing Carthaginian exports of wine and olive oil and by the chance to rob the Carthaginians of their estates.

2. *Elimination of a rival based on irrational fears.* F. E. Adcock and many other modern authors dismiss economic motives, contending that the Senate showed little inclination toward overseas exploitation and that Roman landowners did not build estates on Carthaginian land until many years after the Roman victory. Adcock attributes the Roman decision to the "advent of a phase of that irrational impatience that historians have, if reluctantly, to recognize as a factor in historical causation" (Adcock, 128). In his view, the decision to destroy Carthage marks the unleashing of a "drastic merciless mood of terrorization" in Rome (ibid., 127), which arose as the Romans became more and more fearful about the security of their empire.

A. N. Sherwin-White argues that Rome's "neurosis of fear," as he calls it, was rooted in the real difficulties that emerged when the demands of a culturally heterogeneous and swollen empire began to outstrip Rome's ability to enlist reliable soldiers and maintain a favorable balance of strength against its rivals. Under these conditions, he finds it understandable that the Romans would launch preemptive attacks against irreconcilable enemies as compensation for their insufficient power. Sherwin-White attributes Rome's decision to its fear of a revival of Punic power stimulated by the evidence of Carthaginian prosperity (Sherwin-White, 181).

Adcock and Sherwin-White believe that Rome destroyed Carthage to eliminate a rival and to instill terror in others. They find evidence for their interpretation of Roman motivation in the natural law of empires outlined by Diodorus of Sicily, who said of the Romans, "Those whose object is to gain dominion over others use courage and intelligence to get it, moderation and consideration for others to extend it widely, and paralysing terror to secure it" (Diodorus, 32.2). Modern historians suspect that Diodorus borrowed this maxim from the lost portions of Polybius's history of the Third Punic War.

3. *Elimination of a rival based on rational fears.* Alan Astin rejects the notion that Roman fears of Carthage were entirely baseless. He combines evidence of Carthaginian prosperity and rearmament, self-assertive Cartha-

ginian leadership, and the ease with which Carthage might have gained control of Numidia to make the case that, under the circumstances, the Romans' fears of a Carthaginian revival were justified.

4. *Opportunity for military success, enabling the aristocracy to achieve the higher status and glory required for access to political office and greater wealth.* William Harris rejects Astin's portrait of Carthage as a renascent threat to Roman security and counters with evidence that the Romans set out to push an already-weakened Carthage into war by encouraging Numidia's attacks. He contends that Roman policy rested in the hands of the aristocracy, which needed periodic wars against prestigious foes to earn the status and glory that were prerequisites for political office and access to greater wealth in Roman society. According to Harris, Carthage was the victim of the Roman aristocracy's hunger for power, glory, and booty.

All of the authors included in this review, except for Adcock, believe that the Romans intended to destroy the city of Carthage from the moment they ordered the Carthaginians inland. Adcock raises the possibility that the Romans acted impulsively when they drafted their ultimatum and never expected the Carthaginians to fight back.

What light, if any, do these interpretations shed on Rome's plans for the vanquished Carthaginians? Their one valuable contribution is to highlight the Romans' determination to break the Carthaginians' commercial and military power by forcing them from their strategically valuable location and barring them forever from returning to the coast. Historians have little to say about Roman plans for the Carthaginians once they were conquered. While we attribute part of this omission to the silence of the original sources and other difficulties beyond their control, we are equally struck by the silence of historians generally about the fate of millions of other people who, like the inhabitants of Carthage, vanished from history.

THE CITY OF CARTHAGE†

The population of ancient city-states is very difficult to determine, because of a lack of figures and the different ways of making an estimate. We are told by Strabo that the total population of the city alone (apparently excluding Megara) was 700,000, which is an impossible density. A safer figure

†From B. H. Warmington, *Carthage* (London: Robert Hale Ltd., 1980), 124–27, 196, 199–209. Reprinted by permission.

to work back from is the 50,000 who were the survivors of the three years' siege of 149–146. During this war the walls were defended by 30,000 men and there was another force in the country for a while. This would indicate a total population of some 200,000, including slaves who were freed in the crisis. But it must have been much larger than this at the height of Carthaginian power in the early third century, and it would be surprising if it did not approach 400,000, including slaves and resident aliens, which was the population of Athens in the late fifth century. Strabo's figure may be correct for the population including the Cap Bon peninsula and the area in the immediate vicinity of the city, all of which had a status different from that of the interior whose inhabitants were subject to Carthage. It is unlikely that there were more than 100,000 people of more or less pure Phoenician descent in Africa outside the capital; with such a limited manpower did Carthage face the might of Rome.

Carthage was the city in the Mediterranean in which commerce played the largest part; when a Greek or Roman of Hellenistic times thought of a typical Carthaginian he thought of him as a merchant. It was agreed that it was through her commerce that Carthage had become rich, even the richest city in the world, as some believed. Yet this commerce has left very little traces to be discovered by the archaeologist, and we know that Carthage did not issue coins till the beginning of the third century; indeed if we relied on archaeological evidence alone we would deduce that commercial activity at Carthage played a smaller part than in a number of other Mediterranean cities. This is an illustration of the fact that deductions about trade and commerce from archaeological discoveries must be made with caution. It is obvious that it is primarily artifacts which survive, and that the perishable materials which comprised such a large proportion of ancient trade have left no trace; foodstuffs of all sorts, metal in unworked state, textiles, skins—and slaves. The problem of Carthaginian trade is that much of it was obviously in such goods; her imports and exports of manufactured articles accounted for only a small part of the whole.

It cannot be doubted that till the third century the trade from which Carthage drew the most profit was that with backward tribes, from whom the precious metals, gold, silver, tin, and probably iron (since Carthage manufactured her own weapons) were acquired in exchange for articles of small value. Seeing how little Carthaginian material has been found in the most accessible area of such trade it must be assumed that the most popular exports of Carthage to their tribes were perishables like wine or luxurious robes, both of which are known as articles of Carthaginian trade from literary sources. Much of her trade was in carriage, articles being imported for re-export, and some of the metal acquired was among this.

What part the state played is not known exactly. The report of Hanno shows its participation in a venture which was designed to get control of the West

African gold trade, and some proportion of the imports of gold and silver must have been taken by the Carthaginian treasury which needed vast sums immediately available in order to raise mercenary armies should these be necessary. Carthaginian monopoly of the western Mediterranean not only secured these metals but was a source of profit to her merchants in another way; the products of Greece, Egypt, and Campania, which are found on North African sites and in Sardinia and Spain, must have come in Carthaginian ships.

It was for this reason that while Carthage insisted on preserving her monopoly in the west, foreign traders were allowed to come to Carthage and trade there on the same basis as the Carthaginian citizens themselves; the goods they brought in would be re-exported by Carthaginian merchants. We know that Carthage took stern measures against piracy in the areas over which she had control; her own practice of sinking any foreign ships found in these areas seems to come close to piracy, but the treaties with Rome, discussed more fully later, show that she was able to exact recognition of her claim to a monopoly from other states.

Mention has been made of a period in the fifth century during which the import of foreign goods into Carthage was seriously restricted, and this applies equally to the Phoenician west. Before this date the most obvious import from the Greek world was pottery from Corinth, which probably came by way of Syracuse. At the same time we find numbers of Etruscan bucchero vases in Africa and Sardinia which reflect the commerce with Etruria known from literary sources. These long-lasting remains are only a small trace of a much larger commerce; Selinus grew wealthy from trade with Carthage but in what this consisted is not known. Perhaps foodstuffs played a part, as Carthage must have imported a great deal before her conquest of territory in Africa. No doubt cereals and meat could be obtained from the native peoples but wine and olive oil must have come from outside. In the fifth century itself these products were imported from Acragas. Carthaginian merchants did not cease to frequent the Greek ports and we hear of a number of them established at Syracuse in 398. Continued traffic with Tyre is attested in literary sources, and with Egypt in discoveries in Africa; the objects imported from the latter were mostly of small value, as indeed were the majority of Carthaginian imports; there are none of the finest products of Greece such as were sought after by the Etruscans and which even found their way into central France.

The Carthaginians naturally had industries of their own, some of whose products were exported. There must have been a considerable force of metal workers, in view of the extraordinary production of hundreds of sets of arms per day in the last struggle of Carthage against Rome, but it is difficult to trace their activity in other ways. Few objects of metal which are certainly Carthaginian have been found in Europe and it is probable that much of the exports went to the Libyan and Numidian tribes. The export of these and other products of Carthaginian industry became much commoner in the fourth century, and particularly after the conquests of Alexander. This conquest, and the establishment of the Hellenistic kingdoms, brought about an economic revolution in the eastern Mediterranean and there was a new market for all sorts of cheap manufactured goods which the Carthaginians were well equipped to exploit. They shared with the Phoenicians themselves a lack of artistic talent, at least when compared with the Greeks, and their products lacked individuality, but their mixture of various styles was very suitable for trade in the cosmopolitan cities of the Hellenistic world.

It is not surprising that it was during this period that the Carthaginian merchant became a familiar figure in the east; inscriptions recall their presence at Athens and Delos, two of the greatest markets in the Aegean; but better evidence of their widespread activity is to be found in the fact that there were Greek comedies in which the central character was a Carthaginian trader. These are lost, but the Latin author Plautus wrote a play *Poenulus* based on one of these Greek originals. The scene is in Aetolia and the "hero" is Hanno, a pious trader of small goods searching for his daughter who had been kidnapped from Carthage. In spite of the fact that the play was produced shortly after the Hannibalic war, the Carthaginian is a figure of fun and is not presented as an object of hatred. The articles in his cargo included shoe straps, pipes, nuts and panthers, a list designed to raise a laugh from the fact that a Carthaginian could be expected to trade in anything. Apart from this, we hear of articles made of ivory and textiles for which the Carthaginians had a wide reputation.

But such trade would not account for the wealth of Carthage, and there can be little doubt that from the latter part of the fourth century onwards she exported substantial quantities of corn and other foodstuffs, the import of which into the eastern Mediterranean became increasingly necessary as urbanization increased. A surplus for export is attested for Carthage in the last fifty years of her existence and was undoubtedly available before. Another significant event was the creation of the Hellenistic empire of Egypt under the Ptolemaic dynasty; this included Cyrenaica, Cyprus, and for a while Phoenicia; it adopted the Phoenician standard for its coinage, instead of the Attic which had been general before. This made Carthaginian trade with the area easier, as it was at the same date that Carthage began to issue her own coins on the Phoenician standard. It was in any case impossible to carry on trade with the Greek world without coinage. Imports from the Greek world became common again during these centuries, and to them were added the products of Campania—pottery vessels of all sorts, lamps, terra-cottas and bronzes.

The vigour of Carthaginian commerce is finally attested in the last fifty years
of her existence when, deprived of her sources of metals and her monopoly in
the west, she was nevertheless able to preserve a measure of prosperity while
paying a heavy yearly indemnity to Rome. There can be no doubt that the export
of foodstuffs was more important than ever in this concluding period.

.   .   .   .   .

The Destruction of Carthage

The last fifty years of the existence of Carthage show both
good and bad points in her civilization; the energy, courage and patriotism of
the citizens in times of crisis, and the selfishness and greed of particular sections of the aristocracy.

Two problems in particular faced the city as the effort was made to repair the
damage caused by the war in Africa and the loss of overseas possessions, the
prompt payment of the yearly instalments of the indemnity and the preservation
of Carthaginian territory from the depredations of Masinissa. We know a certain
amount concerning the first of these problems because of its connexion with the
later years of Hannibal. He had remained in command of the remnants of the
army for a few months after the conclusion of peace, but in 200 retired to
private life. The eclipse of his influence was accompanied by an increase in the
corrupt practices of the aristocratic government, which even extended to trying
to pay one of the instalments to Rome in debased silver; it sought to place the
burden of the extra tax which was said to be needed on to the shoulders of the
rest of the community, while much of the state's revenue was appropriated by its
members and their political supporters.

.   .   .   .   .

By their appeal to Rome when attacked by Hannibal the Carthaginian aristocracy had regained power, but it is possible that Hannibal's revelation of the true
state of the finances made it impossible to return entirely to the old ways of
corruption; we find that in 191 Carthage could offer to pay all the remaining
instalments, undoubtedly a vast sum, and make voluntary contributions of corn
on several occasions. Rome refused the repayment in order to maintain in the
Carthaginians a sense of dependence.

But if a measure of financial prosperity returned with a speed which testified
to vigorous trade, probably in foodstuffs, as well as proper administration, it
was not so easy to prevent the gradual erosion of Carthaginian territory by
Masinissa. This prince was 37 years of age at the end of the war with Hannibal
and had a remarkably vigorous constitution. When he died he was survived by

ten out of forty-four sons which had been born to him, the last at the age of eighty-six. In addition he was a man of enormous ambition and diplomatic address, and was no stranger to civilized life as he had spent much of his youth in Carthage. His aim, by no means an unworthy one, was to change the Numidians from a collection of restless and nomadic tribes to a united nation in which an increasing number of the inhabitants lived a settled agricultural life. He fully realized that this meant the introduction of Carthaginian civilization on a large scale, and this was one of the reasons why he continually pressed on their territory; it was largely through his agency that a mixed Numidian and Carthaginian culture became dominant in North Africa until the period of large scale Italian immigration.

By 201 his kingdom already stretched from the Carthaginian boundary to the river Siga, and at the height of his power he envisaged a state stretching from the Atlantic to Egypt with Carthage as its capital. His progress was limited only by his estimate of how far the Romans would let him go; he had the patronage of the Scipionic family and had played a major part in the victory in Africa, nor would it be expected that Rome would be reluctant to see her old enemy weakened still further. But Masinissa was far too intelligent to believe that Rome would always remember him with gratitude, and his long success shows that he had grasped the essential role of a client king in the Roman system; it was to show unconditional obedience to Roman orders, and if possible to anticipate them. If this was done Rome would permit considerable freedom of action.

The Carthaginians, hamstrung by the vindictive clause of the peace of 201 which prohibited them from fighting even a defensive war without Roman permission, could only defend their territory when parts were claimed by Masinissa by appeal to Rome and by outdoing the Numidian in deference and obedience. For this policy, the aristocracy who had called in Rome to get rid of Hannibal was obviously suited, and if it had been successful in obtaining Roman protection would have to some extent justified itself. But Rome, though glad to have a government of such a complexion at Carthage, did not thereby lessen her determination to keep her as weak as possible.

We are not well informed of the precise chronology of Masinissa's encroachments but the information we have shows well enough the attitude adopted by the Romans. In 193 he seized some territory, taking advantage of the fact that Rome's suspicions of Carthage would be aroused by the presence in the city of Hannibal's agent Aristo, and a commission headed by Scipio himself, who of all people could have determined whether Masinissa's claim was justified, either decided in his favour or made no decision at all, which in effect left the territory in his hands. A similar action was taken over another piece of territory in 182.

A more serious attempt was made to damage Carthage in the next decade, though unfortunately the full story is not known owing to gaps in Livy's
narrative. It seems, however, that a Roman commission of inquiry found proved
allegations by Masinissa that the Carthaginian senate had secretly received
envoys from Perseus, king of Macedon, and declared that their denial of an
embassy to Macedon was unconvincing. A war between Perseus and the Romans
seemed at this date to be inevitable, and it is obviously not impossible that he
had sent envoys to see if Carthage might in some way be brought into the
conflict, but the improbability that the Carthaginian senate had anything to do
with such a proposal is heightened by the fact that Rome seems to have taken no
action.

Two years later when Carthage claimed that Masinissa had taken another 70
towns and forts (where is not known), the Romans' answer was slightly more
favourable to her, no doubt because war with Perseus was now in progress and
trouble in Africa had to be avoided. In 171 when Masinissa sent his son to
Rome to defend the action he alleged that Carthage was preparing a fleet ostensibly to help Rome but in fact to help Perseus; this unlikely charge will hardly
have moved the senate. Most serious of all the losses of Carthage was that of the
Emporia, the wealthy district round the Gulf of Gabes, in 161, which Rome
confirmed to Masinissa when appealed to. As a result of this acquisition,
Masinissa's territory now stretched from the river Siga to the borders of Cyrenaica, while Carthage was confined to the north-east of Tunisia; all the settlements
on the North African shore west of Thabarka had certainly been lost by this
date.

After about 160, feeling at Carthage began to grow increasingly bitter about
the circumstances in which the city was placed. In the years immediately preceding the final conflict with Rome, there were three opposing views as to the
policy that ought to be adopted. There was the view of those who had been
prominent since the end of the Hannibalic war, and who still advocated continued deference to Rome in the hope that sooner or later Masinissa would overstep
the mark. It was doubtless owing to the continued support given to the king by
Rome that this policy had been discredited and the governing class had split.
There was a party which our source calls "democratic", which was no doubt
following the policies of the Barcids in obtaining support amongst the mass of
the citizens, though the leaders themselves were men of substance. This party
had nothing particularly constructive to offer but gained in popularity as it was
loudest in denouncing Rome and Masinissa. A third party advocated reaching
an understanding with Masinissa; this was a sensible point of view, because
while any solution of this sort would doubtless mean effective subordination to
the Numidian, it would be materially profitable because of his known attitude

towards the advance of civilization in his kingdom, and could hardly be less dignified than the existing position. It could even be hoped that Numidian and Carthaginian together could defend themselves against the ever growing power of Rome. But the third party failed to win much support because its policy meant the end of a history of five hundred years of independent existence and a cowardly submission to people who had once been subjects; it was the democratic party, which advocated the understandable but dangerous policy of resistance to Masinissa's encroachments, which became dominant.

Between about 160 and 155 one of its leaders named Carthalo made a raid into territory which had been usurped, and there followed several years of minor raids by both sides until the Romans decided as usual in favour of the king. The latter then went on to occupy the Great Plains (around Souk el Kremis) and the territory of Thugga. A Roman commission headed by one of the oldest and most distinguished politicians, M. Porcius Cato, came to Africa in response to a Carthaginian appeal. It insisted that both sides agree to its decision in advance; Masinissa naturally assented but Carthage, remembering the succession of unfavourable decisions by Rome, refused and the commission returned to Rome leaving the dispute unsettled.

Yet this incident had momentous consequences, for the trivial show of independence which Carthage had at last made aroused the strongest emotions in the eighty-one-year-old Cato. He had served in the Hannibalic war and the memory of those fearful years and the hatred of Carthage which they had evoked returned. He set himself to the task of persuading the Roman senate of the danger of a reviving Carthage and the proximity, not the distance, of Africa, which he is said to have illustrated by showing the senators a fig, still fresh, which had been picked in Africa only three days before. He ended all his speeches in the senate, on whatever subject, with the famous words *"ceterum censeo Carthaginem esse delendam"* — "for the rest, it is my opinion that Carthage must be destroyed".

He was opposed by P. Scipio Nasica, who had married a daughter of the great Africanus to whom he was closely related, and a compromise was reached whereby another commission headed by Nasica went to Africa in 152 or 151. Masinissa was forced to yield some of the territory he had seized while the Carthaginian senate also was criticized for building up its armed forces, though hardly its fleet which would have been too obvious a breach of treaty. But the damage was done; Cato worked up sufficient support to bring about drastic action against Carthage if a reasonable excuse should present itself, though it is too much to say as one tradition had it that a secret resolution of the senate to go to war was taken as early as 153, pending a proper *casus belli*; if this had been so there would have been no need for Cato's campaign.

The real motives behind the ultimate support of Cato's policy are hardly so difficult to disentangle as those of the first and second Punic Wars. There is no real evidence of an economic motive; Italian exports to Carthage had been considerable in the last decades, while there is no sign that Carthaginian goods competed with Italian to any degree in other markets; and it was some time before there was any exploitation of the fertile lands of Africa available after the conquest, so it does not seem that greed for land on the part of some senators was a leading motive.

It has been argued that Carthage was destroyed to prevent her falling willingly or unwillingly into the hands of Masinissa now grown too powerful for Rome, but the consistency of our sources in asserting Rome's continued support for Masinissa cannot be overlooked, and there were other ways of achieving such a result. The fact is, as one Roman author saw, that the Romans were willing to believe anything that was said against the Carthaginians, and it is significant that Scipio Nasica agreed with Cato about the strength of Carthage. His argument for not proceeding against her was that Rome would only retain her inner strength, her virile way of life, so long as a potential enemy was in existence, particularly as there were already ominous signs of a degeneration in Roman society. This remarkable viewpoint was not confined to Scipio and was indeed already a commonplace in his day. It seems at this distance incredible that an experienced Roman senator could possibly have considered Carthage to be a possible threat to Rome. It is true that in 151 the final instalment of the indemnity from Carthage would be paid, and Carthage thus freed from a severe burden, that vast quantities of arms were surrendered in 149, and that in spite of this sufficient new arms could be manufactured with great speed and resistance kept up for three years; but Carthage herself knew that she could not resist Rome and the last struggle was a mass suicide.

The fact is that Rome was entering a period when ruthlessness was increasingly used not so much from policy so as to secure her supremacy, as from lack of any policy at all; it was a substitute for the thought and consistency required when dealing with the complicated pattern of states of different races, cultures, and institutions—far more than at present inhabit the Mediterranean coasts—when they refused to recognize the plain fact of Rome's dominance and insisted with intransigence on the old traditions of independence; the destruction of a city was a thing understood everywhere.

The breach of the peace treaty of 201 which gave the legal justification so much desired by the Romans before they went to war came in 151–150. The leaders of the pro-Numidian party in Carthage were exiled at the instigation of the popular party which was now in a dominant position. They went to Masinissa who sent two of his sons to demand their recall. Carthalo prevented their entry into the city and another leader of the popular party, Hamilcar, attacked them on their way home. The Numidian then laid siege to a town called Oroscopa and a Carthaginian army of 25,000 was sent against him under a commander named Hasdrubal. Masinissa was forced by desertions to retreat. It happened that an adopted member of the Scipionic family, Scipio Aemilianus, was in Africa at the time, and the Carthaginians sent to him and offered to surrender all claim to the Emporia, into which they had followed Masinissa, but they refused to hand over the deserters who included two sons of Masinissa. The retention of these would be a good diplomatic card in their hand in view of the advanced age of Masinissa and the likelihood of a break-up of his empire on his death through dynastic quarrels. The struggle continued and Masinissa was able to surround the Carthaginian camp; an epidemic broke out accompanied by increasing shortage of food and in the end the Carthaginians were forced to surrender. A promise was made to pay an indemnity, but the survivors were attacked as they left the camp.

Even before the defeat of the Carthaginian force Rome had begun to raise troops in Italy. It was not said what these were for, but the Carthaginians were not deceived. After the disaster they had suffered they were in the weakest possible position from which to negotiate but they did their best. Those responsible for the war against Masinissa were sentenced to death, though Hasdrubal escaped and raised a force of 20,000 men in the country districts. Envoys to Rome asking how they could obtain pardon received obscure but threatening replies and the preparations for war continued. During this period Utica deserted the Carthaginian cause and surrendered to Rome, following which there seemed no other alternative for Carthage but to give up hope of getting off with a further indemnity or surrender of territory, and to make a formal surrender. Five envoys were sent to Rome with this offer only to be told that war had been declared and that the fleet and army were on their way. However, the surrender was accepted and the Carthaginians were told they would be allowed to retain their freedom, the enjoyment of their own laws, and the possession of their territory and public and private property. On the other hand the Carthaginians were to send as hostages 300 children of members of the senate and obey any further commands of the consuls.

The hostages were handed over and the consuls crossed to Utica with their army. There they demanded that the Carthaginians surrender all the arms that were in the city. This too was agreed to and no fewer than 200,000 sets of arms and 2,000 catapults were handed over. When this had been done the consuls demanded the presence of another embassy to receive their final instructions; these were that the Carthaginians were to leave their city, which the Romans were determined to destroy; they could settle anywhere they liked so long as it was at least ten miles from the sea.

So the final intentions of the Romans were revealed, and the stages of the revelation over the preceding months show a ruthless cunning which would have fitted better with the Roman view of Carthaginian morality. Carthage had been kept in suspense about her fate until she was disarmed so that the chance of resistance was minimized. Popular opinion in Italy gave her very little chance even before this demand (which had naturally been kept secret); 80,000 had quickly volunteered for the campaign which offered easy prospects, though only a few years before it had been found very difficult to raise men to go to fight the warlike Celtiberians in Spain. It should be noted that none of their demands went beyond strict legality as the Romans understood it; the surrender made by Carthage had the same effect as unconditional surrender in modern usage. Assurances were sometimes given before a surrender was made and though this had not been done in the case of Carthage there was a presumption that the city would not be sacked nor the people enslaved. It was the Carthaginians' refusal of the order to leave their city which brought about the final sack and enslavement; the order to leave was not verbally inconsistent with the assurances given after the surrender which had not mentioned the fate of the city itself, since the people could still exist somewhere else.

This was not the view of the Carthaginians. Quite apart from the destruction of their homes and sacred places which were dear enough to them, vast numbers were in effect condemned to death by starvation when they were cut off from the sea or had their workshops destroyed; in any case, once separated from their defences they would fall directly into the hands of Masinissa.

A final appeal was made by one of the envoys but rejected; some, knowing the fierce and stubborn attitude of their fellow citizens when driven too far, took to flight or stayed with the consuls. The rest returned to the city and passed through the waiting crowds to the senate house with expressions which gave away the disastrous nature of their message. When cries of dismay were heard from the senate house, it was invaded by the people, who on learning of the Romans' order stoned to death the unfortunate envoys and others who had advised submission to Rome, and massacred any Italians who could be found. The whole city was gripped with a sense of despairing anger and hatred towards the Romans; if any paused to consider that resistance was bound to be in vain, it must have seemed that to be killed in defence of the city against a vindictive enemy was better than to starve to death in ignominious exile. Since all their arms had been handed over, the temples and public places were turned into workshops in which the citizens worked night and day to manufacture new ones out of the raw material which was to hand; 100 shields, 300 swords, 500 javelins were made every day, besides numerous catapults for the cords of which the women offered their hair. Two generals were chosen of whom one was the

Hasdrubal who had shortly before been condemned to death but who now commanded 20,000 men in the interior. Although six important cities including the ancient foundations of Hadrumetum, Leptis Minor, Thapsus, and Acholla went over to the Romans, Hasdrubal ensured the loyalty of some of the Libyans and got food into the city.

The consuls were slow to advance to the attack, as they believed it would be an easy matter to take it once the initial sense of desperation had worn off, but they underestimated the Carthaginians. An assault was made on a section of the wall bordering the Lake of Tunis, and though a breach was made the Romans were driven out again. When the blockade was begun, one of the two Roman divisions, camped on the edge of the lake, suffered during the heat of the summer from sickness caused by the unhealthy position and its commander, Censorinus, had to move it to the tongue of land separating the lake from the sea, where it got the benefit from the sea-breezes.

During the winter the other consul, Manilius, whose camp was on the isthmus, suffered heavy losses in a sally made by the defenders, and disaster was only averted by the courage of Scipio Aemilianus who was serving in the army with the rank of military tribune. Scipio was also responsible for actions during the winter in which by his resourcefulness he prevented Manilius' incapacity when leading expeditions against Hasdrubal in the interior of the country from having serious results for the Romans. The only success they had was in persuading Hasdrubal's cavalry commander, Himilco Phameas, to desert; this too was Scipio's doing. In the meantime Masinissa had died, apparently full of resentment that his hopes of adding Carthage itself to his empire bad been frustrated by his friends. Scipio was responsible for the division of the powerful kingdom between three of his sons.

The next year, 148, the courage of the Carthaginians was still further rewarded; some Numidian cavalry deserted to them and the sons of Masinissa manifested reluctance to provide help for the Romans. In spite of the Roman fleet blockading the harbour they had been able to get into touch with the Mauretanians and with Andriscus, who was leading a revolt against Rome in Macedonia, though these contacts did more to maintain the morale of the citizens than bring any practical help. The town of Hippo Acra also fiercely resisted an assault after the Romans had ruthlessly sacked Neapolis although it had made a surrender, and Hasdrubal was able to maintain himself in the country and get supplies into the city. There was, however, some division in the city; the general in charge of the defence was another Hasdrubal, through his mother a grandson of Masinissa; for this reason he was apparently suspected of being lukewarm and one day was attacked and killed in the senate house itself. But dissatisfaction in Rome was growing, and it appeared that only Scipio could carry through the siege with the necessary vigour. He was still below the minimum age at which the consulship could be held, but the constitutional requirements were waived for his benefit. He enrolled some fresh troops, and took with him in his entourage two famous Greeks, Panaetius the Stoic philosopher and the historian Polybius; both of these had been his friends for some time, for he was one of those Romans who had an intense admiration for Greek civilization.

His despatch to Africa meant the arrival of a decisive moment for Carthage. It was not only the incompetence of the commanders but also the indiscipline of the Roman soldiers, who had enlisted thinking the campaign would be a promenade, that had delayed action for so long. While Scipio employed himself with the restoration of discipline, the Carthaginians recalled Hasdrubal from the country in case he should be cut off, and he established himself in a fortified post on the isthmus outside but close to the walls; from here he was well placed to threaten any assault which might be made on the formidable defences. This was carried out on a sector apparently on the Sebka er Riana; the Romans broke in through a gate and 4,000 entered; but the ground was favourable to the defenders and they were forced back.

Hasdrubal had meanwhile withdrawn within the walls in the belief that the assault would be decisive and had thus lost his valuable strongpoint. This general was a man of some military talent as his success with limited forces in the country had shown, but was of a cruel and domineering disposition. He adopted the savage tactics used by the mercenary leaders in the Mercenary War, in order to prevent any weakening of the will of the citizens to resist; Roman prisoners were taken on to the walls, mutilated and tortured in the full view of their comrades, and thrown down outside. Those Carthaginians who protested against this needless savagery were killed.

Scipio now devoted his attention to a complete blockade. Elaborate earthworks were built across the isthmus parallel to the Carthaginian defences and carried right round the Roman position. This prevented any possibility of food reaching the city from the remaining Libyan allies. Transport ships still ventured at times to run the blockade of the Roman fleet, so here Scipio after establishing a camp to the south of the city near Le Kram undertook the enormous task of building a mole right across the harbour mouth.

As the work proceeded the defenders planned a counter-stroke. The inner harbour was out of sight of the attackers and in it a fleet of fifty ships was built out of old materials. Meanwhile an alternative exit from the harbour was dug in an easterly direction; it probably was roughly where the modern exit from the inner lagoon has been made. When the fleet was ready a breach was made in the wall and the fleet sailed out. If it had attacked at once with the advantage of surprise it might have destroyed all the Roman ships which were beached on the seaward side of the tongue but the sailors had not the confidence in their ships and rowing. Next day the Romans were ready and a naval battle took place more or less under the walls; the Carthaginians resisted desperately but were outnumbered by the Romans whose ships were in any case much larger, and the survivors were forced back within the harbour. Scipio was able to seize the large quay outside the walls to the east of the original harbour mouth although his siege engines were more than once burnt by courageous sallies of defenders now made desperate by growing hunger.

During the winter of 147–146 the Libyans all submitted to Scipio and in the spring he judged that the defenders had reached the limit of their endurance, as many died from hunger and others gave themselves up. The attack was to be launched from the quay in the direction of the harbours, and to hinder it, Hasdrubal fired all the buildings of the outer port. The Romans got on to the wall however, and Scipio's lieutenant, Laelius, followed it to the region of the inner harbour which fell into his hands with little resistance, as did the market place.

It now remained to assault the defences of the Byrsa, which were on nothing like the same scale as the outer defences of the city; but the Carthaginians turned every house into a fortress and for six days a bitter struggle went on; the description of this scene in Appian, undoubtedly taken from the account of Polybius who was an eyewitness, though rhetorical in parts has the ring of reality about it.

"The streets leading from the market square to the Byrsa were flanked by houses of six stories from which the defenders poured a shower of missiles on to the Romans; when the attackers got inside the buildings the struggle continued on the roofs and on planks crossing the empty spaces; many were hurled to the ground or on to the weapons of those fighting in the streets. Scipio ordered all this sector to be fired and the ruins cleared away to give a better passage to his troops, and as this was done there fell with the walls many bodies of those who had hidden in the upper stories and been burnt to death, and others who were still alive, wounded and badly burnt. Scipio had squadrons of soldiers ready to keep the streets clear for the rapid movement of his men, and dead or living were thrown together into pits, and it often happened that those who were not yet dead were crushed by the cavalry horses as they passed, not deliberately but in the heat of the battle."

On the seventh day some men came out of the Byrsa asking for the lives of those who surrendered; Scipio agreed and 50,000 men, women and children, half starved, filed out of the citadel. Nine hundred deserters from the Romans, who could expect crucifixion as a punishment, continued to resist with Hasdrubal in the enclosure of the temple of Eshmoun until forced to retreat into the building, on the roof of which they took up their final position. At this point the courage of Hasdrubal, who had often proclaimed his determination to fight till death, collapsed, and he came out with his wife and two children to ask for Scipio's mercy. The deserters who saw this asked Scipio for a few moments' respite during which they hurled insults at the Carthaginian general, after which they fired the temple and died in the flames. Hasdrubal's wife also turned on her husband after thanking Scipio for granting their lives, and calling Hasdrubal a coward and traitor threw herself and her children into the burning temple.

For ten days or more the fires raged in the city. Reserving the gold and silver and sacred objects for the state, Scipio allowed his troops to plunder. Those who had surrendered were sold into slavery and all the arms captured were ceremonially dedicated to Mars and Minerva and burned. Finally, everything that was still standing was levelled; Scipio pronounced a curse over the remains, a plough was drawn over the site and salt sown in the furrow, to signify that it was to remain uninhabited and barren for ever.

Such was the end of the city of Carthage after an existence of about six centuries; it remains to be seen what was left of her civilization in Africa in subsequent centuries. There still survived many thousands of people of Phoenician race in North Africa; quite apart from the cities which had made a timely surrender to Rome and who were given a privileged status when the Roman province was established, there were the numerous inhabitants of the coastal cities which had been taken over by Masinissa and now formed part of the kingdoms of his sons, and many who had migrated to Numidian territory in the previous fifty years. For over a century these provided what there was of civilization over most of North Africa, since Roman immigration to the new province was slight and restricted to the immediate hinterland of Carthage. In any case, under the Roman provincial system both at this early stage and later on when it extended over the whole of North Africa local authorities continued to function with the minimum of interference from Roman provincial governors.

The Romans, like most people in antiquity, attached little importance to the idea of race, and the destruction of Carthage did not mean that there was any attempt to root out Carthaginian civilization. The most important known change introduced by them as a deliberate reform of some previously existing custom was the prohibition of human sacrifice; apart from this, religious, social and political institutions continued as before. The position of the Carthaginians in Numidian territory continued to be privileged even after the destruction of the city and the death of Masinissa, and his successors continued to encourage the arts and techniques which had been introduced by Carthage. A remarkable instance of this was the fact that the Romans handed over to the Numidian kings the contents of the libraries of Carthage which fell into their hands at the sack; it is to be presumed that there were many books like that of Mago of immediate practical use in the backward territories. The language of Carthage became the official language throughout North Africa, and there can be no doubt that a large number of Numidians came to learn it.

The religion of the native peoples was greatly influenced by the immigrants and no doubt also by what had been learnt by the numbers of Numidians who served with the armies of Carthage. In the reign of Masinissa there was a tophet at Cirta at which human sacrifices were performed with the same rites as at Carthage itself, though the practice died out fairly quickly.

During the century following the destruction of Carthage many of the more fertile parts of Numidia, particularly those corresponding to eastern Algeria, came to be cultivated by sedentary tribesmen, but at the end of this period, in 46 B.C., two events put a term to the mixed Numidian and Carthaginian civilization; Julius Caesar came to North Africa to complete the destruction of his political enemies, led ironically enough by Cato the Younger, descendant of the man who had brought about the destruction of Carthage; while there, he annexed the eastern part of Numidia to the Roman empire and carried out the rebuilding of Carthage as a colony of Roman citizens, a venture which had been tried once before in spite of the solemn curses on the site but which had not been successful.

Thus a new civilization was planted in North Africa with all the resources and prestige of the greatest empire that had yet existed.

THE EMPIRE OF
THE MONGOLS

Western education tends to ignore the history of Asia, Africa, and South America, except for episodes of European discoveries and conquests. Therefore, we have included rather more material on the empire built by the Mongols under Genghis Khan in the thirteenth century than on some of the other cases. As Saunders points out in his preface, much research remains to be done; but there is now enough material available to make the argument that the genocides practiced by the Mongols were part of a deliberate policy of terror. The frequency, the scale, and the thoroughness of these mass exterminations have ensured them a lasting place in the memory of the victim peoples. Since we have no reports from the Mongols themselves, their history, as reported by their victims, emphasizes their cruelty and destructiveness without giving them credit for their achievements. Saunders has attempted to present a more balanced view. But he leans too heavily on the myths of the Mongols' origin. Christopher Dawson shows that there was considerable continuity between the cultures that had their origin in Central Asia. On the regular cycles of invasions by nomads he writes,

The evidence seems to suggest that the decisive factors were human ones; on the one side the weakening of the resistance of the oasis cultures from political causes, and, on the other, the periodical appearance among the barbarians of some military leader who could unite the barbarians in a movement of expansion and conquest. And whenever such a leader appeared he found an inexhaustible reserve of military material in the nomad horsemen of the steppes, who were the finest light cavalry in the world. . . . Now in almost every case we find that the original starting point of the movement was in North-Western Mongolia, the land beyond the steppes. This forms a kind of oasis of barbarian culture, shut off by the great ranges of the Altai and Khingan Mountains from the rest of Inner Asia. It was here that the great nomad empires of Asia had their centre, from the Huns in the third century B.C. to the East Turks and the Uighurs in the Middle Ages and finally to the Mongols in the thirteenth century. And it is remarkable that all these four empires had their capitals within a few miles of one another in the valley of the Upper Orkhon—where the tombs and inscriptions of the early Turkish and Uighur Khans have been discovered. Thus the empires of the steppes were never quite as barbarous as their victims in the civilized world believed. They had their own ancient traditions of culture which were never entirely lost in spite of all the changes of race and language. Already at the dawn of the Christian era, the tombs of the Hun princes which were discovered in 1924 at Noin Ula near Urga show an extraordinarily wide range of cultural contacts, not only with China but with Iran and Syria and Eastern Europe. . . .

Thus, when Chingis Khan united all the peoples of Mongolia, both Mongol and Turk, and lead them east and west to conquer the world, he inherited a tradition of culture as well as a tradition of empire, and employed the more civilized Kerait and Uighur Turks in the organization and administration of his empire. At the same time he had inherited the highly specialized military tradition of the old warrior peoples of the steppes, who had learned to manoeuvre great masses of cavalry with a speed and discipline which was unknown to the heavy armoured chivalry of the West. [Dawson, ix–x]

In order to maintain perspective, it is important to remember that the Mongols did not discover anything new or innovate in any significant respect. Their genius was confined to doing what others did but doing it much better. This applies even to their genocides. Massacres, wanton cruelty, the destruction of cities, and the devastation of whole regions were commonplace events in Central Asia and Persia as well as in many other areas that they conquered. The Mongols simply killed on a greater scale and as a deliberate part of their policy, a point emphasized by J. A. Boyle in his excellent discussion of the Mongol conquest of Iran (Boyle, 1968, 5:484–88).

Their massacres were intended either as revenge on an opponent who had broken the rules of warfare, such as killing an emissary, or they were part of a deliberate policy of terrorizing real or potential enemies into submission. This policy often allowed them to expand their empire without engaging in warfare. Of course, the victims of their massacres were not the same peoples that they wanted to terrorize into submission. In spite of the Mongols' cruel methods, the peoples of some of the conquered territories welcomed the conquerors. They preferred the harsh but predictable rule of the Mongols, based on their code of laws, to the arbitrary cruelties of their own rulers. The rule of law, even by the severe standards of the Mongols, was thought better than the wanton oppression practiced by most of the feudal lords of the day. Thus W. E. D. Allen (chap. ix) reports that the Georgians had nothing but admiration for the Mongols because of their wisdom and ability, their truthfulness, their impartiality, their justice, and their observance of the excellent laws established by Genghis Khan. This rule of law has become known as the Pax Mongolica. That it really worked is proven by the fact that during their rule and at no other time in history it was safe to travel through Central Asia to China, along the famous "silk route," as Marco Polo did. Since the demise of the Pax Mongolica this has not been possible, even up to our own day.

The Mongols did experience two defeats (both occurred long after the death of Genghis Khan) when they attempted to invade and conquer Japan. However, the Japanese defenders can take only minor credit for these victories. The defeats of the Mongol forces in 1274 and 1281 were almost entirely due to typhoons that destroyed the Mongols' ships and forces (Storry, 40–41).

These experiences were significant factors in the fear of the outside world and its influences which led to and reinforced Japan's exclusion policy, eventually resulting in the massacre of the Japanese Christians in the 17th century (see the readings on Japan).

European historians have often referred to the defeat of the Mongolian army near the outskirts of Vienna. While it is true that their army withdrew and thus saved Europe from further conquests, they had not been defeated. Their withdrawal was caused by an old Mongolian custom: when the Great Khan died, the nobles and the generals had to return to Karakorum, their capital, in order to elect a new khan. Thus did the death of Ogedei save Europe in 1242. One might ask why the Mongols did not return to their conquest of Europe. The answer seems to be too complex to be dealt with here. A simplified version is that, first, the shamans did not approve a propitious date for the renewed campaign, and second, the empire was beginning to lose its unity due to quarrels among the descendants of Genghis Khan, a unity that was essential for raising a large army for a major campaign of conquest.

THE MONGOL CONQUESTS†

Preface

The Mongol conquests of the thirteenth century turned the world upside down; they spanned the globe from Germany to Korea, they destroyed kingdoms and empires wholesale, and left the greater part of the Old

†From J. J. Saunders, *The History of the Mongol Conquests* (London: Routledge & Kegan Paul, 1971), 1–2, 44–45, 52–57, 59–70. Footnotes omitted. Reprinted by permission.

World shaken and transformed. Yet the literature of the subject is surprisingly meagre. Few documented studies (as distinct from popular, romanticizing biographies) exist of the amazing career of Chingis (or, as he is better known, Genghis) Khan; no scholarly life of his famous grandson Kubilai Khan, immortalized by Marco Polo and Coleridge, exists in any Western language, and even the best general histories of the medieval world deal very cursorily with these tremendous events. The reasons for this strange neglect are probably the vast scope of the subject and the daunting character of the linguistic problem. In bulk, the original sources are not unmanageable, but they are extant in so many languages that only a linguistic prodigy could claim a mastery of them all. He who would undertake to write a history of the conquests that fully measured up to the exacting standards of modern scholarship must be fluent in Chinese, Mongol, Japanese, Russian, Persian, Arabic, Armenian, Georgian, Latin and several forms of Turkish. Such a Mezzofanti would be hard to find. However, during the last 200 years or so a small but able band of scholars, who have cultivated intensely small portions of this vast field, have published critical editions, translations, commentaries and learned annotations and so have built up a substantial body of accurate knowledge.

   ·   ·   ·   ·   ·

    In so far as the specialists who have recently examined and reevaluated the contemporary literature on the Mongol conquests have reached a consensus, they may be said to have rejected the old theory of wholesale destruction and to have stressed the more positive and constructive achievements of the last of the great nomad empire-builders. Edward Glanville Browne, writing in the peace and security of late-Victorian and Edwardian England, saw in the Mongol invasions "a catastrophe which changed the face of the world, set in motion forces which are still effective, and inflicted more suffering on the human race than any other event in the world's history" (*A Literary History of Persia*, 1906, II, 426–7), but Wilhelm Barthold replied, in the year of the Russian Revolution, that 'the results of the Mongol invasions were less annihilating than is supposed' (*Mussulman Culture*, Eng. tr. 1934, III), a judgment which is now commonly accepted, for a generation which has lived through world wars and revolutions and genocide on a hideous scale is more impressed by the recuperative powers of human societies than by the destructiveness of armies commanded by fanatical nihilists. Yet however we choose to judge the results, we must still stand amazed at the Mongol military achievement. Our theologically minded ancestors could find no other explanation than that the dreadful "Tartars" were sent by God to punish the nations for their sins: a more secular age, while striving for a more rational judgment, may yet be pardoned for continuing to speak of "the Mongol miracle".

Chingis Khan

Mongolia, which achieved immortal fame as the country of Chingis Khan, had since the expulsion of the Uighurs in the eighth century been peopled almost exclusively by tribes of Mongol speech and primitive manners. They followed the life of hunters and stockraisers; indeed they had no choice, since the land is, or rather was, unsuited for agriculture or mining. The climate of the high plateau is harsh and continental, and in a year of two seasons, only three months can be truly described as summer. From June to August the steppe is a green carpet of grass and flowers, whose growth is promoted by heavy rains; in September the cold is already severe, in October snowstorms sweep across the land, by November the water courses are frozen, and until the following May snowfalls are frequent and winds blow with such ferocity as almost to lift a rider from his saddle. The height and rarified atmosphere sometimes induce giddiness and exhaustion, and the lack of oxygen often obliges the nomad to desist from his attempts to kindle a fire. The monotony of the steppe is notorious; as far as the eye can travel, it sees little but a flat wilderness, broken by occasional ravines and stony hills where no tree is visible. Beyond the steppe, the land rises into lofty ranges; larches and pines flourish on the mountain slopes, the cedar spreads its branches in the valley hollows, and at a lower level, poplars and willows push out along the river courses.

The aboriginal inhabitants of this forbidding land had long been displaced when the name Mongol is first encountered in the Chinese annals. The true Mongols undoubtedly came from the *taiga*, or Siberian forest, the habitat of such fur-bearing animals as the bear and lynx, the fox and squirrel, since the legends of their race, embodied in the famous *Secret History* put together in the imperial age of conquest, trace their descent from the union of a doe and a he-wolf, who met and mated at the source of the Onon river by the holy mountain of Burkan-Kaldun, the home of the sky-god Kökö-Tengri. The first *human* ancestor of the Mongols, Dobun the Wise, married Alan-Koʿa, a woman from a tribe of forest-dwellers settled along the western shores of Lake Baikal. By her he had two sons, but after his death she produced three further sons, as she told the elder ones, by miraculous impregnation by Tengri; the god entered her tent on a moonbeam, caressed her belly, and a ray of light penetrated her womb. The Mongol bards celebrate this divine bastardy, which may be said to have established an intimate connection between the god and his people, whose conquests were later undertaken at the behest and accomplished to the honour of the Eternal Heaven. As the national saga proceeds from legend to history, it links the affairs of the Mongols with the disturbances that followed the fall of the T'ang and the rise of the Chin and the Ju-chen. A Mongol chief died, leaving a widow and seven sons. Nomolun, the widow and the earliest of the spirited dowagers who from time to time governed the Mongol people, held the tribal *tuk*, a banner decked with yak tails, and fought the Jalair, a tribe who had been driven from the Kerulen valley by the Ju-chen and had encroached on Mongol territory. In this war she and six of her sons perished; the seventh, Nachin, survived along with a nephew Kaidu, then a child, who was concealed under a heap of firewood till the enemy had passed. When Kaidu came of age, the uncle loyally recognized him as chief; he gained fame and following as a warrior, and was the first Mongol to be granted by the Chinese about the year 1150 the title of khan. His grandson Kabul was invited to Peking by the Chin Government, who esteemed him a valuable ally against the Ju-chen; he was showered with gifts and recognized as King of the Mongols. Kabul was succeeded by Ambakay, another grandson of Kaidu's, in whose time the Mongols first came in conflict with the Tatars, a people of kindred stock whose name was destined to be for ever linked and confused with theirs.

.   .   .   .   .

In a contest for thé Mongol leadership, Temujin* possessed the double advantage of birth and military prowess; the shamans or sorcerers were granted omens and visions as of a white bull following his wagon and bellowing: "Heaven and earth have decided that the *ulus* [patrimony] shall be Temujin's!" and the clan chiefs decided that the khanate, so long in abeyance, should be revived in the person of Yesugei's son. At a tribal assembly he was offered the throne, and on accepting was raised on a carpet of felt and proclaimed under the title of Chingis Khan. The khan was by tradition a battle warrior rather than an absolute monarch, but Chingis (as we may now style him) had no mind to exercise a limited authority, and his first step, to create a bodyguard (*nököd*) personally devoted and responsible to him, was an earnest of his authoritarian intentions.

.   .   .   .   .

An autumn battle fought near the site of the later Karakorum established the supremacy of the Mongols; after a fierce and hard contest the Naiman were crushed, their king died of wounds, his son Küchlüg fled westwards to the Kara-Khitay, and Jamuka, who had set first the Keraits and then the Naiman against his former *anda*, was captured and put to death. The remnant of the Merkits were subdued by Sübedei, who was to become the most brilliant of Chingis's commanders, and enrolled in the Mongol army; and Chingis, who now reigned unchallenged from the Altai to the Khingan, was proclaimed

*Ed. Note: Temujin was Chingis Khan's given name. *Chingis Khan* is only one of the many spellings of Chengis Khan's name to be found in the literature. *Kuriltai* is the name of the gathering of the nobles who elect the khan.

supreme khan of "all who dwell in tents of felt" at a *kuriltai* on the banks of the Onon in 1206, from which his imperial rule is commonly dated.

The authority of Chingis was now securely based on his personal prowess in war, his hereditary descent from the ancient khans of Mongolia, and an invincible success which betokened to the people the benign approval of heaven. Chingis possessed the full nomad measure of piety or superstition; his devotion to the gods and spirits was exemplary, and he never embarked on a campaign without seeking a personal and private communion with Tengri, whose approval was necessary before the army marched. But as the mightiest prince could commonly learn the will of heaven only through the intermediary of the *shamans*, an unusual degree of power was concentrated in the hands of this primitive clergy, and at the *kuriltai* of 1206 a certain Kokchu, whose father Monglik had once advised Yesugei and married his widow, rode to heaven on a grey horse and returning, informed the assembly that Tengri had consecrated Chingis as universal ruler. Such divine succour, guaranteed from such a source, was doubtless welcome, but Kokchu unwisely presumed on his power, sought to dominate Chingis and set his brothers against him, and expected to usurp a position of influence in the new Mongol government. Chingis was perhaps unaware of his schemes, but Borte warned her husband of the implications, and the new khan, once convinced of a novel and dangerous challenge to his authority and the unity of the ruling family, took ruthless action. As Kokchu emerged from Chingis's tent, he was seized by the guard and his back was broken, a mode of execution common among the Mongols, who were averse to the shedding of human blood on the ground. The fate of the *shaman* terrified the people; it perhaps diminished the fanatical veneration in which these magicians or holy men were held, and it certainly confirmed the unlimited autocracy of Chingis, whose realm was never distracted by conflicts between Church and State.

Once Mongolia was at his feet and the Turco-Mongol peoples had all submitted to his rule, Chingis ventured to strike at the sedentary societies beyond the steppe and desert and the Great Wall, and unlike the earlier barbarian leaders, his aim was conquest rather than simple plunder. Of the three kingdoms into which China was divided, that of the Hsi-Hsia, Tibetan in race and Buddhist in religion, was the smallest and weakest; Chingis, though as yet without the capability of besieging fortified towns, ravaged the open countryside so destructively as to force his enemy to seek terms and acknowledge his suzerainty, and the discomfiture of the Tanguts gave him control of the routes linking China to the west and enabled him to attack his real enemy the Chin from the west as well as the north. The breach with the Chin, the traditional foes of the Mongols, was a natural development. Chingis received an embassy from Peking notifying him of the accession of a new sovereign, upon which as a vassal he was expected to kow-tow before the envoys. Instead, he cried: "Is such an imbecile worthy of the throne and shall I abase myself before him?" and prepared for war, after calling on God to recognize the justice of his cause and avenge the blood of his uncle Ambakay. As usual, he did not move until he was satisfied that the political and diplomatic situation was favourable to him. The Önguts, a Turkish people who guarded the northern frontiers of the Chin empire, were won over to his side, and could be relied on to open the way for the Mongols into the heart of China, and the Ch'i-tan who were of Mongol speech and race, eagerly grasped at the opportunity to revenge themselves on their supplanters in Peking. The campaign against the Chin assumed the character of a national or race war, in which the Turco-Mongol peoples of the north were united against the Tungus-speaking occupants of the northern provinces of China.

The struggle thus opened in 1211 was to continue for twenty-three years, and ended only in 1234, after Chingis's death, with the total destruction of the Chin regime. It began with a series of raids deep into the country south of the Great Wall; a more systematic plan of conquest was then devised, with three armies advancing into Hopei and Liao-ning, and when Peking was threatened, the Chin court decamped southwards to K'ai-feng. This desertion doubtless discouraged the defenders; Chingis had by now enrolled a corps of engineers skilled in siegecraft; Peking was closely blockaded, the governor committed suicide, the walls were breached, and the Mongol army poured into the northern capital (1215). The palaces and public buildings were looted and burnt; many of the inhabitants were massacred; the fate of Ambakay was avenged, and the first out of many civilized capitals felt the savage fury of uncivilized nomads who feared and hated a way of life they could not understand. Thereafter, the war languished; Chingis was drawn away to the west in the campaigns against the Kara-Khitay and the Khwarizmians; the Chin recovered some of the lost territory, and the conflict degenerated into a tedious war of sieges, in which engineers of alien birth were more prized than the native Mongol archers.

The conquest of China was interrupted by developments in Central Asia of which Chingis was obliged to take cognizance lest his own position be undermined. Küchlüg, the ex-king of the Naiman, had taken refuge among the Kara-Khitay, the sinized Mongol aristocracy imposed on the Muslim Turkish peoples of the Altaic steppes who had established their centre at Balasaghun, west of Lake Issik-kul. Under the last of their *yeh-lü*, the Gur-Khan Chi-lu-ku (1178–1211), their power had decayed and their vassals, the Uighurs and the Karluks, had renounced their authority and turned their faces towards the rising sun of Chingis Khan. Küchlüg, a treacherous and incompetent prince, overthrew and supplanted his benefactor the Gur-Khan, who died his captive in 1213, but his rule disgusted his subjects; he provoked a rising in Kashgaria, where he persecuted the Muslims, in Khotan he executed the leading *imam* on a charge of disloyalty, and the prince of Ili was put to death for transferring his allegiance to Chingis. The Mongol chief could scarcely ignore the activities of his old enemy, now in possession of a substantial kingdom, but appeals from his oppressed subjects provided an excuse for intervention. Jebe was sent with 20,000 men against Küchlüg; Balasaghun fell without resistance, the Muslims everywhere welcomed the Mongols as liberators; Küchlüg fled to the Pamir country, where he was killed in 1218, and the former realm of the Kara-Khitay was added to the Mongol empire.

The fall of the Kara-Khitay brought the western boundary of Chingis's realm to the dominions of Muhammad Shah, the ambitious and haughty prince of Khwarizm. Towards this kingdom the Mongol chief at first cherished no hostile intent: indeed he despatched an embassy to Muhammad, proposing that commercial contacts between them could be pursued to their mutual advantage. But the shrewd and clever stratagems of Chingis were becoming widely known, and it was suspected that spies and secret agents were often concealed under the guise of harmless merchants. A Mongol mission, ostensibly concerned only with trade, reached the frontier post of Utrar on the Sir-Darya in 1218; the Khwarizmian Governor, convinced that its purpose was merely to report on the military strength of the kingdom, seized its goods and executed its members, who numbered among them a Mongol diplomatic envoy. Chingis furiously demanded reparation, and on being refused, declared war. For the first time the Mongol military machine was set in motion against a Muslim state, and rivers of blood were destined to flow before Islam, after suffering the most grievous hurts, at last tamed and converted these ferocious pagans.

In this terrible war, in which more lives were lost probably than in any similar conflict of such duration (a mere three years), the advantages once again were wholly on the side of the Mongols. The outrage at Utrar, which involved the slaying of an ambassador, enabled Chingis to appear not as an aggressor but as a redresser of a grievous wrong. His new enemy was powerful only in appearance. The Khwarizmian kingdom was a loose and flimsy structure; the Turkish ruling class was disliked and despised by the Persian subject population; the army was recruited from mercenaries, whose loyalty rarely survived a defeat; the people were oppressed by heavy taxation and the devout were disturbed by the quarrel with the Caliph, and the Sultan, vain, frivolous and incompetent, was neither a statesman nor a soldier, and his soaring ambition to reign as the Great Seljuks had reigned, the leading sovereign of Islam, was belied by his clear unfitness for the role. To him must be ascribed much of the blame for the hideous calamities which fell on the urban centres of eastern Iran. The cold and deliberate genocide practised by the Mongols, which has no parallel save that of the ancient Assyrians and the modern Nazis, perhaps arose from the mixed motives of military advantage and superstitious fears. The Mongols were unaccustomed to fighting in settled and thickly populated lands; however skilled they became in siegecraft, the reduction of fortified places was costly and laborious; as nomads roaming the steppes, they despised the inhabitants of cities and felt constrained and imprisoned within their walls, and by terrorizing the people by massacres they might hasten the surrender of the next town and facilitate the rapid conquest of the region. Yet their material interest was never lost sight of. From the thousands of defenceless civilians who perished at their hands, they always selected a number of useful craftsmen, artisans and engineers who were deported into the heart of the empire and spared to work for their masters. However merciless their rage for destruction, they commonly permitted, after a decent interval, the rebuilding of the cities they had burnt and ruined, since they were satisfied that ruins produced no revenue and that a flourishing trade and manufacture was a source of wealth and prosperity to them.

Chingis prepared for this new conflict with his usual cool deliberation. In the spring of 1219, in the upper Irtish valley, an army was assembled, which, including the Uighurs and Karluks who were now numbered among the Mongol auxiliaries, reached the figure of nearly 200,000 men. The Khwarizmian forces were superior, but as Muhammad distrusted their loyalty, he refused to risk pitched battles in open country and dispersed his troops in garrisons in the principal cities of his empire, trusting to Mongol inability to besiege and capture walled strongholds. The Muslims, says Barthold, displayed much heroism, but all discipline and organization was on the Mongol side. Hostilities opened with the siege of Utrar, the scene of the outrage which had precipitated the war. Two of Chingis's sons, Chagatai and Ögedei, were given charge of this operation; another division under Jochi descended the Sir-Darya to besiege Khojend, while Chingis himself, with his younger son Tolui, made for Bukhara, the richest and most populous city of Transoxiana. The Turkish garrison tried to break out, the citizens surrendered (February 1220), the buildings were systematically pillaged, but the burning of mosques and palaces may have been involuntary and no general massacre was perpetrated. The Persian historian Juvaini narrates that Chingis entered the pulpit of the principal mosque and delivered a political sermon or admonition to the terrified crowd, in which he declared he was 'the flail of God' sent to punish them for their sins. From Bukhara he proceeded to Samarkand, where he was joined by Chagatai and Ögedei who had captured Utrar and punished the perfidious governor by pouring molten gold down his throat. Prisoners taken at Bukhara were driven before them in battle formation so as to give the impression of a vast army. In five days (March 1220) Samarkand capitulated; the inhabitants were ordered to evacuate the city, which was more easily plundered in their absence; the Turkish garrison was put to the sword, the artisans to the number of 30,000 were deported to Mongolia and the clergy were spared, but a great deal of indiscriminate killing went on and only one quarter of the place was reoccupied when the survivors were permitted to return.

Terrified by the avalanche of destruction falling on his kingdom, Sultan Muhammad fled westwards in the hope of raising new armies in Persian Irak, despite the dissuasions of his courageous son Jalal ad-Din, who represented to him that such conduct would appear cowardly desertion in the eyes of his suffering people. Chingis gave orders to Jebe and Sübedei, two of his most valiant captains, to pursue the hapless sovereign from town to town and from province to province; the Mongol cavalry chased him through Tus (where Sübedei burnt the tomb of Harun al-Rashid) and Rayy to Hamadan, where contact was lost, the fugitive managing to reach the shores of the Caspian at Abaskum, near which was a small island where he found (December 1220) asylum and death. The pursuers, doubtless encouraged by this victorious parade through a demoralized and almost defenceless kingdom, continued their advance until they had accomplished a feat never before attempted and rarely imitated since. Riding northwards into Azerbaijan, whose lush pastures attracted every nomad invader, they thrust their way into the Christian kingdom of Georgia, whose army was broken before Tiflis (February 1221), and after ruining the town of Maragha, they turned back to punish a revolt of Hamadan by the total annihilation of the place and its people. Threading their way through the pass of Derbend, they came out on to the steppes north of the Caucasus, to be confronted with a coalition of Alans, Cherkes and Kipchak Turks who sought to bar their approach to the Russian plains. By cunningly pleading Turco-Mongol solidarity, they detached the Kipchaks from this alliance, whose forces they easily routed; the princes of Russia, who laboriously assembled an ill-organized and heterogeneous army, were crushed (May 1222) in the battle of the Kalka, a small river flowing into the Sea of Azov, and after sacking Sudak, a Genoese trading post in the Crimea, they advanced up the Volga to chastise the Muslim Bulghars and the Kangli Turks, and rounding the northern shores of the Caspian, rejoined Chingis and his main army on the steppes beyond the Jaxartes. This astonishing raid, which defeated twenty nations and achieved a complete circuit of the Caspian, produced no immediate political consequences, but set a precedent for the invasion of eastern Europe nearly twenty years later.

Meanwhile Chingis proceeded with the methodical destruction of the Khwarizmian kingdom. Before moving south of the Oxus into Khurasan, he resolved to subdue the homeland of the shahs, the fertile region to the south of the Aral Sea which had for its defensive centre the city and fortress of Gurganj.

His three sons, Jochi, Chagatai and Ögedei, were placed in charge of its siege, and the Mongols, finding a dearth of stones for projectiles, cut down whole groves of mulberry trees, soaked the trunks in water to harden them, and employed them in their siege engines to batter down the walls. The siege was laboriously prolonged for seven months (October 1220–April 1221); the attackers suffered heavy losses, and some blame for this probably attaches to a quarrel between Jochi and Chagatai which forced Chingis to intervene and place them both under the command of Ögedei. When Gurganj finally fell, the Mongols broke the dams and flooded the town, enslaved the women and children, deported the artisans to the number, it is said, of 100,000, and slew the rest. Gurganj was completely ruined, but a new city later arose near its site and received the name of Urgend; the dams were never repaired (perhaps no one could repair them), and the Oxus, having been diverted from its normal course, flowed into the Caspian for 300 years.

Even before Gurganj had fallen, Chingis with his main army had crossed the Oxus and advanced into the rich and populous province of Khurasan. The main forces of the Khwarizmians had been almost destroyed; the defence of the remnant of the kingdom rested on the garrison of the towns, and the fearful massacres which accompanied the progress of the Mongols through eastern Persia were doubtless intended to speed the surrender of these places and save the attackers long and laborious siegework. Not that prompt capitulation always averted the wholesale killing of the civilian population: if the Mongols were provoked by some special circumstances, such as the death in action of one of their leaders, the entire town was likely to suffer fearful retribution. Tirmidh was the first place to be taken and destroyed south of the Oxus, and the chroniclers tell a grim story of how a woman, hoping to be spared, cried out that she had swallowed a pearl, but the merciless butchers merely ripped open her belly and extracted it, and Chingis gave orders that all corpses should be disembowelled lest such treasures should be similarly secreted. Balkh was taken next and spared for the time. Merv fell in February 1221 to Tolui, who butchered 700,000 persons, says the contemporary chronicler Ibn al-Athir, and only eighty craftsmen were spared; Sanjar's tomb was burnt, and a small clan of nomad Turks, who grazed their flocks on the pastures just outside Merv, fled westwards through Irak into Asia Minor, where they were granted asylum by the Seljuk princes there and became the progenitors of the Ottoman Turks. Nishapur was next marked out for vengeance, in particular because the previous year, when Sübedei and Jebe were pursuing the shah, Chingis's son-in-law Tokuchar had been killed by an arrow from its walls. It could therefore expect no mercy and received none. Taken by assault by Tolui in April 1221, it was the scene of a carnival of blood scarcely surpassed even in Mongol annals. Tokuchar's widow presided over the butchery; separate piles of heads of men, women and children were built into pyramids, and even the cats and dogs were killed in the streets. Herat, whose citizens opened the gates to the enemy, was strangely spared, but Bamiyan, in the Hindu Kush, where Chingis's favourite grandson was killed, suffered the fate of Merv. Muhammad's son, Jalal ad-Din, had broken through the Mongol lines and reached Ghazna, where he was striving desperately to raise fresh armies, hampered by the general terror inspired by the Mongols and the jealous quarrels of Turks and Ghurids, on whose joint support he depended. He actually succeeded in routing a Mongol detachment at Parwan near Kabul in Afghanistan, an event which raised many false hopes and led to fatal uprisings against Mongol rule in Merv, Herat and elsewhere in the autumn of 1221. This reverse, the only one suffered by the Mongols in the whole campaign, brought Chingis to the scene; he inspected the site, reprimanded his generals for tactical errors, and marched against Jalal, who retired eastwards to the banks of the Indus. Here was fought (November 1221) the battle which concluded the campaign. Jalal and his paladins performed prodigies of valour, but Mongol discipline and organization prevailed; the presence of Chingis was worth several divisions; when defeat was conceded, the young prince, throwing off his armour, rode his horse into the river and reached the further side, under the admiring gaze of Chingis himself. No pursuit on to Indian territory was attempted; a Mongol patrol penetrated as far as Multan, but the heats of India were too much for these sons of the chilly steppes, who turned aside to inflict condign punishment on those rebels who had dared to rise in arms against them on the morrow of Parwan. Herat was levelled to the ground, after a full week had been devoted to the killing of the inhabitants and the few thousand who had survived at Merv were put to the sword. The stench of death hung over the stricken land.

No attempt was made by Chingis to consolidate Mongol rule in Khurasan or to invade Persian Irak, or to prepare for a possible return from India of Jalal ad-Din, who might in the wake of a Mongol retreat attempt to rebuild his father's kingdom. Chingis might feel that the fearful punishment he had inflicted would leave the region prostrate for many a year, and he may also have deemed unwise a longer absence from Mongolia and China, where his lieutenants were still pursuing the war against the Chin. When military operations ceased after the battle of the Indus, he retired to the pastures south of the Hindu Kush, where he received in May 1222 a visit from the Chinese Taoist sage Ch'ang Ch'un, whom he had summoned to his presence to discuss the philosopher's stone and the problem of immortality. Mellowed perhaps by these philosophical conversations, the conqueror returned to Transoxiana in the autumn of 1222 and at Bukhara required some learned doctors to expound to him the faith of Islam. He listened with interest to their exposition, approved the rites and dogmas of the religion of Muhammad, with one exception: he deplored the annual pilgrimage to Mecca, observing that the whole world and not a single building was the house of God. At Samarkand, where he passed the winter of 1222–3, he ordered the imams to pray for him in the mosques in place of the Khwarizmian prince and exempted the "clergy", that is, the imams and kadis, from all taxation, a concession confirmed by his successors and erected into a general rule for the ministers of all religions. In the spring of 1223 he crossed the Jaxartes and passed a leisurely year or two, hunting animals instead of men in the steppes of western Turkestan where he received Jebe and Sübedei on their completion of the circuit of the Caspian. Only in the spring of 1225 did he set out to return to Mongolia.

After this rest from carnage, the conqueror, before whom all Asia now trembled, found fresh scope for military activity when he returned home after an absence of six years. In China, the Chin were far from subdued, and Mukali, the Mongol general left in command, had died without completing the conquest. The Tangut kingdom of Hsi-Hsia had proved a refractory vassal: when Chingis demanded troops from it for the Khwarizmian war, a Tangut official scornfully observed that if the Mongol leader had not enough soldiers, he had no right to claim the sovereign power. Such an insult must be avenged, and at the close of 1226 Chingis took the field and laid siege to Ning-hsia, the Tangut capital. In the open country, he displayed the same barbarity which had turned eastern Persia into a charnel-house, and the Chinese history mournfully speaks of fields piled with human bones. The last months of Chingis's life (he was now sixty) were darkened by troubles with his eldest son Jochi, who had stayed behind to enjoy his appanage in the Kipchak territory, and the chronicles hint darkly of plots against his father's life. In February 1227 Jochi suddenly died there, at the age of forty or thereabouts, and the succession was doubtless bestowed shortly afterwards on Ögedei, the conqueror's second and favourite son. Chingis did not long survive him. He died in the district of Ch'ung-shui in Kansu province on 25 August 1227; Ning-hsia did not fall till after his death, and in accordance with his wishes, the entire population was put to the sword. His body was conveyed with great funeral pomp to the holy mountain of Burkan Kaldun, at the sources of the Onon and Kerulen rivers in Mongolia, where it was buried at a secret spot, and where in 1229 great sacrifices were held by Ögedei and forty slave-girls and as many horses were despatched to join their master in the next world.

The personal appearance of Chingis is brought but dimly before us by the Persian historian Juzjani, who describes him as "a man of tall stature, of vigorous build, robust in body, the hair on his face scanty and turned white, with cat's eyes, possessed of great energy, discernment, genius and understanding, awe-inspiring, a butcher, just, resolute, an overthrower of enemies, intrepid, sanguinary and cruel". This curious catalogue of physical and moral qualities is typical of the mixture of fear and hate and grudging admiration with which the Islamic world regarded the "accursed one" who had inflicted such dreadful injuries upon it. At a distance of over seven centuries we may judge more objectively this Alexander of barbarism, the nomad who wreaked vengeance on civilization, yet in his best moments rose far above pure destructiveness. I shall first consider his achievement in his double capacity of (1) soldier; (2) administrator.

(1) As the first general of his age, Chingis's ability consisted, not in startling innovations, but in the uncanny power he showed in adapting and improving existing practices. His armies were divided into units of ten, from divisions of 10,000 men to brigades of 1000, companies of 100, and platoons of ten. This decimal system was familiar to the Turks and Mongols, and had hitherto been bound up with the old tribe and clan order; Chingis broke this up, and created new units made up of mixed races and tribes. The army consisted essentially of a cavalry force and a corps of engineers: infantry was hardly ever used, since a nomad fighter without a horse was unthinkable. The heavy cavalry wore armour and was armed with sword and lance: the light cavalry wore no armour and used bow and javelin. The bow was the deadliest and most accurate of Mongol weapons. It was extremely heavy, with a pull of 160 pounds and had a range of from 200 to 300 yards. Each archer carried two or three bows, three quivers, and files for sharpening arrow-heads, which when dipped in redhot brine could pierce armour. The Mongol soldier was well clad to withstand the intense cold of the steppe: in winter he wore a fur cap and coat and heavy leather boots. His food was mostly *yogurt* (curdled milk) or *kumiz* (fermented mare's milk), and a bag of millet meal would last him for days. In addition to his arms, he carried his iron rations, a camp-kettle, and a waterproof pouch with a change of clothing for crossing swamps and rivers. At reviews, the troops' kit was rigorously inspected, and those whose equipment was found deficient were severely punished.

The Mongol battle formation took the form of two ranks of heavy armoured cavalry in front, with three ranks of armourless mounted archers behind. The latter, moving forward through the intervals of the front ranks, poured forth a devastating fire and then withdrew, whereupon the heavy cavalry charged the demoralized enemy off the field. The Mongol horse was small and wiry and perfectly trained and disciplined; it could travel at ten miles an hour, and a short but solidly built stirrup enabled the rider to direct his fire with precision while moving rapidly across country. Chingis, like all outstanding nomad chiefs, understood the value of the medieval equivalent of mechanized warfare, but he alone brought it to the highest pitch of skill. In the days before gunpowder, the walls of fortified places were broken down with stones and other missiles discharged by giant catapults, and various inflammable compounds, usually including naphtha and saltpetre, were poured from tubes or cylinders to set fire to the defences. Under Chingis's orders, his officers sorted out from among their prisoners all artisans, skilled workers and anyone with a pretence to technical knowledge, and drafted them into the engineering corps of the army. Captives whose lives were of no value were employed to fill in moats and put siege-engines and battering rams in position: it did not matter how many of these were killed by arrow fire from the city walls.

Not least among the causes of Chingis's success was his care of maintaining the communications of his expanding empire and his excellent intelligence service. Along the main roads was constructed a series of *yams* or post-houses, each of which was kept provided with food, drink, horses and other supplies. Envoys and messengers arriving at a *yam* showed their passes and were given a meal, rest and fresh mounts to proceed on their journey. Chingis never embarked on a campaign till he had gathered every piece of information he could concerning the size, strength, resources and morale of the enemy. Spies often travelled in merchant caravans, picking up gossip in the bazaars and markets, and relayed what they learnt back to the Khan's camp. Even apparently peaceful trading missions for the Mongols were viewed with alarm and suspicion by foreign princes, and the caravan whose members were killed at Utrar in 1219 may well have contained secret agents sent to spy out the condition of the Khwarizmian defences.

Chingis was an adept at psychological warfare of the most horrific kind. He deliberately set out to create a reputation for ferocious terror, in the expectation (often realized) of frightening whole nations into surrendering without resistance. There is something indescribably revolting in the cold savagery with which the Mongols carried out their massacres. The inhabitants of a doomed town were obliged to assemble in a plain outside the walls, and each Mongol trooper, armed with a battle-axe, was told to kill so many people, ten, twenty or fifty. As proof that orders had been properly obeyed, the killers were sometimes required to cut off an ear from each victim, collect the ears in sacks, and bring them to their officers to be counted. A few days after the massacre, troops were sent back into the ruined city to search for any poor wretches who might be hiding in holes or cellars; these were dragged out and slain. Some modern critics have suggested several reasons for this bloody policy; that the nomads feared and hated walled cities and on taking possession of them were seized with a kind of frenzy of destruction, or that the killings were intended to prevent revolts in the rear as the Mongol army passed on, or that Chingis and his successors, being convinced of their divine mission to conquer the world, treated resistance as an unforgivable crime against God and the Khan. But it is more probable that terror was erected into a system of government to spread fear and panic and demoralize their enemies before a shot had been fired against them.

So impressive were Chingis's victories that his campaigns have been critically studied by modern military planners. Hitler may have owed something to him, for the blitzkrieg and the deep drives into the enemy's defences and the trapping of whole armies, as in the "Barbarossa" campaign against Russia in 1941, are strongly reminiscent of Mongol strategy and tactics. But in many ways the Mongol was cleverer than the Nazi. Hitler took insufficient pains to acquaint himself with the strength and resources of the enemy and provoked a worldwide coalition against him. Chingis's foes were never able to combine against him, partly because owing to his control of the interior lines of Central Asia, they could make no contact with one another, so that China, for example, could not ally with Persia or Russia.

(2) Chingis not only created an empire: he organized it so well that it went on expanding for fifty years after his death. Clearly he was something more than a talented warrior chief: he was also an outstanding civil administrator. This was a surprising achievement for a man of his background. He was an unlettered nomad, who despised farming and hated towns, and viewed settled, civilized lands only as sources of loot and plunder. The free roaming life of the limitless steppes was the only life he knew or wanted: for peasants and workers he had only contempt, the toil they engaged in was fit only for slaves. The Mongols were, after all, remote from the centres of civilized life, and were almost untouched by cultural or religious influences from the cities of eastern and southern Asia. They had no permanent dwellings, no towns or villages, no writing and no manufactures. With an able warrior to lead them, it was no great task to subdue other nomadic or semi-nomadic tribes (this had been done before, by the Huns and Turks among others), but how could an illiterate, barbarous people conquer and hold ancient civilized states? Chingis was intelligent enough to see the value of things outside his normal experiences; like Peter the Great centuries later he realized how backward his people were, and though caring nothing for the arts of civilized existence, he was intensely interested in the technical "know-how" of defence, in whatever could improve military efficiency, and in how the lands he conquered could be made to yield higher revenues. His own Mongols could not help him: hence he enlisted the services of advisers and officials from more advanced societies. He was wholly devoid of race prejudice; his ministers and commanders were recruited from twenty different nations, and there was a general pooling of military and administrative experience which enriched and strengthened his empire.

His first step was to reduce the Mongol language to writing. Like most barbarians, he was impressed by the art of writing, which seemed so permanent, so magical; he marvelled at the facility with which these strange signs could be read and interpreted, and resolved that his own tongue must be written down, so that his laws and decrees could be published in it. Among the prisoners taken by Chingis in his early campaigns was an Uighur named T'a-t'a-t'ong-a, who had been secretary to a local chief; the Khan showed great interest in his documents and seals, and asked him to teach the Mongol princes to write their language in the Uighur script. From this time onwards the Mongol chancery issued all its edicts in the script which the Turks had spread over Central Asia.

Even more useful as a counsellor was Yeh-lü Ch'u-ts'ai, a member, as his title implies, of the imperial family of Liao, who was twenty-five when Peking was taken by the Mongols in 1215 and whose outstanding abilities commended him to the conqueror, who took him into his service and carried him with him on his western campaign of 1219–25. A typical scholar-mandarin, he gained great influence over Chingis and taught him how to organize a civil service; he doubt-less reasoned that by serving the Mongols, he might be better able to protect his countrymen from their excesses. Once, when a Chinese province had been subjugated, one of Chingis's generals observed that the Chinese peasants were of small value as fighting-men and might as well be killed off and their fields turned into pastures for the Mongol horses. Ch'u-ts'ai, hearing of this, knew it would be useless to appeal to the Khan's humanity to avert the threatened massacre: Chingis would be impressed only by practical arguments of a mate-rial kind. He pointed out, with great skill and eloquence, that if he were allowed to organize the province as had been done in the past, land-tax and customs-dues would produce every year 500,000 ounces of silver, 80,000 pieces of silk, and 400,000 sacks of grain. Chingis thought this an excellent idea: Ch'u-ts'ai was commissioned to set the old administrative and revenue system going; nothing more was heard of the 'farms into pastures' plan, and the population was saved. It was Ch'u-ts'ai who organized the *yam* system, set up training schools for officials, fixed the State budget, improved the tax yield, suppressed brigandage, built grain stores, and revived on a bigger scale the old Chinese device of paper money. In short, he applied the traditional techniques of Chi-nese government administration to the expanding Mongol empire, and Chingis seems to have given him more or less a free hand.

Two further traits strengthen Chingis's claim to statesmanship: his policy of religious toleration and his encouragement of international trade.

(1) In his day, the Mongols were untouched by any of the higher religions; they were shamanists, as all the steppe people had once been, with a vague belief in a sky-god *Tengri*, "eternal Heaven"; they had no temples or organized worship; they sacrificed animals, chiefly horses, at stone cairns, and they paid reverent regard to their *shamans*, holy men whose principal function was to

keep in touch with the spirits of their departed ancestors and see that no evil from them befell the tribe. Chingis was firmly convinced that his God had made the Mongols his chosen people and given them a divine commission to conquer the earth: Mongol proclamations were issued in the name of *Tengri* and the Khan, their victories were piously ascribed not to themselves but God. Yet Chingis showed no disposition to force his faith on others. On the contrary, he granted full freedom to all faiths; Christians, Muslims, Jews, Buddhists, all acquired perfect liberty to worship as they pleased and to propagate their tenets anywhere in the Mongol realm provided they did not encroach on the freedom of others. Never had the continent of Asia enjoyed so complete a liberty of conscience, never had it been filled with so many ardent missionaries seeking to push their doctrines. Thus the clergy of all the competing religions tended to preach loyalty to the Mongols, a circumstance which helped to perpetuate their rule.

(2) Chingis was fully aware of the value of international trade, both from the revenue it brought to the Mongol treasury and its role in binding together in a close economic network the many different regions won by the Mongol sword. The Mongols in their homeland in pre-conquest days traded but little; mostly buying arms, clothes and metal goods from the Chinese in exchange for furs and skins. But as Chingis's empire spread and he learnt from men like Ch'u-ts'ai how big a revenue customs duties could bring to the State, everything was done to encourage a brisk commercial traffic: the roads were policed, post-houses established, caravans given armed protection, thieves and robbers put down; the peasants tilling their fields in the fertile oases of Central Asia were guarded against the old curse of peaceful cultivators, raids by nomadic tribesmen. Mongol military power, perhaps we may add Mongol terror, made the highways of Asia safer than they had ever been. Companies of merchants who entered partnership with a prince who provided the capital were given extensive rights and privileges, including exemption from direct taxation, and they journeyed regularly to and fro across the continent from China to Persia and beyond. Such men must have blessed the *Pax Mongolica*, the peace and security the conquerors brought to lands usually torn by war and invasion. When a region was subjugated, Chingis took care to put its economy on a new footing; the ruined cities were rebuilt, and the trading classes encouraged to resume their operation under the protection of the Mongol Army. Profits must have been high, and the influential moneyed men were long among the strongest props of the Mongol Empire.

Chingis aspired to be the lawgiver of his people; at some unknown date subsequent on his assumption of the supreme khanate, he promulgated a code known as the *Yasa*, of which no complete text has come down to us, though we know enough of its contents from the copious extracts given by the chroniclers to get a fair idea of its scope and spirit. It was a curious mixture of enlightenment and superstition: it enacted religious toleration, exempted the clergy of all faiths from taxation, forbade washing or urinating in running water (flowing streams and rivers were held to be "alive" and sacred and were not to be polluted), and prescribed the death penalty for spying and desertion, theft and adultery, the killing of animals in Muslim fashion, and in the case of a merchant, a third bankruptcy! Copies of the code in Uighur script were traced out on great sheets of parchment, and kept in the treasuries of the Mongol princes, to be taken out and consulted as the need arose. The same princes were permitted to issue *yarliks* or decrees in their own domains, but these were never to conflict with the *Yasa*. From a superstitious belief that it contained the secret of the Mongol's success, the *Yasa* attained a wide currency and was adopted in a modified form as far away as Mamluk Egypt.

As administrator and lawgiver, Chingis rose above any other nomad chief known to history, and his fame rests upon this as much as upon his brilliant gifts as a soldier. For the rivers of blood he shed, no forgiveness is possible: the fearful destruction of civilian life in eastern Iran was far worse than anything Attila did in Europe, and he lives in the Muslim chroniclers as the Evil or Accursed One. Yet this man, so contemptuous of human life, was not destitute of finer qualities: he was cool and sensible in his judgments and loyal and faithful to friends and dependants and those who had once rendered service to him. He had a horror of traitors, and often rewarded those who had stood loyally by his enemies. He was receptive to new ideas, dimly grasped some of the merits of civilization, and his imperial ordinances promoted a mingling of cultures such as had never before been seen in Asia.

THE ALBIGENSIAN CRUSADES AND THE KNIGHTS OF THE TEMPLE

The so-called Albigensian Crusades against the Cathars are a difficult case. It has produced, and is still producing, a vast literature. A mass of data is available, though none of it comes to us from the victims, and new analyses are debated in specialist circles by every generation of scholars. We do not pretend to have mastered all of these materials or all of the scholarly arguments based upon them.

The case is included here because the Cathars certainly have disappeared, though it has never been determined how many saved their lives by recanting. Their disappearance as a social group was carefully planned and executed with persistent cruelty. The motive was the suppression of deviance from Roman orthodoxy, a deviation that was perceived as threatening because it had the support of at least some of the ruling elite. During a period of history when conflict between church and state was endemic, a strong pope could not tolerate such a state of affairs.

The difficulties encountered in the suppression of this heresy contributed significantly to the establishment and power of the Inquisition. The king of France was willing to be drawn into this conflict because he saw an opportunity to expand his kingdom into the south. One unanticipated consequence of the crusade was the expansion and strengthening of France and the disappearance of the flourishing, cosmopolitan culture of Languedoc. The king of France and his minister, de Nogaret, were also the first to misuse the Inquisition, destroying the Knights of the Temple and confiscating the order's considerable wealth. The Inquisition thus was an immediate success, both as a tool for the persecution of heretics and as a means of achieving less laudatory ends under the cover of protecting the purity of Christian Europe.

While the very success of the Inquisition did inestimable damage to the Church, its methods of terror and persecution have been used and abused up to the present day. These methods were not only new, but also so successful that they have been copied by totalitarian regimes ever since. The main features of these methods are:

1. Making the denunciation of fellow citizens an obligation that takes precedence over ties of family and kinship;
2. Extracting confessions by imprisonment and torture;
3. Making the naming of fellow conspirators an essential part of confessions;
4. Defining the retraction of extorted confessions as a relapse and therefore a proof of guilt; and
5. In some cases, separating the proof of heresy or opposition from the execution of the penalty. The Inquisition handed over its convicted heretics to the secular arm for punishment just as, hundreds of years later, during Stalin's purges of the Communist party, party members were often deprived of their membership and then handed over to the NKVD for punishment.

THE ALBIGENSIAN CRUSADES: BACKGROUND†

The Albigensian Crusades slash through the history of France and of the Church like a gaping wound. From 1208 to 1226 the papacy sent army after army to the South of France to crush the Albigensian heretics and to punish their supporters. The Albigensian Crusades were religious wars and like all religious wars they were bloody and cruel. They began with a calculated act of terror, the massacre of Béziers; they ended with the establishment of the Inquisition, one of the most effective means of thought control that Europe has ever known. They were completely successful: The losing faith, the Albigensian heresy, was exterminated. The effects of the victory were lasting: The religious unity of Western Europe, the leadership of the Church, and the papal monarchy were preserved for many generations. Except for the Hussites of Bohemia, who lived on the very fringe of the Catholic world, the Church was not again seriously threatened by heresy until the rise of Luther in the early sixteenth century.

Successful wars, however, usually have unexpected consequences, and the Albigensian Crusades were no exception to this rule. For one thing, they made France a Mediterranean power and the greatest power in Europe. Before the Crusades, the king of France had no authority in the southern third of his country, no seaports on the Mediterranean, no direct contacts with Spain or Italy.

†From Joseph P. Strayer, *The Albigensian Crusades*, 8–10, 60–67. Copyright © 1971 by Joseph P. Strayer. Reprinted by permission of Doubleday, a division of Bantam, Doubleday, Dell Publishing Group Inc.

Moreover, he showed no desire to move toward the South. It had been all that he could do to establish his control over the North and he was still consolidating his position there in the early 1200's. It was the Crusades that forced the king to take an interest in the South. The crusading armies were almost entirely composed of men from northern France; their leaders were royal vassals. The king avoided involvement in their campaigns as long as he could, but when the first phase of the Crusades ended in a stalemate he felt that he had to intervene. He did not want princes who were heretics, or at least fellow travelers, as his neighbors, and his own vassals had proved unable to govern the region or to extinguish heresy. So he invaded the South and annexed a great block of territory, running from the Pyrenees to the Rhône. It was this annexation that made France for the next five centuries the most powerful, the wealthiest, and the most populous state in Europe. Neither the pope nor the crusaders who answered his summons had planned to increase the authority of the French king, and yet the aggrandizement of France was one of the most durable results of the Crusades.

Conversely, the success of the Crusades led in the long run to the weakening of the papacy. If religious dissent could be crushed by the sword, then political dissent—disobedience to the pope—could also be crushed by the sword. Thirteenth-century popes were quick to draw this conclusion. They were also quick to draw another conclusion: since the French royal family was responsible for final victory in the Albigensian Crusades, then the French royal family should take responsibility for other wars initiated by the papacy. The French were willing, if they were paid for their trouble, and the Church became dangerously dependent on French support. When, at the end of the thirteenth century, a French king quarreled with Pope Boniface VIII, the pope found that he was helpless. No one came to his aid, even when he was captured and insulted by a French-led gang of conspirators. The successor of Boniface did not dare to live in Italy; he had to take refuge at Avignon, on the borders of France. There the popes remained for over seventy years, improving their administrative apparatus and losing much of their spiritual prestige. They had wiped out heresy, they had defeated most of their political enemies, but they now had only lukewarm support from their friends. The fourteenth-century Church was far weaker, far less influential, than the thirteenth-century Church, and the weakness persisted until the period of the Reformation.

The rise of France, the weakening of the Church, were important events in European history. We would be living in a very different world if France had never acquired a Mediterranean coast; Napoleon, in such a case, almost certainly would not have been a French general. We would be living in a very different world if the Church had not weakened itself in the thirteenth century by becoming addicted to holy wars; in such a case there might not have been a Protestant Reformation. But beyond these obvious conclusions there is a difficult and perplexing problem. The Albigensian Crusades, and their aftermath, the Inquisition, offer one of the classic examples of repression of dissent and of freedom of thought. What effect did this repression have on Western Europe? One unfortunate result was that secular governments learned how easy it was to suppress opposition to their policies. Very few men fought for any length of time in the crusading armies; even fewer men were needed to staff the Inquisition. Yet these small groups were able to wipe out a belief that was held by hundreds of thousands of men and that was viewed with some sympathy by hundreds of thousands of others. Continuing pressure, the use of torture, the imposition of social and economic disabilities, and a nicely graded set of penalties that encouraged the weak to betray the strong in return for immunity or token punishments were the techniques that led to the disintegration of the heretical sects. All these techniques were used by European states of the later Middle Ages. Modern totalitarian governments have made few innovations; they have simply been more efficient.

On the other hand, the cruelty of the Crusades and the injustices of the Inquisition caused large numbers of men to lose faith in both religious and secular institutions. Many good Catholics opposed the Crusades and thought of them as hypocritical excuses for a North French war of conquests. Many good Catholics hated the Inquisition and considered it merely a device for seizing the property of reputable citizens. There was no chance for open rebellion after 1250, but there was plenty of room for obstructionism, cynical political manipulations, and general apathy. When Western European society came under severe strains in the fourteenth century as a result of economic depression, political mismanagement, and plague, a very considerable part of the population made no effort to preserve or reform threatened institutions such as the Catholic Church or the kingdom of France. Instead, they merely tried to save their own status and income. Many forces converged to produce this indifference and this selfishness, but certainly one of the contributing causes was the bitter memory of the Albigensian Crusades. Repression can destroy a faith; it can also produce dangerous decay in the society that uses it.

. . . . .

[The] crusading army had started its march south. It left Lyons on 24 June, and had arrived at Montpellier, one of the few thoroughly Catholic cities of the South, by 20 July. The submission of the count of Toulouse had changed the military objectives of the Crusade; the target was not the lands of the viscount of Béziers rather than Raymond's principality. Raymond Roger of Béziers had at least as bad a reputation for tolerating heretics as Raymond of Toulouse, and his strongholds dominated the region where the Cathars were most numerous. He was the logical man to attack; the only problem was that his strongholds were really strong. One of the basic rules of medieval warfare was never to risk a pitched battle with an invading army while it was fresh and full of enthusiasm. Men who broke this rule, as Harold of England did at Hastings, were running unnecessary and often disastrous risks. The prudent course was to retire before the enemy, concentrate defense forces in a few strongly fortified positions, and wait for the tedium of siege warfare, the inevitable diseases of camp life, and the probable shortage of supplies to weaken the invader. The obvious counterstrategy was for the attacker to seek a quick victory in the field, or, if faced with a siege, to seize every opportunity, no matter how risky, to penetrate the enemy fortress.

The campaign of 1209 offers a classic example of the application of these rules. Raymond Roger did not have much space for maneuver, but he retired to Carcassonne, the most remote and most strongly fortified of his towns. Between Carcassonne and the crusaders lay Béziers, also strongly fortified and well garrisoned. The burghers of Béziers were not entirely happy at being deserted by their viscount, but they were quite confident that they could resist any siege. They were a tough lot; they had assassinated viscount Raymond I in 1167, they had the usual contempt of Occitanians for the clergy, and they had been practically autonomous for many years. They showed their confidence when their bishop, Renaud de Montpeyroux, asked them to turn over 222 heretics to ensure the safety of the city. We have the list of names that he gave, which seems to have included only heads of families, or perhaps only the leaders of the heretics, for Renaud suggested that if the Catholic citizens felt it unsafe to act, they could leave the town and escape the punishment that would be inflicted on the guilty. Some two hundred heretics would not have been enough to terrorize a city of eight to ten thousand people; there must have been many more followers of the two proscribed religions (for Waldensians appeared on the list) and at least an equal number of sympathizers. Whatever the actual figures, the citizens of Béziers refused flatly to betray their unorthodox brethren. As was to be shown again and again during the following decades, the Occitanians felt that the argument between Catholic and heretic was their own private affair, and that the real enemy was the French intruder.

With ordinary prudence, the confidence of the men of Béziers in their ability to resist the crusading army would not have been misplaced. It was almost impossible to storm a fortified town, and if the siege had lasted more than a few weeks the great majority of the crusaders would have fulfilled their obligations and gone home. All that was needed was to sit tight and not provoke the enemy. Instead, the day the siege began (22 July) some of the burghers made a rash and unorganized sortie. In the confused fighting that followed, the defenders were forced back to their gates and the crusaders were able to enter the city along with their fleeing enemies. Once the attackers were inside the walls the gates could not be closed, and more and more men poured in.

There followed one of the most pitiless massacres of the Middle Ages. No one was spared, Catholics and heretics, men and women, clerics and children were all put to the sword. It is not true that the leaders of the Crusade shouted: "Kill them all; God will know his own!" But the German monk who invented this story a few years later accurately reported the mood of the crusading army. In reporting the victory to the pope, the legate Arnaud Amaury said cheerfully that neither age nor sex was spared and that about twenty thousand people were killed. The figure is certainly too high; the striking point is that the legate expressed no regret about the massacre, not even a word of condolence for the clergy of the cathedral who were killed in front of their own altar.

A southern, but Catholic chronicler of the Crusade believed that the massacre was a deliberate act of policy. He says that the leaders had agreed "that in any fortified place that would not surrender, all the inhabitants were to be killed when the place was taken. Then they would find no one to resist them. . . . This is why Béziers was ruined and destroyed, why its inhabitants were slain. All were killed, even those who took refuge in the church. Nothing could save them, neither crucifix nor altar. Women and children were killed, the clergy were killed by those crazy, damnable foot-soldiers. No one escaped; may God, if He will, receive their souls in Paradise. I do not believe that such an enormous and savage massacre ever took place before, even in the time of the Saracens."

It is true that most of the fighting and most of the killing was done by foot-soldiers, camp-followers, and mercenaries. These men were the least disciplined and most brutal element in the crusading army. The mounted men, knights, squires, and barons were the last to enter the city. But this supposedly more chivalrous group of crusaders made no effort to stop the atrocities that were being committed before their eyes. Their indignation was aroused only when the foot-soldiers started looting. This was an infringement on the perquisites of the upper classes and was promptly and swiftly repressed. But if the nobles could stop looting they could have stopped the killing. It is hard not to believe that the massacre was a deliberate act of terror and that the legate was responsible for it. At the very least, he had created an atmosphere of hatred for heretics and their friends which made it easy for the contagion of slaughter to spread.

Deliberate or not, the massacre of Béziers gave the Crusade the quick, initial success that it needed, and broke the resistance of most of the Trencavel lands. The army rested three days in the fields outside Béziers, sharing the booty among the nobles and preparing for the march on Carcassonne. Then the advance began, slowed by the lords who rode in to make their submission and gain the protection of the Church. The great city of Narbonne promised to (and did) take severe measures against its heretics, and dozens of lords surrendered their castles to the army. Others simply abandoned their lands and took refuge in the mountains. The crusaders spent six days in marching the forty-five miles from Béziers to Carcassonne, but it was time well spent. The army now had a solid, well-provisioned base area in the heart of enemy territory.

The city of Carcassonne was not quite as well fortified in the thirteenth century as it was in the nineteenth (thanks to the efforts of that ferocious restorer Viollet-le-Duc), but it was, nevertheless, almost impregnable. Perched on top of a steep hill, surrounded by massive walls, with no cover for the assailants outside the walls, there could be no thought of taking the city by storm. The crusaders settled down to a regular siege, and what should have been a long one. But the siege took place during the warmest part of the summer and Carcassonne, on its hill, began to run short of water. The two suburbs of the city had been taken after hard fighting; refugees from these outposts, added to those who had already fled to Carcassonne as the crusading army advanced, must have terribly overcrowded the city. If viscount Raymond Roger had been able to hold out until fall, it is likely that the besieging army would have melted away, but apparently Raymond Roger feared that prolonged resistance was becoming impossible. He tried to get one of his suzerains, the strictly Catholic king of Aragon, to intercede for him, but Peter of Aragon could secure only a promise that the viscount and twelve of his followers could depart in peace. This was small consolation to a man who knew the fate of Béziers and Raymond Roger decided to act for himself. There are various stories as to the terms on which he entered the crusaders' camp. He must have had some kind of a safe conduct or he could not have negotiated at all; on the other hand, he was treated as a prisoner of war and remained in captivity until his death a few months later.

In any case, Raymond Roger and the men who held the city in his name were able to spare Carcassonne the fate of Béziers. According to the terms of the capitulation, all the inhabitants had to depart; all their property, down to the last penny, was seized as booty; but there was to be no killing. Even the heretics—and there were some notorious Cathar leaders in the city—were allowed to depart in peace. The plundering was systematic and orderly; no houses were destroyed, and many of the Catholic citizens eventually returned and took up their former occupations.

The contrast between the massacre of Béziers and the businesslike occupation of Carcassonne is striking, especially when one remembers that the two events were separated by less than a month. Certainly the crusaders made more of a profit out of the thorough and well-organized confiscation of the goods of the people of Carcassonne than they had out of the wild, unsystematic looting of Béziers. Certainly it must have occurred to some leaders that ruined towns without inhabitants were not a good foundation on which to build new lordships. Certainly the treatment of Carcassonne shows that it was possible to discipline a crusading army and thus strengthens the hypothesis that the massacre at Béziers was a deliberate act of terror. But the essential difference was that Raymond Roger was not at Béziers, and that he was at Carcassonne. He was the lord of the region the Crusade was trying to conquer; he was the archetype of the Occitanian prince who was technically a Catholic but who actually protected and encouraged heresy. Once Raymond Roger had surrendered to the crusaders, he could be made an object lesson to all his fellow-rulers. His lands could be granted to a true Catholic (that is, a Frenchman), and he could be held as a prisoner until death. The crusaders might kill thousands of heretics, but heresy could not be wiped out until the lords of Occitania either moved wholeheartedly to suppress the disease or else were replaced. The calculation was cold and exact; it was worth letting some thousands of heretics go free if Raymond Roger could be kept in prison.

The evidence for this assertion is provided by the events that followed the fall of Carcassonne. The first thought of the legate was to find a new, trustworthy, Catholic viscount of Béziers and Carcassonne. The principality was offered in turn to the duke of Burgundy and the counts of Nevers and St. Pol—probably out of pure politeness, since each of them had all he could do to rule his own lands. It is also likely, though it cannot be proved, that Philip Augustus was opposed to allowing one of his great barons to increase his strength so markedly; after all, it was the accumulation of several large fiefs in the hands of one man that had made the Plantagenets such deadly enemies of the Capetians. In any case, the great lords declined the honor, and, after some discussion, the choice fell on Simon de Montfort. Simon was not powerful enough in France to cause any jealousy, and he had already shown that he possessed two qualities that were essential for a leader of the Crusade, bravery and loyalty to the Church. During the strangely perverted Fourth Crusade, Simon had been one of the few crusaders who had refused to attack the Christian city of Zara; instead, following papal orders, he had gone to the Holy Land. He had fought well there. And he had distinguished himself during the siege of Carcassonne. He was, as it turned out, exactly the right man to finish the job.

THE ALBIGENSIAN CRUSADES†

When in April 1207 Pierre de Castelnau, apostolic delegate and envoy plenipotentiary of Pope Innocent III, was stabbed to death by one of

†From Malise Ruthven, *Torture: The Grand Conspiracy* (London: Weidenfeld and Nicolson, 1978), 75–81, 90–97. Footnotes omitted. Reprinted by permission of Weidenfeld and Nicolson.

the retainers of Count Raymond VI of Toulouse, a train of events was set in motion that destroyed Europe's most brilliant civilization and inflicted a body blow on the Roman Catholic Church from which it was destined never to recover fully. No one, of course, could have foreseen the consequences, either of the murder or of Innocent's reaction to it; nor is it useful to speculate as to whether or not these events would have happened without it. But whether it is seen symbolically, as a solitary act of terrorism that signalled the centuries of terror that were to follow, or as one of those fateful accidents that occasionally tilt the finely-balanced probabilities of action into a new and irrevocable course, the events of that year marked a turning point in the history of the Church. In the struggle against religious dissent, the most powerful of the medieval popes finally abandoned persuasion and diplomacy and initiated a war of destruction. And since the object of his enmity was an idea or series of ideas, rather than the concrete and corporeal manifestations of military power, new and terrible weapons were needed in the campaign. The dazzling military victories initially won by papal arms were no more than the prelude to the battle for hearts and minds waged daily in the tribunals of the inquisition.

For years the Church had been alarmed at the spread and tenacity of heresy in the count of Toulouse's dominions. As early as 1147 St Bernard of Clairvaux, the greatest preacher of his day, had visited Toulouse in order to counteract the dangerous doctrines of a monk called Henry from Lausanne, who had acquired a large following in the area. The situation in the Languedoc had filled St Bernard with despair:

> How much evil has the heretic Henry done, and is still doing, to the Church of God! The Churches are without congregations, congregations without priests, priests without honour, and to sum it all up in one word, there are now only Christians without Christ.

The heresiarch, however, was no match for the saint. The latter challenged him to a public disputation, but Henry refused, either because he knew he would be outclassed by Bernard's renowned eloquence, or because he feared for his own safety. After that, most of Henry's supporters deserted him. He was captured the following year and brought to the bishops in chains, and is believed to have died in prison.

Despite St Bernard's triumph, conditions in the Languedoc did not improve for the Church. In 1178 Count Raymond V appealed to the pope for another mission similar to that of St Bernard:

> Heresy has penetrated everywhere. It has introduced discord into all families, dividing husband and wife, father and son, daughter-in-law and mother-in-law. The priests themselves have been affected. The churches

are deserted and falling into ruin. I myself am doing all I can to stop this plague, but I feel that my powers are not equal to the task. The most important persons in my country have allowed themselves to be corrupted. The masses have followed their example, so that I neither dare nor am able to repress the evil.

We need not suppose that the count was inspired by purely religious fervour in making this appeal to the Church. Although still virtually an independent ruler (he had the advantage of being a vassal of the kings of both England and France), his actual power had been declining. He had lost the contest for Provence to the king of Aragon, who also continued to press him on his western borders. He had backed the wrong side in the struggle between the Emperor Frederick Barbarossa and the pope. Above all, the citizens of Toulouse, his capital, were showing growing signs of independence under their elected consuls. So in seeking to re-establish his credit with the Church, Raymond hoped for support not only against his foreign enemies, but against the powerful burghers of Toulouse whose anti-clericalism and political insubordination sprang from the same source. He was too weak, as he admitted, to act on his own; but if the artillery of the Church could be brought in on his side, there would be worldly benefits as well as spiritual ones.

A mission, led by Cardinal Peter of Pavia and including St Bernard's successor, Abbot Henry of Clairvaux, was duly sent, and for three months established what was the first "real inquisitorial tribunal" ever in Toulouse. Among the first to appear before it was one of the city's richest merchants, described to the tribunal by informants as a "prince" of the "sect", who referred to himself as "John the Evangelist". According to the chronicler who described these events (he was an Englishman, Roger of Hovedene) he was "examined and found to impugn all the articles of the Christian faith". In fact, the text of his confession has survived. At first he denied any heresy, but when he was asked to reaffirm his innocence on oath, he broke down and confessed that he had denied the reality of the Eucharist—his only error. Abjuring his heresy, he begged forgiveness and was sentenced to be flogged naked through the streets of the city and to undertake the pilgrimage to Jerusalem. Meanwhile, all his goods were confiscated.

This ferocious example, we are told, brought many heretics back into the fold who confessed to the cardinal in secret and were treated with mercy. Information about the heretics began to pour in. It was now established, to the satisfaction of the prelates, that they were contending not with Arians (which is what St Bernard had supposed the followers of Henry to be), but Cathars or dualists in the Manichean-Gnostic tradition. Two Manichean "bishops" who had fled to the territories of the viscount of Béziers were summoned to appear. They did so on promise of safe conduct; and, before an impressive assembly of the cardinal, bishops and clergy, and the count of Toulouse and his barons, they were examined on the document they brought with them containing the articles of their faith. According to the chronicler

. . . on the articles of the Christian faith, the men answered on all points as soundly and prudently as though they were thoroughly Christian. But when the Count of Toulouse and others who had previously heard them preaching things contrary to the Christian faith heard this, they were struck with astonishment and kindled with zeal for the Christian faith. Rising to their feet, they proved to the very faces of the men that they had manifestly lied.

They asserted that they had heard from some of them [i.e. the heretics] that there were two gods, one good, the other evil; the good one had created only invisible things, those which could not be altered or corrupted; the evil one had formed the heavens, the earth, mankind and other visible things. Others affirmed that they had heard in their preaching that the body of Christ was not consecrated by the ministry of an unworthy priest or of one who was tramelled by any crime.

The accused heretics denied all these charges, and several others, including the doctrine that men and women who had sexual intercourse could not achieve salvation, or that baptism had no effect on children. They made a complete confession of orthodoxy, stating explicitly that a priest, however wicked, could consecrate the body and blood of Christ. But, says the chronicler, when the cardinal ordered them to swear on their confession ". . . verily, like men of twisted mind and warped purpose, they were still unwilling to abandon their heresy, in which the superficial meaning of any authority seemed to delight their gross and dull minds". They quoted the gospel against swearing; the historian, on weaker ground, cites the Old Testament to refute them. After being convicted by many witnesses, they were urged to repent and accept reconciliation according to the usage of the Church. Thereafter,

The Cardinal and bishops, in the presence of the whole people, together with the bishop of Poitiers and other religious men who were present . . . denounced them as excommunicates and damned them, together with their sponsor the devil, and they commanded the faithful of Christ carefully to shun the aforesaid Bernard and Raymond and their accomplices as excommunicates and men given over to Satan.

The two heretic "bishops" evidently returned to the lands of the viscount of Béziers, for when in 1181 Abbot Henry (who by now had been promoted cardinal) raised a troop of horse and foot and captured the fortress of Lavaur, both were seized and converted back to the faith, and were rewarded by being made canons in two churches in Toulouse.

These measures, however, were not enough to silence the dissidents. They still found protection in the courts of the seigneurs, among whom they are supposed to have made converts, they still walked unmolested through the streets and—to the scandal of the faith—debated openly with Catholics, and with each other. It was not till Innocent III mounted the papal throne in 1198 that a long-term strategy was undertaken. On the one hand the cooperation of the local nobility must be sought to prosecute the heretics in their areas. At the same time, since neglect was obviously the main cause of the trouble, the Church must be reformed, with the help of a sustained campaign of popular preaching of the kind that produced such results for St Bernard.

The second part of the strategy, the campaign of popular preaching spearheaded by the orders of Sts Francis and Dominic whose foundations were authorized by Innocent, was to produce long-term benefits for the Church in the second half of the thirteenth century when heresy notably declined. But in the short term the results were meagre. Dominic himself, who began his ministry in Toulouse in 1204, is only known definitely to have made a single convert. Similarly, a preaching order led by a converted heretic, one Durand of Huesca, yielded very poor results at first.

Meanwhile, the first part of the strategy, to obtain the cooperation of the local nobility, also ran into difficulties. Raymond V had died and was succeeded by his son Raymond VI, an altogether less reliable son of the Church. Although he continually professed his orthodoxy, he made no secret of his hostility to the plans of the papal legate, Pierre de Castelnau, who was seeking to form a league of Catholic barons from among his, Raymond's, vassals in order to wage war on those seigneurs who continued to protect the heretics. Raymond refused to join the league, suspecting rightly that the loyalist vassals would seek their own advantage at his expense. The papal legate responded by publicly excommunicating the count of Toulouse and placing his territories under interdict. Immediately afterwards he left for Rome, and was about to cross the Rhône the following morning when he was stabbed to death by one of the Count's retainers. Whether Raymond had given the order for the murder (which is most unlikely) was immaterial: everyone assumed he bore the responsibility. It was this act that finally hardened Innocent's resolution to deal with the situation by force.

The war which followed has come to be known as the Albigensian crusade after one of the dioceses (Albi) in which the heretics had been established. At first the pope tried to involve the king of France, but without success. But he did find an ardent champion in Simon de Montfort, earl of Leicester, a devout

Catholic and one of the foremost warriors of his time. The army consisted of knights tempted by the rich spoils of the south and the usual spiritual benefits, as well as a moratorium on any of their debts; and an infantry consisting mainly of *routiers* or mercenaries drawn from the toughest criminal elements and lured, no doubt, by the prospect of an unlimited orgy of looting, murder and rape at God's expense (that is to say, any sins incurred in the course of the campaign would not have to be paid for in the next world).

The crusade was dominated throughout by secular interests. Count Raymond vacillated between support for the rebels and loyalty to the Church, uncertain of which side would better serve his interests. Accordingly, he lost out to both: the pope took advantage of his attempts to prove his fidelity by making him give up his best castles, which fatally weakened his capacity to resist. But his leading vassal, the viscount of Béziers, was exasperated, as were the counts of Foix and Comminges, for they correctly judged, as Raymond did not, the extent to which the campaign against heresy was merely the cloak for the worldly ambitions of the northern barons and ultimately, the king of France. The rebels were supported by a majority of the people of the towns and their leaders. Some of these were heretics or sympathizers; but most of them, including many of the Catholic clergy, resisted for purely secular reasons. The rich and varied culture of the south had seen the development of a municipal independence, similar to that which created the political mosaic of northern Italy about the same time. The Church's offensive represented a threat to the economic and commercial life of the greatest city of the region, Toulouse. As in other places at other times, religious and commercial liberty were inextricably bound together.

So it was that Catholics and heretics fought shoulder to shoulder in the struggle. At Béziers the crusaders agreed to raise the siege in return for two hundred and twenty-two named heretics. The citizens indignantly refused—and when the Catholic army breached the city walls, most of them were massacred in consequence. Arnald-Amalric, abbot of Citaux and one of the papal envoys, is supposed to have uttered the famous exhortation: "Kill them all! For God will know his own". After the terror of Béziers, resistance in the region temporarily collapsed. Carcassonne surrendered; other cities—Lavaur, Minerve, Casser, Termes—were rapidly taken. The biggest holocaust was at Lavaur, where four hundred heretics were burned in a single day. Toulouse and Narbonne refused to surrender their heretics, claiming disingenuously that they had none to hide. After the battle of Muret (1213) however, where King Peter of Aragon who supported the rebels was decisively beaten, the council of Lateran (1215) stripped Count Raymond of all his territories west of the Rhône including Toulouse and Montaubon, and gave them to de Montfort. The decision was the signal for a spontaneous rebellion against the pope and the king of France, who was now receiving de Montfort, his vassal, in triumph. The issue of heresy had been pushed even more firmly into the background: it was now a war between two nations and two social systems—the southern Occitan, with its own distinctive language and culture, its self-governing city communes or loosely federated earldoms, against the rigid feudalism of the north, represented by Simon de Montfort and the king of France. When de Montfort arrived to claim his fiefdom, the gates were once more closed against him. He prepared to sit out a long siege. But while supervising the construction of one of the engines used for scaling the walls, he was killed by a stone from a catapult.

The war dragged on for a time under de Montfort's successor Amauri and Louis VIII of France. After the death of Raymond VI, his son Raymond VII realized that outright victory was impossible, and sought a compromise. He promised to extirpate heresy in his dominions, if only he could have them back. He assisted the Dominicans and welcomed the Franciscans in his territories. St Anthony of Padua preached in Toulouse, and created a storm of persecution against the heretics. Raymond was received back into the Church, and he undertook to persecute ruthlessly the heretics and all their followers; the same year, 1229, the inquisition was established at Toulouse.

.   .   .   .   .

Such were the actions with which, from the time they appeared in Toulouse, the inquisitors were obliged to concern themselves. Their procedure was nothing if not thorough, but from the beginning they faced enormous difficulties. The Albigensian war had created a rapprochement between all classes in the Languedoc in the face of French imperialism backed by the moral power of the papacy. The local clergy had divided loyalties, torn between their social ties with the heretics (many of them came from well-known Cathar families) and the demands of their ecclesiastical superiors. The local nobility and public authorities had protected the heretics during the war; many of them, moreover, had themselves become infected —less, perhaps, through the intrinsic attractions of Cathar austerities than because the cause of orthodoxy had come to be identified with the hated foreigner.

The first inquisition after the war was established by the Cardinal-Legate Romanus of St Angelo. Sitting in the council of Toulouse he issued a series of draconian decrees designed to destroy the enemies of Christ—measures which in most of northern Europe had worked well enough. Each parish priest, accompanied by two or three reliable Catholics, was ordered to visit all the houses and suspected hiding places such as barns and caves, where heretics might be found. Similar searches were to be conducted by the seigneurs in their districts, as well as in the towns. Whoever was convicted of allowing a heretic to live in his domain would forfeit it and be handed to his seigneur for summary justice. Bailiffs showing themselves negligent in the pursuit would forfeit their goods and posts. Furthermore, a register was to be made in each parish and everyone over the age of fourteen was required to swear on oath to the bishop or his deputy: anyone refusing the oath would be treated as suspect. The oath had to be renewed every three years, and each person having attained the age of reason had to make three annual sacramental confessions to the parish priest and make his communion at Christmas, Easter and Pentecost. Those who failed to attend Holy Communion incurred suspicion.

Needless to say, without the backing of the local seigneurs, the clergy and the whole-hearted support of the count of Toulouse, the decree was unenforceable. One heretic was burned; another "perfect" recanted in exchange for restoration of his civil rights, and denounced a number of ordinary believers who refused to confess and had to be tried outside the jurisdiction of Toulouse, in the French territory of Orange. Among the most notorious heretics denounced to the cardinal-legate were the three seigneurs of Niort, powerful vassals of the Count of Toulouse who had supported the viscount of Bézier's rebellion against the French. In 1230 they murdered a royal official, a crime which remained unpunished, though they were formally accused, together with the count of Toulouse. Emboldened by this in 1233 they attacked the archbishop of Narbonne, injuring him and assaulting his servants and removing the pallium, the symbol of his authority, before setting fire to the surrounding countryside. After frantic appeals by the archbishop to the pope and the king of France, two of the seigneurs were arrested and an inquisition held by the bishop of Toulouse. There were plenty of witnesses prepared to substantiate the charges which included harbouring up to thirty perfects at one of their castles, and putting down a priest in his own church so that a heretic could preach in his stead. But a large number of witnesses also appeared for the defense—including unimpeachable Catholic dignitaries like the archbishop of Vielmore and the preceptor of the Hospitallers at Puysegur, who swore that the chief of the brothers, Bernard-Otho, had been such a zealous persecutor of heretics that he had been responsible for the deaths of more than a thousand of them. With so many good Catholics prepared to perjure themselves, the case against the brothers collapsed, and it was only in 1235, after the inquisition had been permanently established, that Bernard-Otho and his brother Guillaume were once again brought to book.

Some idea of the popular attitudes towards heresy at the time may be gathered from the notorious case of Jean Tissière, a weaver of Toulouse who, like many of his fellows, found himself the object of the inquisitor's attention. Before his arrest, he ran through the streets of the town shouting

> Listen to me, citizens! I am no heretic! I have a wife and sleep with her, and she has borne me sons. I eat meat, I tell lies and swear, and I am a good Christian. So don't believe it when they say I'm an atheist . . . They'll

very likely accuse you too, as they have me. These accursed villains want to put down honest folk and take the town away from its lawful master!

After this, the inquisitors arrested him and, since he persisted in maintaining his orthodoxy, he was "relaxed" to the secular arm for burning. His arrest caused riots in the streets and the Dominican convent was attacked. But his supporters were soon disillusioned, for during his time in prison he met some Cathar perfects who so impressed him that he asked for the *consolamentum*, which they granted. Before his execution he made an "open confession" of his allegiance to the Cathar church—much to the satisfaction of the inquisitors.

The inquisition as it developed was constructed on three pillars: denunciation, interrogation and secrecy. When the inquisitors visited a district, they first encouraged denunciations by summoning everyone to come forward within a week or so and reveal, on oath, whatever they had heard or known about *anyone*, which might have led them to believe that he or she was a heretic, a defender of heretics, or in any way unusual or unconventional in his behaviour. Failure to heed the summons automatically incurred excommunication. At the same time, a "period of grace", varying from fifteen days to a month, was announced, during which any heretics who came forward spontaneously and confessed, abjured their heresy and denounced their fellow sectaries would be treated with mercy. This usually meant that they would be exempted from "relaxation", the heavier penances such as the pilgrimages to Compostella, Canterbury or Jerusalem, and the confiscation of their property.

Thus, before beginning the interrogation of suspects (who were usually referred to formally as "witnesses") the inquisitors had a substantial body of information before them. To protect the witnesses, the evidence was taken in secret, so that the suspect had little or no idea of the amount of evidence that had accumulated against him. In some districts, such as Narbonne and Béziers, the suspect was even deprived of his right to disqualify hostile witnesses on grounds of personal enmity, since the inquisitors were ordered not to disclose the names of witnesses in any manner whatsoever. Similarly, the Roman prohibitions against witnesses of evil character, such as harlots, convicts and even former heretics, were abandoned; while the Roman law debarring spouses and servants from testifying *against* the accused was entirely inverted: they were allowed to give evidence against him but not on his behalf. Theoretically, the existence of two hostile witnesses was sufficient to have one condemned for heresy, but in practice, most inquisitors insisted on a confession. Even Nicholas Eymeric admitted that witnesses often conspired to ruin an innocent man.

The interrogations were conducted under oath, and were both preceded and followed by abjuration. This, of course, automatically eliminated the true heretics, or *Perfecti*, among the Cathars and Waldensians, although some other sects deemed it lawful to swear falsely to the inquisition. From the start, therefore, the interrogations were directed at the two inferior categories designated by the inquisitors: the *credentes*, or believers, who might or might not have made the covenant to receive the *consolamentum* on their deathbeds, and the *fautores* (protectors) of heresy: those who were not themselves believers who might, in some way or other, have helped or protected them. Voluminous reports of these interrogations survive, but they are summaries, not verbatim records. We do not therefore know exactly by what stages the inquisitors brought their victims to confession and what questions were asked, either before or after the formal introduction of torture. One striking feature, however, is the comparative absence of references to the beliefs of the heretics. Although heresy was an intellectual crime, the locus of which was in the human brain, the inquisitors were usually content to infer it from external acts, such as the breaking of bread, the 'adoration' of perfects, the *covenenza* and the *consolamentum*. In particular, they appear to have been more concerned with obtaining the names of those who attended or took part in these forbidden rites than with the personal guilt of the individual under examination. Before the penitent could expect mercy, it was essential for him to prove his genuineness by denouncing his fellow sectaries. In consequence the records are filled with monotonous catalogues of names, places and dates.

The criteria of guilt were often extremely trivial. In 1244 the council of Narbonne stated that it was sufficient that the accused had shown by any word or sign that he considered the heretics "good men". Inordinate emphasis was placed on "popular repute" and the most unreliable hearsay evidence. In 1254 the council of Albi declared that entering the house of a heretic amounted to "vehement suspicion". According to Bernard Gui, some inquisitors held that visiting heretics, giving them alms or guiding them in their travels was enough for condemnation. A Florentine merchant of unimpeachable orthodoxy found himself in serious trouble for bowing socially to a group of men who subsequently turned out to be heretics—his polite gesture having been taken as an act of "adoration". A priest was once condemned for eating some pears in the company of a group of heretics he met in a vineyard.

Most these measures were designed to attack any form of intercourse between the heretics and the Catholic population, virtually all of whom might, according to the inquisitors' designation, fall into the category of fautors of heresy. The inquisitor of Tarragona, Raymond of Pennaforte, divided these into "defenders", who knowingly defended heretics in words and deed; "receivers" who knowingly welcomed them into their houses several times; "concealers", who did not report heretics when they saw them; and "secretors", who conspired to suppress such reports. The operative principle in these as in many other similar offences was, of course, intention. In a society where heretics or heretic suspects might be one's next-door neighbours or even members of one's own family, it might be impossible to avoid an unwitting transgression. As Innocent III had reminded the authorities at a time when the heresy was at its height, even violent presumptions were not the same as proof. The effect of any such scruples, however, was to ensure that the inquisitors extracted a confession.

Even before the formal introduction of torture in 1252, the inquisitors had at their disposal a number of expedients that were to become familiar once more during the twentieth century: prolonged solitary confinement in dark, festering cells, a starvation diet, the use of "stool-pigeons" (fellow prisoners posing as heretic sympathizers), as well as the "torture of delay"—the agonizingly drawn-out legal proceedings that sapped the morale by keeping the suspect in suspense for months, years or even decades. It was not unusual for five or ten years to elapse between a prisoner's first audience and his final conviction. In one case, a prisoner at Carcassonne was brought to confess after nearly thirty years. The inquisition's vigil was ceaseless, its memory bank almost infinite; and since the concept of innocence did not enter into its scheme of things, there was no such thing as being "cleared" of suspicion, of wiping the slate clean. For all but those with the most determined religious convictions, the best course was to confess and ask for mercy—and then to keep firmly out of trouble, for the penalty for relapse was invariably "relaxation".

The introduction of torture was probably a gradual process and, as with the secular edicts of Frederic II, the bull *Ad Extirpanda* merely gave formal sanction to a practice that was already well established. Harsh prison conditions were consciously used to extract confessions. The *"durus carca et arcta vita"*, consisting of starvation and chains in a narrow dungeon, satisfied all the criteria of torture, and it was fully understood that they weakened resistance. However the process was slow, and in southern France the prisons were already overflowing with penitents sentenced to perpetual imprisonment by the inquisitors. The adoption of the tortures employed by the secular law brought matters to a head much more quickly.

The aim of torture, of course, was to induce denunciations as well as confessions. This is a fact of crucial importance that has surprisingly been overlooked by some scholars. The relevant text from the bull *Ad Extirpanda* is quite explicit:

The podesta or ruler [of the city] is hereby ordered to force all captured heretics to confess and accuse their accomplices by torture which will not imperil life or injure limb, just as thieves and robbers are forced to accuse their accomplices and to confess their crimes, for these heretics are true thieves, murderers of souls and robbers of the sacraments of God.

The introduction of torture led, within thirty years, to a new reign of terror such as the Languedoc had not seen since the days of the Albigensian crusade. Since every heretic suspect was obliged to denounce several others, eventually almost every member of the population found a place in the inquisitors' books. Moreover, zeal for the faith was far from being the only motive of the persecutors. Their own power and influence depended increasingly on the confiscation of heretic property they shared with the municipal authorities. Convents, even cathedrals like the great brick fortress of Albi, were built or enlarged at the expense of wealthy merchants or their descendants whom the inquisitors and their collaborators had every interest in convicting as heretics. Since the heirs of those posthumously condemned as heretics were automatically disinherited, no moderately prosperous family in the region could feel entirely safe, however firm its orthodoxy.

In 1280 the citizens of Carcassonne and Albi protested to the king of France against the cruelty and greed of the inquisitors who they believed were using unspeakable tortures to extract confessions from wealthy but blameless Catholics. The appeal was dismissed for lack of evidence; and in their frustration and fear the consuls of Carcassonne, aided by some senior members of the clergy, may have tried to sabotage the inquisition's records. An appeal to the pope was equally unsuccessful, and merely resulted in a reaffirmation of his support for the inquisitors whom he urged to punish severely all those who stood in their way. This naturally increased the arrogance of the inquisitors who now overreached themselves. When the citizens tried to make an appeal to the new king, Philip the Fair, the inquisitor of Carcassonne, Nicolas d'Abbeville, threw the notary who drew it up into prison. The citizens responded by sending a delegation to the king, and this time their appeal was heard. In 1291 Philip addressed a stern rebuke to the seneschal of Carcassonne condemning the newly invented system of torture by which the living and the dead were fraudulently convicted, and forbidding the royal officials from carrying out arrests for the inquisitors except where the culprits were notorious or confessed heretics. There may have been similar protests from Toulouse, for the following year he prohibited the magistrates from using torture on clerks under the jurisdiction of the bishop.

These restrictions merely encouraged the hatred felt by the people for the inquisitors and the Dominicans, and in 1295 there took place what amounted to a rebellion in Carcassonne. The people took to the streets, Nicolas d'Abbeville was driven from his pulpit and the Dominicans and their supporters were assaulted wherever they dared to appear. The inquisition could not survive without the support of the secular authorities, and for a time, because relations between Philip and the pope were bad, its operations were suspended. After a rapprochement in 1299, however, it was renewed with redoubled virulence. At Albi twenty-five of the wealthiest and most respected Catholic citizens were made to confess to heresy with torture and denounce their accomplices; again, it was widely believed that the victims had been selected entirely because of their wealth and that the extracted confessions had been false. Moreover the inquisitors were accused in some cases, it would seem with justice, of falsifying their own records in order to obtain confiscations.

By 1300 the king had renewed his quarrel with the pope and, posing once more as the champion of his southern subjects, he ordered the fullest investigation into the abuses of the inquisition. After receiving a deputation in Paris, he took the unprecedented step of removing the inquisitor of Toulouse from his post and the bishop and seneschals were informed that among the inquisitor's manifold crimes was the habit of beginning his examinations with unspeakable tortures. His cruelty had threatened to provoke a popular rising among the king's loyal subjects. As well as dismissing the inquisitor of Toulouse, the king introduced a number of reforms. The prisoners were put under the joint control of the bishops and the inquisitors, each of whom had to give their approval for arrests. "We cannot," the king declared, "endure that the life and death of our subjects shall be abandoned at the discretion of a single individual who, even if not activated by cupidity, may be insufficiently informed."

The inquisition did not respond to this insult with Christian meekness. When the king's official removed the twenty-five prisoners of Albi from the jurisdiction of the inquisitor of Carcassonne, the latter promptly excommunicated him for impeding the work of Christ. Nevertheless the king pressed ahead with the reforms. The prisoners were to be visited regularly by royal officials accompanied by the inquisitors. The prisons were to be safe, but not punitive; all inquisitorial trials were to be attended by the bishops as well as the inquisitors. Whatever the immediate effects of the reforms, they do not appear to have lasted. In 1306 the citizens of Carcassonne, Albi and Cordes addressed an appeal to the new pope, Clement V, offering to prove that good Catholics had been forced to confess to heresy by torture and the other pressures of the inquisition. The pope ordered an investigation by two cardinals, during which torture and imprisonment were suspended. Most of the complaints were upheld. At Carcassonne, all but the chief jailer were dismissed, and their replacements were obliged to swear, among other things, not to steal the prisoners' food. At Albi the cardinals ordered new, lighter cells to be built, and gave instructions that the chains which some prisoners had been wearing for up to five years should be removed. They decreed that in future torture should be conducted in the presence of the bishop as well as the inquisitors, in order to safeguard Catholic innocence. These reforms—which became known as the "Clementines"—were incorporated into canon law at the council of Vienne in 1311. They were bitterly resented by inquisitors like Bernard Gui, who argued that they would seriously cripple the efficiency of the inquisition; and they were either ignored or wilfully misrepresented by other inquisitors, or technical loopholes were found which made them nugatory.

Thus in the half-century that torture had been institutionalized in the Languedoc, it had progressed from being an instrument of coercion for use against recalcitrant heretics and their protectors, to a weapon of mass intimidation. The rules of the inquisition had yet to be formalized; as with the later developments in the secular law, the establishment of fixed rules and procedures was prompted by the awareness on the part of the lawyers and inquisitors of the abuses to which the system was liable. As it then stood, the torture system was a weapon of inestimable power in the hands of popes or monarchs. In 1304 King Philip the Fair had found it expedient to attend to his southern subjects' grievances over the exactions of the inquisition. Within three years, however, the same monarch was adapting the system to his own ends in what is perhaps the most celebrated scandal of the Middle Ages, the Affair of the Templars.

THE KNIGHTS OF THE TEMPLE†

The Knights Templars* were an order of military monks established after the capture of Jerusalem in the First Crusade (1099) to protect the pilgrims visiting the Holy City from attacks by Saracens and ordinary bandits. They were founded about the same time as the Hospitallers who provided shelter and medical care for the thousands who arrived sick and exhausted from the journey; they took their name from the quarters they were granted near the Al Aqsa mosque on the site of Solomon's temple. As military pressure on the kingdoms of Outremer increased, the Hospitallers also took up arms, and between them the two military orders remained the principal defenders of Christian Palestine until its final evacuation after the fall of Acre in 1291. The prestige and fame acquired by both the military orders in the East led to a considerable accession of wealth in the West. Combining as they did the finest ideals of medieval chivalry with the rigorous asceticism of the monastic orders, they became the darlings of kings

†From Malise Ruthven, *Torture: The Grand Conspiracy* (London: Weidenfeld and Nicolson, 1978), 98–101, 117. Footnotes omitted. Reprinted by permission of Weidenfeld and Nicolson.

*Ed. note: We are including the famous case of the fate of this order here not because we consider it a genocide: we do not. But it is worthy of our attention because it is a dramatic example of how the newly established Inquisition was used and abused.

and popes alike. From early in the twelfth century, European rulers vied with each other in granting them privileges and making gifts of land for their Houses. King Alfonso I of Aragon even left them each a third of his kingdom, including most of Navarre and a large part of Castile. The will was challenged by his heirs and the knights decided not to involve themselves in a protracted legal struggle — a shrewdly magnanimous gesture that could only increase their prestige. With the general development of trade during the twelfth and thirteenth centuries, the value of their properties rose considerably. The king of France borrowed money from the Templars, and gradually this order took up banking on the grand scale, a function for which its international organization and reputation for probity made it ideally suited. It issued letters of credit to merchants throughout Europe, and managed to circumvent the Church's ban on usury by disguising the interest on the loans it issued as rent. Its houses became safe deposits for crown jewels and other royal valuables, and it was entrusted with the transfer of Church tithes to Rome as well as monies for the Holy Land.

The military orders were entirely autonomous institutions, owing no allegiance other than to the pope himself. They paid no tithes or taxes and enjoyed all the immunities from civil law accorded to those in holy orders; at the same time, the bishops were forbidden to excommunicate them, and were ordered to refer even the local disputes in which they might become involved with them direct to Rome. Naturally these privileges made the Templars and Hospitallers the object of considerable resentment among the bishops and ordinary clergy. The policy of the popes oscillated between unconditional support for the orders and fierce castigations for their pride which, among the Templars especially, began to be notorious. In 1207 Innocent III delivered a stinging rebuke to the fighting élite of Christendom in a bull entitled *De Insolentia Templariorum*, in which, among other things, he accused them of apostasizing from God, scandalizing the Church, and employing doctrines worthy of demons. Although successive popes reconfirmed the orders in their privileges, this polemical attack by the most magnificent of all the princes of the medieval church would not be forgotten. As the military situation in Palestine deteriorated, it was inevitable that the two orders should be blamed for the Christian losses. The charges were exacerbated by the growing rivalry between them. Rumours of treason and corruption began to circulate, fanned by the mutual antagonism. After the loss of the last Christian stronghold at Acre, the Hospitallers regained some of their prestige by conquering the island of Rhodes; the stock of the Templars, on the other hand, was further diminished by a pointless expedition in which they enriched themselves at the expense of the Latin Princes in Greece.

Meanwhile, relations between the Templars and their two most powerful protectors, the pope and the king of France, came under increasing strain as a

result of the refusal of the Grand Master of the order, Jacques de Molay, to agree
to a merger with the Hospitallers. The idea had been mooted ever since the loss
of Palestine, which had been widely attributed to the rivalry between the two
orders. It was indispensable to the ambitious new crusade that Philip was planning to launch. This entailed not only the recovery of the Holy Land, but also
the conversion of the Saracen by a special team of missionaries trained in Arabic who would follow in the wake of the new model army to be commanded by
Philip himself. De Molay's reluctance to go along with the king's wild design,
coupled with his order's apparent inactivity and lack of Christian enthusiasm,
would have been enough to arouse the irritation of both king and pope, without
the additional annoyance of Philip's financial troubles. Like the Tudor monarchy in England, two centuries later, the French kingdom was rapidly outgrow-
ing its financial resources. Philip had begun by taking over some of the Church's
sources of income—a move which had drawn him into conflict with Boniface
VIII; then he devalued the currency, provoking popular riots in Paris. Then, in
1306, he turned on the Jews, who were thrown into prison, their money stolen
and their goods sold for the benefit of the exchequer. Finally, it was the turn of
the Templars: it might have been the Hospitallers, who were just as wealthy, if
not more so. But they were also more powerful, and, what was more important,
they were more popular in France where they carried on their tradition of providing shelter for the poor. The Templars provided a softer and easier target.

Since the inquisition was to be Philip's instrument for the destruction of the
order, the charge he brought against them was heresy—though it was heresy of
an obscure, and peculiarly abominable kind. The proclamation for the arrest of
the knights has survived, and even in translation retains something of its original flavour:

. . . on the report of persons worthy of trust, we have been informed that
the brothers of the military order of the Temple, hiding under the habit of
the order as wolves in sheep's clothing, insulting miserably the religion of
our faith, have once more crucified in our time our Lord Jesus Christ,
already once crucified for the redemption of mankind, and inflicted on him
worse injuries than he suffered on the Cross; when, on entering their order,
they make their vows and are presented with His Image and by a sorrow
—what shall I say, a miserable blindness, they deny Him thrice and by a
horrible cruelty, spit thrice on His face; after which, divested of the clothes
they wore in secular life they are taken naked into the presence of him
whose task it is to receive them and there they are kissed by him, according
to the odious rite of their order, first at the base of the spine, secondly on
the navel, and finally on the mouth, to the shame of human dignity. And
after they have offended against the Divine Law by equally abominable

and detestable acts they oblige themselves, by an oath and fearless of the offence against human law, to deliver themselves one to another, without refusal —and from this time they are required by this vice to enter into an horrible concubinage; and that is why the wrath of God has fallen upon these sons of infidelity. . . .

These odious rites and sodomies were not the only charges brought against the order. According to the detailed instructions given to the commissioners charged with the arrests, an even more sinister significance was attached to the belts the Templars wore over their tunics and which they were never supposed to take off for the whole of their lives. Although it was known only to the Grand Master and the elders of the order, each of these girdles had been secretly consecrated to a heathen idol in the form of the head of a bearded man, which was kissed and adored in each of the provincial chapters. The proclamation was issued in September 1307—though the actual arrests were not carried out for another month. The Templars seem to have had no inkling of the impending catastrophe. The secret was well kept and the *coup de main*, masterminded by Philip's chief minister Guillaume de Nogaret, well coordinated. At daybreak on 13 October, the Templars throughout France were arrested, and the inquisition at once began its work.*

Those who stuck to their confessions were distributed to various monasteries throughout Europe; those who stubbornly maintained their innocence were con-demned to perpetual imprisonment. The order's goods and properties were given to the Hospitallers (but only theoretically in France, where the government had already grabbed the best part of them).

There was a final, heroic scene in this dismal story of royal ambition and papal pusillanimity. The four leaders of the order were brought to the public scaffold in Paris to receive formally their sentences of life imprisonment. Hugues de Pairaud and Geoffroy de Gonville remained silent as the catalogue of abomi-nations was read to them. But Jacques de Molay suddenly and unexpectedly

*Ed. note: The Templars were the victims of persecution in France because the king was desperately looking for money to finance his campaigns in a period when taxation as a means of raising state revenue had not yet been introduced there. The Templars were immensely rich, had become arrogant in the use of their military and financial powers, and had not bothered to find a new raison d'être after the end of the Crusades. The accusation of heresy was a perfect tool of attack because of the secrecy of their rites and because most of them could be made to confess under torture. If they confessed, the most prominent Templars were burned at the stake; if they recanted their confession, they were judged to have relapsed into heresy and were burned at the stake. After much struggle between the disbelieving papacy and the determined king, the order was finally disbanded at the Council of Vienne during the winter of 1310–11.

spoke out, and made before the assembled crowds a last, ringing proclamation of innocence. He was supported by the preceptor of Normandy, Geoffroy de Charnay. Both were sent to the stake without more ado, before the pope or even the bishops had been consulted. But this final act of defiance by the Grand Master did something to vindicate his memory and that of the order his own feeble leadership had played so notable a part in ruining.*

*Ed. note: While it is true that this group has ceased to exist as an order, very few of the knights were killed, and those only in France. In the rest of Europe the charges against the order were not taken very seriously and none were killed; but the papal order to disband was, of course, carried out.

THE CHRISTIANS IN JAPAN

Here is a case on which there is a large literature that is inaccessible, unless you can read Japanese! The materials that are available in English are limited, especially if one is not particularly interested in the martyrdom of individual priests and missionaries.

To understand the ideological basis for Japan's exclusion policy requires not facile generalizations about the geopolitics of an island empire, but a detailed analysis of the history of Japan. The two failed attempts by the Mongols to conquer Japan are only a minor episode in that history—not because Japan was able to defeat them, but because each time a typhoon destroyed the fleet of the Mongols. The much later arrival of European ships generated much interest in Japan. Any such foreign intrusion was, however, met with suspicion because it seemed to have the potential for upsetting the carefully balanced, hierarchical structure of the Tokugawa shogunate that Mikiso Hane describes so well in the excerpt that follows. Even more threatening than trade were the missionaries that arrived with the first ships. They learned Japanese and impressed the Shogun and the nobles with their knowledge of the outside world. Their proselytizing was entirely unwelcome, but they persisted in their missionary zeal. These Iberian world travelers were soon followed by the Dutch, who were interested only in trade. By then it was too late and the success of the missionaries produced a policy that was directed against all foreign contacts.

The surprising aspect of this case is that the Catholic religion, brought by foreign missionaries, should have made such large inroads among the population —among the ruling classes as well as among the peasants. Perhaps it was this very success that eventually spelled its doom. A series of exclusion orders was passed to curb foreign intrusions. It is estimated that by 1610 there were about one million Christians—all in southern Japan. Persecution started with the Jesuit missionaries and then extended to all Christians—European or Japanese converts. Data from Tokugawa records indicate that about 285,000 Christians were martyred between 1587 and 1610. The Shimambara rebellion became the climax of the persecutions of the Christians—not because of the rebellion though. Peasant rebellions occurred frequently in protest against rapacious taxation. They were usually ruthlessly suppressed although the peasants were not exterminated. The Shimabara rebellion also started as a protest against the burden of taxation; what was different was that both the peasants as well as the unemployed samurai (*ronin*) who helped them were predominantly Christian. It was their Christianity rather than their rebellion which led to their extermination.

We have included this case because it is an early example of a purely ideological genocide. It resulted in the strict enforcement of the exclusion orders, which were not relaxed until the nineteenth century.

THE CHRISTIANS IN JAPAN: BACKGROUND†

For more than two centuries before Commodore Matthew C. Perry arrived in Tokyo Bay in 1853, demanding that Japan establish diplomatic relations with the United States, Japan had been virtually sealed off from the outside world, except for a small "opening" at Nagasaki, where the Dutch, Chinese, and Koreans were allowed to come and trade under tight restrictions. During this period, Japan was ruled by the Tokugawa shogunate (Bakufu), which had been established in 1603. Under the Tokugawa rulers, there were about 270 feudal lords (*daimyō*) with domains (*han*) of varying sizes. These lords had autonomous authority over their *han*, but they were in effect vassals of the *shōgun* ("overlord"), and their political conduct was strictly regulated by the Bakufu. The *shōgun* as well as the *daimyō* had their own retainers who, in most instances, were allotted a fixed stipend in return for their services. Unlike the vassals of medieval Europe, the warrior-retainers of Tokugawa Japan were not granted fiefs and did not reside in manorial estates but in "castle towns" where their feudal lords were ensconced. In this sense they were military bureaucrats.

The founders of the Tokugawa shogunate divided the society they ruled into four main classes: the warriors (*samurai*), the peasants, the artisans, and the merchants. At the bottom of society were the outcastes (formerly referred to as *eta* and *hinin*, now as *burakumin*), who may have numbered close to half a million or so by the end of the Tokugawa era. In addition to these strict strata there were the priests, and, at the very top, court aristocrats and, of course, the *daimyō*.

In theory, class divisions were fixed; distinctions between the *samurai* and commoners were strictly observed. Intermarriage was prohibited, although toward

†From Mikiso Hane, *Peasants, Rebels and Outcastes: The Underside of Modern Japan* (New York: Pantheon Books, 1982), 5–7. Footnotes omitted. Reprinted by permission.

the end of the Tokugawa era financially hard-pressed *samurai* sometimes formed marital ties with wealthy merchant houses. Peasants were officially forbidden to leave the land they worked, but those located near towns and cities often did leave their villages in quest of jobs. In general, however, one could say that the official policy of freezing the sociopolitical order was remarkably successful. The peasants, who constituted the vast majority of the population, labored on the land for over two-and-a-half centuries, doing the bidding of the *samurai* class. Only commoners dwelling in towns and cities managed to enjoy some of the benefits of commercial growth.

The peasants were required to turn over to the *daimyō* or Bakufu anywhere from 40 to 50 percent of their harvest as a land tax. As the economic needs of the ruling class became more acute, some *daimyō* collected as much as 70 percent of the yield. In addition to the land tax, a large number of miscellaneous taxes —taxes on doors, windows, female children, cloth, sake, hazel trees, beans, and hemp—were levied on the peasants. The peasants were also called upon to provide corvée to maintain roads, bridges, and other public facilities as well as to repair horse stations along the main roads.

The ruling class regulated the lives of the peasants in minute detail, periodically issuing sumptuary decrees to curb peasant consumption, or proclaiming moral injunctions exhorting them to be frugal, diligent, and self-denying. The ruling class determined what the peasants could plant and grow; what they could eat, drink, and wear; and the kind of houses they could live in. In some instances the *daimyō* even regulated daily work hours. These pronouncements were backed by the sword; little wonder that the ethos and mores of the Japanese peasantry came to be characterized by diligence, frugality, submissiveness, subservience, and self-denial.

However, the peasants could be driven to shatter the psychological barriers of servility and obedience, striking out in blind anger against the authorities, when their situation became desperate enough. In most instances, they sought redress through nonviolent means, submitting petitions to the *shōgun, daimyō*, or other high officials even though they knew they faced certain death because direct appeals to higher authorities were strictly forbidden. When their petitions failed to produce results, which was most often the case, they often turned to mass demonstrations or to violence. Between 1590 and 1867, there were over 2,800 peasant disturbances, most of them erupting in the latter half of that Tokugawa era.

Such uprisings erupted most frequently in years of major famines, when the peasants were literally driven to starvation. There were at least fifteen serious famines during the Tokugawa era, and, just as in the modern age, villagers in the northern areas suffered most severely.

FOREIGN RELATIONS†

I. The Phase of Expansion

Ieyasu . . . was enthusiastic in the promotion of foreign trade, and the first decades of the seventeenth century saw a rapid expansion of Japanese activity abroad. The Bakufu issued licenses for the voyages of Japanese merchant vessels under the Shōgun's vermilion seal, while individual Japanese traders and other adventurers found their way to most countries in the western Pacific and beyond the Malacca Straits to Burma. The number of licenses issued between 1604 and 1635 was of the order of three hundred, or an average of ten voyages out and home each year. This was a fairly large number in a period of very slow transport by sea. In addition to these licensed carriers, Portuguese and Chinese ships carried both imports and exports, while the western daimyos, especially Shimazu, Matsuura, Nabeshima, and Ōmura, traded in licensed vessels on their own account from time to time.

The behaviour of some of the licensed ships was almost piratical. They would attack any ship or place for booty, and they were feared in all parts of South-East Asia. Several countries protested and pressed the Japanese government to take measures of control. At the request of Luzon the visits of the licensed ships were reduced to four a year. Some writers regard this action as a prelude to the exclusion policy developed in the 1640's.

The export cargoes consisted mainly of silver, copper, iron, sulphur, camphor, rice, and other grains, as well as substantial quantities of lacquer goods, fans, and similar works of handicraft. In return traders brought to Japan raw silk (the most important item), silk fabrics of high quality, cotton, shark skin, deer skin, scented woods, dyes, sugar, lead, and tin.

There were Japanese settlements in most parts of eastern Asia, from Formosa and Macao to the Moluccas, the Philippines, Borneo, Celebes and Java, Siam and the Malay Peninsula. The largest were in Luzon, Siam, and Indo-China. Many of the settlers were soldiers who could find no suitable employment at home after the wars. Among them was one Yamada Nagamasa (d. 1633), who lived in the Siamese capital of Ayuthia, where he was trusted as an adviser by the King and appointed to high office. He was able by his military skill to suppress an outbreak of revolt during a succession dispute.

†From George Sansom, *A History of Japan: 1615–1867*, 3:35–45. Reprinted by permission of the publishers, Stanford University Press © 1963 by the Board of Trustees of the Leland Stanford Jr. University and Wm. Dawson & Sons Ltd.

2. The Exclusion Policy

This thriving and promising phase of expansion came to a surprising end upon the issue of certain orders closing the country to foreign trade and travel with a few strictly limited exceptions. These orders, of 1633, 1635, and 1639, are often loosely described as the three Exclusion Decrees. This is not quite accurate, since in form they were not public notices but letters of instruction to provincial officers directing them how to carry out the policy of the central government.

It is of especial interest to examine and compare the contents of these documents, since they show the gradual development of a policy of almost complete isolation—an historical phenomenon which, while simple in appearance, is by no means easily explained. They are akin to the anti-Christian orders issued by Ieyasu in the years 1611–14, but they are much more drastic and much wider in scope.

The order of 1633 is in the form of a memorandum addressed to the two Governors of Nagasaki by the Rōjū Sakai Tadakatsu and three other high officers of the Bakufu. Its main provisions (there are seventeen articles in all) are as follows:

1. It is strictly forbidden for any vessel without a valid license to leave Japan for a foreign country.
2. No Japanese subject may leave for a foreign country in any vessel without a valid license.
3. Japanese subjects who have resided abroad shall be put to death if they return to Japan. Exception is made for those who have resided abroad for less than five years and have been unavoidably detained. They shall be exempt from punishment, but if they attempt to go abroad again they are to be put to death.

The remaining articles deal principally with the search for Christian converts and for missionaries already in hiding in Japan or being smuggled in at Japanese ports. The treatment of foreign vessels applying for entry is to be decided by reference to Yedo.

The order of 1635 is also addressed to the two Governors of Nagasaki. It contains seventeen articles, which resemble those of the 1633 order, but are stated in somewhat more specific terms. Thus Japanese ships are strictly forbidden to make voyages abroad; Japanese subjects may not go abroad, and those who are found secretly taking passage will be put to death, the ship concerned, with its master, to be held pending reference to Yedo. The remaining articles deal chiefly with the search for Christians and with the treatment of cargo. The last article deals with the handling of consignments of raw silk from China. This was the most valuable single item of import trade, and the order provides that the Bakufu, or more specifically the Shōgun, should enjoy a monopoly of the sale of all raw silk. A further provision of interest (Article 14) lays down rules for the treatment of foreign vessels entering Japanese ports, and grants some special privilege to Portuguese and Chinese vessels.

An order of 1636 (not counted separately in our designation of three orders) is substantially the same as that of 1635, except for three clauses dealing with the children and grandchildren of foreigners by Japanese mothers. By another notice of the same year all foreign residents were ordered to move to Deshima, at the head of Nagasaki Bay, where lodgings had been prepared for them. This applied at first only to a few Portuguese, who were expelled from Japan not long afterwards (1638). Later Deshima was to become the permanent home of all Dutch residents in Japan, who moved there from Hirado in 1641. They were confined to a restricted area, and their families were obliged to leave the country.

These documentary orders of 1633–36 together completed the isolation of Japan, except for an indirect contact with the outside world through Chinese, Portuguese, and Dutch ships entering only designated ports and subject to rigorous inspection and control. It will be seen that most of the prohibitions are related to the anti-Christian policy as it had developed since the death of Ieyasu, and it should be noted that in addition to these orders issued to officials in Bakufu domains a clause in the Buke Sho-Hatto of 1635 requires all daimyos strictly to forbid the practice of Christianity in their fiefs.

The third and final measure in the exclusion policy, taken in 1639, seems to have been stimulated by a rising in Kyūshū in 1637–38 which was regarded by the Bakufu as a revolt of Japanese Christians. This was the Shimabara Revolt, in which an army of peasants from the island of Amakusa and the near-by Shimabara peninsula held out for several weeks against a powerful force mobilized by western barons at the order of the Yedo government. The slaughter was dreadful. The insurgents were for the most part poor country people, but they were joined by a number of disaffected samurai and led by some soldiers who had fought under Christian generals in the civil wars. Their total number is usually given as 37,000 and it is said that only a hundred or so escaped. These figures have been challenged, and it is probable that the number of combatants on the rebel side was not more than 20,000. The government forces are put at about 100,000, and their casualties must have amounted to 10,000 or more. They appear to have fought without much courage or skill, and they were not competently led. Their failure to achieve an easy victory seems to indicate a decline in the military spirit during the two decades after the siege of Ōsaka.

The revolt was not primarily a religious uprising, but a desperate protest against the oppressive rule of feudal lords in a remote and backward region. Yet there can be no doubt that many of the insurgents were inspired to feats of courage by the Christian faith of their leaders. Their banners were inscribed with the names of saints and with such legends as "Praise to the Blessed Sacrament." Whatever its true nature, this rebellion led to the end of overt Christian worship in Japan. It doubtless hastened and redoubled the efforts of the authorities to track down believers and to hunt out missionaries; and it must have strengthened the trend towards exclusion which was already apparent in the orders of 1633 and 1635.

The final exclusion order of 1639 was issued over the signatures of the seven senior councillors. It states that in view of the continued arrival of foreign priests and their teaching of the forbidden Christian faith, the formation of leagues plotting against the government (a capital offence), and the fact that prohibited articles from abroad can be sent to priests in hiding and their converts, no galliot (Portuguese vessel) shall from now on be admitted to a Japanese port. Should this order be disobeyed the offending vessel will be destroyed and its crew and passengers put to death. The substance of these orders is to be communicated to Chinese and Dutch vessels arriving at a Japanese port, with a promise of rewards for information regarding persons illegally entering the country.

In spite of this unqualified ban a Portuguese vessel entered Nagasaki Bay in July 1640. The 1639 expulsion had struck a serious blow at the Macao trade, and the Senate of the island had decided to take the great risk of sending a mission to Japan begging the government there to reconsider its policy. But no sooner had the vessel arrived than it was dismantled, and its crew and passengers taken into custody pending the receipt of instructions from Yedo. Early in August the reply came. It was communicated to the Portuguese envoys in a solemn and ceremonial manner. Accused of defying the laws of Japan, the envoys replied that they were not a trade mission and had brought no cargo but only a diplomatic memorial to the Japanese government. The Japanese Commissioners then ordered the sentence to be read to them. It was a sentence of death for disobeying a decree of the Shōgun which had been pronounced for the purpose of putting an end to Christianity in Japan.

Early next morning the envoys, bound and imprisoned, were offered their lives if they would renounce the Christian faith. They all refused, and were thereupon taken to the execution ground, where fifty-seven of their number were decapitated. The remaining thirteen were spared, so that they should carry a report of the punishment to Macao. Their ship was burned.

Evidently the exclusion policy of which this drastic action was a clear display was in some way connected with fear of foreign aggression; yet the texts of the relevant exclusion orders all seem to indicate that their main purpose is the destruction of Christianity in Japan. This view, however, is not easy to reconcile with the condition of Christian evangelism in 1635–39, the years during which the orders were issued. It is therefore worth while to examine the development of anti-Christian policy in Japan from the early days of Ieyasu's government with a view to understanding its motives.

3. The Anti-Christian Movement

It will be remembered that the first anti-Christian pronouncement was made in 1611; this was a notice instructing officials to take steps against converts. It was followed in 1612 by an order to Hasegawa Fujihiro (Sahyōe), Governor of Nagasaki from 1606 to 1614, to punish certain specified offenders. Then came a long decree in June 1613, addressed to all monasteries and shrines, calling upon them to beware of the Evil Sects, which were Christianity and a certain unorthodox branch of the Nichiren or Lotus Sect. Finally in January 1614 the monk Sūden presented a memorial in which he described the evils of Christian belief and the harm done by its teaching to the native religious tradition. This document, in which a certain Confucian flavour can be detected, called for the expulsion of foreign missionaries. It was approved by Hidetada under his vermilion seal, and thus became the law.

It must be said that Ieyasu was quite patient with the foreign missionaries until 1612, and even then his action was relatively mild. He would not allow his officers, the members of the military class, to become Christians, but he did not interfere with the beliefs of the classes beneath them—the farmers, craftsmen, and traders. It is true that in 1613 twenty-seven Japanese evangelists and catechists were executed; but this was punishment for a deliberate breach of the law in the Shōgun's capital by a Spanish missionary named Sotelho, who in 1612 built a chapel in Yedo and publicly celebrated mass. Sotelho was condemned to death, but the sentence was not carried out.

In 1614, however, the ban on Christianity was stated in positive terms. At this time Ieyasu was willing to expel the Jesuits and other missionaries, especially since he could now rely upon Dutch and English traders, who were not subject to missionary pressure. Most of the missionaries now left, but a few remained in hiding and others returned to Japan secretly. It is known that there were several Fathers in the castle at Ōsaka during the siege. Yet despite this flouting of the edicts no foreign priest was punished by death during Ieyasu's lifetime. There is indeed good reason to suppose that Ieyasu, preoccupied as he was with the coming trial of strength at Ōsaka, was not much perturbed by the Christian propaganda in Japan. The decrees issued during his lifetime do not bear the marks of his authorship, and those of 1613 and 1614 were thought by the Jesuits and by the resident English traders to be the work of Hasegawa, the Governor of Nagasaki, who was bitterly anti-foreign and responsible for cruel persecution of Christians in the Arima fief, which he secured by mean trickery in 1614.

Ieyasu was a man of broad mind and calm judgment. He was more interested in the expansion of trade than in the punishment of missionaries. It was not until after his death that stringent action was taken against Christians in Japan. A new edict was issued in October 1616 by the Rōjū. It was addressed to all daimyos and ordered them to prevent all their people, down to the farmers, from adopting the Christian faith. Also in 1616, shortly after Ieyasu's death, certain restrictions were placed on the voyages of Japanese vessels licensed under the vermilion seal. They were to obtain a special approval from the Rōjū.

This measure was the first step in a policy of seclusion which was presently to be rigorously enforced by the Tokugawa Bakufu. In the same year all foreign vessels, except Chinese, were forbidden to enter any ports other than Hirado and Nagasaki. The anti-Christian movement, however, still had not reached its height, and at about this time two Jesuit Fathers, de Angelis in 1618 and Carvalho in 1620, travelled to Yezo and visited newly discovered gold mines. They said mass in settlements of miners brought there from the mainland by a "gold rush" of some 50,000 men a year. In the years from 1618 to 1621 a large number of Japanese Christians, both priests and converts, were executed in Kyoto and Nagasaki—over fifty in 1619—but no foreign Christian was done to death until 1622, which was the year styled in the reports of the missions the year of the Great Martyrdom. At this time Christians were beheaded and twenty-five burned at the stake. Of the latter, nine were foreign priests, the first to suffer the death penalty in Japan.

The tragic scene was described by an eyewitness, the English trader Richard Cocks, a man who had no liking for the "papistical" missionaries. He wrote: "I saw fifty-five of them martyred at one time at Miyako. Among them were little children of five or six years, burned alive in the arms of their mothers, who cried 'Jesus, receive their souls!' There are many in prison who hourly await death, for very few return to their idolatry." No wonder that Cocks called the government of Japan "the greatest and the most puissant tyranny the world has ever known."

In 1624 a number of missionaries from Luzon were allowed entry, but Hidetada refused to approve the requests of an official mission from the Philippines seeking for privileges for Spanish evangelists and traders. In 1625 he forbade Spanish subjects to reside in Japan for purposes of trade, though he did not prohibit trade as such. His order did not, however, prevent the smuggling of missionaries into Japan, and at a somewhat later date Matsukura Shigemasa actually proposed an expedition to destroy what he described as the missionary base in Luzon.

This may have been only a specious excuse for buccaneering voyages, but it is evident that some Bakufu officials were moved by a genuine fear of the influence of Christian doctrine. It is true that most of the converts were poor country people, but there were also among them many samurai and city dwellers. Converts of every kind were subjected to such fierce oppression that in the towns all the Christians seem either to have recanted or to have vanished into obscurity. But the countryfolk clung to their faith and disobeyed the edicts, meaning to resist at the cost of their lives. The Bakufu resorted to cruel persecution, seeking out believers in the remotest corners of the poorest provinces and subjecting them to torture. Yet while some recanted, many withstood the agony inflicted upon them by ruthless pursuers. In some parts of Kyūshū the peasants formed leagues to prolong their revolt, especially in poor regions where religious fervour was strongest.

By 1625 the persecution had reached its peak, and Christianity had been either eradicated or driven underground in most parts of Japan, though there were sporadic revivals and martyrdoms for two or three decades more. In some places the peasants continued to worship in secret, encouraged by missionaries in hiding.

In 1640 a board of enquiry was established in Yedo—a kind of Inquisition —called Shūmon-Aratame, the Examination of Sects. In 1664 all daimyos of 10,000 koku and above were ordered to establish a similar office. The test of trampling on the Cross (*fumie*) was introduced. In order to trace the religious beliefs of the people all monasteries and chapels were ordered to keep a register of persons resident in their parish, with particulars of birth, death, marriage, travel, occupation, and so forth. Thus the Buddhist clergy were called upon to act as police agents for the Bakufu in the pursuit of Christians.

It will be noticed that documents of 1633–39 clearly state that the purpose of the exclusion edicts was the suppression of Christianity in Japan. Since the teachings of the missionaries were incompatible with the feudal principles upon which the power of the Bakufu was based, the persecution of the priests and their converts, though morally evil, might be defended on political grounds; but it could scarcely be argued that it was necessary to close the country altogether in order to keep out the influence of a foreign religion.

Evidently there are some anomalies here. In the first place, the exclusion policy was not thoroughgoing, since it made exceptions for China and Holland, in fact for any country that did not send Christian missionaries to Japan. The Dutch, anxious to capture the Japan trade, had been at pains to warn the Japanese against the Portuguese and the Spanish, whom they accused of planning to seize Japanese territory or at least to use force against Japan. The English traders would not have been excluded, but they had already left Hirado (the centre of their activities) in 1623, before the exclusion orders. Thus the effect desired by the Bakufu could have been secured by the existing ban upon the entry of Portuguese or Spanish persons, whether traders or missionaries.

The Spanish had been denied entry after 1624. And, as mentioned, all foreign residents were ordered in 1636 to move to Deshima at the head of Nagasaki Bay, where lodging was prepared for them. This applied only to a few Portuguese, who were expelled from the country in 1638, following the Shimabara rising. Moreover, by the time of the third and final exclusion order of 1639, Christianity had been all but entirely stamped out, and it would have been possible to prevent the entry of missionaries by a systematic control at the ports. This, however, would have required the collaboration of the daimyos in whose territory the ports were situated; and here we have a further clue to the policy of the Bakufu.

The Tozama daimyos in western Japan and Kyūshū profited by foreign trade, and if they were allowed to continue their trading they might easily grow strong enough to endanger the primacy of the Bakufu and even bold enough to call upon Portuguese or Spanish assistance. The only way of preventing such rivalry was to prohibit all foreign trade at ports other than Nagasaki, which was under the direct jurisdiction of the Bakufu. In this way the Bakufu obtained not only a control of foreign trade but also a monopoly of its profits; and whatever other result was expected from the exclusion policy, it is quite clear that this is exactly what the Shōgun had been aiming at since Ieyasu's day. In retrospect it becomes evident that Tokugawa policy was directed to creating a dictatorship, an authoritarian state, exercising full control over all aspects of the national life, economic as well as social and moral.

Was the Bakufu's fear of Christian propaganda genuine, or was it a pretence by which the exclusion policy was justified? The number of Japanese Christians, probably of the order of 300,000 before the great persecutions, may have fallen by death and apostasy to far less than 100,000 men and women who practised their devotions in concealment. It is hard to believe that a man of the stature of Ieyasu would have been deterred from his policy of expansion by fear of the influence of so small and weak a community as the scattered Christians after 1625. But neither Hidetada nor Iemitsu was cast in the heroic mould, and it is probable that they and their advisers genuinely feared foreign aggression. They were not men to take a great risk. They had no trust in the loyalty of the Outside Lords, and what they had heard of the activities of European states did not encourage them to join in the struggle for territories and trade which was disturbing the Pacific Ocean.

There is an illuminating passage in a report of François Caron, the head of the Dutch trading station in Japan, who had given some lessons in world geography to Iemitsu. Writing in 1641, Caron says that "after investigating the size of the world, the multitude of its countries and the smallness of Japan . . . he [Iemitsu] was greatly surprised and heartily wished that his land had never been visited by any Christian."

Reflecting upon the history of the persecution of Christians in Japan one cannot avoid the question of cruelty. The descriptions of torture to which the converts were subjected are heart-rending, and evoke a detestation of the very memory of those who ordered such atrocities. It appears at first sight that religion calls forth bitter hatreds compared with which secular animosities are almost gentle. In Japan, men, women, and children died after agonies prolonged with a fiendish ingenuity that, it seems, could not be matched elsewhere. But the record of the Christian Church in mediaeval Europe is no less sickening. It even gains an increment of horror from the fact that the pain of the victims was enjoyed. We learn of Savonarola that he suffered "many and assiduous tortures" for many days; and that the Albigensian crusaders burned "innumerable heretics with immense joy—[cum ingenti gaudio]."

It should be noted that the persecution of Christians in Japan was not primarily of religious origin. It was not proposed by the Buddhist Church nor did the Buddhist clergy play an important part in it. The antagonism of the ruling class to Christianity was mainly political. Socially, Christianity was inconsistent with the feudal hierarchy, and ethically it was opposed to the code of the warrior class. It was the faith of potential enemies of Japan.

But it is unlikely that fear of Christianity was the compelling reason for the seclusion policy. There is interesting evidence on this point in an account by a Ming scholar, Huang Tsung-hsi, of his visit to Japan in about 1646, when he sought to obtain help for resistance against the Manchus. He discusses the Japanese seclusion policy and agrees that fear of Christianity and of Europeans was a motive, but says that the underlying reason was the determination of the Tokugawa to secure internal peace and prosperity, and to avoid any foreign involvement likely to jeopardize those aims.

The lengths to which the Bakufu went in enforcing this policy seem to confirm Huang's view. The measures they took were typical of Confucian China, which was always isolationist and preoccupied with internal security, and especially typical of Ming China, which dismantled its navy, closed its ports, and restricted trade to stations where it could be closely regulated.

One point which is often overlooked in considering the seclusion policy is the nature of Japan's foreign trade in the seventeenth century. The Portuguese, Dutch, and English vessels entering Japanese ports did not carry Western goods, but articles from other parts of Asia, principally China. When trade was limited to one port, Nagasaki, Japan was not deprived of any essential articles, since these could still be brought in by Dutch and English vessels and also by Chinese vessels as before. Trade between China and Japan was not interrupted by the Tokugawa Bakufu, although certain articles were at times excluded.

THE WITCH-HUNT
IN EUROPE

For over three hundred years sporadic witch-hunts took place in various locations in Europe. An already huge literature on the subject continues to grow, and not only for scholarly reasons: witches have always been found fascinating because of their esoteric knowledge and their emphasis on sorcery. However, we are not concerned here with benevolent witchcraft, which remained in good repute. The witch-hunts were concerned with discovering and eradicating conspiracy. The trials never dealt with the details of witchcraft; their sole purpose was to identify coconspirators in a pact with the devil. One of the sociologically interesting points about witch trials is their assumption that the devil would deal only with groups; there is no record of a trial of an individual in league with the devil. (Even Dr. Faustus, who has fascinated authors and playwrights, was never tried.)

We consider these witch-hunts a series of important cases because they helped to refine and sharpen the methods of the Inquisition. We are not suggesting that the Great Witch-Hunt was a case of genocide, but that it was the first time a spurious group was persecuted on the basis of a spurious accusation—something that has become less extraordinary only in the twentieth century. Certainly, the groups, that is, the witches' covens, had no basis in reality. There was no way to identify them unless they were accused. That such accusations of conspiracy with the devil were spurious surely will not be doubted these days. The case is particularly important to our study of genocide because it is a precursor of the many twentieth-century cases of ideological killing.

The following selections from Christina Larner's book on the witch-hunt in Scotland raise most of the important questions and present a sophisticated analysis. Larner's major conclusion is that the extermination of thousands of persons falsely accused of demonic witchcraft was part of a process by which the rulers of seventeenth-century Scotland sought to impose the new notion of a nation-state upon a recalcitrant peasant population. Moreover, Larner contends that Scotland's rulers asserted the legitimacy of their new social order and compelled conformity to it by imposing Calvinist Christianity on a peasant population still far from Christianized and by inventing new mechanisms of social control to monitor peasant behavior, enforce orthodoxy, and punish deviance. The core of Larner's argument and some of her evidence are contained in the following selections.

THE WITCH-HUNT IN SCOTLAND†

This [case study] is about the crime of witchcraft in Scotland, and is therefore confined chronologically to the period from 1563, when it became an offence in statute law punishable by death, to 1736, when the crime became officially impossible. It is concerned with the relationship of witch-beliefs in Scotland to witch-beliefs in other cultures, with the relationship of the Scottish witch-hunt to the witch-hunt on the continent of Europe, with the way in which witch-hunting affected peasant life, and with the way in which it reflected the ideological battle current in seventeenth-century Scotland.

The book has three main themes. The first is that witch-hunting was an activity fostered by the ruling class; it was not a spontaneous movement on the part of the peasantry to which the ruling and administrative classes were obliged to respond. This involves some definitions. The term "witch-hunting" is preferred to the more neutral "prosecutions for witchcraft" because it emphasizes that witchcraft suspects were not obvious; they had to be searched for. It also reminds us of common features in the original European witch-hunt and the generally recurring process to which it has given its name: the process whereby the politically powerful pursue a group of persons selected for their beliefs or supposed attributes rather than for anything they have done. A minor disadvantage is that the use of this term draws attention away from the role of witchcraft as an integral part of a criminal code which included many other manifestations exotic to modern jurisprudence of the belief system lying behind it.

Another necessary definition is that of the term "ruling class", which unfortunately evokes strong negative and positive emotional responses. It could be objected to rationally by fellow sociologists on the grounds that it is anachronistic to apply it to a pre-capitalist society, and by historians on the grounds that it ignores the actual complexity of stratification in seventeenth-century Scotland.

†From Christina Larner, *Enemies of God: The Witch-Hunt in Scotland*, 1–5, 25–26, 40–41, 53–59, 100–02. Footnotes omitted. Reprinted by permission of the estate of the author and the Hogarth Press, London, 1981.

To the first I would argue that there is no more convenient term to describe the powerful in relation to the powerless; to the second that, despite considerable gradations of rank among privy councillors, nobles, lairds, grand tenants, lawyers, ministers, and various petty administrators, between all these categories and the peasants from whom 95 per cent of witch suspects were drawn, there was a social, political, and economic gulf. The term "peasant", which is currently the subject of controversy, is likewise used in its most basic sense to mean one who works on the land with family labour to provide no more than subsistence, rent, and other dues.

Witch-hunting was a ruling class activity also because any large-scale pursuit and rounding up of categories of person requires official organization and administration. This does not actually conflict with the proposition that local pressures might have caused witch-hunting in particular areas nor preclude an examination of why certain areas produced suspects when others did not. It does imply, though, that local pressures would need to be felt by the local ruling class. Peasants left to themselves will identify individuals as witches and will resort to a variety of anti-witchcraft measures in self-defence; they cannot pursue these measures to the punishment, banishment, or official execution of even one witch, let alone a multiplicity of witches, without the administrative machinery and encouragement of their rulers. When encouragement is forthcoming, however, they can supply an almost unlimited number of suspects. The actual pattern of witch-hunting in Scotland reinforces this assumption of ruling class control in that witch-hunting crises were nearly always preceded by official expressions of anxiety about witchcraft, and were marked by the simultaneous increase in the supply of suspects from a variety of localities, not all of which are likely to have experienced intolerable internal pressures at the same time in the same way.

The second theme is that witchcraft is an idea, before it is a phenomenon. It is an idea of considerable social flexibility and range. Beyond the basic elements by which we recognize it across cultures—that witchcraft is in general the summation of all evil and in particular the capacity and intention to harm through non-natural means—it may include inversions of any of the positive values peculiar to a given society. Witch-beliefs may therefore encompass a variety of alleged activities, possible and impossible, probable and improbable, and attribute to the performers of these activities a variety of characteristics, all of which serve to highlight local social values.

This emphasis is not directly helpful in excluding or including particular interpretations which focus on the possibility or impossibility of certain types of behaviour most frequently categorized as witchcraft. We may decide that formal cursing, incantation, and the manipulation of objects are possible and well authenticated, that secret meetings are possible but badly authenticated, while the causing of misfortune through incantation and sexual intercourse with the Devil are impossible. This, however, is through the application of other criteria than the one that the evidence for witchcraft relates first and foremost to a set of beliefs rather than activities. The emphasis *is* helpful in analysing the role of witch-beliefs within a complex semi-literate culture. Since most historical evidence comes in literary form we have far more knowledge of the norms and values of past societies than we do of actual behaviour. Historical knowledge is primarily the knowledge of past dominant values; past actions and behaviour emerge in fragmented photographic stills through the distorting mirror of past beliefs. If the idea of a secret, mainly female society is taken as an example, it is not possible to say definitely that such a society could not have occurred or that, although the evidence for it is fragile and based entirely on confession, it did not occur. It is, however, possible to say definitely that a secret society of women was both believed in and feared during the period of the witch-hunt.

While it may be feasible to analyse some aspects of political and military history on the basis of relating fragmented action-stills directly to each other, it is not really possible to treat the witch-hunt in this way. Neither an imperfect nor even a definitive list of executed women has much interest apart from the meaning given to those executions. To treat witch-hunting primarily as an expression of beliefs, however, is to get caught up in general debates of considerable philosophical sophistication which I have neither the space nor the equipment to engage in. I do, however, suggest ways in which European witch-hunting is concerned with these debates. In particular, because the Europe of the witch-hunt had features characteristic both of primitive small-scale societies and of literate, stratified, large-scale societies, there are problems concerning both the issue of relativism—how the modern interpreter should view remote belief systems—and the role of ideology in a stratified society. These again involve questions as to whether ideas have an autonomous life and influence social development; whether they are to be regarded as social products reflecting the socio-economic structure; or whether both these positions can be partially true.

A third, and subordinate theme since the first two have bearing on all types of persecution and all types of belief, is that of the extent to which witch-hunting is to some degree a synonym for woman-hunting. This does not mean that simple overt sex war is treated as a satisfactory explanation for witch-hunting, or that the 20 per cent or so of men who were accused are not to be taken into account. It means that the fact that the accused were overwhelmingly female should form a major part of any analysis. Recent explanations for this female preponderance seem unsatisfactory. The suggestion that more women than men belonged to the ranks of the defenceless poor seems inadequate; even if the proportion of impoverished females to males was the same as that of accused witches it still explains nothing. The suggestion that the stereotype of a witch was always a woman seems tautological.

The identification of the relationship of witch-hunting to woman-hunting is intended to concentrate attention on such questions as why women were criminalized on a large scale for the first time in this period, and whether there is any significance in the simultaneous rise of prosecutions for witchcraft (old women) and infanticide (young women); whether there was any change in the socio-economic position of women in this period; why a female secret society should seem particularly threatening at this juncture; and to what extent the popularization of Christianity, a patriarchal form of religion, was a factor.

These themes of class, ideology, and patriarchy shape the nature of the questions which I think should be asked about the European witch-hunt in general and the Scottish hunt in particular. They cannot provide the answers; for the answers, if there be any, must be inferred from the surviving documentary and secondary material.

A general account of the Scottish witch-prosecutions is at one time both long overdue and distinctly premature. It is long overdue because, despite the ill fame of Scotland as a peculiarly hostile environment for those whose neighbours identified them as witches, an ill fame which has lasted from the sixteenth century to the present, there has been little research and no attempt at a synthesis this century. There has been extensive use of well-known Scottish material, two attempts at enumeration, and a steady supply of retold tales, but no new analysis. Such an analysis seems particularly overdue in that the present emphasis in European witchcraft research is on local studies, and the Scottish experience of witchcraft seems in many respects to occupy an interesting middle position between the English experience on the one hand and that of the European continent on the other. It is, however, premature for two reasons. It is premature first because of the existing state of scholarship on aspects of seventeenth-century Scotland important to an understanding of the witch-trials there. While politics and religion have been relatively well served, little work has been done on the social structure, and almost nothing on crime and the legal history of the period. Lenman and Parker have now provided a hand list of sources for criminological research, but there is as yet no analysis of general rates for crime and misdemeanour against which those for witchcraft can be set. Anyone whose main concern was with Scottish history, rather than with one substantive theme for comparative purposes, would turn to one of these areas. It is premature in the second place because my research was concentrated on the central records. Detailed analysis of all the records local and central for one or more limited areas which might help to answer some of the questions posed in this book has yet to be done.

However, the reasons for publishing an overview at this stage seem more pressing than those for delay. The study of European witchcraft has recently received much stimulation from the work and ideas of Thomas and Macfarlane on English witchcraft and Cohn on the development of the educated demonology behind the European prosecutions. Work is at present being concentrated on detailed local studies. Monographs on south-western Germany, north-west Germany, Switzerland, France, Luxembourg, Massachusetts, and Finland have been produced, and shorter pieces on Russia and Denmark. Further work is in progress on Bamberg and on the very earliest witch trials. Any new overall synthesis of the great European persecution will have to wait until this phase of research has been completed, although it may be that such a synthesis will be overtaken by the developing study of pre-industrial criminology of which witchcraft prosecutions are but a part.

The present book is intended primarily as a contribution to this growing body of local witchcraft studies, and therefore its comparative context and the relationship of its themes to general theories of witchcraft is emphasized. . . .

The title of the book indicates its overall interpretive theme: the significance of ideology in the new post-Reformation regime; the importance attached in new regimes to conformity and discipline as symbols of their legitimacy; and the economy of using the witch figure in this general pattern of increased moral control as a personification of all forms of deviance and revolt. If there was one idea which dominated all others in seventeenth-century Scotland it was that of the godly state in which it was the duty of the secular arm to impose the will of God upon the people. This book is about the women and men (in a ratio of about four to one) who, during this period, were identified by their neighbours, their ministers and elders, their landlords, and the officials of their government, as enemies of God. For the European witch, unlike her* African or American-Indian counterpart, was a transfigured creature who began her career in the farmyard as an enemy of her neighbour, and ended it in the courts as a public person, an enemy of God and of the godly society.

.   .   .   .   .

There now seems to be a consensus that there were a number of factors behind the witch-hunt. Changes in the law were of considerable importance.

*For convenience feminine pronouns embrace masculine in all references to suspected witches.

The development of printing, religious strife, demographic disasters, social stress may have played their part. The most recent analyses have laid the emphasis on the struggle for the minds of the peasantry which was a feature of the late medieval and early modern period.

Delumeau has argued that the peasantry of Europe were Christianized for the first time during the Reformation and Counter Reformation. Both these movements emphasized the importance of lay personal religion in a way previously unknown. In pre-Reformation Europe religious belief and practice were matters for the professionals; lay religion was optional. The idea that individuals were responsible for their own salvation transformed the belief structure. The Reformation and Counter Reformation brought religion, including a sense of sin, to the peasant through preaching and pastoral care. Delumeau relates this to witch-hunting by arguing that the various scourges of famine and disease which afflicted the peasantry began to be seen as the punishment of a just God. The responsibility for sin was seen to lie with the witches. Delumeau also argues that there is a basic antipathy between what he calls "true religion" and magic, and that the witch-hunt was the product of an assault upon the animist mentality of the partly Christianized peasant. Hunting ceased when "true religion" had been well established at parish level.

This interpretation may underestimate the extent to which official religion propagated rather than opposed a belief in the physical power of demonic forces, but it does stress the significance of ideological conformity at the individual level. The whole concept of the Demonic Pact is dependent on the idea of personal responsibility.

The argument that Christianization was an important element in the witch-hunt is set in a wider framework by Muchembled, who sees both as a product of the intensified control by the rulers of newly emergent and shifting political entities. He argues that this involved the imposition of urban values onto the countryside, and suggests that the most persistent witch-hunts took place in border areas where social control was most precarious. Certainly it was a period when the new ruling classes demanded that official ideologies should receive assent from the populace. Collisions between these ideologies and rebellious individuals produced persecutions.

.   .   .   .   .

Social Structure and Social Control

There is some difficulty in writing a synthetic account, however brief, of the social structure of seventeenth-century Scotland, in that very little primary research has been done. Those familiar with recent scholarship on seventeenth-century England would be surprised by the contrast. The political and religious struggles have been well rehearsed, but left relatively unexplored are the formal and informal systems of social stratification, the extent of upward and downward social mobility, the numbers and social origins of the ministers who, together with the lawyers, were the "new men" of post-Reformation Scotland, the social origins of dissident religious groups in the later seventeenth century, the beliefs and culture of the peasantry, the formal powers of criminal jurisdiction and their application in practice, the relative importance of different crimes and the number of cases. Even the lines of live historical controversy have scarcely been laid down. It has not been asked whether the gentry were or were not rising, or whether the poor had any collective consciousness. Only recently has it been suggested by Stevenson that if there *was* a "general crisis" in seventeenth-century Europe Scotland might have been involved in it, and by Foster that Scotland raises peculiar problems for those committed to a Marxist-Leninist interpretation of history. One does not need to share Foster's teleological assumptions about what ought to have been happening, or agree with his assertions about the weakness and short-lived nature of feudalism in Scotland, in order to be grateful for his raising questions about the economic and social structure and the development of capitalism.

No one in particular is to blame for this state of affairs. It is due in part to the relatively small number of people involved in Scottish historical research, in part to the internal tradition of treating Scottish history as local and private, and in part to the habit of emphasizing the known, rather than raising questions about the unknown. It does mean, in practice, that what can be said about social structure and social mobility, and, above all, about the state of law and legal organization in the period is impressionistic, though the situation has been much improved by the recent work of Whyte on agriculture and rural society in this period.

With that proviso there are three main hypotheses to be made in the first part of this chapter. First, non-Gaelic-speaking Scotland can be described as having a peasant economy throughout the period of witch-prosecutions; second, that the social structure was feudal, in that essential relationships were vertical and based on land, payments in kind, and services, including military services; third, this social and economic structure was relatively unchanged for a period a great deal longer at both ends than that covered by the witch-prosecutions, relative, that is to say, to England and parts of the continent. If these suggestions hold, then it follows that the outbursts of witch prosecuting cannot be explained in terms of changes in the basic structure of society, unless it is argued that the very small changes which may have occurred in some of the agriculturally most advanced counties such as Fife, Morayshire, and the Lothians, were sufficient in relative terms to cause the same kind of social stress which is said to have been caused by the enclosure movement in England.

This does not mean that social and economic organization was of no importance. Obviously the way in which the hunts developed and the selection of the people who were hunted were affected by the social order. It merely means that the changes in this aspect of Scottish life prior to and during the period of witch-prosecution were not sufficient in themselves to explain the hunt. There were, however, two major changes in the nature of Scottish society which, while not affecting either the stratification or the economic system except to reinforce them strongly, may have been important factors in the development of a witch-hunt. They followed from the break from Rome and the attempt to develop a nation-state. The first was the strenuous imposition of an entirely new ideology, Calvinist Christianity, on the populace, and the second, closely connected, was the development of a new system of social control by which the behaviour and geographical mobility of large sections of the populace were closely monitored. The new regime asserted its legitimacy by redefining conformity and orthodoxy, and by providing a machinery for the enforcement of orthodoxy and the punishment of deviance which is discussed in the second part of this chapter.

.   .   .   .   .

The initiation and decline of witch prosecuting then were contained well within the limits of a period of little change in economic and social organization. A consideration of the basic components of economic and social structure therefore cannot logically contribute to explanations of why the prosecutions started in the first place: it does, however, help towards an understanding of some of the forms which witch-hunting took. Yet there were real changes in some aspects of social life, which may have been causal factors, and the most notable of these were in the organization and enforcement of religious worship, in the control of geographical mobility, and in the central and local application of the criminal law.

Social Control

If the social structure was static, the methods for controlling it were not. In one sense the Reformation can be described as the biggest reinforcement the feudal system in Scotland ever had, for in the ministers and elders of the Reformed Church the land-owning classes were provided with a police force and civil service.

The term "social control" in this section is used in a sense narrower than the whole social system, but wider than the formal legal system. It refers to the formal and informal mechanisms for creating and enforcing rules, though in practice when dealing with a past society the formal mechanisms are inevitably more visible than the informal. This section deals briefly with the organization of criminal law, and with the activities of the local Kirk sessions as controllers of both crime and lesser misdemeanours, and considers the place of witch prosecution in the general pattern of control.

The larger part of the seventeenth-century machinery for both criminal and civil jurisdictions was a chaotic inheritance from pre-Reformation times. It was observed by Hugo Arnot, the eighteenth-century Edinburgh lawyer and historian, that "there is no determined system of criminal jurisprudence in Scotland. It is a matter of doubt what is a crime in the eye of her law, and what is not, also what is the punishment annexed". If this was true of the eighteenth century it was even more true of the seventeenth. Although some firm statements have been ventured both about seventeenth-century jurisprudence and about the status of the different criminal courts, it is still a largely unknown and unresearched area. In practice judicial outcomes seem often to have reflected the relative power of participants and their capacity to convince. It is not without significance that early legal writers wrote "Practicks" rather than "Institutes".

The organization of criminal justice was complex and overlapping and the areas of competence often ill-defined. The types of jurisdictions can be divided into royal, baronial, and ecclesiastical, though in fact the category of "royal" is a particularly confusing one. It includes not only central government institutions: Parliament, Privy Council, and the Court of Justiciary, plus their local extensions, the hereditary sheriffdoms and the royal burghs, all of which undeniably represented King's law; but also the regalities, which in a sense represented the abandonment of royal control. The regalities were areas where the King's writ was administered by the lord's officials rather than those of the King himself.

The King's writ itself as centrally administered dealt principally with treason and the "four pleas of the crown": robbery, rape, murder, and arson. Witchcraft was added to these after 1597.

·   ·   ·   ·   ·

It would be misleading to suggest that any of this had the effect of improving legal procedures according to some concept of justice, although such concepts did concern lawyers of the period. From the point of view of the accused party justice remained rough, and outcomes could depend, whether at feudal or at central level, on relative power positions. So far as the central courts were concerned it was the opinion of Hugo Arnot that in the seventeenth century the Court of Justiciary was very submissive to government: "its decrees were engines of oppression, the court used often to remit the jury, ordering them to amend their verdict". If that did not work, "the Privy Council, a most tyrannical court, used to interfere with the sentence of Justiciary". The relationship between these courts affected sentencing policy in all those crimes which were centrally controlled.

Yet social control did not end with the formal civil legal provisions. Ecclesiastical law after the Reformation was far more drastically changed than civil law. As in England several ecclesiastical offences were incorporated into statute law, but the greatest change was in organization. Although it took some time for pre-Reformation organizations to be phased out, they were gradually replaced by an entirely different structure.

The Kirk sessions, which by the mid-seventeenth century covered most of non-Highland Scotland and had penetrated Argyll and Invernesshire, consisted of the minister and his elders. They met to arrange not only everything to do with public worship, but also to monitor all the disciplinary aspects of public life. They were the body through which the doctrine that even sinners and the ungodly should be forced to glorify God in their lives was enforced. More prosaically this was identified with suppressing scandalous sexual liaisons, drunkenness, brawling, sabbath-breaking, and backbiting, and with the transference of more serious offences to presbyteries or the secular courts. The penalties open to Kirk sessions were not clearly defined. They could not excommunicate, but in practice they could impose various "degradation rituals", ranging from mere appearance before the session to wearing sackcloth in front of the congregation, and they could fine. On the basis of these fines they supported the poor of the parish, and since fornication was always a major item of business it would be fair to say that the equilibrium of the godly parish was maintained by the lascivious regularly providing for the needy.

.   .   .   .   .   .

Apart from the landowners, the other group which were outside the discipline of the session were the landless labourer and vagabond class. For in addition to controlling behaviour the session also controlled mobility. Not only was it essential for tenant farmers to accept behavioural control, it was an offence for them to take strangers under their roof without permission, and they could not themselves move their domicile and settle elsewhere without a certificate of good conduct from the session to take with them to their new parish. Any unfortunate episodes would be recorded on this certificate, and Janet Anderson in 1650, for example, had to take with her to her new parish the information that she had been suspected of witchcraft nine years previously. This tight control over the mobility of peasants, which was established at this time, may well have been a response to a rising population; it may also have had some influence in holding back industrial growth, and in the high rate of emigration and steady supply of mercenary soldiers to the battlefields of Europe. If those without certificates of godliness were not allowed to settle within Scotland they were perhaps driven outside.

We have then in seventeenth-century Scotland a society which was economically and socially relatively static. There was a considerable degree of stratification with consciousness of rank at all social levels, and it is reasonable to impose on this self-perceived hierarchy a fairly sharp distinction between the ruling class and the rest of the populace. The ruling class proper consisted of the landed and the merchants, but it seems right to include those more marginal groups who administered on their behalf: ministers, lawyers, baillies, and factors. Makey has estimated that a minister would have an income ten times the size of his parishioners, and so it seems likely that there was an economic as well as a social and educational gulf between them.

There was an absence of the peasant unrest seen in parts of France and Germany and of the urban disturbances of the "masterless men" seen in England. Yet of course there was change and turbulence. The Reformation of 1560 had replaced an elite which was tied to France with one which fought among itself for dominance and spoils in the building up of an independent nation-state. The absence of the court in the next century intensified the faction conflict, and the increase of centralization, bureaucracy, and feuferme landholding without the right to hold courts made central rather than local power more attractive. These changes together with the new Reformation ideology can be said to have constituted a social revolution in that the lives of the populace were greatly affected by them. It is in this area that the rise of witch-hunting must be sought.

. . . the pre-Reformation church had left little mark on the beliefs and practices of the peasantry, and . . . for many the preaching of the Reformed clergy was their first contact with Christianity. After the Reformation many former priests who were regarded as too uneducated to be allowed to preach were given the title of reader and made to lead their congregation from a prayer book until a qualified minister became available. But not only was it the first serious encounter with official religion; this was also very thoroughly and systematically taught. In both these aspects Scotland was unlike England. There were no absentee clergy. As the Kirk session system extended itself there were resident educated ministers, preaching every Sunday to a captive parish, there was a literacy drive which appears to have been moderately successful; and the ministers were in constant touch with each other; comparing their successes and failures, preaching at each others' fasts and special occasions, constantly reinforcing each other in their presbytery meetings. It was a very powerful, systematic and effective piece of indoctrination for which parallels can be found in twentieth-century societies which have experienced left-wing revolutions. It was also similar in kind to the religious and moral revivals to be found in other parts of Europe at the same time and with which some witchcraft outbreaks appear to be associated.

It has been observed by Morris that moral and ideological revolutions are a necessary accompaniment of new states and new rulers. The new ideology legitimizes the new regime, and the moral cleansing demonstrates its effectiveness. The pursuit of the witch as a totally evil person, a totally committed enemy to the values of the new society however identified, is, of course, a highly economical way of effecting the moral cleansing of a society.

For post-Reformation Scotland the identification and abolition of witchcraft was only a part of the new pattern of moral endeavour, in which it was the acknowledged duty of the secular arm to ensure that the "crown rights of the Redeemer" were demonstrated in the everyday behaviour of his subjects, yet the drive against witchcraft was in fact a most central crusade. It was not for nothing that witchcraft came to be set beside treason as the two crimes which could not be alienated to regalities. They represented enmity in its purest form to the two swords of God: the secular and the ecclesiastical.

While it is clear that it was possible to prosecute a witch under the old machinery and that from time to time such prosecutions did occur, it is also clear that the witch-prosecutions of the seventeenth century were conducted throughout under those parts of the machinery of social control which were entirely new: the statute of 1563, which made it a civil offence punishable by death, the Order in Council of 1597, which centralized its administration and extended the use of the Privy Council commission, and the Kirk session, where many of the proceedings began and much of the evidence was collected. It was a process which took responsibility from the accusing individual and gave it to the highest powers in the land: the Lords of Privy Council and the Lord Advocate. It was supported by a newly received legal doctrine for which the authority was Canon Law. It was these elements in a socially and economically conservative revolution which nurtured the attack on deviance of which witchcraft was the supreme example.

.   .   .   .   .   .

Labelling theory takes us only so far in suggesting why particular individuals who shared the classic characteristics with many others were selected from them for accusation. It explains the build-up of social reinforcement, but, apart from the selection of daughters of witches, not the beginning of the process. In the last resort it can only be said that these individuals were in the wrong place at the wrong time.

When we turn from the selection of the individual back to the classic characteristics, however, there still remains a problem. What is the relationship between the type of person accused of witchcraft and the growth of witchcraft prosecutions? There is some evidence to suggest that the relationship is a direct one. Witch-hunting *is* woman-hunting or at least it is the hunting of women who do not fulfil the male view of how women ought to conduct themselves. An example from anthropology is that of the Nupe in the nineteen twenties. Nadel describes how the women were money lenders and traders and the men of the Nupe were very often in their debt. These women lived independent lives, took lovers, and rarely had children. They challenged the conventional ideal of women as servicing men and children, and it was they who were accused of witchcraft.

We do not at present have enough evidence to say whether the status of women was radically changing in Europe in the fifteenth, sixteenth, and seventeenth centuries in a manner analogous to the more limited and specific case cited by Nadel. It has been argued that the witch-hunt was an attack by the emergent male medical profession on the female healer. There is a certain amount of evidence for this. In Scotland in 1641 in the ratification of the privileges of the Edinburgh chirurgeons it was noted that unqualified females had been practising chirurgy illegitimately in the city, and a number of witchcraft suspects were identified as midwives. The connection, however, is not direct enough. The main usurpation of midwifery by males took place in the eighteenth century after the witch-hunt was over. The objection to female healers was concentrated in the towns where the emergent male professionals had their strength. While witchcraft prosecutions may sometimes have married conveniently with the suppression of female healing, male professionalization of healing really cannot account for the mass of the prosecutions.

A different argument is that capitalizing agriculture reduced the role of women to that of a mere producer of children rather than a participant in peasant production. Anyone pursuing this argument however is likely to get into difficulties. Not enough is known to support or, what is worse, to make suspect, any large-scale theory on the economic history of women. In particular the timing of that major change seems to have varied greatly in different parts of Europe, and in most areas took place after the end of the witch-hunt. The suggestion that this period saw an increase in the number of unsupported women is, again, difficult to substantiate, and the witch-hunt was not primarily directed against them.

If we turn to the sphere of ideology the case for witch-hunting being seen as a woman-hunt is more convincing. The stereotype of the witch was not that of the child-woman; it was that of the adult, independent woman. The religion of the Reformation and the Counter Reformation demanded that women for the first time become fully responsible for their own souls. Indeed preachers went out of their way to refer to "men and women" in their sermons. The popularization of religion, however, took away from women with one hand what it gave to them with the other, for the particular form of religion was strongly patriarchal. The ritual and moral inferiority of women was preached along with their new personal responsibility. The status of women became ambiguous under the terms of the new ideology.

Witchcraft as a choice was only possible for women who had free will and personal responsibility attributed to them. This represented a considerable change in the status of women in Scotland at least. Up to the time of the secularization of the crime of witchcraft their misdemeanors had been the responsibility of husbands and fathers and their punishments the whippings thought appropriate to children. As witches they became adult criminals acting in a manner for which their husbands could not be deemed responsible. The pursuit of witches could therefore be seen as a rearguard action against the emergence of women as independent adults. The women who were accused were those who challenged the patriarchal view of the ideal woman. They were accused not only by men but also by other women because women who conformed to the male image of them felt threatened by any identification with those who did not.

This explanation is the most plausible of those which identify witch-hunting as woman-hunting because unlike the other explanations the timing seems right. Nevertheless while witch-hunting and woman-hunting are closely connected they cannot be completely identified as one and the same phenomenon. The relationship is at one degree removed. The demand for ideological conformity was simply a much wider one than that aspect of it that concerned the status of women. The present discussion over the direct connection between the alleged uniqueness of English witchcraft and the allegedly unique status of women in England is therefore misconceived. The pursuit of witches was an end in itself and was directly related to the necessity of enforcing moral and theological conformity. The fact that a high proportion of those selected in this context as deviants were women was indirectly related to this central purpose.

DEMONIC WITCHCRAFT AND THE LAW†

In primitive societies two types of witchcraft are identified: white witchcraft or the craft of healing, and black witchcraft or *maleficium*. The distinction was known to Roman law, and dominated all dealings with

†From Christina Larner, *Witchcraft and Religion: The Politics of Popular Belief*, 3–4, 88–91, 127–28. Footnotes omitted. Reprinted by permission of Basil Blackwell, Oxford, 1984.

witchcraft accusations in Europe until the late fifteenth century. It is also common ground in most studies of contemporary primitive societies. Historians of the sixteenth and seventeenth centuries however have to add a third witchcraft which existed only from the fifteenth to the early eighteenth century and which has no contemporary equivalent. It differed from the simple concepts of black and white witchcraft in its origins. Far from being an experience of village life, it was evolved by churchmen and lawyers from Christian theology, canon law and certain philosophical ideas. It differed also in content. Christian witch theorists gave a central position to the idea of the demonic pact. The witch became a witch by virtue of a personal arrangement with the Devil who appeared to his potential recruit in some physical form. At this meeting, in return for renunciation of baptism, services on earth and the soul of the witch at death, the Devil promised material advantages and magical powers. In addition, an integral part of the Christian witch theory was that the witch did not operate alone. Witchcraft involved midnight meetings to worship the Devil, to receive his orders and to have sexual intercourse with him or his subordinate spirits.

The development of this theory in Europe, and its application in witchcraft trials, had a drastic effect on the rate of prosecutions. The change from the isolated local harrying of individuals to a widespread crusade against witchcraft, to a recognisable mania and persecution, began fairly abruptly in northern Italy and southern Germany in the late fifteenth century, and spread widely through the Continent during the following century. There are three main reasons why the introduction of the Christian witch theory had such a catastrophic effect. The first is that it was developed by the ruling classes. If we except the traditional vulnerability of rulers to soothsayers and astrologers, there had previously been a fairly sharp contrast between village credulity and intellectual scepticism. Now the power of the local witch was heavily reinforced by the conviction of the authorities that her power was real and to be feared. At the same time, the capacity to punish her was intensified by the codification of laws against witchcraft, both in canon law and later in the statute law of Protestant countries. The other reasons are connected with the theory itself. The logical conclusion of the idea of the demonic pact was the abolition of the traditional distinction between black and white magic.

The power of the witch sprang from the demonic pact and was therefore evil, whether it was used for healing or harming. This meant that the village healer was as likely to be prosecuted as the local scold. Above all, the idea that witchcraft was organized and that witches worked in groups, was responsible for the way in which witch prosecutions, once initiated, spread rapidly. An accused witch would be invited under torture to name colleagues, and would do so.

Figures for executions for witchcraft in Europe in the sixteenth and seventeenth centuries are not very precise, but estimates are always in thousands.

.   .   .   .   .

When Is a Witch-hunt a Witch-hunt?

The term "witch-hunting" was coined in the United States this century and given two meanings: first, the pursuit of a group of persons for their supposed characteristics or beliefs rather than for anything they have done; and second, the relentless pursuit of an individual by a group through artificial or contrived charges. To what extent is "witch-hunting" an illuminating analogy for these activities?

To answer that question, it is necessary to outline the main features of the European witch prosecutions of the sixteenth and seventeenth centuries. The reasons for the rise and decline of these prosecutions, and the meaning to be attached to them, are still matters of dispute. The interpretation offered here should be read in that light.

The numbers of those accused, tried, acquitted or executed during this period can never be known precisely, but the figures we do have clearly define the areas of most intensive prosecution. These are Germany, Scotland, France and Switzerland, probably in that order. In addition, there were serious isolated outbreaks in Holland, Sweden, the Basque country and America.

In all these countries, the authorities were concerned with the demonological aspects of the crime: the pact with the Devil and the criminal conspiracy of witches against God and the state. Milder prosecutions, in which the authorities were concerned with simple sorcery rather than diabolism, occurred in England, Denmark and Russia. In all countries, the prosecutions were episodic and highly local. Some areas escaped altogether.

Witch-beliefs and witch-hunting were many-faceted, and the European witch prosecutions require a multiple explanation. Necessary preconditions are a peasant (or pre-industrial) economy and near-universal popular witch beliefs. These preconditions, however, obtained long before, and in most of Europe long after, the witchcraft prosecutions. Further requirements were an active belief in the Devil among the educated, a well-developed legal organization with either strong local justice or easy access to central justice, and a degree of lay literacy.

But the crucial factors were the rise of nation-states, and the development of personal religion among the peasantry. In the days of papacy and medieval monarchy, the personal beliefs of the populace were of little interest to rulers and the ultimate fate of their souls the responsibility of religious specialists

—monks and priests. The wandering preachers of the pre-Reformation church, the Reformation, and the Counter-Reformation effectively Christianized the peasantry for the first time.

The rise of nation-states was marked by new regimes establishing more centralized, more secular governments, which demonstrated their independence of the papacy either through direct adoption of the Reformation or through the nationalization (secularization) of areas of ecclesiastical law, including sexual offences and witchcraft.

At the same time it was necessary for these regimes to demonstrate their legitimacy to their peoples, their allies, and their enemies, by appropriating the religious authority previously attributed to the Roman church. The rise of rival versions of Christianity, each with exclusive claims, greatly enhanced the political usefulness of religion to the rulers of early modern Europe. Borders were staked out not with fences but with churches.

Christianity had become a political ideology. It was a political ideology in the sense that a degree of education was required in order for its content to be absorbed. Above all, it was necessary to the governing class that the individual members of the populace adhered to the correct version. In this way the legitimacy of the regime was demonstrated.

In this context, witches represented the most extreme form of deviance. They had renounced their baptism and dedicated themselves body and soul to the Devil in a personal pact—a pact which was consummated by the receipt of the Devil's mark and, in the case of women, by one or more acts of "carnal intercourse". They had conspired with other witches against God, church, state and people. They represented total evil. Neighbours supplied the suspects out of the local world of misfortune, quarrel, sorcery and gossip. Lawyers translated the evidence into political and ideological crime.

Because, within each regime, the preferred version of Christianity represented the whole of Christianity, and because the witch represented enmity to Christianity as such, there was little difference between them in the use they made of witch-hunting. Catholic Germany, Catholic France, Lutheran Sweden, Orthodox Russia, Calvinist Scotland and Calvinist Switzerland, all pursued witches. Areas which escaped the hunt included those which had alternative deviants in racial minorities or organized heretics, and those under armies of occupation where the sanction was force, not legitimacy.

New regimes today have to pursue a variety of offenders in their attempt to demonstrate control of law and order. The Vietnamese closed the brothels; the Iranians stone sexual offenders. A governmental assault on witchcraft was a particularly economical way, unavailable now, of demonstrating control over all deviance. The land that was purged of witchcraft was purged of evil.

Explanations in terms of peasant unrest do not fit the main witch-hunting areas at all satisfactorily. Explanations in terms of social strain are circular. The witchcraft prosecutions in Europe were exactly coterminous with the period during which Christianity was a political ideology. When the establishment of the Kingdom of God ceased to be a political objective and was replaced by the pursuit of liberty, the defence of property, the belief in progress, enlightenment, patriotism and other secular alternatives, the courts ceased to convict.

The belief in witchcraft was not argued out of court at the end of the hunt. Christianity continued to be an important instrument of social control. It simply lost its political vitality.

The description "witch-hunt" for this particular wave of criminal prosecutions was never made at the time. Contemporaries complained of the extraordinary prevalence of witchcraft. Some hinted at too much credulity on the part of prosecutors, but none looked to the latent functions of a witch-cleansing operation. The eighteenth- and nineteenth-century commentators were preoccupied with the horrifying effects of superstition. The term "witch-hunt" was not coined to describe the one historical witch-hunt, but analogous twentieth-century activities.

It seems particularly useful when it is applied to the isolating and labelling of an individual by other members of a social group. In a seventeenth-century village, the identification and labelling of a witch was often built up slowly through association with another reputed witch, often her mother; through a series of quarrels and misfortunes, and through a process of social interaction which frequently resulted in the labelled person accepting the label of witch and the social power that went with it. "If I be a witch," said Katherine Young of Peebles in 1628, "ill may you all thrive this year".

The community, in turn, gained a negative standard of social behaviour and social acceptability. Similarly, modern social groups, whether communities or committees, gain a sense of solidarity by the identification of a fringe or over-powerful individual as eccentric, unsound, unsuitable, deviant.

To apply "witch-hunt" to a wider scene—the pursuit by governments of a whole category of persons—reflects only some aspects of the historical European witch-hunt, but it is nevertheless suggestive. The essentials of a modern witch-hunt are that a government picks on a group and attributes to them certain characteristics and certain beliefs. These characteristics and beliefs are then alleged to make their holders threaten the security of the state. A modern witch-hunt does not represent a simple law-and-order problem: potential treachery and subversion are the issues. Prime examples are the Russian purges, the German extermination of gipsies, Jews and homosexuals, and the Un-American Activities Committee.

The repression of an armed group with overt revolutionary intention is not a witch-hunt. Nor are regimes of pure terror (such as Idi Amin's) witch-hunts. A witch-hunt is selective and ideological. The fact that the original crime of witchcraft was defined by the lawyers in theological terms—apostacy and enmity to God—means we are not likely ever again actually to define ideological deviants as witches; but the parallels are strong. Ayatollah Khomeni has described trade unionists as "enemies of God"—a common sixteenth-century European phrase. The way in which the term "witch-hunt" is applied to contemporary political phenomena plays down some aspects of the historical hunt—notably the fact that about 80 per cent of suspects were women . . . and makes no use of one element in it which does have contemporary parallels. A major feature of the sixteenth-century hunt was the use of torture to extract confession—confession being the ultimate proof in ideological crime. In this respect, the witch-hunt has much in common with the torture-cultures of Latin America.

Barbarism and superfluous repression in the name of the public good are a continual temptation, in all types of regime, to those who fear the loss of power.

.   .   .   .   .

Natural and Unnatural Methods of Witchcraft Control

It is clear from the press that we are, at present, in the middle of a law-and-order crisis. Old ladies go in fear of being mugged; women attend self-defence classes; despite the police force being strengthened the rate of reported crime is soaring. No one in the government or the mass media will pay any attention to sociologists—because it is not what they want to hear—when we say that the law-and-order crisis is an illusion. Reported crime always goes up when police activity increases. The chances for an old white lady of being mugged are in fact extremely low. The present alleged increase in crimes is a statistical distortion caused partly by a reclassification of what counts as a crime. For example, "vandalism" was created a crime last year. Vandalism 1980: zero, Vandalism 1981: 21,758. What we are in fact in the middle of is a law and order *panic*. Definitions change. Levels of attention change. The amount of human behaviour which can be interpreted as criminal remains unlimited. A law and order panic has the latent function for a government of uniting all classes behind it. The rich buy alarm systems; the poor buy dogs.

I want to look today at a seventeenth-century law-and-order crisis, or panic, which affected various countries of Europe but, in particular, southern Germany, northern France, Switzerland and Scotland. It was concentrated on the crime of witchcraft, but other crime rates seem to have gone up and down with the witchcraft rate. The threat from witchcraft for the ordinary peasant affected many aspects of life. Witches could cause illness or death to humans or animals. They could cause crops to wither and milk to dry up. They could affect not only well-being but physical and economical survival. For the ruling class, they represented a different kind of threat; they represented subversion—a conspiracy against the state. But the threat from witchcraft was common and was a uniting force. When the Earl of Haddington complained in 1660 that law and order was not being maintained and that there was a crisis which central government must attend to, he added that his tenants were threatening to leave the land for fear of witchcraft. I think the Earl of Haddington was being disingenuous. There was a land shortage in the Lothians in this period and it is most unlikely that anyone would have voluntarily vacated their bit of infield and outfield; but the tenants' fears will have been real enough.

Although fears of witchcraft are endemic in nearly all preindustrial societies, the witch-hunting epidemic which swept parts of Europe in waves during the sixteenth and seventeenth century was unique and therefore requires an explanation related to the peculiarities of this period. In my recent book on the witch-hunt in Scotland, I argued a case which was intended to be applicable to Europe as a whole and is partly dependent on my argument in lecture 2 that this period in Europe should be seen as the age of faith. In outline it goes thus: the development of printing, the break-up of the universal church and the development of the nation-state led to a new role for Christianity, that of the world's first political ideology. This had the consequence that failures in Christianity—heresy, apostasy, or witchcraft, which had been redefined as a form of apostasy—became political crimes. Witchcraft was particularly economical in a law-and-order crisis (or panic) in that it represented not merely particular misdemeanours or individual crimes but total evil, total hostility to the community, the church, the state, and God.

INDIANS OF THE AMERICAS, 1492 TO 1789

Pre-Spanish Conquest warfare among Indians may have produced the first genocides of the Western Hemisphere, but very little evidence of these killings, if they occurred, has survived the ravages of time. Anthropologists and historians are certain, however, that life in pre-Conquest America was far from the images of the Rousseauean idyl or the paradise of the Noble Savage so popular among English writers at the end of the eighteenth century and persisting to this day (Keen 1971, 306). The Indians did not have to learn about cruelty, warfare, and killing from the Europeans. Aztec society, like many others in the New World, glorified torture and human sacrifice to propitiate the gods. "Blood was necessary to save this world and the men in it," Jacques Soustelle tells us; "the victim was no longer an enemy who was to be killed but a messenger, arrayed in a dignity that was almost divine, who was sent to the gods" (Soustelle, 99). The Aztecs waged perpetual war to secure captives for sacrifices to the gods. As little killing as possible was done on the battlefield; ritual killing on the altars of the gods was preferred (ibid., 100–01).

Among the Aztecs, a city was defeated when invaders had reached its temple and burned the sanctuary of its tribal god (ibid., 211). Tribute was levied on the survivors of the defeat, but the city was not abolished, nor were its language and customs. Soustelle argues that the Aztecs' obsession with wars to obtain sacrificial victims contributed to their downfall. While the Spanish conquistadores killed as many Aztecs in battle as they could, waging total war in accordance with the principles of their monolithic state and religion, the Aztecs deliberately preserved an enemy state—Tlaxcala—at the approaches to their capital because they prized the opportunity it gave their young men to test their valor and to take captives between major military expeditions. By sparing Tlaxcala, the Aztecs inadvertently provided Hernando Cortés with a source of infantry and a secure base for his assault on their kingdom (ibid., 212–15).

But if genocide was alien to Aztec culture, the same cannot be said of every other Indian people. Documented cases of genocide committed by Indians are hard to find, but the deserted thirteenth-century cliff dwellings of the Anasazi of southwestern Colorado and northern New Mexico, with their enigmatic signs of a siege followed by elimination, and the annihilatory assault of the Iroquois on the Hurons in 1649 seriously raise the probability that the Indians of the Americas knew genocide before the coming of the Europeans.

The invasion of the Americas spearheaded by Christopher Columbus in 1492 was the beginning of the end for many of the Western Hemisphere's native peoples. Over the next several centuries, the Spaniards, the Portuguese, the English, and the French built major empires in their new domains and consolidated their rule from the Arctic Circle in the north to Tierra del Fuego in the south. The differing motives of the European colonizers reflected differences in their societies and in the timing of their colonial ventures. In 1492, Spain was a medieval country reveling in its victories over the Moors and imbued with the spirit of the Reconquest. The essence of that spirit was aristocratic, oriented toward warfare and the acquisition of riches by warfare. Projected overseas, these goals were transmuted by the Spaniards into a quest for gold, Indian subjects, land, military title, and souls (Wolf 1959, 152–60). Encountering some relatively dense populations of Indians living in highly complex societies, Spain turned to forced labor, granting land, authority, and tribute rights over the Indians to privileged Spaniards under the provisions of the encomienda system. Hispanicized and Christianized by hundreds of missionaries dispatched to the colonies to save their souls, the Indians found defenders in missionary priests who struggled to bring them under the shelter of Spanish law. However, the legal protection promised the Indians in volumes of Spanish legislation did little good. Natives throughout Spain's empire became subjugated peoples, overworked, abused, and exploited by an aristocratic white class and its allies among the Indians and mestizos (Gibson 1966, 48–67).

France and England, entering the colonial lists in the seventeenth century, brought a more modern, commercial outlook to their colonial ventures than Spain. France's absolute monarchy dictated a colonial policy for New France that emphasized the fur trade and its corollary, good relations with the Indians. Few in number—by 1715, the white population of French Canada stood at only 18,500, compared to over 400,000 in Great Britain's American colonies —the French governors on the St. Lawrence kept their settlers under control and, after decades of fighting the Iroquois, recognized the sovereignty of the Indians in 1701 (Nash 1982, 105–09; Eccles 1972, 95–101). The Jesuits who accompanied the early French explorers cultivated the friendship of the Huron people, who played an important role as middlemen in the fur trade of the St. Lawrence, while to the south, along the Hudson River, France supported the Iroquois as a barrier to Dutch and British participation in the trade (Eccles, 41–45). The French government's highly restrictive immigration policy for New France kept immigration to a minimum and lessened the risk of conflict with the Indians.

In contrast to France's relatively coherent Indian policy, the more pluralistic English parliamentary government veered erratically from one extreme to another, alternating periods of rigid enforcement of mercantilist regulations with periods of so-called salutary neglect (Tepaske 1967, 3). Equally important in explaining the twists and turns of English policy was the difficulty of imposing a single, London-designed formula on thirteen populous American colonies peopled by ambitious settlers more interested in agriculture and industry than trade with the Indians. The main thing that the colonists wanted from the Indians was their land, land for growing their crops, land for lumbering and mining, and land for their children's children.

Compared to those of the colonies of other European powers in the New World, social contacts between Americans and Indians were minimal. Neither the settlers nor the Church of England showed much interest in converting the Indians to Christianity. Unlike the Spanish and French colonies, in which the high proportion of males among the European settlers encouraged intermarriage with the Indians, the British colonies had a settlers' sex ratio that was much more balanced, and few intermarriages took place. When the cost of defending the American colonists against Indian attacks grew too high, the English issued the Proclamation of 1763, temporarily prohibiting settlement of the vast tracts of land across the Appalachian Mountains. George Washington and Patrick Henry were two of the future leaders of the American Revolution who challenged these British restrictions. When he was criticized for allowing the Virginians to stake out claims to Indian land across the Proclamation Line in Kentucky, Governor Dunmore of Virginia drew a portrait of the American settlers that any nineteenth-century American politician could sympathize with: "They do and will remove as their avidity and restlessness incite them. . . . Nor can they be easily brought to entertain any belief of the permanent obligation of Treaties made with those People [the Indians], whom they consider, as but little removed from the brute Creation" (Hagan 1961, 27). Although the Proclamation of 1763 was never enforced owing to the shortage of funds in the English Treasury, London's abortive effort to curtail the theft of Indian land became a cause célèbre in the colonies and one of the justifications for rebellion by the Americans in 1775 (Nash 1982, 64–66, 263).

The native peoples of the New World were devastated by their contacts with Europeans, and the charge of genocide is frequently leveled at the colonial powers. The scale of the Indians' population decline is still being debated by scholars, but whether the losses suffered by the aboriginal population amounted to 50 percent, 95 percent, or some figure in between, the catastrophic demographic impact of the European exploration and settlement of the New World on the Indian peoples is an undeniable fact.

The part played by genocide in the destruction and crippling of so many societies spread over a vast area and colonized by settlers of many different nationalities and social systems is complex and still poorly understood. The opinion of many experts is that genocide was one of five major factors that undermined Indian civilizations; the others were disease, warfare, geographical removals and relocations, and the destruction of traditional Indian ways of life (Thornton 1987, 42–53). Of these major factors, epidemic disease undoubtedly accounted for the greatest number of Indian deaths. Its massive toll began with Columbus's first landing in the Caribbean and rolled on inexorably into the nineteenth century, ending—in the case of North America—only after American settlers had reached the Pacific Ocean and another round of epidemics had devastated the Indians of the West Coast.

The Americas were virgin territory for most Old World and African diseases. European smallpox, typhoid, and measles were the most important killers, but African malaria and yellow fever contributed significantly to the destruction of Indians in the tropical lowlands (Gibson, 64–65; McNeil 1976, 211–13; Thornton, 44). The new diseases spread like wildfire among peoples who had lived in biological isolation and were immunologically defenseless. Epidemics of European diseases could start without the physical presence of a European. A devastating epidemic of measles or smallpox that opened the way for Pizarro's conquest of Peru struck the Inca Empire in 1524–26, six years before Pizarro's first voyage to Peru (Wachtel 1977, 94–95; Hemming 1970, 27). The outbreak was probably started by germs carried down the trade network from the West Indies or Mexico. Population statistics for precolonial and colonial America are highly controversial, but all sides in the debate agree that the demographic impact of the American Indian's vulnerability to disease microbes carried to the New World by Europeans and Africans was profound and deadly.

Diseases introduced from Europe also wrought havoc among Indians trading with New France (Eccles, 21, 44–45). Jesuit missionaries estimated in the early 1600s, at the time of their first contacts with the Huron, that they numbered between 20,000 and 35,000. From 1634 to 1640, the Huron were struck by a wave of epidemics. Smallpox was particularly lethal. According to Thornton, "The Huron soon lost one-half to two-thirds their population as a result of the epidemics; they numbered only about 10,000 by 1640" (Thornton, 73–74).

Given the incredible virulence of smallpox as a destroyer of Indians in the New World, some authors have looked for evidence that the Europeans started epidemics deliberately. William McNeil speculates that the American settlers, who had enjoyed some success in their experiments with inoculation against smallpox since the early eighteenth century (McNeil, 251), may have deliberately encouraged the spread of the disease among the Indians from time to time.

In the one well-documented case cited by McNeil and other authorities, British officers stationed at Fort Pitt (on the site that would become Pittsburgh) gave the Delaware Indians a handkerchief and two blankets from the local smallpox hospital in a desperate effort to halt Pontiac's Revolt (McNeil, 251; Hagan, 25). Sir Jeffrey Amherst, commander-in-chief of the British forces in North America, instructed his subordinate, "You will do well to try to innoculate (*sic*) the Indians by means of blankets as well as to try every other method that can serve to extirpate this exorable race" (Thornton, 78–79). Although there is no proof that this early attempt at germ warfare succeeded, Thornton observes that the Delawares, the Mingo, and the Shawnee were soon gripped by a smallpox epidemic (ibid., 79). The revolt ended in negotiation in 1765.

Whether or not the Americans often had recourse to biological warfare, they were strongly disinclined to take active measures against the spread of epidemics among the Indians. They had inoculated their slaves against smallpox before Edward Jenner's discovery in 1796 that vaccination with cowpox could induce immunity to smallpox, and they had left the Indians in the hands of God and counted the decline in Indian numbers as one of his blessings (Nash 1982, 295).

Among the Portuguese Jesuits working with the Indians of Brazil, the benevolent desire to convert the Indians to Christianity proved as lethal to the Indians as Sir Jeffrey Amherst's malevolent desire to destroy them with smallpox. From the late sixteenth century to the eighteenth century, the Jesuits kept filling their missions with Indian converts despite the fact that disease carried off one cohort after another. "This did not deter them," writes John Hemming:

> The Jesuits were intelligent enough to appreciate that the epidemics were probably imported by Europeans, and that they struck hardest at converts congregated into mission settlements. . . . Some may have believed that it was better for Indians to be baptised but dead than heathen but alive and free. But it often seemed that what really mattered was pride in maintaining the mission system. The Jesuits became obsessed with their personal soul-count. [Hemming 1978, 145]

The devastation suffered by the Brazilian Indians in the Jesuit mission stations gives added force to Francis Jennings's observation that "not even the most brutally depraved of the conquistadors was able purposely to slaughter Indians on the scale that the gentle priest unwittingly accomplished by going from his sickbed ministrations to lay his hands in blessing on his Indian converts" (Jennings, 22).

Ignorant though they were at first of the causes of the epidemics and their cures, the treatment of the native peoples by the European rulers of the New World contributed significantly to their demographic collapse. Although we will never know the exact number, the Spaniards taxed and worked many Indians to death, treating them with a callousness that exceeded even their insensitivity to their serfs in Spain. Fray Toribio de Benavente, known as Motolinia, one of the first Franciscan missionaries to land in Mexico in 1524, gave his own firsthand account of this process: "The tributes demanded of the Indians were so great that many towns, unable to pay, would sell to the moneylenders among them the lands and children of the poor and as the tributes were very frequent and they could not meet them by selling all that they had, some towns became entirely depopulated and others were losing their population" (Todorov 1984, 134).

Bartolomé de las Casas, the Dominican friar who became an outstanding advocate of the Indians' cause, also linked the Spanish system of forced labor to native depopulation:

Thus husbands and wives were together once every eight or ten months, and when they met they were so exhausted and depressed on both sides that they had no mind for marital intercourse, and in this way they ceased to procreate. As for the newly born, they died early because their mothers, overworked and famished, had no milk to nurse them with, and for this reason, while I was in Cuba, 7000 children died in three months. Some mothers even drowned their babies from sheer desperation, while others caused themselves to abort with certain herbs which produced still-born children. [ibid., 134]

Motolinia's description of conditions in the Spanish-operated mines underscores the Spaniards' disregard for the value of Indian lives. He tells of Indians who starved to death while transporting Spanish goods

either at the mines or on the road. . . . The bodies of these Indians and of the slaves who died in the mines produced such a stench that it caused a pestilence, especially at the mines of Guaxaca. For half a league [approximately three miles] around these mines and along a great part of the road one could scarcely avoid walking over dead bodies or bones, and the flocks of birds and crows that came to feed upon the corpses were so numerous that they darkened the sun, so that many villages along the road and in the district were deserted. [ibid., 137–38]

Yet in spite of this evidence of Spanish brutality toward the Indians, genocide —deliberate killing with the intention of destroying the group—played a very small role, if any, in the Spanish Conquest of the New World. The story of Columbus and the Arawaks, a once-numerous group of natives in the West Indies, underscores the point that deliberate annihilation of the Indians was not

Spain's goal. The Spanish monarchs, King Ferdinand and Queen Isabella, valued converting natives to Christianity more than enslaving them. Columbus was responsible for destroying an enormous number of Arawaks by enslaving and transporting them for work in other islands in the West Indies and Spain, where they rapidly fell prey to disease and died. In 1500, when the Spanish sovereigns were informed that Columbus placed his highest priority on enslavement and that he was guilty of mistreating his Indian subjects on the island of Hispaniola (comprised today of Haiti and the Dominican Republic), he was stripped of his colonial offices and taken back to Spain in chains. Although Columbus was eventually freed and given permission to embark on a new voyage, he was never again allowed to set foot on Hispaniola (Stone, 77).

Royal intervention came too late for the Arawaks. Disease, the undermining of native society, and the introduction of new and harsh systems of exploiting the Indians slashed the number of Arawak aborigines on Hispaniola from 60,000 (or even as many as 3 to 4 million if one accepts the higher estimates) in 1492 to nearly zero by 1535 (Cook and Borah 1971, 1:397, 401). Though they did not suffer a genocide, Cook and Borah conclude, the Arawaks of Hispaniola were "for all practical purposes . . . extinct" (ibid.).

The record of France's relations with the Indians is certainly much better than Spain's or the Americans'. Yet the French bear an indirect responsibility for the destruction of the Huron and a direct responsibility for the annihilation of the Natchez of the lower Mississippi region. Although the Huron and the Iroquois were already enemies when the French came to New France, there is no doubt that the struggle for the control of the fur trade between the French and the Dutch raised the viciousness of the warfare among the Indian rivals and that the French did everything in their power to discourage a trade alliance between the Huron and the Iroquois (Eccles, 45). The rivalry finally ended with the defeat of the Huron in March 1649. The Jesuits could not save their Huron allies. The Iroquois burned most of the Hurons in their longhouses. All that the Jesuits could do was to baptize them as they died. Although a few hundred Huron survived, the Huron Confederacy ceased to exist in 1649, and only one of its tribes survived the Iroquois assaults (Eccles, 46–47; Thornton, 74–75; Trigger 1987, 789).

When an Indian people stood in the way of France's quest for wealth, the French were just as ruthless as the Iroquois. The French destroyed an Indian people when it suited their purpose, as in the case of the Natchez in 1731. Arriving in the lower Mississippi region with their own soldiers, women, and black slaves around 1720, the French planned to gain control of the interior of North America. When the Natchez proved intractable and resisted a French ultimatum, hostilities began. Both sides committed massacres until 1731, when the Choctaw joined with the French and destroyed the Natchez stronghold. Then the French avenged the killing of several hundred of their citizens by taking the lives of 1,000 Natchez and selling some 400 of them into slavery in St. Domingue. The Natchez ceased to exist as a people (Nash 1982, 109–10).

Settlers in the British colonies played a major role in the destruction of several native tribes in Connecticut, the Carolinas, Florida, and Virginia, and created conditions that undermined the viability of others. In the seventeenth century, the English Puritans, who had settled in New England for religious reasons, encountered the Pequots, the Narragansetts, and other Indian peoples living in the Connecticut Valley. Already weakened by European diseases acquired through contact with fishermen and traders from across the Atlantic, and divided among themselves by tribal disputes over trade, hunting, and farming rights, the New England Indians offered little resistance to the Puritans; in some cases, they welcomed the Europeans as potential allies against their enemies. Nevertheless, disease and military action decimated the Indians of the New England coast.

The Puritans' annihilation of the Pequots is one genocide against the Indians that can be described in depth. It is examined by Gary Nash in the essay that follows. (For a different interpretation, one which denies that the Puritans attacked the Pequots to obtain their land and argues that Pequots provoked the Puritans, see Alden Vaughn 1979, v–xlv, 134–52. We are persuaded that Nash's interpretation of the Puritans' motives is closer to the truth.). The Pequots were one of the few tribes to escape the epidemics that devastated New England. In 1637, over 500 Pequots were killed when the settlers and their Indian allies attacked them, while the settlers suffered only two fatalities. Nash's account makes it clear that the Puritans murdered noncombatants, prisoners of war, and surrendering warriors. Survivors who had the good fortune to escape or to be absent from the Pequot fort when it was attacked were tracked down, captured, and sold as slaves to other tribes or to planters in the West Indies. In 1638, the Puritans and their Indian allies signed the Treaty of Hartford, which declared the Pequot nation dissolved. The spirit behind this genocide is encapsulated in the victory sermon of Increase Mather, a leading Puritan minister, who asked his congregation to thank God "that on this day we have sent six hundred heathen souls to hell" (Hagan, 13). The poem written by Captain Wait Winthrop in 1675, which follows Nash's essay, illustrates the dehumanized picture of the Indians that arose among the Puritans during their conquest of New England. The cultural bias underpinning the Puritans' perception of the Indians has been described in detail by William S. Simmons (1981).

CULTURES MEET IN
SEVENTEENTH-CENTURY
NEW ENGLAND†

New England could not really remain homogeneous, no matter how many nonconformists were banished from its midst. Nor could the acquisitive instincts which ate at the concept of community be forever dampened. The work ethic inevitably brought material gains, and with worldly success individuals developed the ambition to reach still higher—precisely what the Puritan leaders feared would destroy the stable, harmonious system they were trying to build. Population increase, geographical expansion, and trade with the outside world all worked against the idea of a closed corporate community suffused with religiosity. In spite of the leaders' admonitions that "the care of the public must oversway all private respects," Massachusetts, even in the early years, demonstrated the difficulty, if not the impossibility, of setting down land-hungry immigrants in the New World and expecting them to restrain their appetites and individualistic urges. The centrifugal forces of the environment were more than a match for the centripetal forces of religious ideology.

Puritans and Indians

Given the Puritan ideal of community and the centrality of the idea of reforming the world in their image, it might be thought that the conflict and limited acculturation that characterized Anglo-Indian contacts on the Chesapeake would have been replaced in New England by less hostility and greater interaction. But this was not the case.

Descendants of nomadic hunters who had come to the region 10,000 years before, the Indians of New England lived on the margin of the agricultural zone. Therefore, their economy combined hunting, fishing, and agriculture, though the latter, by the time Europeans arrived, was their primary subsistence activity. Efficiently utilizing their environment according to the season, they engaged in winter hunting, spring stream fishing and clearing of fields, summer cultivation of crops and sea fishing, and autumn harvesting and hunting. "Sea-

†From Gary Nash, *Red, White and Black: The Peoples of Early America*, 2d ed., 74–86. Copyright 1982. Reprinted by permission of Prentice-Hall, Inc., Englewood Cliffs, N.J. (Notes 1–19 correspond to notes 4–22 in the original.)

sonality," writes Neal Salisbury, "provided the basis for a rudimentary but regularly recurrent annual cycle."[1]

The sexual division of labor was marked among the Algonkian tribes of New England. Men hunted but women were responsible for all phases of agriculture —planting, maintaining, and harvesting crops—as well as for fishing and gathering wild plant products. Since agriculture had become the most important component of the economy, a distinct imbalance had evolved in the productivity of the two sexes. This did not lead, as in the case of the Iroquois, to the adoption of a matrilineal kinship system or the conferring of a degree of political power upon women. In New England kinship remained patrilineal, and men continued to dominate political and religious life.

Political leadership of Algonkian tribes in New England was held by single individuals, called "sachems" in the southern region and "sagamores" in the northern region. The sachem's role was to coordinate, at the village level, activities that concerned the group as a whole—hunting, trade, the administration of justice, and diplomacy. The sachem's authority depended heavily on maintaining the consent of his people. This, in turn, depended greatly on the sachem's ability to communicate with the spiritual forces that controlled the fate of the tribe. "Their authority is most precarious," wrote one Frenchman among the Abenaki, "if indeed, that may be called authority to which obedience is in no wise obligatory."[2] Sachems and sagamores were not chiefs or lords whose title was inherited and authority unquestioned, but "coordinators and ceremonial representatives for their people."[3]

In the pre-contact period the Algonkian-speaking people of New England were more densely settled than in the Chesapeake region, probably numbering more than 100,000 between the Kennebec River and Cape Cod. Among them, the most numerous were the Abenaki, Pawtucket, Massachuset, Narragansett, Pequot, and Wampanoag. All of these groups had been in contact with Europeans for many generations. Fishermen who dried their catches and engaged in minor trade had provided the more northerly tribes with knowledge of European culture since the first quarter of the sixteenth century, and short-lived French and English attempts at settlement in the first decade of the seventeenth century gave them further understanding of the people from across the sea.

A series of English exploratory incursions and small-scale attempts at settlement occurred in the early seventeenth century. All of them had to contend with the fact that the French had already established permanent settlements and a trading network that extended from Nova Scotia to Cape Cod. This economic hegemony had been built upon a system of reciprocal relations with the natives of the region. None of the first English attempts at settlement fared well, for the English adopted a far more militaristic stance toward the Indians, typified in John Smith's formula of deception, intimidation, and unbridled force, which he recommended following his voyage to the New England coast in 1614. English expeditions attacked and kidnapped coastal Indians on a number of occasions. In 1614 one of Smith's captains captured more than twenty Indians and sold them into slavery in Malaga, Spain. Such a predatory approach guaranteed that the English, when they came in larger numbers in the 1620s, would not be welcomed as a people with whom amicable relations could be expected.

It was not brute force or superior numbers, however, that paved the way for a permanent English presence in New England. Rather it was disease. In 1616 English fishermen stopped on the coast and triggered a "virgin soil epidemic" — the implantation of viruses into a population with no immunological defense. Tens of thousands of Indians died within a single year along the New England coast. Especially hard hit was the area from Massachusetts Bay to Plymouth Bay where entire towns were swept away or abandoned. Five years later an Englishman moving through the area wrote that the Indians had "died on heapes, as they lay in their houses, and the living that were able to shift for themselves would runne away and let them dy, and let there Carkases ly above the ground without buriall. . . . And the bones and skulls upon the several places of their habitations, made such a spectacle . . . that as I travailed in that Forrest nere the Massachussetts [tribe], it seemed to mee a new found Golgotha."[4] Three-quarters or more of the native inhabitants of southern New England probably succumbed to the disease.

When the Pilgrims arrived in 1620, they disembarked in an area that had suffered catastrophic population losses just a few years before. This was crucial not only in opening up the land for them but also in greatly weakening the Indians' ability to resist the encroachers. It was the further good fortune of the English to encounter Squanto, a Wampanoag who had been kidnapped by an English ship captain in 1614. Squanto had been sold by his abductor in Spain but somehow had made his way to England where he joined an English captain on several trips to the New England coast. On the second of these trips Squanto found that most of his tribe had been killed by the plague, but he remained in the Cape Cod area and was there when the Pilgrims landed. Through Squanto's friendship the Pilgrims were rendered important assistance in the early years.

A decade after the initial settlement, William Bradford, the leader of the Pilgrim colony, wrote that the English had come anticipating the "continual danger of the savage people, who are cruel, barbarous, and most treacherous" — characteristics that made "the very bowels of men to grate within them and make the weak to quake and tremble."[5] But given the record of kidnapping and broken trust which the English had established in their periodic visits to the coast before 1620, the characterization better fitted the English than the local tribes. The local Indians were probably deeply suspicious of the Pilgrims, but no incident of violence at Plymouth occurred until after the newcomers discovered the natives' underground cold-storage cellars and stole as much of the corn, placed there for winter use, as they could carry off. Even then the Indians chose to minimize contact with the settlers, though after death had reduced the Plymouth colony to about fifty persons in the spring of 1621 the vulnerability of the English invited Indian attack.

The need of the local Wampanoags for a military ally to aid them in their struggle with the neighboring Narragansetts probably explains why they tolerated English abuses and even signed a treaty in 1621 that formed the basis for trade and mutual assistance with the precariously situated English. The logic of the Wampanoag diplomacy was revealed when Miles Standish and other Pilgrims aided them in a dispute with their enemies in 1621. The Wampanoags regarded the treaty as an alliance of equals but the English, regarding themselves as culturally superior, saw it as the submission by the Indians to English domination.

This surface amity lasted only a year, however. In 1622 the arrival of about sixty non–Pilgrim newcomers to the colony brought serious friction. The new colonists settled themselves at Wessagusset, some distance from the Pilgrim colony, stole corn from the neighboring Massachusets, and planned attacks on them when they refused to trade with the needy, but arrogant, newcomers. Under cover of a story that the Indians were conspiring against both white communities, Standish, who had long harbored grudges against several insulting Massachusets, led an offensive against the friendly Indians, killing eight of them and impaling the head of the sachem Wituwamet on top of the fort at Plymouth as a symbol of white power. Hearing of the deterioration of relations, John Robinson, formerly the Pilgrims' minister in Holland, wrote Governor Bradford in dismay, asking why the English indulged in needless violence. What was happening to "civilized" men in the wilderness? asked Robinson. Were they beginning to act like "savages," forgetting that they were supposed to represent order and piety? Robinson singled out Miles Standish, the militia captain of Plymouth, who had adopted John Smith's formula of inspiring fear and submission rather than mutual respect and harmonious relations. "It is . . . a thing more glorious, in men's eyes, than pleasing in God's, or convenient for Christians, to be a terrour to poor barbarous people. And indeed I am afraid lest, by these occasions, others should be drawn to affect [this kind of behavior] in the world."[6] As for the Indians, they "could not imagine, from whence these men should come," wrote Thomas Morton, a friend of the Indians, "or to what end, seeing them performe such unexpected actions." From that time on the English colonists were called "Wotowquenange, which in their language signifieth stabbers or Cutthroates."[7]

When the Puritan migration began in 1630, natives of the New England coast had more than a generation of experience with English ways. Little that they had encountered could have rendered them optimistic about future relations, although their own intertribal hostilities continued to make the settlers potentially valuable allies, and their desire for trade goods persisted. As for the Puritans, they were publicly committed to interracial harmony but privately preparing for the worst. The charter of the Massachusetts Bay Company spoke of the commitment to convert the Indians to Christianity. The "principall ende of this plantacion," it pronounced, was to "wynn and incite the natives of [the] country, to the knowledg and obedience of the onlie true God and Savior of mankinde, and the Christian fayth."[8] But the instructions of the Company to John Winthrop revealed more accurately what was anticipated. According to these orders, all men were to be trained in the use of firearms; Indians were prohibited from entering the Puritan towns; and any colonists so reckless as to sell arms to the Indians or instruct them in their use were to be deported to England where they would be severely punished. While ordering that the Indians must be fairly treated, the Company reflected the garrison mentality that settlers, once landed and settled, would manifest even more strongly. No missionary activity was to be initiated for thirteen years.

In the first few years of settlement the Indians did little to arouse Puritan wrath. Their sachems made overtures of friendship; they supplied the colonists with corn during the difficult first winter; and a minor trade was started. It was with surprise that one Puritan leader recounted that during the first winter, when the Puritans "had scarce houses to shelter themselves, and no doores to hinder the Indians access to all they had in them, . . . where their whole substance, weake Wives and little ones lay open to their plunder; . . . yet had they none food or stuffe diminished, neither Children nor Wives hurt in the least measure, although the Indians came commonly to them at those times, much hungry belly (as they used to say) and were then in number and strength beyond the English by far."[9]

This state of coexistence lasted only a few years. Smallpox struck the eastern Massachusetts bands in 1633 and 1634, killing thousands as far north as Maine and as far south as the Connecticut Valley. For the colonists it was proof that God had intervened in the Puritans' behalf at a time when the expansionist impulses of the settlers were beginning to cause friction over rights to land. The town records of Charlestown, for example, state that "without this remarkable and terrible stroke of God upon the natives, [we] would with much more difficulty have found room, and at far greater charge have obtained and purchased land."[10] As in Virginia, it was the need for land that provided the incentive for steering away from rather than toward equitable relations between the societies. That the population buildup came so quickly in Puritan New England only hastened the impulse to regard Indians as objects to be removed rather than subjects to be assimilated.

The Question of Land

Puritan theories of land possession help to clarify this tendency to classify Indians in such a way that only violence rather than assimilation or coexistence could occur. Like other Europeans, Puritans claimed the land they were invading by right of discovery. This theory derived from the ancient claim that Christians were everywhere entitled to dispossess non–Christians of their land. A second European legal theory, called *vacuum domicilium*, bolstered Puritan claims that land not "occupied" or "settled" went by forfeit to those who attached themselves to it in a "civilized" manner. Before he set foot in the New World John Winthrop wrote:

> As for the Natives in New England, they inclose noe Land, neither have any setled habytation, nor any tame Cattle to improve the Land by, and soe have noe other but a Naturall Right to those Countries, soe as if we leave them sufficient for their use, we may lawfully take the rest, there being more than enough for them and us.[11]

Thus, in Puritan eyes, entitlement to the land of New England required nothing more than the assertion that because their way of life did not conform to European norms, the Indians had forfeited all the land which they "roamed" rather than "settled." By European definition the land was *vacuum domicilium* —unoccupied. To this mental picture of an unoccupied land the awful epidemic of 1616–18 had made an important contribution.

Given the slender power of the disease-ravaged coastal tribes of the Massachusetts Bay region and the legal principles invoked under the concept of *vacuum domicilium*, the Puritans were ideally situated to establish their beachhead in the New World. The remnants of the formerly populous Massachuset and Pawtucket peoples were in no position to resist and in fact willingly consented to the settlement of their lands by the Puritan vanguard that inhabited Naumkeag (renamed Salem) in 1629 and the 3,000 settlers who came in the next four years. In return for land, of which they now had a great surplus, the Indians gained the protection of the English against their Micmac enemies to the north. Hence the Puritans quickly acquired the notion that the local Indians were properly regarded as domesticated subjects, who lived in separate villages but were to answer to Puritan concepts of government and law.

Nonetheless, by about 1634 the land question had begun to assume a central place in Puritan–Indian relations. Another epidemic in 1633 had struck down many native people throughout a wide area from the St. Lawrence River to Long Island. Once more the English saw the divine hand intervening in their behalf and Indians trembled at the power of the English God. This may have temporarily lessened the Indian sense of being overwhelmed by the steady flow of English colonists into the area. But pressure on available land resources was mounting rapidly.

The land question also became critical because in 1633 the radical separatist Roger Williams of Salem disputed the claim of the Massachusetts Bay leaders that their royal patent entitled them to occupy Indian land without first purchasing it from the natives. Williams had become immersed in Indian culture shortly after his arrival in 1631—one of the few Englishmen to do so—and by the next year was absorbed in learning their language. Williams argued that the Puritans had illegally and sinfully grabbed Indian land and would have to answer for this before God and the English authorities. He also argued that the natives of the region uséd the land in rational and systematic ways, thus directly challenging the random use of land supposed in the legal concept of *vacuum domicilium*. The Massachusetts magistrates indignantly dismissed these ideas, ceremoniously burned the tract in which Williams advanced his arguments, and shortly thereafter banished him from the colony. Traveling to Rhode Island with some of his followers, Williams was offered land by a Narragansett sachem and found "among the savages," as he wrote, a place where he and his followers could peaceably worship God according to their consciences. Winthrop's response to Williams's argument was that "if we had no right to this lande, yet our God hathe right to it, and if he be pleased to give it us (takinge it from a people who had so long usurped upon him and abused his creatures) who shall controll him or his terms?"[12] By claiming that God directed all Puritan policy, Winthrop thus charged anyone who murmured dissent with opposing not only Puritan policy but God himself.

Nevertheless, the practice of purchasing Indian land progressed slowly as settlement continued. But the purchases were usually made in order to obtain a favorable settlement in a situation where the same tract of land was coveted by rival groups of settlers. In such cases a deed to the land in dispute from an Indian seller was the best way to convince a court of one's claim. Even in those cases where intra–European rivalry necessitated the purchase of Indian land, the sale could be accomplished through a variety of stratagems designed to reduce the cost to the white settler. Turning livestock into cultivated Indian fields over a period of time was an effective way of convincing an Indian that his land was losing its value. Alcohol was frequently used to reduce the negotiating skill of the Indian seller. Another method was to buy the land at a rock-bottom price from an Indian sachem who falsely claimed title to it and then take to court any disputing sachem who claimed ownership. Before an English court, with its white lawyers, judges, and juries, the Indian claimant rarely won his case. Perhaps most effective of all was fining an Indian for minor offenses of English law—walking on the Sabbath or illegally entering a town, for example —and then "rescuing" him from the debt he was unable to pay by discharging the fine in return for a tract of his land. None of these tactics worked in areas where Indian tribes were strong and unified. But among the decimated and divided tribes of southern New England they were highly effective.

The Pequot War

All the factors that operated in Virginia to produce friction between the two societies—English land hunger, a deprecatory view of native culture, and intertribal Indian hostility—were to be found in New England. They were vastly augmented by another factor not present on the Chesapeake —the Puritan sense of mission. For people of such high moral purpose, who lived daily with the anxiety that they might fail in what they saw as the last chance to save corrupt Western Protestantism, the Indian stood as a direct challenge to the "errand into the wilderness." The Puritans' mission was to tame and civilize their new environment and to build in it a pious commonwealth that would "shine like a beacon" back to decadent England. But how could order and discipline be brought to the new environment unless its inhabitants were tamed and "civilized"? Governor William Bradford of Plymouth tellingly described the land he was entering as "a hideous and desolate wilderness full of wild beasts and wild men."[13] Land, beast, and man must all be brought under control. To do less was to allow chaos to continue when God's will was that Christian order be imposed. As Roy H. Pearce has explained, the Indian stood as a vivid reminder of what the English knew they must not become. The native was the counterimage of civilized man, thought to be lacking in what was most valued by the Puritans—civility, Christian piety, purposefulness, and the work ethic. If such people could not be made part of the Puritan system, then the Puritans would have demonstrated their inability to control this corner of the earth to which God had directed them. God would surely answer such a failure with his wrath. So Puritans achieved control of themselves—internal control— through controlling the external world containing forests, fields—and Indians.[14]

The greater one's doubts about the success of this utopian experiment, doubts magnified by internal dissension, the greater the inner need to stifle self-doubt through repression and extension of control. Thus in New England, Indians became obstacles in two senses: as in Virginia and elsewhere they represented a physical barrier since they possessed the land and could not easily be subjugated so as to serve English ends; and they were a psychological obstacle since, while they remained "savages," they threatened the identity of individual Puritans and the collective success of the Puritan Way.

To eliminate "savagism" one did not necessarily have to eliminate the "savages." From their writings it appears that Puritans would have preferred to convert the "heathen" to Christianity. But this could only be accomplished through great expenditure of time and effort. The Spanish and Portuguese had sent hundreds of missionaries along with the conquistadors and settlers. But the Puritans came only with their own ministers and these men had more than enough to do to maintain piety, unity, and moral standards within the white community. Proselytizing the natives of New England never received a high priority. Much was written about foiling Satan, who had "decoyed those miserable savages hither, in hopes that the gospel of the Lord Jesus Christ would never come here to destroy or disturb his absolute empire over them," but little was done in saving the Native Americans from Satan.[15]

Rather than convert the "savages" of New England, the Puritans attempted to bring them under civil government, making them strictly accountable to the ordinances that governed white behavior in Massachusetts. Insofar as Indians were willing to subject themselves to the new white code of behavior, usually out of fear, the Puritans could prevail, keeping a close eye on all Indians within the areas of white settlement and bringing them to court for any offenses against white law. Many of the smaller bands of eastern Massachusetts, disastrously weakened by European disease or living in fear of strong and hostile neighbors, did what was necessary to satisfy the newcomers. But the question of control became a military problem when the Puritans encountered a tribe that was sufficiently strong to resist the loss of its cultural identity and political sovereignty.

Such were the Pequots—a strong and aggressive people who had migrated to southern New England in the century before English arrival. By the 1630s they had built a trading network of tributary groups and viewed the Narragansetts as their main rival in southern New England. The Pequots worked hard to convince the neighboring Narragansetts that only by uniting against the English could either tribe survive. But their arguments went unheard. Following the advice of Roger Williams, the Narragansetts agreed to ally themselves with Massachusetts Bay, leaving the Pequots virtually alone in their determination to resist the English.

Hostilities between the Pequots and English were ostensibly triggered by the murder of two white ship captains and their crews. One of the mariners, John Stone, was cordially hated among the English, for he had attempted to murder Governor Prence of Plymouth and had later been banished from Massachusetts for other misdeeds. Two years alter Stone's death in 1634, John Oldham was found murdered on his pinnace off Block Island. Using these incidents as justification for a punitive expedition against the unsubmissive Pequots, a joint Connecticut–Massachusetts force marched into Pequot country and demanded the murderers (who, as it turned out, were not Pequots) as well as a thousand fathoms of wampum, and some Pequot children as hostages.

The Pequots understood that the issue was broader than the death of several English mariners, that in fact they were embroiled in a complicated set of disputes over land and trade. These were the real causes of the war that shortly would break out. At the center of the tensions was the English–Dutch trade rivalry and intertribal Indian hostilities. Since 1622 the Dutch in New Amsterdam had controlled the Indian trade of New England through their connections to both the Pequot and the Narragansett, the region's two strongest tribes. After the arrival of the English and their rapid expansion in the early 1630s, the Dutch perceived that their trading empire was greatly threatened. Hence, they purchased land on the lower Connecticut River—an area on which several English groups had their eyes—and built a trading post there to defend their regional economic hegemony. Some of the Pequots' discontented client tribes, however, were already breaking away, signing separate trade agreements with and ceding land to the English. Amidst such fragmentation, expansionist New England was ready, with the aid of its Narragansett allies, to drive the Dutch traders from southern New England and to subdue the Pequots who occupied some of the area's most fertile soil. The Pequots first tried to placate the English; when this proved impossible, they chose to resist.

In the war that ensued, the English found the Pequots more than a match until they were able to surround a secondary Pequot village on the Mystic River in May 1637. The English and their Narragansett allies attacked before dawn, infiltrated the town, and set fire to the Pequot wigwams inside before beating a fast retreat. In the meleé about twenty Narragansetts suffered wounds at the hands of the English, who found it difficult to distinguish between Indian enemies and allies. Retreating from the flame-engulfed village, the English regrouped and waited for fleeing survivors from the inferno. Most of the victims were noncombatants since the Pequot warriors were gathered at another village about five miles away. Before the day was over a large part of the Pequot tribe had been slaughtered, many by fire and others by guns. Those who escaped or who were not at the fort were enslaved and sold to other tribes or shipped to the West Indies in chains. One of New England's first historians, William Hubbard, wrote that dozens of captured Pequots were put on board the ship of Captain John Gallup, "which proved [to be] Charon's ferry-boat unto them, for it was found the quickest was to feed the fishes with 'em."[16] One of the militia captains wrote that at Mystic Fort "God . . . laughed [at] his Enemies and the Enemies of his People to Scorn, making them as a fiery Oven . . . [and] filling the Place with Dead Bodies." William Bradford wrote that "it was a fearful sight to see them thus frying in the fire and the streams of blood quenching the same, and horrible was the stink and scent thereof; but the victory seemed a sweet sacrifice, and they gave the praise thereof to God, who had wrought so wonderfully for them, thus to enclose their enemies in their hands and given them so speedy a victory over so proud and insulting an enemy."[17] In 1638, at the Treaty of Hartford, the Pequot nation was declared dissolved. Two generations later Cotton Mather, a pillar of the Puritan ministry, reiterated: "in a little more than *one* hour, five or six hundred of these barbarians were dismissed from a world that was *burdened* with them."[18]

Such savagery as the "civilized" Puritans demonstrated at Mystic Fort was shocking to the Narragansett "savages" who fought with the Puritans. According to one English officer, they came after the victory and "much rejoiced at our victories, and greatly admired the manner of Englishmen's fight, but cried Mach it, Mach it; that is, It is naught, It is naught [bad or wicked] because it is too furious and slays too many men." It was a poignant comment on the different styles and functions of warfare in the two societies.[19]

For the Puritans the extermination of the Pequots was proof of their political and military ascendancy. Its additional function was to provide a response to anxiety and disunity that had become widely diffused throughout the colony. These fears were associated not only with the threat of the Pequots but also with the dissensions within Puritan society. It is well to remember that the war came on the heels of three years of intense internal discord centered around the challenges to the power of the magistrates by Roger Williams and Anne Hutchinson. These challenges, in turn, involved not only theological questions but economic restrictions, the distribution of political power, and competing land claims among English settlers in Massachusetts, Connecticut, and Rhode Island. Their colonies beset with controversy, the Puritan leaders talked morbidly about God's anger at seeing his chosen people subvert the City on the Hill. In this sense, the Puritan determination to destroy the Pequots and the level of violence manifested at Mystic Fort can be partially understood in terms of the self-doubt and guilt that Puritans could expiate only by exterminating so many of "Satan's agents." Dead Pequots were offered to God as atonement for Puritan failings.

Victory over the Pequots decisively established English sovereignty over all the Indians of southeastern New England except the Narragansetts and removed the one remaining obstacle to expansion into the Connecticut River Valley. The tribes of southern New England, reduced to about one quarter of their former population, adjusted as best they could to the realities of Puritan power. The fur trade kept the two societies in touch with each other and provided the means by which English iron goods became incorporated into the material culture of the Indians. But the trade, which flourished in the 1630s, petered out by mid-century as the beaver supply in New England became depleted. In spite of these trade contacts, most of the remnant groups that had survived the coming of the English struggled to maintain their native way of life. Some of the weaker and more demoralized groups followed the handful of missionaries, finally spurred to action in 1643 by English critics, who rightly charged that conversion had been studiously ignored for more than a decade. After ten years of effort less than a thousand Indians of the region were settled in four villages of "praying Indians" and fewer than one hundred of these declared their conversion to the Puritan form of Christianity. Even among these, defections would be numerous in the 1670s when war broke out again in Massachusetts. As in the case of Virginia, the natives incorporated certain implements and articles of clothing obtained in the European trade into their culture, but overwhelmingly, even after major military defeats, they preferred to resist acculturation when it meant adopting English religion, forms of government, styles of life, or patterns of social and economic organization.

For Puritans and non–Puritans who migrated into New England in increasing numbers after mid-century, the Indians served no useful purpose. The rough balance of English males and females eliminated the need for Indian women as sexual partners. The church took only a minor interest in the Indian, who in any event could rarely satisfy the qualifications that Puritans placed upon their own people for church membership. The Indian trade withered to relative unimportance, as fishing, lumbering, shipbuilding, and agriculture became the mainstays of the colonizers' economy. This lack of function within English society, combined with the special tendency of Puritans to doubt the Indians' capacity for meeting the standards required in the New Jerusalem, made close and reciprocal contacts between the two societies all but impossible.

NOTES

1. Neal E. Salisbury, *Manitou and Providence: Indians, Europeans, and the Making of New England, 1500–1643* (New York: Oxford University Press, forthcoming).

2. Reuben Gold Thwaites, ed., *The Jesuit Relations and Allied Documents . . . 1610–1791* (Cleveland: The Burrows Brothers Company, 1896), 2:73.

3. Salisbury, *Manitou and Providence*.

4. Thomas Morton, "New English Canaan," in *Tracts and Other Papers Relating Principally to the Origin, Settlement and Progress of the Colonies in North America.* Peter Force, comp. (Washington, D.C., 1836), II, no. 5:19.

5. William Bradford, *Of Plymouth Plantation, 1620–1647*, ed. Samuel Eliot Morison (New York: Alfred A. Knopf, Inc., 1966), 26.

6. Ibid., 375.

7. Thomas Morton, "New England Canaan," 76, quoted in Neal E. Salisbury, "Conquest of the 'Savage': Puritans, Puritan Missionaries, and Indians, 1620–1680" (Ph.D. dissertation, University of California, Los Angeles, 1972), 86.

8. Nathaniel B. Shurtleff, *Records of the Governor and Company of the Massachusetts Bay in New England*, 5 vols. (Boston: W. White, 1853–54), 1:17.

9. Edward Johnson, "Wonder-Working Providence," quoted in Salisbury, "Conquest of the 'Savage,'" 63–64.

10. Quoted in Alden T. Vaughan, *New England Frontier: Puritans and Indians, 1620–1675* (Boston: Little, Brown and Company, 1965), 104.

11. "Generall Considerations for the Plantation in New England . . ." (1629), in *Winthrop Papers*, 5 vols., ed. Allyn B. Forbes (Boston: Massachusetts Historical Society, 1929–47), 2:118.

12. Ibid., 534n.

13. Bradford, *Plymouth Plantation*, 62.

14. Roy H. Pearce, *The Savages of America: A Study of the Indian and the Idea of Civilization* (Baltimore: The Johns Hopkins Press, 1953), 3–24.

15. Cotton Mather, *Magnalia Christi Americana* (Hartford, Conn., 1853), 2:556.

16. William Hubbard, *A Narrative of the Troubles with the Indians in New England* (1677), quoted in Carolyn T. Foreman, *Indians Abroad, 1493–1938* (Norman: University of Oklahoma Press, 1943), 29.

17. John Mason, "A Brief History of the Pequot War," *Massachusetts Historical Society Collections*, 2d ser., 8 (Boston, 1826): 140–41. Bradford, *Plymouth Plantation*, 296.

18. Cotton Mather, *Magnalia Christi Americana: or, The Ecclesiastic History of New England* (New York: Russell & Russell, 1967), 2:558.

19. John Underhill, "News from America," quoted in Salisbury, "Conquest of the 'Savage'" 81.

A PURITAN VIEW OF THE INDIANS[†]

In July, 1675, colonial militia were seriously mauled by the Narragansett Indians in a fight which took place at the Great Swamp in southern New England. In a poem written to mark the battle, Captain Wait Winthrop prophesied that God would work his wonders to exterminate the Indians (whom

[†]From Douglas Edward Leach, *Flintlock and Tomahawk: New England in King Phillip's War*, 192. Reprinted by permission of W. W. Norton & Co., New York, 1966; original edition, 1958.

he compared to flies, rats, mice, and lice), but only after the prideful New Englanders had mended their sinful ways.

Captain Wait Winthrop's Poem
"Some Meditations"

Late in December, 1675, Captain Wait Winthrop composed a poem which he called *Some Meditations*. After describing the agony of the Great Swamp Fight, and sending up a prayer to God for salvation, he says:

O *New-England*, I understand, with thee God is offended:
And therefore He doth humble thee, till thou thy ways hast mended.

Repent therefore, and do no more, advance thy self so High,
But humbled be, and thou shalt see these Indians soon will dy.

A Swarm of Flies, they may arise, a Nation to Annoy,
Yea Rats and Mice, or Swarms of Lice a Nation may destroy.

Do thou not boast, it is God's Host, and He before doth go,
To humble thee and make thee see, that He His Works will show.

And now I shall my Neighbours all give one word of Advice,
in Love and Care do you prepare for War, if you be wise.

Get Ammunition with Expedition your Selves for to defend,
And Pray to God that He His Rod will please for to suspend.

Thus in poetry . . . the people of New England speculated concerning the sins which had led them to the brink of disaster, and groped for a way to salvation. The idea that God might be angry because of previous mistreatment of the Indians apparently occurred to none of the sin searchers.

INDIANS OF THE UNITED STATES IN THE NINETEENTH CENTURY

The case of the American Indian in the nineteenth century is one of the most complex in the history of genocide. A large number of Indians died in their encounters with white settlers, but, as in the case of Mexico and South America, epidemic disease, not genocide, took the biggest toll on their lives. Nevertheless, genocide and genocidal massacres played an important role in devastating Indian peoples.

When one examines the evidence, it becomes clear that few American leaders wanted to annihilate the American Indian; the government-organized murder of peaceable Indians with the intention of destroying tribes in whole or in part rarely occurred. More often, politicians at the state, local, and national level adopted policies that subordinated the preservation of Indian lives to the higher claims of the myth of progress, the search for material rewards, their own political ambitions, and the relentless demands for more land advanced by white farmers and cattlemen (Moore 1957, chap. 7).

Undeterred by the well-publicized lethal consequences of their policies toward the Indians and supported by the electorate, American political leaders became accomplices in the killing of Indians by repeatedly deporting them from their homelands, failing to provide promised food supplies, and denying the Indians adequate protection from settlers in their new territories and reserves. Moreover, they persisted in harmful acts of commission and omission long after it became clear that their policies emboldened the most unscrupulous settlers, who—left unhindered by the forces of law and order—went on to destroy essential Indian food supplies, to kidnap Indian women and children, and to murder peaceful Indians with impunity.

Soon after the ratification of the Constitution of the United States in 1789, Henry Knox, George Washington's secretary of war and the official responsible for Indian affairs, articulated his vision of American policy toward the Indians. Knox proposed a balanced policy of holding settlers and Indians responsible for maintaining peace on the frontier while taking measures to restrain the settlers and domesticate the Indians. Ethnocide, the destruction of the culture of the

Indians, was at the core of his program, but once their culture was destroyed, he hoped to save the lives of the Indians by convincing them to replace their traditional mixed economy—based on hunting, fishing, and agriculture—with small-scale commercial farming. At its base was Knox's vision that American pioneers would penetrate the Indians' hunting grounds, kill their game, and buy their lands. Knox was one of America's first public officials to advocate private property as a means of "civilizing" the Indians. He foresaw the gradual removal of the Indians as the frontier of white settlement advanced, or, possibly, their absorption into white society (Hagan 1961, 43–44).

Early in his administration, Knox confronted the problem of reserving land for Indian farms. He was unable to set aside land for the Indians because the U.S. government gave priority to the opening of the trans-Appalachian West to vote-wielding American settlers. As William T. Hagan has dryly noted, "Regardless of the century, the reactions of a frontiersman to the sight of good arable land in the possession of an Indian were as easy to predict as the reflexes of Pavlov's dog" (ibid.). Although the new U.S. government interposed itself as a disinterested third party between the Indians and the settlers, it compromised its neutrality many times. By orders issued to the Army in 1799, white squatters were to be granted "all the humanity which the circumstances will possibly permit" (ibid., 44). Hagan describes the effect of this order and others like it: "For Army officers in a civilian-dominated military establishment this was sufficient warning. If Indian and white interests conflicted, the Indian was sacrificed" (ibid.). State governments did not pay any attention to federal measures aimed at protecting the Indians and regulating the pace of their dispossession. In the 1790s, the state of Georgia sold over twenty-five million acres of Indian lands to speculators, ignoring a law that required federal approval for sales of Indian lands (ibid., 48).

By 1800, the demographic collapse of the American Indians produced a fundamental shift in Indian–white relations. Regardless of the debate among scholars about Indian population estimates, it is clear that the Indian population declined dramatically at the same time that the settler population rapidly expanded. Some 600,000 Indians faced a non-Indian population that had grown to over 5 million (Thornton 1987, 90).

The Cherokee Indians were among the first tribes to feel the effects of settler pressure to clear the trans-Appalachian West for white settlement. Their leaders sought friendship with the federal government in a number of ways. Recognizing the growing power of white society, an important segment of the Cherokees adopted a new constitution and a new legal system based on the U.S. Constitution and on elements of Indian law. Many among the Cherokees settled down to farming on permanent homesteads. The Cherokee also cooperated with the U.S. Army to crush resistance among the Shawnee and the Creek indians.

Despite these efforts, the Cherokee were not spared for long. Perhaps their undoing lay in their decision to proclaim their status as an independent nation with sovereignty over Cherokee lands in Alabama, Georgia, North Carolina, and Tennessee. With the discovery of gold and the expansion of cotton planting in the South, the Cherokees were ordered to move by the state of Georgia, which claimed authority over the tribe and its lands. Despite a ruling in their favor by the U.S. Supreme Court in *Worcester vs. Georgia* (1832), the Cherokees were ordered by President Andrew Jackson, who ignored the Supreme Court's decision, to move west of the Mississippi River to the "Great American Desert." Their forced removal, Gary Nash reports, "whose $6 million cost was deducted from the $9 million awarded the tribe for their eastern lands, brought death to perhaps a quarter of the 15,000 who set out" (Nash 1986, 440). Once across the Mississippi River, they joined the remnants of the Chickasaws, Choctaws, and Creeks, who had been deported before them. Was the Cherokee Removal a genocide? Not under the U.N. definition or our own because the element of perpetrator intent is missing. But if we consider the U.S. government's "advertent omission" to preserve Cherokee lives along the Trail of Tears, and accept Whitaker's recommendation that the United Nations include acts of advertent omission in its list of acts of genocide, then an act like the Cherokee deportation would almost certainly be considered an act of genocide today (Whitaker).

A clearer case of genocide is the treatment of the northern Yuki Indians of Round Valley in northern California, located between San Francisco and Eureka, about twenty-five miles from the Pacific Ocean. There were about 5,000 Yuki Indians living at Round Valley when the first Americans stumbled upon it in 1851, three years after the United States took California from Mexico (Cook 1976, 172; Carranco and Beard 1981, 14; Miller, 1979, 98–99). Yuki women and children had been preyed upon for many years by Spanish Californians, who kidnapped them for use as temporary harvest hands, household servants, and camp wives. When the United States assumed control of the area, American hunters and mountain men adopted the practice of seizing Yuki women and children for themselves and for trade with the Spanish Californians. California law provided that citizens could keep Indians as apprentices or indentured servants for as many as ten to fifteen years. Moreover, the kidnappers could not be tried if apprehended unless a white eyewitness was willing to testify against them. The kidnapping and raping of Yuki women also hastened the spread of venereal disease among the Indians and significantly lowered their birth rate (Carranco and Beard, 40, 61).

The coming of American settlers severely depleted the natives' food supply. The Yuki lived by hunting, fishing, and gathering. Their diet included large quantities of acorns, clover, lily bulbs, grass seeds, berries, and the nuts of pine, hazel, and laurel. But the white settlers' cattle consumed the grasses that produced the seeds, and their hogs ate the acorns and other nuts. When the federal government moved the Yuki on to fenced reservations, the settlers tore down the fences to graze their cattle on reservation land (ibid., 18, 20, 55, 59). According to Lynwood Carranco and Estle Beard, "The whites recognized that now the Yuki . . . were prevented from exercising their normal way of life, but they preferred to sacrifice the Indians rather than their livestock" (ibid., 55).

In the period from 1856 to 1858, the settlers at Round Valley appropriated more of the good land for cattle grazing, pushing many Yuki into the mountains, from which they raided the settlers' cattle herds to obtain food. Food intended for the Indians was diverted to white laborers by dishonest federal reservation agents, some of whom operated their own ranches and sawmills. Yuki on the reservation began to die of starvation. As the Yuki killed more cattle in their desperate bid to fend off famine, a number of settlers decided to annihilate them. They mounted their first expedition in 1856, and many others followed over the next five years. One of the worst settler leaders was H. L. Hall, cattle supervisor for the superintendent of the Round Valley reservation. Setting out on one of his many manhunts, Hall was reported to have said that he did not want any man to go with him to hunt Indians who would not kill all he could find, because "a knit (sic) would make a louse." In March 1859, a group of settlers led by Hall killed about 240 Indians in revenge for the killing of a valuable stallion (ibid., chap. 4).

In 1859, the governor of the state of California, John B. Weller, finally intervened, but not on the Indians' side. He granted state commissions to companies of volunteers that excelled in the killing of Indians. The governor acted after receiving a petition signed by a number of leading citizens, including the chief justice of the California Supreme Court, Serranus Clinton, one of the state's most active horse and cattle dealers, who complained to the governor that the federal troops at Round Valley "are the friends of the Indians and appear to be engaged in a campaign against the American citizens settled in this country." Justice Clinton was correct. The army officers wrote reports to their superiors warning them that the companies of volunteers would "hunt the Indians to extermination" and that they had no way of preventing it. Nothing was done. Parallel reports to the secretary of the interior in Washington from a confidential Treasury Department agent, J. Ross Browne, who was appalled by the corrupt diversion of reservation food supplies and by the hunting of Indians as if they were "wild beasts," only led the federal government to cut the number of employees on the reservation and to reduce the allocation of government funds. When the state-commissioned companies of volunteers had finished their work, killing all the Indians they encountered regardless of age or sex, Governor Weller sent his congratulations to their leader for doing "all that was anticipated," and he offered his "sincere thanks for the manner in which it [the campaign] was conducted" (ibid., chaps. 4, 5).

The impact of kidnapping, epidemics, starvation, vigilante justice, and state-sanctioned mass killing on the Yuki of Round Valley is easily measured: from a population of about 5,000 in 1848, their numbers fell by 1880 to some 400 persons (Cook 1976, 105; Miller 1979, 98–99). Special Treasury Agent Browne, an eyewitness to the events described above, gave his judgment on these developments in his report to Washington:

> In the history of the Indian race, I have seen nothing so cruel or relentless as the treatment of those unhappy people by the authority constituted by law for their protection. Instead of receiving aid and succor they have been starved and driven away from the Reservations and then followed into the remote hiding places where they have sought to die in peace, cruelly slaughtered until that a few are left and that few without hope. [Carranco and Beard, 93]

The genocide in this case involves more than "advertent omission" on the part of state and federal officials. The governor of California sanctioned a Yuki genocide.

One of the best-known genocidal massacres in American history may have been the result of a conspiracy between the governor of Colorado and an Army officer looking forward to a new career in politics. At the outbreak of the Civil War in 1861, American settlers in Denver and the mining camps of Colorado violated U.S. treaties with the natives by living on land allocated to the Cheyennes and Arapahos. Rather than irritate the settlers, in February 1861 federal representatives persuaded a number of chiefs to sign a treaty accepting a small reservation in southeastern Colorado. The chiefs renounced the treaty when they realized its full meaning. In November 1863, the governor of Colorado, John Evans, reported to Washington that the Plains Indians planned a full-scale war in the spring of 1864. By August, Governor Evans was authorized by Washington to raise a regiment of men enlisted for one hundred days. This unit was the Third Colorado Cavalry.

The Cheyennes made the governor seem a liar by not attacking in the spring and by even agreeing to peace talks. This news disappointed General Samuel R. Curtis, the commander of all U.S. troops in the region. "I want no peace till the Indians suffer more," Curtis declared in September. "No peace must be made without my direction" (Utley 1984, 90).

Public ire and the political ambition of the key decisionmakers soon pushed public officials and army officers to adopt more aggressive policies toward the Indians. In October and November, Colorado newspapers ridiculed the "Bloodless" Third Regiment and its officers for their inactivity against the Indians.

Governor Evans aspired to a seat in the U.S. Senate. Colonel John Chivington, the military commander of the District of Colorado, was an Indian-hater who had his eye on a seat in the U.S. House of Representatives (Debo 1970, 159; Grinnell 1956, 167; Utley, 91–92). In November 1864, acting on the pretext that the Cheyennes had stolen 175 head of cattle, Chivington led the Third Colorado Regiment into the field. He also seems to have told his men to kill every Cheyenne they found and to take no prisoners (Debo, 159).

One large group of Cheyennes, led by Chief Black Kettle and other chiefs, having signified that they were ready to stop fighting, had moved to the vicinity of Ft. Lyon, an army post, and set up camp on Sand Creek. Living in the encampment were about seven hundred Indians, including five hundred women and children. Chivington led their chiefs to believe that the Army would protect them if they remained at Sand Creek. At dawn on November 29, he and seven hundred of his men attacked the Indians. They killed about one-third of them, most of them women and children, and they took no prisoners. Soon afterward, having mutilated the bodies of those they had killed, Chivington and his enlistees, who were nearing the end of their military service, marched into Denver and were given a hero's welcome. Many of the surrounding tribes, outraged by the reports of the massacre that reached them, went on the warpath. If the attempt to destroy part of the Cheyenne tribe was launched as a genocide of terror, intended to intimidate the surviving Cheyenne and other Indian tribes, it had failed.

The truth about the massacre eventually came out, but by that time Chivington had left the service and could not be court-martialed (Debo, 163). General Nelson A. Miles called the massacre the "foulest and most unjustifiable crime in the annals of America" (Hagan, 108). In October 1865, near the present site of Wichita, Kansas, the U.S. government made treaties with Black Kettle's and Little Raven's Cheyennes and Arapahos. Included in the treaties was an American "confession of war guilt—a reference to 'the gross and wanton outrage' of Chivington—and provision was made for indemnity to the widows and orphans of the massacre" (Debo, 166). Neither Governor Evans nor Chivington ever fulfilled their ambitions for political glory in Colorado.

As early as the 1850s, American politicians began to despair about the failure of their Indian removal policy. Thousands of American settlers who moved into the trans-Mississippi West had proved that the "Great American Desert" was a surmountable barrier. The Indians of the Plains were once again being pressed by the westward movement of American settlers. "A temporizing system can no longer be pursued," Secretary of the Interior Alexander H. H. Stuart declared in 1851. "The policy of removal, except under peculiar circumstances, must necessarily be abandoned; and the only alternatives left are, to civilize or exterminate them. We must adopt one or the other" (Dippie 1982, 75). By "civilize," Stuart meant convincing the Indians to give up their nomadic life style and to settle down and undertake small-scale farming. The first steps in designing a reservation system had been taken by President Millard Fillmore's administration as it grappled with the conflict between the California Indians and white settlers. The federal government promised to keep the California Indians supplied with food, blankets, and luxuries in return for their confinement to designated reserves (Carranco and Beard, 39). This reservation idea was strongly revived for the Plains Indians in 1872 by the commissioner of Indian affairs, Francis Amasa Walker, who advocated coercion to prevent the Indians from obstructing the westward travel of the settlers and strict confinement of the Indians to reservations (Dippie, 152–53).

We have seen how miserably the government implemented its reservation plans where the Yuki were concerned. In the case of the free ranging, horse-mounted Plains Indians, insistence on confinement and the destruction of the buffalo combined to undermine the foundations of Indian life. The Indians depended upon the buffalo for food, clothing, fuel, and housing. As white settlers streamed across the Plains by wagon and train, they joined professional hunters, miners, and railroad crews in slaughtering the buffalo, killing at least 13 million of them by 1883. By 1910, only ten buffalo out of a stock of 60 million remained (Wilson 1986, 14–15).

The federal government welcomed the disappearance of the buffalo. "I cannot regard the rapid disappearance of the game from its former haunts as a matter prejudicial to our management of the Indians," U.S. Secretary of the Interior Columbus Delano wrote in 1872. "As they [the Indians] become convinced that they can no longer rely upon the supply of game for their support, they will return to the more reliable source of subsistence furnished at their agencies" (Nash 1986, 577). The interior secretary's view was more charitable than that expressed by Colonel Richard I. Dodge in 1867 when he advised a group of British hunters at Fort McPherson, Nebraska, not to apologize for their buffalo kill: "Kill every buffalo you can. Every buffalo dead is an Indian gone" (E. Leacock and N. Lurie 1971, 218).

With the passage of the Dawes Severalty Act of 1887, Congress set everything in place for the completion of the ethnocide desired by the American government. The law declared that each Indian family head was eligible to receive a land grant of 160 acres, a homestead intended to encourage the Indians to remain in one place and farm. Reservation lands would no longer be allocated to tribes. This redivision of Indian land left millions of surplus acres that could be sold to white settlers. In presenting the act to Congress, President Chester A. Arthur proclaimed that the act would "have a direct and powerful influence in dissolving the tribal bond, which is so prominent a feature of savage life and which tends so strongly to perpetuate it" (V. Vogel 1972, 176). According to Gary Nash, "Within 20 years of the Dawes Act, Native Americans had lost 60 percent of their lands. The federal government held the profits from land sales 'in trust' and used them for the 'civilizing mission'" (Nash 1986, 577). Reporting to Congress in 1891, President Benjamin Harrison insisted that the Act had helped thousands of Americans to realize the American dream:

> Since March 4, 1889, about 23,000,000 acres have been separated from Indian reservations and added to the public domain for the use of those who desired to secure free homes under our beneficent laws. It is difficult to estimate the increase of wealth which will result from the conversion of these waste lands into farms, but it is more difficult to estimate the betterment which will result to the families that have found renewed hope and courage in the ownership of a home and the assurance of a comfortable subsistence under free and healthful conditions. [V. Vogel, 188]

The U.S. census of 1890 showed a total of 248,253 Indians living in America, down from 400,764 in 1850 (Dippie, 200). Scholars are divided on how the experience of the American Indians should be interpreted. In *Crazy Horse and Custer: The Parallel Lives of Two American Warriors*, Stephen E. Ambrose states his case against those who claim that the United States pursued a policy of genocide toward the Indians:

> The United States did not follow a policy of genocide; it did try to find a just solution to the Indian problem. The consistent idea was to civilize the Indians, incorporate them into the work of the community, make them part of the melting pot. That it did not work, that it was foolish, conceited, even criminal, may be true, but that doesn't turn a well-meant program into genocide, certainly not genocide as we have known it in the twentieth century. [Ambrose, 323]

America's leaders had a higher loyalty than the welfare of the Indians, he argues, and that was "the doctrine of material progress":

> They have believed in that doctrine more than in their Constitution or their treaties or their religion. America's leaders and America's white population have allowed nothing to stand in the path of progress. Not a tree, not a desert, not a river, nothing. Most certainly not Indians, regrettable as it may have been to have to destroy such noble and romantic people. [Ibid., 322–23]

Robert H. Wiebe, on the other hand, in *The Opening of America*, asserts that progress was a two-edged sword: "One side cut the way to an extraordinary vision of human potential: perfectionism. The other side hacked down the people who were obstructing that vision: genocide" (Wiebe 1985, 344). "If the design and acceptance of policies pointing toward the death of an entire people was genocide," he concludes, "white America stood defenseless against the charge" (ibid., 346).

In our view, ethnocide was the principal United States policy toward American Indians in the nineteenth century, but the federal government stood ready to engage in genocide as a means of coercing tribes when they resisted ethnocide or resorted to armed resistance. Ethnocide was at the core of the Indian removals, the reservation system, the Dawes Act, and the schemes for educating native children at boarding schools far from their parents after the Civil War.

Genocide, when it was practiced, could take several forms. The most important was genocide through famine. By encouraging the destruction of the buffalo and driving Native Americans on to marginal agricultural land, the federal government made them more vulnerable to disease, raised their mortality rate, lowered their birth rate, and intimidated those who survived. Tribes that resisted with arms or were thought to be considering resistance were subjected to terrorizing genocides and genocidal massacres intended to teach the lesson that resistance was futile. Such genocides were employed against the Round Valley Indians of California and the victims of the massacre at Sand Creek.

In addition to the clear instances of genocide committed by the U.S. government against American Indians in the nineteenth century, one must also consider those instances of "advertent omission" in which the government showed criminal neglect of the natives' welfare. U.S. leaders had signed treaties binding them to protect the Indians, to guarantee them their lands, and to keep them supplied with food and blankets. By failing to honor these promises, the government did more than dishonor itself and cause untold suffering among the natives: when it tolerated the near annihilation of the Round Valley Yuki in California and abetted the killings at Sand Creek, it became an accessory to genocide by displaying wanton negligence for the lives and safety of the Indians it had sworn to protect.

The discussion of the conflict between natives, settlers, and governments will arise again when we confront the case of the Indians of Brazil in the twentieth century.

THE TASMANIANS

Tasmania, an island off the south coast of Australia, had an indigenous population when the first Europeans visited it and eventually settled there. We know practically nothing about their origin and little about their culture. On the other hand, we know a great deal about what happened to them after the arrival of the Europeans, right up to their disappearance. Why do we know so much about the disappearance of the Tasmanians, when in so many other cases we know little? One wonders what bias there may be because all of the evidence comes from the perpetrators and none from the victims. One may even ask why we have included this as a case of genocide. It is certainly an unusual case. A genocide was planned and intended by the settlers, but its execution was so clumsy that it was unsuccessful in its original aim. What it did achieve was a concerted effort to assure the survival of the remaining Tasmanians. It was this well-intentioned effort to save them that finally spelled their extinction.

The last Tasmanian man died in 1869 and the last Tasmanian woman in 1876. This was the accepted view of Tasmanian history; however, it ignored some little-known facts. In 1881 the reserve system was introduced in Tasmania with the establishment of the Cape Barren Island reserve. The reserve was abolished in 1951 as part of the assimilation policy, which declared that the aborigines had to live "like white people." The existence of the reserve system was not widely known, while the history of the last Tasmanians was very well known. This situation was encouraged by the government; it seems self-evident that one does not need an aboriginal policy, need not deal with the problems of the aborigines, nor provide for a budget if the last Tasmanian died in 1876!

The traditional version of Tasmanian history is correct only in the sense that all present aborigines are the descendants of native women who married white men and whose children intermarried. Regardless of such genealogies, the present community seems to have elected to identify with their aboriginal rather than with their white origins (Ryan 1981, esp. 258–59).

THE FINAL SOLUTION, DOWN UNDER†

"I regret the death of the last of the Tasmanian aborigines," wrote one of the pious mourners when the race had finally become extinct, "but I know that it is the result of the fiat that the black shall everywhere give place to the white."

For many years after the European discovery of Australia, no one realized that Tasmania was an island. To the early navigators it seemed only a protrusion from the southeast corner of the continent, and it was assumed that its flora and fauna must be more or less the same as the rest.

Yet it was in many ways a particularly insular island. Separated from the mainland only by the 150 miles of the Bass Strait, it possessed a character all its own. It was a hilly island, about the size of Ceylon or West Virginia, covered with dense forests of pine, beech, and eucalyptus, sometimes so thickly interwoven with creepers that a man could walk suspended on a web of foliage far above the ground. In the east there was fine rolling downland, fresh and green in the antipodal morning, mauve or golden as the sun went down. In the west impenetrable forest land, tangled with undergrowth, fell away from the central mountains in gorges and fjords to the sea. In many parts the soil was rich. The climate was wet but fresh, rather like Britain's; and indeed there were some corners of the island that looked astonishingly like northern Europe.

Most of the weird marsupials of the mainland were present in Tasmania: kangaroos and wallabies in countless herds, duck-billed platypuses, the black swans that, loitering strangely in the creeks of the southeast, sometimes gave the landscape an inverted look, like a photographic negative. But there were also creatures not found anywhere else. There was *Anaspides tasmaniae*, the shrimp that lived in the high mountain pools of the island and was known elsewhere only as a fossil. There was the huge Tasmanian crayfish, and the minute pygmy possum, like a little gray dormouse with its babies in its pouch, and the water hen, and the yellow wattlebird. There was the Tasmanian devil (*Sarcophilus harrisi*), which looked like a venomous badger, and the Tasmanian tiger (*Thylacinus cynocephalus*), which looked like a great striped dog, walked on its toes, made a noise halfway between a bark and a miaow, carried its babies backward in a pouch beneath its stomach, and could open its jaws so wide that at full stretch they formed almost a straight line from top to bottom.

Strangest of all, there existed, shadowy among the ferns and gum trees, a

†From James Morris, "The Final Solution, Down Under," *Horizon* 14, no. 1 (Winter 1972): 60–71. Illustrations omitted. Copyright 1972 by American Heritage. Reprinted by permission.

race of human beings altogether unique, different ethnically and culturally from the aborigines of the Australian mainland, and living in secluded forest encampments, or along shellfish-strewn shores, unaffected by contact with any other men and women but themselves.

No one knows how many of these original Tasmanians existed when, in 1798, George Bass and Matthew Flinders first sailed through the Strait and discovered Tasmania to be an island. There were probably not more than a few thousand of them, and since they were nomadic hunters, they had no permanent settlements. The Tasmanians never built a village, let alone a town: generally the only traces they left were the middens found here and there along their hunting routes.

Nor does anyone know where they came from. Victorian anthropologists much enjoyed the "Tasmanian problem" and spent many happy evenings debating possible migratory routes and ethnic progenitors. Since the Tasmanians were unquestionably distinct from the mainland aborigines, it was assumed that they had originated in the north or central Pacific and had worked their way southward over the millenniums. Modern theorists mostly suppose they came by way of Australia's east coast, for they had no folk memories of long sea voyages and aborigines of apparently Tasmanian characteristics have been found in Queensland.

They were a smallish but long-legged people, red-brown rather than black, with beetle brows, wide mouths, broad noses, and deep-set brown eyes. The men had rich beards and whiskers and wore their hair tightly curled in ringlets, smeared with red ochre; the women cut their hair short, but they were hirsute, too, and in old age often developed incipient mustaches. Physically, the Tasmanians seem to have lacked stamina: their senses were uncannily acute, but they were not very strong, nor very fast, nor even particularly agile, though they were adept at running on all fours.

Europeans often found them unattractive. Some of the young girls were pretty enough, but they soon faded. "Their forms were generally thin and withered," wrote the Frenchman François Peron in 1807, "their breasts long and hanging; in a word, all the details of their physical constitution were repulsive." Mrs. Augustus Prinsep, writing in 1833, thought they all had a "most hideous expression of countenance"; George Lloyd, nearly thirty years later, found the women "repulsively ugly." To modern tastes, if we are to judge by surviving photographs, they might not seem so disagreeable: they look homely, but oddly wistful, like elves, or perhaps hobbits, and there is something very endearing about their squashed-up, crinkled faces, which seem never to be actually smiling but look suggestively amused all the same.

The Tasmanians did not, by and large, wear any clothes except for loose cloaks of kangaroo skin. Instead, they painted their bodies with red ochre, sometimes all over, sometimes in decorative, wavy lines down their arms and legs. They stuck feathers and berries in their hair, and around their necks they wore necklaces of shells or human bones. They slept in caves or hollow trees, or beneath rough windbreaks of sticks and fronds, stuck with shells on the outside and lined with bark within.

They did not use the boomerangs or womeras of the mainland people, but they were skillful with heavy spears and achieved a remarkably varied diet. Their staple foods were kangaroos and wallabies, but they also ate shellfish, roots and berries, fungi, lizards, snakes, penguins, herons, parrots, and the eggs of ants and emus. Some may have eaten sea fish; others apparently regarded scaled fish as taboo. The Tasmanians made crude boats of bark or logs, but they never ventured far out to sea; instead, they roamed incessantly, pursuing the fugitive marsupials, through the dense bush forests of their island and over its wide downland, or going down to the shingled shore to eat oysters.

A touching sadness surrounds their presence, from our distance of time. They seem an insubstantial people. Polygamous by custom, they were affectionate by disposition, and merry—singing in a sweet Doric harmony and dancing strenuous, hilarious, and frequently lascivious animal dances. But living on the edge of the world, they seem to have been on the edge of reality, too. Their small tribal bands seldom strayed outside their own hunting circuits, and they inhabited a little inconstant world of a few families.

If they met another tribe, they generally fought it, but the moment a man on either side was killed, the battle ended and the tribes withdrew. If they had a religion, it was concerned only with local sprites and goblins; few had any conception of an afterlife, most attached no spiritual importance to the sun or the moon. Some were apparently able to count up to five, others never went farther than two. Their only system of government seems to have been a patriarchal authority tacitly granted to the head of a family or to the bravest hunter of a tribe. Their only visual art consisted of rings chipped out of boulders and striped patterns in red ochre. Even their language was rudimentary, being a series of disconnected words with no linking grammar. This is one of their dancing songs, in a Victorian missionary's translation:

> It's wattle blossom time,
> It's spring-time.
> Bird whistle,
> The birds are whistling.
> Spring come,
> Spring has come.
> Cloud sun,

The clouds are all sunny.
Bird whistle,
The birds are whistling.
Dance.
Everything is dancing.
Spring-time,
Because it's spring-time.
Dance.
Everything is dancing.
Luggarato, Luggarato, Luggarato—Spring,
    Spring, Spring.
Because it's spring-time.

Luggarato, Luggarato, Luggarato! To nearly everything about the Tasmanians there was a haunting naiveté. They lived all by themselves, like children in the woods, and they seem to have thought of life as essentially provisional. The old and the sick they often abandoned when they moved on to new hunting grounds. When someone died, he was usually cremated without ceremony, the tribe seldom staying to watch him burn; or he was placed upright inside a hollow tree, with a spear through his neck to keep him there.

And when a man was gone, he was gone. His name was never mentioned again. It was as though, having lived his short hard life of wandering, having fathered his sons and eaten his feasts of parrot or emu egg—having appeared briefly upon the foreshore of the world—his life had been expunged and he had never existed at all.

Once it was realized that Tasmania was an island, it acquired a peculiar usefulness to the Europeans—more specifically, to the British, the pacemakers of European progress then and the most irrepressible expansionists the world had known. When the war of American independence lost this vigorous people their possessions in the west, they turned to Australia as a usefully remote destination for their castoffs and ne'er-do-wells, and since 1788 they had maintained a penal colony at Port Jackson in New South Wales, the site of Sydney. For this sad settlement, it seemed to the British, Tasmania would be a convenient outstation. It had been discovered in 1642 by the Dutchman Abel Tasman, who called it Van Diemen's Land—a name it was to keep until 1855—and three French expeditions had visited the island; but in September, 1803, a small party of Englishmen, convicts under military guard, sailed from New South Wales to the southern coast of the island, and planting a settlement on the east bank of the Derwent River, hoisted the Union Jack and claimed the area for their own.

Risdon Cove, where Lieutenant John Bowen, his soldiers, and his criminals
pitched their tents, remains much as it was then, and its character is relevant to
our narrative. Across the river the city of Hobart, approached today by a high-
humped concrete bridge, cheerfully surrounds its harbor. There are yachts scud-
ding up and down the fairway, and factories along the shore, and a tumble of
white suburbs spread over the foothills. Incongruously amid this cheerful scene
stands Risdon Cove. Once the city tried to make a memorial park of it, and
there are the remains of a formal entrance with a memorial slab; but it has all
been abandoned, the gum trees crowd down from the hills, and the muddy
water of the creek, oozing through the grassy bottom, makes it all dank. It is not
a scene that speaks of enterprise or adventure; it is a low-spirited place, enervated still, one fancies, by the miseries and squalors of its origins.

One often has this feeling in Tasmania. Though it is a lovely island now, its
landscapes serene and its pride disarmingly genteel, patches of harsh memory
disfigure it. By the 1820s there were European settlements at both ends of the
island. A fine road ran from north to south, and many free settlers were living in
distinctly gentlemanly style in substantial country houses on prosperous estates.
Yet the basis of its society remained punitive: this was a place of exile, a criminal island, and its life was organized around the fulcrum of its penal purpose. In
a suggestive way, it is so still. Though transportation to Tasmania ended in
1853, the most compelling sight on the island remains the celebrated penal
settlement of Port Arthur, on the Tasman Peninsula in the southeast.

This was not the severest of the several prisons on Tasmania. The worst was
at Macquarie Harbour, on the west coast, where the prison buildings stood on a
reef unapproachable by land except at low tide, and recalcitrant convicts were
sometimes confined for weeks at a time on uninhabited rocks in the estuary. The
hinterland there was so terrible that of the hundred-odd prisoners who ever
escaped from Macquarie Harbour, sixty-two died in the bush, many of starvation, and nine were eaten by their comrades. Port Arthur, though, was much
larger and better known, and was a tourist site almost from the start. A tramway
used to take visitors down the steep slope of the Tasman Peninsula, its trucks
pushed along by convicts, and here and there one may still discover the ruts of
its tracks in the bush. At the bottom, then as now, the first thing one saw was the
square English tower of the interdenominational church, looking rural and rooky,
surrounded by English elms and oaks and by the neat verandaed houses of the
governor and his assistants.

Just around the corner, however, beyond a discreet stretch of green with an
ornamental fountain, the granite buildings of the prison were grouped with a
terrible dignity around their harbor. They are mostly ruins now, but they have
lost none of their grim authority. Here is the watchtower, around whose ram-

parts the sentries perpetually tramped, and here the flogging wall, and here the lunatic asylum. In the model prison (to be entered nowadays only with an official guide) the latest techniques of criminal reform were practiced, notably the silence system—a system so absolute that the warders wore felt slippers and the prisoners wore masks in church to preserve their isolation from humankind, and worshiped in single, shuttered cubicles. All the buildings are gray, and a gray suspense hangs over the scene like a vapor, even on bright summer mornings, when the tourists walk cottonfrocked and laughing from block to block, led by a garrulous and facetious guide.

Port Arthur was starkly insulated from the rest of the island. Guard posts with dogs patrolled the narrow spit, Eaglehawk Neck, which was the only land approach to the peninsula, and an elaborate system of sentinels and semaphore towers made it exceedingly difficult for a convict to escape. Some did, nevertheless; many more went to Hobart as assigned servants or ticket-of-leave men. But the very presence of the settlement, with its thousands of helpless men numbed or animalized by despair, pervaded the whole of the island and made society everywhere else coarser by the experience of it.

Many of the settlers were themselves emancipated convicts—very few of those freed in the Australian settlements ever went back to Britain. Nearly all the others employed convict servants. When food ran short in the early years of the settlement, convicts were allowed to go into the bush to forage for themselves; some became bushrangers or bandits, founded a desperado tradition, and graduated often enough into the romantic heroes of island legend. Society was polarized between an authoritarian establishment on the one hand and a huge criminal population on the other, and at either extreme was instinct with violence.

"Our forebears," a Tasmanian lady named Mrs. Charles Meredith wrote in 1852, "were British farmers and country gentlemen, not usually considered a desperately ferocious and blood-thirsty class." The myth has since been assiduously propagated that all the early settlers were either cultivated gentlefolk ("a natural son, I have always been told, of the Duke of Biggleswade") or unfortunates transported for trifling social offenses (riding the squire's horse or poaching hares). It is not true. Most of the convicts were genuine criminals, the toughest products of England's slums and injustices; and the free settlers learned to live as a matter of course with the horrible symptoms of imprisonment.

As the years went by the tone of Tasmanian society grew determinedly respectable, but even in the most idyllic parts of the island one is conscious of this heritage. The country houses of Tasmania are among the best the British built anywhere in their overseas possessions—stone houses, mostly, in a heavy but handsome kind of Georgian style, beautifully set in gardens and lawns and often luxuriantly shaded by English oaks and chestnuts transplanted from the shires. I love to wander around these houses, listening to the queer birds that squawk and chatter anomalously among the oaks, or fondly recognizing the bric-a-brac, the samplers or the Chelsea figures, the auntly water colors and the grandfatherly cricket teams, that are so nostalgically familiar to a visitor from Britain.

Yet always as I linger there, a shadow passes. It is a cloud from the past, a reminder that men in chains built these amiable English homes, that prisoners milked the cows in those fresh, whitewashed dairies, or plowed those Constable fields beside the river, and that the small girls in pantaloons and hair ribbons, so rosy and demure in the portrait above the boudoir desk, grew up in the intimate knowledge of whip and manacle.

Inevitably, this forceful community, gradually spreading from its seashore settlements, came into contact with the elusive aborigines of the forest. It was known from the start that they existed. When Tasman arrived off the southeast coast in December, 1642, he sent a boat into Blackman's Bay (now an archetypal suburban resort ten miles from Hobart); its crew saw nobody, but heard "certain human sounds" and "sounds resembling the music of a trump or a small gong." The races first met face to face more than a century later, when the French navigator Marion du Fresne anchored in the Derwent estuary. His crew found a group of natives on the shore, and an indeterminate squabble ensued; the Tasmanians threw stones and spears, and the Europeans responded with gunfire, killing one aborigine, wounding several others, and sending the rest astonished into the woods, "howling fearfully."

In 1777 the incomparable Captain Cook made a happier contact with a party of natives on the offshore island called Bruny—they seemed, he recorded, neither afraid nor distrustful. Captain Bligh of the *Bounty* also liked them, when he landed on Bruny in 1788, and the Frenchmen of Nicholas Baudin's expedition, in 1802, seem to have been enchanted by them. We read of aborigines clearing paths for their visitors, sharing their food, greeting them with "cries of joy" and "extremely quick stamping of the feet." The only trouble occurred when sailors made advances to native women; at all other times the Tasmanians seemed a shy, hospitable, rather sentimental people. "This gentle confidence of the people in us," wrote Péron, "these affectionate evidences of benevolence which they never ceased to manifest towards us, the sincerity of their demonstrations, the frankness of their manners, the touching ingenuousness of their caresses, all concurred to excite within us sentiments of the tenderest interest."

These were educated observers in the age of Rousseau, yearning for noble savages. Perhaps they were reading too much into the ingenuous caresses and cries of joy—which may have been, so later commentators have suggested, the cries of obscure Tasmanian seabirds, or the cooees of chieftains assembling their followers. Still, these meetings were evidently enjoyable to both sides.

The Europeans felt no threat from the guileless primitives. The aborigines thought the peculiar pale strangers might be the ghosts of their own dead, and may have welcomed their appearance as a break in the immemorial monotony of hunt, sex, and corroboree.

But when Europeans settled in Tasmania, the relationship soon changed. Almost at once the Tasmanians were defined as enemies, actual or potential. One summer day some eight months after the establishment of the camp at Risdon Cove, the convicts and their keepers looked up to the surrounding heights and saw a large group of aborigines, including women and children, advancing in a black semicircle out of the woods. What their intentions were, we shall never know. One eyewitness thought they were merely herding kangaroos, another reported that they were singing and carrying green boughs as tokens of friendship. Still, they must have looked an eerie lot, loping out of the bush into that gloomy gully, and the young lieutenant in charge ordered his soldiers to open fire. Several aborigines were killed, several more wounded, an orphaned black child was brought into camp and hastily baptized, and so, soon after the first European settlement in Tasmania, a precedent of distrust was set.

As the white colony grew in numbers and confidence, the original Tasmanians found themselves treated more and more as predators or vermin. The free settlers wanted land, and ruthlessly drove the nomads from their hunting grounds. The shifting riffraff of bushrangers and sealers used the black people as they pleased, for pleasure or for bondage. By the 1820s horrible things were happening on the island. Sometimes the black people were hunted just for fun, on foot or on horseback. Sometimes they were raped in passing, or abducted as mistresses or slaves. The sealers of the Bass Strait islands established a slave society of their own, employing the well-tried disciplines of slavery—clubbing, stringing up from trees, or flogging with kangaroo-gut cat-o'-nine-tails.

We hear of children kidnapped as pets or servants, of a woman chained up like an animal in a shepherd's hut, of men castrated to keep them off their own women. In one foray seventy aborigines were killed, the men shot, the women and children dragged from crevices in the rocks to have their brains dashed out. A man called Carrotts, desiring a native woman, decapitated her husband, hung his head around her neck, and drove her home to his shack.

"British farmers and country gentlemen" is how Mrs. Meredith remembered her forebears, "[not] by any means disposed to commence hostilities against quiet unoffending people." It is true, of course, that these horrors were generally committed by white men of the lowest sort, many of them criminals. Even so, it was not long before almost the entire European community, even the Mrs. Merediths, behaved little better toward the aborigines. Gone were those sentiments of tender interest. "I well know that these undiscriminating Savages," wrote Governor Collins in a report to his superiors on one fracas, "will consider every White Man as their Enemy." He was right. Despised, debased, and brutalized themselves, their numbers precipitously declining, they were now often the aggressors. Stockmen were murdered. Cattle were speared. Farms were burned. In 1827 the natives actually mounted a raid on Launceston, the second-largest town on the island.

It did not take long for the white community to convince itself that the Europeans were the aggrieved party, threatened by savages who denied them the right to farm and graze their own properties in peace. From time to time humane administrators tried to remind them otherwise. "It [is] no less the duty than it is the disposition of the Lieutenant Governor," proclaimed Governor Sorell in 1817, "to forbid and prevent, and when perpetrated, to punish any ill-treatment of the native people of this island, and to support and encourage all measures which may tend to conciliate and civilize them." "It is undeniable," said another official pronouncement, "that, in many former Instances, cruelties have been perpetrated repugnant to Humanity and disgraceful to the British character, while few attempts can be traced on the Part of the Colonists to conciliate the Native People or to make them sensible that Peace and Forebearance are the objects desired." From London the Colonial Office kept an evangelical watch upon events in the island, and in 1830 a committee of inquiry exposed some of the worst excesses of the sealers and bushrangers.

But the classic settler–native syndrome was already far advanced. The gentlemen in their country houses, the rich merchants in their mansions above the Hobart waterfront, the local administrators preoccupied with penal affairs and orderly government—all were reaching the now-familiar conclusion that life in Tasmania would be much happier if there were no Tasmanians. In language, the decrees of Authority remained irreproachably pious, and frequently warned the colonists that they must not be cruel to the natives. In intent, the announcements became ever less tolerant. The Reverend Thomas Atkins, after a visit to Van Diemen's Land in 1836, conveniently rationalized the attitude in Christian terms. It was a universal law in the divine government, he wrote, that when savage tribes came into collision with civilized races of men, the savages disappeared. This was because they had not complied with the divine conditions for survival—"For God blessed them, and God said unto them, be fruitful and multiply, and replenish the earth and subdue it . . ."

Hobart in 1830 was already a substantial seaport and whaling base, set delightfully in the shadow of Mount Wellington and looking across the wooded estuary of the Derwent southward to the sea. From the sea it looked like a Jane Austen watering place, with the spire of St. David's Church rising gracefully above the roofs and the tidy grid of streets running up the hill behind. On the spot it was more rumbustious. It was full of ambitious merchants, sailors, soldiers, government officials—few of them gentlemen in the English sense of the word, but beginning to fall into patterns of social hierarchy. The big houses of the whaling magnates, often emancipated convicts, stood opulently at street corners or high above the sea at Battery Point, with carriages and stables and convict servants at the door.

Hobart is now a city of 124,000 souls, but one can still recognize the imprint of its early style, in the pattern of the streets and the old town houses that, carefully preserved and pointed out in guidebooks, survive from the first flush of colonial prosperity. Half-concealed behind an office façade in Macquarie Street, for instance, one can glimpse the old red brick of Macquarie House, one of the grandest early houses of Hobart Town. It was built in 1815 in a battlemented, pseudomilitary style, and as it turned out, this was appropriate: in 1830 it served as the headquarters of a military operation, the largest ever conducted against the native peoples of Australia, that was intended to provide a final solution to the problem of the Tasmanian aborigines.

Authority could not, of course, sanction the extermination of the natives. Humanitarianism was a powerful motive of Empire, and public opinion in England would never stomach genocide. Sir George Murray, the Secretary of State for the Colonies, observed in a dispatch to the governor that "the adoption of any line of conduct having for its avowed or for its secret object the extinction of the native race could not fail to leave an indelible stain on the character of the British Government." Anyway, God would doubtless arrange such a consummation in His own time—or as Sir George put it, "[it is] not unreasonable to apprehend that the whole race of these people may at no distant period become extinct."

Meanwhile, what could be arranged with a clear conscience was the removal of the entire race to somewhere else. There were several suitable islands around the coast, and extensive unsettled tracts of mainland, too. "Really it is high time," remarked the Launceston *Advertiser* one day, "they were either removed out of the Island, or driven by force of arms to the uninhabited districts . . ."

First they had to be found. By now they could be counted in the hundreds rather than the thousands, but they were a slippery, will-o'-the-wisp people, moving dappled through the eucalyptus glades or blending indistinguishably with the seashore rocks. Unsuccessful attempts were made to lure them, tribe by tribe, into Hobart and the paternal arms of Authority; in 1830 it was decided that they must be flushed from their nests, like game upon some vast estate, and beaten before an inescapable cordon mile by mile down the length of the island into the Tasman Peninsula at the bottom. There they would be rounded up and taken away to convenient reservations.

Macquarie House bustled with activity. Colonel George Arthur, the governor, himself assumed command of the operation and planned the cordon—"the Black Line"—on the most orthodox military principles (he had fought in the Napoleonic Wars and put down a slave revolt in British Honduras). Upstairs he and his staff officers spread their maps and plotted their dispositions. Downstairs there came and went, saluting and swishing their capes and rattling their swords, the officers of the three regular regiments committed to the operation and an enthusiastic gallimaufry of volunteers who swarmed about the house in a state of belligerent anticipation.

Arthur timed the campaign for the weeks before the harvest, calling upon every farm to send an able-bodied volunteer, and he conscripted ticket-of-leave men, cautiously commissioning police magistrates to be their officers in the field. In all, some 2,500 men were engaged. In case the settlers took the operation too lightly—some of them were, after all, accustomed to chase aborigines in innocent blood-sport—the government publicly warned the participants that it was "not a matter of amusement or recreation, but a cause of the most important and serious kind, in which the lives and property of the whole community are more or less at stake." Martial law was proclaimed against the native population, except for those who "there may be reason to suppose are pacifically inclined," and Arthur himself, ordering his charger saddled and kissing a soldierly farewell to his pregnant wife, rode away from Macquarie House to lead his troops into action.

It was perhaps the most farcical campaign in the history of British imperial arms. The plan called for a steady advance on a front that would begin by being 120 miles long, but would narrow in the course of the march until its two flanks, swinging in an arc around the island, were united like a noose in the peninsula. No man was to be farther than sixty yards from his neighbor, and the beaters were to maintain contact by shouts and bugle calls. Strict military precepts prevailed. Dispatches were sent back to Macquarie House by equerry; requisitions were made for ammunition, food, clothing, and three hundred pairs of manacles. When a skeptical civilian expressed doubts to one officer about this scheme, the colonel replied, "Oh, this is an entirely military manoeuvre, which you, as a civilian, would not understand."

Nothing went right. In that severe terrain the cordon was impossible to maintain. When they came to a defile, the soldiers predictably moved into single file; when they came to a particularly prickly patch of shrub, they naturally avoided it. Soaked through by incessant rains, their clothes torn, their rations inadequate, their muskets often unserviceable, their whereabouts distinctly uncertain, soldiers and volunteers alike soon lost interest in the aborigines and were concerned only with getting themselves dry, fed, and settled at the next bivouac.

Nerves were frayed, tempers rose, volunteers slipped away home, and not even Arthur himself, galloping indefatigably along the line and writing numerous dispatches, could maintain the morale of his exhausted campaigners.

Sometimes they did see an aborigine—once they briefly glimpsed a party of forty. More often they mistook clumps of trees, or black swans, or the rustle of leaves, or kangaroos, for the presence of the black people. For seven weeks the Black Line struggled down the island, until halfway through November, closing upon the southeast corner, the men approached Eaglehawk Neck. Disheartened though they were, they assumed that a mass of black fugitives must be moving somewhere before them, and as they approached the peninsula they repeatedly asked along the way if the natives had passed over the neck to the trap beyond. Educated as they were to the notion of a savage horde always seething out of sight in the bush, they expected to find thousands of refugees, brought to bay at last, caught within the peninsula.

But there was nobody there. Not a single aborigine had crossed the neck. Like ghosts, the black people had slipped through the blundering cordon, crouching in brambles while the soldiers went sweating and cursing past or scuttling away on all fours into the shadows. When the staff officers at Macquarie House made their final assessment, they found that while four British soldiers had been accidentally killed in the course of the operation, only two of the original Tasmanians had been caught. One was a small boy, and the other soon escaped.

There now enters our story a resolute evangelical, George Augustus Robinson, "the Conciliator," whose destiny it was to organize, when all else had failed, the disappearance of the Tasmanian race from the face of the earth.

Robinson was a Londoner, a nonconformist builder who had emigrated to Van Diemen's Land with his wife and seven children and had become well known on the Hobart waterfront for his good works. He was in all ways a man of his time, a Dickensian figure transplanted from *Hard Times* or *Dombey and Son* to this alien environment. He was infinitely pious, humorless, and untiring. One can imagine him running some particularly grim and improving school for indigent children on the outskirts of Manchester, or perhaps supervising, with Mrs. Robinson, a reformatory for reclaimed London prostitutes. He was an uneducated man and correspondingly dogmatic, and his bent was to redeem.

He had entered the government service as an intermediary with the natives. Out he would go into the bush, with a couple of servants, his Bible pack, and a tame native woman, Black Moll, dressed up in gay ribbons to attract attention —they called her Robinson's decoy duck. He learned the aboriginal language, and over many months of wanderings throughout the island he made contact with most of the surviving tribes and gained the confidence of many. He

approached the natives kindly, often entertaining them upon the flute and sometimes spending weeks at a time in their company, for he knew that God had
called him to save them from their sinful ways and lead them toward the Truth.

This was the man to whom a baffled government, after the farce of the Black
Line, turned for an alternative solution. Robinson at once accepted the charge.
He undertook to persuade all the surviving Tasmanians out of the bush and into
government control, and almost single-handed he succeeded. For five years he
came and went, sometimes by boat around the coast, generally on foot, with a
little band of native helpers—notably Truganini, a redeemed sealer's mistress,
who was to become the most celebrated Tasmanian of all. Each year he brought
out a few more aborigines—sixty-three in 1832, forty-two in 1833, twenty-
eight in 1834—until at last there were none left in the bush, and the whole Tasmanian population was safely in the care of Authority.

He had approved for their final destination Flinders Island, in the Bass Strait,
some forty miles north of Tasmania, and in January, 1832, the first of the
expatriates were shipped there. The Hobart *Town Courier*, whose reporter
watched one party embark, declared that the aborigines showed themselves
delighted at the idea of going to the island, "where they will enjoy peace and
plenty uninterrupted." The removal would greatly benefit the island, too: "The
large tracts of pasture that have so long been deserted owing to their murderous
attacks on the shepherds and stock huts will now be available, and a very
sensible relief will be afforded to the flocks of sheep that had been withdrawn
from them and pent up in inadequate ranges of pasture—a circumstance which
indeed has tended materially to impoverish the flocks and keep up the price of
butchers' meat."

Flinders is, as it happens, a singularly beautiful island, at least to northern
tastes. It has not changed much since the 1830s and remains a place of wind-
swept silence, bare on its central hills but thick with aromatic foliage along its
shores. To the aborigines, however, it looked desolate indeed. They may have
seemed happy as they boarded their ship at Hobart, smiling their childlike smiles
and "going through feats of their wonderful dexterity," but eyewitness accounts
of their arrival at Flinders read very differently. "When they saw from shipboard
the splendid country which they were promised, they betrayed the greatest agi-
tation, gazing with strained eyes at the sterile shore, uttering melancholy moans,
and, with arms hanging beside them, trembling with convulsive feeling. The winds
were violent and cold; the rain and sleet were penetrating and miserable . . .
and this added force to their forebodings that they were taken there to die."

So they were. Authority would not admit the fact, even to itself, but like
unwanted old relatives consigned to an institution, the aborigines were taken to

Flinders Island to die. After a couple of false starts they were housed in a settlement on the southwestern shore, named, for them, Wybalenna—Black Man's Houses. It was set on the neck of a promontory, and from the hills above it one could see the sea on either side, and on a clear day make out the hills of Tasmania itself. Wybalenna had its own jetty, convenient for the bishops and governors who occasionally came to observe the progress of the natives' salvation, and its own chapel, and naturally its own cemetery. The natives lived in an L-shaped terrace of cottages, the staff in houses nearby.

Some two hundred Tasmanians were sent to Wybalenna, and there, slowly, far away and out of sight, forgotten by the settlers, guarded by second-rate officials and homesick soldiers, the race wasted away in tedium. At first the aborigines seemed happy enough—they were pleased with the warm clothing the government gave them, and the hot food—but gradually they sank into apathy. They needed to wander, and they pined for the limitless forests and beaches of their larger island. They died by the dozen, of chest complaints, stomach troubles, and plain homesickness: there was nothing for them to do but brood, forlornly dance and sing, listlessly look for opossums and kangaroos, or dig for potatoes in their garden patch.

Presently, Robinson himself, having rounded up every last aborigine, arrived at Flinders Island to preside over their decay, and added to other causes of death a sort of cultural insemination. In his Wesleyan zeal he wanted to redeem them still. He dressed them in Christian clothes. He forbade them their corroborees. He was helped by a catechist named Robert Clark, who had declared it to be one of the dearest objects of his life to disseminate moral and spiritual light among the natives. The two of them worked assiduously to explain the ways of God to those benighted agnostics, Robinson at the same time recommending to the lieutenant governor the construction of a lockup.

Now a Wybalenna Sunday became a day full of purpose: "There is no strolling about, all are expected to attend the public service, none are exempt except through illness, such is the way the Sabbath is kept since I have had the honour to command . . ." Robinson, well though he knew his charges, remained appalled at their religious indifference.

Their mental darkness was truly shocking. Some actually thought they had been created by their own mothers, and one woman believed her brother had done it. As for the afterlife, the aborigines were now inclined to suppose that when a black man died, his soul went to England. But a Sunday school was founded to correct these misconceptions, and a visitor who attended one of Mr. Clark's addresses thought it "very evident from the anxious and searching looks of these people that they are really beginning to know and to feel that there is a God and that God is something powerful."

Here is an extract from one of Robinson's sermons, in his own English version of it:

One good God. One good God. Native good, native dead, go up in sky. God up. . . . Bad native dead, goes down, evil spirit fire stops. Native cry, cry, cry. Good native stops, God sky, no sick, no hungering.

And here are some of the questions, with the prescribed answers, from a Wybalenna catechism class:

Q. What will God do to this world by and by?
A. Burn it.
Q. Who are in heaven?
A. God, angels, good men and Jesus Christ.
Q. What sort of country is heaven?
A. A fine place.
Q. What sort of place is hell?
A. A place of torment.
Q. What do you mean by a place of torment?
A. Burning for ever and ever.

Robinson also inculcated in his wards, dependent for the past few millenniums entirely on hunting and scavenging, a more suitable sense of property. He put English copper coins into circulation, stamped on one side "F.I." for Flinders Island, and he made the aborigines pay for their European clothes and comforts, to teach them the meaning of money. He started a weekly market, every Tuesday at eleven, at which they could sell the game they had caught or the few poor artifacts they had made and in return buy pipes, tea caddies, crockery, fishing rods, or straw hats.

But despite it all, they wasted away, ceased to have babies, and grew thinner and more morose and more helplessly melancholic. The Tasmanians were literally losing heart. Even the Conciliator now complained of their feckless indolence, and Mr. Clark sometimes found it necessary to flog the girls, "in religious anger at their moral offences." By 1847 there were only forty-four aborigines left, and the government, deciding they were no longer a danger to the European community, abandoned Wybalenna and shipped the hangdog survivors back across the strait to die in Tasmania. Mr. Robinson, having thus arranged all things to the divine satisfaction, took his family home to Bath, where he himself died in gentlemanly circumstances in a hilltop villa overlooking the city. He was seventy-eight, and his death certificate, in the column headed "Occupation," describes him simply as "Late Protector of the Aboriginees, Tasmania."

Wybalenna soon crumbled into dereliction; and curiously, hauntingly derelict it remains. Robinson's house is now a farm, and washing flutters in its garden on Mondays, but otherwise there is no sign of human habitation. Yet a suspended animation pervades the scene. On a hill above the settlement an old car has been abandoned and points down the slope perpetually, as though it is about to start moving; and in the hollow it is as if the aborigines are only momentarily out of sight and may still come trailing up from the jetty for dinner. The chapel, built of bilious yellowish brick and propped up with timbers, is now a shearing shed; sea gulls often land on its iron roof and maintain their positions in the blustering sea winds with tinny scratchings of their claws upon the metal. Beside the chapel the remains of the terraces can be seen, all overgrown. In the little cemetery a few graves and memorial slabs illuminate the story. Mr. Clark's son Robert, the first white male child born on Flinders Island, is buried there; and there are slabs erected, long after the event, to the memory of Mannalargenna, "last chief of the Portland tribe," and to remind us of the hundred or so aborigines who lie in unmarked graves thereabouts. The wind blows incessantly, with a soft scent of herbs from the seashore. The gulls slither and rattle on the chapel roof.

Now the end was near for the Tasmanian race. The forty-four survivors—twelve men, twenty-two women, ten young people—were taken to an unused penal settlement at Oyster Cove, twenty-five miles from Hobart and only fifteen miles from the spot where, two centuries before, Tasman's sailors had first heard those "certain human sounds." Though it was swept by bush fires a few years ago, the site is still recognizable; it lies at the end of a dirt road by the water's edge, looking across to Bruny. There the Tasmanians lingered for a last decade. Mrs. Meredith thought their return to Tasmania would "in all probability . . . lead to a renewal of the horrors which, since their removal, have been unknown"; but in fact they no longer posed a threat to anyone, nor even provided hopeful material for the evangelicals, for they were generally drunk and shamelessly immoral. Sometimes people went to look at them and anthropologists, recognizing in them the ultimate specimens of an entire race, measured their skulls and estimated their brain capacities. By 1855 only sixteen Tasmanians were still alive, and all attempts to redeem them had been abandoned. By 1859 Oyster Cove was a slum, the handful of survivors camping in verminous filth among the decaying buildings and sharing their food with their dogs.

A few were adopted by settlers and kept as pets, or curiosities. One pretty girl, almost the last of the young aborigines, was adopted by Lady Franklin, whose husband, Sir John, after great adventures in the Arctic, had come to Hobart as governor. Gaily dressed in European clothes, Mathinna went everywhere with her patroness—highspirited in her carriage on afternoon drives, cossetted by ambitious aides at Government House balls. When the time came for the Franklins to go home to England, Lady Franklin was advised that the sudden change of climate might kill the girl, so Mathinna was placed in an institution called the Queen's Asylum. There the young men at Government House did not call, and the other inmates teased and taunted her. In the end, since she seemed to be wasting away, she was returned to her inebriate and syphilitic relatives at Oyster Cove. We do not hear that Lady Franklin ever wrote to her there, and she soon picked up the local habits, drank heavily, prostituted herself with the timber workers of the surrounding woods, and was eventually found drowned in a creek.

The last male aborigine was an alcoholic whaling man, "King Billy" Lanney, who became a public spectacle in his later years, was shown off at government functions, photographed by scientists, and introduced to Prince Alfred, Queen Victoria's son, when he visited Hobart in 1868. When King Billy died the next year in the Dog and Partridge of chronic diarrhea, he was carried to his grave by four comrades from his old ship, with the ship's flag, an ancient opossum rug, and a clutter of native weapons placed upon the coffin. During the night the grave was reopened and the head snatched—probably at the instigation of the Royal Society of Tasmania, whose savants wanted the skull for their collection.

The last of all was Truganini, Robinson's faithful follower, whose association with the imperial culture had been long and varied. Her mother was stabbed to death by a European. Her sister was kidnapped by sealers. Her intended husband was drowned by two Europeans in her presence, while his murderers raped her. In 1839 she was one of a group of natives taken by Robinson to New South Wales. There, with two other aborigine women and two men she was charged with the murder of two Europeans; the men were found guilty and hanged, the women acquitted and returned to Tasmania.

Long after the end of the settlement at Oyster Cove, Truganini (whose name meant "seaweed") clung to life. For nearly twenty years she lived with a kindly European family in Macquarie Street, a few hundred yards from the former headquarters of the Black Line, and she became a well known and popular figure in the capital. Short and stout, with staring eyes and hairy chin, she liked to wear bright red turbans, and loved a good chat, a glass of beer, and a pipe of tobacco.

She was a demonstrative character. A correspondent of the Hobart *Mercury* remembered meeting her years before at one of Robinson's camps in the bush. She had run after him, clasped him in her arms, and kissed him. "Oh, the outraged modesty of the Tasmanian boy! When I got home, my Ma soundly rated me for my nasty possum-like smell and dirty appearance . . ."

Truganini was terrified that, like King Billy before her, she would be exhumed and dissected after burial. "Don't let them cut me up," she pleaded on her deathbed. "Bury me behind the mountains." So when, seventy-three years old, she died, in May, 1876, her body was taken secretly through the night, in a pauper's coffin on a cart, to the Cascades Female Factory—the women's reformatory, that is—in a cleft in the hills behind Hobart. There she was buried to the tolling of the reformatory bell, in the presence of the premier and the colonial secretary (for in the course of these events Tasmania had graduated to self-government) but without the attendance, we are told, of any of the factory inmates.

She was the very last. Her life had spanned to the year the association between Europeans and Tasmanians. In her own lifetime her people, confronted by the white newcomers from over the sea, had been humiliated, degraded, and eventually extinguished. They buried her privately within the prison compound; but before very long she was dug up anyway, and her skeleton, strung upon wires and placed upright in a box, became for many years the most popular exhibit in the Tasmanian Museum.

Once the aborigines were safely gone, the settlers looked back on the story with remorse. With Truganini, said the *Mercury*, "for the first time in human history, dies out the last of a race, a race . . . which never knew the meaning of suffering, wretchedness and contempt until the English, with their soldiers, bibles and rum-puncheons, came and dispossessed them of their heritage." "With all others who are lovers of their race," wrote another mourner, "I regret the death of the last of the Tasmanian aborigines, but I know that it is the result of the fiat that the black shall everywhere give place to the white."

More recently, the fate of the aborigines, and in particular the exhibition of Truganini's skeleton, has become a protestors' issue—young Tasmanians, being short of present injustices, have seized upon one of the past. Truganini is certainly not forgotten in Hobart. I found her memory everywhere. I looked her up in the library of the *Mercury*, still flourishing in Macquarie Street. I peered through the wooden gates of the Female Factory, now used as a builder's yard, to imagine the premier with his top hat at her funeral, or the body snatchers at work upon her grave. Time and again I found her wrinkled, quizzical face glaring back at me from old photographs, with a coral necklace around her neck and her curly hair cut short—not at all embittered, it seemed to me, by all she had seen of history, but perhaps a little puzzled.

And I went to the museum and asked to see her skeleton, now removed from public show to storage in the basement. They looked embarrassed at the request. Not unless I had a genuine scientific purpose, they said—social science would do. What about an artistic purpose? No, they were sorry: the trustees' instructions were explicit and artistry did not qualify. But I did not really mind, for though I was professionally curious to see those last bleached bones of a vanished people, in my better self I preferred to leave the old soul undisturbed.

THE ZULU
UNDER SHAKA

Shaka ruled the Zulu kingdom in Southern Africa from 1818 until his assassination in 1828. This was a time of enormous population pressure and land hunger among the African peoples of the region, triggered by the northward migration of European settlers from the Cape of Good Hope. In the course of his brief but brilliant career, Shaka conquered the peoples of over three hundred chiefdoms, annihilating some and fusing others into one Zulu nation.

Shaka's success was based on terror. He was the first African state leader to wage a war of complete annihilation in Southern Africa. As in the case of the Mongols, this method struck fear into his enemies and brought many peoples under his sway without a struggle. To maintain the security of his empire, Shaka surrounded it with traffic deserts—devastated areas in which anyone found trespassing was automatically killed. Shaka's exterminatory campaigns—known as the *Mfecane*, or the great crushing—triggered a mass exodus of African peoples fleeing his reign of terror. To this day, peoples in Zimbabwe, Malawi, Zambia, Tanzania, Kenya, and Uganda can trace their descent back to the refugees who fled from Shaka's warriors.

The following selection focuses on Shaka's destruction of the Ndwandwe people at the conclusion of the Third Ndwandwe war in 1826. Shaka's *impi* —the Zulu word for a force of armed warriors—were reported to have killed "nearly every human being of the tribe, man, woman, and child," a devastation estimated to have cost the lives of at least 40,000 persons.

One problem with this case (and with many others) is the dearth of reliable sources. With the exception of a few survivors of shipwrecks, the first literate people to live among the Zulu arrived only in 1824, years after the Zulu kingdom and its forerunners were established and close to the end of Shaka's reign. The earliest written accounts of the Zulu empire were produced by traders such as Henry Francis Fynn (who arrived in 1824) and Nathaniel Isaacs (1825), and some of the early missionaries, who came in the 1830s. The oral traditions of the Zulu were not given serious attention until the arrival of A. T. Bryant, a Catholic missionary, who came to the Zulu area in 1883. The historian Leonard Thompson (1969, 336–37) encourages us to use these major primary sources with caution:

223

The original diary of Fynn, who came to know far more about northern
Nguni society than any other trader, was buried by Nguni in his brother's
grave, and what we have is a later reconstruction, much of it heavily worked
over by the author, with the help of others, towards the end of his life.
Isaacs was a young man while in South Africa and there is reason to believe
that his account has many distortions. . . . Though Bryant's voluminous
writings constitute most valuable compendia of northern Nguni history,
they were compiled two generations and more after the foundation of the
kingdoms.

In spite of these difficulties, which underscore the need for further work on this
case, Eugene Victor Walter has succeeded in constructing a composite account
of Shaka's mass killings that summarizes the available evidence and raises the
important issues.

THE TERROR UNDER SHAKA†

Terror of Arms

There were two turning points in the development of Shaka's
practice of violence: first, after the defeat of the Ndwandwe around 1819, when
the internal system of terror was apparently initiated; second, after the death of
his mother in 1827, when the terror seemed to be out of control, exceeding all
limits and threatening to devour the society. Before the system of terror was
established within the state, however, Shaka had committed himself to a policy
of military terrorism, from which he never wavered, having discarded the limited
warfare of Dingiswayo's era for the *impi ebomvu* — literally, "red impi" — or war
of extermination. The chroniclers say that as a regimental commander under
Dingiswayo, Shaka had chafed at the policy of limited warfare and in the councils
of war had unsuccessfully argued for the strategy of *impi ebomvu*. In any single
battle, the technique resembled, to some extent, immemorial Nguni hunting
methods: the crescent formation or "horns" of the Zulu impi encircled the enemy
— similar to the way in which lines of hunters enclosed the prey — and killed
every living thing caught within the circle. Bryant suggested that Shaka had

†From Eugene Victor Walter, *Terror and Resistance: A Study of Political Violence*, 137–
43. Footnotes omitted. Copyright © 1969 by Oxford University Press, Inc. Reprinted
by permission.

adopted the policy of extermination as soon as he became chief of the Zulu, even
before Dingiswayo was out of the picture. Early in his career, Shaka

> after overcoming the Butelezis had conceived the then quite novel idea of
> utterly demolishing them as a separate tribal entity by incorporating all
> their manhood into his own clan or following, which brilliant manoeuvre
> immediately reduced his possible foes for all time by one and at the same
> time doubled the number of his own army.

Admitting the young warriors into his regiments, he usually destroyed women,
infants, and old people. Sometimes he spared the girls, who, presumably, entered
the royal seraglios, and the stout lads, who became herd boys, baggage carriers,
and, ultimately, Zulu warriors. All who were admitted into Zulu society in this
way were absorbed as individuals, giving up their formal tribal loyalties and
assuming a Zulu identity. The case was somewhat different for the communities
of chiefs who voluntarily became tributaries and were permitted to remain intact.
Nevertheless, it is clear that the Zulu system was quite different from those
"conquest states" such as the Matebele (Ndebele) which maintained a caste
structure.

One element in Shaka's strategy was to create a vast artificial desert around
his domain. The area was depopulated and anything that might serve as food
was destroyed. There are several descriptions of this wasteland on record and,
Shepstone observed, "The object, of course, was to render existence impossible within the reach of his arms, except under his rule." Bryant added that "to
make the destruction complete, organized bands of Zulu murderers regularly
patrolled the waste, hunting for any stray men and running them down like
wild-pig." The desolation not only made escape from Shaka's domain precarious, to say the least, but also would have imposed an equally difficult logistic
problem for invading warriors. Fynn reported that a belt of more than 25 miles
around Natal was uninhabited except for a few living skeletons who stayed alive
by eating roots and who played the antelope to the Zulu lion. An area 200 miles
to the north of the center of the state, 300 miles to the west, and 500 miles to
the south was ravaged and depopulated. Some people turned to cannibalism,
and one narrator recalled fleeing through the wasteland to a deserted village
where crops were still intact, but "They found the gardens all cultivated, and
the crops ripe; but the cannibals had been there, had eaten the cultivators, and
placed their skulls on the top of their huts." Robert Payne, as he said in his book
on terrorism, believed that "The German Army under Keitel invented the 'traffic
desert,'" but it is clear that in this respect as well as others, Shaka had anticipated the Nazis.

Shaka responded to resistance of any kind with destruction, and the only alternative he offered a community that refused swift capitulation and enthusiastic subordination was total war. Flight was impeded by the determination of people beyond his domain to defend their territories against invasion, and in the later period the possibility of escape was reduced further by the presence of the traffic desert. In the earlier campaigns, it seems, after a Zulu attack, Shaka held out the captured women and cattle as inducements for the fugitives to return and enter the ranks of the Zulu. Bryant believed that in this stratagem lay the secret of Shaka's military success:

> If a foe were worth conquering at all, he was worth crushing out of existence once and for all. Whatever was to fear in the tribe must be eternally removed; whatever was good and serviceable must be appropriated by the victor as a reward of triumph and applied as a further strengthening of his own position. In this way something could be gained and then securely held. Shaka's army, therefore, would charge the enemy, and, when it fled in panic, as inevitably it would, they would follow it vigorously home, kill its chief, and return with its cattle and women as booty. Thus reduced, without a head, without women, without cattle, a vanquished clan had no recourse but to avail itself of the "clemency" offered it of incorporation with the victor's own people.

In his later campaigns, Shaka grew more destructive. Sometimes explicit instructions were given to spare no one. Fynn witnessed such an order after Shaka was stabbed in an attempted assassination. It was supposed that the assassins had been sent by Zwide, Shaka's distant but only powerful enemy, who may have been gathering forces to reoccupy the homeland from which the Ndwandwe had been expelled. Bryant speculated that Zwide may have actually died at this time, and the attempted assassination may have been part of his *ihlambo* ceremony: the "washing of the spears" in blood that concluded a month of mourning after the death. When Shaka recovered from his wound, an impi was mustered against the Ndwandwe. The chief induna, Mbikwane, made a speech urging revenge, and the order to march was given. The warriors, Fynn reported, "were directed to spare neither man, woman, child, nor dog. They were to burn their huts, to break the stones on which their corn was ground, and so prove their attachment to their King." The opportunity to find and exterminate the Ndwandwe arrived soon enough.

Zwide was succeeded by his son, Sikunyana, who led the revitalized Ndwandwe back to the Zulu frontier in 1826. Shaka forced a small detachment of Englishmen to accompany him as musketeers as he marched an army of 50,000, according to Fynn's reckoning, to engage Sikunyana in the Third

Ndwandwe War. In a battle that did not last more than an hour and a half, the
Ndwandwe threat was extinguished. According to Fynn's report, their numbers,
including women and children, "could not have been less than 40,000." He
looked on as "The remnants of the enemy's army sought shelter in an adjoining
wood, out of which they were soon driven. Then began a slaughter of the women
and children. They were all put to death." Isaacs also noted that Shaka appeared
"to have destroyed in this last encounter nearly every human being of the tribe,
man, woman, and child."

Soon after this battle, Shaka, enraged at the crime of Michael and John, two
Hottentots who had raped the young wife of an important Zulu chief while in
the service of the Englishmen, insisted that to make amends for the offense and
to avert a general execution of all the foreign visitors, a detachment of ten
muskets march with an impi against Beje, chief of a Kumalo segment. This
small community formerly pursued by Zwide had also eluded the Zulu for years
by hiding in the rocks. Isaacs, who was severely wounded in this conflict,
reported that when Shaka instructed them in the mode of attack, he commanded
them

> not to leave alive even a child, but exterminate the whole tribe. We remon-
> strated against the barbarity and great impropriety of destroying women
> and children, who, poor unoffending innocents, were not culpable, and
> could do no injury. "Yes they could," he said; "they can propagate and
> bring children, who may become my enemies. It is the custom I pursue not
> to give quarter to my enemies, therefore I command you to kill all."

That this practice was a matter of policy and not the product of an adventitious
rage, was indicated again in an argument with Fynn, in which Shaka maintained that the Cape colonists were foolish to deal with the frontier tribes on a
friendly basis. He argued, "By destroying a tribe entirely, killing the surviving
chiefs, the people would be glad to join you on your own terms."

In an interesting essay comparing the Zulu and the Spartan systems, W. S.
Ferguson, the classical historian, described Shaka's practice of total war, correctly observing that he waged war "not against the armed forces of the enemy
alone, but against his entire moral and material resources." It is clear, however,
that there were two parts to his military policy: first, the destruction of any tribe
engaged in combat; second, the effects that the violence—or even the reputation of this violence—had on the emotions of people within striking range. The
violence was wrought by highly disciplined impi, similar to hoplite formations,
executing massed attacks in precise evolutions, using the short, stabbing asse-
gai. The combination, which was a revolution in weaponry and military technique, could not be defeated by anything less than firearms, and was powerful

enough, as the Zulu War proved half a century later, to give a modern British army serious resistance. The secondary effects of this violence were skillfully used by Shaka, like other marauding conquerors known to history, to spread the terror of his name. Fynn testified that "the barbarous cruelties he practised struck terror into many who had never seen his force and fled at his name." Likewise, Shepstone declared that his new mode of warfare caused such terror that chiefdom after chiefdom gave way at his very approach to their frontiers. Ferguson, in his careful assessment of the Zulu system, wrote:

> In summary, we may say that the Zulu impis owed their irresistibility among the surrounding natives, and their successes over the whites, to the following characteristics:
>
> 1. The merciless discipline maintained by Chaka.
> 2. The high training of the men in physical endurance and effecting mass movements.
> 3. The use of the stabbing assegai and hand to hand fighting.
> 4. The tactics of surrounding the enemy and thus destroying him utterly.
> 5. The well organized system of espionage.
> 6. Their reputation for invincibility and the terror which their pitiless massacres of the entire population of the enemy inspired.

There is evidence that Shaka considered the terror process at least as important in his strategy as the ability of his impi to overcome antagonists by force of arms. Although he recognized the superiority of firearms, if the English should invade his territory, he told Fynn, "they would be terror-struck at the magnitude of his army." Shaka's English friends registered doubts that the Zulu prowess, apart from the success of their technique, was inherently superior to that of other communities. Fynn believed that the Zulu were confident in their system as long as they were successful, but that a few defeats would have demoralized them. Near the end of Shaka's career, in the campaign against the amaMpondo, Fynn listened to speeches made by a number of chiefs to Ngomane, then chief induna, in the course of which

> One in particular said that the whole army, during such time as they had served under Shaka, every time a war was proposed had expected to be defeated, but, under his command, they had become so used to conquering and to seeing the enemy entirely defeated on every occasion, that they were now ready to face whatever the enemy might offer, and that as soon as possible.

Isaacs noted that Shaka had struck the surrounding communities with terror and that they were alarmed at the sound of his name, but that the Zulu tended to avoid direct confrontation wherever possible and to rely on terror and deception. The soldiers of Shaka, he said, "knew full well that their renown was enough to make their enemies crouch before them, and they gained more by the terror of their name, than they achieved by their prowess in arms." Moreover, "It is not the Zoola's system of warfare to meet their enemy openly, if they can avoid it: they like to conquer by stratagem, and not by fighting; and to gain by a ruse what might be difficult for them to achieve by the spear."

THE HEREROS OF
SOUTH-WEST AFRICA
(NAMIBIA)

Several of the preconditions for genocide crystallized in the midst of the late nineteenth- and early twentieth-century contacts between European colonizers and indigenous peoples. The sense of mission and paternalism of Europeans at home and in the colonies could turn hard and vengeful when peoples like the Hereros rose in armed rebellion. The revolt of the Hereros lasted from 1904 to 1907. In the following selection, Horst Drechsler contends that the German war to crush the rebellion amounted to a genocide against the Hereros. In our view, the core of the genocide was the German killing of Herero noncombatants after their warriors had been defeated.

Otto von Bismarck's motives for extending Germany's empire to South-West Africa in the 1880s are still widely debated: rivalry with other European states; pressure from German manufacturers, traders, and bankers; domestic politics; and the element of chance and contingency are all well supported in the historical literature. Whatever Chancellor Bismarck's precise motives, in 1892 the first German colonists arrived in South-West Africa, and the struggle for control of the land began. While it is true that the Germans eventually discovered diamonds and that these became a profitable export, precious gems were not discovered until 1908 and are not part of this story.

Most of the 4,500 German settlers in South-West Africa when the Herero revolt began were cattle ranchers. Their prosperity rested on railroad lines linking their inland ranches with the coast. Since the German government compensated the railroad companies for their investment by granting them title to broad strips of land and valuable water rights along the line of rail, the construction of each new rail line shrank the quantity of land available to the cattle-keeping Herero people.

In 1903, just as German officials announced their plans for new rail lines, the Herero learned of plans to move them to reservations. If the German governor, Major Theodor von Leutwein, thought that his plan would reassure the Hereros, he was sadly mistaken. Moreover, Herero resentment was further fueled at just this moment by the intensified collection of debts by German traders and the continued refusal of the courts to punish Germans for raping and murdering Hereros.

At the outbreak of the revolt, in 1904, there were about 80,000 Hereros; in 1911, four years after the crushing of the revolt, only 15,000 remained. Of the 65,000 Hereros who vanished, no more than a thousand escaped to British territory. The rest had died, some killed in battles with German troops, many more as the victims of gruelling working conditions and disease in prisons and labor camps, and still more in the desert, where thirst or German patrols finished them. The underlying racism of the Germans expressed itself as fully during the war as it had before the rebellion began.

The consequences of the genocide for the few Herero survivors were devastating. Their spirit was broken. Karla Poewe, an anthropologist who has worked among their descendants, reports that the survivors "simply rejected any inner involvement with the past—as if it had died" (Poewe 1985, 77–78). Thousands of them converted to Christianity. "In my research," she observes, "I was unable to find any living Herero who could remember those times or remember having been told about them" (Poewe, 69).

By 1914, lured by government assistance and dreams of striking it rich, 14,000 Germans had settled in South-West Africa. As in the earlier cases of the Pequot Indians and the Tasmanians, the Herero were the victims of a perpetrator who killed those who blocked his access to wealth. In this type of genocide, the perpetrator's definition of the victims as economically useless and hopelessly primitive reinforced their exclusion from the universe of human obligation. The impetus to settlement was quite different in each of the colonial genocides we have presented thus far. But did the original aims of settlement of the Puritans, the British, and the Germans really matter to the victims, since the outcome for the Pequots, the Tasmanians, and the Hereros was virtually the same? And why was genocide the result of these cases of colonization, but not of many others? These are questions that remain to be answered.

THE HERERO UPRISING[†]

Now I should like to make a few observations regarding the subdivision of South-West Africa's history into periods in the years between 1884 and 1915.

†From Horst Drechsler, *"Let Us Die Fighting": The Struggle of the Herero and the Nama against German Imperialism (1884–1915)*, trans. Bernd Zollner, 6–7, 17, 132–34, 142–44, 148, 153–57, 213–17. Footnotes omitted. Reprinted by permission from Zed Books. Copyright 1980; original German edition 1963, Akademie-Verlag.

The first stage, lasting from 1884 to 1892, is characterized by the fact that both the Herero and the Nama [also known as Hottentots] failed to realize that the coming of the Germans had changed the situation in South-West Africa. The changes were hardly discernible in the eighties because the presence of the German colonial masters was limited to a handful of Imperial civil servants. The Herero and the Nama continued the battle between themselves for supremacy in South-West Africa as though there were no German colonialists in the country. It was not until the early nineties, when more and more German soldiers were despatched to South-West Africa and the Imperial Commissioner Heinrich Goering and Captain Curt von François began to interfere openly in their affairs, that the black population began to look upon the German colonialists as their chief enemy. The result was that the Herero and Nama, after having been locked in struggle throughout the 19th century, made peace at the end of 1892 in order to meet the new situation created by the German penetration.

The second stage, comprising the period from 1893 to 1903, opened with the German raid on Hornkranz, marking the beginning of the war against the Witboois. Between 1893 and 1903 the land and the cattle of the Herero and Nama passed gradually into the hands of German settlers. Since the South-West Africans did not meekly put up with expropriation, the period 1893–1903 was one of bitter struggle by the Herero and Nama against German imperialism. The common feature of their resistance was, however, that it took the form of uncoordinated local uprisings which their colonial masters found relatively easy to crush. Governor Theodor Leutwein pursued a shrewd policy of divide and rule, playing off Africans against Africans. When the construction of the Otavi railway was undertaken in 1903, it became clear to the Herero that their expropriation was about to be consummated.

The third stage covers the period from 1904 to 1907 during which the great rebellions of the Herero and Nama took place, born of sheer desperation. The outcome of the conflicts was hardly in doubt, given the Germans' superiority in weaponry and their possibilities of unlimited supply. So it was all the more surprising that the South-West Africans offered heroic resistance for such a long time that the military prestige of their German oppressors began to wane. The war against the Herero and Nama was the first in which German imperialism resorted to methods of genocide, thus earning unenviable notoriety in later years.

The crushing of the great Herero and Nama uprisings marks the beginning of the fourth and last stage of South-West African history under German colonial rule. This lasted from 1907 to 1915. It was only now that the German imperialists achieved their aims of transforming South-West Africa into a German

colony where they had a completely free hand and of relegating the Herero and
Nama to the status of forced labour.

.   .   .   .   .

South-West Africa's monopolistic exploitation by German imperialism came
to an abrupt end in 1915 when the colony passed into the hands of Great
Britain, later becoming a territory mandated to the Union of South Africa.

The Peoples of South-West Africa

South-West Africa (Namibia) is one of the most inaccessible
regions of Africa. Along the coast is the Namib, a sandy desert 50 to 70
kilometres wide, that makes it difficult to reach the interior, and in the eastern
part the Kalahari desert has the same effect.

South-West Africa is not the territory's name, but a description of its geographical location. Within its boundaries, which were artificially fixed by the
imperialists in the late 19th century, it contains—from north to south
—Ovamboland, Hereroland (or Damaraland) and Namaland.

Even by African standards South-West Africa is extremely sparsely populated, but for once this is not attributable to the barbaric slave trade. As the
names of the regions mentioned suggest, the principal population groups are the
Ovambo, the Herero and the Nama.

The Ovambo can be more or less left out of consideration here because they
remained outside the German sphere of influence throughout the era of German
colonial rule in South-West Africa. Indeed, their area has not become part of
the so-called Police Zone to the present day. As a matter of fact, the area inhabited by the Ovambo was cut in two by the arbitrary delimitation of the border so
that a part of them now live in Angola and the rest in Namibia. The Ovambo
living in Namibia constitute the largest population group in that country. At the
end of the last century their numbers were estimated at 100,000 to 150,000.

The central region of Namibia is peopled by the Herero, who are a Bantu-
speaking people just like the Ovambo. The Herero comprise the Mbandjeru
and the Tjimba (or Tsimba). No accurate data are available about their numerical strength in the late 19th century. However, most experts agree that approximately 80,000 Herero inhabited the area at the beginning of German colonial
rule in South-West Africa.

The Herero are nomadic herdsmen who, unlike all other Bantu tribes, do not
engage in crop raising. The soil was common property of the tribe. Yet, as
Heinrich Loth rightly pointed out, it would be an oversimplification to classify

the stage of socio-economic development which South-West Africa had attained in the 19th century as primitive-communism. The tribal system was fast breaking up in the 19th century, with an influential aristocracy typical to the early phase of feudalism assuming control of the tribes. The process of social differentiation had progressed so far that the contours of a class society had become clearly visible. The relationships of dependence that were emerging showed distinct traits of a feudal system of exploitation. However, this was not based on landed wealth, but on ownership of cattle, which was the chief form of private ownership of the means of production. Loth described the phase of social development briefly sketched here as the stage of transition to an early type of pastoral feudalism.

The region to the south of Hereroland is inhabited by the Nama, or to give them their own name, the Khoikhoin. They are made up of the Nama proper and the Orlam tribes, who entered South-West Africa from across the Orange River as late as the beginning of the 19th century to escape annihilation by the Boers. The Nama, too, are nomadic herdsmen who do not till the land. In socio-economic terms, what has been said here about the Herero also applies to the Nama. The principal distinction between Herero and Nama at the close of the last century was that the latter's herds were much smaller and that, generally speaking, cattle did not dominate to the same extent as among the Herero. It is estimated that there were about 20,000 Nama towards the end of the 19th century.

The Causes of the Uprising

To the total surprise of the Germans, a great uprising of the Herero broke out on 12 January 1904. The Herero rose as one man under the leadership of their Supreme Chief Samuel Maharero, who thus reversed the ill-conceived policy he had pursued thus far in a turn-about due largely to the pressure brought upon him by the lesser chiefs.

There can be no doubt about the reasons behind the insurrection. It was the systematic expropriation of the Herero and their consequent status of rightlessness that impelled them to their national uprising against German imperialism. They neither could nor would live any longer under these conditions. They preferred to die arms in hand rather than wait in resignation until their last possessions had been taken away from them.

Paradoxically, measures such as the establishment of reserves and the July 1903 statute of limitations on contracts, designed to remedy abuses, had the opposite effect. The creation of reserves made it clear to the Herero that the

amount of land still left to them was dwindling rapidly while the decree establishing a 12-month time limit for the enforcement of claims on Africans caused
traders to press even harder for the repayment of their debts. These measures
were factors that hastened the outbreak of the rebellion.

Another factor acting as a catalyst was the construction of the Otavi railway.
The building of the railway line from Swakopmund to Windhoek, which affected
"only" the southern part of Hereroland, had soon left no land suitable for
farming anywhere along its length. Even more worrying for the Herero was the
projected construction of the Otavi line, which was to cut right across Hereroland.
The Otavigesellschaft, the company which was financing the undertaking,
demanded that the Herero cede not only the land directly required for the construction of the railway, but also a 20-kilometre-wide strip on either side of the
track plus all water rights within this area. In direct negotiations with Samuel
Maharero, Governor Theodor Leutwein finally persuaded the Supreme Chief to
give up free of charge the land needed for laying the track. But Maharero was
not prepared to make any further concessions. In a letter to the banker Adolph
von Hansemann, Leutwein wrote about the outcome of his talks with Maharero:
"It will not be possible to obtain a cession of land on the scale envisaged by the
company. The kapteins have even asked that the natives inhabiting areas that
would be crossed by the railway line should not be forced to evacuate these
areas altogether, but only as far as is necessary. The experience gathered in
building the government railway suggests, however, that the natives, who seem
to abhor life in proximity to major routes of communication, will in time withdraw from the areas in question of their own free will, provided they find adequate water supplies elsewhere." At any event, it was not difficult for the Herero
to foresee that the construction of the Otavi line would set off an unprecedented
rush of German settlers to Hereroland.

A serious problem that has so far gone unmentioned but that went a long way
towards bringing matters to a head was the state of rightlessness to which the
Africans had been reduced by the Germans. Displaying a blatantly racist attitude, the Germans described the Africans as baboons and treated them accordingly. The gamut of the high-handed measures they inflicted on them ranged
from doses of "paternal care" (i.e., whipping) to plain murder. To explain such
outrageous behaviour they often pleaded diminished responsibility due to "tropical frenzy", a term specifically invented for this purpose. When a German was
put on trial—an event of extremely rare occurrence—the judge would, as a
rule, dismiss the charges or impose very light sentences. As a matter of principle, courts tended to call in doubt the credibility of African witnesses. Indeed,
these were the days when the German Colonial League demanded that the testimony of seven Africans should be deemed equivalent to that of one white man.

Deprived of all their rights, Africans had the feeling of being slaves in their own country.

To make matters worse, the Germans completely ignored the solemn promise they had made in Article 3 of the so-called treaty of protection and friendship with the Herero that they would respect the latter's habits and customs. Governor Theodor Leutwein believed that "the bulk of the whites here were ignorant of the protection treaty with the Herero." The Herero, for their part, had not forgotten the provisions of the agreement, but with the Germans persistently violating them, they decided in January 1904 that they, too, were no longer bound by the terms of the treaty. The Herero were full of complaints that the Germans were flouting their customs and habits and raping their women and young girls. Although this was not denied by the Germans, it is symptomatic that not a single case of rape came before a court in South-West Africa before the Herero rising. The Germans looked upon such offences as mere peccadilloes.

A graphic description of what happened when an African had the temerity to protest against the rape of his wife was given by *Berner Tagwacht*, a Social Democratic paper published in Switzerland: "The overseer of the kraal, a German, and two of his cronies had locked themselves in with the wife of a native, probably after having administered a heavy dose of schnapps to her. Her husband, who had got wind of the matter, rushed to their house, hammering at the door and demanding the release of his wife. Thereupon one of these heroes came out to give the black man a good hiding, a practice which, albeit forbidden, is fairly commonplace here. However, the black man offered resistance and, after having himself struck a blow, fled into his hut. The whites, blazing with anger, dragged him out and maltreated him, subsequently bundling him off to the police station where he was given fifty lashes into the bargain for having assaulted a white man." This report, which a Swiss railway worker had sent to the paper, makes it abundantly clear why no case of rape was ever brought before a court in South-West Africa.

.   .   .   .   .

The Herero Conduct of the War

The Herero uprising had doubtless been planned long in advance. But since time was not on their side, with their plight deteriorating further from year to year and the construction of the Otavi railway raising the spectre of total expropriation, the moment to act had come at the beginning of 1904. Circumstances were rather favourable at the time because three out of the four German companies of troops were operating in the far south of the country or were on their way there to deal with the uprising of the Bondelswarts so that Hereroland was practically devoid of German troops. Despite the careful planning, the decision to move into action was taken at short notice; this can be deduced from the fact that the 600 or so Herero engaged in the building of the Otavi railway were not notified in time. The internment of these Herero labourers at the outset of the insurrection deprived the insurgents of 600 fighting men.

Leading the insurgents was Samuel Maharero, Supreme Chief of the Herero. In all likelihood, the uprising was preceded by arguments and discussions for which we do not possess any written evidence. However this may be, Samuel Maharero's brave act marked a break with his previous misguided policy. Since it was the Supreme Chief who ordered the uprising, all the Herero responded. In a letter to Hendrik Witbooi, Samuel was able to report proudly: "I am not battling alone, for we are all fighting together: Kaptein Zacharias, Otjimbingwe; Kaptein Michael, Omaruru; and Kaptein David, Waterberg." The joint uprising of all Herero against German imperialism signified an initial significant success for them.

Yet from the first the uprising was in the nature of a desperate rearguard action. The Herero were keenly aware that the opposing sides were unevenly matched owing to the inadequacy of their own weapons and equipment and the technical superiority of their colonial masters, who were able to rely on unlimited supplies from Germany. But the Herero preferred to die rather than live under the German yoke any longer. Samuel Maharero wrote in a letter: "Let them [the Germans] kill us all, let them all come here. There is no other way." And the son of Chief Zacharias of Otjimbingwe later stated in evidence: "He [Chief Zacharias] knew that if we rose in revolt we would be wiped out in battle because our men were almost unarmed and without ammunition. The cruelty and injustice of the Germans had driven us to despair, and our leaders and the people felt that death had lost much of its horror in the light of the conditions under which we were living."

Samuel Maharero displayed considerable political shrewdness by attempting, before the outbreak of the uprising, to unite all South-West Africa for the struggle against German imperialism. In early 1904, just as in 1896, Hendrik Witbooi was the factor that tipped the scales. If he set up the standard of revolt, all Nama kapteins would follow his example. Therefore, in a letter dated 11 January 1904, Samuel informed him that he was planning an insurrection against the Germans and invited him to join in the rebellion. In another message to Witbooi he said: "All our obedience and patience with the Germans is of little avail, for each day they shoot someone dead for no reason at all. Hence I appeal to you, my Brother, not to hold aloof from the uprising, but to make your voice heard so that all Africa may take up arms against the Germans. Let us die fighting rather than die as a result of maltreatment, imprisonment or some other calamity. Tell all the kapteins down there to rise and do battle." Neither of these messages, however, reached its destination. Samuel Maharero sent them to Hermanus van Wyk, kaptein of the Rehoboth tribe, with the request that he pass them on to Witbooi. Instead, van Wyk transmitted them to the Germans together with two similar letters addressed to himself. In fact, even if the letters had reached Hendrik Witbooi, they would hardly have induced him to change his mind. It was nothing short of a tragedy that the Herero and Nama took up arms successively rather than simultaneously against the hated German yoke.

At the beginning of the insurrection Samuel Maharero issued the following order: "In my capacity as Supreme Chief of the Herero I hereby decree and resolve that none of my people lay their hands upon the English, the Bastaards, the Berg Damara, the Nama and the Boers. We shall not lay violent hands on any of these. I have made a solemn pledge not to make this known to anyone, including the missionaries."

This order is remarkable in two ways. For one thing, the uprising was directed only against the Germans whereas Britons and Boers were expressly excluded, so there could be no question of a "racial war". This decision was yet another sign of the political shrewdness displayed by a Supreme Chief who did not want to make himself more enemies than was necessary. In issuing this directive, Samuel did, in a manner of speaking, neutralize the British and the Boers. For another thing, it is interesting to note that he delivered a clear warning regarding the missionaries. He appears to have been in no doubt that, if the missionaries had had advance knowledge of the Herero's plans, they would have betrayed their cause. The isolation of the missionaries made sure that the secret was kept. There was no traitor among the Herero.

As a matter of fact, Samuel Maharero's order does not tell the whole story. The conduct of the war and testimony given later by subchief Daniel Kariko showed that the uprising was exclusively directed against German *men*. Kariko stated: "At our clandestine meetings our chiefs decided to spare the lives of all German women and children. The missionaries, too, were to be spared. . . . Only German men were regarded as our enemies."

The day when the Herero rose up in arms was 12 January 1904. At one fell swoop they seized all of Hereroland (except for the fortified places which came under siege) and the bulk of the German settlers' livestock, with more than 100 German settlers and soldiers meeting their deaths.

The Herero rising marked the beginning of "Germany's bloodiest and most protracted colonial war." In the initial stages the Herero were superior to their opponents. But since they failed to take advantage of their temporary superiority to storm the fortified places of their colonial masters, they gradually saw the initiative pass to the enemy. Being Africans, they disliked the idea of taking buildings by assault. Rather, their intention was to bring about a decision in open battle. The Germans, however, were unwilling to take the risk of such a battle before the arrival of reinforcements had given them a clear position of superiority. They knew only too well that time was on their side. While the situation for the Herero remained unchanged, the Germans were able to strengthen their position step by step through a constant influx of manpower and *materiel*.*

.   .   .   .   .

When Berlin learned about this step of Leutwein's there was already speculation that he was about to enter into negotiations with the Herero. The Director of the Colonial Department, therefore, lost no time in sending Leutwein a cable instructing him to "refrain from any bilateral negotiations with the Herero and to demand unconditional surrender." It said that negotiations, "whatever the circumstances, may be opened only with the permission of His Majesty."

Leutwein hurriedly prepared a lengthy report to the Colonial Department to justify his action. The report is of considerable interest because it constitutes an outline of the Governor's basic stance on the Herero issue. He wrote: "Colonial policy is not only a matter of leadership, but also of diplomacy. The insurgents must know that there is an alternative to death. Otherwise, we will only drive them to despair, bringing on an endless war that will be to our disadvantage. After all, the natives have nothing to lose now but their lives—and they are doomed anyway—while we suffer setback after setback due to the cessation of our work of colonization. The Spanish have won one 'victory' after another in Cuba only to lose that island in the end.

"As regards the future terms for subjugation, I share the Department's view that after all the outrages the Herero have committed nothing short of unconditional surrender will have to be enforced. On the other hand, I do not concur with those fanatics who want to see the Herero destroyed altogether. Apart from the fact that a people of 60,000 or 70,000 is not so easy to annihilate, I would consider such a move a grave mistake from an economic point of view. We need the Herero as cattle breeders, though on a small scale, and especially as labourers. It will be quite sufficient if they are politically dead. If this is practicable, they should be denied any form of tribal government and confined to reserves adequate for their needs . . .

"Those on *werfs* not involved in the conflict will also have to allow themselves to be disarmed and placed in reserves. All prisoners of war will have to

*Ed. note: After underestimating the strength of the Herero forces, Leutwein wrote a letter to Samuel Maharero in February 1904. The letter was actually a ruse intended by Leutwein to elicit accurate information on the location of Maharero's main force.

be court-martialled and, if found guilty of having looted farms or murdering innocent people, be sentenced to death without exception. There can be no other form of punishment, considering the severity of the atrocities that have been perpetrated. For the rest, I shall consult the Department once again before reaching an agreement with the insurgents. The only favour I beg of you now is to give me a free hand concerning the diplomatic methods to be used to bring the negotiations to a close."*

.   .   .   .   .   .

On 11 June 1904 General Lothar von Trotha arrived in South-West Africa. Only five days later he asked Leutwein to come and see him at Okahandja, where the first meeting between the two men took place. Leutwein's son later reported that his father had advised the new Commander-in-Chief "to conduct the war in such a way as to ensure the survival of the Herero nation. General von Trotha listened calmly to these words and then replied: 'Your remarks have been of great interest to me, but you will have to allow me to conduct the campaign as I see fit.' " This, at least, is Leutwein's version.

About six months later von Trotha described his first encounter with Leutwein in a communication to the Imperial Chancellor: "When I took over as Commander-in-Chief, Governor Leutwein handed me a proclamation, ready for the press, that was to be issued to the Herero. Astutely phrased, it condemned them for what they had done, but promised clemency if they showed repentance and were prepared to mend their ways. I objected immediately that I was, as a matter of principle, against dealing with the rebellion in that way and expressed my firm belief that such a course of action was running counter to the intentions of His Majesty the Emperor." For his part, Leutwein did his best to play down the differences between him and General von Trotha in an optimistically worded cable sent to the Foreign Office in Berlin.

Both Leutwein and von Trotha were pursuing the same aim: to end the uprising forthwith, to force the Herero to surrender unconditionally, and to take away their last possessions. But while the goal of the two men was the same, they differed on the means of achieving it. In seeking to gain his ends, Leutwein always showed a concern for the future of the colony after the crushing of the rebellion whereas von Trotha did not. The Governor was acutely aware that after a campaign of extermination against the Herero the colony would have lost most of its value for German imperialism. Hence his demand to spare the country's

---

*Ed. note: In April 1904, Herero attacks and an outbreak of typhoid among the German forces compelled Leutwein to suspend major military operations. During the resulting lull, Wilhelm II named Lieutenant-General Lothar von Trotha commander-in-chief of the German troops in South-West Africa.

most important productive force—the people—and the cattle as well. Thwarted in his plans by the hysterical mood prevailing in South-West Africa towards the indigenous population and faced with the failure of his strategy against the Herero, he was quite content to relinquish his post as military leader.

In marked contrast General von Trotha was a soldier and nothing else. He had gained his "baptism of fire" by resorting to ruthless methods in suppressing popular uprisings in East Africa (notably the Wahehe rising in 1896) as well as the Boxer Rebellion in China in 1900–01. His one overriding ambition was to be able to report to the Kaiser that the revolt had been quelled. In a letter to Leutwein he wrote somewhat later: "I did not receive any instructions or directives on being appointed Commander-in-Chief in South-West Africa. His Majesty the Emperor only said that he expected me to crush the rebellion by fair means or foul and to inform him later of the causes that had provoked the uprising."

Von Trotha made a point of providing a pseudo-scientific rationale for his brutal and primitive concept of warfare in Africa. Thus he wrote: "I know enough tribes in Africa. They all have the same mentality insofar as they yield only to force. *It was and remains my policy to apply this force by unmitigated terrorism and even cruelty. I shall destroy the rebellious tribes by shedding rivers of blood and money.* [emphasis added] Only thus will it be possible to sow the seeds of something new that will endure."

The Battle in the Waterberg: The Genocide of the Herero

After reinforcements had been moved up, von Trotha made preparations for a decisive assault on the Herero south of the Waterberg. The German Commander-in-Chief ordered the Waterberg to be surrounded by his troops. But there could be no question of encircling and destroying the Herero given the vastness of the territory and the lack of a sufficient number of men to seal off the whole area of the Waterberg. The odds were that the Herero could not be prevented from breaking out at some point or other. They were, in any case, determined to confront the enemy for the final battle rather than avoid such an encounter by crossing the border as was assumed in the German camp right up to the last moment.

On 4 August 1904 von Trotha announced his "Directives for the Attack on the Herero". This order is of special interest because it clearly spells out the General's aim of annihilating the Herero and because it provided for a rather peculiar disposition of his forces. Even someone ignorant of military matters cannot fail to notice that the six German detachments spread out all around the Waterberg greatly differed in size, the smallest contingent (under Major von der Heyde) having taken up position to the southeast. As Colonel Deimling's force, which was easily the largest, had received orders to attack the Herero from the west, there can be little doubt about the tactics being pursued: the Herero, finding their way eastward and southward blocked by the comparatively strong contingents commanded by von Estorff and Mueller, would overrun the small force under Major von der Heyde and break through in a southeasterly direction.

Paul Leutwein, the Governor's son, later reported that both Major von Estorff and his father had warned against such a disposition of the German troops. He said that the Governor "foresaw the breakthrough of the Herero and their resulting flight into the sandveld or across the border. He realized that in both cases the entire people would be lost. In another conversation he expressly warned von Trotha against carrying out this plan, suggesting that von der Heyde's and Deimling's detachments be simply switched around. But von Trotha could not bring himself to make such a concession."

As a matter of fact, it was not—as Leutwein's son presumed—incompetence on the part of the General that led to this arrangement of the German forces; rather it was a well-thought-out plan that the Herero should break through towards the south and perish in the desert there. A study prepared by the General Staff is quite explicit on this point: "If, however, the Herero were to break through, such an outcome of the battle could only be even more desirable in the eyes of the German Command because the enemy would then seal his own fate, being doomed to die of thirst in the arid sandveld." Von Trotha had but one aim: to destroy the Herero nation. He believed that the easiest way of achieving it was to drive the Herero into the Omaheke Desert. But such a crime can only be described as genocide.

The date fixed by the General for the German assault was 11 August 1904. After two days of fierce fighting, in which the Germans brought into action 30 pieces of artillery and 12 machine-guns, the Herero had to yield to the Germans' superiority in weaponry. In their attempt to pierce the German lines they ultimately discovered the only weak point—von der Heyde's unit southeast of the Waterberg—and achieved a breakthrough there as von Trotha had anticipated in his sinister scheme. Stretching out before them was the sandy waste of the Omaheke Desert. The study of the General Staff noted laconically: "The arid Omaheke was to complete what the German Army had begun: the extermination of the Herero nation."

Contrary to what is often alleged, it is not true that the Herero were destroyed by the fighting in the Waterberg. Rather, the losses sustained during the battle were relatively slight. The annihilation of the Herero was due to the militarily unjustifiable measures taken by von Trotha after the fighting in the Waterberg.

Von Trotha immediately set off in pursuit of the Herero, bent as he was on their total destruction. To achieve this objective, it was quite sufficient to make it impossible for them to escape in a different direction. When part of the Herero tried to turn northeastward, their way was barred at once by a German unit. The study of the General Staff mentions this fact, observing on a rather complacent note: "With several of our contingents in hot pursuit, they too [the Herero] were pushed southeastward toward the arid, waterless Omaheke." Another attempt by the Herero to escape in a southern direction was prevented by German troops through a sweeping outflanking movement. By 20 August or so, the German forces had driven the Herero to the western edge of the Omaheke sandveld. Through constant harassment they forced them to flee into the sandveld itself. German units and patrols tracked down the Herero to the last water-hole and drove them away from there. Von Trotha then ordered the Omaheke to be sealed off by a 250-kilometre cordon in the west and southwest, making it virtually impossible for anyone to escape from the desert. This cordon was maintained until about mid-1905. The bulk of the Herero met a slow, agonizing death. The study of the General Staff noted that the Omaheke had inflicted a worse fate on the Herero than "German arms could ever have done, however bloody and costly the battle."

Von Trotha's Conduct of the War

Von Trotha's "conduct of the war", culminating in genocide, will now be considered in some detail. First of all, let us take a look at his notorious proclamation, known as the "Extermination Order", which, significantly enough, is not mentioned at all in the study of the German General Staff. The proclamation reads:

Osombo-Windimbe, 2 October 1904

"I, the Great General of the German Soldiers, address this letter to the Herero people. The Herero are no longer considered German subjects. They have murdered, stolen, cut off ears, noses and other parts from wounded soldiers, and now refuse to fight on out of cowardice. I have this to say to them: Whoever turns over one of the kapteins to one of my garrisons as a prisoner will receive 1,000 Marks and he who hands over Samuel Maharero will be entitled to a reward of 5,000 Marks. *The Herero people will have to leave the country. Otherwise I shall force them to do so by means of guns. Within the German boundaries, every Herero, whether found armed or unarmed, with or without cattle, will be shot. I shall not accept any more women and children. I shall drive them back to their people—otherwise I shall order shots to be fired at them.* These are my words to the Herero people.

Signed: the Great General of the Mighty Kaiser, von Trotha.

"This order shall be made known to the troops at the roll-call together with the additional provision that soldiers capturing a kaptein are also entitled to the reward offered and that the firing of shots at women and children means firing over their heads to drive them away. *I am in no doubt that as a result of this order no more male prisoners will be taken,* but neither will it give rise to atrocities committed on women and children. These will surely run away after two rounds of shots have been fired over their heads. I trust that our force will always bear in mind the good reputation that the German soldier has acquired.

The German Command

Signed: Lieutenant-General von Trotha."

.   .   .   .   .

Commenting on his order to drive the Herero women and children back into the Omaheke, General von Trotha hinted a few years later that he, the "hero" of the Waterberg, had already been at the end of his tether. Apologetically, he claimed that no other option had been open to him: "My force was on the verge of disaster. If I had made the small water-holes accessible to the womenfolk, I would have run the risk of an African catastrophe comparable to the Battle of the Beresina."*

One dimension of German war strategy in South-West Africa was to "eliminate" or "attack" the *werfs*, to use the stereotype expressions found in von Trotha's reports. In plain language this meant that African settlements were raided and destroyed and their inhabitants put to death. This was done both in the hinterland and near the front line. It was irrelevant whether those attacked had been involved in the war or not and whether they were Herero, Bergdamara or San ("Bushmen")—the German soldiers were anyway incapable of distinguishing between them. Anyone with a dark skin was considered fair game. In a brochure entitled *Was soll aus den Herero werden?* (What is to become of the Herero?) the missionary J. Irle was particularly scathing in his criticism of this aspect of the German policy of extermination.

.   .   .   .   .

The butchery at Ombakaha ruled out any further negotiations, which suited von Trotha very well. Indeed, the word "negotiations" did not exist in his vocabulary. This was also reflected in a report to the Chief of the Army General Staff in which he wrote: "The crucial question for me was how to bring the war against the Herero to a close. The Governor and some other 'old Africans' on the one hand and myself on the other are poles apart on this issue. The former

---

*Ed. note: The Battle of Beresina was the crucial battle of Napoleon I's retreat from Russia in 1812. Napoleon's tactics saved the last remnants of his Grand Army from complete annihilation by the Russian forces.

have long advocated negotiations, describing the Herero nation as a labour reservoir that will be needed in future. I take a completely different view. As I see it, the nation must be destroyed as such and, should this prove impossible to achieve by tactical moves, they will have to be forced out of the country through a long-term strategy. It will be possible, by occupying all sources of water supply from Grootfontein all the way to Gobabis and by maintaining high mobility of our columns, to track down and gradually obliterate the small bands of people flocking westward. To pursue the main contingents of the nation with their kapteins right into the Omaheke sandveld and to capture and annihilate them is not feasible at the moment. On the question of provisions I have already passed the limits of what is reasonable. Only time will show to what extent it will be possible for the Estorff unit left behind in Osombo-Ovondimbe to drive them [the Herero] back from any water-holes they may find and to force them to seek refuge in Bechuanaland. If this is impracticable, everything will depend on whether the Herero are capable of holding their own in the Omaheke sandveld until the onset of the rainy season, whether they will attempt to cross into British territory, or whether they will try to regain their traditional grazing grounds through force or total submission. Since I neither can nor will come to terms with these people without express orders from His Majesty the Emperor and King, it is essential that all sections of the nation be subjected to rather stern treatment. I have begun to administer such treatment on my own initiative and, barring orders to the contrary, will continue to do so as long as I am in command here. My intimate knowledge of so many Central African tribes—Bantu and others—has made it abundantly plain to me that Negroes will yield only to brute force, while negotiations are quite pointless. Before my departure yesterday I ordered the warriors captured recently to be court-martialled and hanged and all women and children who sought shelter here to be driven back into the sandveld, handing them a copy of the proclamation drawn up in Othihererro. . . . To accept women and children who are for the most part sick, poses a grave risk to the force, and to feed them is out of the question. For this reason, I deem it wiser for the entire nation to perish than to infect our soldiers into the bargain and to make inroads into our water and food supplies. Over and above this, any gesture of leniency on my part would only be regarded as a sign of weakness by the Herero. They will either meet their doom in the sandveld or try to cross into Bechuanaland. This uprising is and remains the beginning of a racial struggle, which I foresaw for East Africa as early as 1897 in my reports to the Imperial Chancellor."

.   .   .   .   .   .

Taking stock of the losses which the South-West African people suffered between 1904 and 1907 as a result of the German policy of annihilation, one can give a relatively accurate answer to the crucial question as to how many Herero and Nama survived German captivity. The answer is found among the records of the Imperial Colonial Office in a "Report on the Mortality in Prisoner-of-War Camps in German South-West Africa" drawn up by the High Command of the "Protective Force". Summing up, the report states: "According to despatches covering the period *from October 1904 to March 1907 a total of 7,682 of the approximately 15,000 Herero and 2,000 Hottentots, or 45.2 per cent of all prisoners, have died.*" [emphasis added] In other words, almost half of them were wiped out.

However, as not all Herero and Nama had been captured, the number of prisoners who survived is not identical with the number of those who actually escaped the German policy of extermination. In a report made in December 1906 Deimling put the number of Africans not in German captivity at about 15,000. They included the Bondelswarts, the Berseba community, the Keetmanshoop tribe and the so-called Field Herero. When the 9,300 surviving prisoners are added to Deimling's estimate, one arrives at a total of 25,000 Herero and Nama who had escaped with their lives.

To compute the losses which the South-West African population sustained in human terms between 1904 and 1907 owing to the savagery of the German methods of warfare, the official census taken in 1911 can be the basis. *It shows that in 1911 there were a mere 15,130 Herero left out of an original 80,000 and 9,781 Nama out of an original 20,000. No fewer than 80 per cent of the Herero and 50 per cent of the Nama had thus fallen victim to German colonial rule.* In addition, one-third of the Berg Damara, who had not joined in the uprising, were killed simply because the German troops were unable to tell them from the Herero. Such was the staggering human cost of German colonial rule in South-West Africa. To this one has to add the plunder which accompanied the killing.*

. . . . . .

Within two months of this, Hans Tecklenburg, Deputy Governor of South-West Africa, came up with a detailed report outlining the standpoint of the Colonial Administration on the expropriation of the South-West African population. He said, *inter alia*: "The tribal property of the tribes fully or partly involved in the rebellion will be subject to confiscation. Whether they have

*Ed. note: The acquisition of African lands by colonial powers was generally cloaked in the mantle of laws. In May 1905, the German Colonial Department asked the authorities in Windhoek to draft a scheme for the confiscation of native lands. By the same letter, the authorities conveyed a copy in French of the sequestration order issued for Algiers in October 1845. The French colonial order was included because it contained "many a valuable hint for the draft solicited by Berlin."

carried out, or aided and abetted, warlike acts will make no difference. *It would be a sign of weakness, for which we would have to pay dearly, if we allowed the present opportunity of declaring all native land to be Crown territory to slip by.* Only the territory of the Rehoboth Bastaards must remain in the possession of the natives for the time being. . . . The non-rebellious section of tribes partly involved in the uprising (e.g., the Berseba Hottentots) may be granted the free use of part of their former tribal area by the Governor for the lifetime of their kaptein or as long as political considerations make this necessary . . .

"*With the confiscation of their land, the natives will be deprived of the possibility of raising cattle.* All objections notwithstanding, they must not, as a matter of principle, be allowed to own cattle because they cannot be conceded the grazing lands required for this purpose. For the moment, however, the non-rebellious natives and especially the Bastaards, will be allowed to keep their cattle and horses nor will these be taken away from the Berseba Hottentots.

"The reserves established by Imperial Decree of 10 April 1898 will *have to be confiscated by all means.* This plan will be relatively easy to put into execution as few reserves have been created thus far. . . . The reserves can be abolished without difficulty with one stroke of the pen. The only tribal area to remain, apart from Ovamboland, would be that of the Rehoboth Bastaards. Besides, the area of the Berseba Hottentots would also be spared for the time being. Some kind of locations would be created for the other natives, *but any form of tribal organization would be eliminated and the treaties concluded with the former tribes annulled.* The natives would be settled on individual *werfs* in proximity to the places of residence of the whites. Those living on such *werfs* will serve as labourers to individual farmers. . . . *Werfs* in outlying areas not subject to police control will not be tolerated. They would only provide a nucleus keeping alive memories of the tribal system and land ownership. No major community of natives must be left to their own devices lest they form a self-contained unit. Freedom of movement will be abolished and passes will be introduced as a compulsory measure. Some districts have already made a move in this direction. The natives have been given an identification tag with a number, the name of the district and the Imperial Crown imprinted on it. The introduction of the tag, which is seen as the 'Emperor's sign', has proved quite a success. In due course it will be possible to register the natives so identified—or rather the men to begin with—and to keep a closer watch on their movements and activities. Any native found without a tag can then be arrested as a person of no fixed abode. . . .

"I frankly admit that my proposals are of a very draconian nature. Yet halfway measures would only cause resentment without breaking resistance once and for all and ruling out another rebellion. . . . Here in this settler colony the natives must never be allowed to forget for a single moment that they are in a country ruled by the white man and that they are subject to German legislation. All the sacrifices made in terms of blood and gold will then not have been made in vain."

On the basis of Tecklenburg's report, the Colonial Department, acting in conjunction with the Imperial Ministry of Justice, spent the next few months working out the Imperial Decree that was to provide the legal foundation for the dispossession of the Herero and the Nama. On 24 December 1905, Chancellor Bülow transmitted the draft to the Kaiser, who endorsed it two days later. What thus became the "Imperial Decree of 26 December 1905 Pertaining to the Sequestration of Property of Natives in the Protectorate of South-West Africa" afforded the Governor a legal instrument that enabled him to "sequester" the land of Africans at his discretion. Indeed, Lindequist promptly declared the whole of Hereroland Crown land. A few months later, after the expiry of a hypothetical "deadline for appeals", the Governor reported smugly that the decree had become unassailable: "All legal impediments have thus been removed that stood in the way of granting the numerous applications made for the acquisition of farms and homesteads in Hereroland."

.   .   .   .   .   .

Following the intervention of the Social Democratic Party, the Reichstag on 30 May 1906 adopted a resolution calling on the Government to hand back to the Nama and Herero as much land as they needed to make a living. The Government, however, in a demonstration of its contempt for the German Parliament, completely ignored this resolution. In December 1906 Lindequist observed sarcastically during a meeting of the Budgetary Committee that the resolution had been impracticable "because without cattle the Herero have no use for the land."

THE ARMENIANS
IN TURKEY

The Armenians are a very ancient people who seem to have lived in the same area throughout their history. They survived a large number of migrations that have washed over the Middle East, and they have maintained their ancient culture and language in spite of frequent pressures to adapt to the cultures of their conquerors. They adopted Christianity very early and have adhered to it to the present day. In the Ottoman Empire they were tolerated as a "people of the book," but they were never considered as fully equal. During the nineteenth and early twentieth centuries toleration degenerated into frequent persecutions, often escalating into massacres.

The genocide of the Armenians in 1915 was the first of the modern ideologically-motivated genocides. It occurred during World War I, after the Ottoman Empire had been experiencing a steady decline. The decline, combined with ideas spreading from Western Europe, gave rise to a new ideology of nationalism that emphasized a homogeneous nation with one language and one religion. Through the writings of Ziya Gökalp this new ideology, with its rejection of minority rights and individual liberties, found an audience among the Young Turks, a factious movement that sought to overthrow the Sultan and modernize the Turkish state. Its emphasis on a common culture and language, shared by all Turkic-speaking people, led to a Pan-Turkism that excluded all minority groups. When the Committee of Union and Progress under Talaat and Enver came to power, Gökalp was a member of the Central Committee. After the end of the war he was arrested together with other leading members of the Committee of Union and Progress and was found guilty of his part in the genocide and exiled from the country.

Unlike the racial theories of the Nazis, the nationalism of the Young Turks was not based on a racial determinism. In Turkey, members of minorities could become members of the majority by adopting its language, culture, and religion —which few did voluntarily. There was another difference between the two genocides. Hitler announced his ideas and especially his anti-Semitic views in *Mein Kampf*, which was dictated while he was in prison in 1924, and which by the fall of 1933 had one million copies in circulation. The book was widely circulated in Germany, though few Germans, or Jews, took it seriously. When the Nazis did implement Hitler's ideas, it came as a surprise to almost everyone. In Turkey, because Gökalp's ideas had not nearly the same wide distribution, their implementation came even more unexpectedly.

Comparisons between the Armenian genocide and the Holocaust come readily to mind, and many of them are discussed in the literature (see, for example, Dadrian 1988). Both events have been vigorously denied, but from very different quarters. The denial of the Armenian genocide is an official policy of the Turkish government, supported by considerable financial resources and the connivance of intellectuals and academics who cherish the attention of those in power. (For a review of this phenomenon, see, for example, Terrence Des Pres' "Introduction" to Hovannisian 1986.) The denial of the Holocaust, in contrast, is loudly publicized by a small number of unreconstructed Nazis and anti-Semites in spite of the admission of guilt by the perpetrator countries' governments.

In order to do original research in this area, a scholar requires not only the relevant technical training, but also considerable linguistic skills. However, the available materials for the Armenian case, even in English, are quite extensive. The "deniers" have questioned the reliability of much of these materials, even though the evidence from Armenian sources and from foreign observers is overwhelming. Since the Turkish government does not permit access to the relevant archives to outside scholars, research on their side of the debate is seriously handicapped—which seems especially curious since the present Turkish government was not the perpetrator of the genocide. This only goes to prove once again that historical truth is far less important than the socioeconomic and geopolitical games that nation-states play.

THE HISTORICAL DIMENSIONS OF THE ARMENIAN QUESTION, 1878–1923[†]

The genocide of the Armenian minority in the Ottoman Empire during World War I may be viewed in the context of the broader Armenian Question, which had both internal and international aspects. Indeed, it was to rid themselves of this question and to create a new, homogeneous order that the Turkish dictators organized the deportations and massacres of the Armenian population. Through death and destruction they eliminated the Armenians from

†From Richard G. Hovannisian, ed., *The Armenian Genocide in Perspective*, 19–32, 38–41. Copyright © 1986 by Transaction Publishers. Reprinted by permission.

most of the Ottoman Empire, including all of the historic Armenian homelands, and radically altered the racial and religious character of the region. An overview of the Armenian Question in the Ottoman Empire should help to place the [matter] . . . into perspective.

Although tracing their lineage, according to epical-biblical traditions, to Noah, whose ark was said to have rested on Mount Ararat, the Armenians actually passed through a long era of formation and emerged as an identifiable people sometime around the sixth century before Christ. Their lands lay between the Black, Caspian, and Mediterranean seas, in an area now referred to as Eastern Anatolia and Transcaucasia, on both sides of the current Soviet–Turkish frontier. For the next two thousand years, they were led by their kings, nobles, and patriarchs, sometimes independently and often under the sway of powerful, neighboring empires of the East and West. Located on perhaps the most strategic crossroads of the ancient and medieval worlds, the Armenians managed not only to survive but also to develop a rich, distinctive culture by maintaining a delicate balance between Orient and Occident. Adopting Christianity as the state religion at the turn of the fourth century A.D., however, the Armenians were often persecuted because of their faith by invaders and alien overlords. By the end of the fourteenth century, the last Armenian kingdom had collapsed, the nobility had been decimated in constant warfare, and the Armenian plateau had fallen under foreign subjugation. Most of the country ultimately came under Turkish rule, except for the eastern sector, which came first under Persian and then in the nineteenth century under Russian dominion.

In the Ottoman Empire, which by the seventeenth century pressed to the gates of Vienna, the Armenians were included in a multinational and multireligious realm, but as a Christian minority they had to endure official discrimination and second-class citizenship. Inequality, including special taxes, the inadmissibility of legal testimony, and the prohibition on bearing arms, was the price paid to maintain their religion and sense of community. Down through the centuries, many thousands eventually converted in order to be relieved of these disabilities as well as the sporadic violence that fell most heavily upon the defenseless Armenian peasantry. The *devshirme*, or child levy, was occasionally imposed, and in many districts in Western Anatolia the Armenians were not allowed to speak their own language except in the recitation of prayers. This is not to say that there were not prosperous merchants, traders, artisans, and professional persons throughout the empire, for it is well known that the minority populations played a most important role in international commerce, as interpreters and intermediaries, and in the highly skilled professions. Nonetheless, most of the Armenian population remained rooted in its historic homeland, becoming, in large part, tenant farmers or sharecroppers under the dominant Muslim feudal-military elite.

Despite their second-class status, most Armenians lived in relative peace so long as the Ottoman Empire was strong and expanding. But as the empire's administrative, financial, and military structure crumbled under the weight of internal corruption and external challenges in the eighteenth and nineteenth centuries, intolerance and exploitation increased. The breakdown of order was accelerated by Ottoman inability to compete with the growing capitalistic system in the West and to modernize and reform. The legal and practical superiority of one element over the other groups continued, and the lavish and uncontrolled spending of the Ottoman court led to even more oppressive taxation, including the infamous method of tax farming, that is, the sale of the privilege to exact as much tax as possible from a particular district in return for an advance lump-sum payment. The wasteful ways of the ruling elite drew the empire into bankruptcy in the 1870s and opened the way for direct European financial supervision, beginning in 1881.

The decay of the Ottoman Empire was paralleled by cultural and political revival among many of the subject nationalities, which were swept by the European winds of romanticism and revolt. The national liberation struggles, supported at times by certain European powers, contributed to Ottoman loss of most Balkan provinces in the nineteenth century and constituted one aspect of the Eastern Question, namely, what was to become of the decrepit empire. The rivalry among the European powers and their economic exploitation of the Ottoman Empire led to efforts to preserve it as a weak buffer state and a lucrative marketplace. The British, in particular, fearing that dissolution of the empire would threaten their mastery of the seas, came to the conclusion that it could be saved only if the worst abuses of government were eliminated and fundamental administrative changes implemented. A growing circle of Ottoman liberals was also persuaded that survival depended on reform. These men became the movers behind the several major reform edicts issued during the so-called *tanzimat* period from 1839 to 1876.[1] Yet time and again the supporters of reform became disappointed and disillusioned in the face of the entrenched vested interests that resisted change. The *tanzimat* era, for all its fanfare, brought virtually no improvement in the daily life of the common person.

Of the various subject peoples, the Armenians perhaps sought the least. Unlike the Balkan Christians, they were dispersed throughout the empire and no longer constituted a majority in much of their historic homelands. Hence, Armenian leaders did not think in terms of separation or independence, but, professing loyalty to the sultan and renouncing any separatist aspirations, they petitioned for the protection of their people and property from corrupt officials and from marauding bands often linked with those officials. It was not inappropriate, therefore, that the Ottoman sultans should have referred to the Armenians as their "faithful community." The Armenians nonetheless also passed through a long period of cultural revival. Thousands of youngsters enrolled in schools established in the nineteenth century by U.S. and European missionaries and hundreds of middle-class youth traveled to Europe for higher education. Many of these men returned home, imbued with the social and political philosophies of contemporary Europe, to engage in teaching, journalism, and literary criticism. Gradually a network of Armenian schools and newspapers spread from Constantinople (Istanbul) and Smyrna (Izmir) to Cilicia, and eventually to many towns in the primitive eastern provinces, that is, Turkish Armenia. As it happened, however, this Armenian self-discovery was paralleled by heightened administrative corruption, economic exploitation, and physical insecurity. It was this dual development—the conscious demand for security of life and property on the one hand, and the growing insecurity of both life and property on the other—that gave rise to the Armenian Question as a part of the larger Eastern Question.

Widespread dissatisfaction with inadequate implementation of the several reform edicts of the *tanzimat* period, the aggravated plight of the Asiatic Christians, and, above all, the severe Turkish reprisals against a rebellious Balkan Christian population brought renewed European pressure on the Sublime Porte [Ottoman government] in 1876. In a maneuver to undermine the international conference summoned to deal with the crisis, Sultan Abdul-Hamid II (1876–1909) promulgated a liberal constitution drafted by sincere advocates of reform.[2] Had the sultan been as sincere in implementing the constitution, it could have removed the major grievances of the subject peoples, the Armenians included. But having warded off the European diplomats, Abdul-Hamid soon suspended the constitution and the parliament for which it had provided. Instead of abating, the tribulations of the Armenians multiplied. Robbery, murder, and kidnapping became commonplace in a land where even the traditional feudal protective system had broken down.

In the aftermath of the Russo-Turkish war of 1877–78, the leaders of the Armenian community, or *millet*, put aside their customary caution and conservatism and appealed to the victorious Russian commander-in-chief to include provisions for the protection of the Armenians in the forthcoming peace treaty.[3] That treaty, which was signed at San Stefano in March 1878, granted independence to Serbia, Montenegro, and Rumania, and autonomy to a large Bulgarian state. No such provision was either sought or executed for the Armenians. On the contrary, the Russians agreed to withdraw their armies from most of Turkish Armenia, while annexing the border districts of Batum, Ardahan, Kars, Alashkert, and Bayazid. The Armenian leaders were not entirely disappointed, however, because Article 16 of the treaty stipulated that Russian withdrawal would be contingent upon the implementation of effective reforms in Turkish Armenia:

As the evacuation by the Russian troops of the territory which they occupy in Armenia, and which is to be restored to Turkey, might give rise to conflicts and complications detrimental to the maintenance of good relations between the two countries, the Sublime Porte undertakes to carry out into effect, without further delay, the improvements and reforms demanded by local requirements in the provinces inhabited by the Armenians, and to guarantee their security from Kurds and Circassians.[4]

General M. T. Loris-Melikov was to stand firm in Erzerum until this condition was met.

The aftermath of the Treaty of San Stefano is familiar to students of European history. Prime Minister Benjamin Disraeli and especially Foreign Secretary Robert Salisbury believed that the interests of the British Empire were jeopardized by the treaty. Enlisting the support of other European powers, they intimidated Russia with threats of joint action, not excluding war. The outcome was the convening of a European congress in Berlin in mid-1878 to review and revise the treaty. An Armenian delegation also traveled to Berlin with the goal of persuading the six European powers to arrange for a specific Armenian reform program, rather than simply general reforms, past instances of which had proved most disappointing. Using the administrative statute for Lebanon as a model, the Armenians asked that Turkish Armenia be granted a Christian governor, local self-government, civil courts of law, mixed Christian–Muslim militias, voting privileges for all tax-paying adult males, and the allocation of most local tax revenues for local improvements.[5]

The sympathetic expressions of the European diplomats aside, the Berlin congress revised the Treaty of San Stefano in conformity with the guidelines of the British negotiators. Several provinces were taken back from the newly independent and autonomous states in the Balkans, and on the Caucasus frontier the districts of Alashkert and Bayazid were restored to Ottoman rule. Moreover, insofar as Armenian reforms were concerned, the coercive aspect of Article 16 in the Treaty of San Stefano was superseded by the stipulation in Article 61 of the Treaty of Berlin that the Russian armies should withdraw immediately, and that the sultan would simply pledge to take it upon himself to implement the necessary reforms and to report to the European powers collectively about the progress.[6] The effect of the inversion of Article 16 at San Stefano to Article 61 at Berlin was trenchantly caught in the Duke of Argyll's cryptic observation, "What was everybody's business was nobody's business."[7]

As payment for services rendered to the sultan, Great Britain exacted, through secret agreement, control over the strategic island of Cyprus, and Austria-Hungary gained the right to administer Bosnia and Herzegovina, which had been taken back from Serbia. In the eastern provinces, meanwhile, horrified

Armenian peasants witnessed the evacuation of Loris-Melikov's army. As had been the case during the Russian withdrawal from Erzerum in 1829, thousands of Armenians departed with the Russian troops to resettle in the Caucasus. Yet, despite the setback, the Armenian religious leaders did not lose hope and declared that they still had faith in the Ottoman government and in its introduction of the necessary reforms. Armenian patriarch Nerses Varzhapetian swore fidelity to the sultan and emphasized that efforts to overcome Armenian misfortunes would be made within the established legal framework of the Ottoman homeland. At a time when several of the Balkan nationalities had won independence, the Armenians still shunned talk of separatism.[8]

The Treaty of Berlin elevated the Armenian Question to the level of international diplomacy, but the Armenians gained no advantage from that status. On the contrary, Kurdish tribesmen, organized and armed by the sultan's government, spread havoc over the eastern provinces, particularly in the districts from which the Russian army had recently withdrawn. Neither the petitions of the Armenian patriarch nor the establishment of more European consular posts in Turkish Armenia helped to improve the situation. European consuls at Kharput, Erzerum, Van, and other interior centers could do little more than relay frequent dispatches describing the rapacious acts to which the Armenians were subjected. For two years the European powers, outwardly cooperating under the joint responsibility of Article 61, issued collective and identic notes reminding the Sublime Porte of its treaty obligations. But by 1881, these powers had become too involved in the scramble for empire elsewhere to worry further about the Armenians. They silently shelved the Armenian Question and turned away from Armenian troubles.[9]

Feeling abandoned and betrayed, a growing number of Armenians began to espouse extralegal means to achieve what they now regarded as the right and moral duty to resist tyrannical rule. Instead of meeting its obligation to protect its subjects, the Ottoman government had become the instrument of exploitation and suppression. Some Armenians came to believe that, like the Balkan Christians, they too would have to organize, perhaps even take arms. Local self-defense groups that had coalesced in the 1880s gradually gave way to several broadly based secret political societies in the 1890s. Still, few among those who called themselves revolutionaries were prepared to expound national independence as a goal. Rather, they sought cultural freedom and regional autonomy, equality before the law, freedom of speech, press, and assembly, unhindered economic opportunity, and the right to bear arms.[10]

Thus, while the patriarch in Constantinople continued supplications to the Sublime Porte, exponents of the new political mentality preached resistance. Under such influence the rugged villagers of the Sassun district in the province of Bitlis refused to continue paying an extortionary protection tax to Kurdish chieftains. In 1894 the Kurds, unable to subdue their former clients, accused Sassun of sedition and appealed to Ottoman officials. Regular Turkish regiments joined the irregular Kurdish Hamidiye cavalry units and, after weeks of siege and combat, forced the Armenians to lay down their arms in return for the promise of amnesty. Instead, however, Sassun was plundered and several thousand Armenians were put to the sword without regard to age or sex. European consuls and Christian missionaries raised their voices against the outrage, and soon the newspapers of Europe and the United States were again demanding intercession on behalf of the Armenians. After nearly fifteen years of silence, the European powers were drawn back to the Armenian Question, but now only Great Britain, France, and Russia were willing to address the Sublime Porte on the subject. European representatives attached to an Ottoman commission of inquiry reported that the Armenians of Sassun had been forced to take arms for their own protection and that the gratuitous acts of cruelty by the sultan's regular and irregular troops and the irresponsibility of the Ottoman officials and commanders were reprehensible. There had been no rebellion, and even if the facts had proved otherwise, the unbridled, indiscriminate brutality could in no measure be justified.[11]

The Sassun crisis revived the European call for Armenian reforms. In May 1895 a joint British, French, and Russian plan was submitted for the consolidation of the Armenian provinces into a single administrative region, the release of political prisoners and the repatriation of exiles, the making of reparations to the people of Sassun and other victims, the disarming of the Hamidiye corps in time of peace, and the creation of a permanent control commission to oversee the reforms. Diplomatic exchanges continued through the summer and autumn of 1895 until at last, in October, Sultan Abdul-Hamid assented to a reform program based on, but far less inclusive than, that proposed by the three European governments. Once again, a ripple of optimism emanated from Constantinople.[12]

As before, however, European intercession unsustained by force only compounded the troubles of the Armenians. Even as Abdul-Hamid seemed to acquiesce in the reform program in October 1895, the Armenians in Trebizond were in the throes of massacre. In the following months, systematic pogroms swept over every district of Turkish Armenia. The slaughter of between 100,000 and 200,000 Armenians, the forced religious conversion of the population of scores of villages, the looting and burning of hundreds of other settlements, and the coerced flight into exile of countless Armenians were Abdul-Hamid's actual response to European meddling.[13] His use of violent methods was a desperate attempt to preserve the weakening status quo in the face of enormous external

and internal challenges to it. In this regard, the major difference between Abdul-
Hamid and his Young Turk successors was that he unleashed massacres in an
effort to maintain a state structure in which the Armenians would be kept in
their place without the right to resist corrupt and oppressive government, whereas
the Young Turks were to employ the same tactic in 1915 on a grander scale to
bring about fundamental and far-reaching changes in the status quo and to create an entirely new frame of reference that did not include the Armenians at all.

In the years following the calamities of 1894–96, disillusion weighed heavily upon the Armenians, yet some comfort was found in the fact that other
elements, too, were organizing against the tyrannical rule of Abdul-Hamid. In
Geneva, Paris, and other emigre centers, reformists and revolutionaries of all
the Ottoman nationalities conceived programs of change and envisaged a new,
progressive government for their common homeland. In 1902 the first congress
of Ottoman liberals, attended by Turkish, Armenian, Arab, Greek, Kurdish,
Albanian, Circassian, and Jewish intellectuals, convened in Paris and joined in
demands for equal rights for all Ottoman subjects, local self-administration,
and restoration of the constitution, which had been suspended since 1877. A
second congress in 1907 pledged its constituent groups to a united campaign to
overthrow Abdul-Hamid's regime by the swiftest means possible and to introduce representative government.[14]

Within the Ottoman Empire itself, Turkish opposition elements, especially
among the junior military officers and the faculty of the technical institutes,
merged into the Committee of Union and Progress (Ittihad ve Terakki Teshkilati),
popularly referred to as the Young Turks. Thereafter, events moved quickly
toward confrontation. When Young Turk army officers in Macedonia were about
to be exposed by the sultan's agents in 1908, they led their regiments toward
Constantinople in a defensive maneuver and, as the mutiny spread, demanded
the restoration of the constitution. Lacking loyal units to crush the rising, Abdul-
Hamid bowed to the ultimatum in July and acquiesced in the formation of a
constitutional monarchy. The Armenians hailed the victory of the army and its
Young Turk commanders; at this historic moment manifestations of Ottoman
Christian and Muslim brotherhood abounded.[15]

One of the most unexpected and, for the Armenians, most tragic metamor-
phoses in modern history was the process, from 1908 to 1914, that transformed the seemingly liberal, egalitarian Young Turks into extreme chauvinists,
bent on creating a new order and eliminating the Armenian Question by eliminating the Armenian people. European exploitation of Turkish weaknesses contributed to this process. In the immediate aftermath of the Young Turk revolution, Austria-Hungary annexed Bosnia-Herzegovina, Bulgaria asserted full
independence, Crete declared union with Greece, and Italy forcibly pursued

claims to Tripoli and the Libyan hinterland. The impact of these troubles emboldened Turkish conservative elements to stage a countercoup to restore the sultan's
authority. Although the movement was suppressed and Abdul-Hamid was deposed
and exiled, the turmoil did not abate without renewed tragedy for the Armenians. Throughout Cilicia, Armenian villages and city quarters were looted and
burned and some 20,000 Armenians were massacred. While there was evidence that Young Turk sympathizers, too, had been among those who incited
the mobs, the party's leaders moved to placate the Armenians by ascribing the
bloodshed to the Hamidian reaction and by conducting public memorial services for Muslim and Christian sons of a common fatherland who had fallen in
defense of the revolution.[16]

The abortive countercoup prompted the Young Turk cabinet to declare a state
of siege and to suspend normal constitutional rights for the next four years, until
1912. It was during this period that the concepts of Turkism and exclusive
nationalism captivated several prominent Young Turks, who began to envisage a
new, homogeneous Turkish state structure in place of the enervated and exploited
multinational Ottoman Empire.[17] In a new coup in 1913 the ultranationalistic
faction of the Young Turk party seized control, and thereafter, until the end of
World War I in 1918, the government was dominated by a triumvirate composed of Enver, minister of war; Talaat, minister of internal affairs and subsequently grand vizier; and Jemal, military governor of Constantinople and later
minister of the marine.[18]

The Young Turk revolution of 1908 allowed Armenian political parties to
emerge from the underground and to operate clubs and newspapers and vie for
the parliamentary seats allotted the Armenians. The most influential of those
parties, the Dashnaktsutiun, was in fact linked in an alliance with the Young
Turks. Despite increasing signs of Turkish extremism, the Dashnaktsutiun
resolved to remain loyal during the troubled years preceding the outbreak of
World War I. Yet the seeming gains in the postrevolutionary period did little to
diminish the hardships of the rural population. Armed marauding bands in the
eastern provinces became all the more audacious when the Armenian youth
went off to fight for the Ottoman homeland during the Balkan wars of 1912–13.
European consuls in the region filled their dispatches with descriptions of the
deadly anarchy. In Constantinople the petitions of the patriarch were answered
with promises of action, but effectual measures did not ensue.

As a result of renewed international interest in the Armenian Question following the Balkan wars, the European powers once again raised the issue of
reforms. Great Britain, France, and Russia on the one hand, and Germany,
Austria-Hungary, and Italy on the other, ultimately reached a compromise settlement. Trebizond and the six Turkish Armenian provinces—Erzerum, Sivas,

Kharput, Diarbekir, Bitlis, and Van—would be combined into two administrative regions with broad local autonomy, under the guarantee of the European powers and the supervision of inspectors-general selected from citizens of the small European nations. Without detailing the extensive diplomatic correspondence and the final provisions of the compromise plan of February 1914, let it suffice to say that the reform measure was the most comprehensive and promising of all the proposals put forth since the internationalization of the Armenian Question in 1878.[19]

The outbreak of world war in the summer of 1914 jeopardized implementation of the reform program and deeply alarmed Armenian leaders. Should the Ottoman Empire enter the conflict on the side of Germany, the Armenian plateau would become the inevitable theater of another Russo-Turkish war. In view of the fact that the Armenian homelands lay on both sides of the frontier, the Armenians would suffer severely no matter who might eventually win the war. For these reasons, Armenian spokesmen implored their Young Turk associates to maintain neutrality and spare the empire from calamity. When pressured to organize an Armenian insurrection in the Caucasus against Russia, the leaders of the Dashnaktsutiun declined, again urging neutrality but making it known that if war did engulf the region the Armenians would dutifully serve the government under which they lived.[20]

Despite the advice and appeals of the Armenians, the Germanophile Young Turk faction, led by Enver and Talaat, sealed a secret alliance with Germany in August 1914 and looked to the creation of a new Turkish realm extending into Russian Transcaucasia and Central Asia. Turkey's entrance into the war voided the possibility of solving the Armenian Question through administrative reform. Rather, the Young Turk leaders were drawn to the newly articulated ideology of Turkism, which was to supplant the principle of egalitarian Ottomanism and give justification to violent means for transforming a heterogeneous empire into a homogeneous state based on the concept of one nation, one people. Any vacillation that still may have lingered after Turkey's entrance into the war was apparently put aside as the result of the tragic Caucasus campaign, in which Enver Pasha sacrificed an entire army to his militarily unsound obsession to break through to Baku and the Caspian Sea in the dead of winter, as well as the subsequent Allied landings on the Gallipoli peninsula in April 1915 in an abortive maneuver to capture Constantinople and knock Turkey out of the war.[21] The major Turkish military setback and parallel Allied threat to the capital allowed Young Turk extremists to make Armenians the scapegoats by accusing them of treachery and persuading reluctant comrades that the time had come to settle the Armenian Question once and for all. In *Accounting for Genocide*, Helen Fein has concluded: "The victims of twentieth-century premeditated genocide—the

Jews, the Gypsies, the Armenians—were murdered in order to fulfill the state's design for a new order. . . . War was used in both cases . . . to transform the nation to correspond to the ruling elite's formula by eliminating the groups conceived of as alien, enemies by definition."[22]

On the night of April 23/24, 1915, scores of Armenian political, religious, educational, and intellectual leaders in Constantinople, many of them friends and acquaintances of the Young Turk rulers, were arrested, deported to Anatolia, and put to death. Then in May, Minister of Internal Affairs Talaat Pasha, claiming that the Armenians were untrustworthy, that they could offer aid and comfort to the enemy, and that they were in a state of imminent nationwide rebellion, ordered their deportation from the war zones to relocation centers—actually the deserts of Syria and Mesopotamia. In fact the Armenians were driven out not only from the war zones but from the width and breadth of the empire, with the exception of Constantinople and Smyrna, where there were many foreign diplomats and merchants. The whole of Asia Minor was put in motion. Armenians serving in the Ottoman armies, who had already been segregated into unarmed labor battalions, were now taken out in batches and murdered. Of the remaining population, the adult and teenage males were, as a pattern, swiftly separated from the deportation caravans and killed outright under the direction of Young Turk officials and agents, the gendarmerie, and bandit and nomadic groups prepared for the operation. The greatest torment was reserved for the women and children, who were driven for weeks over mountains and deserts, often dehumanized by being stripped naked and repeatedly preyed upon and abused. Many took their own and their children's lives by flinging themselves from cliffs and into rivers rather than prolonging their humiliation and suffering. In this manner an entire nation melted away, and the Armenian people were effectively eliminated from their homeland of nearly three thousand years. Countless survivors and refugees scattered throughout the Arab provinces and Transcaucasia were to die of starvation, epidemic, and exposure. Even the memory of the Armenian nation was intended for obliteration; churches and monuments were desecrated, and small children, snatched from their parents, were renamed and farmed out to be raised as Turks.[23]

The Turkish wartime rationalizations for these deeds were roundly refuted by statesmen and humanitarians such as Henry Morgenthau, Arnold Toynbee, James Bryce, Henry Adams Gibbons, René Pinon, Anatole France, Albert Thomas, and Johannes Lepsius.[24] It was not Armenian treachery, Lepsius declared, but the exclusivist nationalism adopted by the Young Turk extremists that lay at the root of the tragedy. Elimination of the Armenians would avert continued European intervention in the name of a Christian minority and would remove the major racial barrier between the Ottoman Turks and the Turkic peoples of the Caucasus and Transcaspia, the envisaged new realm of pan-Turkish champions.[25] Gibbons described the Armenian massacres as "The blackest page in modern history," and Ambassador Morgenthau wrote: "I am confident that the whole history of the human race contains no such horrible episode as this. The great massacres and persecutions of the past seem almost insignificant when compared to the sufferings of the Armenian race in 1915."[26]

While the decimation of the Armenian people and the destruction of millions of persons in Central and Eastern Europe during the Nazi regime a quarter of a century later each had particular and unique features, historians and sociologists who have pioneered the field of victimology have drawn some startling parallels.[27] The similarities include the perpetration of genocide under cover of a major international conflict, thus minimizing the possibility of external intervention; conception of the plan by a monolithic and xenophobic clique; espousal of an ideology giving purpose and justification to chauvinism, racism, exclusivism, and intolerance toward elements resisting or deemed unworthy of assimilation; imposition of strict party discipline and secrecy during the period of preparation; formation of extralegal special armed forces to ensure the rigorous execution of the operation; provocation of public hostility toward the victim group and ascribing to it the very excesses to which it would be subjected; certainty of the vulnerability of the intended prey (demonstrated in the Armenian case by the previous general massacres of 1894–96 and 1909); exploitation of advances in mechanization and communication to achieve unprecedented means for control, coordination, and thoroughness; and use of sanctions such as promotions and the incentive to loot, plunder, and vent passions without restraint or, conversely, the dismissal and punishment of reluctant officials and the intimidation of persons who might consider harboring members of the victim group.

News of the deportations and massacres evoked expressions of sympathy and outrage in many countries. On May 24, 1915, when the first reports had reached the West, the Allied Powers declared: "In view of this new crime of Turkey against humanity and civilization, the Allied Governments make known publicly to the Sublime Porte that they will hold all members of the Turkish Government, as well as those officials who have participated in these massacres, personally responsible."[28] In December 1916 the *Manchester Guardian* summarized the sentiments of most British leaders: "Another word remains—Armenia—a word of ghastly horror, carrying the memory of deeds not done in the world since Christ was born —a country swept clear by the wholesale murder of its people. To Turkey that country must never and under no circumstances go back."[29] A year later Prime Minister David Lloyd George declared that Mesopotamia would never be restored to Turkish tyranny, adding: "That same observation applies to Armenia, the land soaked with the blood of innocence, and massacred by the people who were bound to protect them."[30] In his war aims, delivered in January 1918, Lloyd George reiterated that "Arabia, Armenia, Mesopotamia, Syria and Palestine are in our judgment entitled to a recognition of their separate national condition."[31] And in August, shortly before the end of the war, he told an Armenian delegation: "Britain will not forget its responsibilities toward your martyred race."[32]

Similar statements were issued in France, as Prime Minister and Foreign Minister Aristide Briand declared in November 1916: "When the hour for legitimate reparations shall have struck, France will not forget the terrible trials of the Armenians, and in accord with her Allies, she will take the necessary measures to ensure for Armenia a life of peace and progress."[33] His successor, Georges Clemenceau, wrote to an Armenian leader in July 1918: "I am happy to confirm to you that the Government of the Republic, like that of Great Britain, has not ceased to place the Armenian nation among the peoples whose fate the Allies intend to settle according to the supreme laws of Humanity and Justice."[34] The Italians, too, expressed determination that the Armenian people would have a secure collective future. Prime Minister Vittorio Orlando declared: "Say to the Armenian people that I make their cause my cause."[35]

In the United States, incredulity and indignation were the reactions to the Turkish atrocities. The country rallied to assist the "Starving Armenians" through an outpouring of private charity. Until the Ottoman government broke diplomatic relations with the United States in April 1917, U.S. officials tried to assist the Armenian survivors as best they could. In the wake of the massacres, leaders of both parties and of all branches of government pledged themselves to the goal of caring for the survivors and restoring them to their ancestral lands. One of President Wilson's Fourteen Points for peace read: "The Turkish portions of the present Ottoman Empire should be assured a secure sovereignty, but the other nationalities which are now under Turkish rule should be assured an undoubted security of life and an unmolested opportunity of autonomous development."[36] This statement reflected a recommendation by the United States Inquiry, a special commission charged with the formulation of a U.S. peace program: "It is necessary to free the subject races of the Turkish Empire from oppression and misrule. This implies at the very least autonomy for Armenia and the protection of Palestine, Syria, Mesopotamia and Arabia by the civilized nations."[37]

NOTES

1. See, for example, Roderic H. Davison, *Reform in the Ottoman Empire, 1856–1876* (Princeton: Princeton University Press, 1963); A. Schopoff, *Les Réformes et la protection des Chrétiens en Turquie, 1673–1904* (Paris: Plon-Nourrit, 1904); Edouard Engelhardt, *La Turquie et le tanzimat*, vol. 1 (Paris: Cotillion, 1882); Bernard Lewis, *The Emergence of Modern Turkey* (London: Oxford University Press, 1961).

2. Great Britain, Parliament, House of Commons, Sessional Papers, 1877, vol. 112,

command 1739, Turkey no. 16, *Reports by Her Majesty's Diplomatic and Consular Agents in Turkey respecting Conditions of the Christian Subjects of the Porte, 1868–1875*; Sessional Papers, 1876–77, vol. 91, c. 1641, Turkey no. 2, *Correspondence respecting the Conference at Constantinople and the Affairs of Turkey, 1876–1877*; Sessional Papers, 1877, vol. 91, c. 1738, Turkey no. 15, *Further Correspondence respecting the Affairs of Turkey*, and vol. 92, c. 1806, Turkey no. 25, *Further Correspondence. . . .* ; Great Britain, Foreign Office, *British and Foreign State Papers*, 1875–76, vol. 68, 683–98, "Constitution de l'Empire Ottoman, promulguée le Zilhidjé 1293 (11/23 Décembre 1876)," and vol. 68, 1114–11207, "Protocols of Conferences between Great Britain, Austria-Hungary, France, Germany, Italy, Russia, and Turkey . . . , Constantinople, December 1876–January 1877."

3. Leo [A. Babakhanian], *Hayots hartsi vaveragrere* [Documents on the Armenian question] (Tiflis, 1915), pp. 56–58.

4. Great Britain, Sessional Papers, 1878, vol. 83, c. 1973, Turkey no. 22, *Preliminary Treaty of Peace between Russia and Turkey Signed at San Stefano 19th February/ 2nd March, 1878*, and c. 1975, Turkey no. 23, *Maps Showing the New Boundaries under the Preliminary Treaty between Russia and Turkey Signed at San Stefano.*

5. Leo, *Hayots hartsi vaveragrere*, pp. 63–69; Gabriel Lazian, *Hayastan ev hai date (vaveragrer)* [Armenia and the Armenian question (documents)] (Cairo: Houssaper, 1946), pp. 86–88.

6. Great Britain, Sessional Papers, 1878, vol. 83, c. 2083, Turkey no. 39, *Correspondence relating to the Congress of Berlin with Protocols of the Congress*, and c. 2108, Turkey no. 44, *Treaty between Great Britain, Germany, Austria, France, Italy, Russia, and Turkey for the Settlement of Affairs in the East, Signed at Berlin*. See also W. N. Medlicott, *The Congress of Berlin and After* (London: Methuen, 1938).

7. Duke of Argyll [George Douglas Campbell, 8th Duke], *Our Responsibilities for Turkey* (London: J. Murray, 1896), p. 74.

8. Leo, *Hayots hartsi vaveragrere*, pp. 113–33; A. O. Sarkissian, *History of the Armenian Question to 1885* (Urbana: University of Illinois Press, 1938), pp. 89–90.

9. For documents relating to conditions after the Treaty of Berlin and to the diplomatic notes and correspondence about the introduction of reforms in the Armenian provinces, see, for example, Great Britain, Sessional Papers, 1878, vol. 81, c. 1905, Turkey no. 1; 1878–79, vol. 79, c. 2204, Turkey no. 53, and c. 2205, Turkey no. 54, vol. 80, c. 2432, Turkey no. 10; 1880, vol. 80, c. 2537, Turkey no. 4, vol. 81, c. 2574, Turkey no. 7, and c. 2611, Turkey no. 9, vol. 82, c. 2712, Turkey no. 23; 1881, vol. 100, c. 2986, Turkey no. 6. See also *British and Foreign State Papers*, 1877–78, vol. 69, 1313–47, and 1880–81, vol. 72, 1196–1207.

10. See Louise Nalbandian, *The Armenian Revolutionary Movement* (Berkeley and Los Angeles: University of California Press, 1963); Mikayel Varandian, *H. H. Dashnaktsutian patmutiun* [History of the Armenian Revolutionary Federation], vol. 1 (Paris: Navarre, 1932).

11. France, Ministère des Affaires Etrangères, *Documents diplomatiques: Affaires arméniennes; Projets de réformes dans l'empire Ottoman, 1893–1897* (Paris: Imprimerie

Nationale, 1897); Great Britain, *Sessional Papers*, 1895, vol. 109, c. 7894, Turkey no. 1, pt. 1, *Events at Sassoun and Commission of Inquiry at Moush*, and pt. 2, c. 7894–1, *Commission of Inquiry at Moush: Procès-verbaus and Separate Depositions*. See also E. M. Bliss, *Turkey and the Armenian Atrocities* (Boston: H. L. Hastings, 1896); Victor Bérard, "La Politique du Sultan," *La Revue de Paris* (December 15, 1896):880–89.

12. Great Britain, *Sessional Papers*, 1896, vol. 95, c. 7923, Turkey no. 1, *Correspondence respecting the Introduction of Reforms in the Armenian Provinces of Asiatic Turkey*; France, *Affaires arméniennes*, nos. 43, 57; Germany, Auswärtiges Amt, *Die grosse Politik der europäischen Kabinette, 1871–1914* (40 vols.; Berlin: Deutsche Verlagsgesellschaft für Politik und Geschichte, (1922–27), vol. 9, nos. 2184–89, 2203–12, vol. 10, nos. 2394–2444; Schopoff, *Les Reformes et la protection des Chrétiens en Turquie*, pp. 475–526.

13. For reports and diplomatic correspondence relating to the Armenian massacres of 1895–96, see, for example, Great Britain, *Sessional Papers*, 1896, vol. 95, c. 7927, Turkey no. 2, vol. 96, c. 8108, Turkey no. 6, and c. 8273, Turkey no. 8, and 1897, vol. 101, c. 8305, Turkey no. 3; France, *Affaires arméniennes*, nos. 116–235, and *Supplément, 1895–1896* (Paris: Imprimerie Nationale, 1897), no. 1–178; Germany, *Grosse Politik*, vol. 10, nos. 2410–76 *passim*, and vol. 12, nos. 2883–2910, 3065–3113 *passim*. Of the hundreds of books and eyewitness accounts relating to the massacres, see, for example, Johannes Lepsius, *Armenia and Europe* (London: Hodder & Stoughton, 1897); Georges Clemenceau, *Les Massacres d'Arménie* (Paris: n.p., 1896).

14. Ernest E. Ramsaur, Jr., *The Young Turks* (Princeton: Princeton University Press, 1957), pp. 65–76, 124–29; Paul Fesch, *Constantinople aux derniers jours d'Abdul-Hamid* (Paris: M. Riviere, 1907), pp. 366–76.

15. Ramsaur, *The Young Turks*, pp. 130–39; Feroz Ahmad, *The Young Turks* (Oxford: Clarendon Press, 1969), pp. 1–13; Charles R. Buxton, *Turkey in Revolution* (London: T. F. Unwin, 1909), pp. 55–73.

16. For findings of the Armenian member of the inquiry commission sent to Cilicia, see Hakob Papikian, *Adanayi egherne* [The Adana calamity] (Constantinople: Kilikia, 1919). See also Duckett Z. Ferriman, *The Young Turks and the Truth about the Holocaust at Adana in Asia Minor, during April, 1909* (London: n.p., 1913); Georges Brézol, *Les Turcs ont passé là: Receuil de documents sur les massacres d'Adana en 1909* (Paris: L'Auteur, 1911); René Pinon, *L'Europe et la Jeune Turquie* (Paris: Perrin, 1911); M. Seropian, *Les Vêpres ciliciennes* (Alexandria: Della Roca, 1909).

17. See Uriel Heyd, *Foundations of Turkish Nationalism: The Life and Teachings of Ziya Gökalp* (London: Luzac, 1950), esp. pp. 71–81, 104–48. See also Arnold J. Toynbee, *Turkey: A Past and a Future* (New York: George H. Doran, 1917), pp. 15–40; Victor Bérard, *La Mort de Stamboul* (Paris: A. Coller, 1913), pp. 259–398.

18. Ahmad, *The Young Turks*, pp. 92–120; Wilhelm Feldmann, *Kriegstage in Konstantinopel* (Strassburg: K. J. Trübner, 1913), pp. 106–71.

19. See Roderic H. Davison, "The Armenian Crisis, 1912–1914," *American Historical Review* 53 (April 1948):482–504; Russia, Ministerstvo Inostrannykh Del, *Sbornik diplomaticheskikh dokumentov: Reformy v Armenii* (Petrograd: Gosudarstvennaia Tipografiia, 1915); Germany, *Grosse Politik*, vol. 38, nos. 15283–15434 *passim*; *British*

Documents on the Origins of the War, 1898–1914, ed. G. P. Gooch and Harold Temperley (11 vols.; London: H.M.S.O., 1926–38), vol. 10, pt. 1 *passim*; Leo, *Hayots hartsi vaveragrere*, pp. 342–57.

20. V. Minakhorian, *1915 tvakane* [The year 1915] (Venice: St. Lazarus, 1949), pp. 66–71. See also Johannes Lepsius, *Der Todesgang des armenischen Volkes* (Potsdam: Tempelverlag, 1930), pp. 178–79.

21. W. E. D. Allen and Paul Muratoff, *Caucasian Battlefields* (Cambridge: Cambridge University Press, 1953), pp. 240–84; N. Korsun, *Sarykamishskaia operatsiia na kavkazskom fronte mirovoi voiny v 1914–1915 godu* (Moscow: Gosudarstvennoe Voennoe Izdatel'stvo, 1937). See also Winston Churchill, *The World Crisis* (2 vols.; New York: Scribner's, 1929), vol. 2, *1915;* Trumbull Higgins, *Winston Churchill and the Dardanelles* (New York: Macmillan, 1963).

22. Helen Fein, *Accounting for Genocide* (New York: Free Press, 1979), pp. 29–30.

23. For archival sources and published studies on the Armenian genocide, see Richard G. Hovannisian, *The Armenian Holocaust: A Bibliography Relating to the Deportations, Massacres, and Dispersion of the Armenian People, 1915–1923* (Cambridge, Mass.: Armenian Heritage Press, 1980).

24. For Turkish rationalizations, see, for example, Ahmed Rustem Bey, *La Guerre mondiale et la question turco-arménienne* (Berne: Staempfli, 1918); Turkey, *Aspirations et agissements révolutionnaires des comités arméniens avant et après la proclamation de la constitution ottomane* (Constantinople: n.p., 1916).

25. Lepsius, *Todesgang,* pp. 215–29. See also Toynbee, *Turkey,* pp. 20–27, 30–31.

26. Henry Morgenthau, *Ambassador Morgenthau's Story* (Garden City, N.Y.: Doubleday, Page, 1918), pp. 321–22.

27. See especially Vahakn N. Dadrian, "The Structural-Functional Components of Genocide," in *Victimology*, vol. 3, ed. I. Drapkin and E. Viano (Lexington, Mass.: D. C. Heath, 1974), and "The Common Features of the Armenian and Jewish Cases of Genocide," in *Victimology,* vol. 4, ed. I. Drapkin and E. Viano (Lexington, Mass.: D. C. Heath, 1975).

28. Richard G. Hovannisian, "The Allies and Armenia, 1915–18," *Journal of Contemporary History* 3, no. 1 (1968):147.

29. *Manchester Guardian,* 29 December 1916, p. 4.

30. Great Britain, Parliament, House of Commons, *The Parliamentary Debates,* 5th series, 1916, vol. 100, col. 2220.

31. Carnegie Endowment for International Peace, Division of International Law, *Official Statements of War Aims and Peace Proposals, December 1916 to November 1918* (Washington, D.C.: Carnegie Endowment, 1921), p. 231.

32. *Armenia's Charter* (London: Spottiswoode, Ballantyne, 1918), p. 9.

33. *Le Temps,* 7 November 1918.

34. *Armenia's Charter,* pp. 14–15.

35. Archives of Republic of Armenia Delegation to the Paris Peace Conference (now housed in Boston, Mass.), File 344/1, *H. H. Hromi Nerkayatsutschutiun ev Italakan Karavarutiune, 1918* [Republic of Armenia Rome Mission and the Italian Government, 1918].

36. U.S. Department of State, *Papers Relating to the Foreign Relations of the United States*, 1918, Supplement 1: *The World War*, 2 vols. (Washington, D.C.: G.P.O., 1933), vol. I, 16.

37. Ibid., 1919: *The Paris Peace Conference*, 13 vols. (Washington, D.C.: G.P.O., 1942–47), vol. 1, 52.

PROVOCATION OR NATIONALISM: A CRITICAL INQUIRY INTO THE ARMENIAN GENOCIDE OF 1915[†]

Surely one of the most salient and deplorable features of our era is its history of massacre and genocide. Millions of innocent noncombatants have been slaughtered by states, mostly their own, usually in the name of preposterous worldviews. Among the most terrible of these catastrophes—caused by human intervention, not by natural forces—have been the widespread massacres of Ottoman Armenians in 1894–96 and again in 1915. Indeed, the violence that was visited upon the Armenians in 1915 has been called the first modern genocide, and it is with this event that we are here concerned.[1]

Our aim in this essay is to raise three questions: What happened? Why did it happen? And what might be learned from the Armenian case that might shed some light on others as well? Given the complexity of the problem, the answers that this essay will suggest must necessarily be tentative. Within the perspectives of political science, relying on the work of historians and scholars in other disciplines, the best one can hope for is more or less convincing, more or less credible formulations.

Against a number of historians who have argued that the reason for the genocide derives from Armenian provocations, in this essay we suggest that the reason may be found in the context of Armenian–Turkish relations and in the motives and worldview of the Committee of Union and Progress, the ruling party of the time. If there was a necessary condition for the genocide, it may have derived from the military and political disasters of 1908–1915 that isolated the Armenians and stimulated Turkish nationalism. It was this newly experienced nationalism that not only transformed Turkish identity but changed as well the image of the Armenians from that of a loyal *millet* into that of a threat-

†From Robert Melson, "Provocation or Nationalism: A Critical Inquiry into the Armenian Genocide of 1915," in *The Armenian Genocide in Perspective*, ed. Richard G. Hovannisian (New Brunswick, N.J.: Transaction Publishers, 1986), 61–84. Reprinted by permission.

ening and alien minority. In that sense it can be said that disaster and ideology estranged Armenians from Turks and made them available for extermination. The discussion that follows is divided into four parts. The first is a brief synthesis of some of the evidence pertaining to the Armenian genocide. The second critically examines the thesis that alleges that the genocide stemmed from the provocations of the victims themselves. The third proposes an explanation that includes the independent motives, the worldview, and the situation of the Committee of Union and Progress preceding the killings. The fourth suggests some parallels between the Armenian genocide and other cases, especially the Holocaust of European Jews.

The Genocide

Many scholars who are concerned with the Young Turks and the Committee of Union and Progress (CUP), which led the revolution of 1908 against Sultan Abdul-Hamid II and which directed Turkey from 1908 to 1918, would agree with Davison's judgment that although it failed in the short run, "In the long run, it not only transmitted to the future the progress made in the preceding hundred years, but also contributed to the institutional, ideological, and social development that underlay the emergence of the modern Turkish nation and Turkish republic."[2] In this essay, since we are not concerned with the salutary effects that the Young Turks might have had on Turkish progress but with their effects on the Armenians, it can be said without hesitation that the Young Turk regime, especially in its later phases, was an unmitigated disaster for the Armenian people.[3] Significantly, it was the Committee of Union and Progress, headed by Talaat Pasha, minister of the interior, and Enver Pasha, minister of war, that was responsible for the deportations leading to the genocide of 1915.

So many years after the tragedy, a detailed recapitulation of the genocide remains to be written, and one of the best sources in a Western language is still Toynbee.[4] Relying explicitly on that account, we shall briefly describe in this first section of our paper the course of events constituting the genocide of 1915. It should be noted, however, that there exists a sharp controversy pertaining to the motives of the actors, the extent of the destruction, and the actual course of events.[5] Within this limited space, it is impossible to resolve all such quarrels, some of which are tendentious in the extreme. Indeed, the best we can do here is to make note of the controversy and steer the reader to accounts that differ from our own. In the next two sections, however, we shall take up the controversy directly in the hope of clarifying some of the issues.

The killings began in the spring of 1915 with the deportation of the total Armenian population from the *vilayets*, or provinces, of the East to the Syrian desert at Aleppo in the south. Portents of what was to come, however, became apparent by February 1915, when Armenian troops serving with the Ottoman forces were disarmed, demobilized, and grouped into labor battalions. Concurrently, the Armenian civilian population was also disarmed, with each community required to produce a specified number of weapons. Indeed, the search for weapons became an occasion to destroy the local leadership. When community leaders were not able to come up with the required number they were arrested for withholding arms; when they did come up with the required number they were arrested for conspiring against the government.

The deportations were coordinated between Talaat Pasha's Ministry of the Interior, which was in charge of the civilian population, and Enver Pasha's Ministry of War, which was in charge of the disarmed labor battalions. On 8 April 1915, when the deportations commenced from Zeitun and other population centers, the Armenian labor battalions were rounded up by troops of the regular army and massacred.[6]

As to the deportations, these began with the killing of the able-bodied men and the deporting of the remainder. Toynbee summarizes the process as follows:

On a certain date in whatever town or village it might be . . . the public crier went through the streets announcing that every male Armenian must present himself forthwith at the Government Building. In some cases the warning was given by the soldiery or gendarmerie slaughtering every male Armenian they encountered in the streets . . . but usually a summons to the Government Building was the preliminary stage. The men presented themselves in their working clothes. . . . When they arrived, they were thrown without explanation into prison, kept there a day or two, and then marched out of the town in batches, roped man to man, along some southerly or southeasterly road. They were starting, they were told, on a long journey—to Mosul or perhaps to Baghdad. . . . But they had not long to ponder over their plight, for they were halted and massacred at the first lonely place on the road. The same process was applied to those other Armenian men . . . who had been imprisoned during the winter months on the charge of conspiracy or concealment of arms. . . . This was the civil authorities' part. . . .[7]

Except for Bitlis, Mush, and Sassun, where the total population was marked out for extermination by the army, presumably because these population centers were close to Van, the women and children and the surviving men in other population centers were deported.

As columns of defenseless Armenians were marched through towns and villages they would be set upon again and again, sometimes by brigands but more often by Turkish or Kurdish villagers.[8] The gendarmerie from the Ministry of the Interior, which was ostensibly there to "protect" the deportees, far from discouraging such attacks, joined in the violence.[9]

With the deserts beyond Aleppo as their final destination, Toynbee draws the following pattern in the timing of the deportations:

The months of April and May were assigned to the clearance of Cilicia; June and July were reserved for the east; the western centres along the railway were given their turn in August and September; and at the same time the process was extended, for completeness' sake, to the outlying Armenian communities in the extreme southeast. It was a deliberate, systematic attempt to eradicate the Armenian population throughout the Ottoman Empire, and it has certainly met with a large measure of success.[10]

An extensive massacre or genocide always leads to a controversy over the number of victims. Those who would deny it minimize the number; those who would affirm it maximize the number. Clearly no precise measures can be cited. To gauge the extent of the destruction, Toynbee estimates the predeportation population, the number who escaped the deportations, and the number who perished during the deportations.

If one takes the Armenian Patriarchate figures as a bench mark, the mid-nineteenth century Armenian population in the Ottoman Empire was 2.5 million. Presumably due both to emigration and massacre it became 2.1 million by 1914. Toynbee, however, is more conservative. Suggesting that the Patriarchate figures may be inflated, he averages these with the Ottoman census figures, which claimed that the Armenian population of the day was 1.1 million. This gives him a predeportation figure of 1.6 million (the average of 2.1 and 1.1).[11]

Toynbee estimates that some 600,000 Armenians escaped the deportations. Among these were 182,000 who fled as refugees into the Russian Caucasus, and 4,200 who fled into Egypt. Significantly, he points out that the Armenian populations of Smyrna and Constantinople were not deported, and nominally at least, Armenian Catholics, Protestants, and converts to Islam were also not deported. But, "It is impossible to estimate the numbers in these categories . . . for the conduct of the authorities in respect of them was quite erratic."[12]

Toynbee estimates that the number of refugees plus the populations of Smyrna and Constantinople who escaped the deportations was 350,000, and the number of non-Apostolic (Gregorian) Armenians, plus converts to Islam, plus those who may have escaped in hiding was 250,000. This gives him a figure for the number who escaped or were spared at 600,000.[13]

Combining the predeportation figure with the figure of those who escaped gives Toynbee 1 million Armenians who were deported.[14] Of these he estimates some 50 percent perished due to massacre or other causes:

A large combined convoy, for instance, of exiles from Mamouret-ul-Aziz and Sivas, set out from Malatia 18,000 strong and numbered 301 at Viran Shehr, 150 at Aleppo. In this case, however, the wastage appears to have been exceptional. We have one similar instance of a convoy from Harpout which was reduced on the way to Aleppo from 5,000 to 213, a loss of 96 percent: but in general the wastage seems to fluctuate, with a wide oscillation, on either side of 50 percent.

This should give Toynbee a figure of some 500,000 who perished, but this he revised upward and suggests a final figure of 600,000.

We can sum up this statistical enquiry by saying that, as far as our defective information carries us, about an equal number of Armenians in Turkey seem to have escaped, to have perished, and to have survived deportation in 1915; and we shall not be far wrong, if in round numbers, we estimate each of these categories at 600,000.[15]

Toynbee's description and analysis stops with the winter of 1915 and the spring of 1916, by which time the bulk of the Armenian population had been killed or deported. As valuable as it is, this work cannot take into account what subsequently happened to the deportees in 1916 nor can it take into account the Armenians who were deported from some of the major urban areas after 1916.[16] Thus, Aram Andonian's translator notes:

Three great massacres took place after 1916. . . . Men, women, and children from Constantinople and the surrounding district, from the Anatolian railway line and Cilicia, were driven into the desert, where they met people from the six Armenian provinces and from the shores of the Black Sea, but this latter contingent consisted only of women, girls and boys of seven and under, as every male over seven had been slaughtered. All these were the victims of the three massacres. The first massacre was that of Res-ul-Ain, in which 70,000 people were killed; the second took place at Intilli, where there were 50,000 people assembled, most of them working on a tunnel of the Baghdad Railway; and the third, which was the most fearful of all, at Der Zor, where Zia Bey slaughtered nearly 200,000 Armenians. . . . These figures only give the numbers of people killed by massacre. If we add to their numbers the victims of misery, sickness and hunger, especially in Res-ul-Ain and Der Zor, the number of Armenians who were slain or died in the desert will exceed a million.[17]

Leaving out further killings of Armenians such as occurred in Smyrna in 1922, after the conclusion of World War I and after the demise of the CUP, we are still left with close to 1 million people killed. This amounts to nearly half of the Armenian population if we take the Patriarchate figures, and more than half if we take Toynbee's estimate for the initial population. The figure of about 1 million killed is independently arrived at by Johannes Lepsius.[18]

Unlike the massacres of 1894–96, where the connection between Sultan Abdul-Hamid II and the violence had to be constructed on conclusive but nonetheless circumstantial evidence, in the case of the deportations the orders were clearly given by the CUP headed by Talaat and Enver.[19] Indeed when the U.S. ambassador, in trying diplomatically to intercede on behalf of the Armenians, attempted to separate the mass killings of the Armenians from the real intentions of the CUP, he was rebuffed by no less a figure than Enver Pasha:

> In another talk with Enver I began by suggesting that the Central Government was probably not to blame for the massacres. I thought this would not be displeasing to him.
>
> "Of course, I know that the Cabinet would never order such terrible things as have taken place," I said. "You and Talaat and the rest of the Committee can hardly be held responsible. Undoubtedly your subordinates have gone much further than you have ever intended. I realize that it is not always easy to control your underlings."
>
> Enver straightened up at once. I saw that my remarks, far from smoothing the way to a quiet and friendly discussion, had greatly offended him. I had intimated that things could happen in Turkey for which he and his associates were not responsible.
>
> "You are greatly mistaken," he said. "We have this country absolutely under our control. I have no desire to shift the blame on to our underlings and I am entirely willing to accept the responsibility myself for everything that has taken place. The Cabinet itself has ordered the deportations. I am convinced that we are completely justified in doing this owing to the hostile attitude of the Armenians toward the Ottoman Government, but we are the real rulers of Turkey, and no underling would dare proceed in a matter of this kind without our orders."[20]

Adding shading to an already sinister picture, no sooner had the Armenian population been physically removed or liquidated and replaced by a Turkish or Kurdish one, than all symbolic, cultural traces of the former inhabitants such as churches and place names were destroyed and eradicated. It was as if the Committee of Union and Progress had wanted to obliterate even the memory of Armenian existence.

In contemporary Turkey, as Michael Arlen remarked: "The Armenian connection" has been erased, "as though by an act of will."[21] It is not only the
extent of the destruction, it is this "act of will," this desire to wipe the slate
clean, that convinces us that genocide was perpetrated against the Armenians.
The question that needs to be raised is, "Why?"

The Provocation Thesis

A number of influential historians continue to argue that the
reason for the Armenian genocide derives from Armenian provocations, that is,
from the intolerable threat that the Armenians presented to Turkey and to the
Committee of Union and Progress. A most succinct and influential statement of
the provocation thesis is that of Bernard Lewis.[22] We have chosen to focus on
his explanation because it both attempts to be fair and is part of what has become
a classic study of the history of modern Turkey. Other explanations that rely on
the provocation thesis may be more verbose and more strongly felt but they are
not more convincing.

Referring to the rise of Armenian nationalism in the latter half of the nineteenth century, Lewis points out:

For the Turks, the Armenian movement was the deadliest of all threats.
From the conquered lands of the Serbs, Bulgars, Albanians, and Greeks,
they could, however reluctantly, withdraw, abandoning distant provinces
and bringing the Imperial frontier nearer home. But the Armenians, stretching across Turkey-in-Asia from the Caucasian frontier to the Mediterranean
coast, lay in the very heart of the Turkish homeland—and to renounce
these lands would have meant not the truncation, but the dissolution of the
Turkish state. Turkish and Armenian villages, inextricably mixed, had for
centuries lived in neighbourly association. Now a desperate struggle between
them began—a struggle between two nations for the possession of a single
homeland, that ended with the terrible holocaust of 1915, when a million
and a half Armenians perished.[23]

For Lewis, then, the matter of the Armenian genocide seems to be a clear-cut
case of two nationalisms in conflict. Armenians were a Christian, national minority living, unfortunately for them, on both sides of the Turkish-Russian border.
Like the other minorities of the Ottoman Empire they came to be caught up in
the nationalism of the nineteenth and early twentieth centuries. Hence, like the
Serbs, Bulgars, Albanians, and Greeks they might have been expected to want

to secede. Whereas the secession of the latter nationalities might have been a blow to the power and prestige of the Ottoman state, the secession of Armenia would spell its demise, for the Armenians lived in the very heartland of Turkey. Thus Armenians posed a deadly threat. Presumably Lewis does not advise genocide in cases such as this, indeed he refers to the Armenian genocide as a "holocaust" in clear allusion to the Jewish genocide and cites a figure of a million and a half dead, which one presumes to be based on the Armenian Patriarchate statistics. The problem with the Lewis analysis does not lie in its insensitivity to the moral issue. The problem with the Lewis analysis is that it moves too easily by analogy from Turkish nationalism to that of the Armenians and, paradoxically, argues for a historical treatment that ignores Armenian history.

Let us consider his assumptions one at a time: to say that there were two nations locked in a desperate struggle for the possession of a single homeland without adding qualifying remarks is to impute a level of equality of force and self-consciousness that is unwarranted by any evidence. Clearly, without knowing more about the situation, one would be under the impression that the Armenians, like the Turks, were in possession of a government, of an army, or of some other centralizing, directing agency representing a monopoly of legitimate forces. One would also expect them to be armed and in some way powerful. The truth of the matter is that the Armenians were not united under a single agency, even under a single political party, and they certainly did not have any army or a police force either to conquer the Turks or to defend themselves. Beyond an assumption of equality of power, the "two-nations-same-land" argument assumes that Armenian national sentiment was somehow symmetric or equivalent to Turkish national sentiment. That there was Turkish nationalism can be assumed from Lewis's work itself. That it had not as yet found its proper boundaries in the manner of Kemal Ataturk is something else again, but that it existed in the manner of Ziya Gökalp and that it had broken with Islam and Ottomanism are Lewis's major point. That such an evolution or transformation of identity and ideology occurred for the Armenians as well, however, is to beg the question, What was Armenian nationalism? How did it differ from fealty to the millet? What boundaries and powers did it claim for itself? And how did it differ from other nationalisms, including Turkish, in the disintegrating Ottoman Empire?

Finally, to state that "for the Turks the Armenian movement was the deadliest of all threats" is to be ambiguous in the extreme. What is meant? Is it meant that the Turks *perceived* the Armenians to be a deadly threat? Or is it meant that the Armenians were *in fact* a deadly threat? If the first is meant, there can be no quarrel. Talaat and Enver have themselves clearly stated that they feared the

Armenians as a deadly threat to the integrity of Turkey. Indeed, given the drastic situation of the Young Turks, where the secession of minorities was joined to military defeat on a large scale, one might assume that their perceptions and judgments were not clear. The question remains, however, whether their fear of the Armenians rose out of the actions and capabilities of the Armenians or whether it rose out of other sources including their own desperate situation and their newfound faith in Turkish nationalism?

In addressing oneself to the reality of the Armenian threat—Were Armenians the threat that the Young Turks thought they were?—it is important to make clear what time and which Armenians one is talking about. Two Armenian political parties, the Hnchakist and the Dashnaktsutiun, especially following the massacres of 1894–96, were in league with the Young Turks and therefore may have been a threat to the regime of Abdul-Hamid—a point that has been touched on elsewhere.[24]

As to being a threat to the Young Turks themselves, neither the Armenian population as a whole nor any of its parties was either a threat or seen to be a threat in 1908 when the "revolution" first broke out. Quite the contrary, Armenians took great satisfaction in the victory of the army and its CUP commanders, as well they might. The downfall of the sultan and the restoration of the constitution of 1876 was everything and more that they and their parties such as the Dashnaks had hoped for. Their long years of active participation in the liberal wing of the Young Turk movement had finally borne fruit, and Lewis himself writes of the enthusiasm of the hour: "The long night of Hamidean despotism was over: the dawn of freedom had come. The constitution had once again been proclaimed and elections ordered. Turks and Armenians embraced in the streets."[25] One assumes, therefore, that in 1908 Armenians as a whole and Dashnaks in particular were not a "deadly threat" to the Ottoman Empire and were not perceived to be such. What intervened that might have made them seem to be a deadly threat?

Though it is questionable that the regime should be blamed for the Adana massacres of 1909, where it is estimated that fifteen to twenty thousand Armenians perished, these massacres plus the increasing harshness of the CUP and the continuing insecurity of Armenian peasants in the face of Kurdish depredations did strain relations between the Young Turks and the Armenians. As one of the more careful scholars of the period notes:

> Armenian disillusionment sprang from the massacres of 1909, the so-called "Cilician Vespers," in Lesser Armenia for which the Young Turks must bear a goodly share of responsibility. More lasting troubles came with Kurd depredations in Greater Armenia. . . . Wandering Kurds or

Muhajirs had seized the lands of many Armenians who had been massacred or had fled in 1895. When some of the refugees returned in 1908,
the Kurds would not restore the lands. . . . From 1909 on there was what
the French vice-consul in Van described as real war between the two
peoples.[26]

The Armenian response was to ask for greater autonomy in internal matters
and for greater government protection against Kurdish depredations. The pre-
cariousness of the Armenian situation was taken note of by Russia, which in
1912 once more reopened the Armenian Question. Since Britain and Russia
had come to terms in 1907 by concluding the Eastern settlement, Russia once
more felt the temptation to expand her influence. Here it found some support
among the Armenian leadership in the National Assembly, which wanted to use
Russia as leverage against the CUP. Russian moves were checked by Hans von
Wangenheim, the German ambassador, but by 8 February 1914, an accord was
reached between the powers and the CUP that called for the appointment of
European inspectors-general in the eastern *vilayets* whose duties were in large
part to oversee intercommunal relations.[27]

One can only imagine the sense of humiliation and rage felt by the Turkish
nationalists at this proposed interference. Nevertheless, even at this late date, it
cannot be said that there ensued a "struggle between two nations." For the
Armenians were not struggling to destroy the Turks, nor were they even struggling to secede or to join Russia. As Davison notes: "The peasant mass was not
very vocal. Higher classes of Ottoman Armenians wished rather for a regener-
ated and orderly Turkey and thought that autonomy would be possible only
within Turkey and not under Russian domination."[28] Turning to the Dashnaks,
easily the leading Armenian party, which by 1907 claimed for itself a membership of 165,000, Davison writes: "Their program was essentially one of reform
within the Ottoman Empire. They did not believe that Russian occupation would
bring them more freedom."[29] On the contrary, continues Davison, they did believe
that "a complete separation of Armenia from Turkey was ethnographically and
geographically impossible." Indeed, as late as 1913 when the CUP had become
more authoritarian and intolerant, "on the whole Dashnaksouthium [*sic*] seems
not yet to have favored separatism or Russian occupation, but to have pursued a
policy of waiting and pressure for reform and autonomy."[30] If in the prewar
period Armenians came to be seen as a deadly threat, it was not necessarily
because of anything they did or did not do. The perception of threat did not
emanate only from changes in the object. Could it have been engendered by
changes in the context in which the object was perceived or in changes that the
perceiving subject experienced?

Provocation and Scapegoating

The provocation thesis argues that something in the actions or demeanor of the victim causes the perpetrator, the provoked party, to react with violence. The causal connection, though not explicit, assumes a flow from the victim to the perpetrator, from the provocateur to the provoked. If the Armenians had behaved differently, if they had acted less threateningly, the Committee of Union and Progress would not have decided on genocide in 1915. If there had been fewer Jewish communists, or bankers or department store owners, or journalists or beggars, there would have been no Holocaust.

The principal weakness of the provocation thesis is that it neglects the independent predispositions, perceptions, and actions of the perpetrators. It may be that Mr. A killed Mr. B because Mr. B taunted him, but it also may be that Mr. A killed Mr. B because he wanted to rob Mr. B or because A hated B or even because he mistook B for C. Indeed, taking a clue from gestalt psychology, we know that a perception of an object not only depends on the object itself but depends as well on the context in which the object is perceived and depends on the predispositions of the perceiver. Thus if A found B threatening it may be that A was paranoic or it may be that he saw B in a threatening context.

To argue against the provocation thesis does not at all imply that the victim was a pure scapegoat whose motives and actions played no role in the violence. It is to argue that both the perpetrator and victim and their relations must be examined for a complete explanation.

Turkish Disaster and Armenian Genocide

We come closer to the truth of why the Armenians were seen as a deadly threat, leading to genocide, when we move away from the intentions and alleged provocative actions of the victims and examine, on the one hand, the context of Armenian–Turkish relations, and on the other hand, the experiences and views of the perpetrators. Both the context of relations and the views of the CUP were drastically altered when between 1908 and 1915 the Young Turks were not able to stem further defeat in battle or the secession of minorities.[31] The retreat of the empire from Europe to Anatolia was nothing less than a military and political disaster for the Turks, but it was a disaster that had even more serious consequences for the Armenians. Not only did the retreat isolate this minority, thereby making it more conspicuous, it produced a crucial shift from Ottoman pluralism to narrow Turkish nationalism in the ideological perspective and worldview of the ruling party. These two consequences, we propose, gave rise to the view that the Armenians were a deadly threat to which a deadly response seemed appropriate.

Turning first to the disasters on October 5, 1908, some three months after the Young Turk revolution, Bulgaria proclaimed her complete independence, and on October 6, 1908, Austria annexed Bosnia and Herzegovina, which she had occupied since 1878. Due to the rapaciousness of the Great Powers and the weakness of Turkish arms, the empire was to experience still greater losses: in 1911, the Italians captured Libya, and the next year the Balkan states effectively eliminated Turkey from Europe.

Out of a total area of approximately 1,153,000 square miles and from a population of about 24 million, by 1911 the Turks had lost about 424,000 square miles and 5 million people. By 1913, when Talaat and Enver were already in power, the Ottoman government had lost all of its European territory except for a strip to protect the straits of Istanbul itself. As Feroz Ahmad has noted, "The significance of these losses is difficult to exaggerate."[32]

Of profound significance for the Armenians was the fact that the loss of the European provinces, in effect, destroyed the multinational and multireligious character of the Ottoman Empire. The Greeks and then the Balkan Christians had seceded, leaving the Armenians as the last of the great Christian minorities still under Ottoman rule. Moreover, the Armenians were not just any minority. Though they had experienced the full measure of Ottoman contempt for dhimmis and infidels—tolerance did not mean equality under the empire[33]—they had throughout the nineteenth century undergone a process of social, economic, cultural, and political development that has been called a renaissance.[34] It has been proposed elsewhere that it was this social mobilization that was a contributing factor to the massacres of 1894–96 under the regime of Abdul-Hamid.[35] Our suggestion is that the sultan's regime committed or tolerated the massacres not as a measure to exterminate the Armenians but to teach them a lesson, to keep them in their assigned place in the millet system, to abort their renaissance, and to restore an old order.

The coming of the Young Turks with their emphasis on renewal and modernization seemed like a new opportunity to the Armenians and they invested their energies in the new regime. Ironically and tragically for them, however, by 1912, as the new regime became increasingly less tolerant and more nationalistic, the very aptitude of the Armenians for modernization must have made them appear as a threat to the CUP.

In sum, the disastrous loss of territory and population that the empire experienced between 1908 and 1912 isolated the Armenians, made them more salient and exposed than they wished to be. Meanwhile, their ongoing social mobilization challenged Turkish and Muslim supremacy. But this was not all.

It should be kept in mind that after the Turkish disasters the bulk of the Armenian population was not located just anywhere in the remaining Ottoman regions. The great mass of Armenian peasants lived in eastern Anatolia, an area claimed to be the heartland of Turkey, bordering on Russia, Turkey's traditional enemy. Beyond that a sizable Armenian population lived across the border in Russia itself. Here there were parties that evinced irredentist sentiments. Even a benign regime devoted to pluralism might under these circumstances cast an uneasy glance in the direction of the Armenians. But, by 1912, certainly by 1915, the Young Turks were not particularly benign, nor were they dedicated to pluralism.

Had the Young Turks clung to the ideology of Ottomanism, which made legitimate the presence of minorities among them, military disaster and transformations in the geopolitical context need not automatically have produced a corresponding change in Armenian–Ottoman relations. But, as Lewis has noted, the Young Turks themselves, partly in response to the crisis of 1908–12, were to experience and help to engender a radical change in identity and ideology that came to replace Ottomanism with nationalism. Indeed, he begins his masterful work by noting:

"The Turks are a people who speak Turkish and live in Turkey." At first glance this does not seem to be a proposition of any striking originality, nor of any revolutionary content. Yet the introduction and propagation of this idea in Turkey, and its eventual acceptance by the Turkish people as expressing the nature of their corporate identity and statehood, has been one of the major revolutions of modern times, involving a radical break with the social, cultural, political traditions of the past.[36]

The point that he makes here and that he develops so ably throughout his book is that the heirs of the Ottoman Empire, the Young Ottomans, the Young Turks, Kemal Ataturk himself, had to preside over a major revolution in perception and identity as well as in politics in order to create a modern Turkey. It is my contention that the genocide of the Armenians, the first genocide of our modern era, was at one and the same time a product of this nationalist revolution and a stage in its development.

Ottomanism and Pan-Islam

To understand Turkish nationalism and how it might have helped to engender genocide, we need briefly to contrast it with two competing orientations that lost out. These were Ottomanism and Pan-Islam.

During the *tanzimat*, the nineteenth century reform period, when it seemed that the millet system could still be adapted to the exigencies of empire, the dominant ideology was Ottomanism, whose tenets were embodied in the reform constitution of Midhat Pasha.[37] Ottomanism had hoped to maintain the integrity of the empire by allowing greater autonomy to the minority millets and by introducing certain liberal reforms and rights that were to be used equally by all Ottomans regardless of religion and national origin. It will be recalled that under Abdul-Hamid, Ottomanism had to go underground where it found its supporters among the minorities such as the Armenian Dashnaks and in the liberal wing of the Young Turk movement led by Prince Sabahaddin. With the overthrow of the sultan, Ottoman liberalism and pluralism came into its own for a brief period, but its success was short-lived. It was abandoned by some of the minorities who preferred self-determination over its proffered autonomy and protofederalism. Above all it was undermined, as we have noted, by the crushing military defeats that pared the empire down to the Anatolian core. In a sense, except for the Armenians, these defeats solved the minority problem by excising most of the minorities from the empire. But by eliminating the minorities, such defeats at the same time undermined the very *raison d'être* for the doctrine of Ottomanism and gave rise to two competing orientations, which were Pan-Islam and Turkish nationalism.

One should bear in mind that Abdul-Hamid had already been unsuccessful in his attempts to preserve the empire by making appeals to Pan-Islam. After 1908, however, Pan-Islam once again came into vogue, but with the successful revolt and secession of Muslim nationalities, especially in Albania and Macedonia, the hope that Islam could serve as a basis for imperial unity was seriously undermined. Still later it was to be dashed by the Arab revolt. As Davison has noted, "The crowning blow to Pan-Islamism was the wartime attitude of the Arabs within the Ottoman domains." When the Arabs, on the side of Britain, began to attack their Turkish rulers, it became clear that "Islamic unity was a mirage, and Pan-Islam was worthless as a political doctrine."[38] Having abandoned Ottomanism and Pan-Islamism by 1914, the Young Turks increasingly turned to Turkish nationalism.

Integral Nationalism

Though it was to be Mustafa Kemal who would finally nail down the boundaries of the Turkish state, thereby defining the territorial and social scope of Turkish nationalism, in the first instance this ideology took the form of a rather nebulous doctrine, a kind of Pan-Turkism called Turanism.[39] According to this belief system, ardently adhered to by Enver Pasha until his end, all Turkic-speaking peoples share a common culture and should be unified into a political entity. Since Turkic-speaking peoples were present as far afield as the Russian Caucasus,

Central Asia, Kazan, and the Crimea, in theory Turanism aspired to a size rivaling that of the Ottoman Empire but without that empire's annoying minority problems. In practice Turanism had little chance of succeeding, but its primary result was to "increase a sense of Turkishness among Ottoman Turks."[40] By the same token it was to decrease the sense that minorities such as the Armenians had a right to exist in the newly valued entity.

As expressed in the thought of Ziya Gökalp, "the father of Turkish nationalism," and in some of the public statements of Talaat and Enver, Turkish nationalism had close parallels to the ideology of organic or integral nationalism enunciated by such figures as Herder and Fichte in continental Europe.[41] In its rejection of minority rights and individual liberties implicit in liberal nationalism, and in its glorifying the ascriptive and "primordial sentiments" of the majority group, it had certain affinities to *Volkism* and racism as well.[42]

Classifying Turkish nationalism under the rubric of "integral nationalism" does not imply that European movements and ideologies were imported by some kind of ideational processes unrelated to the very real political and military conditions of Turkey. Far from it. As we have seen, the Turkish crisis, especially after 1911, gave rise to a felt need for a new direction, a new ideology, and a new identity, which came to be satisfied by a homegrown nationalism. Indeed, in the case of Ziya Gökalp it was neither Herder nor Fichte who were influential, but Durkheim! More precisely it was Gökalp's reading of Durkheim and his adapting Durkheim to the political landscape that proved to be seminal.

It should be noted that when the Young Turk revolution first took power in 1908, in addition to the integral nationalism that was to succeed, there did exist another tendency, namely, that of liberal nationalism led by Prince Sabahaddin. That it failed in holding onto power set the conditions for the Armenian genocide; that it existed, however, indicates that this catastrophe was not a foregone conclusion in 1908.

Gökalp

To illustrate how integral nationalism came to be used in the Turkish context, it may be instructive to quote from Ziya Gökalp, about whom Heyd, his intellectual biographer, has noted, "He laid in his writings the foundation of the national and modern state which was eventually established by Mustafa Kemal."[43] Beyond his intellectual influence on Talaat and Enver, when the CUP took power Gökalp was a member of the Central Council and was designated to investigate the conditions of minorities, especially the Armenians. Heyd notes rather cryptically, "A considerable part of his suggestions were accepted by the Party and

carried out by its Government during the First World War."[44] In 1919, when the
Allied forces entered Constantinople, he was arrested together with other members of the Committee of Union and Progress. When he was placed on trial for
his part in the genocide,

> Gökalp denied that there had been any massacres, explaining that the Arme-
> nians had been killed in a war between them and the Turks whom they had
> stabbed in the back. He admitted, however, without hesitation that he had
> approved of the expulsion of the Armenians. The Military Court sentenced
> him and his friends to be exiled from the country.[45]

In trying to assess the consequences of Gökalp's thought, Heyd notes without
irony: "The Turkish Republic tried to achieve Gökalp's ideal of a homogeneous
Turkish nation. The majority of the Greek population was exchanged against
the Turks, and the bulk of the Armenians left Turkey gradually."[46]

According to the doctrine of integral nationalism, one familiar to most students by now, the primary units of historical and political action are not social
and economic forces such as classes, nor for that matter are they dynasties or
heroic personalities. They are nations. In all essentials unchanged from time
immemorial, such nations have their origins in a dim but glorious past, a Golden
Age. Since the beginning, the history of nations, and hence the history of humankind, is one of ceaseless struggle of one nation over another for power and
territory, with the result that in some cases nations become militarily defeated
—usually through inner corruption or treachery—wherein they run the risk of
being physically eliminated. But, their elimination, or rather their temporary
submergence, can also be accomplished by the stifling of the national culture
and the national language.

For his part Gökalp saw in the Turkish past, not in the Ottoman past, a Golden
Age that predated the coming of Islam. He gloried in the military exploits of
such "Turkish" conquerors as Attila, Jenghis Khan, and Timur Babur. He contrasted their times with the weakness and decadence of the present. He emphasized the national affinities between Turks and such ancient peoples as the
Scythians, Sumerians, and Hittites, among whom he found the same moral qualities that distinguished the Turks from other peoples. These were "open handed
hospitality, modesty, faithfulness, courage, uprightness. . . . Especially praise-
worthy was their attitude to the peoples subdued by them. Strong as was their
love for their own people . . . they did not oppress other nations."[47] He lamented,
however, that "the sword of the Turk and likewise his pen have exalted the Arabs,
Chinese, and Persians. He has created a history and a home for every people.
He has deluded himself for the benefit of others."[48] In a poem, Gökalp wrote,

We succeeded in conquering many places
But spiritually we were conquered in all of them.[49]

According to Heyd, Gökalp defined the nation as

a society consisting of people who speak the same language, have had the
same education and are united in their religious, moral and aesthetic
ideals—in short, those who have a common culture and religion.[50]

On the surface this definition is innocuous enough, but in the context of Ottoman pluralism, on the basis of religion, history, and descent it excludes Armenians as well as other minorities from the newly valued Turkish entity. "Greeks,
Armenians and Jews who lived in Turkey were Turks only in respect of citizenship but not of nationality . . . they would remain a foreign body in the national
Turkish state."[51] For Gökalp, as for all integral nationalists, the nation is not
merely an analytic construct but a basic principle of moral action. As Heyd
notes, "replacing the belief in God by the belief in nation," for Gökalp, "nationalism had become a religion."[52] Simply put, the good without limit is the good
of the nation and for its sake all is permissible.

I am a soldier [the nation] is my commander
I obey without question all its orders
With closed eyes I carry out my duty.[53]

Given Gökalp's identification of the good with the good of the nation and
given his exclusion of Armenians from the nation, it follows that he excluded
Armenians from his moral concerns. It should be noted that this kind of integral
nationalism was quite distinct from Ottomanism, which not only accorded minorities a place in the empire but also defined certain moral and political responsibilities of the ruling classes toward them and toward all millets. A once recognizable, if not valued, community under the old Ottoman regime, from the novel
perspective of integral nationalism, Armenians came to be regarded as a group
of strangers. In this sense it might be said that Gökalp's formulations aided in
the estrangement of Turks from Armenians and set the stage for their destruction.

That in the minds of Talaat and Enver the Armenians were fully a stranger
group beyond the moral ken can be seen readily from conversations recorded by
the U.S. ambassador, Henry J. Morgenthau, when he tried to intervene on behalf
of the Armenians. Thus when at the height of the deportations and the killings
Morgenthau inquired of Talaat why the supposedly disloyal Armenians could
not be separated from those who had remained loyal, Talaat replied: "We have
been reproached for making no distinction between the innocent Armenians and
the guilty; but that was utterly impossible, in view of the fact that those who

were innocent today might be guilty tomorrow."[54] In an even more chilling passage that reveals Talaat's attitude, Morgenthau recalls:

One day Talaat made what was perhaps the most astonishing request I had ever heard. The New York Life Insurance Company and the Equitable Life of New York had for years done considerable business among the Armenians. . . . "I wish," Talaat now said, "that you would get the American life insurance companies to send us a complete list of their Armenian policy holders. They are practically all dead now and have left no heirs to collect the money. It of course all escheats to the State. The Government is the beneficiary now. Will you do so?"[55]

The ambassador refused, but how astonishing was the change from the traditional Muslim and Ottoman view of the Armenians as "people of the book," as the "most loyal millet" who had a vital role to play even under Abdul-Hamid, to that of Talaat, in which the Armenians had become so alien that, even in death, their sole function was to be exploited for their money.

Lewis's insight that the idea "the Turks are a people who speak Turkish and live in Turkey" had profound consequences for Turks can now be expanded to include profound consequences for non-Turks, especially Armenians, as well. For a transformation of identity in the majority group implies a change in how this group views minorities. Once Turks became Turks, nationalists like Gökalp, Talaat, and Enver saw Armenians in a new, fresh light, not as an ancient millet but as strangers who did not belong among them. Moreover, these strangers were seen as part of a dangerous context: They were the last of the Christian minorities—the others had seceded—who still remained within the newly valued boundaries; there had been national stirrings among them; and in the midst of war, it was said that they favored the Russian side. No wonder Armenians were seen as a "deadly threat."

The genocide of the Armenians, we believe, should be understood not as a response to "Armenian provocations" but as a reaction to Turkish disasters and a stage in the Turkish national revolution. As many historians have noted, that revolution was successful in creating a new Turkey, but it came close to destroying an ancient people in the process.

Conclusion

In this conclusion we would like to summarize briefly the major points of this essay and to draw certain parallels from the Armenian case to other cases such as the Holocaust of European Jews.

In contrast to several historians who have argued that the reason for the Armenian genocide of 1915 derives from the provocative behavior of the victims themselves, we have proposed that in addition to inquiring into the activities of the Armenians, it is also important to consider the context of Armenian–Turkish relations and the motives of the Turkish state.

It was noted that the context of Armenian–Turkish relations was dangerous for this minority because there was an Armenian population on both sides of the Russo-Turkish border, because the Armenians were the last of the Christian millets that had not seceded from the Ottoman Empire, and because for more than a century preceding the genocide they had experienced a period of ethnic renewal and growing self-confidence. Taken together, these factors increased the saliency of the Armenians and made them seem threatening at a time when Turkey was on a collision course with Russia.

Such a context of relations may have led even a secure and pluralist regime to view the Armenians with some suspicion, but as has been pointed out, the CUP was neither secure nor pluralist. Quite the contrary. After a sequence of military and political disasters, by 1912 leading members of the CUP had become radical Turkish nationalists who rejected Ottoman pluralism and who came to view the Armenians not only as threatening but as alien. Hence, from the embattled and exclusivist perspective of the CUP, the Armenians had to be eliminated.

We would suggest that four factors preceding the Armenian genocide may be at work in other cases as well. First, the victimized group is a communal minority that was tolerated but was by no means considered as equal to the majority. Indeed, it was a communal group that had historically experienced some persecution and contempt at the hands of the larger society. Second, despite this history—or perhaps because of it—for some years preceding the genocide, the group that will come to be victimized adapts with relative success to the modern world and undergoes progress in the social, economic, cultural, and political spheres. This social mobilization creates new tensions between this minority and segments of the majority who find its progress to be both illegitimate and threatening to the old order, which was based on inequality. Third, the victimized group comes to be identified, either geographically or ideologically, with the enemies of the larger society and state. This identification may be real or may be imputed to the minority, but a link is established between an external and an internal threat. Fourth, the larger society and the state experience a series of significant military and political disasters that undermine their security and worldview.

Together these factors allow for the emergence of an ideology that links the crisis of the state and the majority to the social mobilization or progress of the minority and to its outside connections with the state's enemies. The progress of the minority is seen as having been gained at the expense of the majority and the targeted group is blamed for the disasters engulfing the state and the larger society. In the grip of its new ideology the state radically redefines its identity and decides to eliminate the offending communal group from the social structure.

It is this fateful convergence of a minority's renaissance and its connections to the outside world with the majority's disasters, fear of external aggression, and transformation of ideology and identity that seems to us to be at the core of both the Armenian and Jewish genocides. Once the state has become convinced that a minority is alien and that it is a deadly threat to its existence, by administrative fiat or by legalistic means it geographically segregates the targeted group and disintegrates it from the social structure. By means of propaganda and reeducation it supplants a worldview that was more or less tolerant of the minority with one that is chauvinistic and that blames the minority for the disasters of the larger society. Once the minority has been socially segregated and culturally alienated and the instruments of destruction have been readied, the state waits for an opportunity to eliminate the offending minority from the social structure.

It is no accident that the opportunity for both the Armenian and Jewish genocides appeared in the context of a general war. Wartime conditions heighten feelings of threat, permit administrative measures that would not be tolerated otherwise, and provide a cover from external interference and condemnation.

It is suggested that with some adaptation the process described above fits the Armenian and Jewish cases and may be pertinent to state-sponsored domestic genocide in general. In other cases in which a settler regime confronts a technologically less advanced or "primitive" people, where from the first the targeted groups are seen as existing outside the social and moral order of the perpetrators, the genocidal process may be simpler. In such cases, like, for example, the Achés of Paraguay, neither the state nor society needs to demolish a worldview that had once tolerated the prospective victims.[56]

NOTES

1. The term *genocide* was first coined and used by Raphael Lemkin in 1944 to refer to the partial or total destruction of a nation or an ethnic group. The concept recurs in the indictment of the major German war criminals at Nuremberg in 1945. Most recently and significantly the term has been used by the United Nations in its Convention on Genocide, which was approved by the General Assembly on December 9, 1948. An insightful discussion of the concept and of the efforts of the UN to apply the Genocide Convention

is provided by Leo Kuper in *Genocide: Its Political Uses in the Twentieth Century* (New Haven and London: Yale University Press, 1982). A trenchant critique of the too casual use of terms such as *genocide* and *holocaust* is provided by Lucy S. Dawidowicz in *The Holocaust and the Historians* (Cambridge: Harvard University Press, 1981). Yehuda Bauer suggests that the term *holocaust* be reserved for instances of extermination. In his view the Armenian genocide of 1915 is one such instance. See Yehuda Bauer, "The Place of the Holocaust in Contemporary History," in *Studies in Contemporary Jewry*, ed. Jonathan Frankel (Bloomington: Indiana University Press, 1984), pp. 201–24.

2. Roderic H. Davison, *Turkey* (Englewood Cliffs, N.J.: Prentice-Hall, 1968), p. 109.

3. For precursors and background to the Young Turks, see Serif Mardin, *The Genesis of Young Ottoman Thought* (Princeton: Princeton University Press, 1962); Bernard Lewis, *The Emergence of Modern Turkey* (Oxford: Oxford University Press, 1961); Feroz Ahmad, *The Young Turks* (Oxford: Clarendon Press, 1969); Ernest E. Ramsaur Jr., *The Young Turks* (Beirut: Khayats, 1965).

4. Arnold J. Toynbee, "A Summary of Armenian History up to and including 1915," in *The Treatment of Armenians in the Ottoman Empire: Documents presented to Viscount Grey of Fallodon, Secretary of State for Foreign Affairs* (London: H.M.S.O., 1916), pp. 591–653. For recent accounts that complement the Toynbee study, see Richard G. Hovannisian, *Armenia on the Road to Independence* (Berkeley and Los Angeles: University of California Press, 1967); Christopher J. Walker, *Armenia: The Survival of a Nation* (London: Croom Helm; New York: St. Martin's Press, 1980). For insightful attempts to set the Armenian genocide in a sociological framework, consider especially Vahakn N. Dadrian, "The Structural and Functional Components of Genocide: A Victimological Approach to the Armenian Case," in *Victimology*, ed. Israel Drapkin and Emilio Viano (Lexington, Mass.: D. C. Heath, 1975), and "A Theoretical Model of Genocide with Particular Reference to the Armenian Case," *Armenian Review* 31 (1979):115–36. For a discussion and critique of the Dadrian approach, see Kuper, *Genocide*, pp. 40–56, and Irving Louis Horowitz, *Genocide: State Power and Mass Murder* (New Brunswick, N.J.: Transaction Books, 1977), pp. 45–48. For a useful bibliography on the Armenian genocide, consider Richard G. Hovannisian, *The Armenian Holocaust: A Bibliography Relating to the Deportations, Massacres, and Dispersion of the Armenian People, 1915–1923* (Cambridge, Mass.: Armenian Heritage Press, 1980).

5. Among writers who disagree with the Toynbee description or interpretation are Stanford J. Shaw and Ezel Kural Shaw, *History of the Ottoman Empire and Modern Turkey*, vol. 2, *Reform, Revolution, and Republic: The Rise of Modern Turkey, 1808–1975* (Cambridge: Cambridge University Press, 1977); William L. Langer, *The Diplomacy of Imperialism* (New York: Alfred A. Knopf, 1935); and Bernard Lewis, *The Emergence of Modern Turkey*. For a critique of the Shaws' approach, see Hovannisian, "The Critic's View: Beyond Revisionism," *International Journal of Middle East Studies* 9 (August 1978):337–86. For a reply, see Stanford J. and Ezel K. Shaw, "The Authors Respond," ibid., pp. 386–400. See also Gwynne Dyer, "Turkish 'Falsifiers' and Armenian 'Deceivers': Historiography and the Armenian Massacres," *Middle Eastern Studies* 12

(1976):99–107. For a critique of Dyer, consider Gerard J. Libaridian, "Objectivity and the Historiography of the Armenian Genocide," *Armenian Review* 31 (Spring 1978): 79–87.

6. Toynbee, "A Summary of Armenian History," p. 640.

7. Ibid.

8. Especially in the eastern *vilayets*, some of the Muslim villagers themselves had been driven out of Russia. This is an important point because it might shed some light on the motives of these villagers. See Hovannisian, *Armenia*, p. 13, and Shaw and Shaw, *Reform, Revolution, and Republic*, p. 203.

9. Toynbee, "A Summary of Armenian History," p. 643. Consider as well the testimony of survivors such as Kerop Bedoukian, *The Urchin: An Armenian's Escape* (London: J. Murray, 1978), pp. 34–35. Compare such accounts with the following from the Shaws, *Reform, Revolution, and Republic*, p. 315: "Specific instructions were issued for the army to protect the Armenians against nomadic attacks and to provide them with sufficient food and other supplies to meet their needs during the march and after they were settled . . . the Armenians were to be protected and cared for until they returned to their homes after the war." It should be noted that this description is given without any discussion of disconfirming evidence, including that of Toynbee above.

10. Toynbee, "A Summary of Armenian History," p. 648.

11. Ibid., p. 649. In a private correspondence, Professor Alan Fisher of Michigan State University has suggested that the Ottoman census may have underestimated the total population of whatever group because the census counted number of households only. Thus the 1.1 million figure that Toynbee uses may be low, both because of the Ottoman desire to underestimate the size of the Armenian *millet* and because of the reasons cited by Fisher.

12. Ibid. That there were categories of Armenians who were spared the deportations and the massacres was a point stressed by Professor Yehuda Bauer in "Unique and Universal: Some General Problems Arising out of Holocaust Research," an undated mimeographed publication from Hebrew University. He used the point to suggest that the Armenian genocide was less inclusive than that suffered by the Jews under the Nazis. Later Bauer changed his mind, referring to both events as "holocausts." See Bauer, "The Place of the Holocaust in Contemporary History." Moreover, Aram Andonian, in *The Memoirs of Naim Bey*, (London: Hodder & Stoughton, 1920), suggests that a significant part of the population of Constantinople was not spared, and we know from Marjorie Housepian, *The Smyrna Affair* (New York: Harcourt Brace Jovanovich, 1966), that the population of Smyrna was massacred in 1922. Neither of these facts was available to Toynbee, who in his work was acquainted with reports no later than the spring of 1916.

13. Toynbee, "A Summary of Armenian History," p. 650.

14. Ibid.

15. Ibid., p. 651.

16. In his later works such as *The Western Question in Greece and Turkey* (London: Constable, 1922) and *Acquaintances* (London: Oxford University Press, 1967), Toynbee

was to repudiate some of his own denunciations of the Young Turk regime, and like Bernard Lewis, *The Emergence of Modern Turkey*, he came to see why the CUP felt threatened by Armenian self-determination. Nevertheless, he never denied the validity of his earlier findings: "In Turkey . . . in 1915 . . . the deportations were deliberately conducted with a brutality that was calculated to take the maximum toll of lives *en route*. This was the CUP's crime; and my study of it left an impression on my mind that was not effaced by the still more cold-blooded genocide, on a far larger scale, that was committed during the Second World War by the Nazis" (*Acquaintances*, pp. 241–42). For an interesting discussion of Toynbee's position regarding the Armenian genocide, see Norman Ravitch, "The Armenian Catastrophe," *Encounter* 57 (1981):69–84.

17. Aram Andonian, *The Memoirs of Naim Bey* (London: Hodder & Stoughton, 1920; second reprinting, Armenian Historical Research Association, 1965), pp. xiii–xiv.

18. Johannès Lepsius, *Le Rapport secret sur les massacres d'Arménie* (Paris: Payot, 1918; reprint 1966). Dickran Boyajian, in *Armenia: The Case for a Forgotten Genocide* (Westwood, N.J.: Educational Book Crafters, 1972), p. 287, and others dispute the 1 million figure and suggest that 1.5 million Armenians perished. It may be suggested that this higher figure reflects all of the victims from 1915 to 1923.

19. Robert Melson, "A Theoretical Inquiry into the Armenian Massacres of 1894–1896," *Comparative Studies in Society and History* 24 (1982):481–509.

20. Henry Morgenthau, *Ambassador Morgenthau's Story* (Garden City, N.Y.: Doubleday, Page, 1918), pp. 351–52.

21. Michael J. Arlen, *Passage to Ararat* (New York: Ballantine Books, 1975), p. 201.

22. Lewis, *The Emergence of Modern Turkey*.

23. Ibid., p. 356.

24. Melson, "Theoretical Inquiry into the Armenian Massacres," pp. 481–509.

25. Lewis, *The Emergence of Modern Turkey*, pp. 210–11.

26. Roderic H. Davison, "The Armenian Crisis, 1912–1914," *American Historical Review* 53 (1948):482.

27. Hovannisian, *Armenia*, pp. 38–39.

28. Davison, "The Armenian Crisis," p. 483.

29. Ibid., p. 484.

30. Ibid., pp. 484–85.

31. Ahmad, *The Young Turks*.

32. Ibid., p. 153.

33. Roderic H. Davison, "Turkish Attitudes Concerning Christian–Muslim Equality in the Nineteenth Century," *American Historical Review* 60 (1953–54):844–64.

34. Hovannisian, *Armenia*, p. 1.

35. Melson, "A Theoretical Inquiry into the Armenian Massacres," pp. 505–9.

36. Lewis, *The Emergence of Modern Turkey*, p. 1.

37. Roderic H. Davison, *Reform in the Ottoman Empire, 1856–1876* (Princeton: Princeton University Press, 1963).

38. Davison, *Turkey*, p. 117.

39. For works on Pan-Turkism and Turanism, see, among others, Ahmed Emin, *Turkey in the World War* (New Haven: Yale University Press, 1930), pp. 87–100; Alexander Henderson, "The Pan-Turanian Myth Today," *Asiatic Review* (January 1945):88–92; Gotthard Jäschke, "Der Freiheitkampf des türkischen Volkes," *Die Welt des Islams* 14 (1932):6–21; Jacob M. Landau, *Pan-Turkism in Turkey* (London: C. Hurst, 1981). For a discussion relating "Pan" movements to racism, and in the European context to anti-Semitism, see Hannah Arendt, *The Origins of Totalitarianism* (New York: Meridian Books, 1958).

40. Davison, *Turkey*, p. 112.

41. Salwyn J. Schapiro, *The World in Crisis* (New York: McGraw-Hill, 1950), pp. 134, 136–37; Anthony D. Smith, *Theories of Nationalism* (London: Duckworth, 1971), p. 16.

42. George Mosse, *The Crisis of German Ideology: The Intellectual Origins of the Third Reich* (New York: Grosset & Dunlap, 1964).

43. Uriel Heyd, *Foundations of Turkish Nationalism: The Life and Teachings of Ziya Gökalp* (London: Luzac, 1950), p. 29.

44. Ibid., p. 36.

45. Ibid., p. 37.

46. Ibid., p. 132.

47. Ibid., p. 113.

48. Ibid., p. 111.

49. Ibid.

50. Ibid., p. 63.

51. Ibid., p. 132.

52. Ibid., p. 57.

53. Ibid., p. 124.

54. Morgenthau, *Ambassador Morgenthau's Story*, p. 336.

55. Ibid., p. 339.

56. Eric R. Wolf, "Killing the Achés," in *Genocide in Paraguay*, ed. Richard Arens (Philadelphia: Temple University Press, 1976.)

THE USSR UNDER STALIN

The infamous rule of Stalin is a very special case, particularly from the point of view of documentation. Very tight control over all forms of communication is being exercised in the Soviet Union and facts are periodically altered to fit the prevailing political line. Most of the primary material has never been opened up for research purposes. Much of the Russian material that has become available in the West is also available in translation. A large part of the available data comes from expatriate Russians, the major exceptions being the limited materials that became available after the Twentieth Congress of the Communist party in 1956. One hopes that *glasnost* under Mikhail Gorbachev will in the future provide greater access to the relevant materials.

In the first selection, the historian Robert Conquest summarizes the long-neglected history of the man-made famine in the Ukraine and the human costs of Stalin's dekulakization drive. Conquest's essay also highlights the persistent hostility to the peasantry embedded in the Soviet Marxist tradition, a factor that helps to explain the behavior of Stalin and his officials.

The excerpts from Khrushchev's secret report to the twentieth party congress are particularly interesting because they provide an insider's view of Stalin's regime. Khrushchev comments on Stalin's invention of a pseudo-group of victims — "enemies of the people." The chief advantage of this category to Stalin lay in its infinitely expandable boundaries, which could be stretched to include anyone from a political rival to randomly chosen scapegoats for economic failures. Khrushchev also describes the methods by which confessions were extorted and points to some of the real groups that were victimized: the military and party elites and some nationalities.

It was also after the time of the party congress that Antonov-Ovseyenko was able to gather much of his evidence. We are using selections from his book not only because they represent another view from the inside, but also because he is one of those authors who shows that the terror was often not random, but was frequently directed at well-defined groups.

We shall probably never know the exact number of Stalin's victims in the Great Purge, but we include Robert Conquest's brief attempt to estimate them because it gives some idea of the available information and the difficulties of using it.

The Soviet Union presents us with several different cases of genocide and massacre for analysis; not all of them are discussed in these readings. While they offer an opportunity for comparative analysis, access to sufficient data represents a real challenge. (Legters, 1984)

NO GRAIN OF PITY†

Just over fifty years ago the Ukraine and its neighboring areas, the Don, the Volga, and the Kuban—a great stretch of territory inhabited by about forty million people—resembled a vast Belsen. One-quarter of the rural population lay dead or dying, the rest in various stages of debilitation with no strength to bury their families or neighbors. As at Belsen, well-fed squads of police and government officials supervised the victims.

This was the climax of the "revolution from above," as Josef Stalin put it, in which the Soviet leader and his associates crushed two elements seen as irremediably hostile to the regime: the Soviet peasantry as a whole and the Ukrainian nation in particular.

Stalin's campaign had begun in 1929. Although the Ukraine was under Communist control, the population was unreconciled to the system. Historically, Ukrainians are an ancient nation which has survived through terrible calamities. They have their own language, their own culture, and a cementing history of persecution.

By 1929, having outwitted and crushed the right wing of the Communist party, Stalin was at last ready to give effect to his hostility against what he saw as centrifugal tendencies in the countryside. He began with a double blow: dekulakization and collectivization.

Vladimir Ilyich Lenin, the father of the Soviet Union, envisioned the kulak —literally, "fist"—as a rich, exploiting class against whom, after the removal of the landlords proper, peasant hatred could be equally directed. A kulak was a village money-lender and mortgager, of whom there was usually one in a village or group of villages. Any rich peasant might make an occasional loan, indeed, would be expected to. Only when money-lending became a major source of income and of manipulation was he seen as a kulak by the villagers.

In practice, then, dekulakization meant the killing or deportation to the Arctic of millions of peasants with their families—in principle the better-off, in practice the most influential and most resistant to the party's plan.

†From Robert Conquest, *Harvest of Sorrow*. Copyright © 1986 by Robert Conquest. Reprinted by permission of the author.

Collectivization, the second measure, meant the effective abolition of private property in land, and the concentration of the remaining peasantry in collective farms under party control.

Stalin seems to have realized that only a mass terror throughout the body of the nation—that is, the peasantry—could really reduce the country to submission. In 1932–33, accompanied by an attack on all Ukrainian cultural and intellectual centres and leaders, as well as on the Ukrainian churches, came what may be described as a terror-famine. It was inflicted on the collectivized peasants by setting grain quotas far above the possible, while removing every handful of food and preventing outside help—even from other areas of the Soviet Union—from reaching the starving.

Nationalism was blamed explicitly for the supposed contumacy of the Ukrainian peasants in not surrendering grain they did not have, all of which was in accord with Stalin's dictum that the national problem was in essence a peasant problem. In fact, one of the aims of collectivization in the Ukraine had been stated officially as "the destruction of Ukrainian nationalism's social base—the individual land-holdings." The Ukrainian peasant thus suffered in double guise, as a peasant and as a Ukrainian.

In normal circumstances, the Ukraine and the North Caucasus provided half the Soviet Union's total marketable grain. In the good harvest of 1930, the Ukraine's share was 7.7 million tons (33 percent). In 1931, the same 7.7 million tons was demanded of the Ukraine out of a harvest of only 18.3 million tons: that is, 42 percent. Only 7 million tons were actually collected. Thus, what amounted to a famine was affecting the Ukraine in the late spring of 1932.

In July of that year, the vital decisions were taken that led to the holocaust of the next eight months. Stalin again ordered a delivery target of 7.7 million tons out of a total harvest that collectivization and poor weather had reduced to 14.7 million tons, two-thirds of that of 1930. It was obvious that the proposed levels of requisition were not merely excessive but impossible. After considerable argument, the Ukrainians managed to get the figure reduced to 6.6 million tons, but this too was far beyond the feasible.

The position was bad in July 1932, but it was to grow worse. The first procurements were carried out in August, and in many areas, by great effort, the targets were met. This virtually exhausted the countryside. From then on, the inhabitants of the twenty thousand villages of the Ukraine awaited an even more menacing future.

On October 12, 1932, two senior Russian apparatchiks—A. Akulov, who had been deputy head of the OGPU (Stalin's secret police), and M. M. Khatayevich, who had been prominent in Stalin's collectivization of the Volga

—were sent from Moscow to strengthen the local party. At the same time, a second procurement was announced, though there was now almost nothing available.

By November 1, the delivery plan had been fulfilled only to the level of 41 percent and people were already dying. Far from relaxing its demands, Moscow launched into a crescendo of terror by hunger.

A decree passed the previous August had ordered that all collective farm property such as cattle and grain should henceforth be considered state property, "sacred and inviolable." Those guilty of offences against the decree were to be considered enemies of the people, to be shot unless there were extenuating circumstances, in which case the penalty must be imprisonment for not less than ten years, with confiscation of property.

One peasant was shot for possession of twenty-five pounds of wheat, gleaned in a field by his ten-year-old daughter. A woman was sentenced to ten years for cutting one hundred ears of ripening corn from her own plot a fortnight after her husband had died of starvation. In the village of Mala Lepetykha, peasants were shot for eating a buried horse.

Some party activists, even ones with bad personal records, tried to get fair treatment for the peasantry. One activist explained: "In some cases they would be merciful and leave some potatoes, peas, corn for feeding the family, but the stricter ones would take not only the food and livestock, but 'all valuables and surpluses of clothing,' including icons from their frames, samovars, painted carpets and even metal kitchen utensils that might be silver—and any money they found stashed away."

In the larger villages, where such things could be better concealed, women would be procured for the party officials by their need for food. At the district level, there was even luxury. A dining hall for party officials in Pehrybyshcha is described: "Day and night it was guarded by militia keeping the starving peasants and their children away from the restaurant. . . . In the dining room, at very low prices, white bread, meat, poultry, canned fruit and delicacies, wines and sweets were served to the district bosses. . . . Around these oases, famine and death were raging."

In many areas, brigades would now make complete formal searches every couple of weeks, and not to be in a starving state was to be the object of suspicion. The activists would then make an especially careful search, assuming some food had been hidden.

One activist, after searching the house of a peasant who had failed to swell up, finally found a small bag of flour mixed with ground bark and leaves, which he then poured into the village pond. There are a number of reports of brutal

brigadiers who insisted on carrying the dying as well as the dead to the cemetery to avoid the extra trip, and of children and old people lying in mass graves,
still alive, for several days.

But one activist recalls: "With the rest of my generation, I believed firmly
that these ends justified the means. Our great goal was the universal triumph
of communism, and for the sake of that goal everything was permissible—
to lie, to steal, to destroy hundreds of thousands and even millions of people,
all those who were hindering our work or could hinder it, everyone who stood
in the way. With the others I emptied out the old folks' storage chests, stop-
ping my ears to the children's crying and the women's wails. For I was convinced that I was accomplishing the great and necessary transformation of the
countryside."

As the winter of 1932 wore on, famine in the Ukraine countryside grew
steadily worse. On November 20, a government decree withheld the distribution of any grain at all to the peasants in payment for their work on collective
farms until Stalin's grain delivery quota had been met.

Villages that could not meet the demands were literally blockaded. A month
later, a list was published of whole districts "to which supplies of commercial
products have been halted until they achieve a decisive improvement in fulfillment
of grain collective plans." Inhabitants of these blockaded districts were deported
en masse to the north.

As the government's brigades of thugs and idealists probed houses and yards
for grain in the later months of 1932, the peasants invented methods of finding
and preserving something to eat.

There were public attacks on hiding grain in the straw by inadequate thresh-
ing, which took place on a number of collective farms. If the peasant took this
grain to the local nationalized mill, it would go to the government, so local
artisans built hand mills. Party newspapers reported that they were discovered
by the hundred—two hundred in one district, seventy-five in one month in
another. When they were found, maker and user were both arrested. With or
without such implements, extraordinary "bread" was made—for example,
sunflower oil cake soaked in water, with millet and buckwheat chaff and a little
rye flour to hold it together.

There were local rebellions in the Ukraine throughout the winter and spring.
The peasants were usually infuriated into revolt because there was grain available often within miles of where they starved. Not all the grain was exported or
sent to the cities or the army. Local granaries held reserves for emergencies such
as war: the famine itself was not sufficient occasion for their release. Food
available on the spot but denied to the starving constituted an unbearable
provocation—particularly when grain and potatoes were piled up in the open

and left to rot. In the Lubotino area, several thousand tons were held in a field surrounded by barbed wire. When they began to go bad, they were transferred from the Potato Trust to the Alcohol Trust, but were left in the fields until they were useless even for that.

At the height of the famine in the spring of 1933, peasants in Mikolaiv province attacked an already-rotting dump of grain and were machine-gunned by the guards of OGPU. In Poltava province, villagers looted a grain warehouse but some, too weak to carry the corn home, died on the way back, and the rest were arrested next day. Many were shot, the rest given sentences between five and ten years.

At the beginning of 1933, a third grain levy was announced and a further assault on the now nonexistent reserves of the Ukrainian peasantry took place. People had been dying throughout the winter, but death on a mass scale really began early in March 1933.

"People had swollen faces and legs and stomachs . . . and now they ate anything at all," one observer wrote. "They caught mice, rats, sparrows, ants, earthworms. They ground up bones into flour, and did the same with leather and shoe soles; they cut up old skins and furs to make noodles of a kind, and they cooked glue. And when the grass came up, they began to dig up the roots and eat the leaves and the buds; they used everything there was: dandelions, and burdock, and bluebells, and willowroot, and sedums and nettles."

Murder became commonplace. In the village of Bilka, Denys Ischenko killed his sister, his brother-in-law, and their sixteen-year-old daughter in order to obtain their thirty pounds of flour. Ischenko also murdered his friend Petro Korobeynyk, who was carrying four loaves of bread he somehow had obtained in the city. There are innumerable reports of suicide, almost invariably by hanging; mothers frequently put their children out of their misery.

The most horrifying result was cannibalism. "Some went insane," wrote novelist Vasily Grossman. "There were people who cut up and cooked corpses, who killed their own children and ate them. I saw one. She had been brought to the district centre under convoy. Her face was human, but her eyes were those of a wolf. These are cannibals, they said, and must be shot."

But not all were shot. In the late 1930s, 325 of the cannibals—75 men and 250 women—were reported to be still serving life sentences in Baltic-White Sea Canal prison camps.

Driven by desperation, large numbers of those who could still move left their villages. If they could not reach the cities, they hung around the railway stations. If unable to reach the stations, they went to the railway lines and begged bread from the passing trains. Even skilled workers in Ukrainian cities found themselves existing on black bread, potatoes, and salt fish. As early as the summer of 1932, Kiev office workers' daily bread ration of 1 pound had been cut in half, while industrial workers' rations were reduced from 2 pounds to 1-½ pounds.

At the bread shops, there were lineups more than four hundred meters long, the people so weak that they were able to stand only by holding on to the belt of the person in front. Each would receive from less than a pound of bread to less than half a pound of bread, the last few hundred perhaps getting nothing but tickets or chalked numbers on their hands to present the next day.

The peasants flocked to the cities to join these lineups, to buy from those who had managed to get bread, or simply under a vaguely understood compulsion. Although road blocks and controls were set up to keep them out, many managed to get through. In the towns, eerie scenes took place. People hurried about their affairs in the normal way, although "there were starving children, old men, girls, crawling about them on all fours," hardly able to beg, mainly ignored.

In Kiev, Kharkov, Dnipropetrovsk, and Odessa it became routine for the local authorities to go round the town in the early morning clearing the corpses. In 1933, about 150 dead bodies a day were gleaned in the streets of Poltava.

The Soviet intelligentsia generally took two contrary views of the peasantry. On one hand, they were the People incarnate, the soul of the country, suffering, patient, the hope of the future. On the other, they appeared as the "dark people," backward, mulish, deaf to argument, an oafish impediment to progress. There were elements of truth in both views, and some of the country's clearest minds saw this. In the nineteenth century, writer Alexander Pushkin praised a peasant's many good qualities, such as industry and tolerance. Soviet memorist Nikitenko called him "almost a perfect savage" and a drunkard and a thief into the bargain, but added that he was nevertheless "incomparably superior to the so-called educated and intellectual. The muzhik [peasant] is sincere. He does not try to seem what he is not."

Philosopher Alexander Herzen held, if rather sanguinely, that intermuzhik agreements needed no documents and were rarely broken. In the peasant's relationship to the authorities, on the other hand, his weapon was deceit and subterfuge, the only means available to him—and he continued to use it in Communist times, as can be seen in the work of all schools of Soviet writers from Mikhail Sholokhov to Alexander Solzhenitsyn.

But for the Utopian intellectual, it was one or the other, devil or angel. The young radicals of the 1870s, by the thousands, "went to the people"—stayed for months in the villages and tried to enlist the peasants in a socialist and revolutionary program. This was a complete failure, producing negative effects on both sides. Bazarov, the hero of Ivan Turgenev's *Fathers and Sons,* gives some of the feeling: "I felt such hatred for this poorest peasant, this Philip of Sidor, for whom I'm to be ready to jump out of my skin, and who won't even thank me for it." Even Bazarov didn't suspect that in the peasants' eyes, he was "something of a buffooning clown."

It would not be true to say that all the intelligentsia suffered this revulsion, and early in the next century the Socialist Revolutionary Party took up the peasant cause in a more sophisticated manner. Marxism, meanwhile, had won over a large section of the radicals, and they were given an ideological reason for dismissing the peasantry as the hope of Russia. This change of view was, of course, little more than a transfer of hopes and illusions from an imaginary peasant to an almost equally imaginary proletarian.

But as regards the "backward" peasantry, one now finds expressions of hatred and contempt among the Marxist, and especially among the Bolshevik, intellectuals going far beyond Marxist theoretical disdain; and one can hardly dismiss this accounting for the events that followed the October Revolution.

The townsman, particularly the Marxist townsman, was not even consistent in his view of what was wrong with the peasantry, seeing them as varying between "apathetic" and "stupidly greedy and competitive." Playwright and social critic Maxim Gorky, giving a view shared by many, felt that "the fundamental obstacle in the way of Russian progress toward Westernization and culture" lay in the "deadweight of illiterate village life which stifles the town," and he denounced "the animal-like individualism of the peasantry and the peasant's almost total lack of social consciousness." He also expressed the hope that "the uncivilized, stupid, turgid people in the Russian villages will die out . . . and a new race of literate, rational energetic people will take their place."

The founder of Russian Marxism, Georgi Plekhanov, saw them as "barbarian tillers of the soil, cruel and merciless, beasts of burden whose life provided no opportunity for the luxury of thought." Karl Marx had spoken of "the idiocy of rural life," a remark much quoted by Vladimir Lenin. (In its original context it was in praise of capitalism for freeing much of society from this "idiocy.")

Lenin himself referred to "rural seclusion, unsociability and savagery." In general, he believed the peasant "far from being an instinctive or traditional collectivist, is in fact fiercely and meanly individualistic." While, of a younger Bolshevik, Nikita Khrushchev tells us that "for Stalin, peasants were scum."

Josef Stalin had a profound grasp of what Adolf Hitler approvingly called the Big Lie. The terror famine with which the Soviet leader killed millions in the Ukraine and other regions in the early 1930s was the first major instance of the exercise of this technique of influencing public opinion. Every effort was made to persuade the West that no famine was taking place, and later that none had taken place.

Even in 1932 it was not feasible to keep all foreigners out of the famine areas, and a number of true accounts reached western Europe and the United

States. In most cases, journalists could not both keep their visas and reveal the facts, although Malcolm Muggeridge, writing for the *Manchester Guardian*, sent some of his reports sub rosa through the British diplomatic bag. "The battlefield is desolate," he reported,

> as in any war and stretches wider . . . on the one side, millions of starving peasants, their bodies often swollen from lack of food; on the other, soldier members of OGPU (Stalin's secret police) carrying out the instructions of the dictatorship of the proletariat. They had gone over the country like a swarm of locusts and taken away everything edible; they had shot or exiled thousands of peasants, sometimes whole villages; they had reduced some of the most fertile land in the world to a melancholy desert.

In the Soviet Union, no word about the famine was allowed to appear in the press or elsewhere. People who referred to it were subject to arrest for anti-Soviet propaganda, usually being sentenced to five or more years in labor camps.

In 1933, a soldier serving in Fedoslya in the Crimea received a letter from his wife describing the deaths of neighbors and the miserable condition of herself and their child. The local political officer seized the letter and next day had the soldier denounce it as a forgery. The wife and son did not survive.

One agronomist, bullied for sending a sick messenger, replied that the whole village was starving. The response was: "There is no starvation in the Soviet Union."

Writer Arthur Koestler, who was in Kharkov in 1932–33, reported that it gave him a most unreal feeling to read the local papers full of pictures of young people smiling under banners but "not one word about the local famine, epidemics, the dying out of whole villages. . . . the enormous land was covered with a blanket of silence."

Outside the Soviet Union, the denials were hot and strong. The Soviet Embassy in Washington claimed the Ukraine's population had increased by 2 percent per annum during the early 1930s, and it had the lowest death rate of any Soviet republic.

Stalin also was abetted by many Westerners who for one reason or another wished to deceive or be deceived. In the huge work *Soviet Communism: A New Civilization?* by Sidney and Beatrice Webb which followed their visit to the Soviet Union in 1932 and 1933, one finds a general hostility toward the peasantry matching that of the Bolsheviks. The Webbs wrote of the peasants' "characteristic vices of greed and cunning, varied by outbursts of drunkenness and recurrent periods of sloth." They also spoke approvingly of turning these backward characters "into public-spirited co-operators, working upon a prescribed plan for the common product to be equitably shared among themselves."

In a significant statement at the time, M. M. Khatayevich, a leading Communist, told a party activist, "A ruthless struggle is going on between the peasantry and our regime. It's a struggle to the death. This year was a test of our strength and their endurance. It took a famine to show them who is master here. It has cost millions of lives, but the collective farm system is here to stay. We've won the war."

With the "victory" won, however, Moscow realized that the disastrous agricultural situation could hardly be allowed to go on indefinitely. In February 1933, a "seed subsidy" was authorized for the next harvest, with 325,000 tons to go to the Ukraine. In the following month, the grain collection in the Ukraine was officially halted at last.

The debilitated peasants were now launched on a new harvest campaign. Neither they nor their surviving horses were capable of hard labor, yet the Ukrainian government called for harder work. The sowing of 1933 was accomplished in various ways. The inadequate local work force was supplemented from outside. Students and others from the towns were "mobilized" to reap the harvest, and army squads were sent to help. In one village, where the whole population had either died or left, troops were kept in tents away from the village and told, as others had been, that there had been an epidemic.

The central fact of the whole famine is that the Soviet Union's total grain crop for 1932 was no worse than that of 1931, and was only 12 percent below the 1926–30 average. It was far from famine level, but procurements were up by 44 percent. There was no way in which local readjustments could have prevented the crisis and the famine, and it can be blamed quite unequivocally on Stalin and the Moscow leadership.

There has never been an official investigation of the rural terror in the Ukraine and neighboring territories in 1930–33; no statement on the loss of human life has been issued, and archives have not been opened to independent researchers. Nevertheless, we are in a position to make reasonably sound estimates of the number who died.

The casualty rate varied considerably by area and even by village, from 10 percent to 100 percent. In villages of three to four thousand people (Orlivka, Smolanka, Hrabivka), often fewer than one hundred were left. Nowadays, the term *genocide* is often used rhetorically, but it certainly appears that such a charge can be leveled against the Soviet Union for its actions in the Ukraine.

It was the view of Nikolai Bukharin, a Bolshevik leader executed in 1938

Table 1. Death Toll Estimate, 1930–37

Peasants	11.0 million
Arrested in this period, dying in camps later	3.5 million
Total	14.5 million

Breakdown	
Dead as a result of dekulakization	6.5 million
Dead in the Kazakh catastrophe	1.0 million
Dead in the 1932–33 famine:	
Ukraine	5.0 million
N. Caucasus	1.0 million
Elsewhere	1.0 million
Total	14.5 million

during a Stalin purge, that the worst result of the events of 1930–33 was not so much the sufferings of the peasantry, frightful though these were. It was the "deep change in the psychological outlook of those Communists who participated in this campaign and, [who,] instead of going mad, became professional bureaucrats for whom terror was henceforth a normal method of administration, and obedience to any order from above a high virtue," diagnosing a "real dehumanization of the people working in the Soviet apparatus."

The main lesson seems to be that the Communist ideology provided the motivation for an unprecedented massacre of men, women, and children, and that this ideology, perhaps a set-piece theory, turned out to be a primitive and schematic approach in matters far too complex for it. Sacrifices of millions of people were made and they were in vain.

The events that took place in the Soviet Union in the early 1930s cannot be shrugged off as too remote to be of any current significance. So long as they cannot be seriously investigated or discussed in the country where they took place, it is clear that they are in no sense part of the past but a living issue very much to be taken into account when considering the Soviet Union as it is today. The present rulers remain the heirs and accomplices of that dreadful history.

KHRUSHCHEV'S SECRET SPEECH ON
STALIN'S CRIMES†

Stalin, on the other hand, used extreme methods and mass repressions at a time when the Revolution was already victorious, when the Soviet state was strengthened, when the exploiting classes were already liquidated and socialist relations were rooted solidly in all phases of national economy, when our party was politically consolidated and had strengthened itself both numerically and ideologically.

. . . . .

Stalin originated the concept "enemy of the people." This term automatically rendered it unnecessary that the ideological errors of a man or men engaged in a controversy be proved; this term made possible the usage of the most cruel repression, violating all norms of revolutionary legality, against anyone who in any way disagreed with Stalin, against those who were only suspected of hostile intent, against those who had bad reputations. This concept "enemy of the people" actually eliminated the possibility of any kind of ideological fight or the making of one's views known on this or that issue, even those of a practical character. In the main, and in actuality, the only proof of guilt used, against all norms of current legal science, was the "confession" of the accused himself; and, as subsequent investigation proved, "confessions" were secured through physical pressures against the accused. This led to glaring violations of revolutionary legality and to the fact that many entirely innocent persons, who in the past had defended the party line, became victims.

We must assert that, in regard to those persons who in their time had opposed the party line, there were often no sufficiently serious reasons for their physical annihilation. The formula "enemy of the people" was specifically introduced for the purpose of physically annihilating such individuals.

. . . . .

The way in which the former NKVD workers manufactured various fictitious "anti-Soviet centers" and "blocs" with the help of provocatory methods is seen from the confession of Comrade Rozenblum, party member since 1906, who was arrested in 1937 by the Leningrad NKVD.

During the examination in 1955 of the Komarov case Rozenblum revealed the following fact: When Rozenblum was arrested in 1937, he was subjected to terrible torture during which he was ordered to confess false information concerning himself and other persons. He was then brought to the office of Zakovsky,

†From Nikita Khrushchev, Secret Speech to the Twentieth Communist Party Congress, February 24–25, 1956. Reprinted from the *New York Times*, June 5, 1956, pp. 13–16.

who offered him freedom on condition that he make before the court a false confession fabricated in 1937 by the NKVD concerning "sabotage, espionage and diversion in a terroristic center in Leningrad."

(*Movement in the hall.*)

With unbelievable cynicism, Zakovsky told about the vile "mechanism" for the crafty creation of fabricated "anti-Soviet plots."

"In order to illustrate it to me," stated Rozenblum, "Zakovsky gave me several possible variants of the organization of this center and its branches. After he detailed the organization to me, Zakovsky told me that the NKVD would prepare the case of this center, remarking that the trial would be public. Before the court were to be brought 4 or 5 members of this center: Chudov, Ugarov, Smorodin, Pozern, Shaposhnikova (Chudov's wife) and others together with 2 or 3 members from the branches of this center. . . .

". . . The case of the Leningrad center has to be built solidly, and for this reason witnesses are needed. Social origin (of course, in the past) and the party standing of the witness will play more than a small role.

"'You, yourself,' said Zakovsky, 'will not need to invent anything. The NKVD will prepare for you a ready outline for every branch of the center; you will have to study it carefully and to remember well all questions and answers which the Court might ask. This case will be ready in four-five months, or perhaps a half year. During all this time you will be preparing yourself so that you will not compromise the investigation and yourself. Your future will depend on how the trial goes and on its results. If you begin to lie and testify falsely, blame yourself. If you manage to endure it, you will save your head and we will feed and clothe you at the Government's cost until your death.'"

These are the kind of vile things which were then practiced.

.   .   .   .   .   .

When Stalin said that one or another should be arrested, it was necessary to accept on faith that he was an "enemy of the people." Meanwhile, Beria's gang, which ran the organs of state security, outdid itself in proving the guilt of the arrested and the truth of materials which it falsified. And what proofs were offered? The confessions of the arrested. And the investigative judges accepted these "confessions."

And how is it possible that a person confesses to crimes which he has not committed? Only in one way—because of application of physical methods of pressuring him, tortures, bringing him to a state of unconsciousness, deprivation of his judgment, taking away of his human dignity. In this manner were "confessions" secured.

When the wave of mass arrests began to recede in 1939, and the leaders of territorial party organizations began to accuse the NKVD workers of using methods of physical pressure on the arrested, Stalin dispatched a coded telegram on 20 January 1939 to the committee secretaries of *oblasts* and *krais*, to the Central Committees of republic Communist parties, to the People's Commissars of Internal Affairs and to the heads of NKVD organizations. The telegram stated:

> "The Central Committee of the All-Union Communist Party (Bolsheviks) explains that the application of methods of physical pressure in NKVD practice is permissible from 1937 on in accordance with permission of the Central Committee of the All-Union Communist Party (Bolsheviks) . . . It is known that all bourgeois intelligence services use methods of physical influence against representatives of the socialist proletariat and that they use them in their most scandalous forms.
>
> "The question arises as to why the socialist intelligence service should be more humanitarian against the mad agents of the bourgeoisie, against the deadly enemies of the working class and of the kolkhoz workers. The Central Committee of the All-Union Communist Party (Bolsheviks) considers that physical pressure should still be used obligatorily, as an exception applicable to known and obstinate enemies of the people, as a method both justifiable and appropriate."

Thus, Stalin sanctioned in the name of the Central Committee of the All-Union Communist Party (Bolsheviks) the most brutal violation of socialist legality, torture and oppression, which led as we have seen to the slandering and self-accusation of innocent people.

Not long ago—only several days before the present Congress—we called to the Central Committee Presidium session and interrogated the investigative judge Rodos, who in his time investigated and interrogated Kossior, Chubar and Kosaryev. He is a vile person, with the brain of a bird, and morally completely degenerate. And it was this man who was deciding the fate of prominent party workers; he was making judgments also concerning the politics in these matters, because, having established their "crime," he provided therewith materials from which important political implications could be drawn.

The question arises whether a man with such an intellect could alone make the investigation in a manner to prove the guilt of people such as Kossior and others. No, he could not have done it without proper directives. At the Central Committee Presidium session he told us: "I was told that Kossior and Chubar were people's enemies and for this reason, I, as an investigative judge, had to make them confess that they are enemies."

(Indignation in the hall.)

He could do this only through long tortures, which he did, receiving detailed instructions from Beria. We must say that at the Central Committee Presidium session he cynically declared: "I thought that I was executing the orders of the party."

In this manner, Stalin's orders concerning the use of methods of physical pressure against the arrested were in practice executed.

.　　.　　.　　.　　.

Very grievous consequences, especially in reference to the beginning of the war followed Stalin's annihilation of many military commanders and political workers during 1937–1941 because of his suspiciousness and through slanderous accusations. During these years repressions were instituted against certain parts of military cadres beginning literally at the company and battalion commander level and extending to the higher military centers; during this time the cadre of leaders who had gained military experience in Spain and in the Far East was almost completely liquidated.

The policy of large-scale repression against the military cadres led also to undermined military discipline, because for several years officers of all ranks and even soldiers in the party and Komsomol cells were taught to "unmask" their superiors as hidden enemies.

.　　.　　.　　.　　.

All the more monstrous are the acts whose initiator was Stalin and which are rude violations of the basic Leninist principles of the nationality policy of the Soviet state. We refer to the mass deportations from their native places of whole nations, together with all Communists and Komsomols without any exception; this deportation action was not dictated by any military considerations.

Thus, already at the end of 1943, when there occurred a permanent breakthrough at the fronts of the Great Patriotic War benefiting the Soviet Union, a decision was taken and executed concerning the deportation of all the Karachai from the lands on which they lived.

In the same period, at the end of December, 1943, the same lot befell the whole population of the Autonomous Kalmyk Republic. In March, 1944, all the Chechen and Ingush peoples were deported and the Chechen-Ingush Autonomous Republic was liquidated. In April, 1944, all Balkars were deported to faraway places from the territory of the Kabardino-Balkar Autonomous Republic and the Republic itself was renamed the Autonomous Kabardian Republic. The Ukrainians avoided meeting this fate only because there were too many of them and there was no place to which to deport them. Otherwise, he would have deported them also.

(Laughter and animation in the hall.)

Not only a Marxist-Leninist but also no man of common sense can grasp how it is possible to make whole nations responsible for inimical activity, including women, children, old people, Communists and Komsomols, to use mass repression against them, and to expose them to misery and suffering for the hostile acts of individual persons or groups of persons.

.　　.　　.　　.　　.

It was determined that of the 139 members and candidates of the party's
Central Committee who were elected at the Seventeenth Congress, 98 persons,
i.e., 70 per cent, were arrested and shot (mostly in 1937–1938).
The same fate met not only the Central Committee members but also the
majority of the delegates to the Seventeenth Party Congress. Of 1,966 delegates with either voting or advisory rights, 1,108 persons were arrested on
charges of revolutionary crimes, i.e., decidedly more than a majority. This very
fact shows how absurd, wild and contrary to common sense were the charges of
counterrevolutionary crimes made out, as we now see, against a majority of
participants at the Seventeenth Party Congress.

THE TIME OF STALIN†

From the Author's Preface

The literature on Stalin published in the West is generally
unavailable to Soviet historians. I have had the good luck to read several basic
studies and some of the memoir literature from the West. My primary concern,
however, has been to present information that was previously unknown or known
only to a limited circle. In the case of first-hand witnesses or participants, I have
by no means named *all* my sources, or given the names of all authors of unpublished memoirs. For obvious reasons. Moreover, some information is not accessible to formal documentation or verification: many official archives are sealed,
and much evidence has been destroyed or lost.

However, nothing in my book has been made up. I have striven for truthfulness, and not only from a historian's sense of responsibility. There are no fabri-
cations in this book. What would be the need? The truth is horrendous enough.

In my portrait of Stalin I have tried to expose his criminal essence, to reveal
the gangster and hoodlum that he was. I may be accused of painting the picture
too darkly. But can Stalin and the crimes of his rule really be presented too
darkly? Perhaps the book will seem overburdened with bloody scenes from
those terrible times. If so, the reader might bear in mind that I felt obliged to
leave out many pages, even though they told of crimes that should be known.

Perhaps the author has not sufficiently restrained his personal feelings as a
survivor of the terror. I have heard such reproaches from my friends. But it is

†From Anton Antonov-Ovseyenko, *The Time of Stalin: Portrait of a Tyranny*, trans. George
Saunders. Copyright © 1981 by Harper & Row, Publishers, Inc. Reprinted by permission.

hard to be brief and "restrained" when you are trying to restore a canvas of criminality on such a scale.

My father, the revolutionary Vladimir Antonov-Ovseyenko, fought against the tsarist regime, took part in the October insurrection, and commanded several battlefronts in the civil war. He did not do this so that a filthy criminal could entrench himself in the Kremlin. Stalin murdered my father, just as he murdered thousands of other revolutionaries. My mother committed suicide in one of Stalin's prisons. I spent my youth in his prisons and camps.

It was late in life, terribly late, that I came to realize Stalin's true place in history, and in the life of our society. Once I learned about it, however, I felt I had to speak out. It is the duty of every honest person to write the truth about Stalin. A duty to those who died at his hands, to those who survived that dark night, to those who will come after us.

I understood that to remain silent about Stalin today is to betray. And I resolved to do my duty as a human being.

Moscow

May 1979

[On the Famine]

In 1921 the whole country came to the aid of the Volga region. Twelve million poods of seed and more than thirty million of grain were distributed to the starving villages from government reserves. The Soviet government readily accepted aid from foreign workers and bourgeois governments. Railroad cars with food from the United States, the gift of the American Relief Administration, arrived in the Volga region.

In 1932 the areas hit by famine did not receive a single kilogram of grain from the government. Stalin did not have on his conscience a single child saved from death by starvation. Not one.

It wasn't enough, however, to organize a famine. The gains had to be consolidated. Stalin began to *export* grain. In 1929, 13 million centners; in 1930, 48.3 million; in 1931, 51 million. And in the year when famine was everywhere, grain exports were still 28 million. Not a huge amount. But the very fact . . .

.   .   .   .   .

Millions of deaths by starvation lie at his door. Different sources give different figures—from three to six million dead. Altogether the campaign for forced collectivization, liquidation of the kulaks, and the Stalin-organized famine cost the growers of grain twenty-two million lives. Experienced Soviet statisticians arrived at this figure. We thank these honest specialists and place the figure against the Big Chief's account. We have yet to draw the final balance.

It is not hard to prove that this figure reflects the real situation. An important monograph was published in 1969, *The Population of the USSR* by A. Gozulov and M. Grigoryan. The authors give summary data for the Ukraine. The population declined from 31.2 million in 1926 to 28.1 million in 1939. Three million disappeared. But what about the natural increase? Let's call it 2 percent (which is rather low for an average yearly increase). This would give 600,000 a year, or about 9 million over 14 years. Adding the initial figure of 3 million, we get a total of 12 million. Where did those 12 million Ukrainians go? And remember, the famine that accompanied forced collectivization reaped its harvest among the populations of the Northern Caucasus, the Volga region, and Central Asia as well.

[On the Party Elite]

How did he treat the heroes of October, the leaders of the armed insurrection in Petrograd? In the forties Grigory Petrovsky was working in the Museum of the Revolution, one of a handful of surviving party veterans. Stunned by the deaths of all of Lenin's old comrades, someone asked Petrovsky: "What's going on, Grigory Ivanovich? Explain it to me. What's happening?" "Read the history of the great French revolution," answered Petrovsky.

The man who asked the question was fairly well informed, but he reread the history of the French revolution and compiled some statistics. Here's what he found: of the twenty top leaders of the French revolution, including Robespierre, Danton, Saint-Just, Couthon, and Barnave, seventeen were guillotined within a few years of the revolutionary outbreak. The rate of butchery for the French revolution, then, was 85 percent.

The data for the October revolution had to be taken after 1935. In the Russian revolution eighteen years passed before Thermidorian terror began. Some people, of course, managed to die before that. Others perished in the fighting during the revolution and civil war.

Nevertheless, out of the twenty members of the Petrograd Military Revolutionary Committee, which led the insurrection, only one came through the Stalinist terror unharmed. That was Nikolai Podvoisky, who was mentally unbalanced and incapable of holding a job. No one from the Moscow Military Revolutionary Committee survived.

Only one member of the Presidium elected by the Second Congress of Soviets, which proclaimed Soviet power and adopted the first Soviet government decrees, survived—Aleksandra Kollontai. Stalin not only destroyed Lenin's closest collaborators, such as Trotsky, Zinoviev, Kamenev, and Rykov, and all three members of the first Soviet government's Committee for Army and Navy Affairs —Antonov-Ovseyenko, Krylenko, and Dybenko—he also killed the leaders of

the Left SRs who were elected to the Presidium at the Second Congress of
Soviets—Maria Spiridonova, Vladimir Karelin, and Boris Kamkov.
Twelve members of the first Soviet government lived to see 1937. Stalin
wiped out eleven of them, and he himself was the twelfth. A 100-percent record.
This was an advance over the French counterrevolution. He achieved a substantially higher rate of butchery—95 percent, as against the 85 percent achieved
in Paris. (Meanwhile, we should keep in mind the 100-percent record in relation to the Central Committee elected at the Sixth Party Congress.)

The first and most immediate aim of Stalin's campaign was to eliminate those
who had made the revolution and defended it in combat. His ultimate aim was
to transform the party, bled white and paralyzed with fear, into the central stronghold of his personal dictatorship. The statistics on the various Central Committees elected at party congresses illustrate plainly the process by which he
destroyed the central core of party activists. I will leave out the earlier congresses
and begin with 1925.

Year	Congress	Number elected to Central Committee	Number killed in 1936–38
1925	Fourteenth	106	80
1927	Fifteenth	121	96
1930	Sixteenth	138	111
1934	Seventeenth	139	98*

*This figure was given by Khruschchev in his secret speech to the Twentieth Congress. Some Soviet
historians, including Roy Medvedev and Pyotr Yakir, have placed the figure at 110.—Trans.

On the average, three out of four were cruelly murdered. And what a group it
was! For example, out of the 121 Central Committee members and candidate
members elected at the Fifteenth Congress, 111 (or 92 percent) had joined the
party before 1917. The Central Committee delivered a steady stream of Lenin's
fellow fighters to the Lubyanka. There was no more regular clientele for the
Lubyanka torturers.

The Great Woodcutter not only selected the mighty oaks and pines to be
felled; he also attended to the underbrush. He was not too proud for that.

Nothing delineates his nationwide tree-cutting spree so clearly as the plain
black-and-white of statistics. These figures are taken from the reports of the
credentials committees at twelve party congresses.

The Eighteenth Congress was the only one the party came to with such
losses—300,000 Communists. That's how many were purged in 1934. How-

Year	Congress	Number of Party members (in thousands)
1918	Seventh	170
1919	Eighth	313
1920	Ninth	611
1921	Tenth	732
1922	Eleventh	612
1923	Twelfth	532 (after the party purge)
1924	Thirteenth	736
1925	Fourteenth	643 (after the purge)
1927	Fifteenth	887
1930	Sixteenth	1,261
1934	Seventeenth	1,872.5
1939	Eighteenth	1,589

ever, approximately two million new members had joined in the intervening five years. Thus, well over two million Communists disappeared between 1934 and 1939. These same statistics give us a no less important qualitative picture of the extermination campaign.

Invariably delegates who had joined the party before the revolution, or at least during the civil war, predominated at all congresses until the Eighteenth. The president of the credentials committee at the Fourteenth Congress, Konstantin Gei, reported that the number of party members with prerevolutionary records was declining on the average by 3 percent from one congress to the next, which in view of the age of these veteran members was a natural development. At the Fourteenth Congress he reported a decline of 3.6 percent.

Here are the data for subsequent congresses.

At the Fifteenth Congress, delegates who had joined the party before 1920 constituted 71 percent.

At the Sixteenth Congress, they constituted 82 percent.

At the Seventeenth Congress, 80 percent.

At the Eighteenth Congress, 19 percent.

The main blow fell on them, the Leninist cadres.

[On the Military Elite]

Stalin's war of extermination against his own people could not pass over the army, leaving it untouched. He feared the military command as a force capable of leading a rebellion. Quite often cowardice and ferocity are combined in the same person. Stalin's fearfulness, compounded by his suspicious nature, had prompted him long before to prepare to move against the army.

The operation had to begin in the summer of 1937, no sooner and no later. By then the people had been warmed up enough by the spy hysteria to accept it. Delaying the destruction of the officer corps meant risking everything that had been achieved. The mass arrests of veteran party leaders might shake the confidence of even the most loyal officers. It would be one thing if Gorky interfered (the "Stormy Petrel" had been removed in timely fashion), or Bukharin, or that hysterical old woman, Krupskaya. It would be quite another if the military leaders started to grumble.

.   .   .   .   .

In less than two years, Stalin sent virtually the entire high command and almost all the senior officers to prisons and labor camps. Later, General Aleksandr Todorsky, who himself spent many years in Stalin's camps, put together some figures. If you add up all the officers lost in wars by the various belligerent countries over the past two centuries, this comes to only half the number of officers murdered by Stalin. Lefortovo prison alone ground up fifty-three corps commanders in the course of two years—more than all the country's wars together. Of the five Soviet marshals, Stalin liquidated three—Tukhachevsky, Blyukher, and Yegorov. Out of four fleet commanders, he also liquidated three —Vladimir Orlov, Mikhail Viktorov, and Aleksandr Sivkov.

In October 1957, Marshal Malinovsky said, at a meeting of the party activists in the Ministry of Defense, it was as though the *Beria clique* had picked up a giant crystal vase containing 82,000 of the best, most experienced, and qualified commanders and political workers in the army and navy, and smashed it on the rocks. "On the eve of the war, we found ourselves decapitated," Malinovsky concluded.

.   .   .   .   .

True to form, Stalin interpreted the suicide of Yan Gamarnik, the head of the political directorate of the army, as the cowardly act of "an enemy who got entangled in his own web," and that is how it was explained to the people. After that, "without further ado," as the saying went, the entire top staff of the directorate, eighty-two people, were jailed. Nor did the Master forget about his beloved Red Army band. In 1937, the band musicians played in Paris. The leading musicians were arrested as soon as they returned home to Moscow, right in the railway station.

In early 1938, after liquidating 82,000 commanders (a mere trifle on the scale of totalitarian terror), Stalin could stop and catch his breath. He indicated to the few commanders who still survived (for how long?) that his thirst for blood had been appeased to a certain extent and that the mass arrests were over.

Pavel Dybenko, the commander of the Leningrad military district, was echoing the Master when he assured party members at the artillery academy in a meeting at the end of January that from then on the NKVD would not arrest any member of the military without a careful investigation. Dybenko himself was seized a month after this meeting. In a forty-eight-hour period, they arrested nine hundred commanders and political workers in the Leningrad military district.

. . . . . .

By the end of 1938, Stalin had not left a single proven commander alive.

CASUALTY FIGURES†

No exact numbers can yet be given of those who suffered in the Great Purge. In general Soviet citizens speak of "millions of lives" broken, of "millions of innocent people in camps and prisons." . . . The evidence will naturally lack precision until the NKVD archives are available for examination.

Nevertheless, there is much material which bears on the question. And without attempting to deduce from it a rigour which it will not at present support, we can list the main points which lead to the type of conclusion I have come to.

This can suitably be done under five main heads. First, the number arrested can be considered. Second, the number of these condemned to death, or at least executed. Third, the numbers in the labour camps. Fourth, the death rate in those camps. The figures for each of these depend to some degree on the others, but there is in every case a body of evidence directly bearing on the special point. Fifth and additionally, we can consider, looking back from the most recent Soviet census, the population deficit produced by the Purge. I have thought it best to give each train of evidence separately, and not make any explicit attempt to collate them. The extent to which they confirm each other, and the areas of uncertainty too, will be fairly apparent.

A. Arrests

1. We know from the Stalin-Molotov Secret Instruction of 8 May 1933 that there were at that time 800,000 persons in "places of detention . . . *not* counting labour camps and colonies", that is, prisons. All accounts

†From Robert Conquest, *The Great Terror*. Copyright © 1968 by Robert Conquest. Appendix A, pp. 525–35. References omitted. Reprinted by permission.

agree that crowding was much greater in 1937–38 than at any previous period: we can take 1,000,000 as a minimum, at any rate.

It fits with direct evidence from the cells. The Butyrka held about 30,000 prisoners. If we conservatively allow another 20,000 for the other Moscow prisons, plus those of the towns of Moscow province, that would imply a total in the whole country of 950,000: Moscow province, with about 9 million inhabitants, had about one-nineteenth of the total population. Moscow is, indeed, not entirely typical. Its high concentration of Party members and Government officials was particularly liable to arrest; on the other hand, ordinary citizens are usually reported to have suffered less than the norm, and in general these factors are believed to balance out. (Leningrad, with a province population of about 6 million, reportedly had some 40,000 prisoners in 1940.) A figure around a million might still be an underestimate of the number actually held in prisons proper at a given moment in 1937–38.

2. An estimate which has found much support is that the average prisoner, over the whole two-year period, stayed in jail about three to four months. This would give a total arrest figure for the two years of 6–8 million, if we accept an average jail population of only a million.

A complementary figure, given by an NKVD interrogator himself under arrest, is that there were 3,000 interrogators in Moscow alone. If they concluded a case a week on the average—not a heavy demand—this would be at the level, for the whole country, of 6 million for the two years of "political" prisoners only.

3. Dr Alexander Weissberg, the physicist, who was in the Kharkov prisons from March 1937 till February 1939, estimates that about 5.5 per cent of the population of the area feeding these jails were arrested during this period. Among other indications, a check was kept by following the numbers on the receipts given prisoners for their goods confiscated on arrest—money, braces, etc. But this was confirmed by other methods. (Avtorkhanov, a high official in the North Caucasus, estimates that about 4 per cent of the population of that region was arrested in 1937 alone, though he appears to grant that this is a higher figure than for the USSR as a whole.)

It has been objected to Dr Weissberg's figures that Kharkov too may not be representative. But Weissberg in fact compared the local figure with those made by prisoners who had done the same computation in other parts of the country,* and found that 5–5½ per cent was regularly reported. (Another prominent academic prisoner who conducted the same researches concluded that 5 per cent was a minimum figure for arrests.)

*As another prisoner remarks: "Every cell possesses at least one statistician."

Applied to the population total as given in the 1939 census,† this would mean about 8½ million arrests.

4. It can be estimated that during the most crowded period in the winter of 1937, over 4,000 men a week went from the Butyrka prison, mainly into camps, and were replaced. For the whole of Moscow province one might postulate 7,000. If the average over the two years was of the lower order of c. 4,000, we get a total for the two years of 416,000; which applied to the whole country would give just under 8 million as the total number of arrests.

5. In 1934, at the XVIIth Party Congress, there were 2,817,000 members and candidate members of the Party. Under the then regulations, candidates could not retain that intermediate position for more than three years. That is, by the XVIIIth Congress in 1939, they should all have been promoted—or expelled. The full membership in 1939 was 1,568,000, and of these c. 400,000 had not been in the Party at all in 1934. That is, there is a deficit of c. 1,640,000. About 300,000 had been expelled in 1934, when comparatively non-incriminating reasons were common. But the rest, including the 1935 expellees,* formed the first and hardest-hit target of the whole Purge. We can scarcely allow that a quarter of them escaped arrest. This would give a figure for party arrests of not far short of a million.

Another careful estimate is that about 850,000 expulsions took place in the eighteen months January 1937–June 1938, which accords with the above estimate.

The figure most commonly found of the proportion of non-Party to Party arrests runs at 7–9 to 1. This would give some 7–9 million arrests.

6. Other estimates are of the same general type. A Yugoslav estimate is that there were about 7 million arrests in 1936–38. An estimate by a responsible Party official is also 7 million arrests. In fact all our chains of evidence (treated,

†One of the difficulties is that we do not know what to make of the 1939 census. The census taken in January 1937 was suppressed, and publicly though vaguely denounced, for "gross breaches of the elementary bases of statistical science". The Census Board is believed to have been shot. But what it was that proved unsatisfactory in their results is unknown. An NKVD rumour had it that the total population fell far below what was expected and required (a figure of 147 million instead of the 170 million reported in January 1939 was bruited). On the other hand, the published total seems on the face of it compatible with the known and estimated population trends, and a quite different motive for the stifling of the 1937 figures—unsatisfactory social distribution—has been suggested. Even so, in the circumstances, we can hardly repose unreserved confidence in any aspect of the 1939 census.

*A typical description of the reasons for expulsion being that they were "*kulaks*, White Guards, Trotskyites, Zinovievites, and all other filth".

in general, somewhat conservatively) lead, though without any real precision, to some such figure.

B. Executions

1. Of the number of death sentences the impression of careful observers is that "they did not exceed ten per cent of the whole." An analysis of reports on 471 random arrests in the period 1936–40 (relatives of 2,725 Soviet citizens later defecting to the West) included 52 known death sentences—around 10–11 per cent. On the arrest figures we have, this would give c. 700,000 "legal" executions.

The Party official who estimates 7 million arrests suggests that the death sentences amounted to about 500,000.

2. We are told by a Soviet writer that in the Lefortovo, as early as August 1937, they were shooting seventy men a day. The rate for the first five months of 1937 must have been a good deal lower; but, on the other hand, things were worse over the winter of 1937–38. If we take a total of 40,000 over the two years, we shall probably not be far wrong. This would give a figure of around 800,000 for the whole country if all the remaining prisons in it accounted for twenty times as many executions, which seems conservative even allowing for the special circumstances of the Lefortovo. Then again, local NKVD branches in the provinces were ordered on occasion simply to execute a given number of "enemies of the people" in their hands, that is, not prisoners held by GULAG in camps, but by the local authorities in prisons. For example, a former NKVD officer reports one telegram of which he was personally aware, and which is doubtless representative of others sent regularly throughout the Union, such is its air of routine formality: this was from Yezhov to the NKVD chief at Frunze, capital of Kirghizia:

You are charged with the task of exterminating 10,000 enemies of the people. Report results by signal.

The form of reply was:

In reply to yours of . . . , the following enemies of the people have been shot,

followed by a numbered list. One order to the city NKVD of Sverdlovsk called for 15,000 executions. Another, to a small town near Novosibirsk, ordered 500, but the NKVD there could find only petty offenders available. In the end they had to shoot priests and their relatives, all who had spoken critically of conditions, amnestied former members of White Armies and so on—mostly people who would have ordinarily qualified for five-year sentences or less. One example of this type of massacre has become known in physical detail. Mass graves were discovered in Vinnitsa, in the Ukraine, in 1943 when the area was under German occupation, and were examined—like the Katyn graves—by an international commission of medical experts. The number of corpses, all killed by shots in the back of the neck, except for a few cases of braining with gun butts or clubs, was over 9,000. 1,670 corpses were examined. These shootings seem to have taken place in 1938. The identifications made by relatives give the latest arrests in June that year. The bodies were buried actually within the city limits in an orchard, a cemetery and a section of the municipal park. This implies a far greater likelihood of discovery than in the (presumably more natural and usual) selection of more isolated spots. The discovery was, in fact, made because various inhabitants had heard or seen suspicious actions. There is thus a presumption—as indeed can be deduced from Katyn—that other similar massacres remained undiscovered. (But we can also note in the selection of such sites that the NKVD in 1938 is shown as arrogantly sure of itself in its treatment of the population.)

The population of Vinnitsa before the war was about 70,000, and of the province about 1,000,000. If these 9,000 were the only executions in Vinnitsa, if they represented the entire province, and if the same proportion applied throughout the country, we get a figure of c. 1½ million executions. The same calculation applied to the (less solidly authenticated) Frunze and Sverdlovsk massacres mentioned above gives a countrywide figure of over a million, from these one-shot operations alone.

3. Very significantly to estimates derived from known death sentences, there was also a sentence of forced labour "without right of correspondence". No ex-prisoner ever met anyone serving such a sentence. Moreover, when the mass grave at Vinnitsa was examined, a number of relatives identified corpses whose sentence had been notified to them as of (usually) ten years "without right of correspondence". We can conclude that this phrase was no more than a method of concealing the execution rate. We have no means of estimating the numbers of deaths thus misrepresented. But the employment of this ruse was pointless unless it had substantial application, and one Moscow informant notes several out of his own limited acquaintance. An ex-NKVD officer says that it was quite a normal procedure.

4. Mass executions were also ordered at this time in the camps. These were almost always carried out somewhat furtively. Prisoners would disappear to special centres, and thus not be reckoned by their mates among the camp death-rate estimates. Genuine old Trotskyists, of whom a few still survived even in 1938,

were usually given a formal, if rapid, "trial", but this was exceptional. An account from the central isolation prison of the Baikal-Amur railway group of camps, where executions were entirely clandestine and without sentence, estimates that in the two years 1937–38 some 50,000 people were executed here in this fashion. In addition to such operations, death sentences for sabotage and anti-Soviet propaganda were routine in camp.

5. It will be seen that no exact estimate of total executions can be made, but that the number was most probably something around a million. One officer (of the central NKVD estimates about two million "liquidations" in 1936, 1937 and 1938. An official Yugoslav statement estimated, as we have seen, that the total "killed" in 1936, 1937 and 1938 was 3 million. These seem high figures and perhaps include estimated camp deaths other than by shooting.

C. Numbers in the Camps

We are not able to give exact figures in this field any more than in the others. But there are methods of estimating which are sound in principle and cannot give answers that are far wrong, if carefully applied. Though arising independently, they tally with each other. And the results are in adequate accord with those deduced at the other end of the process—the rates of arrest.

1. First, we have a set of figures, authentic in themselves, but needing interpretation, for the forced labour resources expected by the NKVD to be available in 1941. These come in the secret "State Plan for the Development of the National Economy of the USSR in 1941". The version available is incomplete. From its list of the amount of production allotted one can make certain deductions on the amount of forced labour in lumbering, coal-mining and other spheres. But it omits gold-mining, agriculture and certain other branches, and, in particular, gives no figures for the out-contracting in construction work done by the NKVD for other Commissariats, one of its major spheres. Professor Swianiewicz, in a careful and conservative estimate based on this, arrives at a total of just under 7 million. It should be noted that late 1940 was a comparatively low period for camp population: Wiles, estimating 8 million for 1939, gives 6½ million for 1940.

2. The second method is also sound in theory—that based on prisoners' reports. Dr Julius Margolin, for example, was imprisoned in several camps of the Baltic–White Sea group from 1940 on. He found that the group contained a Division 28, that each division had at least 10 to 15 sites, and that these held a range from a few hundred to a few thousand prisoners. A rough deduction gives several hundred thousand prisoners for the whole. (The true total is believed to

be about 300,000.) Obviously such individual estimates can give no more than a rough result. But when a considerable number of such reports are collated, plainly a very reasonable approximation can be attained. This was done, over the whole range of camps, by Dallin and Nicolaevsky in the mid-forties, and their conclusion warrants considerable confidence. (Many of the survivors of the c. 440,000 Poles sent to labour camps in 1939–41, and allowed to leave the USSR in 1942–43, gave useful indications.) Calculations so based give a figure, for the 1940–41 period, of 8–12 million.

3. There are various odd points in Soviet statistics published in the late thirties which have seemed to researchers to give indications of a possible labour-camp figure. For example, there is a discrepancy between the aggregate payroll for the whole economy and the total wage bill on the basis of official labour statistics, amounting to 18.5 per cent of the total payroll. Part of this is accounted for by the Army, but it has been estimated that 13.5 million involuntary workers remain after that has been done. These would include the large category of those doing "forced labour" at the place of employ, then a common penalty though a short-term one.

Again, the author of the most authoritative study of the Soviet population (Lorimer) was puzzled by a residue of 6,790,000 unaccounted for in terms of employment, pensions, Army, etc., plus just under 1¼ million labelled "social group not indicated". Similarly, an analysis applying to the 1939 figures the proportion of population to labour force of the 1926 census—a point not given in that of 1939—left a residue of 10 million.

Thus, those who take these approaches as genuinely significant can deduce from them figures of the right sort of magnitude. But the formal difficulties are great, and in none of these cases is it possible to say that the apparent anomaly is not accountable in some other way.

It is clear, again, that the 1939 census does *not* list the prisoners in the areas which actually contained them. Komi, for example, is given as having c. 319,000 population, half of them of the local nationality, and Magadan as a mere 173,000 (these figures are probably adequate to cover the free staff of the camp complexes, and their surroundings). Nor is it possible to establish whether or not the census contains the prisoners in any other way.

We must leave it that neither the census nor any other published Soviet statistics of the period have yet yielded any sound basis for an estimate; though it is worth noting that the expected population for 1937, as given in the preface, prepared in 1936, to *The Second Five Year Plan for the Development of the National Economy of the USSR* (English ed., New York, 1937), was 180,700,000, as compared with the census result of 170,467,000 two years later.

4. Other evidence is simply by report, but deserves consideration because it must often represent official leakage or at worst informed guesswork. The general estimate in the camps themselves over 1938–41 was from 15 million upwards, and this was shared by many NKVD officers themselves under arrest. It was also the common rumour in official circles. GULAG officials arrested in 1938 gave about 10 million as their own estimate. There are a few lower estimates, such as that of an official who gave 6 million "with a strong upward trend" in early 1941. A colonel connected with the inspectorate of camp guards from 1934 to 1941 said there were between 12 and 14 million just before the war.* That these estimates run several million higher than those arrived at by other methods is probably due to the inclusion of those charged under other articles of the Code than 58—that is, "common criminals" such as bandits, small peculators, breakers of labour discipline, etc. Most of these did not go through the processes described above but were held at detention centres attached to the police stations (Moscow had eleven prisons in addition to the five named in the Purge literature). There, their cases, involving simple and genuine facts, were processed in two or three days; and they went straight off to camp.

5. No exact computation being possible, one can see that these figures, together with those for arrests and executions, are compatible with a highly conservative solution of the following type—not including "criminals", as not specifically victims of the purge—for the end of 1938:

In jail or camp already January 1937	c. 5 million
Arrested January 1937–December 1938	c. 7 million
	c.12 million
of which executed	c. 1 million
died in camp 1937–38	c. 2 million
	c. 3 million
In captivity late 1938	c. 9 million
of which in prison	c. 1 million
in camps	c. 8 million

*After the war there was certainly an increase. NKVD functionaries imprisoned in 1948 spoke of 12 million. The commandant of a "repatriation camp" feeding the labour camps spoke of the post-war total as 15–17 million.

D. Death in the Camps

We are typically told that "during the first year about one-third of the prisoners die", mainly of exhaustion. That is, those physically most unfitted to the extreme conditions of the camps went quickly. Taken as applying to the newly arrested of 1937–38, it would imply a loss of about 1 million of them each year, over the period immediately following admittance.

This 30 per cent death rate for the new intake is not of course the death rate for the camp population as a whole. A careful study of this has produced a rate in camps, in 1933, of about 10 per cent per annum. In 1938 it had risen to about 20 per cent. This variation is compounded by another difficulty—that our information usually comes from particular areas, and there was much variation in conditions. Kolyma, as we have seen, had a death rate of up to 30 per cent. If we take its average population as 500,000, possibly an underestimate, this camp area alone probably accounted for over 2 million deaths up to 1950. Lumber work, and others in the far north—especially on the Vorkuta railway—were also dangerous employments. But in general, leaving aside a few very bad and a few notably moderate camps, the total impression is that the ration was always and everywhere insufficient to the work, and until 1950 always produced a death rate of a minimum of 10 per cent per annum.

An estimate in the broad scale, though still not a precise one, can be made in the case of the Polish prisoners of 1939–42. Of 1,060,000 Poles taken to labour camps, prisoner of war camps, or forced settlement, about 270,000 died. Of these, the great majority perished in the labour camps, which accounted for about 440,000 of the total detainees. Even allowing for the executions at Katyn and elsewhere, and starvation in a number of free settlements, it seems that not less than 40–50 percent of the labour-camp inmates of Polish citizenship must have died during an average incarceration of around two to two and a half years.

Release was very rare. Moreover, in the late forties, as is now admitted, those who had been released were all rearrested. Thus, the average prisoner had to go through bad years as well as fair, and except in a few favoured camps was most unlikely to survive. Of 3,000 Kursk "collaborationists" sent to camp after the recapture of that city in 1943, only sixty were alive in 1951.

After 1950 the death rate, at least in the main zones of northern Russia, became little higher (except for "disciplinary" deaths) than the local civilian rate. The physical possibility of surviving a sentence existed, though the prospects at the time seemed poor, for, as the well-adjusted "Ivan Denisovich" could say:

Maybe you could last ten years and still come out of it alive, but how the hell could you get through twenty-five?

Fortunately, these later victims did not have to wait so long. But the average camp inmate arrested in the period before 1950 had usually been through killing years, as with the men from Kursk. The 1937–38 victims who did not go under in the first wave of deaths often survived right up to the war. But the bad years then ensuing killed the vast majority of them. They are only reported most exceptionally in the post-war evidence.

Taking the conservative figures of an *average* over the period 1936–50 inclusive of an 8 million population of the camps and a 10 per cent death rate per annum, we get a total casualty figure of 12 million dead. To this we must add a million for the executions of the period, certainly a low estimate. Then there are the casualties of the pre-Yezhov era of Stalin's rule, 1930–36: this includes as its main component the 3½ million who perished in the collectivization itself plus the similar number sent to camps where virtually all died in the following years: again, minimal estimates. Thus we get a figure of 20 million dead, which is almost certainly too low and might require an increase of 50 percent or so, as the debit balance of the Stalin regime for twenty-three years.

Addendum: The Soviet Census of January 1959

The total figure of 208,827,000 was some 20 million lower than Western observers had expected *after* making allowance for war losses —even though the first losses of the Purge, or such of them as may be registered in the 1939 Census, had also been taken into account. On the other hand war losses had probably been underestimated, and this remains to some degree an imponderable.

But the main point arises from a consideration of the figures for males and females in the different age groups:

Age (15 Jan. 1959)	Numbers (thousands)		Per cent	
	Male	Female	Male	Female
0– 9	23,608	22,755	50.9	49.1
10–19	16,066	15,742	50.5	49.5
20–24	10,056	10,287	49.4	50.6
25–29	8,917	9,273	49.0	51.0

Age (15 Jan. 1959)	Numbers (thousands)		Per cent	
30–34	8,611	10,388	45.3	54.7
35–39	4,528	7,062	39.1	60.9
40–44	3,998	6,410	38.4	61.6
45–49	4,706	7,558	38.4	61.6
50–54	4,010	6,437	38.4	61.6
55–59	2,906	5,793	33.4	66.6
60–69	4,099	7,637	34.9	65.1
70 and older	2,541	5,431	31.9	68.1
Age not given	4	4	–	–
Total	94,050	114,777	·45.0	55.0

Many women died as a result of the war and the purges. But in both cases the great bulk of the victims was certainly male. From neither cause should there be much distinction in the figures for the sexes for the under-30 age groups in 1959. Nor is there. For the 30–34 block the proportion of 453 men to 547 women is a comparatively small difference, presumably indicating the losses of the young Army men in their late teens during the war. In the 35–39 group, which could have been expected to take the major war losses, we find figures of 391 men to 609 women. One would have thought that these men, in their early twenties in the war, would have had the highest losses.* But the proportion then gets worse still, and for the 40–44, 45–49 and 50–54 remains a set 384 to 616. Even more striking, the worst proportion of all comes for the 55–59 age group (334 to 666: in fact in this group alone there are almost exactly twice as many women as men). The figures for the 60–69 group (349 to 691) and for the 70 and over group (319 to 681) are also much worse than the soldiers' groups.† Now all authorities agree that the Purge struck in the main at people "between thirty and fifty-five"; "generally, arrested people are all thirty or over. That's the dangerous age: you can remember things." There were few young or

*This obvious point is backed by one of the few available age analyses of actual deaths in war. Losses in the German Army in World War I in proportion of age groups were distributed as follows: 15–19, 2.81 per cent; 20–24, 15.25 per cent; 25–29, 22.9 per cent; 30–34, 15.48 per cent; 35–39, 11.6 per cent; 40–44, 5.38 per cent; 45–49, 3.49 per cent.
†It is true that losses in the First World War and the Civil War have some effect on this group, but in the census of 1926 there is none with a deficit of males of more than 10 per cent.

old, most of them being "in the prime of life". Add twenty years for the 1959 position.

Precise deductions are not possible. Older men died as soldiers in the war. But on the other hand, the mass dispatch to labour camps of prisoners of war returned from Nazi hands in 1945 must have led to an extra, and non-military, death rate among the younger males. So must the guerrilla fighting in the Baltic States and the Western Ukraine, which lasted for years after the war; and so must the deportations from the Caucasus and the general renewal of Purge activities in the post-war period. But in any case, the general effect of the figures is clear enough. The wastage of millions of males in the older age groups is too great to be masked, whatever saving assumptions we may make. We here have, frozen into the census figures, a striking indication of the magnitude of the losses inflicted in the Purge.

THE HOLOCAUST

THE ULTIMATE IDEOLOGICAL GENOCIDE†

For many of us, interest in the study of the history and sociology of genocide is a direct consequence of the Holocaust, Hitler's war to destroy the Jewish people and most of the Romanies, or Gypsies. It took decades for the world to fathom the extent and significance of the Holocaust. For some scholars, the enormity of the Holocaust is so great that they reject categorizing it with other cases of mass killing. They argue that the Holocaust is the only case in history of the attempted destruction of an entire people. All other cases of mass killing, in their view, were attempts to destroy an old rival, to win a war, or to eliminate a culture by destroying some of its bearers. For them, earlier and later cases of genocide pale into insignificance next to the Holocaust.

We strongly believe that the Holocaust is part of a larger category of genocides and that it must be compared with earlier cases of mass killing before its origins, its significance, and the measures needed to prevent its recurrence can be understood. Indeed, only by comparing the Holocaust with other cases of genocide can one fully grasp the fact that the Holocaust was the most carefully conceived, the most efficiently implemented, and the most fully realized case of ideologically motivated genocide in the history of the human race and that it represents a type of genocide that is characteristic of aberrant quests for a "perfected" society in our time (Cohn 1957 and 1967).

Nevertheless, we respect the argument that the Holocaust belongs in a category all its own. The Holocaust was unique among genocides in several vital respects that must be recognized. First among these was Hitler's definition of the Jews as members of a subhuman race and his insistence that they be annihilated immediately and totally in order to save Germany and the Aryan race from racial pollution and death. Nothing in their past encounters with European anti-Semitism and discrimination prepared the Jewish people for this all-encompassing

†From a paper presented by Frank Chalk at "Remembering for the Future: The Impact of the Holocaust and Genocide on Jews and Christians," an International Scholars Conference held at Oxford, England, 10–13 July 1988.

assault on their most precious right—their right to live; even veteran anti-Semites found it hard to imagine that the Nazi regime seriously intended to make the Jewish people extinct.

The incredulity of Jews and their fellow citizens in Europe and America was reinforced by a further special characteristic of the Holocaust: its roots in Germany, one of the most scientifically and industrially advanced countries of Europe. That Germans perpetrated the Holocaust in the twentieth century, long after the dawn of the Enlightenment was assumed to have raised Western civilization beyond barbarism, still raises serious questions about our understanding of Western society. As worshippers of Western culture, Jews had convinced themselves that human nature was fundamentally benevolent and rational. Richard Rubenstein argues that the mass slaughter that occurred in the trench warfare of World War I foreshadowed the coming of the Holocaust, but this is true only in retrospect. Nothing about the killing of soldiers by other soldiers allowed the West to anticipate the Holocaust, a catastrophe in which the full might of a modern industrialized state was mobilized for the total annihilation of a group of men, women, and children living under the supposed protection of their own government, as in the case of the German Jews, or under the provisions of international conventions governing a military occupation, as in the case of Jews in other parts of Europe. Warning signs such as the Turkish genocide against the Armenians, which bears many similarities to the Holocaust, or the mass brutalities directed against civilians in the Balkans would have been dismissed as irrelevant by European Jews, had they been considered at all. Jews viewed the Turks and the peoples of southern Europe as living in premodern, less advanced societies that were more vulnerable than the civilized West to outbreaks of collective violence.

Germany's outstanding progress in science, industry, and administration gave Hitler the tools to carry out the most thorough and pervasive genocide in history. This third unique characteristic of the Holocaust, especially its modern bureaucratic organization, is unlike any previous mass killing in history. Consider Hitler's weapons for carrying out the Holocaust in Occupied Europe: special registers and identity papers for Jews; mass deception of the victims through skillful propaganda designed to lull them into a sense of security; centrally directed and highly specialized mobile killing squads; the concentration of Jews in ghettos; deliberate starvation and unchecked diseases; recruitment of anti-Semitic allies to kill Jews in almost every country; the death camps with their specially developed gas chambers; medical experimentation upon the victims; numbers tattooed on the forearms of concentration camp inmates; a continentwide bureaucracy dedicated to tracking down and killing every single survivor; and participation in the running of the machinery of mass murder by every highly skilled professional group in German society, including railroad administrators and crews, diplomats and lawyers, engineers and military personnel, scientists and physicians, and economists and anthropologists. Individually, a few of these features of the Holocaust are detectable in earlier cases of genocide, but no people in history had ever been attacked by such an array of scientific, industrial, and administrative weapons in a program specifically designed to insure its complete and immediate biological destruction.

While we contend that the Holocaust belongs to the larger history of genocide, we recognize that, unlike all previous genocides, it represents a unique challenge from within to Western society and especially, to use Alan Rosenberg's phrase, to "the most sacred of the Enlightenment ideals—the goal of perfection itself." Rosenberg captures the essence of this challenge in his interpretation of the Holocaust as an assault on Western values:

> [The Holocaust] became a deliberate scientific undertaking, a project for remedying the errors of the past by removing the causes of these errors, aimed at improving the nation's racial stock and bringing about a better and more secure future for all. . . . These consequences of the Enlightenment, of the Industrial and Technological Age, were scarcely foreseen or foreseeable. But can we deny them as we look back in frustration and despair? [Rosenberg 1985, 6]

Rosenberg's warning echoes Saul Friedlander's call for Western scholars to "note the simultaneity and the interaction" of entirely different phenomena in the Nazi Holocaust: "messianic fanaticism and bureaucratic structures, pathological impulses and administrative decrees, and archaic attitudes within an advanced industrial society" (Friedlander 1984, 50).

The Holocaust has a special meaning for Western civilization: unlike the dead of ancient genocides, unlike the Cathars, the Japanese Christians, the Pequots, and the Hereros, unlike the Armenians and the victims of Stalin's terror, the Jews and the Gypsies were murdered in post-Enlightenment Europe by a people steeped in Western culture and rich in scientific knowledge. "No assessment of modern culture can ignore the fact," Irving Greenberg writes, "that science and technology—the accepted flower and glory of modernity—climaxed in the factories of death" (quoted in Rosenberg 1985, 6). We agree that in the challenge it poses to Western values from within our own society, the Holocaust stands alone in the history of the West and in the history of genocide.

THE UNIQUENESS
OF THE HOLOCAUST:
NEGLECTED ASPECTS AND
THEIR CONSEQUENCES†

Whenever the word *genocide* is mentioned, whether in the context of a news item, a film, or a book, it is almost inevitably associated with the Holocaust. Even the terminology is revealing: the term *genocide* is a modern invention, coined in response to the victimization of the Jews, but since being incorporated into the UN Convention is applied to the extermination of any group. The term *Holocaust*, which has its roots in antiquity, is reserved for the Nazi's program to exterminate the Jews. This terminological distinction draws attention to the uniqueness of the Holocaust and to the generic qualities of genocide. But in what sense was the Holocaust a unique event? We have discussed some of these above, but there exists on this topic a growing body of literature that we recommend to the attention of the interested reader. Here we propose to discuss several aspects of the Holocaust's uniqueness that have received somewhat less attention, but that are of relevance to the comparative study of genocides. These aspects concern the consequences of the Holocaust rather than the event itself.

a. The first of these aspects concerns the behavior of the perpetrator country. West Germany, created as a result of the division of Germany after the war, is the first country in modern history to admit that a genocide was committed and to agree to a modest form of reimbursement to some of the survivors. In spite of this precedent, West Germany's is the only case in which a perpetrator has admitted guilt. It is true that in his famous secret speech in 1956 Khrushchev tried to admit at least a part of what had occurred under Stalin. It was not a popular move at the time. New efforts to set the record straight seem to be under way under Gorbachev's initiative; to what extent he will succeed remains to be seen. The action of West Germany has had the opposite effect on most cases of post–World War II genocides: perpetrator countries not only continued to deny that a genocide had been carried out, but even copied the now well-known methods of secrecy, control of information, the great lie, and the staged visit of dignitaries to support their contrived version of events. One might even speculate on the extent to which the UN Convention has discouraged perpetrators from following West Germany's example since a guilty plea now exposes the

†Revised version of a paper presented by Kurt Jonassohn at the annual meeting of the International Studies Association, St. Louis, 29 March–2 April 1988.

perpetrator country to the sanctions foreseen in the various conventions dealing with genocide and human rights violations.

After all, the United Nations is a club whose membership consists of sovereign nations, and most post–World War II cases of genocide have been perpetrated by these same nations. When one of these nation-states commits a genocide it is always intended as the solution to a perceived problem. To the extent that the genocide is successful (complete success is rare), it will have solved this problem. But if a nation-state were to admit its guilt it would thereby generate a whole series of new problems for itself. The perpetrator state would presumably be tried by an international court under several applicable UN conventions. It would lose the case; it might have to give up for imprisonment or execution those of its citizens that were found guilty of having played a responsible role; it probably would have to give up considerable amounts of money to pay reparations; it might even have to cede some of its territory to the victim group; and it would presumably lose prestige. Why would any perpetrator country voluntarily expose itself to such consequences? It is for such reasons that the UN conventions have failed to have their intended results. A critic might argue that these mechanisms should be put into motion even if the perpetrator does not admit guilt. But who among this family of nations would volunteer to throw the first stone, and who would deliver the proofs of a perpetrator's guilt? It seems that the real question should be not one of punishing the guilty, but of preventing future genocides.

b. The Jewish survivors of the Nazi Holocaust also were unique. Traditionally, the victims of genocide have collaborated in the "collective denial" by which most such events went unrecorded and/or unreported. It seemed as if the victims accepted their fate; they seemed to share the view that theirs was the lot of the weak and of the losers and was somehow ordained. The Jewish survivors of the Holocaust were the first victims of genocide to refuse to accept such a fate. They not only voiced their sorrow, but also gave expression to their outrage at such monstrous violations of common decency, human rights, and civilized values. They expressed their outrage in several art forms, such as painting, sculpture, poetry, memoirs, and novels as well as in the recording of oral histories, the preservation of records, and in lobbying for human rights. Tremendous resources were and still are being devoted to the preservation of the memory of what happened and to the quest for understanding and future prevention.

It might be objected that this is not a unique aspect of the Holocaust because the suffering of the Armenians in 1915 had already produced an outpouring of literature from both Armenian and non-Armenian sources. This "breaking of the silence" happened after both cases, the genocide of the Armenians and that of the Jews. However, events must not be taken in isolation; their meaning derives from their context. The literature of the Armenian genocide has had much less impact because it continues to fire the debate on questions of historical fact. This is so because Turkey denies that the genocide ever took place. The literature on the Holocaust had a completely different impact because neither of the two Germanies ever denied that the Holocaust had occurred. The Holocaust-denial literature, which originates from circles of so-called revisionist historians, lacks the credibility it might otherwise have, and it does not generate a serious debate about what really happened. Thus, the Holocaust literature is directed at remembering, understanding, and preventing a recurrence by emphasizing the role of human rights, while much of the literature on the Armenian genocide still addresses matters of historical fact—almost three-quarters of a century after the events of 1915. Another difference is that German authors are participating in the examination of what happened, whereas Turkish authors are still trying to deny that a genocide occurred.

c. The accumulation of thousands of years of diaspora persecution had, by the end of the nineteenth century, led to the rise of Zionism—the movement based on the idea that Jews need their own state in order to defend themselves against persecution by host states, that is, to bring about the end of the diaspora. While individual idealists did move to Palestine, none of the powers concerned were eager to allow a Jewish state to arise in Palestine. After World War II, the world was shocked by the revelations of what had happened under the Nazis. However, the shock was not so great that any countries were eager to absorb the survivors. Instead, the abused and homeless survivors were confined to so-called displaced persons camps. These displaced persons were caught in a cruel dilemma: either they did not want to return to their country of origin and/or their country of origin was not prepared to take them back. Under the pressure of so many Jews whom nobody wanted, and aided by the embarrassed conscience of many UN member countries, the United Nations finally voted the new state of Israel into existence in 1948. Since it is not at all clear that the Zionist dream would have gained sufficient support to be realized if the Holocaust had not happened, one can argue that another unique aspect of the Holocaust is that it facilitated the birth of the state of Israel. Jewish survivors of the Holocaust, and also Jews everywhere, are better protected by having a state of their own in which they are all entitled to citizenship by right. This is one of the unintended and unanticipated consequences of the Holocaust.

d. A fourth result of the Holocaust's uniqueness derives from the perpetrator's admission of guilt and from the victim's speaking out: this concerns the effects these new developments had on the victims of other genocides. Many victim groups whose survivors suffered their fate in the privacy of their hurts and their losses were amazed at the initiatives carried out by Holocaust survivors. The success of the initiatives outside of Jewish groups convinced other victim groups to break their silences. They started to publicize their fate and the injustices they had suffered by organizing publications, meetings, lobbying groups, and the commemoration of anniversaries. This clearly is not yet true of all victim groups. It is true only for those groups whose survivors take such initiatives themselves; if they do not do so, the traditional silence persists and can be overcome by outsiders only with the greatest difficulty. While traditional public opinion has tended to side with the victor, modern public opinion increasingly sympathizes with the victim; this too encourages the victims to speak out. It is to be hoped that, together with several other developments, this change will strengthen support for the rule of law and for the enforcement of human rights codes.

e. The final aspect of the Holocaust's uniqueness to be mentioned here concerns its effect on the social sciences and on the humanities. Although these fields of study have paid attention to many aspects of the social world, they seemed to share the collective denial by ignoring past and present genocides. Of course, the intellectuals of the social sciences and humanities establishment had quite different reasons from those of the victims for maintaining silence: First, they were not members of the victim groups; moreover they often collaborated with the perpetrators by providing theoretical, technological, and policy support. This collaborator role receives very little attention, even when the historical record is subjected to scholarly scrutiny. Such scholarly scrutiny is another one of the unanticipated consequences of the Holocaust. It took the shock of the Holocaust to initiate research on the Holocaust in particular and on genocide in general. The need to understand the preconditions and the processes of extermination has only recently led a small group of scholars to engage in serious research—research that is essential if future genocides are to be predicted and prevented.

None of these consequences had been planned or anticipated by the perpetrators. But their effect has been dramatic. They have contributed much to the passing of various bills and conventions on human rights, on the outlawing of torture, and on the crime of genocide by the United Nations and by many of its member countries. These bills and conventions have not been notably effective; that would be too much to expect after a history of thousands of years of genocide. But they have achieved the breaking of the silence and a growing emphasis on human values and human worth—surely an essential first step.

THE TRAINING OF
THE NAZI ELITE†

Late in the fall of 1937, in Frankfurt, I had occasion for an
extended discussion with a leading SS man from Vogelsang Castle—a discussion that continued over several afternoons.

It should be noted that Vogelsang, in the Eiffel Mountains, was one of three
castles—*Ordensburg* is the German term—where the new Nazi elite was to be
incubated. *Ordensburg* really describes a castle belonging to a medieval order,
such as the Knights Templar—and that is how the Nazis thought of their elite.
At the *Ordensburg*, young men chosen with care were trained for several years
under an austere regimen of consecration.

My discussion with the SS officer was very frank on both sides. It dealt with
such questions as the meaning of German history, the role of the Third Reich,
and the racial theories of the SS. The contrast between the views expressed was,
of course, extreme and gave me a wealth of insight, confirming much that I had
already suspected. The SS officer was by no means stupid, indeed he had a
superior intellect, for all that he was a thoroughgoing fanatic. He made three
remarkable statements:

What we trainers of the younger generation of Führers aspire to is a
modern governmental structure on the model of the ancient Greek city
states. It is to these aristocratically run democracies with their broad economic basis of serfdom that we owe the great cultural achievements of
antiquity. From 5 to 10 per cent of the people, their finest flower, shall
rule; the rest must work and obey. In this way alone can we attain that peak
performance we must demand of ourselves and of the German people.

The new Führer class is selected by the SS—in a positive sense by
means of the National Political Education Institutes (Napola) as a prepara-
tory stage, of the Ordensburgen as the academies proper of the coming
Nazi aristocracy, and of a subsequent active internship in public affairs; in
a negative sense by the extermination of all racially and biologically inferior elements and by the radical removal of all incorrigible political opposition that refuses on principle to acknowledge the philosophical basis of the
Nazi State and its essential institutions.

†From Eugen Kogon, *The Theory and Practice of Hell*, trans. Heinz Norden, 1–2.
Reprinted by permission of Farrar, Straus and Giroux, Inc., New York, 1984; original
edition 1950.

Within ten years at the latest it will be possible for us in this way to dictate the law of Adolf Hitler to Europe, put a halt to the otherwise inevitable decay of the continent, and build up a true community of nations, with Germany as the leading power keeping order.

HITLER'S ANTISEMITISM†

It is reasonable to ask in what way antisemitism may be seen as "central" to Nazism. The key, I think, lies with Hitler himself. About the centrality of anti-Jewish commitment in his own worldview, there seems little doubt. The Jews not only appear in virtually everything that ever concerned Hitler, but are at the very basis of his conception of the historical process—the idea of struggle. Adopting the crudest perversion of the familiar Darwinian view, Hitler saw history as a great arena in which peoples forever engaged in ruthless competition. These confrontations were not limited, as with sporting contests or the highly ritualized warfare of the eighteenth century. Nations, like individuals, Hitler believed, had to struggle desperately for their very existence. "The idea of struggle is as old as life itself," he said in a 1928 speech, "for life is only preserved because other living things perish through struggle. . . . In this struggle the stronger, the more able, win, while the less able, the weak, lose. Struggle is the father of all things. . . . It is not by the principles of humanity that man lives or is able to preserve himself above the animal world, but solely by means of the most brutal struggle." "Ultimately this struggle, which is often so hard, kills all pity," Hitler wrote in *Mein Kampf*, the book that was supposed to describe his personal odyssey as well as that of his people. "Our own painful struggle for existence destroys our feeling for the misery of those who have remained behind."

Hitler claimed to have first discovered the Jews in Vienna, where he lived for five years before the First World War. In the pages of *Mein Kampf* he presented this discovery as an earth-shattering revelation. His eyes were opened to Marxism and Jewry, "whose terrible importance for the German people" he previously did not understand. "In this period there took shape within me a world picture and a philosophy which became the granite foundation of all my acts. In addition to what I then created, I have had to learn little; and I have had to alter nothing."

†From Michael R. Marrus, *The Holocaust in History*, 13–14. Footnotes omitted. © 1987. Reprinted by permission of the University Press of New England, Hanover, N.H.

Hitler consistently portrayed Jews as the most determined and sinister enemies of the Germans and all other nations as well. Jews constantly undermined
a people's capacity for struggle, weakened and subverted its racial purity, poisoned its institutions, and corrupted its positive qualities. The Jews themselves
were not a race, but an antirace; they had no culture of their own, but purveyed
instead such doctrines as democracy or parliamentarianism which perverted or
degenerated previously sound societies. Jews were continually mingling with
other cultures, seeking to dissolve their structures and their institutions. Marxism was but one additional means by which Jewry conducted its relentless assault
upon the societies and peoples of the world. Capitalism was another. In a world
dominated by struggle, the Jews could be fiendishly successful and were a perpetual threat to the existence of all healthy societies.

Jews posed a particular danger to the German people, for whom Hitler claimed
to be a prophetic spokesman. Indeed, as he excoriated German society and its
institutions during the *Kampfzeit*, Hitler associated the degeneration of his country with the triumph of Jewry. "In Germany today," he wrote in 1928, "German interests are no longer decisive but rather Jewish interests." Undermined
and weakened by the Jews at home, Germany at the same time confronted world
Jewry abroad. Committed in the long run to securing *Lebensraum*, or living
space in the east, Germans were locked in an uncompromising conflict with
Bolshevism, itself a Jewish invention. Jewry, Hitler believed, "has taken over
the leadership of all areas of Russian life with the Bolshevik revolution." What
emerged from that upheaval was a regime that had a single aim: "to carry over
the Bolshevist poisoning to Germany." Finally, according to Hitler, the situation
was desperate. Germany was sunk in decay and decadence. Jewry had triumphed
in 1918, with the defeat of the Wilhelmenian Reich, and was closing in for the
kill. To do nothing would be to assure catastrophe. "The German people is
today attacked by a pack of booty-hungry enemies from within and without.
The continuation of this state of affairs is our death."

THE EVOLUTION OF NAZI
JEWISH POLICY, 1933–1938†

Mein Kampf, the holy writ of the Nazi movement, had a tremendous influence. In his biography of Hitler, Robert Payne wrote:

†From Yehuda Bauer, *A History of the Holocaust*, 83–84, 85, 87–109. Copyright ©
1982 by Yehuda Bauer. Reprinted by permission of the publisher, Franklin Watts.

It is a great book in the sense that Machiavelli's *The Prince* is a great book, casting a long shadow. The Renaissance word *terribilita* implies superb daring, immense disdain, an absolute lack of scruples, and a terrifying determination to ride roughshod over all obstacles, and the book possesses all these qualities. The author says: "This is the kind of man I am, and this is what I shall do," and he conceals nothing, as though too disdainful of his enemies to wear a disguise. The armed bohemian describes in minute detail how he will stalk his prey. . . . There is no evidence that Baldwin, Chamberlain, Churchill, Roosevelt, Stalin, or any of the political leaders most directly affected did anything more than glance at it. If they had read it with the attention it deserves, they would have seen that it was a blueprint for the total destruction of bourgeois society and the conquest of the world. . . . Just as Hitler's speeches lack any sense of progression, for he is continually circling round a small, hard core of primitive ideas announced with complete conviction, so in *Mein Kampf* he disdains any reasoned argument but repeats his ideas *ad nauseam*, loudly, firmly, unhesitatingly, until the reader becomes deafened. . . . The ideas he expresses—hatred for the Jews, the insignificance of men, the necessity of a Fuehrer [leader] figure possessing supreme authority, the purity of the German race so immeasurably superior to all other races, the need for living space in the East, his absolute detestation of Bolshevism—all these are announced with manic force.[6]

But, as Payne pointed out, Hitler's analysis of the receptivity of large masses of people to the blandishments of propaganda is a classic. The masses, Hitler says, are essentially "feminine," that is, in his view, feelings and emotions are far more important than logical, reasoned thought. Successful propaganda must concentrate on a few points only and hammer at those points incessantly. His purpose, Hitler said, was to concentrate on one enemy only and through him attack all others. That one enemy: the Jew.

.   .   .   .

Underneath a veneer of prosperity and liberalism, Germany harbored disappointment and discontent. Defeat in the war had not been accepted by the nationalistic upper and middle classes. The republic was seen as an artificial import forced on Germany by the Allies. Still largely monarchistic, the bureaucracy despised the new democratic rulers, as did the army officers in the Reichswehr and those former officers who were now unemployed. Disaffected and bitter

6. See Robert Payne, *The Life and Death of Adolf Hitler* (New York, 1973), pp. 197–198.

Table 4.1. *Reichstag Representation, 1919–1932*

	1919	1920	May 1924	December 1924
Total seats	421	459	478	493
Left				
Communists	—	4	62	45
Independent Socialists	22	84	—	—
Social-Democrats	165	102	100	131
Total	187	190	162	176
No. of seats lost or gained	—	+3	−28	+14
Center and Right				
Catholic Center party	91	85	81	88
National party	19	65	45	51
Economic party	—	—	10	17
Nationalist party	44	71	95	103
Miscellaneous	5	9	25	12
Total	159	230	256	271
No. of seats lost or gained	—	+71	+26	+15
Democrats	75	39	28	32
No. of seats lost or gained	—	−36	−11	+4
National Socialists	—	—	32	14
No. of seats lost or gained	—	—	—	−18

Source: Documents on the Holocaust, 31.

members of the working class supported the communist party. Old hatreds persisted.

In 1929 the New York Stock Exchange collapsed. As the economic crisis spread worldwide, unemployed millions struggled bitterly for a piece of bread, a sack of coal. The German people yearned for strong leadership that would end the misery and degradation rampant in the land. Between 1929 and 1933 political crises followed one upon another, expressing the reality of a deeply divided people. Beginning in the elections of September 1930, no possible coalition of parties received a parliamentary majority (table 4.1). Of 547 seats in 1930, the

1928	1930	July 1932	November 1932
491	547	599	572
54	47	89	100
—	—	—	—
153	143	133	121
207	190	222	221
+31	−17	+32	−1
78	87	97	90
45	30	7	11
23	23	2	—
78	41	37	52
23	49	—	—
247	230	143	153
−24	−17	−87	+10
25	20	4	2
−7	−5	−16	−2
12	107	230	196
−2	+95	+123	−34

National Socialists won 107 seats, the Nationalists 41 and the Communists 47—35.6 percent of the Reichstag representatives were committed to the overthrow of the republic. The Social Democrats, the Catholic Centrists, and the Democrats, who were committed to maintaining the republic, had 250 seats, or 40 percent, not enough for a majority. In the subsequent elections of July and November 1932, the situation did not improve. With 7 million unemployed, the validity of the free-enterprise system and of democracy itself seemed denied.

.   .   .   .   .   .

Yet the fact of the matter is that the economic crisis hit the United States and Britain no less than it did Germany. In both these countries, democracy emerged victorious. Yet in January 1933, the Nazis came to power in Germany.

Table 4.2. *Industrial Production in Germany, 1932 (1928 = 100)*

	1st quarter	2nd quarter	Aug.	Sept.	Oct.	Nov.
Index	55.0	57.7	52.3	56.3	59.9	62.9

Source: Karl D. Bracher, *Die Auflösung der Weimarer Republik* (Villingen, 1960), 226.

The 1930–32 governments tried to stem the tide of economic crisis by budgetary cuts and other stringent measures that only deepened the misery of the masses. The president of the republic, the old hero—real or supposed—of the late war, Marshal Paul von Hindenburg, was enamored of neither the republic nor the democratic idea. Using a suitable paragraph in the constitution, he enabled three chancellors—the Catholic leader Heinrich Brüning (1930–32), the Catholic aristocrat Franz von Papen (1932), and the former army general Kurt von Schleicher (1932–33)—to rule by decree in his name. Parliamentary democracy, in effect, was thus rendered impotent more than two years before Hitler's accession.

The Nazi party grew stronger, feeding on the discontent of the middle and lower-middle classes. The working class did not abandon the warring factions of the Social Democrats and the Communists. Nor did the Catholic voters join the Nazis; even the right-wing Nationalists held their own, more or less, against the Nazi onslaught. But the moderate right and the Democratic party collapsed. Millions of new voters—many of them middle-class and unemployed Germans who had not bothered previously to vote and people voting for the first time —cast their ballots for the Nazis.

The Nazis were still a minority, however, when Hitler came to power. Of the 585 seats contested in the Reichstag elections of November 1932, the Nazis won 196 (33.1 percent of the vote, or 33.5 percent of the seats). They actually lost 2 million votes (34 seats and more than 4 percent of the popular vote) as compared to the previous elections, whereas the Communists and the right-wing Nationalists registered important gains.

In the early months of 1932 the economic crisis in Germany had reached its nadir. During the summer months industrial production was stabilized, and later in the year production was on the rise (table 4.2). Although economic recovery did not begin as early in other countries, neither did it have as far to go (table 4.3).

Hitler came to power, therefore, as the strength of the Nazi party was beginning to wane and Germany was beginning to emerge from the depth of the economic crisis. The right-wing politicians surrounding Hindenburg no longer trusted the Catholic Center party; nor would they ally themselves with social democracy; their experiment with a progressive army general (Schleicher) had failed. Hitler, it seemed, could provide a mass following as well as a deterrent to

Table 4.3. Industrial Production in Developed Countries (1929 = 100)

	Germany	United States	Great Britain	France
1st quarter	54.2	58.8	85.1	72.3
2nd quarter	56.9	51.4	84.3	67.3
October	59.1	55.1	78.1	68.0
November	62.0	—	—	—

Source: Karl D. Bracher, *Die Auflösung der Weimarer Republik* (Villingen, 1960), 227.

the growing Communist movement. As a front for the right-wing nationalists, he could be controlled. After much wavering, Hindenburg accepted the idea. A government with only three Nazis (Hitler; Wilhelm Frick, minister of the interior; and Göring, minister for Prussia) among a conservative majority would be a safe solution. Hitler became chancellor in January 1933.

Nazi Antisemitism

The Nazi propaganda of 1929–33 stressed unemployment, social security, tariffs on agricultural products, war reparations to foreign nations, Germany's status among nations, and the territories it lost in World War I. At that time, antisemitism itself was not the main focus.

The Nazis did not add any new elements to antisemitism—except for their determination to implement it—but the full-blown antisemitic ideology that eventually developed combined elements of both traditional Christian and pseudoscientific nineteenth-century antisemitism. The Protocols of the Elders of Zion, containing the Jewish world-conspiracy theory, were adopted as an article of faith. The concept of the satanic Jew was taken over from Christianity, as only a people possessed by Satan could have killed the Messiah. But whereas traditional Christian antisemitism viewed the Jew as a human being possessed by the Devil, Nazi ideology viewed the Jew as the Devil himself. The Medieval Church hoped to save Jewish souls through baptism, and stopped short of planned mass murder, though popular Christian antisemitism had not been limited to the deprivation of all civil and most economic rights, as the many murderous outbreaks show. Nevertheless, it remained for the National Socialists to turn the symbol of the Devil, the Jew, into content: the Jew *was* the Devil, in Nazi eyes.

An "International World Jewry," a kind of Jewish world government, actually existed, according to the Nazis, and they attempted throughout the Holocaust period to discover its location and the identity of its members and leaders. In support of their "world Jewish domination psychosis," the Nazis cited an imaginary Jewish "control" of the Western "plutocracies" and Russian bolshevism. In the Nazi mind, the illogical concept of Jewish "control" of both bolshevik Russia and the capitalist West was rationalized by the attribution of demonism to the Jew.

Hitler classified countries as enemy or friend by the measure of supposed Jewish control in their administrations. France, for example, was considered under Jewish control and therefore an enemy. England, however, struggling against "Jewish domination," was a friend, a potential German ally. (Hitler refused to believe until the last moment that "Aryan" England would enter the war against Germany.)[7]

To establish a historical basis for his analysis of the Jewish "plot" to rule the world, Hitler contended that the Jews had introduced into civilization unnatural concepts—humanism, Christianity, equality, liberalism, compassion, conscience —to weaken the resistance of other peoples to their rule. Did not Christianity, introduced into the all-powerful Roman empire by the Jews, weaken and ultimately destroy Rome? The survival of the human race depended not on humanitarian, egalitarian Judaical concepts but on natural, pagan, hierarchical strength and force.

Nineteenth-century racism, that is, the superiority of one race over another, was appropriately congruent with Nazi ideology. The Germanic peoples were a superior part of the "Aryan" race and were, therefore, along with other nations of similar "blood," the rightful rulers of the world. Indeed, they were the only true humans. Because of the Germanic "blood" in their veins, certain nations (e.g., the Scandinavians and the British) might become Germany's allies. Other Europeans (e.g., Latins and Slavs), although they were "Aryans," too, would be ruled by Germany because of their lack of Germanic blood. Due to past contacts between Germans and Slavs, the latter had absorbed some Germanic "blood," which was to be "rescued" by kidnapping blue-eyed, blond-haired Slav children, and by permitting Poles with German names or German ancestry (real or supposed) to be considered Germans. The other Slavs were often termed "subhuman,"[8] and though there never was any plan to annihilate completely any of the Slav nations, their leadership was to be eliminated along with their

7. *Hitler's Secret Book* (New York, 1961), pp. 146–159, 215; Joachim C. Fest, *Hitler* (New York, 1973), pp. 594–603.

8. Himmler's Memorandum, "Reflections on the Treatment of Alien Races in the East", handed to Hitler 5/25/1940, IMT, Nuremberg Trial Document NO–1880. German original in: Vierteljahreshefte für Zeitgeschichte, 1957, Vol. 2, pp. 196–198.

religious and educational institutions. With their culture reduced to a primitive level, the Czechs, Poles, Russians, and others were to assume the mantle of slaves to serve the aims of the superior Teutons.[9]

Whereas the Slavs were subhuman, the Jews were nonhuman. Hitler saw the Jews as a kind of anti-race, a nomadic mongrel group. Because contact with Jews would corrupt German blood and culture, Jews would be segregated,[10] a segregation that led to the possibility of annihilation. In segregating the Jews, the Nazis followed the traditional Christian policy that viewed the Jew, the "Other," as essentially different and somehow inherently dangerous, a danger to be avoided. In elaborating their concept of the Jews as nonhuman, the Nazis described them as parasites, viruses, or loathsome creatures from the animal and insect world (rats, cockroaches). As a parasitic force, the Jews corroded, and would ultimately destroy, the cultures of their host nations.

To the Nazis, the "Jewish problem" was a problem of cosmic importance. Human survival itself depended on the fate of the 17 million Jews inhabiting the globe. Should the Jews be successful in their quest for world domination, the Nazis said, they would deny existence to all others. Human survival depended, therefore, on the victory of the forces of light (Aryans) over the forces of darkness (Jews). In the Nazi *Weltanschauung* (ideology, world view), the Germanic Aryans, not the Jews, had been commissioned by Providence to rule the world.[11] This Manichean juxtaposition of Jews and Germanics shows that their contradictory racist ideology really served as a rationalization for that central pillar in their world view: antisemitism. In addition, it must be emphasized that the Nazis, that is in effect the German intellectual elite supporting them, actually believed in this nonsense.

In a memorandum on the Four-Year Plan in 1936, Hitler wrote:

Since the beginning of the French Revolution the world has been drifting with increasing speed towards a new conflict, whose most extreme solution is named Bolshevism, but whose content and aim is only the removal of those strata which gave the leadership to humanity up to the present, and their replacement by international Jewry. . . . Germany has a duty to make its own existence secure by all possible means in face of this catastrophe and to protect itself against it; a number of conclusions follow from this necessity, and these involve the most important tasks that our nation

9. Ibid.

10. Conference at Hermann Göring's Headquarters, 11/12/1938, IMT, Nuremberg Trial Document, PS–1816.

11. Josef Ackermann, *Heinrich Himmler Als Ideologe* (Göttingen, 1970), pp. 178–194 (esp. p. 194).

has ever faced. For a victory of Bolshevism over Germany would not lead to a Versailles Treaty but to the final destruction, even the extermination, of the German people.[12]

The Nazis, then, accused the Jews of wanting to do what they, the Nazis, were out to do themselves: control the world and annihilate their enemies. In this inverted picture of themselves, they described the Jews as the demonic force of evil that Nazism itself was. In doing this, they dehumanized themselves first, and that enabled them to strip the Jews, in their own minds, of any human quality. This was a necessary ideological prelude to a gradual political development that turned ideology into murderous reality. The very fact that the process, as we shall see, was gradual, indicates that it might have been stopped somewhere on the way. Once, however, the victim became completely devoid of humanity in the perpetrator's eye, he could be killed. Annihilation followed.

.   .   .   .   .

Rank-and-file Germans who voted for the Nazi party in 1932 were voting for a regeneration of the German people, for new and decisive leadership, and for an economic revival to be initiated by a new national sense of purpose. They did not vote for the extremist positions of the party. As with all political parties on the assumption of office, it was expected that the power and responsibility of governing would dampen Nazi extremism and produce rational compromises with reality. The writing on the wall was soon there for all to see, however.

On February 27, 1933, the Reichstag burned down. Marinus van der Lubbe, a Dutch anarchist, was accused by the Nazis of heading a Communist plot to set the fire. Others claim that the Nazis themselves burned down the Reichstag in order to blame the Communists, or that van der Lubbe did it himself. Still another version suggests that both the Nazis and van der Lubbe, unaware of the other's plan, set fire to the building simultaneously. Regardless of the fire's origin, however, the burning of the Reichstag served the Nazis well. Using it as a pretext, they arrested Communist leaders and Reichstag deputies.

On February 28, they persuaded President von Hindenburg to issue a decree, "for the protection of the People and the State" (supposedly from the Communist menace), suspended the constitutional guarantees of personal liberty, the right of free expression of opinion, including freedom of the press; and the rights of assembly and association. The privacy of postal, telegraphic, and telephonic communication was no longer guaranteed, and warrants for house searches

12. *Documents on German Foreign Policy, 1918–1965*, Series E (1933–1937), Vol. 5, 2 (Göttingen, 1972), pp. 793–795 (in German). Also quoted in: Yehuda Bauer, "Genocide: Was it the Nazis' Original Plan," in: *The Annals of the American Academy of Political and Social Science*, July 1980, vol. 450, p. 38.

and orders for confiscations of, as well as restrictions on, property were also permissible beyond the legal limits otherwise prescribed.[1]

To eliminate both their Communist opposition and their right-wing bedfellows, the Nazis called for new elections on March 5, 1933. Again using the burning of the Reichstag as a pretext, the Nazis denied the Communist party inclusion on the ballot. Despite the official elimination of the Communists (who nevertheless voted for the illegal Communist party) and a widespread reign of terror on election day, however, the Nazi party was unable to achieve a parliamentary majority. Of 647 seats, the Nazis gained 288. With the support of right wingers, however, Hitler pushed through the "Law for Removing the Distress of People and Reich," the so-called Enabling Act, on March 23, which removed the power of legislation from the Reichstag and gave it to the Nazi-controlled government. By the time the Law expired in 1937, the Nazi dictatorship was complete. Authorized by the Enabling Act, the dictatorship ruled Germany until its defeat in 1945.

During the spring of 1933, the other political parties were forced out of existence by a combination of threats, force, and cajoling. On July 14, a law was enacted declaring the Nazi party (NSDAP) the only legal party in Germany. On December 1, 1933, the "unity of Party and the State" was officially decreed. In effect, the government as such ceased to function. All authority emanated from the Führer, Adolf Hitler, and the various ministers became his executive officers.

After Hindenburg's death on August 3, 1934, Hitler combined the presidency and Reichskanzlership and assumed the title of Führer and Reichskanzler. In June 1934 the leadership of the SA (Storm Troops) was purged. SA leader Ernst Röhm had demanded that the SA become a part of the Reichswehr, the official German army, hoping to become its main force. Röhm and the SA, who supported an anti-aristocratic, populist version of Nazi doctrine, stood in stark contradiction to Hitler's careful wooing of the propertied classes and the aristocratic caste of mainly Prussian military. Röhm might become a dangerous rival. The rebuilding of the army as an instrument of Nazi policy demanded, at that stage at least, an alliance with the military rather than a surrender to social demagogy. On June 30,1934, after much wavering, Hitler agreed to the murder of his loyal SA commanders, including Röhm. The opportunity was also used to rid the regime of other opponents, particularly right-wing opposition leaders such as Schleicher, Hitler's predecessor.

Following the June 30 assassinations, the SS (Schutzstaffel, the Defense Corps), a special elite corps under SA stewardship, became independent. Control of the concentration camps was also in SS hands. Heinrich Himmler, the

---

1. William L. Shirer, *The Rise and Fall of the Third Reich* (London, 1962), p. 194.

leader of the SS since 1929, gained complete control of the police by 1936 and became Reich Leader (Reichsführer) of both the SS and the Police. The SD (Sicherheitsdienst, the Intelligence branch of the SS) was established in 1934 with Reinhard Heydrich at its head.

By late 1932 and particularly early 1933 the German economy, as previously noted, had passed its lowest point and was experiencing an upturn. The effort of the new government's economic policies, which included a lowering of wages, the commencement of great public works (the autobahns, for example), rearmament, and the gradual elimination of unemployment, was less important than the economic upturn already in progress.

With the abolition of trade unions and the establishment of a Labor Front (May 1933), wages were no longer negotiated but determined by the state. Under the slogan "Joy through Work," workers were treated to state-organized pastimes to take their minds off "dangerous" thoughts.

Similarly, the spiritual and artistic life of Germany was regimented. Reich Propaganda Minister Josef Goebbels directed the press, literature, arts, and science in accordance with Nazi thought. Books written by Jews and those deemed dangerous to Nazi ideology were removed from public libraries. In May 1933 such books were publicly burned in Berlin and elsewhere. Artists and scientists who refused to adhere to the Nazi line either emigrated or were silenced. However, large numbers of creative people accepted the Nazi line, sometimes reluctantly at first, and allowed themselves to be used in Nazi propaganda both at home and abroad.

Special emphasis was placed on the education of youth. Dissident teachers were gradually removed. New textbooks were written in the spirit of Nazism — for example national-socialist physics, national-socialist chemistry — and soon young people joined Nazi youth movements — the Hitler Youth (Hitlerjugend, HJ) for boys and The League of German Girls (Bund deutscher Mädel, BdM) — where blind obedience and loyalty to Hitler and the regime were propagated.

German Foreign Policy

Because the weakness of the German army in 1933 delayed Hitler's demand for *Lebensraum* (living space) for supposedly overpopulated Germany in the East (Russia), he appeared at first as the apostle of peace in Europe, whose sole aim was to recoup losses unjustly suffered by Germany at Versailles. Gradually, however, the underlying principles of Nazi foreign policy unfolded. The Nazis took the first offensive step in October 1933 when they withdrew from the League of Nations. With the signing of a treaty of neutrality with Poland in February 1934, the eastern flank was protected and the Franco-Polish treaty, which was directed toward the encirclement of Germany, was negated. In accordance with provisions of the Versailles treaty, a plebiscite in the Saar region in 1935 determined by an overwhelming majority to return the region to Germany. A region of great mineral wealth and industry, the Saar served as a site for the rearmament of Germany. In a parallel development, the 1935 Naval Agreement with Great Britain allowed Germany to build up a fleet equal to 35 percent of the British fleet's tonnage—a vast building program that soon turned Germany into a major naval power.

In March 1936, with the rearmament program successfully underway, Hitler started bluffing his way through Europe. The Rhine province, a demilitarized zone, was occupied by the as yet unprepared German army. At the slightest sign of French opposition, the troops were to withdraw. But the French did not react, and the occupation, in defiance of the Versailles provisions, stood.

In his quest for allies, Hitler achieved a binding agreement with Italy, which had become isolated following its aggression and conquest of Ethiopia in 1936. The weaknesses of the Italian fascist dictatorship were not apparent, and in 1936 the Berlin-Rome Axis appeared to be a strong combination in the European power game. In defiance of the St. Germain treaty between the Allies and Austria, the Nazis forced the *Anschluss* (annexation) of Austria by a combination of threats and propaganda in March 1938. To Britain, Nazi Germany was a bulwark against European communism and a countervailing force to French power on the Continent. The blindness of British politicians was matched by the weakness of the French state. Finally, using the grievances of the German minority in the Sudeten borderlands against the Czech majority of the democratic Czechoslovak republic, Hitler demanded and, after difficult negotiations with British Prime Minister Neville Chamberlain, obtained the annexation of the Sudetenland to Germany, in an agreement signed in late September 1938 at Munich by Germany, Britain, France, and Italy. The hapless Czechs surrendered without fighting. The conquest of the Sudetenland eliminated the powerful Czech army, whose main fortifications lay in the Sudeten region, and effectively dismantled the Czechoslovak republic, thereby giving the Nazis a predominant position in Central Europe. Hungary and Poland used the dismemberment of Czechoslovakia to obtain portions of Czech territory as well and in the process became Germany's allies. Chamberlain returned to London from Munich with the belief that he had secured "peace in our time." On March 15, 1939, Hitler repudiated the Munich agreement by occupying the Czech lands of Bohemia and Moravia. Declaring them a German Protectorate, he forced the Slovak fascists to declare the independence of the Slovak state.

During these maneuvers, appearances to the contrary, the German Army was still unprepared for war. Tanks and armored vehicles became mired in the spring mud as they entered Austria. During the Sudeten negotiations, German generals offered to rebel against Hitler if the British would not sign the agreement. But the British were not interested; they preferred to rely on Hitler's promises.

On November 5, 1937, Hitler informed his chief generals and confidants that Germany was to be prepared for war within the next few years, that Czechoslovakia and Poland would be eliminated, and that Germany would expand into Russian territory (as recorded in the protocols by officer Friedrich Hossbach). In the course of such a policy, Hitler was prepared to face the Western Powers as well. During 1938 and 1939, consequently, preparation for war intensified. After the repudiation of the Munich agreement in March 1939, Britain understood that appeasement was not possible. Faced with British and French guarantees to Poland, Hitler decided to isolate the struggle against Poland as far as possible and to avoid a two-front struggle by reaching an understanding with the Russians. The Russians, who had followed a straight anti-Nazi line since 1933, were concerned by British prevarications. To the Soviets, Britain and France seemed to want a war between Germany and the Soviet Union, in which the Western Powers would watch while Germans and Soviets killed each other. Stalin thus agreed to turn the tables on the West and on August 23, 1939, signed a neutrality pact (the Molotov-Ribbentrop pact) with the Germans. The agreement guaranteed the Germans the import of essential raw materials from the Soviet Union and effectively neutralized the USSR in the coming struggle against Poland. In addition, in a secret protocol attached to the pact, the Germans agreed to another partition of Poland, in which Latvia and Estonia (and by a later addition Lithuania as well) would come under the Soviet sphere of influence. These previously independent states were subsequently annexed by the Russians in 1940.

Nazi Antisemitic Policy

Affected by the development of both their domestic and their foreign policies, the realization of the Nazi antisemitism evolved gradually, and was marked by considerable vacillations.

Upon the Nazi accession to power, the SA and the SS began their campaign of terrorism by invading apartments, offices, and stores to arrest Jews, in particular lawyers, doctors, and other professional people. They were later released, after being tortured and upon signing a statement that they had been treated well. Nazi brutality turned against political opponents, especially leftists and particularly Jewish leftists. Detailed reports of maltreatment published in the

Western press were quickly defined by the Nazis as "Jewish atrocity stories." In retaliation for such "anti-Nazi propaganda," the Nazis announced an economic boycott of the Jews to start on April 1, 1933. The extremists were Goebbels, Julius Streicher, the Franconian area leader (Gauleiter) and publisher of the pornographic antisemitic weekly "Der Stürmer," and others. These viewed the boycott as an opportunity to rid the German economy of the Jews altogether. Along with the devastation of German Jewry, a permanent boycott would have shattered, perhaps, the illusions indulged in by large numbers of Jews as to the transitory nature of their troubles. But this was not to be.

To protest the Nazi persecution of the Jews, a mass rally was organized for March 27 at Madison Square Garden in New York City by Rabbi Stephen S. Wise, leader of the American Jewish Congress and American Zionism. Threatened by Göring with dire reprisals if the rally was not stopped, German Jewish liberals and Zionists appealed to their American brethren and even to the American Embassy in Berlin to cancel the rally, but to no avail. The rally raised the consciousness of Americans and thoroughly frightened conservative Reich cabinet ministers, who cited the adverse results a war of "international Jewry" would have on the German economy. They pleaded with the Nazi hierarchy to stop the boycott. On March 31 Goebbels announced a one-day boycott for Saturday, April 1, a day on which many Jewish shops and offices were closed in any case. Both the Nazis and their right-wing allies thus fell victim to their own ideology. In the Madison Square Garden rally they saw the expression of that mysterious international Jew they had invented, their all-consuming fear. In calling off the permanent boycott in fear of the counterreaction of the Jews, the Nazis yielded, in effect, to the figment of their own imagination.

Nevertheless, the April 1 boycott was implemented with much brutality by party members. The attitude of the population in general left much to be desired from a Nazi point of view, which indicated the need the Nazis felt to intensify their antisemitic propaganda.

On April 7, 1933, the Law for the Re-establishment of the Professional Civil Service, which provided for the dismissal of "non-Aryans," was promulgated. The few exceptions—those who had been serving since August 14, 1914, or prior to that date, those who had fought at the front for Germany (or one of its allies), and those whose fathers or sons had died in the German cause—a concession to Hindenburg, were abolished after his death. The importance of the law lies in its definition of "non-Aryan": In practice the term non-Aryan applied only to Jews. By a subsequent definition of April 11, a person who had one Jewish parent or one Jewish grandparent was identified as "of non-Aryan descent." One can see how confused Nazi racism was when Jewish grandparents were defined by religion rather than so-called racial criteria.

Although detailed anti-Jewish legislation had not been prepared prior to the Nazi accession to power, the general proposals contained in Heinrich Class's book *Wenn Ich der Kaiser wär* (If I Were the Kaiser, Berlin 1913) were to be translated into action: elimination of Jews from public life, from the armed forces, from state education, from influence on the press, from the management of corporate banks, and from the ownership of rural property. Jews who had acquired German citizenship were to be denaturalized and Jewish names that been translated into German were to be nullified.[2] Internal memoranda show that the decision to implement these proposals was clear before 1933.

A series of laws and administrative orders promulgated or issued between April and October 1933 translated these proposals into reality. Jews were excluded from such occupations as assessors, jurors, and commercial judges (April 7): a *numerus clausus* law limiting Jewish students in institutions of higher learning to 1.5 percent of new admissions was promulgated on April 25. In the professional sphere, the establishment of a Reich Chamber of Culture (September 29, 1933) provided a means for excluding Jews from entertainment enterprises (art, literature, theater, movies); the National Press Law (October 4, 1933) excluded Jews from the press. Jewish ritual slaughter was forbidden; Jews could no longer farm land; and on July 14, the Law on the Revocation of Naturalization and Annulment of German Citizenship deprived Jewish immigrants, especially those of East European background, of German citizenship.

Pressure from the party rank and file and from the SA especially to go beyond these legal restrictions was resisted on several grounds. First, the conservatives were opposed, especially those like Hjalmar Schacht, the minister responsible for the restoration of the German economy. To them, any such action was likely to disrupt economic recovery. Schacht and others like him opposed drastic anti-Jewish actions because Jews were considered an important middle-class element in Germany and a powerful force abroad. Second, what the next step should be was not clear. The Nazis wanted the Jews to leave Germany, but they were not quite sure how to achieve their goal. . . . Third, in 1934 the Nazi party was facing serious internal problems (e.g., the purge of SA leadership and other opponents), and the "Jewish problem" had a lower priority.

The relative quiet of 1934 acted as a dangerous sedative on the Jewish community, lulling many into a false sense of security. Insofar as Jews were not members of opposition groups, they were not arrested. But an unofficial boycott and public humiliation continued, and life for Jews, in many small places especially, was becoming unbearable. Although about 20 percent of German Jews had lost their livelihood, according to JDC [Joint Distribution Committee] esti-

2. Lucy S. Dawidowicz, *The War Against the Jews, 1933–1945* (New York, 1975), pp. 57–58; see also pp. 59–60.

mates, the mood prevalent among German Jews was that Hitler's rule could not last, that the country of Goethe and Schiller, Beethoven and Schubert would soon shake off the barbarians who had temporarily gained control.

In 1935 ominous signs appeared. The increasingly violent hate articles appearing in Julius Streicher's *Der Stürmer* (The Attacker) were echoed in Goebbels' *Der Angriff* (The Attack) and another party magazine in Berlin, *Der Judenkenner* (The Jew-Expert). The exclusion of Jews from German life altogether was demanded. On May 21, 1935, Jews were excluded from the armed forces. Goebbels and the party apparently linked their attacks on the Jews with their desire to eliminate centers of conservative power. On July 16, 1935, shops were destroyed and Jewish passers-by were beaten up on Berlin's main thoroughfare, the Kurfürstendamm. The next day, *Der Angriff* carried the headline: "Berlin is being cleansed of Communism, Reaction and the Jews." The beatings and destruction of property continued about a week.

But there were other views in the party as well. Frick and Bormann intervened against the disorder, and the conservatives, led by Schacht, warned the party leadership energetically against excesses. Schacht spoke publicly on August 18 and convened a conference of experts on August 20, although a unanimous stand was not achieved. On June 18, 1935, the German-British Naval Agreement was signed, and economic negotiations were begun on June 17 with France. There was no point in proving at that point that disorder and insecurity were reigning in Germany.

Hitler, apparently, had kept aloof from these developments. However, after the signing of the Anglo-German and French-German accords he intervened, because he saw that the situation was ripe for a legal disenfranchisement of the Jews. Disenfranchisement would gratify party activists, especially if accompanied by dramatic acts of humiliation; and the conservatives would see it as an end to insecurity, a legal definition of the rights of second-class citizens.

Various laws designed to disenfranchise the Jews had been prepared earlier, but what became known as the Nuremberg laws resulted from a direct order by Hitler on September 13. The two laws promulgated at the Reichstag in Nuremberg on September 15, 1935, and the first decree to the Reich citizenship law of November 14 are usually included in what is known as the Nuremberg laws.

The Reich citizenship law of September 15 says in part:

1. (1) A subject is anyone who enjoys the protection of the German Reich and for this reason is specifically obligated to it.
    (2) Nationality is acquired according to the provisions of the Reich and state nationality law.
2. (1) A Reich citizen is only that subject of German or kindred blood who

proves by his conduct that he is willing and suited loyally to serve the
German people and the Reich.

(2) Reich citizenship is acquired through the conferment of a certificate
of Reich citizenship.

(3) The Reich citizen is the sole bearer of full political rights as provided
by the laws.[3]

The Law for the Protection of German Blood and German Honor, passed on
the same day, says in part:

Imbued with the insight that the purity of German blood is a prerequisite for
the continued existence of the German people and inspired by the inflexible
will to ensure the existence of the German nation for all times, the Reichstag
has unanimously adopted the following law, which is hereby promulgated:

1. (1) Marriages between Jews and subjects of German or kindred blood are
   forbidden. Marriages nevertheless concluded are invalid, even if
   concluded abroad to circumvent this law.

   (2) Only the State Attorney may initiate the annulment suit.
2. Extramarital intercourse between Jews and subjects of German or kindred
   blood is forbidden.
3. Jews must not employ in their households female subjects of German
   or kindred blood who are under 45 years old.
4. (1) Jews are forbidden to fly the Reich or national flag and to display the
   Reich colors.

   (2) They are, on the other hand, allowed to display the Jewish colors.
   The exercise of this right enjoys the protection of the state.[4]

The decree of November 14, which defined so-called *Mischlinge*, or persons
of "mixed blood," is perhaps more indicative of Nazi ideology than the others.
It reads, in part:

2. (2) A Jewish "Mischling" is anyone who is descended from one or two
   grandparents who are fully Jewish as regards race, unless he is deemed a
   Jew under 5, Paragraph 2. A grandparent is deemed fully Jewish without
   further ado, if he has belonged to the Jewish religious community.
3. Only a Reich citizen, as bearer of full political rights, can exercise the
   right to vote on political matters, or hold public office. The Reich
   Minister of the Interior or an agency designated by him may, in the

3. Lucy S. Dawidowicz, *A Holocaust Reader* (New York, 1976), p. 45.
4. Dawidowicz, *Holocaust Reader,* pp. 47–48.

transition period, permit exceptions with regard to admission to public office. The affairs of religious associations are not affected. . .

5. (1) A Jew is anyone descended from at least three grandparents who are fully Jewish as regards race. Paragraph 2, Sentence 2 applies.

(2) Also deemed a Jew is a Jewish Mischling subject who is descended from two fully Jewish grandparents and

a. who belonged to the Jewish religious community when the law was issued or has subsequently been admitted to it;

b. who was married to a Jew when the law was issued or has subsequently married one;

c. who is the offspring of a marriage concluded by a Jew, within the meaning of Paragraph 1, after the Law for the Protection of German Blood and German Honor of September 15, 1935 took effect;

d. who is the offspring of extramarital intercourse with a Jew, within the meaning of Paragraph 1, and will have been born out of wedlock after July 31, 1936.[5]

Believing that the laws would allow the establishment of a bearable relationship with the Germans, the Jews accepted their status as second-class citizens.

To create a good impression on visitors to the Olympic Games in 1936, the Nazis splashed a coat of whitewash on Berlin. Anti-Jewish signs disappeared from shops, theaters, and the town gates. Jewish sportsmen and sportswomen were invited to participate in the games. The international community sent athletes from the world around, ignoring not only the Nuremberg laws and the other anti-Jewish measures but also the military occupation of the Rhineland—in contravention of the Versailles peace treaty—by Nazi forces in March 1936, three months before the games. The effect of the Nuremberg laws did not appear until the games were over, when the Jewish situation began to deteriorate. As in 1934, the 1936 Olympic Games episode tended to delude the Jews into a false sense of relative stability, if not security.

The fate of the Jews was linked to Hitler's preparation for war. As early as the end of 1935 at a meeting of Gauleiters, Hitler reported that war would be launched in four years when preparations were complete.[6] As we have seen already, Hitler prepared a memorandum outlining his program for Hermann Göring, who assumed responsibility for the Nazi Four-Year Plan in September 1936.

The war was to insure the dominance of Europe by the Aryan race and through

5. Dawidowicz, *Holocaust Reader,* p. 46.

6. Bernhard Lösener, "Als Rassereferent im Reichsministerium des Innern," (As Race Experts in the Reich Ministry of the Interior), *VJHfZ* (Vierteljahreshefte für Zeitgeschichte), 9 (1961): 264–266.

it the dominance of the world as well. To accomplish this goal, Germany would have to eliminate the Jews within the four-year period of preparation, for if Germany did not eliminate the Jews under their control, the Jewish Satan, still residing in Germany, would, according to Hitler, eliminate the German people. Clearly, therefore, as war approached Nazi policies toward the Jews became more extreme.

These developments took place at a time when Jews were not leaving Germany fast enough. On October 14, 1937, the SS journal *Das Schwarze Korps* stated that Jewish businesses should "disappear," that is, be confiscated. In February 1938, Economic Affairs Minister Hjalmar Schacht, who had objected to anti-Jewish measures out of economic considerations, was replaced by Walther Funk. Funk's first task was to remove the Jews from the German economy. An SD internal report of January 1938 demanded the removal of all the poor Jews. A similar line was taken by the *Das Schwarze Korps* in February, although more radical laws proposed by extreme Nazis in various ministeries and supported by Hitler were shelved.[7]

The annexation of Austria on March 13, 1938, increased the Jewish population by approximately 200,000.[8] The Jewish communities of Germany and Austria were quite different. Jews in Austria were, for the most part, a relatively new group, having arrived over the past one hundred years from Polish Galicia, Bukovina, and the Czech lands. In Vienna, where the overwhelming majority of Austrian Jews lived, they engaged in trade—mostly small businesses—and the professions. In 1937, the Jewish proportion of various industries was: advertising, 90 percent; furniture manufacturing, 85 percent; newspapers and shoe manufacturing, 80 percent. Of the doctors and dentists, 51.6 percent were Jewish, as were 62 percent of the lawyers. In the slums of Vienna, 30 percent of the Jews lived in great poverty, many dependent on charity, and 35.5 percent of the Jewish working population were unemployed.[9]

Early in the twentieth century Vienna had been the hotbed of a populist, Christian-Socialist antisemitism, personified by Mayor Karl Lueger. After the dissolution of the Habsburg monarchy, dislike of the stranger—in the Jewish case both visible and vulnerable—increased rather than decreased. At the same time, social democracy was a powerful factor and the Social-Democrats opposed

7. Uwe D. Adam, *Judenpolitik im Dritten Reich* (Jewish Policy in the Third Reich), (Düsseldorf, 1972), pp. 159–166.

8. Official population figures: 185,246 Jews. The inclusion of converts to Christianity, or people not declaring for any religion, would add 15,000 and possibly more persons of Jewish origin.

9. Yehuda Bauer, *My Brother's Keeper* (Philadelphia, 1974), pp. 222–223.

antisemitism. Socialism—the universalist ideas of a working-class movement that promised security and brotherhood to the outsiders—quite naturally appealed to the Jews, who contributed such leaders as Otto Bauer, Viktor Adler, and Friedrich Adler. In early 1934, however, with the defeat of a socialist uprising against the dictatorship of Christian-Socialist Engelbert Dollfuss, the Socialist party disappeared.

The Jewish community—the Israelitische Kultusgemeinde (IKG)—was organized on party lines: the Unionists, who were the Austrian equivalent of the liberal, assimilationist Central-Verein in Germany, and the Zionists, who were in the majority.

When the Nazis marched into Austria in 1938, the Austrian population, especially the Viennese, rallied to them with great enthusiasm. The arrest of political opponents was accompanied by massive action against the Jews. The process of degradation, terror, and expropriation that had taken five years in Germany was completed—indeed surpassed—in a few months in Austria. Men and women were forced to scrub streets on their knees, while crowds of Viennese stood by and cheered; shops were invaded, robbed, and their owners beaten; arbitrary arrests deprived families of fathers who were never seen again.

In Germany, the legal campaign against the Jews continued. On April 22, 1938, a law against "hiding" the identity of Jewish businesses was enacted. On April 26 an order was issued requiring the registration of all Jewish businesses worth more than 5,000 marks. Such businesses were officially identified on June 14. Until then, although deprived of governmental or public posts, Jews could operate private businesses and pursue legal and medical professions, albeit under increasingly difficult conditions that included unofficial boycott. Jewish artisans and laborers could still work if they could find someone willing to employ them. In the spring of 1938, however, the laws took on a new character.

On March 28, 1938, the German Jewish communities were deprived of the right to act as legal personalities (i.e., own property, etc.). As of September 30, Jewish doctors could no longer treat Aryans, although they were allowed to function as medical orderlies for their Jewish patients; Jewish lawyers were forbidden to practice law as of November 30. On August 17 a law was issued requiring that all male Jews assume the name Israel and all females the name Sarah by January 1, 1939. On October 5, a law was issued requiring all Jewish passports to be marked with the letter "J" (for "Jude," Jew)—which originated with the head of the Swiss Alien police, Dr. Heinrich Rothmund, who wanted to limit the entry of Jews into Switzerland.[10]

On June 9, 1938, the synagogue in Munich was set on fire. On June 15 some

10. Bauer, *Brother's Keeper,* pp. 97–98.

1,500 Jews who had police records (including traffic violations) were put into concentration camps. Until then, Jews had not been systematically incarcerated in such camps whose overall population in late 1937 was about 7,000.

On August 10, Julius Streicher destroyed the Nuremberg synagogue. Meanwhile in Austria, anti-Jewish attacks tended to be more extreme than in Germany itself. By September 1938, 4,000 Austrian Jews had been sent to concentration camps. Suicides multiplied. In some small communities (Horn in Lower Austria and the Burgenland) expulsions took place in September and early October. Berlin canceled a plan to expel all the Jews from three Viennese districts on October 5, Yom Kippur, the Day of Atonement, the holiest of Jewish holidays, a day of repentance and fasting.[11]

To prevent Polish Jews who were living in Vienna from fleeing to Poland after the annexation of Austria on March 13, a Polish law was promulgated on March 25 decreeing that Polish citizens who had not visited Poland for five consecutive years would be deprived of their citizenship. In June it was reported that Polish Jews affected by this regulation who nevertheless returned to Poland would be put into a concentration camp for political prisoners (at Bereza Kartuska).

Of the 98,747 non-German Jews in Germany in 1933, 56,480 were Polish nationals. On October 6, 1938, the Polish government declared that citizenship would be denied to those whose passports were not renewed by October 29. On October 26 the German Foreign Office requested the Gestapo to deport as many Polish Jews as possible. The Gestapo was eager to comply. On the night of October 27–28, some 18,000 Jews were put on special trains and sent to the Polish border. Denied entrance into Poland, many were nevertheless forced across the border illegally by the Nazis; others, some 5,000, were forced to camp in a tiny Polish frontier village, Zbazsyn. When Hershel Grynszpan, a 17-year-old student living in Paris, received a letter from his father telling him what had happened to his family in Zbazsyn, he went to the German Embassy in Paris on November 7 to kill the ambassador. Instead, he shot a third secretary of the embassy, Ernst vom Rath, who was not a Nazi; he died on November 9. Grynszpan's action triggered the Kristallnacht (Night of the Crystal Glass) pogrom.

Vom Rath's death was a convenience for the Nazis, allowing them to justify mass action against the Jews as revenge for the German diplomat's death, but mass arrests actually had been planned long before the shooting in Paris —barracks to accommodate tens of thousands of Jews had been built in concentration camps.

Hitler and Goebbels discussed their strategy in Munich on the night of November 9 as Nazi leaders assembled to celebrate the anniversary of Hitler's 1923

---

11. Herbert Rosenkranz, *Reichskristallnacht* (Vienna, 1968).

putsch. In an attempt to seize control of the Jewish question from his Nazi competitors, Göring and Himmler, Goebbels activated the SA and tens of thousands of loyal party members to burn all the synagogues in Germany, destroy and loot Jewish shops, and physically abuse large numbers of Jews. Ninety-one Jews were reported dead. But the German population at large did not respond enthusiastically to the pogrom. Although little help was extended to the victims, neither was there a joyous participation in the orgy of destruction. Most Germans were shocked or disinterested. Himmler and Heydrich quickly regained control and emphasized their own anti-Jewish hallmark: cold, "scientific," unemotional brutality. SS units were ordered to capture Jewish archives, to insure the confiscation, not the looting, of individual and community property. In a major action, they arrested and sent to concentration camps some 30,000 Jewish men at least.

Three major points emerge from the documentation: (1) the details of a new Jewish policy were worked out *after* the Kristallnacht, not before; (2) the Jews had to pay the Nazis a so-called indemnity (for the death of vom Rath) of 1 billion reichsmarks, as well as insurance benefits for their destroyed property, which came to another 250 million reichsmarks; and (3) following the Kristallnacht, the Jews were finally and totally evicted from German economic life. By January 1, 1939, a Jew could be employed only by a Jewish organization. As businesses were taken over by "Aryan" Germans ("aryanized"), employees were fired. The ultimate goal, the eviction of all Jews from Germany, was within reach. Those in concentration camps were released, provided frantic relatives arranged for emigration. A mass panic and mass exodus ensued to anywhere, at any price. Of the approximately 500,000 Jews in Germany and 200,000 Jews in Austria, about one-half had emigrated by the outbreak of war.

EUGENICS AND NAZI RACE THEORY IN PRACTICE†

The transition from theory to practice in Nazi Jewish policy provided the indispensable background to the "final solution of the Jewish question." Those involved—victims and persecutors alike—could not have envisaged the unprecedented mass murder which lay at the end of this policy, even after the harsh turn of the winter of 1937. When Hitler first in secret issued the verbal order for the practical execution of the final solution sometime during the

†From George L. Mosse, *Toward the Final Solution: A History of European Racism* (Madison: University of Wisconsin Press, 1987; original ed. 1978), 215–20. Footnotes omitted. Reprinted by permission of author.

late spring of 1941 and designated the SS to carry it through, there was some astonishment among the SS leadership. Yet there should have been no doubt that Hitler took racism seriously, even if the will to push it to its logical conclusion was only implicitly evident until the Führer regarded the time as ripe.

The law of July 14, 1933, to prevent the bearing of hereditarily sick offspring was a eugenic measure in which sterilization was defined as voluntary except in certain very precisely described circumstances. But before the law was a year old, sterilizations had become compulsory and it was no longer necessary to obtain the victim's consent. What kind of hereditary sickness would warrant sterilization was discussed in terms of the victim's ability to cope successfully with the exigencies of life and the likelihood of his being able to face the dangers of war. Both these considerations had nothing to do with the usual definitions of sickness, but instead were related to the sick individual's usefulness to society.

The congenitally sick were thought to be unproductive and . . . productivity played a large part in racist thought. The superior race was always considered productive, while the inferior races had nothing tangible to show for their labor. The one book which most impressed Nazi eugenicists centered on this very problem; the congenitally sick and those who had lost their will to work should be killed because the community must be freed from the burden of caring for its useless members. The lawyer Karl Binding and the physician Alfred Hoch wrote their *The Release of Unworthy Life in Order that It Might Be Destroyed (Die Freigabe der Vernichtung Lebensunwertes Lebens*, 1920) during the postwar economic crisis. To keep alive those who had lost their usefulness to themselves and society meant wasting the will to work and the fortunes of healthy and productive people. They contrasted the sacrifice of youth in war with the waste of nursing such useless existences. Euthanasia, the book concluded, was based upon respect for "everyone's will to live."

Binding and Hoch were not racists, and no argument based upon racial eugenics can be found in their book. But the concept of usefulness to society, of the ability to work and, last but not least, the thought that some had to be killed so that others could live to the full, were easily assimilated into racial arguments. The qualities Binding and Hoch praised were also those which characterized the "master race." Euthanasia thus became the necessary consequence of attempts to improve the race by doing away with its parasites.

In fact, the killing of those with mental deficiencies and physical peculiarities had already taken place when, on September 1, 1939, Adolf Hitler gave over increased authority to the physicians and laymen chosen to administer the Nazi program. The euthanasia decree was predated by Hitler himself to the first day of the outbreak of the Second World War—a gesture more significant than the

administrative decree itself. Hitler saw the victory of the Aryan as the overriding purpose of the conflict; not only was it necessary to put lesser races in their
place, but also to free the Aryans of any potential weakness. Euthanasia and the
war were interrelated as closely as the war and the final solution. During December 1939, every asylum in Germany was obliged to fill out a questionnaire
identifying each patient and the length of time he had been in the asylum.
Anyone who had stayed five years or more was closely scrutinized. Was he or
she criminally insane, schizophrenic, or senile? They would then have to be
transferred to those institutions like Grafeneck or Hadamar that were supposed
to be secret, but where in fact everyone knew that euthanasia took place. The
list of diseases which led to the transfer was constantly revised, but all of them
were illnesses difficult to define accurately. Only one "disease" was precise: all
Jewish patients were to be killed, regardless of medical findings. The Jewish
mental patients and neurologically ill were the vanguard of the 6 million who
were to die. A new questionnaire was devised in 1940, which now openly
asked whether patients were able to work. At the same time, physicians not
trained in psychiatry were allowed to take part in the selection process.

There was resistance. Some of Germany's most famous institutions for the
insane refused to fill out the questionnaire and got away with it. But there were
also a few parents who asked that their sick children be killed. Euthanasia could
not be kept secret. It took place in institutions near population centers, and
parents and relatives were soon suspicious of the all too sudden deaths. The
churches took the lead in protesting euthanasia. The Protestant bishop Theophile
Wurm was one of the first to protest, and so was Bishop Konrad von Preysing of
Berlin. Yet it was Bishop Clemens August Galen of Münster who created the
most attention when he publicly exposed the program on August 31, 1941. If
so-called unproductive people can be killed like animals, then "woe to us all
when we become old and feeble," he exclaimed. Such exposure was only the
climax of a feeling of insecurity which euthanasia had spread throughout the
population.

The Nazis attempted to popularize euthanasia as a sacrifice that would prove
a blessing for the victim. They used the medium of film in order to spread this
message, and in *I Accuse (Ich klage an*, 1941) tried to demonstrate the innocence of a physician who had killed his incurably sick wife. Reference was
made to heroic Roman times when such deaths had been permitted, and to the
ancient Germans, who had allowed mercy killings. Only at one point in the film
was the killing of the insane obliquely referred to, and then in the context of
Hoch and Binding, to point out the supposed absurdity of maintaining a huge
staff and many buildings in order to keep "a few miserable creatures" alive.
This film did not have a great impact. But the Nazis in their striving for totality

whenever possible used film to propagate their policies through visual statements, always so much more important for them than the written word. Thus the roundup of Jews in 1940, wherever it occurred, was accompanied by a showing of an anti-Semitic film, *Jud Süss* (1940), that was highly successful. Süss Oppenheimer was a seventeenth-century court Jew who was executed for his supposed exploitation and corruption of the German state of Württemberg. This was vastly more popular than *I Accuse*, perhaps because its subject did not touch the daily life of the average German and the racial stereotype had been well prepared.

In spite of all propaganda for euthanasia, shortly after Bishop Galen's sermon, Hitler gave the order to halt the program; a combination of ecclesiastical protest and adverse public opinion convinced him that the time was not ripe for such measures. Nevertheless, euthanasia continued sporadically in secret.

The opposition which officially ended the program was nowhere to be found when it came to the final solution of the Jewish question. There too the Nazis transgressed the "laws of God and nature" in ignoring the sacrament of baptism by killing converted Jews. But few parishioners were involved, no aunt or uncle was suddenly taken by death, and thus no feeling of insecurity spread within the German population. Euthanasia affected all Germans, while the deportation and death of the Jews affected only a minority that had already been "pushed into a corner," as Hitler put it, and separated from the population as a whole.

The euthanasia program killed some 70,000 people, among them a high percentage of babies and children. At first the victims were shot, but soon they were killed by gas in rooms disguised as showers. The connection between euthanasia and the eventual method of the Jewish mass murder is obvious here. But the link between euthanasia and the destruction of Jews was closer still. Putting euthanasia into practice meant that the Nazis took the idea of "unworthy" life seriously, and a life so defined was characterized by lack of productivity and degenerate outward appearance. Lombroso's psychology underlay much of the selection process of euthanasia: physical deformity was taken as a sign of mental sickness. While the ideas of unproductivity and physical appearance were both constantly applied to Jews, euthanasia showed for the first time Hitler's determination to destroy such unworthy life. Ominously, the definition applied to the mentally sick and to the Jews was very similar.

At the same time, the régime believed, the Aryan race itself must constantly be improved. Even as "unworthy life" was snuffed out, Heinrich Himmler attempted to initiate programs which would transform into reality the utopias of racial breeding that had fascinated racial theoreticians ever since the beginning of the twentieth century. Racial screening in the SS became thorough, demanding not only the presentation of a genealogy but photographs of the applicants as well. The *Lebensborn* (literally, "the source of life") was instituted in 1936 so that mothers bearing pure racial offspring might get the best medical care, even if they happened to be unmarried. All liaisons between racially valuable SS men and racially pure women were encouraged; but the bourgeois values of Himmler restrained such attempts at selective breeding. For him marriage was the answer, and unmarried SS members would never get promotions, while those with many children could count on his goodwill. Eventually, the planned settlements of German peasants in the Slavic lands would serve as Aryan stud farms (among their other duties as outposts of defense), providing the kind of isolated Aryan paradise of which men like Willibald Hentschel had dreamed.

Euthanasia was part of the reciprocal relationship between an unworthy life and one considered especially worthy of continuation. It was built upon the images of inferior and superior races that have filled the pages of this book. But the Jews were not only singled out because of so-called signs of physical degeneration, or their so-called lack of productivity, but also because of their supposed criminality. The Nazis based their concept of criminality on the theories of Cesare Lombroso, for whom the habitual criminal was "an atavistic being who reproduced in his person the ferocious instincts of primitive humanity and the inferior animals." This degeneration (as Lombroso called it) was proved by physical deformities of the skull, though the whole body could be deformed as well. Phrenology had added to this concept not only the assertion (taken from Gall) that "the heads of all thieves resemble each other more or less in shape," but also that criminals, because they are "immoderate," are rootless "and relapse into nomadism." Lombroso had believed that habitual criminals could not be rehabilitated since their very physical appearance was involved in their actions, and that they must therefore suffer the death penalty. The Jews because of their race were regarded as habitual criminals by the Nazis and therefore rightly doomed to destruction.

This concept of criminality has been ignored by scholars of the holocaust, although Nazi literature and films are full of it. There is no doubt that belief in this theory of criminality made it easier to accept the murder of the Jews, because it had sunk so deep into popular consciousness. It was not just a part of Volkish and Nazi writings, but also of the popular literature, with its decisive separation of good and evil, and its criminals who in their very appearance reflected their opposition to the law. In a manner of speaking, such stories perpetuated the evil mental and physical characteristics that earlier writers like Balzac and Eugène Sue had thought typical of the underworld. For some at least, the Jews were similarly degenerate characters; if they did not originate in the sewers of Paris, they were nevertheless compared to rats. Indeed, this was how the Jews had been pictured in the highly successful film *Jud Süss* as they scurried into the city of Stuttgart after the duke of Württemberg had delivered his state into their hands through his minister Süss Oppenheimer. Even as the film was being shown, real-life Jews were being rounded up and deported to the east.

THE ANATOMY OF THE HOLOCAUST†

In the middle of the war a remarkable man by the name of Franz Neumann, who worked in the Office of Strategic Services and the Department of State, wrote a book about Nazi Germany called *Behemoth*. The first edition came out in 1942, the second in 1944. Each edition was written without the benefit of any original documents, any of the captured materials which became available after the collapse of Germany and which constitute the major source of our knowledge about the destruction process. Franz Neumann worked from newspapers, from published decrees, from journal articles that were somehow transmitted across the ocean, through Switzerland to the United States. He worked intuitively, and he analyzed the structure of the Nazi regime with singular insight. He called Germany a "non-state," a "behemoth" but not a state. He identified four hierarchical groupings as operating virtually independently of one another, and occasionally coming together to make what he sarcastically called "social contracts." Those four hierarchies were the veritable pillars of modern Germany, as they have occasionally been described by German constitutional lawyers and historians: the German civil service, the German army, the later emergent industrial conglomeration of various giant enterprises, and finally, the Nazi Party and its machinery.

Several years later, when the war crimes trials were begun in Nuremberg, most particularly after the very first one, more and more documents were turned up here and there, a paper residue of a vast bureaucracy. The primary problem was to make a few piles of them so that one could at least break down this mass of tens of thousands and even hundreds of thousands of materials into manageable quantities. The records were labeled roughly by subject matter: "NG," "NI," "NO," and "NOKW." "NG" stands for Nazi government, in the main correspondence produced by the civil service; "NI" is Nazi industry; "NO," Nazi organizations, that is to say, Party documents; and "NOKW" stands for Nazi

†From Raul Hilberg, "The Anatomy of the Holocaust," in *The Holocaust: Ideology, Bureaucracy, and Genocide. The San José Papers,* ed. Henry Friedlander and Sybil Milton (New York: Kraus International Publications, 1980), 85-102. Reprinted by permission.

Oberkommando der Wehrmacht, the high command of the armed forces. Independently of Franz Neumann, the archivists and researchers preparing the Nuremberg trials had developed the identical scheme of things as they looked at these documents. They, too, concluded that there were four major hierarchies.

Fortunately, I came under Neumann's influence very early, while I was a beginning graduate student at Columbia University. Neumann was not a very approachable man, and I did not want to tell him that I was about to embark on the study of the destruction of the Jews. Therefore I said that I wanted to investigate the role of the German civil service in that destruction. He nodded his head, and that was as much conversation as he made because he was hard of hearing. Actually, I was preparing to do more—I was going to write about all the other hierarchies as well, because somehow I felt that each was involved in the destruction process in some way. And then I realized that I would have to write four stories, paralleling one another. That wouldn't do. Consequently I had to come upon another scheme, another anatomy, to describe that development. At that very moment I came across an analysis by an extraordinarily shrewd observer who was in Hungary during the war. Rudolf Kastner, a Jew who made audacious attempts to negotiate with the Germans in 1944 for ransoming the Jews of Hungary (efforts that by and large failed), wrote an affidavit on his experiences and perspectives at Nuremberg right after his liberation. In that 18-page summation he said words to the effect: For years, we sat there in Hungary surrounded by other Axis countries. We watched the Jews disappear in Germany. We watched them disappear in Poland. We watched them disappear in Yugoslavia and many other places. And then we noticed—meaning in essence *he* noticed—that everywhere the same events seemed to be happening, that certain steps followed in sequence. In a crude way he outlined these steps. And it suddenly occurred to me that the destruction of the Jews was a process.

In the administrative process, the path of a bureaucracy is determined, not by blueprints or strategies, but by the very nature of the undertaking. Thus, a group of people, dispersed in a larger population over an entire continent, will not be concentrated or seized until after they have been identified and defined. One step at a time, and each step dependent on the preceding step. The destruction of the Jews transpired in this manner; it had an inherent logic, irrespective of how far ahead the perpetrators could see and irrespective of what their plans were. They could have stopped at any one moment and at any one place, but they could not have omitted steps in the progression or "escalation" of the process. They had to traverse all of these routines. They had to sever, one by one, the relations and ties of the Jewish community with the surrounding population in every region of German-dominated Europe. Step one, in the analytical scheme of things, was thus the undertaking of defining Jews as such. It would appear to have been a simple matter, but it was not. There is a Jewish definition of the term "Jew," but that would not serve the Germans. To them, an adherence to the Jewish religion, or descent from a Jewish mother, was not decisive because there might have been recent converts to Christianity, or half-Jews with a Jewish father who were not Jewish in Jewish eyes but who could not be German in the Third Reich. Above all, if Jewry were defined in accordance with religious criteria alone, Jews might convert overnight and, by doing so, immunize themselves from the effects of the destruction process, a medieval approach adequate enough in an earlier age, but one that was not proper in a racial environment. Yet everyone knew that Jews could not be identified in every case by physiognomy. Definition could not rest on measurements of faces. The whole notion of race had an ideological tinge, but very little administrative utility.

It was an official in the Interior Ministry (originally in the customs administration) who wrote the final version of the definition decree that we associate with the Nuremberg Laws. The original Law, the very first in which measures were taken against Jews, the Law for the Restoration of the German Civil Service, had specified "non-Aryan." The phrase had come down from the nineteenth century. It resulted in a protest by the Japanese government, which felt insulted. The Germans replied, "Wait. We do not mean that different races are necessarily different in quality. They are just different in kind." But even with this explanation, that concept was in trouble.

Non-Aryan, at any rate, was any person with a single Jewish grandparent. That grandparent only had to belong to the Jewish religion. A person with a Jewish grandparent could be dismissed from a post in the civil service or from the teaching profession. Yet in the escalating destruction process, such a definition, embracing individuals who were three-quarters German, was too harsh. It was up to Bernhard Lösener, the customs official transferred to the Interior Ministry, to define the term Jew. He had to do so urgently because at Nuremberg a law had been issued, a criminal law, in which "Jews" were forbidden to marry Germans, and "Jews" were forbidden to have extramarital intercourse with Germans, and "Jews" were forbidden to employ in their household German women under the age of 45. And Jews were not defined in that criminal law.

Thus, an implementation decree had to be issued that would contain that missing definition. It was to provide that a person was to be considered Jewish if he had three or four Jewish grandparents. That person was Jewish regardless of his own religious adherence. He could have been brought up as a Christian, his parents might have been Christians, but if most of his grandparents were Jewish by religion, then he was Jewish in accordance with this new definition. If an individual had two Jewish grandparents, he would be classified as Jewish only if he himself belonged to the Jewish religion at the time of the issuance of the decree, or if—at that moment—he was married to a Jewish person. The critical factor in every case was in the first instance the religion of the grandparents. That is the reason for a new profession that came into being all over Germany, the *Sippenforscher*, specialists in genealogy who were providing evidence of the religion of grandparents by means of records found in state offices or baptismal certificates furnished by churches.

The definition decree had the effect of targeting the Jews automatically in that it precluded them from doing anything at all to change their status and thereby to escape from the impact of all the destructive measures that were to come. The very next step in the unfolding destruction process was economic, primarily the expropriation of Jewish business firms, a process known as "Aryanizations."

At the beginning, the "Aryanizations" were "voluntary." German companies, aided by regulations of the Economy Ministry, would bid for Jewish enterprises, always at levels below market value. Still, we can clearly see a struggle being waged by Jewish owners attempting to obtain a meaningful price, and by German interests competing for Jewish property against each other, attempting to enlarge their over-all strength or influence in a sector of the economy. However, this phase of acquisition came to an end, by and large, at the end of 1938 with the firing of the synagogues. At that point the Aryanizations were no longer voluntary, but compulsory. Jewish firms could be sold or liquidated by German "trustees" and Jewish employees in these concerns lost their jobs.

The very next step was concentration, the physical separation and the social isolation of the Jewish community from the German. Actually the very first Nuremberg decree prohibiting new marriages between Jews and Germans was an initial step in that direction. There followed others, including measures that placed the machinery of the Jewish community under German command. Henceforth, in the Reich as well as in newly conquered territory, the Germans would employ Jewish leaders and Jewish community personnel for housing segregation, personal property confiscation, forced labor, and even deportations. In the wake of the violence and the arrest waves of November 1938, Hermann Göring and several other Nazi personalities discussed the question of whether one ought to form ghettos inside Germany. The idea was rejected, most particularly by that expert policeman Reinhard Heydrich, who was to head the German Security Police and Security Service, on the ground that so long as the Jews were not inside a wall, out of sight of the German population, every German could act as an auxiliary policeman, every German could watch the Jews, every German could keep track of them.

Less than one year after that conference, war broke out. Poland was invaded, and several million additional Jews came under German jurisdiction. A concentration process in Poland began almost immediately; the medieval ghetto came into existence once more. The largest was the Warsaw ghetto, the second largest was the ghetto of Lodz, and there were hundreds of others. All were captive city-states, with a variety of functions including mundane as well as extraordinary tasks. That is a history so varied, so diversified, so complex as to demand attention in and of itself. In the great work of Isaiah Trunk, *Judenrat,* you may discover the history not only of the Jewish Councils, but of the entire structure of the ghettos, their social, economic, and political problems under the Nazis.

There was an ambiguity in the very formation of the ghettos. What was going to happen to the Jews inside the walls? The death rates slowly began to climb. We have detailed statistics from Lodz and from Warsaw, though not from most of the other ghettos. Because those two ghettos were very different, the Lodz ghetto having been stratified and centralized under a kind of Jewish dictatorship, even as the Warsaw ghetto remained laissez-faire with private enterprise, it is instructive to note that in both starvation and illness they were roughly comparable, and that the death rates rose at an almost uniform rate to 1 percent of the population per month.

By 1940 the Germans attacked the western countries: France, Belgium, Holland. They won a quick, decisive victory on the ground and contemplated a peace treaty with England. Were that treaty to have come into being, it would automatically have been made also with France, and France was to have ceded the African island of Madagascar to the Germans. That island was to have been governed by the police, and all the Jews of Europe would have been shipped there. Such, at least, was the fantasizing in certain sections of the German Foreign Office. But the British did not make peace. When that fact began to sink in, toward the end of 1940, there was a transition period of greatest importance in German thinking. Up to that moment there really had been only two policies in all history against the Jews, the first being the conversion of the Jews to Christianity, the second being the expulsion of the Jews from a country in which they lived. Expulsion was now becoming impossible. In the middle of a war, millions of people cannot be expelled. Forced emigration was no longer feasible. Hence the idea of "a territorial solution" emerged. How? What form was it to take? That was not spelled out in 1940 or even in early 1941. Everyone was waiting with some anticipation for a decision.

Then came the planning of "Barbarossa" (the attack on the Soviet Union). The onslaught was being contemplated in a military conference held as early as July 22, 1940, and plans were taking shape in directive after directive, order of battle after order of battle, and in negotiations with Axis partners. In the course of these preparations a document was being drafted in the High Command of the Armed Forces. The order contained a cryptic sentence to the effect that the armed forces would be accompanied by special units of the SS and Police, which were to carry out certain state-political tasks in occupied territory. That was the beginning of the first massive killing operation. It has its origin in a social contract, as Neumann would have called it, between the German army and the SS and Police. The arrangement was hammered out in a series of agreements between the Quartermaster General of the German Army, Edward Wagner, and representatives of the Security Police, particularly Heydrich and Schellenberg. On June 22, 1941, when the German armies spilled into Russia, the Security Police units—called *Einsatzgruppen*—also moved in and started killing Jews on the spot.

The *Einsatzgruppen* sent daily reports to Berlin. In consolidated form, this revealing material was routed to many recipients, but only one set of copies was discovered after the war. As for the original reports from the field, very few are still around. From the Soviet Union came one report of a single commando that operated in Lithuania. A commando was a company-sized unit augmented by native helpers. The commando of which I speak killed 135,000 Jews in its area between June 1941 and January 1942.

The occupied territories of the U.S.S.R. were the scenes of massacre after massacre. Sometimes the *Einsatzgruppen* commanders would return to the same place again and again, shooting Jews en masse. In White Russia, a substantial number of victims fled to the woods; few were the survivors of roundups and shootings in the Ukraine.

But shooting operations had their problems. The Germans employed the phrase *Seelenbelastung* ("burdening of the soul") with reference to machine-gun fire or rifle fire directed at men, women, and children in prepared ditches. After all, the men that were firing these weapons were themselves fathers. How could they do this day after day? It was then that the technicians developed a gas van designed to lessen the suffering of the perpetrator. It was simply a vehicle, or a van, strictly speaking, with an exhaust pipe turned inward so the carbon monoxide would kill the seventy people inside even while they were being driven to their graves. The gas vans began operating in the east for women and children, but the unloading was very dirty work.

In 1941, some six weeks after the attack on the Soviet Union, a letter was written by Hermann Göring to Reinhard Heydrich, charging Heydrich with the Final Solution of the Jewish problem in Europe. I have always regarded that letter as the signal for the total destruction of European Jewry, the decisive step across the threshold. Although Göring was not specific about the time or manner in which his directive was to be implemented, his words implied finality and irreversibility.

How was the killing set into motion? As of November 1941, there was some thinking about deporting Jews to the *Einsatzgruppen* so they could be killed by these experienced shooters. That is why German Jews were transported to Minsk, Riga, and Kovno. In the long run, however, the shooting of millions would be an insurmountable problem; there would be too many witnesses, too many bodies, too many soul-burdened members of the SS and Police. Some of the deportees were consequently sent to the crowded ghettos of Poland. The ghettos themselves were to be dissolved soon. In various parts of the occupied Polish territory, the Germans were erecting facilities for the silent killing of Jews—the gas chambers. There were pure killing centers, including Kulmhof, Treblinka, Sobibor, and Belzec, the object of which was nothing except the gassing of people on arrival. A more complex camp was Auschwitz because it had industry as well as killing facilities. At Auschwitz, death was administered by hydrogen cyanide. The crystals were poured from a canister by an SS man wearing a gas mask with a special filter. In the crowded chamber the solid material became a gas.

The Jews had to be transported from all over Europe, always to the "East." We now know of the very expensive preparations that were required for these deportations. The Foreign Office negotiated and actually made treaties with satellite countries promising, as it were, that the Jews would be leaving for good, but that their property would be left behind. Some of the countries allied with Germany would not agree. The Romanians, although at first very enthusiastic killers in Russia, balked, and by the fall of 1942 rescinded an agreement to hand over their Jews, while Bulgaria procrastinated, allowing the deportation of Jews from Bulgarian occupied territories in Yugoslavia and Greece, but not permitting the deportation of Jews from Bulgaria itself.

The French Vichy regime adopted a compromise: negotiations were conducted with a view to protecting Jews of French nationality, while foreign Jews were surrendered to the Germans. "How can an occupied country," said French Premier Pierre Laval, "be a country of asylum?" The Italians not only did not deport their Jews, they refused to allow the deportation of Jews under Italian jurisdiction in other Mediterranean regions, including France, Greece, and Yugoslavia. The Germans never let up. You may find correspondence about twelve Jews in Liechtenstein. "What are they doing there?" Or Monaco. Several hundred Norwegian Jews were being deported from Oslo and Trondheim; they were gassed in Auschwitz.

It was wartime, and transport itself was a problem. Movement to killing centers took place by railroad for the most part, occasionally over long distances, as in the case of deportations from southern France or southern Greece. For the Transport Ministry, the movement of the Jews was a financial as well as an operational matter. In principle, each passenger transport had to be paid for. Jews were "travelers" and the Gestapo paid the railroads one-way fare (third class) for each deportee, half price for each transport of more than four hundred. The railroads were accommodating that way. The Gestapo on its part attempted to collect the necessary funds from the Jewish communities themselves. Although such "self-financing" took place in contravention of normal budgetary procedure, the Finance Ministry acquiesced in the practice.

The operational problem was even more complex. For each death transport, central and regional railway offices had to assign scarce rolling stock and time on tracks. Yet these transports seldom had a priority rating. A classification would have identified them for what they were. Instead they were being dispatched whenever possible. The timetables, written for each of them, placed them behind and ahead of regularly scheduled trains. Thus it was that with the intensification of the war, and even after the climax of Stalingrad, the Germans were pursuing ever more relentlessly and ever more drastically the one operation they were bound and determined to finish. They were going to solve the Jewish problem in Europe once and for all.

By the end of 1942, the death camp of Belzec had fulfilled its mission and was dismantled. Six hundred thousand Jews had died in Belzec; there was but one known survivor. At Sobibor and Treblinka there were uprisings. The survivors numbered in the dozens, but the dead of these two camps were about one quarter of a million and three quarters of a million, respectively.

The one camp that remained in operation throughout was Auschwitz. It was the farthest west, not in the path of the advancing Red Army. It was maintained, and even built up, in 1944. The year 1944 is of interest to us because no one could pretend not to know what was going on at that moment. The Jews knew. The Germans knew. The British knew, the Americans knew, everyone knew. There had already been escapes from the Auschwitz camp, and information was gathered also by the War Refugee Board in the United States. Despite that dissemination, no serious ransom negotiations were attempted by the Allies, no strategy of psychological warfare was developed, and no bombs were dropped on the gas chambers.

The Germans continued to destroy the European Jews, even under bombing, even while the Soviet forces were breaking into Romania and eastern Poland, and even as Allied landings were begun in France. To the end, we see the alignment of the German army, the German SS, the German Transport Ministry, the German Foreign Office, as well as financial agencies, all completing the work of solving the "Jewish problem" in Europe. Now we see the results. Here they are, in plain statistics.

I believe the Jewish death toll to be slightly above five million. I arrive at this figure not by subtracting the postwar population from the prewar figures, but by adding numbers that I find in German documents, and extrapolating from them the unreported data. The deaths in camps were roughly three million. Auschwitz had over a million dead; Treblinka on the order of seven hundred to eight hundred thousand; Belzec about six hundred thousand; Sobibor, two hundred to two hundred fifty thousand; Kulmhof, one hundred fifty thousand; Lublin (also known as Maidanek) some tens of thousands. In addition, tens of thousands of Jews were shot by the Romanians in camps between the Bug and Dniester rivers, thousands of Jews were killed at Semlin and other places in Yugoslavia. There were a number of additional camps where Jews suffered heavy losses, but in Holocaust statistics, thousands and even tens of thousands may be lost in footnotes.

About one million four hundred thousand Jewish victims were shot or died in mobile operations of one sort or another. Six hundred thousand died in ghettos.

The heavy concentration of dead is in Eastern Europe. Polish Jewry has virtually disappeared; dead are three million. Soviet Jewry, which was subject to shooting, lost seven hundred thousand within pre-1939 boundaries of the Soviet Union and another two hundred thousand in the Baltic area. In Western Europe the number of dead was proportionally smaller—in France, Belgium, and Italy, the survival rate was relatively high.

Today, the distribution of Jews is radically changed. The United States now has the largest Jewish population in the world, followed by almost equally sized Jewish communities in Israel and Russia. In these three countries live three-quarters of all the Jews remaining in the world. Europe is, for Jewry, a graveyard, and this, after a presence, on that continent, going back to the Roman Empire, of some two thousand years. That is the anatomy. And that is the statistic.

"MASTERING THE PAST": GERMANS AND GYPSIES[†]

In the vast body of Holocaust literature, the story of the Gypsy extermination has become an almost forgotten footnote to the history of Nazi genocide. Under Hitler's rule, approximately half a million European Gypsies

[†]From Gabrielle Tyrnauer, " 'Mastering the Past': Germans and Gypsies," in *Genocide and Human Rights: A Global Anthology*, ed. Jack Nussan Porter (Washington, D.C., 1982), 178–92. Reprinted by permission of University Press of America and the author.

were systematically slaughtered. Yet there was no Gypsy witness at the Nuremberg trials and no one was accused of the crime. Neither the scholars who provided the data, nor the officials who formulated the "final solution to the Gypsy problem," nor the bureaucrats and military men who executed it were ever called to account. The Gypsies became the forgotten victims of the Holocaust.

But all this is changing in the Federal Republic of Germany. Thirty-four years after the end of World War II, the victims have at last broken their long silence. In a dramatic reversal, German ministers of state were summoned to the former death camps for negotiations with one-time inmates and their children. A Gypsy civil rights movement had sprung, phoenix-like, out of the ashes of the Holocaust to demand an accounting for the past and to call attention to continued discrimination against Gypsies in Germany. A new chapter in the historic process of *Vergangenheitsbewältigung* (mastery of the past) is under way.

The Legacy of Persecution

Centuries of prejudice and persecution in Germany and elsewhere prepared the ground in which the seeds of genocide were planted. Since the Gypsies' first appearance in Europe in the early 14th century, they were regarded with a blend of fear and fascination by the sedentary peoples among whom they moved. Their language and their appearance were strange. They were not farmers or laborers, their women told fortunes and they all seemed to have a special relationship with the supernatural. They were treated as vagrants, criminals and spies by the secular powers, often as witches, heretics, and pagans by the Church, even when they were nominally Catholic. A 16th century Bishop's edict in Sweden, for example, forbade the priests to administer the sacraments to the Gypsies.[1]

Gypsies were imprisoned, expelled and enslaved by the princes through whose territories they passed. There were also some early attempts to forcibly settle them. The best known of these was that of the 18th century Austro-Hungarian empress, Maria Theresa, who wanted them to become God-fearing peasants and proceeded to forbid them nomadism, the use of their language and most of their traditional occupations. They were given land and called "New Hungarians," while their children were taken away from them to be raised by more "civilized" foster parents.[2]

At the same time, Gypsies became an important part of the European cultural scene. Individual dancers, musicians and circus performers acquired legendary reputations among the *gaje*, or non-Gypsies. With the advent of the Romantic

movement, their unfettered life style became attractive to a restless young generation. There were elements of envy as well as contempt in the composite stereotype. It led to a curious ambivalence in the attitudes of the settled peoples
towards the colorful nomads in their midst.[3]

It was in the Nazi concentration camps that this ambivalence assumed its
most bizarre forms. The Commandant of Auschwitz, Rudolf Höss, expressed
his fondness for the Gypsies in his charge. They were his "best-loved prisoners," "trusting as children." He ordered special rations of salami for them en
route to the gas chambers and built a playground for their children a month
before their final liquidation.[4] Dr. Mengele never failed to bring the Gypsy
children candy before taking them from their parents to perform his deadly
experiments. SS officers organized Gypsy orchestras in Auschwitz and other
concentration camps.[5] Academic researchers whose work provides the foundation for the system, immersed themselves, like good anthropologists, in the
language and culture of the people they helped to destroy.

The real *Zigeunerfrage* (Gypsy Question) was only formulated, according to
one German historian, about the time of German unification in the late 19th
century. Since then, successive German governments have worked diligently at
its solution. Under the monarchy, data collection on the Gypsies began, first
with the establishment in 1899 of a "Gypsy Information Service" (*Zigeuner-*
nachrichtendienst). In 1905 the government of Bavaria started a "Gypsy Book"
(*Zigeunerbuch*) in which acts and edicts related to Gypsies in the years
1816–1903 are compiled as guidelines for the continuing battle against the
"Gypsy Plague" (*Zigeunerplage*). Matters did not improve for Gypsies under
the Weimar Republic, when a variety of legislation aimed at *"Zigeuner,*
Landfahrer und Arbeitsscheue" (Gypsies, Travellers, and Malingerers) was
passed. In 1926, a "Gypsy Conference" was held in Munich to bring some
uniformity to the legislation of the different provinces (*Länder*). In fact, laws
against Gypsies were so harsh during this period, that the Nazis continued to
use them for their own purposes.[6]

The Third Reich and the "Final Solution"

While the Weimar laws sufficed for the first few years of
National Socialist rule, soon new legislation, consistent with Nazi racial ideology, was sought. At the Party's 1935 convention in Nuremberg, the new racial
laws were announced. These made Gypsies as well as Jews *"artfremd"*, "alien
to the German species." It followed that both could be deprived of their German
citizenship.

There began a period of unprecedented government support for research intended to provide the "scientific" underpinnings for future policy. The *Rassenhygienische und Bevölkerungsbiologische Forschungsstelle* was founded in 1936 as a part of the Ministry of Health. By 1942, Dr. Robert Ritter had collected over 30,000 genealogies by means of which he classified almost all the Gypsies of the Reich as either of "pure" or "mixed" race. He designated the "mixed race" Gypsies as "asozial" and recommended their sterilization, as did his student, Eva Justin. For those of "pure blood" who—to the embarrassment of Nazi ideology—were closer to the "Aryans" than any other people of Europe, these two scholars recommended a kind of "reservation."[7]

By 1942, Gypsies had been removed from the "normal" criminal procedures and delivered wholly to the jurisdiction of Himmler's SS. The distinctions among them were abandoned as orders were issued for mass deportation to the concentration camps of the "eastern territories." According to a record book hidden by an inmate of the Gypsy camp in Auschwitz, 20,967 Gypsies from all over Europe were transported to the Nazis' most notorious death factory. The first contingents arrived in several cattle cars attached to Jewish transports in February, 1943.[8] A year and a half later, about 4,000 remained and these were, on Himmler's orders, exterminated in a single night. Commandant Höss describes the matter routinely in his prison autobiography:

There remained until August, 1944 ca. 4,000 Gypsies, who must still go to the gas chambers. Up to this time they did not know what awaited them. They only noticed it when they were taken barrack by barrack to Crematorium V. It was not easy to get them into the gas chambers.[9]

The next morning, there were no Gypsies left in Auschwitz.

The Past Becomes Present

On October 27, 1979 a group of German Gypsies, or Sinti, as they call themselves, gathered at the former concentration camp of Bergen Belsen to honor their Holocaust victims and call attention to the continuing discrimination against them in the Federal Republic. The event was organized by three groups: the *Verband Deutscher Sinti* (Federation of German Sinti), a national organization, the *Romani Union*, an international organization recognized by the United Nations in 1979, and a non-Gypsy support group, *Die Gesellschaft für Bedrohte Völker* (The Society for Threatened Peoples). Roma (as the Gypsies are now known internationally) representatives from France, England, Switzerland, the Scandinavian countries, Belgium and the Netherlands, Yugoslavia, Greece and Italy were there. For the first time German government officials paid homage to the other victims of the "Final Solution."[10] The guest of honor was the president of the Council of Europe, Simone Veil, herself a survivor of Bergen-Belsen, who declared her personal solidarity as well as the support of the Council of Europe.[11] The wreath was laid by the charismatic young Sinti Romani Rose, who has taken over the leadership of the *Verband Deutscher Sinti* from his uncle, Vinzenz Rose. Thirteen members of Rose's immediate family died in the concentration camps of Hitler's Germany.

The next and still more powerful expression of the Sintis' rendezvous with history was a hunger strike at Dachau—the first concentration camp—on April 4, 1980. In the presence of more than 100 German and foreign journalists and several television crews, fourteen hunger-strikers, including one German social worker (the only non-Sinti), began their fast on Good Friday, following an ecumenical service in the chapel. Their objectives included official recognition of the Nazi crimes against the Roma and Sinti, appropriate restitutions,[12] an end to legal discrimination and police harassment, and the establishment of a Sinti cultural center at Dachau. The strike continued for eight days until satisfactory negotiations were initiated with government officials. Members of all three major political parties represented in the Bundestag and representatives of church groups also took part in the negotiations. While Rose proclaimed a "victory" for the Sinti, in fact their demands were met more with supportive rhetoric than real concessions. The city of Dachau vigorously opposed the establishment of the cultural center, expressing the fear that the "unjust" prejudices against the Sinti would be transferred to the city of Dachau if such an institution existed, adding to the burden it already carries through its past association with the concentration camp.[13]

Between these two powerfully symbolic events, Sinti, or as they are still more widely known, Zigeuner (Gypsies), burst into the German consciousness with the force of a 35-year time bomb. Within the next year, there was an unprecedented media boom and half a dozen German universities were conducting research on some aspect of past and present Sinti problems.[14] An event which really triggered the explosion, according to many German observers, was the telecasting of the American TV dramatization entitled "Holocaust." For a generation, particularly one which had little or no knowledge from home or schools of the Nazi period, it became a powerful catalyst to questioning and probing of what remains little more than a common cliché, "die unbewaltigte Vergangenheit," the "unmastered" past. It was estimated by newspaper surveys that 48% of the German population over the age of fourteen saw it. Although it contained only fleeting references to the fate of Gypsies, it created an atmosphere in which the Nazi past in all its facets could be reexamined by a new generation. For many Sinti it meant "coming out of the closet" to publicly acknowledge their ethnic identity, past persecution, and hopes for the future. Many could for the first time share their remembered sufferings and individual terrors with members of their own community and outsiders.

In the course of the next two years in almost every city with a concentration of Sinti, an organization came to life. The largest of these are *The Verband Deutscher Sinti* and *The Sinti Union*. In Hamburg there is a unique association of Sinti *and* Roma, the Gypsies from eastern Europe who play a prominent role in the international organization. Many of the Roma have only recently come to Germany with the waves of immigrant workers or *"Gastarbeiter."* They are culturally and linguistically distinct from the Sinti, who have been mostly sedentary and partly assimilated to German culture for centuries. The Sinti attitude towards the Roma ranges from indifference to outright hostility, particularly when their sporadic encounters with the police carry over in the popular mind to Sinti.[15] So a joint association, like that in Hamburg, is unusual.

The best-known product of this association is the "Duo-Z," two young Gypsy musicians, who have developed a repertoire of bitter satirical songs and a national reputation.[16] The duo was among the hunger strikers at Dachau for the first few days, but it was generally decided that their media work was of greater importance to the movement and that their concerts should not be cancelled.

Several Gypsy jazz groups in the tradition of the late Django Reinhardt have been popular for years and are increasingly becoming openly engaged in the Sinti, as well as the international Roma, movement.[17] They are much in demand at universities, festivals, and concerts throughout Germany. They can reach a wider audience than can the political leaders, and on a number of musical occasions during the past two years have effectively carried the political message.[18]

The Underlying Factors

The rediscovery of the Holocaust is a historic event for both Germans and Gypsies, which has been made possible by the conjunction of a number of factors. Some of the most important of them are as follows:

I. A post-war generation of Sinti who have grown up in an increasingly, though unintentionally, pluralistic society as waves of foreign workers transformed Germany during the past two decades into an immigrant society.[19] Better educated and more militant than their elders, they are no longer content to choose between assimilation and dissimilation but are proclaiming their ethnic identities and persuading many of their elders to follow suit. These elders, as Romani Rose remarked in explaining his own leadership position, are often broken in spirit as well as in body from their experiences in the Third Reich. "We cannot expect them to carry the burden."[20]

In addition to the social milieu in which the post-war Sinti have grown up, there is a psychological dimension, which has recently acquired a name in the studies of the second generation Jewish Holocaust survivors. Dr. William B. Niederland, a psychiatrist, claims to have coined the term "survivors' syndrome" after extensive study of Holocaust survivors. The survivors live constantly with their memories and their fears which are conveyed to their children, who in reaction often exhibit strong tendencies to seek positive action or resistance to compensate for their parents' passivity.[21]

2. Continuing popular prejudice and official discrimination, recently accentuated by the ever-increasing number of immigrants and an economic recession which often makes them competitors for scarce resources. The discrimination, of course, reinforces the Sinti consciousness of minority status and minority rights. This has deepened their historical consciousness (which is conspicuously absent in the culture of most Gypsy groups in other countries) so that they quickly relate present discrimination to past persecution climaxing in the Holocaust. It also makes them more sensitive than most members of the population (with the exception of Jews) to any stirrings of neo-Nazism. Reactions have ranged from street demonstrations against SS reunions,[22] civil disobedience against exclusion from camping places[23] to the dramatic hunger-strike at Dachau which demanded remembrance of the past, just restitution for its victims and the dismantling of institutions, such as special police offices for "Travellers," as well as destruction of data collected by Nazi officials and researchers. They maintain (and their claims can be substantiated) that the new wave of xenophobia has led to stricter enforcement of existing laws applying to foreigners, especially to "migrants" or "travellers." Some of these laws dating back to the Nazi period or still earlier, were largely ignored (though in many cases, never abolished) in the post-war years. Also, deadlines and legal technicalities related to applications for restitution (*Wiedergutmachung*) and citizenship have been enforced more rigidly, so that there are cases of Sinti whose grandparents were German citizens but who must themselves carry a foreigner's identification (*Fremdenpass*), with restrictions on work and residence.[24] This has led to increasing resentment and fears that "the Nazis are coming back" or, in some cases, never left. One dramatic instance of

this is the case of an Auschwitz survivor who drove into a camping place with his trailer and family. When the local official in charge saw the concentration camp number still tatooed on his arm, he said to him, "This place is not for you."[25] Another, even more shocking incident was that of a woman, also an Auschwitz survivor, who was sterilized under Nazi law and when she applied for restitution in the city which had always been her home, found herself, at the required physical examination, face-to-face with the physician who had performed the sterilization operation.[26] The Sinti's new eagerness to speak publicly about the Nazi past and their experiences in it grows out of their escalating fears of its repetition, perhaps in altered form.[27]

3. The support of key non-Gypsy groups has been an important factor in the whole difficult process—particularly so for a people still largely illiterate and powerless—of remembering the past and organizing for the future. These groups can be divided into religious organizations, ad hoc citizens' groups, social workers and secular leftist groups some of which have grown out of the student movement of the late 1960s. There have also been committed unaffiliated individuals in the press and at various universities, some of whom have come together for more effective action. These groups have given moral, financial, and technical support. They have sponsored and helped to organize congresses and issued publications, in almost all of which the Holocaust figures as the central historical experience of Gypsies in Germany.[28]

4. The existence of an international Gypsy organization known as the Romani Union and admitted to membership of the Economic and Social Council of the United Nations as a non-Governmental organization. The fact that the most recent Congress (the third since the organization's founding in 1971) was held on German soil (in Göttingen, May, 1981) and that Romani Rose, the German Sinti leader, was elected vice-president of the organization suggests the importance of this international connection for German Sinti.

5. Continuing war crimes trials and the controversy over the statute of limitations. The five and a half year Maidanek trial, in which one of the defendants was a naturalized American citizen (the only one sentenced to life imprisonment) who was extradited for the trial, was to recent German history what the Eichmann and the Auschwitz trials were to the generation coming to maturity in the early and middle sixties. It was well covered by the German media and remained a constant reminder that the past was not yet "mastered." While it created guilt feelings in some young people who

had no personal experience of that past, it raised a wall of anger and hostility in many of the older people who wanted to hear no more about it. In either case, it kept the past in the foreground of the news.

6. A similar polarized effect resulted from the showing on German television of the American Holocaust dramatization, as mentioned previously. The videotape and the instructional materials which accompanied it were used extensively in the schools, sometimes by teachers who had not wanted or had not dared teach their pupils the history of the Third Reich. It also stimulated spontaneous and organized group discussions throughout Germany. The impact on the Sinti, who are avid television watchers, was powerful. Now, they felt, their story too could be told.

Conclusion

All these elements combined to create, in the late 1970s, an awareness and a movement that had been gestating for more than three decades. The elders broke their long silence and spoke publicly about things that had only been whispered in the presence of close family members since the end of World War II. One elder Sinti whose entire family was murdered in Auschwitz, whose wife was sterilized by Dr. Mengele, while her family too was killed, makes a pilgrimage to Auschwitz annually, sometimes twice a year. When asked why, his wife replied simply, "Because my whole family is there. I go there to pray." Her husband has, during the past two years, lectured at clubs, schools and churches.

Thus, in the twilight of the twentieth century, a new generation of Germans and Gypsies are coming together to wrestle with their still "unmastered" past, trying to assure that the forgotten victims of the Holocaust will be remembered and that their children can live as full and equal citizens of the Federal Republic.

NOTES

1. Donald Kenrick and Grattan Puxon, *Sinti und Roma, Die Vernichtung eines Volkes im NS-Staat*, Göttingen: Die Gesellschaft für Bedrohte Völker, 1981, p. 24. The first edition of this book was in English; *The Destiny of Europe's Gypsies*, London: Chatto-Heinemann-Sussex, 1972.

2. Ibid., p. 45.

3. The traditional ambivalence springing from the conflict between the Romantic cult of individual freedom and the Protestant ethic of hard work and postponed gratification was reflected in much of the literature which appeared in Europe during the 19th century.

A recent survey of such literature in relation to Gypsies was called "Bürgerfluch und Bürgersehnsucht: Zigeuner in Vorstellungsbild (The Imagination of the Literary Intelligentsia) in Hohmann, Schop and others, *Ziegeunerleben*, Darmstadt, 1979.

4. Jerzy Ficowski, "Die Vernichtung" in Tilch, op. cit., (pp. 91–112), p. 109.

5. Two particularly shocking stories among the many survivors' accounts of the SS staff's "music appreciation" are recounted by Kenrick and by Streck. The first concerns the Auschwitz Gypsy Orchestra organized by SS Officer Broad. On the 25th of May, 1943 a concert was given for the SS. It was however, interrupted in the middle, the musicians sent back to the barracks while on special orders a thousand prisoners were gassed. (Donald Kenrick, "Das Schicksal der Zigeuner im NS-Staat" in Donald Kenrick, Grattan Puxon, Tilman Zulch (eds.) *Die Zigeuner, Verkannt—Verachtet—Verfolgt* Hannover: Niedersächsischen Landeszentrale für politische Bildung, 1980, pp. 37–74, pp. 68–69. The second story comes from a death camp in Bosnia, Jasenovac, and was first related by a Franciscan priest who served as chaplain in the German Wehrmacht. "Each 12 man Gypsy ensemble played one month, from the first day until the last. A month with 31 days was luck, a gift for the 12 Gypsies. One day more, 24 hours. They played until noon, they played in the evening and on the last day until morning . . . After dinner the electric light was switched off and only candles were lit . . . now each of the 12 Gypsies prayed that the Kommandant would not become sleepy. When the Kommandant began to grow tired and the night began to glide away, he would point to one of the Gypsy musicians. He would have to lay down his instrument and would walk through the candlelit room to the door of the Casino where his escort already waited to take him into the forest. When the shot from the forest came—one could hear it even while the music played in the room—the next one prepared himself. But he continued to play until the Kommandant pointed to him." (Bernhard Streck, "Das Ende der Musik: Zigeuner hinterm Stacheldraht" in Georgia A. Raklemann, *Zigeuner,* Materialien für Unterricht und Bildungsarbeit, Gesellschaft für entwicklungspolitische Bildung: 1980). A grim photograph shows prisoners being led to the gallows accompanied by musicians. The prescribed song for the occasion was "All the little birds are here." (Ibid.)

6. Bernhard Streck, "Die Bekämpfung des Zigeunerwesens". Ein Stück moderner Rechtsgeschichte in Tilman Zulch (ed.) *In Auschwitz Vergast, bis Heute Verfolgt.* Hamburg: Rowohlt Taschenbuch Verlag, 1979, pp. 64–87.

7. Alwin Meyer, "Holocaust der Zigeuner" in *Zeichen* (Mitteilungen der Aktion Sühnezeichen/Friedensdienste), No. 3, Sept. 1979, p. 6.

8. Ibid.

9. Ibid.

10. Karl-Klaus Rabe, "Zigeunerische Personen sind Asozial" in *Zeichen,* no. 3, September 1979, p. 16.

11. Her speech is reproduced in a special publication documenting the occasion, *Sinti und Roma im ehemaligen KZ Bergen Belsen am 27. Oktober 1979,* Göttingen, 1981, pp. 49–57.

12. There has been a long history of controversy over the subject of "Wiedergutmachung" for European Gypsies who survived the Holocaust. In the post-war period,

the continued fear of official persecution and the lack of required documentation resulted in a situation where few Gypsies exercised their rights and official deadlines for applications passed. Many applications were rejected after a statement by the Minister of the Interior of Baden-Württemberg in 1950, circulated to judges who were concerned with such applications, reminding them that Gypsies were, in the early years of the war, not persecuted on "racial" grounds (which was the legal basis of *Wiedergutmachung*), but on the basis of an "asocial and criminal past" and a security threat. After 1959, when the first Wiedergutmachung law expired, and was renewed, the situation improved somewhat. Today individual Gypsies can receive DM 5 per day they spent in a concentration camp and some additional money for damage to health. Sterilization was not classified as such a damage. (Grattan Puxon, "Verschleppte Wiedergutmachung," in *In Auschwitz Vergast, Bis Heute Verfolgt*, pp. 149–157, Documents, ibid., pp. 168–171.

13. *Dachauer Neueste Nachrichten*, May 7, 1980.

14. Academics, for the most part, approached the subject with extreme caution because of the unhappy past involvement of German scholars with the "Gypsy Question." With the exception of an older scholar, Hermann Arnold, who has become the subject of a storm of controversy, most of the present "Tsiganologues" are young and politically committed and engaging in "action research."

15. A recent example of this was a well-reported incident involving a group of Roma alleged to have been involved in a large number of burglaries. The police rounded them up in their trailers and broadcast an appeal for witnesses. The *Nürnberger Nachrichten* reported that the police rounded up a "100 head Sinti clan" (July 1, 1981).

16. The name of the duo was chosen ironically. "Z"—for "Zigeuner" was the symbol Gypsies had stamped on their papers by the Nazi officials. Their theme song is a grim parody of a traditional German folk-song called "Lustig ist das Zigeuner-leben" (Merry is the Gypsy Life) which describes the Gypsies' life in Auschwitz and Buchenwald. The son of a Sinti leader in the Nürnberg area who wanted to perform it for a school festival was prohibited from singing it by his teacher, who explained that it was "too sharp."

17. The names are confusing and reflect the schisms normal among culturally diverse groups attempting to unite politically. Even in the framework of an international congress of the "Romani Union" the Sinti have insisted on retaining their name. The outgoing president of the Union, Czech émigré Dr. Jan Cibula, now living in Switzerland, urged all Gypsies to adopt the term "Rom" as a generic title. But the Sinti were not persuaded and all posters at the Congress in Göttingen (May, 1981) referred to "Roma and Sinti." Thus, today the term *Roma* may designate either a particular ethnic group of mainly Balkan Gypsies or, as used by Romani nationalists, it may refer to all Gypsies.

18. Hans'che Weiss, for example, one of the best known of the Gypsy jazz musicians, has popularized a Romanes song entitled "Let us demand our Rights." The program notes for a Gypsy music festival in Darmstadt in 1979, were in fact, essays on the past genocide and present persecution of the Gypsy people written by some of the politically engaged young "Tsiganologues" from Giessen University.

19. Friedrich Heckmann, "Socio-Structural Analysis of Immigrant Worker Minorities:

The Case of West Germany," *Mid-American Review of Sociology*, 1980, vol. V, no. 2: 13–20.

20. Interview, May 29, 1981.

21. "Das Überlebendensyndrom der Opfer und ihre Kinder," *Zeichen*, 3, p. 14.

22. As an example of this might be cited the demonstration in Würzburg on September 18, 1976, a meeting of former SS men, which escalated into a fight resulting in some minor injuries and prosecution of seven demonstrators, six of whom were Gypsies.

23. Inge Britt, "Zigeunern ist die Benutzung des Campingplatzes untersagt," *Zeichen*, 3, pp. 18–20.

24. The Nazis stripped Gypsies, like Jews, of their German citizenship. Some Sinti even served in the armed forces until the order came in 1942 that all Gypsies must be sent to Auschwitz. (e.g., Julius Hodost, "Wir werden Euch vertilgen wie die Katzen" *Zeichen*, no. 3, p. 7). After the war, many of these stateless Gypsies did not have the necessary documentation to regain their citizenship.

25. Personal communication, July 5, 1981, Erlangen Folk Festival.

26. Personal communication, May 29, 1981, Frankfurt.

27. This feared continuity under a changed name is illustrated by a recent cartoon which shows a police official speaking to his two subordinates who are rifling through mountains of disorderly files. "Have you found something on 'Landfahrer' yet?" he asks. "No," one of them replies, "only on Zigeuner, Herr Minister."

28. Some of the most important of the religious groups are the Catholic Caritas, the Evangelischer (Lutheran) Aktion Sühnezeichen, Innere Mission, Diakonisches Werk, Jewish organizations such as the Berlin Jewish congregation, its leader, Heinz Galinski, and the well-known Jewish Nazi hunter Simon Wiesenthal; in the last 2 years, probably the most active group, the liberal secular Gesellschaft für bedrohte Völker; der Verband der Verfolgten des Nazi regimes, individuals and groups close to the Social Democratic Party, journalists such as Anita Geigges and Bernard Wette, social workers associated with the Deutsche Verein für öffentliche und private Fürsorge, etc. Information about the work of a few of these groups can be found in C. Freese, M. Murko, G. Würzbacher, *Hilfen für Zigeuner und Landfahrer*, Stuttgart, Kohlhammer, 1980.

INDONESIA*

Background

Indonesia, the most improbable country to arise out of the ashes of colonialism, consists of about 13,700 islands, some 12,700 of which are uninhabited and about 7,600 of which do not even have names. They are scattered over an area of Southeast Asia that stretches 3,400 miles in an east–west direction and 1,000 miles in a north–south direction. The biggest of these islands are Kalimantan (Borneo), Sulawesi (Celebes), Java, Sumatra, and the western half of Irian Jaya (New Guinea). Java is important because it contains the capital, Jakarta (Djakarta), and the densest population. West Irian is important because it has a land border with Papua–New Guinea, while Kalimantan is shared with Malaysia and Brunei. These are the only land borders with other countries. Indonesia, with its 2 million square kilometers and over 185 million people (in 1988) is a poor country of enormous diversity. Life expectancy is 58 years and infant mortality is 83 per thousand (in 1988). It consists of over 300 ethnic groups of which the Javanese are the largest with about 45 percent of the population. They speak over 250 distinct languages, Bahasa Indonesia being the official language. Almost every religion of the world is represented, although 87 percent of the people are Muslims. The per capita gross national product in 1988 was US$ 450 and the rate of natural increase was 2.0 percent.

The modern history of Indonesia started in the seventeenth century when the Dutch East India Company established economic and political control over most of these islands, but particularly Java, because it valued them for their resources. The Moluccas were often simply referred to as the Spice Islands because of that particular form of wealth. While they were a source of great wealth to the Dutch traders, the native population suffered and in 1927 formed the Indonesian

*This summary is based on Anderson and McVey (1971), Crouch (1978), Hughes (1968), and Vittachi (1967) in addition to background data from several encyclopedias and demographic series of the United Nations and the Population Reference Bureau and a personal communication from Benedict R. Anderson. All quotations are reprinted from Harold Crouch, *The Army and Politics in Indonesia*, © 1978 by Cornell University. Used by permission of the publisher, Cornell University Press.

National Party (PNI) under the chairmanship of Sukarno. Almost all of Indonesia was conquered by Japan during 1942 and remained under its control until the end of World War II. In August 1945, following Japan's surrender to the Allies, Sukarno declared independence. The Dutch did not think much of this move and tried to reassert control. Their effort resulted in much bitter fighting. In the end, it was only under the pressure of world opinion and the American threat to cut off Marshall aid that the Dutch finally agreed to transfer sovereignty to the new nation in 1949. President Sukarno has been much criticized for his political and economic policies at various times, but his main goal was to form a modern nation out of this diverse collection of islands and peoples. In this goal he succeeded beyond the expectations of most observers. He followed no ideological line consistently and honored foreign commitments only if it suited his primary goal. He avoided the trap of language conflict by making a minority language, Bahasa Indonesia, the official language—rather than his own Javanese—and he built a national army. The army gained much credibility and power because of its efficient handling of several rebellions and because it held the country together under central control.

After independence, there were four major political parties in addition to several minor ones. These were the PNI, the Indonesian Communist Party (PKI), which had been founded in 1920, the Masjumi, which was the major Moslem party, and the NU, which was the party of the Moslem theologians. After the rebellions of 1957–58 Masjumi was banned while the other parties expanded considerably. In 1959 President Sukarno proclaimed "guided democracy," and the PKI acquired much influence in spite of great hostility from the army. The impression one gets is that Sukarno played off the two major sources of power, the PKI and the army, in order to follow his own initiatives. At the same time he also was able to play off against each other the foreign interests focused on his country. Indonesia, then and now, plays an important role in the foreign policy of many countries. To some it is of interest because of its great natural resources; to others it represents a great market for military hardware; and in addition it is of great strategic importance to the great powers, all of whom have tried hard to gain influence in its internal affairs. The United States has probably been more successful than most due to its virtual monopoly of the advanced training of Indonesian army officers and is exercising and maintaining its influence.

The Coup

Against this background, a coup took place under the leadership of a Lieutenant-Colonel Untung during the night of 30 September–1 October 1965. The situation and the circumstance, the purpose and the sponsorship of the coup remain shrouded in mystery and controversy. Under Untung's command six generals were killed and their bodies were thrown down a well. Two important generals, Nasution and Suharto, escaped being killed and rapidly organized the army's response. The coup was short-lived and failed. In the present context it is not important to establish the facts, even if that were still possible. What is important is that the army took control of the country and that the army blamed the PKI for having planned and carried out the abortive coup. Most of the army was bitterly opposed to the PKI because of its influence with Sukarno and because of its penetration of much of the air force and the navy. Over the next three years, Suharto gradually took power. While he gained effective power in 1965 after the coup, Sukarno became a virtual prisoner in his palace although he was not formally deposed. In 1967 Sukarno was finally deposed and Suharto became acting president; in 1968 Suharto was elected president. In March 1966 the PKI was formally outlawed.

Harold Crouch (1978, 346) has pithily summarized the history of the army's monopolization of power:

As the army's power grew, its rivals were neutralized one after another. The non-Communist political parties had been largely discredited together with the parliamentary system in the 1950's, leaving the PKI as the main organized civilian counterweight to the army during the first half of the 1960's. The intense competition between the army and the PKI after 1963 culminated in the coup attempt and army-instigated massacres of 1965, in which the army used its physical power to eliminate the PKI as a political force. In the aftermath, President Sukarno was left as the main obstacle to army domination. In the drawn-out maneuvering between October 1965 and March 1967, the army leaders gradually divested the president of his allies, while Sukarno held back from forcing a showdown that might have thrown the nation into civil war. After the elimination of the PKI and the dismissal of Sukarno, the army's domination of the government was unchallenged, and in the following years the remaining centers of independent power in the political parties and other civilian organizations were completely subjugated.

The Genocide

After the coup, the mass slaughter of PKI members started. During the first few weeks, this was an action by the army against the mostly unarmed PKI cadres and supporters. Then the army encouraged civilian groups to become involved. The motivations of the latter differed widely; in some cases personal jealousies led to ethnic victimizations of supposedly disloyal foreigners (that is, Chinese); in other cases fanatical Muslims were bent on clearing out atheists. Over the next five months the slaughter of Communists escalated into a "holy war." The usually friendly and placid people of Indonesia practiced excesses of savagery. The victims' bodies often were mutilated and exhibited on poles along roads or thrown into rivers. Their possessions were looted and their houses often burned. Eventually, the army used its authority to reestablish order. Nobody kept count of the casualties, but the consensus of informed opinion sets the number killed at about 500,000 and the number arrested also at 500,000.

Crouch (1978, 155) has described the various attempts to estimate the number of victims in the killing that followed the coup:

Although the worst of the killing was over by December, executions continued on a diminished scale well into 1966. Estimates of the total number killed varied from 78,500, suggested by a Fact-Finding Commission appointed by the president at the end of December, to one million, based on an army-sponsored survey conducted by students from Bandung and Jakarta. The Fact-Finding Commission, which made brief visits to only East and Central Java, Bali, and North Sumatra, noted a tendency on the part of officials "to hide or minimize the number of victims reported," and estimated that 54,000 had been killed in East Java, 10,000 in Central Java, 12,500 in Bali, and 2,000 in North Sumatra (Report of the Fact-Finding Commission). While the Fact-Finding Commission's estimate is universally regarded as too low, the estimate of a million appears to be too high. According to the survey, 800,000 were killed in Central and East Java and 100,000 in Bali, with the remaining 100,000 spread through the other provinces. (Information from Frank Palmos. An example of overestimation is the report's estimate that "one-third of the population" was killed in the Boyolali-Solo-Klaten "triangle." If it is assumed that half the population were children, this would mean that two-thirds of all adults were killed. Possibly one-third of adult men were killed, or about 8 percent of the total population, and a much smaller percentage of adult women.) Although there is no way of knowing, the most commonly accepted estimate was between 250,000 and 500,000. (In 1976 the head of the Kopkamtib, Admiral Sudomo, estimated that between 450,000 and 500,000 had been killed, according to *Tempo*, 10 July 1976.) In addition, the Fact-Finding Commission reported that 106,000 supporters of the PKI had been interned in prison camps, of whom 70,000 were in

Central Java, 25,000 in East Java, and 11,000 in North Sumatra, while
the number taken prisoner in Bali was apparently too small to note. Later
the attorney general estimated that some 200,000 people had been arrested
throughout Indonesia. [*Harian Kami*, 27 July 1976]

While this genocide was directed at a political party, it had curious overtones
of an ethnic, religious, and economic character. Ethnic because the attacks
spread to many Chinese, who were seen not only as foreigners, but also as
representatives of communist China; religious because the Muslims and also
some Christians saw the Communists as enemies of God; and economic because
on the one hand Chinese traders were accused of growing rich by exploiting the
poor masses and on the other hand because the PKI advocated the confiscation
of landed estates and their redistribution to poor peasants. When these massacres were finally stopped by the army, the PKI remained outlawed and the army
was in full control of the military and political situation.

According to Crouch (1978, 344), Indonesia's army has always played a role
in politics:

> The Indonesian army differs from most armies that have seized political
> power in that it had never previously regarded itself as an apolitical organi-
> zation. From the army's beginning in 1945 as a guerrilla force to combat
> the return of Dutch colonial rule until the consolidation of its political
> power under the New Order, Indonesian army officers have always con-
> cerned themselves with political issues and for most of the period actively
> played important political roles. Having participated fully in the nationalist
> struggle against Dutch rule, most officers continued to feel that their voices
> should be heard in postindependence political affairs. After the imposition
> of martial law in 1957, their right to participate was given formal recogni-
> tion through appointments to the cabinet, the parliament, and the adminis-
> tration. During the Guided Democracy era, the army became one of the
> two major organized political forces, which, with President Sukarno, domi-
> nated the politics of the period. Finally, the army's drive against the PKI in
> 1965 and its success in easing President Sukarno out of office left it as the
> dominant force in Indonesian politics.

The government was fully aware that the PKI at its height had many more
members than were actually killed in 1965–66. So, persecution and arrests
continued for several years. Periodic massacres continued to occur, particularly
in the remoter regions. Arrests of PKI leaders and members also continued,
some of whom were brought before military courts and sentenced to death or to
long periods of imprisonment. The prison camps were strong on political indoctrination and forced labor. The number of surviving prisoners remains uncertain

because no reliable figures are available. But the camps for political prisoners continue to exist. Many of the Communists were released in 1978–79, mainly as a result of the Fraser Amendment (a human rights amendment) to the U.S. Foreign Assistance Act.

Crouch (1978, 135) emphasizes the importance of the genocide to the army's powerful position:

> The crucial condition for the army's increasing dominance was the elimination of the PKI. While it was not clear that the army leaders intended that the postcoup massacres should reach the level of ferocity experienced in areas like East Java, Bali, and Aceh, they no doubt consciously exploited the opportunity provided by the coup attempt to liquidate the PKI leadership, both in Jakarta and at the provincial and district levels. In the rural areas of Java and elsewhere, army officers cooperated with members of anti-Communist civilian organizations to murder several hundred thousand PKI activists, resulting in the party's loss of its organized mass base of support. The PKI, which had been organized for agitation rather than warfare, was in no position to defend itself against the army-backed offensive.

As a result of these events, Indonesia has since the coup been firmly in the camp of the West, especially of the United States, which sees it as a bulwark against Communism in Southeast Asia. The army is still in control in Indonesia and the PKI is still outlawed; it eliminated a political group that was perceived as a threat and it allowed and encouraged popular participation in the massacres in order to legitimate its actions by demonstrating popular support. By our definition this action qualifies as a genocide; but Indonesia would deny this. An element of controversy will always be associated with these events because the facts will remain hard to ascertain. No exact records were kept. Such records as existed have been lost or are not accessible to scholars. The participants and witnesses tend to slant their evidence in accordance with their interests and loyalties. So, many questions will probably remain unanswered. But the overall picture is clear enough to permit the conclusion that a genocide has occurred here.

BURUNDI

The following reading by Stanley Meisler was a particularly fortunate find.₅ It presents in a clear, summary fashion the relevant facts concerning a genocide that took place relatively recently. That is a considerable achievement because this case has received very little publicity—in part because much of the information was suppressed and has become available only in bits and pieces that were difficult to evaluate and put together.

We have included the section entitled "World Reaction" to show that the perception and reporting of contemporary genocides is still affected by what we have, in part I, referred to as *collective denial*, as well as by political and racial bias. We suggest that this case is of particular relevance to a discussion of an early warning system and of the possibilities of the prevention of future genocides. For more detailed discussion of this case, the writings of Réné Lemarchand are indispensable.

The new massacres in Burundi in 1988 may not qualify as a genocide. However, they illustrate in a most disheartening way how little has changed either in Burundi or in the reactions of the outside world.

HOLOCAUST IN BURUNDI, 1972[†]

In 1972, the government of Burundi, controlled by the minority Tutsi tribe, tried to eliminate the entire modern class of the majority Hutu people. All those with some education, government jobs or money were to be killed. The Hutus then made up 85 percent of the population in this central African country. But they offered little resistance. The government probably killed somewhere between 100,000 and 200,000 Hutus that year.

[†]From Stanley Meisler, "Holocaust in Burundi, 1972," in *Case Studies on Human Rights and Fundamental Freedoms: A World Survey*, vol. 5, ed. Willem A. Veenhoven (The Hague: Martinus Nijhoff, 1976), 227–32. Reprinted by permission of Kluwer Academic Publishers, Dordrecht, The Netherlands.

It was not easy for the rest of the world to find out what was going on. But the news did seep out. Six months later, there could be no doubt of the enormity of the horror. Yet, even when the facts were beyond dispute, the rest of the world did little to condemn Burundi or to prevent more violence. In 1973, in fact, new massacres began.

The situation was a complex one, and several questions need to be considered. What were the forces that pushed the government of Burundi to such large scale murder? What happened? Why did the rest of the world simply turn away?

I. Historical Background:
Burundi and Rwanda

The history of Burundi cannot be separated from that of its neighbour, Rwanda. There had been mass tribal killing in Rwanda and Burundi for more than a decade, the killing on one side sometimes provoking the killing on the other. The two neighbours have similar traditions and problems. Each about the size of the American state of Maryland, each with almost four million people, Burundi and Rwanda are the most densely populated countries in Africa and among the poorest in the world. Their people graze cattle and farm on a myriad of lovely, verdant hills along Lake Kivu and Lake Tanganyika. In colonial days, the two countries were ruled together as Rwanda-Urundi, a colony of the Germans from 1885 until World War I and a mandate and trust territory of the Belgians from then until independence. Both were feudal kingdoms with masses of Hutu people ruled by Tutsi lords and kings.

More than four hundred years ago, the Tutsi people (better known by the African plural, Watutsi) came down to Rwanda and Burundi from the north, probably Ethiopia. They were cattle people, probably Hamitic, with slender features and skin somewhat lighter than most other Africans. The Tutsis were tall, some well over six feet. Rwanda and Burundi were already inhabited then by a few pygmies and by many Hutu people. The Hutus were farmers who lived by their hoes. They were Bantu people, short, stocky, dark, with negroid features.

Over the years, the small group of Tutsi immigrants subjugated the masses of Hutus into a kind of feudal system by exchanging their cattle for subservience. Much as in medieval Europe, a pyramid developed with Tutsi lords giving their own loyalty to more important Tutsi lords in exchange for protection. A mwami, or Tutsi king, ruled at the top of the pyramid in each country.

There were all kinds of variations in the basic feudal scheme. But one thing was clear. Centuries of tradition made the Tutsis feel like a privileged, superior people and the Hutus feel like a subjugated, inferior people. The Tutsis looked on themselves as intelligent people capable of leadership and scorned the Hutus as no more than hard-working and dumb peasants. The Hutus tended to agree. The Tutsi attitude, nurtured by tradition, was expressed to the writer after the massacres by a young American-educated Tutsi of Burundi, the son of a lord. "I know the Hutus," he said. "They will never take over. The Hutu peasant does not care anything about politics. And, what if he took over the government? He could never run it. Throughout the world, the ruling class is always made up of no more than one to five percent of the population. Why should it be different in Burundi?"

Such feelings of innate Tutsi superiority and the feudal structure of Rwanda and Burundi were challenged in the early 1960s by many of the ideas generated during the rush to independence in black Africa. Only 15 percent of the population in Burundi and 10 percent in Rwanda, the Tutsis began to feel deep fears about their place in societies where power might go to the majority tribe. The feelings of inferiority by the Hutus and of fear by the Tutsis probably account for most of the terrible bloodshed.

The first troubles took place in Rwanda. In early 1961, the Hutu leaders, with the connivance of Belgian colonial officials, overthrew the mwami of Rwanda. Rwanda became independent in 1962 as a republic run by Hutus. This revolution was accompanied by continual persecution of the Tutsi minority which reached its peak in 1963 and 1964. At that time, the late English philosopher Bertrand Russell called the killings "the most horrible and systematic human massacre we have had occasion to witness since the extermination of the Jews by the Nazis." It is probable that since the mwami of Rwanda was overthrown, the Hutus have killed more than 20,000 Tutsis and forced 200,000 to take refuge in neighbouring Uganda, Zaire and Burundi.

This could hardly reassure the Tutsis of Burundi. Unlike Rwanda, Burundi became independent in 1962 as a kingdom with a mwami still ruling. But he lasted only four years. He was overthrown in 1966, not by Hutus, but by Tutsi army officers from a non-royal clan led by Michel Micombero, now president. Since independence, Hutu rebels have tried to take over Burundi in a succession of coups, plots or uprisings. Each attempt has been met by Tutsi reprisals. The most terrible reprisal came in 1972 after the most serious Hutu uprising.

II. The Great Killings of 1972

It would be misleading to blame all of the 1972 killing on a savage frenzy of Tutsi fear. Some Hutus were killed in wild, indiscriminate rampages. Others were victims of personal vendettas. But most were wiped out in a cold and calculated way by a Tutsi government that seemed to make the decision that it could guarantee itself power for at least another decade by eliminating all potential leaders of the majority tribe. It is this coldness that made the events of Burundi different from the earlier bloodshed in Rwanda.

The killings began in late April, reached their height in May and ended, more or less, by August. The government did not try to deny that great killing had taken place. But it issued a self-serving interpretation of the events. According to a government white paper, issued in June, a force of 25,000 Hutus, many led by former Congolese rebels in exile in East Africa, had attacked four sectors of Burundi on the night of April 29th. Their aim, according to the Tutsi government, was genocide of the Tutsi people.

The government said that bands of Hutus pillaged the countryside and murdered Tutsis. The Hutus, according to the white paper, were armed with poisoned machetes, clubs, automatic rifles, and Molotov cocktails. The invaders and rebels were drugged into a state of ferocious excitement. They were convinced their skin was impermeable, that bullets coming at them would turn to water. Before the Burundian army could defeat them, the government insisted, the Hutu rebels massacred 50,000 people, almost all Tutsis.

President Micombero said that his army found lists of Hutu plotters on the defeated rebels. These lists, he said, were used by the government to track down and execute the plotters. "Only the guilty have been punished," he said, "The innocent were not troubled at all." The president estimated that the death toll could have reached 100,000.

The government's version of the events, however, was rejected by all foreign sources in Burundi who spoke to the writer several months later. Many foreigners were reluctant to talk with a visiting newsman. They were afraid of expulsion, fearful of being overheard by government security men. They sometimes used the euphemism of "talls and smalls" to describe the Tutsis and Hutus. But, reluctant or not, all foreign sources said that the government had not sought out plotters. Instead, it had attempted a systematic elimination of the modern Hutus.

Many sources agreed that the troubles began with some kind of Hutu uprising. But they said that the Hutu rebels killed a few thousand Tutsi at most, not 50,000. The uprising, the sources went on, became a trigger or an excuse for the government onslaught.

A few sources, in fact, speculated that the government knew about the intended uprising but did not try to prevent it. The Tutsis wanted an excuse, according to these sources, to begin their long-planned drive against the Hutus. Victor D. Du Bois has suggested that the Hutu revolt was, in fact, provoked by the Tutsis.

According to most sources, the government had lists of intended victims. The lists were not exclusive. More Hutus died than were listed. But the lists were taken seriously. There are stories of Hutus begging Tutsi friends to check the lists in government offices to see which Hutus were on it. One source said a Tutsi official tried to reassure the wife of a missing Hutu by showing her a government list without her husband's name on it. But he had been killed anyway.

Although many Hutus were taken away from their homes at night, a large number simply received a summons in an orderly way to report to the police at a certain time. In Bujumbura, the capital, many victims were killed in prison. Many foreigners later had all kinds of grisly stories about the methods of execution, all difficult to verify. But most sources agreed with a diplomat who said, "They did not use many bullets."

The bodies were thrown on trucks that drove from the city to a field near the airport. In the first few days, the trucks rumbled through town in daylight. But the government later decided to try to hide what it was doing. The trucks were shifted to night runs. Under heavy lighting, bulldozers dug mass graves at night and covered them over.

There seemed to be three kinds of victims. First, the government tried to kill almost every Hutu who had a government job, including Hutu soldiers. Many of the death lists were simply lifted from civil service rolls that evidently had been prepared a few months earlier.

Second, the government tried to kill all Hutus who had enough wealth for potential leadership. Wealth is a very relative term in Africa. Many sources said that the so-called wealthy Hutus were any who owned a shop, had a bank account, or lived in a house with a corrugated iron roof instead of a thatched one.

Finally, the government tried to kill all educated Hutus. Education was probably defined differently by officials in different parts of the country. But almost all Hutu university students, many Hutu secondary school students, and perhaps half the country's Hutu teachers were killed. In one incident, six women teachers were killed in front of their students.

The categories of victims explained why a visitor later could hardly find a Hutu inside Bujumbura but could see many trudging along the roads in the countryside, their hoes on their shoulders. Bujumbura, a city of 70,000, was never a Hutu city. The Tutsis, who controlled the wealth and power of Burundi, dominated the capital. But there were thousands of Hutus living there, the Hutus who had left their traditional peasant life in the countryside to join the modern world of the big town. These modern Hutus—all in the money economy, some educated, many in government jobs—were the prime targets of the onslaught.

It is difficult for an outsider to understand how the government was able to inflict so much punishment on the Hutus in a tiny country where they make up the great bulk of its population. They outnumbered the Tutsis almost six to one. Yet the Hutus were cowed by an army that numbered no more than 4,000 at the start of the troubles and far less after it had purged itself of Hutus.

75,000 Hutus fled Burundi and took refuge in Zaire, Tanzania and Rwanda. But thousands more remained behind and took their punishment without much resistance.

There were stories of Hutus accepting their summonses and reporting to the police at the scheduled time even though they knew death awaited them. There were other stories of officials loading Hutus on trucks and, when the trucks were full, ordering the remaining Hutus to come back the next day. The Hutus obeyed. One Hutu minister was overseas when the troubles erupted, yet flew home to his execution. Some Hutus escaped, according to one story, only after Europeans forced them against their will into a truck and drove them across the border.

Some observers said that even Hutus trying to escape did so half-heartedly. "They were pathetic," said one foreigner who had worked with Hutus for many years. "Any kid with a third-grade education in the United States has read enough funny books to know how to escape. But they would walk to the border down the main road. If one gendarme stopped them, they would turn back."

Foreigners who knew the Hutus well blamed their strange acquiescence on a strong streak of fatalism in the Hutu personality and an intense psychological dependence on their Tutsi lords. Much like the serfs in medieval Europe, the Hutus for centuries had given their loyalty to the Tutsis in exchange for protection. Caught in a terrifying crisis in 1972, most did as they were told.

III. World Reaction

The reaction by outsiders to this killing was feeble. Missionaries kept quiet or muted their concern. Most foreign governments refused to protest in public. Two African countries even rushed military help to Micombero's government. Almost all foreign aid continued to flow. European businessmen kept playing golf in Bujumbura.

It is not difficult to imagine the outcry in the rest of the world if the whites who run the government of South Africa had decided to put down a rebellion and guarantee their continued control by killing all black South Africans with some education, wealth or potential for leadership. Yet the events in Burundi, roughly analogous, provoked few protests. It was almost as if all foreigners had banded together in a conspiracy of silence.

Actually there was no conspiracy. For a variety of reasons, all institutions that might have protested—churches, governments, international organizations —made separate decisions to look the other way. Each decision seemed logical and right to those who made it. But, as a result, the Burundi government escaped any punishment or even condemnation.

Missionaries and other religious leaders showed the most surprising restraint, for, in the past, they have been in the forefront of those exposing injustice in Africa. During the Nigerian and Sudanese civil wars, for example, church groups played a major role in publicizing the pains of Biafra and the southern Sudan.

Burundi is one of the most Christian countries in Africa, for more than half of its population is Christian, mostly Catholic. It might seem that this strength would make churchmen forthright in their condemnation of the killing. But it actually made most missionaries hesitant. They were afraid that if they spoke out they might lose their hold on Burundi. They believed that silence was the price they had to pay to expand Christianity. Some reasoned that protest would have been futile anyway. In the long run, they told themselves, their silence and the spread of Christianity might give them more influence to prevent the recurrence of such a holocaust.

Some of the tortuous reasoning came through in an interview that an American Protestant missionary reluctantly granted. He said that Protestant missionaries were in a precarious position in Burundi. Government leaders, mainly Catholic, suspected them of stirring up troubles among the Hutus. He paid tribute to the American embassy in Bujumbura for trying to keep stories about the massacres away from the American press when they began. He said that if the news had been splashed in American newspapers, the Burundi government might have blamed the 100 American Protestant missionaries in Burundi and expelled them.

Yet, a few minutes later, the missionary deplored the fact that the rest of the world had ignored what had happened in Burundi. The inconsistency was quickly pointed out. How could he praise the U.S. embassy for withholding the news and then deplore the fact that the news was ignored? The missionary shrugged.

He was asked how he could continue to work in Burundi. Many victims had been Protestant. The government had slaughtered Hutus that he had trained for years. Why convert people to Christianity and educate them in a country that might slaughter them just because they were educated? Put on the defensive, the missionary laughed nervously. "I suppose you could say that's our job," he said, "preparing people to die."

Catholic leaders also found themselves caught between their conscience and politics. Much of the Catholic clergy was Tutsi. Almost all the Tutsi leaders of government, including the president, who came to confession several times a week, were Catholic. The Catholic clergy did not remain silent, but it did not say very much either.

Soon after the killing began, the Bishop of Bujumbura, a Tutsi, urged the government to be judicious in punishing those Hutus accused of plotting against the government. A few weeks later, Pope Paul VI, speaking to a Sunday crowd at St. Peter's Square, called for a solution to the "pitiless and ferocious strife." The Papal Nuncio in Bujumbura delivered a note to the Burundi government urging restraint. In January 1973, the five bishops of Burundi—two Tutsi, two Hutu, and one Belgian—issued a pastoral letter describing the country as "drowned in blood" but blaming the troubles on "the egoism of both Hutu and Tutsi elites," not tribalism. Against the enormity of what happened in Burundi, all these Catholic pronouncements seemed ineffectual.

The reaction of the U.S. government to the events was typical of most foreign governments. Ambassador Thomas P. Melady believed that his first responsibility was protection of the 150 Americans in Burundi, mostly missionaries. When the massacres began, the U.S. embassy in Kenya, receiving reports from Melady, began briefing American correspondents on what was going on. The correspondents, based in Nairobi, had been unable to obtain visas for Burundi. Melady immediately rebuked the embassy in Nairobi and demanded that it stop the briefings. He feared that news reports in American newspapers would be traced easily by the Burundi government to the U.S. embassy in Bujumbura and its main sources, the American missionaries. The clamp down on the news became so tight that Senator Edward M. Kennedy complained in June that the State Department was withholding its information on the massacres from Congress.

The U.S. government never publicly rebuked the Burundi government. In the fall of 1972, Assistant Secretary of State David Newsom secretly called the Burundi ambassador to the State Department and expressed American concern over the troubles. But this concern was never communicated in person in Bujumbura to President Micombero by either Melady or his successor, Ambassador Robert L. Yost. Melady, in fact, accepted an award from Micombero before he left Burundi in late May 1972 to become Ambassador to Uganda.

According to a report by the Carnegie Endowment for International Peace, a State Department officer did propose that the United States, as a sign of its displeasure, stop buying coffee from Burundi. An American firm, Folgers, buys more than 80 percent of Burundi's coffee, its main export, accounting for 65 percent of Burundi's earnings of foreign exchange. The officer proposed that the U.S. government either place an embargo on purchases of coffee or persuade Folgers to stop buying on its own.

But this proposal, according to the Carnegie report, was dropped without even serious consideration. American policy-makers were persuaded that protest was futile in any case and that the troubles ought to be treated as an African problem. If African governments chose to ignore the massacres, the U.S. officials reasoned, why should the American government make an issue of it?

The United States did suspend a fund of $25,000 that the office of the ambassador had available for small self-help projects within Burundi. But the U.S. government supplied $300,000 worth of relief in 1973, mostly in surplus food. American officials insisted that this food was distributed only to the widows and orphans of the victims. But, according to the Americans actually distributing the food, it went to all people of all tribes throughout the country without discrimination.

Belgium was the only western country to react differently from the United States. The former colonial power in Burundi, Belgium was the largest donor of foreign aid and had the most nationals living there, about 3,000. In May, Premier Gaston Eyskens denounced the massacres as "veritable genocide." His government announced it would review continuation of its four and a half million dollars a year foreign aid programme. This set off a storm of anti-Belgian invective from the Burundi government, which even accused the Belgians of starting all the troubles in the first place.

In the end, Belgium did not carry out its threat. It withdrew 35 advisers from the Burundi army, but this was less to punish Burundi than to placate Belgian public opinion. It was hard to justify keeping advisers in an army that was killing the elite of the majority tribe. The Belgians also refused to replace 50 technicians who were expelled by the Burundi government after the massacres, evidently because they had expressed disapproval of what was going on.

But, in general, Belgium neither withdrew nor substantially cut its foreign aid. It may have decided against planning new programmes, but that is something that Burundi would not perceive as a rebuke. Belgian officials took the view of most foreigners involved in foreign aid in Burundi. They insisted that punishing the government by withdrawing aid would only hurt the masses. "Foreign aid must be maintained," said a Belgian official. "This, with Rwanda, is the poorest country in the world." "If we cut foreign aid," said a foreign aid official from another country, "you will only have more misery here. If you put a curtain around this country, it will be worse." As a result, the United Nations, France, the Common Market, and West Germany all maintained their foreign aid programmes.

Almost all African governments reacted in a predictable way. As usual in cases of African disorder, the governments either ignored the massacres or pledged support to the government. Deluded by the claim that the original Hutu uprising had been led by former Congolese rebels now exiled in Tanzania, President Mobutu Sese Seko of Zaire (the former Congo) even sent troops to

Bujumbura and President Julius Nyerere of Tanzania sent ammunition. In May, Diallo Telli, then secretary-general of the Organization of African Unity (OAU), flew to Bujumbura and announced "the total solidarity of the secretary-general of the OAU with President Micombero." At its annual summit conference in June, the OAU refrained from any public statement on the massacres.

Only Rwanda departed from the African line. In June, President Gregoire Kayibanda of Rwanda sent a letter to Micombero asking him to "halt the killing that does Africa no good." But the Burundi government, without making the letter public, described it as an endorsement of the government's policies. Rwanda then dropped the matter.

While governments and institutions kept quiet about the massacres, most of the 6,000 foreigners in Burundi also made little protest. Few demonstrated their disgust by leaving. They, like their governments, probably felt that protest was futile.

Some foreigners also reported that it was possible to ignore what was going on. Most of the killings and arrests took place at night far from the offices where expatriates worked. Trucks went through streets at night, but only a few whites actually saw the bodies in them. Expatriates were often not on close terms with Africans anyway. Seven workers might disappear from an office one week. That would be terrible and regrettable but not heart-rending. Moreover, the government was careful not to harm foreigners. For a white expatriate, it was possible to remain in Burundi and keep playing golf. There was another reason for the lack of outcry. Most westerners and their governments reacted to the disorders as if they believed slaughter was a way of life in this part of Africa, best ignored, at least until time and civilization tamed the savages. The slaughter of thousands of blacks by blacks was not really considered a holocaust by most white governments. Ironically, African governments seemed to agree.

BANGLADESH*

Bangladesh is located on the Bay of Bengal and has borders with India and with Burma. While its low-lying territory is very fertile it is also ravaged by periodic typhoons. With about 144,000 square kilometers of land and a rapidly growing population (115 million in 1988) it is one of the most densely populated countries in the world (800/sq. km.). Over 85 percent of the population profess Islam; several of the tribal peoples in the Chittagong Hill Tracts are Buddhists; the rest are Hindus. The language of the country is Bengali, with some dialect variations from region to region. This already dense population has one of the highest birthrates in the world (43/1,000), and a high death rate (15/1,000); infant mortality is also high (138/1,000), and life expectancy is 52 years, according to 1988 data. As such data indicate, poverty and illiteracy are widespread.

The country's history goes back at least five thousand years, but we are concerned only with the modern period, starting with India's independence. When the British left after World War II, they thought that a united India would be one of their most cherished legacies to the newly independent country. This was not to be because Moslems and Hindus did not want to live under the same rule. The negotiations leading to partition were characterized by bitter disagreements and accompanied by much bloodshed. What finally emerged was a most unlikely new state—Pakistan—which consisted of two halves that were over one thousand miles apart and had nothing in common but their religion. The separation of Pakistan from India created a great deal of suffering, bloodshed, and lasting hostility. Millions of Moslems migrated to the new state and millions of Hindus left it. But the separation of the two religious groups was not perfect: about 40 million Moslems remained in India, and about 1½ million Hindus remained in Pakistan.

The newly created Pakistan had its well-wishers and its critics. The well-wishers argued that with modern means of travel and communication the distance between West Pakistan and East Pakistan should not present great difficulties

*This summary is based on Chaudhuri, Choudhuri, International Commission of Jurists (1972), Kuper (1981), Rahman, Sethi as well as several encyclopedias.

to the new community, especially since it was organized around the integrating factor of a common religion. The critics pointed out that this belief was in fact the only thing they had in common. They spoke different languages; they did not share a common history or tradition; they ate and dressed in distinctive fashion; they did not intermarry or enjoy the same sports; and they were politically oriented in opposite directions—West Pakistan toward the Middle East and East Pakistan toward Southeast Asia. And as to bridging the one-thousand-mile gap with modern technology, that was a viable possibility only for a small elite, not for the poor masses.

Predictably, the two did not get on very well. The country was established as a democracy with the capital and the government in the West and the poor, but export-producing farmers in the East. The sharing of power and resources soon lost its appeal, and a military government took over. Perhaps the greatest source of friction and dissatisfaction was the unequal economic development. Although the East produced the bulk of the exports that brought in foreign currency, the West developed much more rapidly. The East felt that colonial exploitation had not really ended; it had just exchanged one colonial master for another. Such views became crystalized in the Awami League, which agitated for a return to democracy and for regional autonomy.

Without going into the details of the political life of Pakistan, we can now jump to December 1970, when a general election was finally held. To the great consternation of the government, this election produced a majority for the Awami League. President Yahya was reluctant to call the Constituent Assembly into session, and on March 1, 1971, he announced that it was suspended indefinitely. This produced a crisis. It meant that military government would continue and that the long-promised democracy was postponed again. Sheikh Mujibur Rahman, the charismatic leader of the Awami League, reacted by calling for a general strike in what he now called Bangladesh. Efforts to negotiate were carried on by phone until March 17, when Yahya Khan came to Dacca, the capital of East Pakistan, in order to negotiate a compromise. The Awami League held firm in insisting on the six points that were the crux of its Manifesto, which asked that Pakistan become a federation in which each of the federating units was to have full autonomy on the basis of the following six points: "(1) The character of the Government shall be Federal and Parliamentary, . . . (2) The Federal Government shall be responsible only for defence and foreign affairs and, subject to the condition in (3) below, currency. (3) There shall be two separate currencies mutually and freely convertible in each wing for each region, or in the alternative a single currency, subject to the establishment of a Federal Reserve System in which there will be regional Federal Reserve Banks which shall devise measures to prevent the transfer of resources and flight of capital from one region to another. (4) Fiscal policy shall be the responsibility of the Federating Units. . . (5) Constitutional provisions shall be made to enable separate accounts to be maintained of the foreign exchange earnings of each of the Federating Units, under the control of the respective Governments of the Federating Units. . . (6) The Government of the Federating Units shall be empowered to maintain a militia or para-military force in order to contribute effectively towards national security" (Rahman 1978, Appendix D).

We cite these six points of the Awami League program in order to indicate how central a role economic exploitation played in its perception of the situation and how much of its authority its leaders expected the central government to surrender. During the general strike the Awami League not only prepared for conflict and for forming the government, but also engaged in a good deal of violence and killing of opponents. During these disorders the negotiations continued until they eventuated in concerted face-to-face talks on March 17–23, but without much progress, and on the twenty-fourth they broke down. On the twenty-fifth Yahya Khan left for West Pakistan. On the same day he denounced Mujib and his men as traitors, and the massive military attack began to "reoccupy" East Pakistan. On the twenty-seventh the military government in Islamabad actually declared war on Bangladesh. The West Pakistan army was first cleared of Bengalis, then it killed an undetermined number of people, concentrating on Hindus (because they were accused of loyalty to India), military and paramilitary personnel, journalists, teachers, students, and cadres of the Awami League. Killing, looting, rape, and arson were quite general, and whole villages were emptied of their population and destroyed. To indicate the attitude of the military junta, we quote the reply given by General Tikka Khan, the military governor of East Bengal during this period, when he was reminded that he was administering a majority province of Pakistan: "I will reduce this majority into a minority" (Sethi 1972, 28).

The devastation wrought by the Pakistani military was enormous, although estimates of casualties vary widely. Between one million and three million were killed; about two million were rendered homeless; and about ten million fled across the border to India, where they had to live in conditions of unimaginable hardship in spite of India's best efforts. On April 15 the Provisional Government of the People's Republic of Bangladesh was formed, and resistance to the military forces of West Pakistan continued in spite of the great inequality of training and equipment. By summer, the *Mukti Bahini* (Liberation Forces) were losing the unequal contest and retreated to India for more training and weapons. Choudhury (1974, chap. 8) argues that India had always wanted to interfere and used the plight of the Mukti Bahini and of the refugees, many of them Hindus, as a pretext to complete the dismemberment of Pakistan. In December

1971 India invaded East Pakistan and on the sixteenth forced the Pakistani army to surrender. The new state of Bangladesh had become reality, but at tremendous costs in terms of lives and destruction.

The case of Bangladesh is in many ways an interesting one that is accompanied by many debates and surprises. It is the only twentieth-century case in which a secessionist movement has been successful, although some may argue that it might not have succeeded without the intervention of India. It is also the only case in which the victims of a genocide have won out over the perpetrator. Even the events that we have characterized as genocide are subject to controversy. Bangladesh has its "deniers," who claim that there was a civil war between the government in power and a rebellious and traitorous region. Others have argued that civil unrest, accompanied by rioting, looting, and killing, had broken out and that the troops merely tried to reestablish order. Some concede that the discipline of the troops may not always have been exemplary, but that no mass killing occurred. And there is even the extreme view that it was the Awami League that was engaged in a genocide that was stopped by the Pakistani military. International reaction was equally diverse. It ranged all the way from the intervention by India to the refusal by the United Nations to even discuss the case. The relations between the participants in this tragedy have not changed; they are still quite unfriendly between India and Pakistan, while they are quite warm between India and Bangladesh.

For the scholar, this case is particularly puzzling. It seems to involve such a mixture of motives that it is hard to decide whether this was an ideological genocide, or a genocide to eliminate a threat, or one to preserve access to economic goods. Perhaps we need another category in our typology: genocides intended to abort secession movements (see Kuper's typology, discussed on pp. 17–18 above). Additional cases that might qualify for inclusion into this category are Ethiopia, Sri Lanka, and the Sudan. What would be particularly distinctive about such a category is that the victim groups also engaged in killing, though less successfully than the perpetrators.

CAMBODIA*

Background

Cambodia, as Kampuchea was known until a new regime, the Khmer Rouge, came to power in 1975, is a small country situated in the southwest part of the Indochinese Peninsula. At its greatest extent, it spans 350 miles in an east–west direction and 280 miles in a north–south direction. It has borders on the east and southeast with Vietnam, on the northeast with Laos, on the west and northwest with Thailand, and on the southwest with the Gulf of Thailand. With its 69,900 square miles (about the area of Oklahoma) and 7 millon people (in 1971), Cambodia had a population density of about 100 persons per square mile, one of the lowest in Southeast Asia; it was considered underpopulated by the standards of the region. By contrast, North and South Vietnam had estimated population densities in 1975 of 385 and 311 persons per square mile, respectively, and estimated total populations of 20 and 23 million persons. Among the countries of Southeast Asia, only Laos, with 3 million persons, and Singapore, with 2 million, had smaller populations. Life expectancy was only 50 years (in 1961), and the per capita gross national product in 1969 was US$ 120.

Although an underdeveloped country, Cambodia rarely experienced famine. Together with South Vietnam, it was one of the major granaries of Indochina. Before the South Vietnamese invasion of Cambodia in 1970, the Cambodians exported large quantities of rice every year. This staple crop was grown on 85 percent of the country's cultivated land. Until the Vietnam War swelled the streets of the cities with refugees from the countryside, only 10 percent of its people lived in urban areas of 10,000 or more inhabitants. Phnom Penh, its capital city, with a population of nearly 480,000 persons, housed the bulk of the country's urban population.

Most Cambodians lived in small villages of less than 300 persons, where

*This summary is based on Becker (1986), Burton (1984), Chandler and Kiernan (1983), Chandler (1983), Kiernan (1986), Ponchaud (1978), Szymusiak (1986), and Willmott (1981), in addition to background data from several encyclopedias.

they clustered around a market, a primary school, some small shops, and a few Buddhist temples. The family was the basic social unit of the village. Prewar Cambodia had few big landlords. Eighty-four percent of rural Cambodians were owner-cultivators of their land and only 6 percent were tenants. The remainder were artisans, shopkeepers, monks, teachers, and merchants. The inhabitants of a typical village were nearly all of Khmer ethnic origin. Indeed, the Khmer, almost all of whom were Buddhists, accounted for 90 percent of the nation's population. Among the nations of Southeast Asia, Cambodia displayed a homogeneity that was unique.

Nevertheless, Cambodia had a number of important minority ethnic groups, including the Chinese, the Vietnamese, and the Muslim Cham-Malays. Chinese entrepreneurs controlled Cambodia's commercial life, serving as moneylenders, investors, merchants, and transporters. Yet there was little animosity toward the Chinese. When he traveled throughout Cambodia in the early 1960s, sociologist W. E. Willmott found that the higher standard of living and different functions of the Chinese were perceived by the Cambodian peasantry as "part of a foreign *culture* rather than as an aspect of exploitation" (Willmott 1981, 222–23). The Vietnamese minority was in a far worse position. Relations between the Khmer and the Vietnamese were poisoned by hundreds of years of hostility and suspicion.

Much of the hostility between the Khmer and the Vietnamese can be explained by Cambodia's early history. The great Khmer kingdom that reached its peak in the twelfth century, with its impressive capital at Angkor and its magnificent system of irrigation canals and roads, ruled the lands that we know today as Vietnam, Thailand, and Laos. However, the Thais and the Vietnamese soon recovered, rebelled, and broke the Khmer hold on their lands. In 1444, the Khmer fled from Angkor, marking the start of a nearly two-hundred-year-long period of incessant warfare between the Khmer and the Thais. The accession to power of Barom Reachea IV in 1603 with Thai support launched a new stage, in which weak Khmer kings were forced to depend for protection on either Siam (Thailand) or Vietnam. For several years in the mid-1800s, this process went so far that the Vietnamese exercised total control over the country. This was the situation until 1863, when France declared a protectorate over Cambodia.

French rule fell more lightly on Cambodia than on Vietnam, but the Khmer rose in a major revolt in 1884, when the French tried to usurp the power of the Cambodian monarch. In spite of their resistance to colonial rule, the Khmer rescued many Frenchmen from the Japanese during World War II. The truth is that they resented the Vietnamese even more than the French. Two of the most commonly heard grievances voiced against French rule by the Khmer after the war were that the French had used Vietnamese officials to rule Cambodia and that they had given Cochin China (southern Vietnam)—called the cradle of Cambodia and sometimes identified as Kampuchea Krom (lower Cambodia) by many Khmer—to the Vietnamese.

After achieving independence from France in 1953, Prince Sihanouk's government concentrated on developing schools and teachers. Improved access to education was especially significant for a country in which children under fifteen constituted 46 percent of the population. From 1953 to 1969, school enrollment grew rapidly, soaring from about 300,000 to about 1,000,000 at the elementary level, from 6,000 to 120,000 at the secondary level, and from over 100 to 9,000 at the university level. Many of the future leaders of the Khmer Rouge movement started their working careers as teachers in the burgeoning school system. They were among the first Khmer sent to study in Paris by the French.

In 1945, in one of the many ironies of Cambodia's history, the French government had reversed its custom of sending Cambodia's best students to Hanoi for university study because of fears that they might be seduced by the radical ideas of Ho Chi Minh's Vietminh movement. But in Paris the students were attracted to an equally heady brew incorporating the ideas of French Communists and Chairman Mao Zedong. This was the same atmosphere that produced radical intellectuals like Frantz Fanon, who argued that only violence and armed revolt could cleanse the minds of Third World peoples and rid them of their colonial mentalities. Blended with their already strong Khmer nationalism, this intoxicating mixture of radical concepts ultimately led the future leaders of the Khmer Rouge to spectacularly misdiagnose the sources of Cambodia's ills. They came to believe that the majority of Khmer peasants would welcome with open arms an armed revolutionary movement dedicated to the abolition of high rents and usury, evils that the peasants were barely acquainted with.

The leading members of the Cambodian student radical elite became active participants in Cambodia's political life in the 1960s. Among them were Kim Trang, born in Cochin China, who changed his Vietnamese-sounding name to Ieng Sary, the name by which he was known when he became deputy premier in charge of foreign affairs in the government of Democratic Kampuchea; Son Sen, another Khmer from Cochin China, who would later become deputy premier in charge of defence in the Khmer Rouge government; Khieu Samphan, the author of a moderate doctoral dissertation examining the Cambodian economy and problems of industrialization, who would become Kampuchea's head of state; Saloth Sar, better known by his nom de guerre, Pol Pot, who would become the dominant and most famous Kampuchean to emerge from this group of students; and Hou Youn, the author of a doctoral dissertation on the Cambodian peasantry and modernization, who disappeared just before the fall of Phnom

Penh, probably killed by his comrades because he opposed the deportation of the capital's residents to the countryside.

In the late 1950s and early 1960s, many of the students returning to Cambodia became teachers in Cambodia's best schools, where their strong advocacy of an end to the corruption that pervaded Prince Sihanouk's government and the country's urban centers earned them the respect of their students and colleagues. Persecuted by the prince's security police, several of the radical teachers chose to go underground. Their numbers remained small until March 1970, when Lon Nol, the brutal, ambitious, and militantly anti-Vietnamese head of the Cambodian army and police, led a coup that overthrew the government of the still popular Prince Sihanouk, driving the prince and his many followers into the arms of the radical ex-teachers and their allies in the world of clandestine politics. During the next five years, organizing themselves under the name Khmer Rouge, aided by the Vietnamese Communists, and strengthened by Prince Sihanouk's popularity among the peasants, the Khmer Rouge radicals and their peasant followers became first-class soldiers. Lon Nol's army was steadily weakened by its clashes with North Vietnamese units protecting the Ho Chi Minh trail, Hanoi's vital supply route to South Vietnam. On April 17, 1975, after a long siege, Khmer Rouge troops overran Lon Nol's troops and captured Phnom Penh.

Military victory only strengthened the leadership's commitment to a misguided class analysis of Cambodian society. W. E. Willmott argues persuasively that the Khmer Rouge's ability to win the support of the peasants had little to do with class struggle, but rather was due to three quite different factors: "the popularity of Sihanouk, the [South] Vietnamese invasion in 1970, and the American bombing of Kampuchea" (Willmott, 224–26). To these factors should be added one other that contributed to their victory and foreshadowed their behavior once in power: the utter ruthlessness of Khmer Rouge battle tactics. The best account of these tactics is offered by Elizabeth Becker, who covered the war in Cambodia for the *Washington Post*. She writes:

> The Khmer Rouge approached battle as they approached all other matters, devoted to achieving an objective at whatever cost, devising drastic strategies, willing to use people as expendable commodities. . . . From the inside, at the junior commander level, their methods were perceived as "savage," the word used by Hem Samin, a dissident returnee from Vietnam who later fled to Vietnam.
>
> "They would say we should attack right away no matter how many got killed, as long as we won, not to worry about how many got killed because it didn't matter," Samin stated. In practice this meant ordering attack en

masse. If the attack failed, the military officer in charge would be "liquidated" and a junior officer considered loyal to the party selected to regroup
and reengage. If that were to fail, another attack was mounted. "Once
there was some path of attack, that would be it. There would be that single
path of attack," he said. [Becker 1986, 171–72]

The Genocide

Once in power, the Khmer Rouge embarked on a vast experi-
ment in social engineering that would have the most devastating consequences
for Cambodia. From 1975 to 1978, they carried out the largest mass political
killing of the post–World War II era. One to two million Cambodians were
murdered by their own government. The victims were shot by firing squads,
tortured to death, worked to death, and starved to death. They were not the
casualties of local vigilantes set loose by the devastating American bombing of
Cambodia, but rather the victims of Pol Pot and the Kampuchean Communist
Party, which he led. Charles Burton explains the case for holding the leaders of
the government and the party responsible:

Pol Pot's literal reading of "bourgeoisie" as "those who live in cities," and
his attempt to eliminate them by turning the entire populace into "poor
peasants" through forced rustification, was not accompanied by an attempt
to build a constituency of supporters from within the poor peasants themselves. The latter were less than enthusiastic about the abolition of religion, private plots, monetary exchange, and even family life (through the
institution of communal eating). In the absence of popular support, local
cadres were given the power of life and death over the people through the
control of food distribution and the right to execute more or less at will.
Because the central authorities tolerated and indeed encouraged this state
of affairs . . . they are ultimately morally responsible for its consequences.
[Burton 1984, 532–33]

The regime's understanding of the peasantry was no better than its analysis of
the "bourgeoisie." W. E. Willmott describes how the Khmer Rouge reacted
when their prophecies failed:

Because their social analysis convinced them that they could expect widespread support for revolutionary change, the KCP [Kampuchean Communist Party] were not prepared for the growing opposition and could define it
as nothing else than counter-revolutionary. Consequently, no criticism was

tolerated, and even the mildest opposition was punished severely. . . . Inexperienced cadres could think of no better solution to failing support than to punish or kill those who lacked enthusiasm for their programme. Their leaders are most to blame; not only did they lack any sense of Khmer history, they criminally failed to understand their own society. "Democratic Kampuchea," therefore, stands as a forlorn monument to the horrible consequences of any socialist revolution that ignores its own history and culture. [Willmott 1981, 226–27]

The first victims of the Khmer Rouge were the residents of Phnom Penh. Many attempts have been made to explain the Khmer Rouge's fateful and controversial decision to evacuate Phnom Penh. Ieng Sary has claimed that the "prospect of an inevitable famine was the prime motivation for the evacuation." He says,

We had estimated the population of Phnom Penh at two million, but we found almost three million people in the city when we entered it. The Americans had been bringing 30,000 to 40,000 tons of food into Phnom Penh daily. We had no means of transporting such quantities of supplies to the capital. So the population had to go where the food was. We had to feed that population and at the same time preserve our independence and our dignity without asking for help from any other country. [Sary, as quoted in Ponchaud, 36–37]

François Ponchaud, a French priest who worked in Cambodia right up to the fall of Phnom Penh, contests this explanation. He shows that of the two and a half million people in the city when it fell more than a million and a half were peasants who had fled the fighting during the previous five years. They were eager to return to their homes; no force was needed. As for the natives of Phnom Penh, Ponchaud maintains that the stocks of rice accumulated during the fighting could have fed them for two months and could have been supplemented with the several thousand tons of rice that lay rotting in the port of Sihanoukville (Kompong Som) during the first months following the revolution (ibid., 36–37).

The Khmer refused all forms of foreign help, regarding it as an unjustifiable interference in Kampuchea's domestic affairs and as an insult to the country's independence and sovereignty. When the UNICEF representative offered his organization's assistance to help care for Khmer children, Ponchaud relates, he was rebuffed with the claim that "our Angkar has everything it needs." The Khmer Rouge also refused to accept a planeload of medicine that was offered by the French government (ibid., 52) and, in 1976, they ignored OPEC's offer of a loan of 3 million petrodollars repayable in twenty-five years (ibid., 106). A rational approach to feeding Phnom Penh would have included maximum utilization of foreign aid and the mobilization of existing rice reserves while the peasants returned to their homes and planted a new crop of rice.

What then is the real explanation for the brutal deportations organized by the Khmer Rouge? "The deeper reason," contends Ponchaud, "was an ideological one, as we saw later on when we learned that the provincial towns, villages and even isolated farms in the countryside had also been emptied of their inhabitants." If Ponchaud is correct, the deportations were nothing less than an attack on the very idea of a city, which was repugnant to the Khmer Rouge leadership. Nor was this a new tendency in Khmer Rouge thinking; it had been evident in their military operations since 1972 (ibid., 36–37).

Once in power, the Khmer Rouge leaders began to murder all those who fit into certain social and political categories. In the weeks following the capture of Phnom Penh, they killed the bulk of the former civilian and military establishments (ibid., 45). Those who were regarded as corrupted by their education, class, or employment—civil servants, doctors, lawyers, soldiers, and teachers—were identified and eliminated. The Khmer Rouge leaders paid no attention to the fact that by virtue of their own education, overseas experiences, and urban background they were identical to the very people they were destroying (ibid., 62–63). The killing of soldiers' wives and children is also alleged to have occurred frequently. A Khmer Rouge slogan advanced the maxim that "Their line must be annihilated down to the last survivor" (ibid., 70).

The inhabitants of Phnom Penh who survived the exodus to the country, as well as the deported inhabitants of the other towns of Cambodia, were branded with the label "new people" and treated as enemies by the Angkar (ibid., 74). Refugees who managed to leave Cambodia after the Communist-style election of the Representative Assembly of the People that took place on March 20, 1976, reported that in many villages housing deportees only the revolutionary soldiers were allowed to cast ballots because new people were regarded as prisoners who had forfeited their civic rights (ibid., 126–27).

Khmer Rouge acts of annihilation went beyond the notion of destroying categories of people who might contribute to the organization of an armed opposition to the regime. This "total purge," Ponchaud maintains, "is, above all, the translation into action of a particular vision of man: a person who has been spoiled by a corrupt regime cannot be reformed, he must be physically eliminated from the brotherhood of the pure" (ibid., 69). This is borne out by slogans broadcast over the radio by the Khmer Rouge: "What is infected must be cut out," "What is rotten must be removed," and "What is too long must be shortened and made the right length" (ibid., 70).

Unlike the revolutionaries of China and Vietnam, who sometimes tried to indoctrinate captured soldiers and civil servants, the central Khmer Rouge leadership thought this was impossible. In Khmer Rouge parlance, the "people" (*pracheachon*) meant factory-workers and peasants, but the broader use of the term by the leadership included the Khmer Rouge armed forces and civil servants. Those who were defined as "enemies of the people," as well as Khmer Rouge who made mistakes, were called "subpeople" (*anoupracheachon*). According to the Khmer Rouge view of the world, townspeople were not really part of the people and had no claim on the people's resources (ibid., 108–09).

Fortifying the Khmer Rouge in their repressive outlook was the simple fact that they had too few militants to openly control Cambodia. According to Elizabeth Becker's estimate, in April 1975 the Khmer Rouge army numbered 68,000 troops, and the party had only 14,000 members (Becker, 179). The regime's insecurity also explains the fact that throughout its first two years in power it carefully concealed the identities of all its top leaders and their commitment to Communism. Pol Pot delayed until September 28, 1977, the revelation of the existence of the Kampuchean Communist Party and its control of the government. Up to then, the Khmer Rouge hid behind the popularity of Prince Sihanouk, whom they were actually holding under house arrest in the royal palace (Chandler 1983).

Becker's figures underscore refugee reports indicating that life in the countryside was thoroughly regimented by the Khmer Rouge. The entire population was split up into groups (*krom*) of ten to fifteen families with a chairman at the head of each group. A tract of forest land was allotted to each family. The new people had to clear the land, plant, and tend crops. In most cases, the rice paddies were taken away from the villagers and nationalized. At crucial points in the agricultural cycle, particularly planting and harvest times, the regime drafted large groups of new people to work in the rice paddies. No trading was allowed outside the membership of a single ten-family group (Ponchaud 74, 109).

The social norms of the population were assaulted by the Khmer Rouge. For example, parents no longer had authority over their children. Marriage, which had required parents' permission, now depended on approval by the heads of the boys' and girls' groups in the village (ibid., 145). Under the new regime, parents were to honor their children, whose spirit was held to be pure and unsullied by the corrupt past of the adults (ibid., 143). As in Mao Zedong's China during the Cultural Revolution, science was subordinated to the wisdom of the peasantry. One radio broadcast reported, "The young are learning their science from the workers and peasants, who are the sources of all knowledge" (ibid., 141–43).

The drive to impose new social norms was accompanied by a massive propaganda campaign rich with Orwellian language and images. At the same time, Buddhism was treated as a reactionary religion and was therefore forbidden. The Khmer Rouge killed a number of the country's leading monks because they had too much influence over the people. The rest were put to work in the country building dams and working on other collective projects (Ponchaud, 147–48).

Displaying the same ruthlessness in peacetime that they had shown during the war, the Khmer Rouge let no scruples about the value of human life block their way. Hundreds of thousands of Cambodians in the countryside died, succumbing to the toll taken by extreme hard labor, chronic malnutrition, and the total lack of sanitary equipment and medical care. The deportees from large cities were particularly vulnerable to malaria, sleeping sickness, dysentery, beri-beri and other fevers (ibid., 82).

After the Khmer Rouge took power, food allowances plummeted. The ration throughout most of the country was 1 tin of rice (180 grams) per person every two days. According to Ponchaud, Cambodians should have been receiving from 2.7 to 4.4 tins of rice per day in order to avoid malnutrition and its long-term effects.

Survivors of this period recall how the Khmer Rouge supervisors prohibited the new people to pick the fruits growing around them in abundance on pain of death even while they were starving. When the supervisors relented in order to maintain the supply of forced labor, they banned sharing the fruits with those already too sick to work, thus condemning them to death (Szymusiak 1975, 64, 75). Throughout the postwar famines, Khmer Rouge soldiers and officials ate well. Their attitude seems to have been, "We went hungry for five years. Now it's your turn!" (Ponchaud, 80–81).

Added to the toll exacted by man-made famine and attendant disease was the daily toll of officially conducted killings. Terror and summary executions were endemic to the Khmer Rouge regime. It killed anyone who deviated from the path it had laid down. (ibid., 84) Refugee testimony seems unanimous that people would disappear almost every evening, summoned to the "Angkar Leu," or higher organization (ibid., 86). Summarizing the consequences of these conditions, Ponchaud says, "A large part of the deported population appears to have been sacrificed. Its role in the history of Democratic Kampuchea will thus have been to build up the country's economic infrastructure with its own flesh and blood" (ibid., 92).

The Khmer Rouge also singled out ethnic and religious groups as victims. In November 1975, the Muslim Cham in the village of Trea (north of Kompong Cham) rebelled. According to a refugee report, the Khmer Rouge annihilated the villagers (ibid., 153). The Buddhist clergy too were selectively murdered

by Khmer cadres. These two cases, which fall under the UN definition of genocide, are described more fully by David Hawk (1984).

When the Cambodian economy failed to recover, the Khmer Rouge leadership turned against its own cadres and blamed the impending disaster on "sabotage" by foreign agents. Khmer Rouge regional leaders, some of whom resisted
the party's most socially and economically irrational orders, were forced to
confess under torture that they were agents of the Soviet KGB *and* of the American CIA and to give the names of their fellow conspirators. Mythical networks
of spies and traitors were meticulously invented by the interrogators of the
security apparatus, who granted the loyal militants the peace of the grave only
after they had furnished the system with the names of fresh victims. A sample
of the lists found at Tuol Sleng, just one of the regime's many killing centers,
includes the names of 1,000 Khmer Rouge soldiers, 324 workers from various
factories, 206 officers of the prerevolutionary army, 113 teachers and professors, 87 foreigners (mainly from Thailand and Laos), 148 highly educated
Khmer who returned voluntarily from overseas to serve their country, and 194
students, doctors, and engineers (A. Barnett and J. Pilger 1982, 115). The
cycle of torture, denunciation, and murder was brought to an end only by the
Vietnamese army's invasion of Kampuchea in December 1978.

The genocide in Cambodia represents an explosion of viru-
lent ideologically motivated killing. The world cannot afford to ignore this form
of genocide simply because most of its victims were not selected as members of
racial, religious, or ethnic groups. The definition of genocide must be broad
enough to encompass the case of the Khmer Rouge in Kampuchea. Assessing
the consequences for Cambodia of Khmer Rouge Communism, Ponchaud calls
the genocide they instigated and managed "a perfect application of an ideology
pushed to the farthest limit of its internal logic" (Ponchaud, 214).

EAST TIMOR*

Timor is an island east of Java that has historically been of interest to many trading peoples because of its great stands of sandalwood. The Portuguese started trading there about 1520, and in 1613 the Dutch also established themselves there. It was only in 1860 and in 1914 that these rivals finally signed treaties that effectively divided the island into two colonies.

East Timor, the former Portuguese colony, is the larger half of the island with about 19,000 km² — which is less than one-half the size of Holland or Switzerland. Before the withdrawal of Portugal, it had a population of about 680,000 people; the average life expectancy was about 40 years. Its people speak several languages, with the Tétun language serving as a lingua franca, and they were mostly animists, although both Moslem and Christian missionaries were making inroads. Infant mortality is very high, and gross national product figures are not available for this largely undeveloped area. The country is mountainous, and three-quarters of it is forest lands. This geography facilitates the coexistence of a large number of small kingdoms and a history of local raids and rebellions.

The entire island of Timor was occupied by Japan during World War II. In 1950 the former Dutch colony in the western part of the island became part of the newly independent Indonesia. The Portuguese stayed on in East Timor, where they had been for so long that they were hardly perceived as foreigners by the native population. However, they did little to prepare an indigenous group for eventual independence and self-administration. This led to special difficulties when, in April 1974, the government in Portugal was overthrown; for the Portuguese colonies it opened possibilities for decolonization and independence that

*The following summary is largely based on Budiardjo (1984), Cultural Survival (1981), and Joliffe (1978) in addition to background data from several encyclopedias and the demographic series of the United Nations, and of the Population Reference Bureau, and a personal communication from Benedict R. Anderson.

were encouraged by the new government, while many of the small cohort of intellectuals in East Timor wanted Portugal to stay on to facilitate a gradual transition to independence.

At this point there existed three political parties in East Timor: two of them were for independence, and the third, the smallest of the three, was pro-Indonesian. In June 1974 Indonesia's foreign minister gave written assurance that Indonesia respects East Timor's right to self-determination. In August 1975 civil war raged in Dili, the capital of East Timor, among those who wanted integration with Indonesia and those who wanted independence. The Frente Revolucionário de Este Timor Independente (FRETILIN), the leading proinde-pendence group, emerged as the dominant force. However, the Portuguese gov-ernor abandoned Dili for the safety of Atauro island, which used to be an offshore penal colony. FRETILIN wanted him to return to complete the decolo-nization process, but he refused. An appeal to the United Nations was ignored, and on November 28 FRETILIN declared independence, making immediate efforts to establish an infrastructure.

U.S. President Gerald Ford and Henry Kissinger were in Djakarta in Decem-ber 1975, and the day after their departure (December 7) Indonesia bombarded Dili and invaded East Timor. On December 12 the United Nations General Assembly called for Indonesia's withdrawal, but the United States, with Japan and Australia, blocked effective action. Over the next ten years, the General Assembly, the Security Council, and the Human Rights Commission condemned the human rights abuses committed by Indonesia a dozen times and voted to support East Timor's right to self-determination. All of these votes were ignored by the Indonesian government and served no other purpose than to underline the impotence of the United Nations.

On May 31, 1976, an Indonesian-sponsored "people's assembly" unani-mously decided to integrate East Timor as a province of Indonesia. Neither side recognized the legitimacy of the other, and (at the time of this writing) the war of conquest and of resistance continues, in spite of Indonesia's superiority in personnel and equipment. Indonesian methods have become increasingly brutal and costly.

Father Leoneto De Rega, a Portuguese priest who lived in East Timor during the invasion and was captured and exiled in July 1979, recently described Indonesian military activities in East Timor from 1975 to the present—search-and-destroy missions and saturation bombing of fields, hamlets, and homes—and the constant flight of the civilian population who were unable to plant and harvest their food crops. On the basis of his personal observation and extensive contacts with the East Timorese, Father

Leoneto concluded that cultivated areas were deliberately destroyed and the civilian population starved to force them out of their mountain villages, where they provided support for resistance fighters. Father Leoneto testified that, contrary to State Department reports, Indonesian bombing intensified since 1977, when it became clear that Indonesian ground forces could not rout the widespread resistance to annexation.

Furthermore, the priest has seen evidence that refugees in Indonesian "relocation" camps are prevented today from planting and harvesting food crops. The fact that the government of Indonesia would not permit relief organizations to provide food aid to thousands of starving East Timorese until resistance areas had been devastated is further confirmation that Indonesia used hunger as an instrument of pacification in East Timor. [Cultural Survival 1981, 36]

Since East Timor is an island it has been very easy to control the movement of people, materials, and information. But from a variety of sources it is clear that Indonesia uses aerial bombing of both people and crops to starve the population into submission, that it kills opposition members without trial, that it uses torture to elicit information about the resistance, and that it relocates whole villages into camps where food is deliberately withheld.

If humanitarian needs went unaddressed because of callous indifference, the disregard of civil and political rights appears to have been calculated. In the early days of the occupation, hundreds of civilians were summarily executed in Dili. Numerous reports evidence the disappearance of East Timorese, often the educated and those with leadership ability. Journalists also report that people who had surrendered under the presidential amnesty in 1977 have since disappeared and are believed to have been killed.

A report issued by the Australian Council for Overseas Aid in 1979 estimated that there are approximately forty prisons scattered throughout East Timor—three prisons in each of twelve administrative centres. A Timorese dignitary told a visiting *New York Times* reporter that in four detention camps, prisoners are held incommunicado (two in Dili, one in Baucau, and one near Maliana).

The conditions in the prisons are reported to be seriously sub-standard. Diseases, including tuberculosis and malnutrition, are alleged to be rampant. Thus far, the ICRC [International Committee of the Red Cross] has not been permitted by Indonesian authorities to carry out its normal function of prison visitation in East Timor. [Cultural Survival 1981, 13]

It is quite impossible to obtain accurate information on casualties; estimates run as high as one-half of the population: "Refugees interviewed have described a regular charade which occurs when foreign visitors are in Timor. Bombers are grounded, soldiers become civilians and war material is hidden and the population is forbidden on pain of imprisonment from speaking to foreign visitors" (Cultural Survival 1981, 20).

Relief workers who have been admitted to East Timor report that famine among children is so severe that one-half of all children will be permanently mentally retarded. At the same time as large areas are being depopulated in these ways, Javanese settlers are being moved in to facilitate East Timor's integration into Indonesia.

The world is forgetting East Timor—if it ever knew about it. Too little information is available and too much is happening in other parts of the world. For the United States, the alliance with Indonesia is so important that it does not want to rock the boat over East Timor. The United States considers Indonesia a major bulwark against Communist expansion in Southeast Asia. Therefore, it continues to send aid and arms to this country, in violation of its own laws prohibiting aid to those who violate human rights. In addition, it wants to protect its considerable trade and investments.

Canada has voted against the United Nations resolutions on self-determination and humanitarian assistance to East Timor. It is more interested in expanding its foreign trade. Canadian businessmen are among the largest Western investors in Indonesia. Canada has also been promoting the sale of Canadian arms to the Indonesian military, and the Department of External Affairs sponsored Canada's first arms show in Indonesia in November 1984.

The defense of human rights and freedoms does not seem to rank high on anyone's agenda when it interferes with power politics and international trade and when the victims are a small and isolated people in an almost unknown corner of the world.

What is perhaps most interesting about this case from a theoretical perspective is Indonesia's own history of rebelling against colonialism and exploitation. From 1945 to 1949 it fought for its independence with the support of the United Nations and especially of the Americans. Having succeeded in its own struggle, it now behaves even worse than its erstwhile colonial oppressors.

THE INDIANS OF
THE AMAZON, AN
IMPERILED PEOPLE*

Brazil is an enormous country (the fifth largest in the world) of 3.2 million square miles, richly endowed with natural resources. Its new civilian government, installed in 1985 after two decades of military rule, has brought hope to most of its 138 million people. There is little hope, however, among the Indian tribes of Brazil's Amazon region, home to three-quarters of its 225,000 Indians. Representing a mere 0.1 percent of the country's population, the Indians are more imperiled today than at any time in their history.

The biggest threat to their survival is the invasion of the Amazon region by hundreds of thousands of settlers fleeing from the poverty of northeast Brazil and the slums around Brazil's big cities. The magnets drawing the immigrants to Amazonia are land, gold, and timber. The federal government of Brazil has played a major role in this massive influx. Brazil's economic planners look to the rain forests of the northwest as a safety-valve for the pressure building up in Brazil's slums and squatter suburbs.

Starting in 1973, the federal government bulldozed roads through the rain forest to connect the most overpopulated states with the sparsely inhabited wilderness. The results have been tragic for the Indians. The new farmers clear the land with fire, axes, chain saws, and bulldozers. They have no respect for the boundaries of Indian reservations, and there are too few police and Indian agents to control their destructive activities. The farmers and miners kill Indians who obstruct the opening of the land, chase away the game on which the Indians depend for an important part of their diet, spill toxic mercury from their gold ore separators into rivers and streams, and infect the biologically vulnerable Indians with diseases they have never encountered before.

Many tribes have disappeared and others have been decimated. The Yanomami,

*Information for this essay was gathered from a number of sources, including Burger (1987); Chernela (1988); Davis (1977); Ellis (1988); McIntyre (1988); and Vesilind, (1987). Articles in the *Gazette* [Montreal] are from the Reuter news service and appear in local newspapers across North America and Great Britain.

one of the biggest aboriginal tribes left in the Amazon, has a population of
9,000, but they are outnumbered on their own lands by 40,000 gold diggers
and prospectors (*Gazette* [Montreal], December 1, 1988, A14). Disease and
violent clashes with white men are bringing the life of the Yanomami to an end.
News dispatches regularly tell of attacks on isolated Indian tribes like the Tukuna,
who suffered an attack by a group of white timber exploiters with rifles and
submachine guns in March 1988 that killed fifteen Indians, including six children (*Gazette* [Montreal], April 1, 1988, A12).

The impact of Brazil's ambitious hydroelectric projects poses another threat
to the survival of the Indians and their culture. Funded by the World Bank, the
dams at Balbina in the state of Amazonas and at Tucurui in the state of Para
have proven disastrous to the Waimiri-Atroari and the Parakaná, native tribes of
these regions. The forced resettlement of the Waimiri-Atroari in 1981 brought
them into contact with new diseases that reduced their population from 1,000
to 400. The flights of the Parakaná from the rising floodwaters of the Tocantins
River exposed them to large landholders who shot them as trespassers and to
diseases such as river blindness and snail parasite infestations of their visceral
organs (Chernela 1988, 21–22). The federal government, disclaiming any intent
to commit genocide, buttresses its case by pointing to the work of FUNAI (the
National Foundation for the Indian), an agency dedicated to saving the lives of
the Indians and protecting their cultures. Yet the real intent of the government
can be imputed from the patent consequences of its actions. Indian tribes are
destroyed with each advance of the frontier of development and the government
—far from trying to stop the process—knowingly repeats the same measures
that led to the last devastation. This failure to protect the tribes and their way of
life speaks louder than official denials of the government's intention to sacrifice
the tribes for the sake of development.

The criminal negligence of the development planners first manifested itself in
their roadbuilding plans. In the early 1970s, ignoring Brazil's limited capacity
to police such a vast area as the Amazon region, they designed a nine-hundred-
mile, ruler-straight road, the BR-364, running between Pôrto Velho and Cuiabá,
the capital of Mato Grosso state. A trip from one end of the new state of Rondônia
to the other had taken up to thirty days before the road was paved; now it took
two days. When the paving of the highway was completed in 1984, immigration took off, with migrants entering the area at the rate of 150,000 a year.
Rondônia's capital city, Pôrto Velho, once a tiny outpost in the wilderness, now
has a population of 450,000 and that of the state is said to have reached one
million people.

The government of Brazil and the World Bank undertook the construction of
the BR-364 as part the Polonoroeste scheme—a comprehensive plan for the

economic development of the region. Brazil's National Institute of Colonization and Agrarian Reform (INCRA) distributed thousands of plots of land ranging from 125 to 250 acres to poor peasants participating in the scheme. According to Dr. Philip Fearnside, an ecologist with the National Institute for Research in the Amazon, located in the city of Manaus, "Once you build highways into those areas, then there's a process that is outside the control of the government. That leads to clearing of the area. Building roads in Brazil is something that's decided by a handful of people in Brasilia. But you can't control what thousands of small farmers and squatters are going to do after they follow the road into the forest" (Ellis 1988, 785–86).

The World Bank and the government of Brazil now admit that they erred when they opened the northwest region to a massive influx of miners, lumbermen, and settlers. The bank is readying a $200 million loan to Brazil for environmental damage control. In October 1988, Brazil's president, José Sarney, responding to foreign critics, proclaimed a dramatic turnaround in his government's policies and introduced new measures aimed at halting the destruction of the rain forest. Sarney announced restrictions on subsidies to farmers in the Amazon, proclaimed a total ban on log exports, and promised to curtail cattle raising in the area (*New York Times,* October 13, 1988, A6; *Gazette* [Montreal] October 13, 1988, F15). A month earlier, for the first time in Brazil's history, the federal government brought charges of committing genocide before a federal court. Five men were accused of intending to "exterminate or eliminate an ethnic group or race," in this case the Xacriaba Indians, a tribe numbering about 4,000 persons that lives in the state of Minas Gerais (*Gazette* [Montreal], September 27, 1988, B6).

Despite these favorable developments, the Indians of northwestern Brazil are still disappearing, and the situation remains out of control. The government agencies charged with protecting the Indians and the environment are underfunded and understaffed, and they receive little political support. An observer with the Conselho Indigenista Missionário, Gilio Brunelli, estimates that the Indian population of Rondônia has declined from 30,000 in 1950 to 5,000 today. Disease and hired gunmen are still taking their toll among the aborigines. Orlando Villas Boas, one of the Indians greatest defenders, is almost ready to give up. "All we can do," he says, "is pick up the hat of a drowning man and marvel that we lived to witness the last days of Eden." If Brazilians do not implement and enforce their newfound conservation policies, the tragedy of the Indians in the American West will be repeated along the banks of the Amazon.

SOME CONSEQUENCES OF GENOCIDE FOR THE PEOPLE OF THE PERPETRATOR STATES*

Genocide is a new word for an ancient crime that has been practiced from antiquity to the present day. In this chapter I do not want to deal with definitions and typologies, important as these are (Jonassohn and Chalk, 1987). Instead, I want to explore an avenue for the prevention of genocides that does not require their prediction in specific places at specific times.

In the last few years several scholars have been working on schemes of prediction and prevention. It is not clear that they are making significant progress. While it is certainly important for an understanding of the genocidal process to study the social systems and social situations that appear to predispose to genocide, this is still a long way from predicting future genocides. Considering the conspicuous failure of the social sciences to predict much of anything, it seems unduly optimistic, if not downright foolhardy, to wait for their prediction of genocides before investigating possibilities of prevention. It is for these reasons that this chapter proposes an avenue that would contribute to prevention without being predicated on prediction.

The occurrence of genocides throughout history in all parts of the world raises many important questions. Surely the most important of these are, Why have genocides happened so often? Why have they recurred in such widely differing situations and under such diverse conditions? The answer seems to lie in their efficacy. They do, in fact, solve a perpetrator's problem so efficiently that it not only is solved, but also stays solved—at least in those cases in which the genocide has been carried out successfully. The costs of such solutions are borne by the victims; but since historically the victims are located outside the perpetrator society, such victim costs need not enter into any cost-benefit calculation by the perpetrator. Thus, the perpetrator society reaped enormous benefits while bearing only minimal costs.

*Revised version of a paper presented by Kurt Jonassohn at the 6th International Symposium on Victimology, Jerusalem, Israel, 28 August–1 September, 1988.

This sketchy analysis seems to hold true until the Middle Ages, when a new type of genocide was invented. This new type is ideological genocide, committed to enforce conformity to a belief, theory, or ideology (Chalk and Jonassohn, 1988). What is particularly new about ideological genocide is that it is most often practiced on members of the perpetrator's own society. While other types of genocide have decreased in frequency, this new type has increased dramatically in the twentieth century. It is with this new type that I am concerned in this chapter because it radically changes the cost-benefit calculation—a calculation that may be performed by scholars, though hardly ever by the perpetrators themselves. I hope to argue convincingly that if the results of such calculations were known to the peoples of perpetrator states, they might actively oppose their leaders' plans instead of remaining inactive bystanders. The reason is that in ideological genocides both the benefits and the costs have to be absorbed by the perpetrator society.

In ideological genocides the benefits to the perpetrators are hard to measure. In all other types of genocides they are easily measured in terms of economic gains, eliminated enemies, or terrorized opponents. In ideological genocides the only possible benefit is the enforcement of an ideological imperative—a benefit mainly in the eyes of the adherents to the perpetrator's ideology—which in actual cases is hardly ever achieved. The costs, on the other hand, are very easy to measure; since the victim groups are contained within the perpetrator society, the latter also has to bear the costs. These costs of ideological genocide, unlike the benefits, are easily measured in terms of the human and material effects on the perpetrator society.

An empirical study of the relevant cases will show not only that the costs of ideological genocides to the perpetrator societies are enormous, but also that it takes a very long time to recover from them. At the same time it is also true that individuals will have enriched themselves at the expense of the victims. This may sound contradictory; but the empirical data confirm that in almost every case individuals have enriched themselves while their society paid heavily. Thorough research in this area remains to be done. Some preliminary results are presented below; they should motivate a series of intensive case studies whose results ought to be widely disseminated. Such publicity may convince potential perpetrators that ideological genocides can be performed only at enormous costs to their own societies and that historical beliefs about the benefits of genocides have been invalidated by more recent events. However, there is little evidence that perpetrators are open to such rational assessments of empirical evidence. Much more important would be if the people of potential perpetrator societies were to realize the consequences of the proposed actions of their rulers. In that case they are much more likely to oppose such proposed actions. That such opposition can have an effect even in a totalitarian state was demonstrated by the opposition that Hitler's euthanasia program evoked in Germany.

The following brief sketches of some cases are intended to convey an idea of the direction of the argument by presenting some typical cases; the list is not meant to be exhaustive.

The *Albigensian Crusades* (see Madaule; Oldenbourg; Wakefield) took place in the first half of the thirteenth century in the Languedoc, which at that time (when Berlin was just beginning to be founded) was probably the richest area in Europe in terms of agriculture, trade, culture, and the standard of living of its people; it also was not yet included in the realm of the king of France. Several heresies flourished and found an interested hearing even among the aristocracy and especially at the court of the Count of Toulouse. This tolerance was not shared by the papal authorities, who shortly called for a crusade to wipe out this threat to their authority. The king of France fielded the required troops and reaped the benefits of enlarging his kingdom.

The crusaders not only killed the heretics and their sympathizers, but also uprooted the vineyards and cut down the orchards. The crusade was too successful: while it exterminated the heresies, it also ruined agriculture and commerce so thoroughly that the area has not fully recovered to this day.

The *Albigensian Crusades* were a transitional case in the sense that the victims were a group outside the perpetrator state (as had been true of historic genocides) while the motive was to enforce conformity to a belief system (which is an early case in the transition to the ideological genocides so common in the twentieth century). I include this case to highlight the main point of this paper. When the victims were located outside the perpetrator state, it was obvious that the victim society/state suffered enormously—this was so obvious that nobody seriously questioned it. It was also taken for granted that the perpetrator state reaped benefits in terms of wealth and acquisition of territory. When the victim group is located inside the perpetrator state a great deal of this cost and suffering does not simply disappear—it is now located inside the perpetrator state and cannot be confined to the victim group. This phenomenon has received little attention, although the proposition that a state can victimize and exterminate one of its constituent parts without damage to the whole seems on the surface implausible. This important point should become clearer through an examination of several cases in which the perpetrator state victimizes one of its constituent parts. These cases occur most frequently in the twentieth century and involve most often an ideological genocide.

The *Spanish Inquisition* (see Kamen; Llorente; Roth) is not usually considered a genocide at all because the nonbelievers were given a choice of emigrating or converting to Christianity. The goal was to create a homogeneous Catholic realm. The converts were, however, never fully accepted; even after several generations they were referred to as New Christians and suspected of secretly practicing their former religion. Such accusations were impossible to disprove, and the victims were severely punished, including by burning at the stake. Many had to flee for their lives. Before the expulsion of the Jews and the Moors and the persecution of the Conversos (or Marranos, as converted Jews were referred to) and Moriscos (converted Moors) Spain flourished, not only economically. It was a seat of learning, philosophy, and the arts. Arabic, Greek, Hebrew, and Latin language and literature interacted through translation and enriched one another. Spanish culture and learning influenced much of Europe.

The expansion of trade and the establishment of colonies by both Spain and Portugal took place during the same period. Iberian ships sailed to the ends of the world. But even here the motives were not purely economic. While trade and the acquisition of wealth financed the journeys, spreading the gospel and saving souls justified them. The proselytizing was done so successfully that in the early seventeenth century it caused Japan to pass several exclusion acts that effectively closed that country to the rest of the world until the nineteenth century.

After the purification of Spain from all non-Catholic influences it began to stagnate. For a while the newly acquired colonies kept it afloat economically. The cultural decline was much more rapid. In both areas Spain has not recovered to this day. Its economy is still one of the poorer ones in Europe; its cultural and intellectual life has still not produced a world-class university. It seems clear that the cost of enforcing conformity to a homogeneously Catholic society has been very high.

The *Armenians* (see Hovannisian; Dadrian, 1986; Trumpener) were the victims of a genocide carried out during World War I by Turkey, which then was an ally of Germany. The Ottoman Empire had been declining for some time, and Turkey was trying to orient itself toward a nationalistic ideology centered on the image of a Turkic state in which there was no room for a foreign, non-Moslem group. While the Armenians were predominantly peasants, they also played a major role in skilled trades, commerce, and the professions. Their elimination had both short-term and long-term consequences. The former became almost immediately felt during the war. A couple of illustrations must suffice here.

The completion of the Berlin-Baghdad railroad, which had been started before the war, was considered of prime strategic importance, especially since there were few all-weather roads in Turkey. The German embassy and the railroad company's management tried very hard to convince the Turkish rulers that the completion of the railroad was a top priority within the overall war effort — without success. The majority of the workers were Armenians and they were slaughtered. The result was that the railroad was not completed. Another illustration comes from a military hospital full of wounded Turkish soldiers and staffed almost entirely by Armenian doctors and nurses. Again, in spite of pleading by the staff, the Armenians were eliminated, and the hospital was left with almost no staff to care for the wounded.

The long-range costs of the genocide of the Armenians are more diffuse and not quite as easy to demonstrate. In addition to losing the war, Turkey had also lost much of its skilled labor force, its professionals, and its commercial and trading resources. This has dramatically retarded its development, the effects of which are observable to this day.

The people of the USSR (see Antonov-Ovseyenko; Conquest, 1968; Mace) experienced a great deal of persecution under Stalin's reign of terror. Scholars disagree about which of his several campaigns should be considered genocidal—a debate that will not be addressed in this paper. What is relevant here is that it is quite easy to demonstrate the enormous costs of these genocidal campaigns to Soviet society. Thus, in the 1930s Stalin decided to eliminate the so-called class of kulaks. Many were killed outright, many more died in the Gulag, and the survivors acquiesced to collectivized agriculture. What had been an agriculture that without modern equipment like tractors and combines had produced a large surplus for export became an agriculture that has not recovered to this day; the USSR has been an importer of foodstuffs ever since.

A little later Stalin decided that the military were not to be trusted. He proceeded to wipe out almost the entire officer corps. When Germany attacked in spite of Stalin's pact with Hitler, the Soviet war effort was in the hands of inexperienced and rapidly promoted junior officers. It seems reasonable to suppose that there might have been fewer defeats and lower casualties if the senior officers had remained in command.

Even the authorities in Moscow have lately begun to acknowledge the excesses of the Stalin regime and the costs to their society. Therefore, there is no need to go into the other genocidal persecutions of the Stalin era.

The case of *Nazi Germany and the Holocaust* is a special one, in this context as well as others: first, because Germany has openly acknowledged its guilt, and second, because German scholars themselves have started to look at the costs to Germany. (For such views see Baum; Engelmann; Haffner; Yavner; Müller-Hill; Weinreich.) These costs may be roughly divided into those incurred up to the end of World War II and those continuing to be exacted since then.

In the first category may be cited the loss of human resources in those areas where the Jews excelled. But even when Jews were used only as slave labor in factories associated with concentration camps, it was more important to kill them than to let them work. Thus, the I. G. Farben synthetic rubber plant near Auschwitz had by the end of the war not produced a single pound of rubber. It has also been suggested that the extensive use of rail transport during the Holocaust interfered with sending troops and materiel to the front. In the extreme case, it has been argued, though it is impossible to prove, that without the costs of the Holocaust Germany might have won the war.

In the second category of costs, those incurred after World War II, one would start with the enormous loss of talent and expertise that is clearly observable in those areas where the Jews had excelled. One might also point to the loss of international prestige as the information about what had happened spread throughout the world. The division into the two Germanies is considered a major loss by most Germans. Certainly, one might write a whole book about the many ways in which the world, particularly the Western world, would have been a different place had the Holocaust and its costs not changed it in so many ways.

Cambodia, now called *Kampuchea* (see Chandler and Kiernan; Etcheson; Szymusiak), will be the last case to be mentioned. Here we have an almost pure case of ideological genocide. Pol Pot and his cohorts sacrificed a significant proportion of their country's population to their image of an ideal society. In this process, they not only killed millions of their own people, but they also destroyed the web of social relations, the cities, the educational and health system, etc. in order to erase so-called Western influences. In a few short years they managed to reduce the country to a state of primitiveness and poverty. There is no question that the genocide reduced the perpetrator society to total bankruptcy in both human and material terms. No people should have to bear such costs.

Finally, there is one consequence of genocide for the perpetrator society that all cases seem to have in common: an enormous increase in corruption. As daily existence and survival become increasingly difficult for some of the people, there will be more and more other people who will see this as an opportunity to enrich themselves. Unavailable goods and services will become available at a price. Once such practices become established, they are unlikely to disappear, and the perpetrator societies will continue to be subject to such practices long after the genocide has become history.

The list could be continued. But I think that the point is quite clear. Genocides that victimize a part of the population of the perpetrator country impose a huge cost on the perpetrator society. These costs are paid by many succeeding generations.

The lesson of history was, and still seems to be, that genocides produce material benefits for the perpetrator. This was undoubtedly the case when the victims of genocides were a people outside the perpetrator society. But the process works differently in ideological genocides when the victims are located within, and are part of, the perpetrator society. In that case there are no benefits. Instead, there remain only enormous costs.

In attempting to make connections between historical events it is, of course, always difficult to establish proof. These examples of the deleterious consequences of genocides may have been the result of quite different factors. Thus, it can be argued, for example, that the continued failure of Soviet agriculture is the result of collectivization. Since it is safe to say that all historical events are the result of multiple causation, it is probably the case that Stalin's massacre of the kulaks and the drive to collectivize were both factors in the failure of agriculture. Instead of proof, one has to rely on the weight of the evidence and the plausibility of the argument.

For those of us who are committed to the prediction and the prevention of genocide the argument presented in this chapter seems to open up another possible avenue of action. If further research will confirm these conclusions, and if we can publicize this finding sufficiently, we may eventually be able to change the outdated lesson of history about the benefits of genocide. The new lesson will be that genocides can be carried out only at enormous costs to the perpetrator society and that even the potential ideological benefits are never realized.

Such analysis should be incorporated into the curriculum of the many courses on genocide, the Holocaust, and human rights that are being established. In North America such course materials are being introduced in high schools, colleges, and universities. Curriculum proposals seem to generate heated debates about cases to be included or excluded. However, there is little debate about how to cover prediction and prevention—in part because as yet there is so little known in this area. If the above analysis is confirmed by detailed case studies, the results should be added to the curriculum so that eventually this knowledge may attain the status of conventional wisdom.

With such conventional wisdom in wide currency it seems likely that the incidence of genocides will decline dramatically. Even if potential perpetrators would be tempted to test this finding on their own society, their own people would not support them in such plans; and without a minimum of such support, a genocide can hardly be carried out. This latter point is crucial for the prevention of future genocides; the carrying out of a massive genocide does not necessarily require the active support of the population, but it does minimally require their passive acquiescence—and even that is hardly likely to be forthcoming when the prospect of the enormous costs has acquired the status of conventional wisdom.

If the above argument sounds at all plausible, I hope that some colleagues will join me in doing the research to buttress this finding and in spreading the results.

THE UNITED STATES RATIFIES THE GENOCIDE CONVENTION*

There is jubilation in human rights circles that the United States has finally, after a delay of forty years, ratified the Genocide Convention. Amnesty International has good reason to congratulate itself on the success of the vigorous campaign it conducted for ratification. The long delay in the ratification is particularly startling, given the dominant role of the United States in the early years of the United Nations. It was not only that the United States had the wealth, and the generosity of spirit, to assist in the reconstruction of the shattered states of Europe. It also possessed the atom bomb. And it had been spared the destruction of war on its own territory.

This early dominant role of the United States is manifest in the Universal Declaration of Human Rights, adopted by the United Nations General Assembly on 10 December 1948. The declaration is clearly informed by the natural law of human rights. It expresses a democratic credo, with its emphasis on the inherent rights of the individual. Thus the preamble opens with the recognition of the inherent dignity and of the equal and inalienable rights of all members of the human family as the foundation of freedom, justice and peace in the world. And Article 1 declares that all human beings are born free and equal in dignity and rights.

In the tortuous debates on the Genocide Convention, in which the participating states responded to their particular experience of genocide, it was the United States which dominated the discussions, and negotiated and approved the final compromises, as for example on the exclusion of political groups from the "protection" of the Convention. The final form of the Convention, adopted in December 1948, was shaped, in many significant aspects, by the American contribution. It becomes difficult then to interpret the long delay, and the obvious reluctance of the United States to ratify the Genocide Convention. Did it

*Leo Kuper, "The United States Ratifies the Genocide Convention." Issued by International Alert, Los Angeles and London; reprinted from *Internet on the Holocaust and Genocide*, no. 19 (February 1989), Special Supplement. Reprinted by permission.

fear that it might be held responsible, retrospectively, for the annihilation of Indians in the United States, or its role in the slave trade, or its contemporary support for tyrannical governments engaging in mass murder?

The American approach to the international surveillance of human rights is all the more disturbing and confusing in the context of the American failure to ratify other basic human rights covenants and conventions. The list includes the following: The Convention against Torture and Cruel, Inhuman or Degrading Treatment or Punishment; The International Covenant on Civil and Political Rights; The International Covenant on Economic, Social and Cultural Rights; The American Convention on Human Rights; The Convention on the Elimination of All Forms of Discrimination Against Women.

How is this failure to be explained? Was the American record on human rights so exemplary that it would have been superfluous to bind the American people to the obligations of the human rights conventions and covenants? Or was the explanation quite simply that the American government did not have sufficient public support for these international commitments from such influential bodies as the American Bar Association!

In any event, whatever the explanation, Amnesty International USA has decided to give priority to a campaign for ratification of these remaining key human rights instruments by the American government. In some ways this seems a strange decision. One can readily appreciate the contribution that the U.S. ratifications could make to the advancement of human rights within the United States. And one can also envisage a contribution to the extension of domestic jurisdiction to the punishment of international crimes. But given the horrifying destructive nature of the crime of genocide, so deeply embedded in the history of human society, one would surely also need to ask whether ratification of the Genocide Convention is meaningful in itself, and if not, how it can be used to contribute to the prevention of genocide.

Now clearly, ratification is in itself quite without significance. The Genocide Convention has been ratified by almost one hundred states, yet it is totally inoperative, and has been inoperative from its very inception. If it has been honored at all, it is in the breach, not the observance. The Convention is described as a Convention on the Prevention and Punishment of the Crime of Genocide, but there have been so many genocides since the adoption of the Convention, and almost no punishment. The problem lies in part in the provisions of the Convention, but more particularly in the nature of the body entrusted with its enforcement.

The emphasis in the Convention is on the punishment of the crime, to which five articles are devoted. Jurisdiction to punish the crime vests in a "*competent tribunal of the State in the territory of which the act was committed, or by such international penal tribunal as may have jurisdiction with respect to those Contracting Parties which shall have accepted its jurisdiction.*" No international penal tribunal has yet been established, and it seems unlikely that it will be established in the foreseeable future. The only states that might conceivably support the establishment of such a tribunal are states that feel confident they could not possibly be involved in genocidal conflicts. This then leaves only the jurisdiction of tribunals in the country in which the crime was committed. But genocide is a crime committed generally by, or with the condonation of, governments. So it would be governments that are called upon to punish themselves, which is to say, that it is only in cases where the government is overthrown that the successor regime might institute criminal action against its predecessor. Thus Macias, in Equatorial Guinea, was found guilty of genocide and executed, and in Cambodia, Pol Pot and his deputy prime minister were tried and found guilty of genocide in absentia. And even when governments are overthrown, the murderous leaders are likely to find sanctuary.

Thus the provisions for punishment of the crime are by no means realistic. There remain then the possibilities for preventive action. Only two articles deal with prevention. Any of the contracting parties can submit a dispute concerning the interpretation, application or fulfillment of the Convention to the International Court of Justice. But many states, as for example, the USSR, have excluded the jurisdiction of the International Court, and this is a precedent the United States has followed. Perhaps it might still be possible for the United States to appeal to the International Court as a complainant. But this would hardly be consistent. This leaves then the further preventive measure referred to in the Convention, namely, a call on the competent organs of the United Nations to act as they consider appropriate for the prevention and suppression of acts of genocide. But this is a possibility available to the United States in any event as a Member State, and as a member of the Security Council. It would seem that the U.S. ratification of the Convention has not made a significant change in the potentialities for action in the United Nations under the provisions of the Genocide Convention.

Turning then to the domestic, the national arena, what steps can be taken within the United States to render the ratification of the Genocide Convention meaningful for preventive action against the mass killing of racial, ethnic, religious, and national groups. Clearly, a prerequisite is an informed public, with significant pressure groups to campaign for preventive action in specific cases of threatened or incipient genocidal conflict. And this is dependent on an effective educational program to raise the level of awareness of genocide, the establishment of networks of committed organizations for the actual campaigning, and a research unit based on academics with area interests and on human rights' organizations in the field.

In regard to the means available for preventive action, the provision of aid has been a traditional American inducement for improved performance on human rights, as for example during the Carter regime, and the human rights record is still relevant, however erratically applied, in the extending of aid to other governments. Aid may be used positively as an inducement to promote group conciliation, or negatively as a sanction against gross and threatening violations of human rights. In appropriate cases, a combination of aid as sanction and aid as inducement may be effective. So too where trade relations are maintained, restraints on trade may be used as a sanction and the extension of trade as an inducement. Indeed, there are many inducements and sanctions available to a superpower with the resources of the United States. If, then, it becomes possible to promote a national commitment to the prevention of genocide, this commitment is certain to have repercussions in the United Nations and other intergovernmental organizations, thus permitting a coordination of national and International Initiatives. By this means, the U.S. ratification of the Genocide Convention would cease to be a reluctant and compromised and pro forma response to skillful and persistent campaigning by Amnesty International and its supporters, and become instead a serious commitment to the prevention of genocide, for which the United States campaigned so vigorously in promoting the Nuremburg trials and as a leading participant in the framing of the Genocide Convention.

BIBLIOGRAPHIES

Introduction

The selected bibliographies in this part are organized alphabetically by topic. We have included certain cases that some authors have considered to be genocides, although we disagree with their classification (for example, Nigeria). For further discussion of which cases fit our definition, see parts I and II of the present volume. We have also included bibliographies on a number of cases that are not mentioned at all in our discussions. In these controversial cases, a potential genocide appears to have been averted (for example, Iran) or a genocide seems to be in the making (for example, Sudan). Brief bibliographies on a few such cases are included for readers who wish to explore on their own.

Two major exclusions need to be mentioned: we have not dealt with the history of genocide in China or India in the text or in the bibliography. These are two areas on which much research remains to be done: such research is especially arduous due to the obstacles impeding access to sources—particularly linguistic barriers and governmental restrictions.

These selected bibliographies are intended as introductions to the relevant literature on specific cases. They are to be thought of as "starter kits" for readers interested in further exploration and research. In no case are they or can they possibly be exhaustive. To give just one example of why this is so, by 1965 there were already two bibliographical volumes on the Knights of the Temple (Neu and Dessubré)!

Thus, these brief bibliographies are intended to serve as introductions to the literature. Researchers will find them helpful as preliminary guides to primary and secondary sources and to expand their reading in the direction of specific interests. If these bibliographies facilitate this task, they will have served the purpose for which they were intended.

We have generally tried to limit the bibliographies to easily available books written in English. A few exceptions have been made for important books, even if they have not yet been translated. We have also given preference to books with good bibliographies and/or discussions of the literature, and to published bibliographies. No other bias is intended, except that the literature by "deniers" and "revisionists" is not included. Only a few journal articles have been included;

rather than including a great many specific articles, we have indicated some of the journals in which relevant materials regularly appear.

Conceptual and Background Materials

Arendt, Hannah. *The Origins of Totalitarianism.* 2d enl. ed. Cleveland: World Publishing, 1958.

Ashworth, Georgina, ed. *World Minorities.* 3 vols. London: Minority Rights Groups, 1977, 1978, 1980.

Bauer, Yehuda. "The Place of the Holocaust in Contemporary History." In *Studies in Contemporary Jewry,* vol. 1, ed. Jonathan Frankel. Bloomington: Indiana University Press, 1984.

Bernard, Jessie. *American Community Behavior.* New York: Dryden, 1949.

Braudel, Fernand. *Capitalism and Material Life: 1400–1800.* New York: Harper and Row, 1967.

Chalk, Frank, and Kurt Jonassohn. "The History and Sociology of Genocidal Killings." In *Genocide: A Critical Bibliographic Review,* ed. Israel Charny. London: Mansell, 1988.

Charny, Israel, ed. *Genocide: A Critical Bibliographic Review.* London: Mansell, 1988.

———. *Toward the Understanding and Prevention of Genocide.* Boulder, Col.: Westview Press, 1984.

Chorover, Stephan L. *From Genesis to Genocide: The Meaning of Human Nature and the Power of Behavior Control.* Cambridge: MIT Press, 1979.

Clastres, Pierre. "De L'Ethnocide." *L'Homme* 14 (July–December 1974): 101–10.

Cohn, Norman. *The Pursuit of the Millennium.* 1957. Rev. and exp. ed. New York: Oxford University Press, 1970.

Dadrian, Vahakn N. "A Typology of Genocide." *International Review of Modern Sociology* 5 (Fall 1975): 201–12.

Davies, Nigel. *Human Sacrifice in History and Today.* New York: Morrow, 1981.

Drost, Pieter N. *The Crime of State.* 2 vols. Leyden: A. W. Sythoff, 1959.

Fein, Helen. "Scenarios of Genocide: Models of Genocide and Critical Responses." In *Toward the Understanding and Prevention of Genocide,* ed. Israel W. Charny. Boulder and London: Westview Press, 1984.

Hohenberg, John. "The Crusade that Changed the U.N." *Saturday Review* 9 (November 1968): 86–87.

Horowitz, Irving Louis. "Genocide and the Reconstruction of Social Theory: Observations on the Exclusivity of Collective Death." *Armenian Review* 37 (1984): 1–21.

———. *Genocide: State Power and Mass Murder.* New Brunswick, N.J.: Transaction Books, 1976.

———. *Taking Lives: Genocide and State Power.* New Brunswick, N.J.: Transaction

Books, 1980.

International Commission of Jurists. "Bangladesh." *The Review* 11 (1973): 30–33.

———. *The Trial of Macias in Equatorial Guinea*. Report by Alejandro Artucio. Geneva: International Commission of Jurists, 1978.

Jonassohn, Kurt, and Frank Chalk. "A Typology of Genocide and Some Implications for the Human Rights Agenda." In *Genocide and the Modern Age*, ed. Isidor Wallimann and Michael Dobkowski. Westport, Conn.: Greenwood Press, 1987.

Kinder, Hermann, and Werner Hilgemann. *The Penguin Atlas of World History.* 2 vols. New York: Penguin Books, 1974.

Kuper, Leo. *Genocide: Its Political Use in the Twentieth Century.* New York: Penguin Books, 1981.

———. *International Action against Genocide*. Report no. 53. London: Minority Rights Group, 1982.

———. *The Pity of It All: Polarisation of Racial and Ethnic Relations*. London: Duckworth, 1977.

———. *The Prevention of Genocide*. New Haven: Yale University Press, 1985.

Lang, Berel. "The Concept of Genocide." *The Philosophical Forum* 16 (1984–85): 1–18.

Langbein, John E. *Torture and the Law of Proof: Europe and England in the Ancien Regime*. Chicago: University of Chicago Press, 1977.

Lemkin, Raphael. *Axis Rule in Occupied Europe*. Washington, D.C.: Carnegie Endowment, 1944.

Lerner, Gerda. *The Creation of Patriarchy.* New York: Oxford University Press, 1986.

McEvedy, Colin, and Richard Jones. *Atlas of World Population History.* New York: Penguin Books, 1978.

Porter, Jack Nusan, ed. *Genocide and Human Rights: A Global Anthology.* Washington, D.C.: University Press of America, 1982.

Robinson, Nehemia. *The Genocide Convention*. New York: Institute of Jewish Affairs, 1960.

Ruthven, Malise. *Torture: The Grand Conspiracy.* London: Weidenfeld and Nicolson, 1978.

Savon, Hervé. *Du cannibalisme au génocide*. Paris: Hachette, 1972.

Smith, Anthony D. *The Ethnic Origins of Nations*. Oxford: Basil Blackwell, 1986.

Smith, Roger. "Human Destructiveness and Politics: The Twentieth Century as an Age of Genocide." In *Genocide and the Modern Age: Etiology and Case Studies of Mass Death*, ed. Isidor Wallimann and Michael Dobkowski. Westport, Conn. : Greenwood Press, 1987.

United Nations. *Convention on the Prevention and Punishment of the Crime of Genocide*. Paris, 9 December 1948. London: Her Majesty's Stationery Office, March 1966. (See part I.)

Van Boven, Theo C. "Introduction." In *Political Killings by Governments*. London: An Amnesty International Report, 1983.

Walzer, Michael. *Just and Unjust Wars: A Moral Argument with Historical*

Illustrations. New York: Basic Books, 1977.

Wedgwood, C. V. *The Thirty Years' War.* 1938. Reprint. London: Jonathan Cape, 1971.

Whitaker, Ben. *Revised and Updated Report on the Question of the Prevention and Punishment of the Crime of Genocide.* United Nations Economic and Social Council, Commission on Human Rights (E.CN.4.Sub.2.1985.6: 2 July 1985).

For additional literature see the reports and bulletins of Amnesty International; Cultural Survival (Cambridge, Mass.; *Cultural Survival Quarterly*); International Alert (London); the International Commission of Jurists (*The Review*); Institute of the International Conference on the Holocaust & Genocide (Jerusalem; *Internet on the Holocaust and Genocide*); and the Minority Rights Group (London).

For reactions to and analyses of current events see especially the *New York Times*; the *New York Review of Books*; the *Manchester Guardian*; *Der Spiegel*; *Le Monde*; and *L'Express*.

Antiquity

The Bible. Translated out of the original tongues by the commandment of King James the first anno 1611. New York: AMS Press, 1967.

Ceram, C. W. *Gods, Graves, and Scholars: The Story of Archeology.* 1949. Reprint. Toronto: Bantam Books, 1980.

————. *The Secret of the Hittites: The Discovery of an Ancient Empire.* Translated by Richard Winston and Clara Winston. New York: Alfred A. Knopf, 1956.

Ebeling, E., and B. Meissner, eds. *Reallexicon der Assyriologie.* 1928. Reprint. Berlin: Walter de Gruyter, 1971.

Edwards, I. E., C. J. Gadd, and N. G. L. Hammond, eds. *The Cambridge Ancient History.* Vol. 3: *The Assyrian Empire.* 1925. Reprint. Cambridge: Cambridge University Press, 1970.

Gurney, O. R. *The Hittites.* 1952. Reprint. London: Book Club Associates, 1975.

Homer. *Iliad.* Translated by E. V. Rieu. Middlesex: Penguin, 1981.

Jastrow, Morris. *The Civilization of Babylonia and Assyria.* 1915. Reprint. New York: Benjamin Blom, 1971.

Josephus. *The Jewish War.* Translated by G. A. Williamson. Middlesex: Penguin Books, 1970.

Macqueen, J. G. *The Hittites and Their Contemporaries in Asia Minor.* London: Thames and Hudson, 1975.

Maspero, G. *History of Egypt, Chaldea, Syria, Babylonia and Assyria.* 13 vols. London: Grolier Society, 1904.

Saggs, H. W. F. *Everyday Life in Babylonia and Assyria.* London: B. T. Batsford, 1965.

————. *The Greatness That Was Babylon: A Survey of the Ancient Civilization of the Tigris-Euphrates Valley.* New York: Praeger, 1969.

Speiser, E. A. "Ethnic Movements in the Near East in the Second Millennium B.C."
   Annual of the American School of Oriental Research 13 (1931–32): 13–54.
Wiseman, D. J. *Chronicles of the Chaldean Kings (626–556 B.C.)* in the British
   Museum. London: Trustees of the British Museum, 1961.

The Armenians in Turkey

Anderson, M. S. *The Eastern Question, 1774–1923: A Study in International
   Relations.* London: Macmillan, 1966.
Boyajian, Dikran H. *Armenia: The Case for a Forgotten Genocide.* Westwood, N.J.:
   Educational Book Crafters, 1972.
Bryce, Viscount James, ed. *The Treatment of the Armenians in the Ottoman Empire:
   Documents Presented to Viscount Grey of Fallodon, Secretary of State for Foreign
   Affairs.* Toronto: Hodder and Stoughton, 1915.
Chaliand, Gérard, and Yves Ternon. *The Armenians: From Genocide to Resistance.*
   Translated by Tony Berrett. London: Zed Press, 1983. Original edition, 1981.
Dadrian, Vahakn N. "The Convergent Aspects of the Armenian and Jewish Cases of
   Genocide: A Reinterpretation of the Concept of Holocaust." *Holocaust and
   Genocide Studies* 3 (1988): 151–70.
———. *The Methodological Components of the Study of Genocide as a Sociological
   Problem: The Armenian Case.* Cambridge, Mass.: Armenian Heritage Press,
   1972.
———. "The Naim-Andonian Documents on the World War I Destruction of Ottoman
   Armenians: The Anatomy of a Genocide." *International Journal of Middle East
   Studies* 18 (1986): 311–60.
———. "The Role of Turkish Physicians in the World War I Genocide of Ottoman
   Armenians." *Holocaust and Genocide Studies* 1 (1986): 169–92.
Findley, Carter V. *Bureaucratic Reform in the Ottoman Empire: The Sublime Porte,
   1789–1922.* Princeton: Princeton University Press, 1980.
Heller, Joseph. "Britain and the Armenian Question, 1912–1914: A Study in Real
   Politik." *Middle Eastern Studies* 16 (1980): 3–26.
Hovannisian, Richard G. *Armenia on the Road to Independence: 1918.* Berkeley:
   University of California Press, 1967.
———. *The Armenian Holocaust (A Bibliography).* Cambridge, Mass.: Armenian
   Heritage Press, 1978.
———. "The Critics' View: Beyond Revisionism." *International Journal of Middle
   East Studies* 9 (August 1978): 379–88.
———. The Republic of Armenia. 2 vols. Vol. 1: *The First Year, 1918–1919.* Vol.
   2: *From Versailles to London, 1919–1920.* Berkeley: University of California
   Press, 1971, 1982.
———, ed. *The Armenian Genocide in Perspective.* New Brunswick, N.J.:
   Transaction Books, 1986.

Melson, Robert. "A Theoretical Inquiry into the Armenian Massacres of 1894–1895." *Comparative Studies in Society and History* 24 (1982): 481–509.

———. "Provocation or Nationalism: A Critical Inquiry into the Armenian Genocide of 1915." In *The Armenian Genocide in Perspective*, ed. Richard G. Hovannisian. New Brunswick, N.J. and Oxford: Transaction Books, 1986.

Morgenthau, Henry. *Ambassador Morgenthau's Story.* New York: Doubleday-Page, 1918.

Nalbandian, Louise. *The Armenian Revolutionary Movement.* Berkeley: University of California Press, 1967.

Ravitch, Norman. "The Armenian Catastrophe: Of History, Murder and Sin." *Encounter* 57 (1981): 69–84.

Suakjian, Kerork Yeghia. *Genocide in Trebizond: A Case Study of Armeno-Turkish Relations during the First World War.* Lincoln: University of Nebraska Press, 1981.

Toynbee, Arnold J. *Armenian Atrocities: The Murder of a Nation.* Toronto: Hodder and Stoughton, 1915.

Trumpener, Ulrich. *Germany and the Ottoman Empire: 1914–1918.* Princeton: Princeton University Press, 1968.

Walker, Christopher J. *Armenia: The Survival of a Nation.* New York: St. Martin's Press, 1980.

Zamir, Meir. "Population Statistics of the Ottoman Empire in 1914 and 1919." *Middle Eastern Studies* 17 (1981): 85–106.

For additional literature on the Armenian genocide, see the *Armenian Review* and *Middle Eastern Studies.*

Bangladesh

Bangla Desh: Documents. New Delhi: Ministry of External Affairs, n.d.

Bertocci, Peter J. *Bangladesh History, Society, and Culture: An Introductory Bibliography of Secondary Materials.* East Lansing: Asian Studies Center, Michigan State University, 1973.

Bhatnagar, Yatindra. *Bangla Desh: Birth of a Nation.* Delhi: Indian School Supply Depot, Publication Division, 1971.

Chaudhuri, Kalyan. *Genocide in Bangladesh.* Bombay: Orient Longman, 1972.

Choudhury, G. W. *The Last Days of United Pakistan.* Bloomington: Indiana University Press, 1974.

Chowdhuri, Subrata Roy. *The Genesis of Bangladesh: A Study of International Legal Norms and Permissive Conscience.* New York: Asia Publishing House, 1972.

International Commission of Jurists. *The Events in East Pakistan.* Geneva: ICJ Secretariat, 1972.

Levak, Albert E. "Provincial Conflict and Nation Building in Pakistan." In *Ethnicity and Nation Building: Comparative, International, and Historical Perspectives*, ed.

Wendell Bell and Walter E. Freeman. Beverly Hills, Cal.: Sage, 1974.
———. "Discrimination in Pakistan: National, Provincial, Tribal." In *Case Studies on Human Rights and Fundamental Freedoms: A World Survey*, vol. 1, ed. Willem A. Veenhoven. The Hague: Martinus Nijhoff, 1975.
Mascarenhas, Anthony. *The Rape of Bangladesh*. Delhi: Vikas Publications, 1971.
Payne, Robert. *Massacre*. New York: Macmillan, 1973.
Rahman, Matiur. *Bangladesh Today: An Indictment and a Lament*. London: News and Media Ltd., 1978.
Satyaprakesh, comp. and ed. *Bangla Desh: A Select Bibliography*. Gurgaon: Indian Documentation Service, 1976.
Sethi, S. S. *The Decisive War: Emergence of a New Nation*. New Delhi: Sagar Publications, 1972.

Burundi

Bowen, Michael, Gary Freeman, and Kay Miller. "No Samaritan: The U.S. and Burundi." *Africa Report* 18 (1973): 32–39.
———. *Passing By: The United States and Genocide in Burundi, 1972*. New York: Carnegie Endowment for International Peace, 1973.
Du Bois, Victor D. *To Die in Burundi*. American Universities Field Staff Reports, Central and Southern African Series, vol. 16, no. 4 (September 1972).
Greenland, Jeremy. "Ethnic Discrimination in Rwanda and Burundi." *Case Studies on Human Rights and Fundamental Freedoms: A World Survey*, vol. 4, ed. Willem A. Veenhoven. The Hague: Martinus Nijhoff, 1976.
Kuper, Leo. *The Pity of It All: Polarisation of Racial and Ethnic Relations*. London: Duckworth, 1977.
Lemarchand, Réné. "Ethnic Genocide." *Issue* 5 (Summer 1975): 9–16.
———. *Rwanda and Burundi*. New York: Praeger, 1970.
Lemarchand, Réné, and David Martin. *Selective Genocide in Burundi*. Report no. 20. London: Minority Rights Group, 1974.
Meisler, Stanley. "Holocaust in Burundi, 1972." *Case Studies on Human Rights and Fundamental Freedoms: A World Survey*, vol. 5, ed. Willem A. Veenhoven. The Hague: Martinus Nijhoff, 1976.
Melady, Thomas Patrick. *Burundi: The Tragic Years*. Maryknoll: Orbis Books, 1974.
Morris, Roger, Michael Bowen, Gary Freeman, and Kay Miller. "The United States and Burundi in 1972." *Foreign Service Journal* 50 (1973): 8–15, 29–30.
République du Burundi. *Livre blanc sur les evènements survenus au mois d'avril et mai 1972*. Bujumbara: Ministère de l'Information, 1972.
Weinstein, Warren, and Robert Schrire. *Political Conflict and Ethnic Strategies: A Case Study of Burundi*. Syracuse: Syracuse University Press, 1976.

Cambodia

Barnett, Anthony, and John Pilger. *Aftermath: The Struggle of Cambodia and Vietnam*. New Statesman Report no. 5. London: New Statesman, 1982.

Barron, John, and Anthony Paul. *Peace with Horror*. London: Hodder and Stoughton, 1977.

Becker, Elizabeth. *When the War Was Over: The Voices of Cambodia's Revolution and Its People*. New York: Simon and Schuster, 1986.

Burchett, Wilfred. *Twentieth Century Slave Society*. London: Zed Press, 1981.

Burton, Charles. Review of *Revolution and Its Aftermath in Kampuchea*, edited by David P. Chandler and Ben Kiernan. *Pacific Affairs* 57 (Fall 1984): 532–33.

Caldwell, Malcolm, and Tan Lek. *Cambodia in the Southeast Asian War*. New York: Monthly Review Press, 1973.

Carney, Timothy Michael. *Communist Power in Kampuchea (Cambodia): Documents and Discussions*. Ithaca, N.Y.: South East Asia Program, Cornell University Press, 1977.

Chandler, David. "Revising the Past in Democratic Kampuchea: When Was the Birthday of the Party?" *Pacific Affairs* 56 (Summer 1983): 288–300.

Chandler, David P., and Ben Kiernan, eds. *Revolution and Its Aftermath in Kampuchea: Eight Essays*. New Haven: Yale University Southeast Asia Research Monograph no. 25, 1983.

Correze, Françoise. *Choses vues au Cambodge*. Paris: Les éditeurs français réunis, 1979.

Debré, François. *Cambodge: La révolution de la forêt*. Paris: Flammarion, 1976.

Etcheson, Craig. *The Rise and Demise of Democratic Kampuchea*. Boulder, Col.: Westview Press, 1984.

Hawk, David. "Pol Pot's Cambodia: Was It Genocide?" In *Toward the Understanding and Prevention of Genocide*, ed. Israel W. Charny. Boulder and London: Westview Press, 1984.

Hildebrand, George, and Gareth Porter. *Cambodia: Starvation and Revolution*. New York: Monthly Review Press, 1976.

Kamm, Henry. "The Agony of Cambodia." *New York Times Magazine*, November 10, 1977, pp. 40–43, 142–52.

Kiernan, Ben. *Cambodia: The Eastern Zone Massacres*. New York: Center for the Study of Human Rights, Columbia University, 1986.

———. *How Pol Pot Came to Power: A History of Communism in Kampuchea, 1930–1975*. London: Verso, 1985.

Kiernan, Ben, and Boua. Chanthou, eds. *Peasants and Politics in Kampuchea: 1942–1981*. London: Zed Press, 1982.

Lacouture, Jean. *Survivre le peuple cambodgien*. Paris: Le Seuil, 1978.

May, Someth. *Cambodian Witness: The Autobiography of Someth May*. Edited by James Fenton. London: Faber and Faber, 1986.

Ponchaud, François. *Cambodia Year Zero*. Translated by Nancy Amphoux.

Harmondsworth: Penguin, 1978.
Shawcross, William. *The Quality of Mercy: Cambodia, Holocaust and Modern Conscience.* New York: Simon and Schuster, 1984.
Szymusiak, Molyda. *The Stones Cry Out. A Cambodian Childhood, 1975–1980.* Translated by Linda Coverdale. New York: Hill and Wang, 1986.
Vickery, Michael. *Cambodia, 1975–1982.* London: Allen and Unwin, 1984.
Willmott, W. E. "Analytical Errors of the Kampuchean Communist Party." *Pacific Affairs* 54 (Summer 1981): 209–27.

Carthage and Rome

Adcock, F. E. " 'Delenda est Carthago.' " *Cambridge Historical Journal* 8 (1946): 117–28.
Astin, Alan E. *Cato the Censor.* London: Oxford University Press, 1978.
———. *Scipio Aemilianus.* London: Oxford University Press, 1967.
Caven, Brian. *The Punic Wars.* London: Weidenfeld and Nicolson, 1980.
Diodorus of Sicily. 12 vols. Translated by C. H. Oldfather. The Loeb Classical Library. London: Heinemann, 1933.
Dio's Roman History. 9 vols. Translated by Earnest Cary. The Loeb Classical Library. London: Heinemann, 1914.
Dorey, T. A., and D. R. Dudley. *Rome against Carthage.* London: Secker and Warburg, 1971.
Hallward, B. L., and M. P. Charlesworth. "The Fall of Carthage." In *Rome and the Mediterranean: 218–133 B.C.* Vol. 8 of the *Cambridge Ancient History*, 12 vols., ed. S. A. Cook, F. E. Adcock, and M. P. Charlesworth. Cambridge: Cambridge University Press, 1930.
Harris, William V. *War and Imperialism in Republican Rome: 327–70 B.C.* Oxford: Clarendon Press, 1979.
Hopkins, Keith. *Conquerors and Slaves.* Cambridge: Cambridge University Press, 1977.
Polybius. *The Histories.* 6 vols. Translated by W. R. Paton. The Loeb Classical Library. London: Heinemann, 1922.
Ridley, R. T. "To Be Taken With A Pinch of Salt: The Destruction of Carthage." *Classical Philology* 81 (April 1986): 140–46.
Rostovtzeff, Michael. *Rome.* 1927. Reprint. Translated by J. D. Duff. Edited by Elias J. Bickerman. London: Oxford University Press, 1960.
Sherwin-White, A. N. *Racial Prejudice in Imperial Rome.* Cambridge: Cambridge University Press, 1967.
———. "Rome the Aggressor?" Review of *War and Imperialism in Republican Rome: 327–70 B.C.* by William Harris. *Journal of Roman Studies* 70 (1980): 177–81.
Warmington, B .H. *Carthage.* London: Robert Hale, 1960.

Westington, N. *Atrocities in Roman Warfare to 133 B.C.* Ph.D. diss., University of
Chicago, 1938 (Private Edition, Distributed by the University of Chicago Libraries,
1938).

The Hereros

Bley, Helmut. *South West Africa Under German Rule, 1898–1914.* London:
Heinemann Educational Books, 1971.
Bridgman, Jon. *The Revolt of the Hereros.* Berkeley: University of California Press,
1981.
Dewaldt, Franz, ed. *Native Uprisings in Southwest Africa.* Chapel Hill, N.C.:
Documentary Publications, 1976.
Drechsler, Horst. *"Let Us Die Fighting": The Struggle of the Herero and the Nama
against German Imperialism (1884–1915).* Translated by Bernd Zollner. London:
Zed Press, 1980. Original German edition, Akademie-Verlag, 1966.
Esterhuyse, J. H. *South West Africa: 1880–1894.* Capetown: Rustica Press, 1968.
Poewe, Karla. *The Namibian Herero: A History of Their Psychosocial Disintegration
and Survival.* Lewiston, N.Y. and Queenston, Ont.: Edwin Mellen Press, 1985.
Wellington, John H. *South West Africa and Its Human Issues.* Oxford: Oxford
University Press, 1967.

Heresies, Witch-Hunts, and the Inquisition

Barber, Malcolm. *The Trial of the Templars.* New York: Cambridge University Press,
1978.
Ben-Yehuda, Nachman. "The European Witch Craze of the 14th to 17th Centuries: A
Sociologist's Perspective." *American Journal of Sociology* 86 (1980): 1–31.
Berne-Lagarde, Pierre de. *Bibliographie du catharisme languedocien.* Toulouse: Institut
des études cathares, Collection de textes et documents, 1957.
Campbell, George Archibald. *The Knights Templar: Their Rise and Fall.* New York:
AMS Press, 1979.
Cohn, Norman. *Europe's Inner Demons: An Inquiry Inspired by the Great Witch-hunt.*
New York: Basic Books, 1975.
Delumeau, Jean. *La peur en occident (XIVe–XVIIe siècles): une cité assiégée.* Paris:
Fayard, 1978.
Dessubré, M. *Bibliographie de l'ordre des Templiers: Imprimés et manuscrits.* 1928.
Reprint. Nieuwkoop: B. de Graaf, 1966.
Dupont-Bouchat, Marie-Sylvie, Willem Frijhoff, and R. Muchembled. *Prophète et
sorciers dans les Pays-Bas.* Paris: Hachette, 1978.
Duvernoy, Jean. *L'Histoire des cathares.* Toulouse: Privat, 1979.
Emery, Richard Wilder. *Heresy and Inquisition in Narbonne.* 1941. Reprint. New

York: AMS Press, 1967.

Guiraud, Jean. *The Medieval Inquisition.* New York: AMS Press, 1979.

Hamilton, Bernard. *The Albigensian Crusade.* London: The Historical Association, 1974.

———. *Reform, Catharism, and the Crusades (900–1300).* London: Variorum Reprints, 1979.

Kamen, Henry. *The Spanish Inquisition.* London: White Lion, 1976.

Larner, Christina. *Enemies of God: The Witch-Hunt in Scotland.* London: Chatto and Windus, 1981.

———. *Witchcraft and Religion: The Politics of Popular Belief.* Oxford: Basil Blackwell, 1984.

Llorente, Juan Antonio. *History of the Spanish Inquisition.* New York: G. C. Morgan, 1826.

Luchaire, Achille. *Social France at the Time of Philip Augustus.* New York: Harper Torchbooks, 1967.

Madaule, Jacques. *The Albigensian Crusade.* Translated by Barbara Wall. New York: Fordham University Press, 1967.

Martin, Edward James. *The Trial of the Templars.* New York: AMS Press, 1977.

Melia, Pins. *The Origin, Persecutions, and Doctrines of the Waldenses.* New York: AMS Press, 1978.

Muchembled, Robert. *Culture populaire et culture des élites dans la France moderne, XVe-XVIIIe siècles: essais.* Paris: Flammarion, 1977.

———. *La sorcière au village.* Paris: Gallimard, 1979.

Neu, Heinrich. *Bibliographie des Templer-Ordens, 1927–1965.* Bonn: Verlag Wissenschaftliches Archiv, 1965.

Nickerson, Hoffman. *The Inquisition: A Political and Military History of Its Establishment.* 1932. Reprint. Port Washington, N.Y.: Kennikat Press, 1968.

Oldenbourg, Zoé. *Massacre at Montségur: A History of the Albigensian Crusade.* New York: Pantheon, 1961.

Ollivier, Albert. *Les templiers.* Bourges: Seuil, 1974.

Roth, Cecil. *The Spanish Inquisition.* 1937. Reprint. New York: Norton, 1964.

Ruthven, Malise. *Torture: The Grand Conspiracy.* London: Weidenfeld and Nicolson, 1978.

Schmidt, Charles Guillaume Adolphe. *Histoire et doctrine de la secte des Cathares ou Albigeois.* 2 vols. New York: AMS Press, 1979.

Shannon, Albert Clement. *The Popes and Heresy in the Thirteenth Century.* New York: AMS Press, 1979.

Strayer, Joseph R. *The Albigensian Crusades.* New York: Dial Press, 1971.

———. *The Reign of Philip the Fair.* Princeton: Princeton University Press, 1980.

Sumption, Jonathan. *The Albigensian Crusade.* London: Faber and Faber, 1978.

Turbeville, A. S. *Medieval Heresy and the Inquisition.* London: Archon Books, 1964.

Wakefield, Walter L. *Heresy, Crusade and Inquisition in Southern France, 1100–1250.* London: Allen and Unwin, 1974.

440   BIBLIOGRAPHIES

The Holocaust

Arad, Yitzhak. *Belzec, Sobibor, Treblinka: The Operation Reinhard Death Camps.*
Bloomington: Indiana University Press, 1987.
Arendt, Hannah. *Eichmann in Jerusalem: A Report on the Banality of Evil.* Revised
and enlarged edition. New York: Penguin, 1977. Original edition, 1964.
Avni, Haim. *Spain, the Jews, and Franco.* Translated by Emanuel Shimoni.
Philadelphia: Jewish Publication Society of America, 1982.
Barnadac, Christian. *L'Holocauste oublié: Le massacre des tsiganes.* Paris:
France-Empire, 1979.
Bauer, Yehuda. "Trends in Holocaust Research." *Yad Vashem Studies on the European
Jewish Catastrophe and Resistance* 12 (1977): 7–36.
———. *The Holocaust in Historical Perspective.* Seattle: University of Washington
Press, 1978.
———. *A History of the Holocaust.* New York: Franklin Watts, 1982.
———. "The *Kristallnacht* as Turning Point: Jewish Reactions to Nazi Policies." In
Western Society after the Holocaust, ed. Lyman H. Legters. Boulder, Col.: Westview
Press, 1983.
Baum, Rainer C. *The Holocaust and the German Elite: Genocide and National Suicide
in Germany, 1871–1945.* London: Croom Helm, 1981.
Bracher, Karl Dietrich. *The German Dictatorship: The Origins, Structure, and Effects
of National Socialism.* Translated by Jean Steinberg. New York: Praeger, 1970.
Browning, Christopher R. *Fateful Months: Essays on the Emergence of the Final
Solution.* New York: Holmes and Meier, 1981.
———. *The Final Solution and the German Foreign Office: A Study of Referat DIII of
Abteilung Deutschland.* New York: Holmes and Meier, 1978.
Cohn, Norman. *Warrant for Genocide: The Myth of the Jewish World Conspiracy and
the Protocols of the Elders of Zion.* 1967. Reprint. Chico, Cal.: Scholars Press,
1981.
Davidowicz, Lucy S. *A Holocaust Reader.* New York: Behrman, 1976.
———. *The War against the Jews: 1933–1945.* New York: Holt, Rinehart and
Winston, 1975.
Dicks, Henry V. *Licensed Mass Murder: A Psychological Study of Some SS Killers.*
New York: Basic Books, 1972.
Engelmann, Bernt. *Germany without Jews.* Toronto: Bantam Books, 1984.
Fein, Helen. *Accounting for Genocide: National Responses and Jewish Victimization
during the Holocaust.* New York: Free Press, 1979.
Freeman, Michael. *Atlas of Nazi Germany.* London: Croom Helm, 1987.
Friedlander, Henry, and Sybil Milton, eds. *The Holocaust: Ideology, Bureaucracy and
Genocide. The San Jose Papers.* Millwood, N.Y.: Krauss International Publishers,
1980.
Friedlander, Saul. "From Anti-Semitism to Extermination: A Historiographical Study
of Nazi Policies towards the Jews and an Essay in Interpretation." *Yad Vashem*

Studies 16 (1984): 1–50.

Friedman, Philip. *Their Brothers' Keepers: The Christian Heroes and Heroines Who Helped the Oppressed Escape the Nazi Terror.* 1957. Reprint. New York: Crown, 1978.

———. *Roads to Extinction: Essays on the Holocaust.* Edited by Ada June Friedman, with an introduction by Salo Wittmayer Baron. New York & Philadelphia: Conference of Jewish Social Studies, The Jewish Publication Society of America, 1980.

Gilbert, Martin. *The Holocaust: A History of the Jews of Europe during the Second World War.* New York: Holt, Rinehart and Winston, 1985.

———. *The Macmillan Atlas of the Holocaust.* New York: Macmillan, 1982.

Gordon, Sarah. *Hitler, Germans, and the Jewish Question.* Princeton: Princeton University Press, 1984.

Gutman, Yisrael. *The Jews of Warsaw, 1939–1943: Ghetto, Underground, Revolt.* Brighton, Sussex: Harvester Press, 1982.

Haffner, Sebastian. *The Meaning of Hitler.* New York: Macmillan, 1979.

Hallie, Philip P. *Lest Innocent Blood Be Shed: The Story of the Village of Le Chambon and How Goodness Happened There.* New York: Harper and Row, 1979.

Hilberg, Raul. *The Destruction of European Jewry.* Revised. 3 vols. New York: Holmes and Meier, 1985. Original one-volume ed., 1961.

———, ed. *Documents of Destruction: Germany and Jewry, 1933–1945.* Chicago: Quadrangle Books, 1971.

Hirschfeld, Gerhard, ed. *The Policies of Genocide: Jews and Soviet Prisoners of War in Nazi Germany.* London: Allen and Unwin, 1986.

International Auschwitz Committee. *Nazi Medicine: Doctors, Victims, and Medicine in Auschwitz.* New York: Howard Fertig, 1986.

Jäckel, Eberhard. *Hitler's World View: A Blueprint for Power.* Translated by Herbert Arnold. Cambridge: Harvard University Press, 1981.

Kenrick, Donald, and Gratton Puxon. *The Destiny of Europe's Gypsies.* New York: Basic Books, 1972.

Kogon, Eugen. *The Theory and Practice of Hell.* Translated by Heinz Norden. New York: Farrar, Straus and Giroux, 1984. Original edition 1950.

Kren, George and Leon Rappoport. "Failures of Thought in Holocaust Interpretation." In *Towards the Holocaust,* ed. Michael N. Dobkowski and Isidor Wallimann. Westport, Conn.: Greenwood, 1984.

———. *The Holocaust and the Crisis of Human Behavior.* New York: Holmes and Meier, 1980.

Levi, Primo. *Survival in Auschwitz: The Nazi Assault on Humanity.* Translated by Stuart Woolf. New York: Collier Books, 1961.

Lifton, Robert J. *The Nazi Doctors: Medical Killing and the Psychology of Genocide.* New York: Basic Books, 1986.

Marrus, Michael. *The Holocaust in History.* Toronto: Lester and Orpen Dennys, 1987.

Marrus, Michael R., and Robert O. Paxton. *Vichy France and the Jews.* New York:

Schocken Books, 1983.

Mosse, George L. *Toward the Final Solution: A History of European Racism.* New York: Harper and Row, 1978.

Müller-Hill, Benno. *Murderous Science: Elimination by Scientific Selection of Jews, Gypsies, and Others, Germany, 1933–1945.* Translated by George R. Fraser. Oxford: Oxford University Press, 1988.

Poliakov, Léon. *The Aryan Myth: A History of Racist and Nationalist Ideas in Europe.* Translated by Edmund Howard. New York: Basic Books, 1974. Original edition, 1971.

———. *Harvest of Hate: The Nazi Program for the Destruction of the Jews of Europe.* Syracuse: Syracuse University Press, 1954.

Reitlinger. Gerald. *The Final Solution: The Attempt to Exterminate the Jews of Europe, 1939–1945.* New York: Barnes, 1961.

Rhodes, James M. *The Hitler Movement: A Modern Millenarian Revolution.* Stanford, Cal.: Hoover Institution Press, 1980.

Robinson, Jacob, and Philip Friedman. *Guide to Jewish History under Nazi Impact.* New York: Institute for Jewish Research, 1960.

Robinson, Jacob. *And the Crooked Shall Be Made Straight: The Eichmann Trial, the Jewish Catastrophe, and Hannah Arendt's Narrative.* New York: Macmillan, 1965.

Robinson, Jacob, and Yehuda Bauer. *Guide to Unpublished Materials of the Holocaust Period.* 6 vols. Jerusalem: Hebrew University, Institute of Contemporary Jewry, 1970–.

Rosenberg, Alan. "An Assault on Western Values." *Dimension: A Journal of Holocaust Studies* 1 (Spring 1985): 5–11.

———. "Was the Holocaust Unique?: A Peculiar Question?" In *Genocide and the Modern Age: Etiology and Case Studies of Mass Death,* ed. Isidor Wallimann and Michael Dobkowski. Westport, Conn.: Greenwood Press, 1987.

Rubinstein, Richard L. *The Cunning of History: Mass Death and the American Future.* New York: Harper and Row, 1975.

Schleunes, Karl A. *The Twisted Road to Auschwitz: 1933–1939.* Urbana: University of Illinois Press, 1970.

Sereny, Gitta. *Into That Darkness: From Mercy Killing to Mass Murder.* New York: McGraw Hill, 1974.

Tal, Uriel. "On the Study of the Holocaust and Genocide." *Yad Vashem Studies of the European Jewish Catastrophe and Resistance* 13 (1979): 7–52.

Tyrnauer, Gabrielle. *Gypsies and the Holocaust: A Bibliography and Introductory Essay.* Montreal: Interuniversity Centre for European Studies and Montreal Institute for Genocide Studies, 1989.

Weinreich, Max. *Hitler's Professors.* New York: YIVO, 1946.

Yavner, Robert Simon. "I. G. Farben's Petro-Chemical Plant at Auschwitz." M.A. thesis, Old Dominion University, 1984.

For additional literature and book reviews on the Jewish Holocaust see *Holocaust and Genocide Studies; Simon Wiesenthal Center Annual; Patterns of Prejudice; Yad Vashem Studies on the European Jewish Catastrophe and Resistance.*

The Indians of Canada and the United States

GENERAL

Ashburn, Percy M. *The Ranks of Death: A Medical History of the Conquest of America*. New York: Coward-McCann, 1947.

Axtell, James. *The Europeans and the Indian: Essays in the Ethnohistory of Colonial North America*. New York: Oxford University Press, 1981.

Berkhofer, Robert F. *The White Man's Indian*. New York: Alfred A. Knopf, 1978.

Bolt, Christine. *American Indian Policy and American Reform: Case Studies of the Campaign to Assimilate the American Indians*. London: Allen and Unwin, 1987.

Canny, Nicholas P. "The Ideology of English Colonization: From Ireland to America." *William and Mary Quarterly* 30 (1973): 575–98.

Debo, Angie. *A History of the Indians of the United States*. Norman: University of Oklahoma Press, 1970.

Dippie, Brian W. *The Vanishing American: White Attitudes and U.S. Indian Policy.* Middletown, Conn.: Wesleyan University Press, 1982.

Dobyns, Henry F. *Native American Historical Demography: A Critical Bibliography.* Bloomington: Indiana University Press, 1976.

———. *Their Numbers Became Thinned: Native American Population Dynamics in Eastern North America*. Knoxville: University of Tennessee Press, 1983.

Hagan, William T. *American Indians*. The Chicago History of American Civilization. Chicago and London: University of Chicago Press, 1961.

Leacock, Eleanor Burke, and Nancy Oestreich Lurie, eds. *North American Indians in Historical Perspective*. New York: Random House, 1971.

McNeil, William H. *Plagues and Peoples*. Garden City, N.Y.: Doubleday, 1976.

Moore, Arthur K. *The Frontier Mind*. Lexington: University of Kentucky Press, 1957.

Murdock, George P. *Ethnographic Bibliography of North America*. Human Relations Area File. 4th ed. New Haven: Yale University Press, 1975.

Nash, Gary, et al. *The American People: Creating a Nation and a Society.* New York: Harper and Row, 1986.

Prucha, Francis Paul. *A Bibliographical Guide to the History of Indian-White Relations in the United States*. Chicago: University of Chicago Press, 1977.

———, comp. *Documents of United States Indian Policy.* Lincoln: University of Nebraska Press, 1975.

Russell, Don. "How Many Indians Were Killed? White Man Versus Red Man: The Facts and the Legend." *American West* 10 (4): 42–47, 61–63.

Sheehan, Bernard W. *The Seeds of Extinction*. Chapel Hill: University of North Carolina Press, 1973.

TePaske, John J., ed. *Three American Empires*. New York: Harper and Row, 1967.

Thornton, Russell. *American Indian Holocaust and Survival: A Population History since 1492*. Norman and London: University of Oklahoma Press, 1987.

Vogel, Virgil J., ed. *This Country Was Ours: A Documentary History of the American Indian*. New York: Harper and Row, 1972.

Washburn, Wilcomb E. *Red Man's Land, White Man's Law: A Study of the Past and Present Status of the American Indian*. New York: Scribner, 1971.
Wiebe, Robert. *The Opening of American Society: From the Adoption of the Constitution to the Eve of Disunion*. New York: Vintage Books, 1985.
Wilson, James. *The Original Americans: U.S. Indians*. Minority Rights Group Report no. 31. London: Minority Rights Group, 1986.

CANADA

Devreux, E. J. "The Beothuk Indians of Newfoundland in Fact and Fiction." *Dalhousie Review* 50 (1970): 350–62.
Eccles, W. J. *France in America*. New York: Harper and Row, 1972.
Fisher, Robin, and Kenneth Coates, eds. *Out of the Background: Readings on Canadian Native History*. Toronto: Copp Clark Pitman Ltd., 1988.
Rowe, Frederick W. *Extinction: The Beothuks of Newfoundland*. Toronto: McGraw-Hill Ryerson, 1977.
Surtees, Robert J. *Canadian Indian Policy: A Critical Bibliography*. Bloomington: Indiana University Press, 1982.
Tobias, John L. "Canada's Subjugation of the Plains Cree, 1879–1885." *Canadian Historical Review* 64 (December 1983): 519–48.
Trigger, Bruce. *The Children of Aataentsic: A History of the Huron People to 1660*. 2d ed. Kingston and Montreal: McGill-Queen's University Press, 1987. Original edition, 1976.
Upton, Leslie F. S. "The Beothuks: Questions and Answers." *Acadiensis* 7 (Spring 1978): 150–55.
———. "The Extermination of the Beothuks of Newfoundland." *Canadian Historical Review* 58 (June 1977): 133–53.

NEW ENGLAND AND THE PEQUOT INDIANS

Carroll, Peter N. *Puritanism in the Wilderness: The Intellectual Significance of the New England Frontier, 1629–1700*. New York: Columbia University Press, 1969.
Ceci, Lynn. "The First Fiscal Crisis in New York." *Economic Development and Cultural Change* 28 (1980): 839–47.
Cook, Sherburne F. *The Indian Population of New England in the Seventeenth Century*. Berkeley: University of California Press, 1976.
DeForest, John William. *History of the Indians of Connecticut from the Earliest Known Period to 1850*. 1851. Reprint. Hamden, Conn.: Archon Books, 1964.
Eisenger, Chester M. "The Puritans' Justification for Taking the Land." *Essex Institute Historical Collections* 84 (1948): 131–43.
Hirsch, Adam J. "The Collision of Military Cultures in Seventeenth-Century New England." *Journal of American History* 74 (1988): 1187–1212.
Jennings, Francis. *The Invasion of America: Indians, Colonialism and the Cant of*

Conquest. Chapel Hill: University of North Carolina Press, 1975.

Leach, Douglas Edward. *Flintlock and Tomahawk: New England in King Philip's War.* New York: Norton, 1958.

Nash, Gary B. *Red, White, and Black: The Peoples of Early America.* Englewood Cliffs: Prentice-Hall, 1974.

Pearce, Roy H. "The 'Ruines of Mankind': The Indian and the Puritan Mind." *Journal of the History of Ideas* 13 (1952): 200–17.

Salisbury, Neal. *The Indians of New England: A Critical Bibliography.* Bloomington: Indiana University Press, 1982.

———. *Manitou and Providence: Indians, Europeans, and the Beginnings of New England.* New York: Oxford University Press, 1982.

Simmons, William S. "Cultural Bias in the New England Puritans' Perception of Indians." *William and Mary Quarterly* 38 (1981): 56–72.

Thomas, G. E. "Puritans, Indians, and the Concept of Race." *New England Quarterly* 48 (1975): 3–27.

Thomas, Peter A. "Contrastive Subsistence Strategies and Land Use as Factors for Understanding Indian-White Relations in New England." *Ethnohistory* 23 (1976): 1–18.

Vaughn, Alden T. *The New England Frontier: Puritans and Indians, 1620–1675.* Rev. ed. New York: Norton, 1979.

Washburn, Wilcomb, ed. *The Indian and the White Man.* New York: Doubleday, 1964.

Willison, George F. *Saints and Strangers.* New York: Reynal and Hitchcock, 1945.

THE SOUTH

Bridenbaugh, Carl. *Jamestown: 1544–1699.* New York: Oxford University Press, 1980.

Cotteril, R. S. *The Southern Indians: The Story of the Civilized Tribes before Removal.* Norman: University of Oklahoma Press, 1963.

Crane, Verner W. *Southern Frontier: 1670–1732.* Ann Arbor: University of Michigan Press, 1956. Original edition, 1929.

Craven, Wesley Frank. *White, Red, and Black: The Seventeenth Century Virginian.* Charlottesville: University Press of Virginia, 1971.

Fogelson, Raymond. *The Cherokees: A Critical Bibliography.* Bloomington: Indiana University Press, 1978.

Foreman, Grant. *Indian Removal.* Norman: University of Oklahoma Press, 1932.

Jahoda, Gloria. *Trail of Tears: The Story of the American Indian Removals, 1813–1855.* New York: Holt, Rinehart and Winston, 1976.

Morgan, Edmund S. *American Slavery, American Freedom: The Ordeal of Colonial Virginia.* New York: Norton, 1975.

Nash, Gary B. "The Image of the Indian in the Southern Colonial Mind." *William and Mary Quarterly* 29 (1972): 197–230.

O'Donnell, James H. *Southeastern Frontiers: Europeans, Africans, and American Indians, 1513–1840.* Bloomington: Indiana University Press, 1982.

Sheehan, Bernard W. *Savagism and Civility: Indians and Englishmen in Colonial Virginia*. Cambridge: Cambridge University Press, 1980.

Washburn, Wilcomb. *The Governor and the Rebel: A History of Bacon's Rebellion in Virginia*. Chapel Hill: University of North Carolina Press, 1957.

Wright, James Leitch, Jr. *The Only Land They Knew: The Tragic Story of the American Indians in the Old South*. New York: Free Press, 1981.

For more literature on the southern Indians see the *Journal of Cherokee Studies*.

THE WEST

Ambrose, Stephen E. *Crazy Horse and Custer: The Parallel Lives of Two American Warriors*. Garden City, N.Y.: Doubleday, 1975.

Bancroft. Hubert H. *History of California*. 7 vols. San Francisco: The History Co., 1884–90.

———. *The Native Races of the Pacific States of North America*. 5 vols. San Francisco: A. L. Bancroft, 1874–75.

Brown, Dee. *Bury my Heart at Wounded Knee: An Indian History of the American West*. New York: Holt, Rinehart and Winston, 1971.

Carranco, Lynwood, and Estle Beard. *Genocide and Vendetta: The Round Valley Wars of Northern California*. Norman: University of Oklahoma Press, 1981.

Coffer, William E. "Genocide of the California Indians." *The Indian Historian* 10 (1977): 8–15.

Connell, Evan S. *Son of the Morning Star: Custer and the Little Big Horn*. San Francisco: North Point Press, 1984.

Cook, Sherburne F. *The Conflict between the California Indians and White Civilization*. Berkeley: University of California Press, 1976.

Dollar, Clyde. "The High Plains Smallpox Epidemic of 1837–38." *Western History Quarterly* 8, no. 1 (1977): 15–38.

Grinell, George Bird. *The Fighting Cheyennes*. 2d ed. Norman: University of Oklahoma Press, 1956.

Miller, Virginia P. "Whatever Happened to the Yuki?" *Indian Historian* 8, no. 2 (1975): 6–12.

———. *Ukomno'm: The Yuki Indians of Northern California*. Sorocco, New Mexico: Ballena-Press, 1979.

Utley, Robert M. *The Indian Frontier of the American West, 1846–1890*. Albuquerque: University of New Mexico Press, 1984.

———. *The Last Days of the Sioux Nation*. New Haven: Yale University Press, 1963.

The Indians of the Caribbean, Mexico, and South America

GENERAL

Burger, Julian. *Report from the Frontier: The State of the World's Indigenous Peoples*. London: Zed Press, 1987.

Casas, Bartolomé de las. *Bartolomé de las Casas: A Selection of His Writings.*
Translated and edited by George Sanderlin. New York: Alfred A. Knopf, 1971.
————. *The Devastation of the Indies: A Brief Account.* Translated by Herma Briffant.
New York: Seabury Press, 1974.
Cook, Sherburne F., and Woodrow W. Borah. *Essays in Population History: Mexico
and the Caribbean.* 2 vols. Berkeley and Los Angeles: University of California
Press, 1971.
Denevan, William M., ed. *The Native Population of the Americas in 1492.* Madison:
University of Wisconsin Press, 1976.
Dominguez Ortiz, Antonio. *The Golden Age of Spain: 1516–1659.* Translated by
James Casey. London: Weidenfeld and Nicolson, 1971.
Friede, Juan, and Benjamin Keen. *Bartolomé de las Casas in History: Toward an
Understanding of the Man and His Work.* DeKalb: Northern Illinois University Press,
1971.
Gibson, Charles. *Spain in America.* The New American Nation Series. New York:
Harper and Row, 1966.
Gongora, Mario. *Studies in the Colonial History of Spanish America.* Cambridge:
Cambridge University Press, 1975.
Hanke, Lewis. "A Modest Proposal for a Moratorium on Grand Generalizations: Some
Thoughts on the Black Legend." *Hispanic American Historical Review* 51 (1971):
112–27.
————. *Aristotle and the American Indians: A Study in Race Prejudice in the Modern
World.* London: Hollis and Carter, 1959.
————. *The First Social Experiments in America: A Study in the Development of
Spanish Indian Policy in the Sixteenth Century.* 1935. Reprint. Gloucester, Mass.:
Peter Smith, 1964.
————. *The Spanish Struggle for Justice in the Conquest of America.* Philadelphia:
University of Pennsylvania Press, 1949.
Haring, Clarence H. *The Spanish Empire in America.* New York: Oxford University
Press, 1947.
Keen, Benjamin. "The Black Legend Revisited: Assumptions and Realities." *Hispanic
American Historical Review* 49 (1969): 703–19.
————. "The White Legend Revisited: A Reply to Professor Hanke's 'Modest
Proposal.'" *Hispanic American Historical Review* 51 (1971): 336–55.
Parry, J. H. *The Age of Reconnaissance.* London: Weidenfeld and Nicolson, 1963.
————. *Europe and a Wider World: 1415–1715.* London: Hutchinson's University
Library, 1949.
————. *The Spanish Theory of Empire in the Sixteenth Century.* Cambridge:
Cambridge University Press, 1940.
Simpson, Leslie Byrd. *The Encomienda in New Spain.* Berkeley and Los Angeles:
University of California Press, 1950.
Steward, Julian H., ed. *Handbook of South American Indians.* 7 vols. New York:
Cooper Square, 1963.

Todorov, Tzvetan. *The Conquest of America: The Question of the Other.* Translated by
    Richard Howard. New York: Harper and Row, 1984. Original edition, 1982.
Villamarin, Juan A., and Judith E. Villamarin. *Indian Labor in Mainland Colonial
    Spanish America.* Latin American Studies Program Occasional Papers and
    Monographs, no. 1. Newark, Del.: University of Delaware Press, 1975.

THE CARIBBEAN

Henige, David. "David Henige's Reply [to Zambardino]." *Hispanic American
    Historical Review* 58 (1978): 709–12.
————. "On the Contact Population of Hispaniola: History as Higher Mathematics."
    Hispanic American Historical Review 58 (1978): 217–37.
Newson, Linda. *Aboriginal and Spanish Colonial Trinidad.* London: Academic Press,
    1976.
Stone, Edward T. "Columbus and Genocide." *American Heritage* 26, 6 (1975): 4–7,
    76–79.
Williams, Eric. *From Columbus to Castro.* New York: Harper and Row, 1970.
Zambardino, R. A. "Critique of David Henige's 'On the Contact Population of
    Hispaniola: History as Higher Mathematics.' " *Hispanic American Historical Review*
    58 (1978): 700–08.

MEXICO

Borah, Woodrow W., and Sherburne F. Cook. *The Aboriginal Population of Central
    Mexico on the Eve of the Spanish Conquest.* Berkeley and Los Angeles: University
    of California Press, 1963.
————. *The Population of Central Mexico in 1548.* Berkeley and Los Angeles:
    University of California Press, 1960.
Cook, Sherburne F., and Woodrow W. Borah. *The Indian Population of Central
    Mexico: 1531–1610.* Berkeley and Los Angeles: University of California Press,
    1960.
Cook, Sherburne F., and Leslie Byrd Simpson. *The Population of Central Mexico in
    the Sixteenth Century.* Berkeley and Los Angeles: University of California Press,
    1948.
Hu-DeHart, Evelyn. *Yaqui Resistance and Survival: The Struggle for Land and
    Autonomy, 1821–1910.* Madison: University of Wisconsin Press, 1984.
Keen, Benjamin. *The Aztec Image in Western Thought.* New Brunswick, N.J.: Rutgers
    University Press, 1971.
Morley, Sylvannus G. *The Ancient Maya.* Stanford: Stanford University Press, 1956.
Prescott, William H. *History of the Conquest of Mexico.* 1843. Reprint. New York:
    Random House, 1936.
Soustelle, Jacques. *The Daily Life of the Aztecs on the Eve of the Spanish Conquest.*
    Translated by Patrick O'Brian. London: Weidenfeld and Nicolson, 1961. Original

French edition, 1955.
Vaillant, George. *Aztecs of Mexico: The Origin, Rise and Fall of the Aztec Nation.* Garden City, N.Y.: Doubleday Doran, 1941.
Wolf, Eric. *Sons of the Shaking Earth.* Chicago: University of Chicago Press, 1959.

SOUTH AMERICA

American Friends of Brazil. *Supysaua: A Documentary Report on the Conditions of Indian Peoples in Brazil.* Berkeley: Indigena, Inc. and American Friends of Brazil, 1974.
Arens, Richard, ed. *Genocide in Paraguay.* Philadelphia: Temple University Press, 1976.
Bodard, Lucien. *Green Hell: Massacre of the Brazilian Indians.* New York: Dutton, 1974.
Brooks, Edwin, et al. *Tribes of the Amazon Basin in Brazil, 1972. Report by the Aborigines Protection Society on a Mission Led by Edwin Brooks.* London: Charles Knight, 1972.
Chernela, Janet M. "Potential Impacts of a Proposed Amazon Hydropower Project," *Cultural Survival Quarterly* 12, 2 (1988): 20–24.
Cook, Noble David. *Demographic Collapse: Indian Peru, 1520–1620.* Cambridge: Cambridge University Press, 1981.
Cowell, Adrian. *The Tribe That Hides from Man.* London: Bodley House, 1973.
Davis, Shelton H. *Victims of the Miracle: Development and the Indians of Brazil.* Cambridge: Cambridge University Press, 1977.
Dostal, W., ed. *The Situation of the Indians in South America: Contributions to the Study of Inter-Ethnic Conflict in the Non-Andean Regions of South America.* Geneva: World Council of Churches, 1972.
Ellis, William S. "Rôndonia: Brazil's Imperiled Rain Forest." *National Geographic* 174 (December 1988): 772–79.
Goodland, R. J. A., and H. S. Irwin. *Amazon Jungle: Green Hell to Red Desert.* New York: Scientific, 1973.
Gross, Daniel, ed. *Peoples and Cultures of Native South America.* New York: Doubleday, 1973.
Hemming, John. *Amazon Frontier: The Defeat of the Brazilian Indians.* Cambridge: Harvard University Press, 1987.
———. *The Conquest of the Incas.* New York: Harcourt Brace Jovanovich, 1970.
———. *Red Gold: The Conquest of the Brazilian Indians.* Cambridge: Harvard University Press, 1978.
Hopper, Janice, ed. *Indians of Brazil in the Twentieth Century.* Washington: Institute for Cross-Cultural Research, 1967.
Junqueira, Carmen. *The Brazilian Indigenous Problem and Policy: The Example of the Xingu National Park.* Copenhagen/Geneva: AMAZIND/INGIA Documaen, 1973.
Lewis, Norman. *Genocide: A Documentary Report on the Conditions of Indian*

Peoples. Berkeley: Indigena and the American Friends of Brazil, 1974.

Mahar, Dennis J. *Frontier Development Policy in Brazil.* New York, 1979.

McIntyre, Loren. "Urueu-Wau-Wau Indians: Last Days of Eden." *National Geographic* 174 (December 1988): 800–17.

Munzel, Mark. *The Aché Indians: Genocide in Paraguay.* Copenhagen: Iwgia, 1973.

Prado, Caio. *The Colonial Background of Modern Brazil.* Translated by Suzette Macedo. Berkeley: University of California Press, 1967.

Prescott, William H. *History of the Conquest of Peru.* 1847. Reprint. London: J. M. Dent and Sons, 1963.

Robock, Stephan H. *Brazil: A Study in Development Progress.* Toronto: Lexington Books, 1975.

Steward, Julian, ed. *Handbook of South American Indians.* 7 vols. New York: Cooper Square, 1946–59.

Vesilind, Pritt J. "Brazil: Moment of Promise and Pain." *National Geographic* 171 (March 1987): 349–85.

Wachtel, Nathan. *The Vision of the Vanquished: The Spanish Conquest of Peru through Indian Eyes, 1530–1570.* Translated by Ben Reynolds and Siân Reynolds. New York: Barnes and Noble Books, 1977. Original French edition, 1971.

Wagley, Charles. *Amazon Town.* New York: Alfred A. Knopf, 1964.

Wauchope, Robert, ed. *Handbook of Middle American Indians.* 16 vols. Austin: University of Texas Press, 1964–76.

Indonesia

THE COUP OF 1965 AND ITS AFTERMATH

Anderson, Benedict R., and Ruth T. McVey. *A Preliminary Analysis of the October 1, 1965, Coup in Indonesia.* Ithaca: Cornell University, Southeast Asia Program, 1971.

Brackman, Arnold. *The Communist Collapse in Indonesia.* New York: Norton, 1969.

Budiardjo, Carmel. "The Abuse of Human Rights in Indonesia." In *Case Studies on Human Rights and Fundamental Freedoms: A World Survey.* vol. 3, ed. Willem A. Veenhoven. The Hague: Martinus Nijhoff, 1976.

Caldwell, Malcolm, ed. *Ten Years of Military Terror in Indonesia.* Nottingham: Spokesman Books, 1975.

Crouch, Harold. *The Army and Politics in Indonesia.* Ithaca: Cornell University Press, 1978.

Griswold, Deirdre. *The Bloodbath That Was.* New York: World View Publishers, 1975.

Hughes, John. *The End of Sukarno.* London: Angus and Robertson, 1968.

———. *Indonesian Upheaval.* New York: D. McKay, 1967.

Jones, Howard. *Indonesia: The Possible Dream.* New York: Harcourt Brace Jovanovich, 1971.

Kroef, J. M. van der. *Indonesia after Sukarno*. Vancouver: University of British Columbia Press, 1971.
Legge, John D. *Sukarno: A Political Biography.* New York: Praeger, 1972.
Palmier, Leslie. *Communism in Indonesia*. New York: Doubleday, 1973.
Sloan, Stephen. *A Study in Political Violence: The Indonesian Experience*. Chicago: Rand McNally, 1971.
Taylor, J., et al. *Repression and Exploitation in Indonesia*. London: Spokesman Books, 1974.
Vittachi, Tarzie. *The Fall of Sukarno*. New York: Praeger, 1967.

EAST TIMOR

Amnesty International. *Submission to the U.N. Decolonization Committee*. Amnesty International, 1983.
Budiardjo, Carmel, and Liem Soei Liong. *The War against East Timor.* London: Zed Books, 1984.
Cultural Survival. *East Timor: Five Years after the Indonesian Invasion. Testimony Presented at the Decolonization Committee of the United Nations General Assembly, October 1980*. Cambridge, Mass.: Cultural Survival, 1981.
Centre for Defense Information. *A World at War.* Washington, D.C., 1983.
Jolliffe, Jill. *East Timor: Nationalism and Colonialism*. St. Lucia: University of Queensland Press, 1978.
Ramos-Horta, José. *Funu: The Unfinished Saga of East Timor.* Trenton, N.J.: Red Sea Press, 1987.

For additional literature on Indonesia and East Timor see *Briarpatch* (Regina, Saskatchewan); *Inside Indonesia: Bulletin of the Indonesian Resources and Information Programme* (Australia); and *Tapol Bulletin* (Great Britain; Indonesia Human Rights Campaign).

Iran

Bahkash, Shaul. *The Reign of the Ayatollahs: Iran and the Islamic Revolution*. New York: Basic Books, 1984.
Benard, Cheryl, and Zalmay Khalilzad. *"The Government of God": Iran's Islamic Republic*. New York: Columbia University Press, 1984.
Cooper, Roger. *The Baha'is of Iran*. Minority Rights Group Report no. 51. Rev. ed. London: MRG, 1982.
Green, Jerrold D. *Revolution in Iran: The Politics of Counter-Mobilization*. New York: Praeger, 1982.
Hiro, Dilip. *Iran under the Ayatollahs*. London: Routledge and Kegan Paul, 1985.
Keddie, Nikki R., ed. *Religion and Politics in Iran: Shi'ism from Quietism to Revolution*. New Haven: Yale University Press, 1983.

Lenczowski, George, ed. *Iran under the Pahlavis*. Stanford: Hoover Institute Press, 1978.

Japan

Adachi, Ken. *The Enemy That Never Was: The History of Japanese Canadians*. Toronto: McClelland and Stewart, 1976.
Boxer, C. R. *The Christian Century in Japan*. London: Cambridge University Press, 1951.
Hane, Mikiso. *Peasants, Rebels and Outcastes: The Underside of Modern Japan*. New York: Pantheon, 1982.
Kennedy, Malcolm D. *A History of Japan*. London: Weidenfeld and Nicolson, 1963.
Sansom, George B. *A History of Japan: 1615–1867*. 1963. Reprint. Folkestone, Kent: Wm. Dawson, 1978.
———. *Japan: A Short Cultural History*. 1943. Reprint. New York: Appleton-Century-Crofts, 1962.
Storry, G. Richard. *A History of Modern Japan*. Middlesex: Penguin, 1960.

Melos

Adcock, F. E. *Thucydides and His History*. Cambridge: Cambridge University Press, 1963.
Aristophanes. *Three Comedies: The Birds; The Clouds; The Wasps*. Translated by William Arrowsmith and Douglass Parker. Ann Arbor: University of Michigan Press, 1969.
Connor, W. Raymond. *Thucydides*. Princeton, N.J.: Princeton University Press, 1984.
Durcey, P. *Le traitement des prisonniers de guerre dans la Grèce antique*. Paris: E. de Boccard, 1968.
Ferguson, W. S. *Greek Imperialism*. 1913. Reprint. New York: Biblo and Tannen, 1963.
Finley, M. I. *The Ancient Economy*. Berkeley: University of California Press, 1973.
———. *Ancient Slavery and Modern Ideology*. New York: Viking Press, 1980.
———, ed. *Slavery in Classical Antiquity*. Cambridge: W. Heffer and Sons, 1960.
Garlan, Yvon. *War in the Ancient World: A Social History*. London: Chatto and Windus, 1975.
Hasebroek, J. *Trade and Politics in Ancient Greece*. 1933. Reprint. Translated by L. M. Fraser and D. C. Macgregor. New York: Biblo and Tannen, 1965.
Kagan, Donald. *The Outbreak of the Peloponnesian War*. Ithaca and London: Cornell University Press, 1969.
Littman, Robert. *The Greek Experiment: Imperialism and Social Conflict, 800–400 B.C.* London: Thames and Hudson, 1974.

Meiggs, Russell. *The Athenian Empire*. Oxford: Oxford University Press, 1972.

Pritchett, W. Kendrick. *The Greek State at War*. Berkeley: University of California Press, 1974.

Renfrew, Colin, and Malcolm Wagstaff, eds. *An Island Polity: The Archeology of Exploitation in Melos*. Cambridge: Cambridge University Press, 1982.

Sagan, Eli. *The Lust to Annihilate: A Psychoanalytic Study of Violence in Ancient Greek Culture*. New York: Psychohistory Press, 1979.

Starr, Chester E. *Economic and Social Growth of Early Greece*. New York: Oxford University Press, 1977.

―――. *The Origins of Greek Civilization*. New York: Alfred A. Knopf, 1961.

Ste. Croix, G. E. M. de. *The Origins of the Peloponnesian War*. London: Duckworth, 1972.

Thucydides. *The Peloponnesian War*. Translated by Rex Warner. Harmondsworth, Middlesex: Penguin Books, 1954.

Vernant, J. P. *Problèmes de la guerre en Grèce ancienne*. Paris and The Hague: Mouton, 1968.

The Mongols

Allen, W. E. D. *A History of the Georgian People, from the Beginning Down to the Russian Conquest in the Nineteenth Century*. New York: Barnes and Noble, 1932 (see esp. chap. 9, "The Monarchy under the Mongols: Giorgi IV to David VI").

Ayalon, David. "The Great Yasa of Chingiz Khan: A Re-examination." Parts I and II. *Studia Islamica* 36 (1972): 8–158 and 38 (1973): 107–56.

Bartol'd, V. V. *Histoire des turcs d'Asie Centrale*. Translation by M. Donskis. Paris: Adrien-Maisonneuve, 1945.

Bosworth, C. E. *The Medieval History of Islam, Afghanistan and Central Asia*. London: Variorum Reprints, n.d.

Boyle, John Andrew. *The Mongol World Empire: 1206–1370*. London: Variorum Reprints, 1977.

―――, ed. *The Cambridge History of Islam*. Vol. 5: *The Saljug and Mongol Periods*. Cambridge: Cambridge University Press, 1968.

Brent, Peter. *Genghis Khan: The Rise, Authority and Decline of Mongol Power*. New York: McGraw-Hill, 1976.

Chambers, James. *The Devil's Horsemen: The Mongol Invasion of Europe*. New York: Atheneum, 1979.

Dawson, Christopher Henry, ed. *The Mongol Mission: Narratives and Letters of the Franciscan Missionaries in Mongolia and China in the Thirteenth and Fourteenth Centuries*. Translated by a nun of Stanbrook Abbey. New York: Sheed and Ward, 1955.

Elias, Ney, ed. *A History of the Moghuls of Central Asia: Being the Tarikh-i-Rashidi of Mirza Muhammad Haidar, Dughlat*. 1895. Reprint. London: Curzon Press, 1972.

Hodgson, Marshall. *The Venture of Islam*. 3 vols. Chicago: University of Chicago Press, 1974.

Iwamuru, Shinobu. "Mongol Invasion of Poland in the Thirteenth Century." The Memoirs of the Research Department of the Toyo Bunko (Oriental Library, Tokyo), 10 (1938): 103–57.

Jenkins, Gareth. "A Note on Climactic Cycles and the Rise of Chinggis Khan." *Central Asiatic Journal* 18 (1974): 217–26.

Joveynī, Alā al-Dīn Aṭā-Malek. *The History of the World-Conqueror*. 2 vols. Translated by J. A. Boyle. Manchester: Manchester University Press, 1958.

Langlois, J. D., Jr., ed. *China under Mongol Rule*. Princeton: Princeton University Press, 1981.

Martin, Henry Desmond. *The Rise of Chingis Khan: His Conquest of North China*. 1950. Reprint. New York: Octagon Books, 1971.

Pelliot, Paul, and Louis Hambis, eds. and trans. *Histoire des campagnes de Gengis Khan*. Vol. 1. Leiden: E. J. Brill, 1951.

Pelliot, P., ed. and trans. *Histoire secrète des mongols*. Paris: Librairie d'Amérique et d'Orient, 1949.

Polo, Marco. *The Travels of Marco Polo*. 1854. Reprint. London: J. M. Dent, 1926.

Pokotilov, Dimitri. *History of the Eastern Mongols during the Ming Dynasty from 1368–1631*. Translated by Rudolph Lowenthal. Perspectives in Asian History no. 1. Philadelphia: Porcupine Press, 1976.

Rashid al-Dīn Tabīb. *The Successors of Genghis Khan*. Translated by John Andrew Boyle. New York: Columbia University Press, 1971.

Sansom, George. *The History of Japan to 1334*. 1958. Reprint. Folkestone, Kent: Wm. Dawson, 1978 (see chap. 20 for the Mongol invasions of 1274 and 1281.)

Saunders, J. J. *A History of Medieval Islam*. London: Routledge and Kegan Paul, 1965.

———. *The History of the Mongol Conquests*. London: Routledge and Kegan Paul, 1971.

Sinor, Denis. *Inner Asia and its Contacts with Medieval Europe*. London: Variorum Reprints, 1977.

Spuler, Bertold. *History of the Mongols: based on Eastern and Western accounts of the thirteenth and fourteenth centuries*. Translated by Helga Drummond and Stuart Drummond. Berkeley: University of California Press, 1972.

———. *The Mongols in History*. Translated by Geoffrey Wheeler. New York: Praeger, 1971. Original edition, 1961.

Vernadsky, George. *The Mongols and Russia*. New Haven: Yale University Press, 1953.

———. "The Scope and Content of Chinggis Khan's Yasa." *Harvard Journal of Asiatic Studies* 3 (1938): 337–60.

Vladimirstov, B. Ya. *The Life of Chingis Khan*. Translated by Prince D. S. Mirsky. New York: Benjamin Blom, 1930.

———. *Le régime social des mongols: La feodalisme nomade*. Translated by Michel Carsow. Paris: A. Maisonneuve, 1948.

Nigeria

Africa Report 13 (February 1968). Special issue on the Nigerian Civil War.

Balogun, Ola. *The Tragic Years: Nigeria in Crisis, 1966–1970.* Benin City: Ethiope, 1973.

Coleman, James. *Nigeria: Background to Independence.* Berkeley: University of California Press, 1962.

Dudley, B. J. *Instability and Political Order: Politics and Crisis in Nigeria.* Ibadan: Ibadan University Press, 1973.

Kirk-Greene, A. H. M. *Crisis and Conflict in Nigeria.* London: Cambridge University Press, 1971.

Luckham, Robin. *The Nigerian Military: A Sociological Analysis of Authority and Revolt, 1960–1967.* Cambridge: Cambridge University Press, 1971.

Melson, Robert, and Howard Wolpe, eds. *Nigeria: Modernization and the Politics of Communalism.* East Lansing: Michigan State University Press, 1971.

Mezu, S. O. *Behind the Rising Sun.* London: Heinemann, 1971.

Nafziger, E. W., and W. L. Richter. "Biafra and Bangladesh: The Political Economy of Secessionist Conflict." *Journal of Peace Research* 13 (1976): 91–109.

O'Brien, Connor Cruise. "Biafra: Genocide and Discretion." *The Listener* 30 (January 1969): 129–31.

———. *Herod: Reflections on Political Violence.* London: Hutchinson, 1978.

O'Connell, James. "Political Integration: The Nigerian Case." In *African Integration and Disintegration: Case Studies in Economic and Political Union,* ed. Arthur Hazelwood. London: Oxford University Press, 1967.

Olorunsola, Victor A., ed. *The Politics of Cultural Sub-Nationalism in Africa.* Garden City, N.Y.: Doubleday, 1972.

Panter-Brick, S. K., ed. *Nigerian Politics and Military Rule: Prelude to the Civil War.* London: Athlone Press, 1970.

St. Jorre, John D. *The Brothers' War: Biafra and Nigeria.* Boston: Houghton Mifflin, 1972.

Oceania

Abbie, A. A. *The Original Australians.* London: Frederick Muller, 1969.

Clark, C. M. H. *A History of Australia.* 3 vols. Melbourne: Melbourne University Press, 1962.

———, ed. *Select Documents in Australian History, 1788–1850.* Sydney: Angus and Robertson, 1950.

Inglis, K. S. *The Australian Colonists: An Exploration in Social History, 1788–1870.* Victoria: Melbourne University Press, 1974.

Jones, Lancaster F. *The Structure and Growth of Australia's Aboriginal Population.* Aborigines in Australian Society no. 1. Canberra: Australian National University, 1970.

Moorehead, Alan. *The Fatal Impact: An Account of the Invasion of the South Pacific, 1767–1840.* London: Hamish Hamilton, 1966.

Morris, James. "The Final Solution, Down Under." *Horizon* 14 (1969): 60–71.

Price, Grenfell A. *White Settlers and Native Peoples: An Historical Study of Racial Contacts between English-Speaking Whites and Aboriginal Peoples in the United States, Canada, Australia and New Zealand.* Cambridge: Cambridge University Press, 1950.

Robson, Lloyd. *A History of Tasmania.* Vol. 1: *Van Diemen's Land from the Earliest Times to 1855.* Melbourne: Oxford University Press, 1983.

Rowley, Charles Dunford. *Aboriginal Policy and Practice.* 3 vols. Vol. 1: *The Destruction of the Aboriginal Society.* Canberra: Australian National University, 1970.

Ryan, Lyndall. *The Aboriginal Tasmanians.* Vancouver and London: University of British Columbia Press. 1981.

Stone, Sherman N. *Aborigines in White Australia: A Documentary History of the Attitudes Affecting Official Policy and the Australian Aborigine, 1697–1973.* London: Heinemann Educational Books, 1974.

Travers, Robert. *The Tasmanians: The Story of a Doomed Race.* Melbourne: Cassell Australia, 1968.

Sri Lanka

Amnesty International. *Sri Lanka: Some Recent Reports of Extra-Judicial Killings, September 1985 to March 1986.* London: Amnesty International, April 30, 1986.

Fernando, Tissa, and Robert N. Kearney, eds. *Modern Sri Lanka: A Society in Transition.* Syracuse: Syracuse University Press, 1979.

International Alert. *Emergency: Sri Lanka, 1986.* London: International Alert, 1986.

Leary, Virginia A. *Ethnic Conflict and Violence in Sri Lanka: Report of a Mission to Sri Lanka in July-August 1981.* 2d ed. Geneva: International Commission of Jurists, 1983.

McGilvray, Dennis B., ed. *Caste, Ideology and Interaction.* Cambridge: Cambridge University Press, 1982.

Schwarz, Walter. *The Tamils of Sri Lanka.* Minority Rights Group Report no. 25. London: Minority Rights Group, 1983.

Sieghart, Paul. *Sri Lanka: A Mounting Tragedy of Errors.* London: International Commission of Jurists, 1984.

Tambiah, S. J. *Sri Lanka: Ethnic Fratricide and the Dismantling of Democracy.* Chicago: University of Chicago Press, 1986.

Wilson, A. Jeyaratnam. *Politics in Sri Lanka: 1947–1979.* 2d ed. London: Macmillan, 1979.

Sudan

Albino, Oliver. *The Sudan: A Southern Viewpoint.* London: Oxford University Press,
1970.
Bechtold, Peter K. *Politics in the Sudan: Parliamentary and Military Rule in an
Emerging African Nation.* New York: Praeger, 1976.
Beshir, Mohammed Omer. *The Southern Sudan: Background to Conflict.* Khartoum:
Khartoum University Press, 1970.
————. *Revolution and Nationalism in the Sudan.* New York: Barnes and Noble,
1974.
Eprile, Cecil. *War and Peace in the Sudan, 1955–1972.* Newton Abbot: David and
Charles, 1974.
Mahjub, Muhammed Ahmad. *Democracy on Trial: Reflections on Arab and African
Politics.* London: Deutsch, 1974.
Morrison, Godfrey. *Eritrea and the Southern Sudan.* Minority Rights Group Report no.
5. 2d ed. London: Minority Rights Group, 1976. First edition, 1971.
O'Ballance, Edgar. *The Secret War in the Sudan: 1955–1972.* Hamden, Conn.:
Archon Books, 1977.
Oduho, Joseph, and William Deng. *The Problem of the Southern Sudan.* London:
Oxford University Press, 1963.
Voll, John Obert. *Historical Dictionary of the Sudan.* London: Scarecrow Press, 1978.
Wai, Dunstan M., ed. *The Southern Sudan: The Problem of National Integration.*
London: Frank Cass, 1973.
Warburg, Gabriel R., and Uri M. Kupferschmidt, eds. *Islam, Nationalism, and
Radicalism in Egypt and the Sudan.* New York: Praeger, 1983.

For additional literature see *Cultural Survival Quarterly.*

The USSR

Abramovitch, Raphael R. *The Soviet Revolution: 1917–1939.* New York: International
Universities Press, 1962.
Andics, Helmut. *Rule of Terror: Russia under Lenin and Stalin.* New York: Holt,
Rinehart and Winston, 1969.
Ammende, Ewald. *Human Life in Russia.* London: George Allen and Unwin, 1936.
Antonov-Ovseyenko, Anton. *The Time of Stalin: Portrait of a Tyranny.* Translated by
George Saunders. Introduction by Stephen F. Cohen. New York: Harper and Row,
1981.
Bailes, Kendall. *Technology and Society under Lenin and Stalin.* Princeton: Princeton
University Press, 1978.
Broido, Vera. *Lenin and the Mensheviks: The Persecution of Socialists under
Bolshevism.* Boulder, Col.: Westview Press, 1987.

Carynnyk, Marco. "The Famine the *Times* Couldn't Find." *Commentary* 76 (November 1983): 32–40.

Carynnyk, Marco, Lubomyr Y. Luciuk, and Bohdan S. Kordan, eds. *The Foreign Office and the Famine: British Documents on Ukraine and the Great Famine of 1932–1933.* Kingston, Ont., and Vestal, N.Y.: Limestone Press, 1988.

Chamberlin, W. H. *The Ukraine: A Submerged Nation.* New York: Macmillan, 1944.

Cohen, Stephen. *Bukharin and the Bolshevik Revolution: A Political Biography, 1888–1938.* New York: Knopf, 1973.

Commission on the Ukraine Famine. *Investigation of the Ukraine Famine: 1932–1933. Report to Congress.* Washington, D.C.: Government Printing Office, 1988.

Conquest, Robert. *The Great Terror: Stalin's Purge of the Thirties.* New York: Macmillan, 1968.

———. *The Harvest of Sorrow: Soviet Collectivization and the Terror-Famine.* New York: Oxford University Press, 1986.

———. *Kolyma: The Arctic Death Camps.* New York: Oxford University Press, 1978.

———. *The Nation Killers: The Soviet Deportation of Nationalities.* New York: Macmillan, 1970.

Dallin, David. *Forced Labor in Soviet Russia.* New Haven: Yale University Press, 1947.

Davies, R. W. *The Industrialization of Soviet Russia.* Vol. 1: *The Socialist Offensive: The Collectivization of Soviet Agriculture, 1929–1930.* Vol. 2: *The Soviet Collective Farm, 1929–1930.* London: Macmillan, 1980.

Dekker, Nikolai., and Andrei Lebed, eds. *Genocide in the U.S.S.R.: Studies in Group Destruction.* New York: Scarecrow Press, 1958.

Dunham, Vera. *In Stalin's Time.* Cambridge: Cambridge University Press, 1976.

Dushnyck, Walter. *Fifty Years Ago: The Famine Holocaust in Ukraine—Terror and Human Misery as Instruments of Soviet Russian Imperialism.* New York and Toronto: World Congress of Free Ukrainians, 1983.

Getty, J. Arch. *Origins of the Great Purges: The Soviet Communist Party Reconsidered, 1933–1938.* Cambridge: Cambridge University Press, 1985.

Ginzburg, Eugenia. *Journey into the Whirlwind.* Translated by Paul Stevenson and Max Hayward. New York: Harcourt, Brace, 1967.

Gouldner, Alvin W. "Stalinism: A Study of Internal Colonialism." *Telos* 34 (1977–78): 5–48.

Ivanov-Razumnik, Vasil'evick. *The Memoirs of Ivanov-Razumnik.* Translated by P. S. Squire. London: Oxford University Press, 1965.

Kravchenko, Victor. *I Chose Freedom: The Personal and Political Life of a Soviet Official.* New York: Scribner's, 1946.

Leggett, George. *The Cheka: Lenin's Political Police.* Oxford: Oxford University Press, 1981.

Legters, Lyman H. "The Soviet Gulag: Is It Genocidal?" In *Toward the Understanding and Prevention of Genocide*, ed. Israel Charny. Boulder, Col.: Westview Press, 1984.

Lewin, Moshe. *Russian Peasants and Soviet Power: A Study of Collectivization.* London: George Allen and Unwin, 1968.

———. "Society and the Stalinist State in the Period of the Five Year Plans." *Social History* (Great Britain) 1 (May 1976): 139–75.

Mace, James. "The Man-Made Famine of 1933 in the Soviet Ukraine: What Happened and Why?" In *Toward the Understanding and Prevention of Genocide*, ed. Israel Charny. Boulder, Col.: Westview, 1984.

Manning, C. A. *Ukraine under the Soviets.* New York: Bookman Associates, 1953.

Medvedev, Roy A. *Let History Judge: The Origins and Consequences of Stalinism.* New York: Alfred A. Knopf, 1972.

Nekrich, Aleksandr M. *The Punished Peoples: The Deportation and Fate of Soviet Minorities at the End of the Second World War.* New York: Norton, 1978.

Pethybridge, Robert W. *The Social Prelude to Stalinism.* London: Macmillan, 1974.

Serbyn, Roman, and Bohdan Krawchenko, eds. *Famine in Ukraine, 1932–1933.* Edmonton: Canadian Institute of Ukrainian Studies, University of Alberta, 1986.

Shanin, Teodor. *The Awkward Class: Political Sociology of the Peasantry in a Developing Society—Russia, 1910–1925.* Oxford: Clarendon Press, 1972.

Solzhenitsyn, Aleksander M. *The Gulag Archipelago.* 3 vols. Harper and Row, 1973–74, 1975, 1978.

Tucker, Robert, ed. *Stalinism: Essays in Historical Interpretation.* New York: Norton, 1977.

Ulam, Adam. *Stalin: The Man and His Era.* New York: Viking, 1973.

Volin, Lazar. *A Century of Russian Agriculture: From Alexander II to Khruschev.* Cambridge: Harvard University Press, 1970.

Von Laue, Theodore H. *Why Lenin? Why Stalin?: A Reappraisal of the Russian Revolution, 1900–1930.* 2d ed. New York: Harper and Row, 1971.

Wolfe, Bertram D. *Khrushchev and Stalin's Ghost: Text, Background and Meaning of Khrushchev's Secret Report to the Twentieth Congress on the Night of February 24–25, 1956.* New York: Praeger, 1957.

For additional literature on the Ukrainian famine see *Journal of Ukrainian Studies* (Toronto); *Ukrainian Quarterly*; and *Ukrainian Review* (Great Britain).

The Zulu under Shaka

Chanaiwa, David. "The Zulu Revolution: State Formation in a Pastoralist Society." *African Studies Review* 23 (December 1980): 1–20.

Gluckman, Max. "The Kingdom of the Zulu of South Africa." In *African Political Systems*, ed. M. Fortes and E. E. Evans-Pritchard. London: Oxford University Press, 1955.

———. "The Rise of a Zulu Empire." *Scientific American* 202 (April 1960): 157–68.

Hammond, Dorothy, and Alta Jablow. *The Africa That Never Was: Four Centuries of British Writing about Africa*. New York: Twayne Publishers, 1970.

Krige, Eileen Jensen. *The Social System of the Zulus*. Pietermaritzburg: Shuter and Shooter, 1936.

Marks, Shula. "The Nguni, the Natalians and Their History." *Journal of African History* 8 (1967): 529–40.

Morris, Donald. *The Washing of the Spears: A History of the Zulu Nation under Shaka and Its Fall in the Zulu War of 1879*. New York: Simon and Schuster, 1965.

Omer-Cooper, J. D. *The Zulu Aftermath: A Nineteenth Century Revolution in Bantu Africa*. Evanston: Northwestern University Press, 1966.

Thompson, Leonard. "Cooperation and Conflict: The Zulu Nation and Natal." In *The Oxford History of South Africa*. Vol. 1: *South Africa to 1870*, ed. Monica Wilson and Leonard Thompson. Oxford: Clarendon Press, 1969.

Walter, Eugene Victor. *Terror and Resistance: A Study of Political Violence with Case Studies of Some Primitive African Communities*. Oxford: Oxford University Press, 1969

On the Prediction and Prevention of Genocide

Bazyler, Michael J. "Reexamining the Doctrine of Humanitarian Intervention in Light of the Atrocities in Kampuchea and Ethiopia." *Stanford Journal of International Law* 23 (1987): 547–619.

Charny, Israel W. "Intervention and Prevention of Genocide." In *Genocide: A Critical Bibliography*, ed. Israel W. Charny. New York and London: Facts on File and Mansell Publishing Ltd, 1988.

Charny, Israel W., ed. *Toward the Understanding and Prevention of Genocide: Proceedings of the International Conference on the Holocaust and Genocide*. Boulder, Col.: and London: Westview Press, 1984.

Clay, Jason W., and Bonnie K. Holcomb. *Politics and the Ethiopian Famine 1984–1985*. Cultural Survival Report 20. Rev. ed. Cambridge, Mass.: Cultural Survival Inc., 1986.

Deutsch, Eberhard P. "International Covenants on Human Rights and Our Constitutional Policy." *American Bar Association Journal* 54 (1968): 238–45.

"Biafra, Bengal, and Beyond: International Responsibility and Genocidal Conflict." *American Journal of International Law* 66 (September 1972): 89–107.

Gayner, Jeffrey. "The Genocide Treaty." *Journal of Social and Political Studies* 2 (Winter 1977) : 235–45.

Goldberg, Arthur J., and Richard N. Gardner. "Time to Act on the Genocide Convention." *American Bar Association Journal* 58 (February 1972): 141–45.

Harff, Barbara. *Genocide and Human Rights: International Legal and Political Issues*.

Monograph Series in World Affairs, Graduate School of International Studies. Denver: University of Denver, 1984.

Howard, Rhoda E., and Jack Donnelly. "Human Dignity, Human Rights, and Political Regimes." *American Political Science Review* 80 (September 1986): 801–17.

Kuper, Leo. *International Action against Genocide.* Report no. 53. Rev. ed. London: Minority Rights Group, 1984.

———. *The Prevention of Genocide.* New Haven, Conn.: Yale University Press, 1985.

Schwelb, Egon. "Crimes against Humanity." *The British Yearbook of International Law* 23 (1946): 178–226.

Sanford, Nevitt, Craig Comstock, and Associates. *Sanctions for Evil.* San Francisco: Jossey-Bass, 1973.

For additional literature on prediction and prevention, see *Cultural Survival Quarterly* and *Internet on the Holocaust and Genocide.*

Printed in the USA
CPSIA information can be obtained
at www.ICGtesting.com
LVHW091534241223
767349LV00005B/677

9 780300 044446